THE DIOCESAN SEMINARY IN THE UNITED STATES

NOTRE DAME STUDIES IN AMERICAN CATHOLICISM

Sponsored by the
Charles and Margaret Hall Cushwa Center
for the Study of American Catholicism

The Diocesan Seminary in the United States:

A History from the 1780s to the Present

Joseph M. White

University of Notre Dame Press
Notre Dame, Indiana

Library of Congress Cataloging-in-Publication Data

White, Joseph Michael.
  The diocesan seminary in the United States : a history from the 1780s to the present / Joseph M. White.
      p.   cm. — (Notre Dame studies in American Catholicism)
  ISBN 0-268-00865-5
  1. Theological seminaries, Catholic—United States—History. 2. Catholic Church—Education—United States—History. I. Title. II. Series.
BX905.W47   1989
207′.73—dc20   89-40383

To my parents

Contents

Preface

Catholic teaching proclaims the high dignity of the priest appropriate to his functions as minister of the sacraments that are considered essential to salvation. The priest's high status contrasts sharply with the low level of interest in the historical study of topics related to the priesthood and seminary in American Catholic life. Without question church historians have produced a steady stream of biographies of prominent bishops and priests, but historical inquiries into the collective experience of ordinary priests or the practice of priestly ministry in the United States have been rare. The lack of scholarship directed to the priesthood extends to the Catholic seminary. The individual seminary's history published for an anniversary occasion has been the most common approach to the history of clerical training. These volumes seldom treat more than institutional events. Dissertations on selected aspects of the seminary have occasionally appeared, though the general history of the diocesan seminary has not emerged.

The publication of *The Catholic Priest in the United States: Historical Investigations* (Collegeville, Minnesota: St. John's University, 1971), edited by John Tracy Ellis, was a milestone in the historical study of the American Catholic priest. This collection of essays provides a useful introduction to seminary education, priests' relations with bishops, the status of priests belonging to religious orders, and the priest's intellectual isolation. In the recent *Tradition and Transformation in Catholic Culture: The Priests of Saint Sulpice in the United States from 1791 to the Present* (New York: Macmillan, 1987), Christopher J. Kauffman advances the historical study of the priesthood and seminary with an interpretation of the most influential community of seminary educators.

The following study aims at a historical survey of the institutional patterns and major issues related to diocesan seminaries of the Latin rite in the United States from the 1780s to the present. It focuses on seminaries training diocesan priests, because this aspect of the Catholic seminary tradition originated with the Council of Trent's seminary decree of 1563, which

ix

addresses only the training of diocesan clergy and not priests of religious
orders. A study of seminary training among religious orders would require
an examination of the institutional histories and specific traditions of many
individual orders. However, for the purposes of the study I include those
seminaries conducted by religious orders for training diocesan priests as
well as the seminaries under the direct control of dioceses. In the course
of focusing on the preparation of diocesan priests, I found it useful to
depart from an exclusive concern with American diocesan seminaries to
include the related issue of American colleges founded abroad for training
diocesan clergy and the role of the Catholic University of America in relation to the diocesan priesthood and seminaries.

In addition to the differences between diocesan seminaries and those
of religious orders, two types of Catholic seminary institutions had developed in the United States by the 1960s, the six-year minor or preparatory
seminary for students of high school and junior college and the six-year
major seminary for students of philosophy and theology. The study treats
the major seminary program with particular reference to the years of the
seminarian's theology studies.

The formal preparation of Protestant clergy is usually described as
"theological education." This term does not seem suitable to describe the
spiritual, academic, and professional training or formation of candidates
for the Catholic priesthood, and, thus, I avoid its use. Formal theological
study is but one, albeit important, aspect of the diocesan seminary's function. I do not attempt a history of Catholic theology or of the content
of theology taught in the diocesan seminary except in the most general
fashion. The content of theological learning in the seminary will only become clear when historians of Catholic theology explore the treatment of
issues in the textbook literature used in seminaries.

In offering this survey, I am aware that many topics taken up here
deserve more thorough study. Other topics scarcely addressed should be
studied, such as the collective experience and background of seminarians,
the growth of the network of minor seminaries in the twentieth century,
and the content of each of the disciplines in the seminary curriculum. It
is my hope that others will take up further inquiries into aspects of the
priesthood and seminary.

When establishing a diocesan seminary in the United States was first
seriously considered in the 1780s, the idea of the seminary was less than
two and a half centuries old. The American diocesan seminary was naturally an heir to a tradition that had developed in Europe. The Prologue
treats the "Rise of Seminaries" from the era of the Council of Trent (1545–
1564) to the late eighteenth century. The council's strong restatement of

the theology of the priesthood that sets the priest apart from the unordained provides the basis for the subsequent development of the methods of seminary training. The Tridentine seminary decree of 1563 provided the institutional model of the local bishop taking responsibility for forming clerics at a school attached to his cathedral. The figures associated with the seventeenth-century "French School" of spirituality had a profound impact in informing the general Catholic approach to the priest's spiritual life as the basis of seminary training. These influences were brought to the United States by the many influential French clergy engaged in seminary activities in the nineteenth century.

From the 1780s to 1884, church leaders faced the challenge of organizing Catholic life and institutions for a Catholic community continuously enlarging under the impact of immigration. Part I on "Forming Traditions" focuses on seminary foundings during this century of rapid organizational development. While the Tridentine seminary decree provided for one type of diocesan seminary, several types of institutions emerged in the American church. At Baltimore, the first diocese established in the United States, emigré priests of the French Society of St. Sulpice assumed responsibility for launching several diocesan seminaries. As dioceses multiplied, most bishops until the middle of the nineteenth century sponsored short-lived seminaries for a handful of students in affiliation with, or "mixed" with, their own household, the cathedral, or a local academy for boys. As these local seminaries closed because of lack of funds or students, several large dioceses formed seminaries operating without the support of an affiliated enterprise to sustain them, such as an academy. Thus at the middle of the century, the type of seminary that later came to be known as "freestanding" develops. The interests of a few religious orders on behalf of developing a diocesan clergy resulted in the founding of their mixed seminaries with lay colleges. The dependence of American Catholics on the services of priests recruited from Europe stimulated proposals to establish American seminaries there. These proposals resulted in the formation of American colleges at Rome and Louvain, Belgium.

Through this century the missionary character of the Catholic church required a rapid seminary course for candidates for the priesthood rather than a close attention to the quality of training. The era ends as the American bishops, meeting in the Third Plenary Council of Baltimore of 1884, took steps to raise the standards of American seminaries and to establish a graduate school for advanced studies.

Part II on "The Americanist Era" deals with the period from 1884 to 1910, in which church leaders identified as "Americanists" were influential advocates for an accommodation of Catholicism to American thought and institutions. Their ideas on clerical formation were directed to improving the professional qualities of priests, lengthening the seminary course, and supporting the new Catholic University of America. New freestanding seminaries at major dioceses arose to fulfill the expectations for improved standards. The era was brought to a close as Roman authority sought to control the intellectual content of Catholic theology with the condemnation of modernism in 1907 and the imposition of the oath against modernism in 1910. The condemnations had the effect of curbing interest in ongoing reform of seminary life and learning.

Part III, the "Roman Period" from 1910 to 1962, saw an unprecedented assertion of the Holy See's control over aspects of Catholic life, including the seminary. The Code of Canon Law of 1918 provided a new universal church legal code that for the first time outlines how the diocesan seminary should operate. Roman authority issued a steady stream of supplementary decrees based on the code and exhortations touching all aspects of seminary activities. While responding to the requirements of church authority, bishops greatly expanded the pattern of freestanding diocesan seminaries as the American Catholic community grew. Challenged by the rapid growth of the Catholic seminary network, seminary educators by the 1950s began to share ideas to improve the quality of seminary studies in order to meet the standards of modern education. They formulated an agenda that included obtaining accreditation and improving the professional preparation of seminary faculties. Their aim, to bring the seminary out of its isolation from the modern educational world, formed an agenda of reform for the 1960s and 1970s.

The history of seminaries since the opening of Vatican Council II in 1962 is too recent to warrant more than a brief "Epilogue" on the obvious developments. Vatican II provided a charter of reform in its decree *Optatam Totius* to relate the seminary to contemporary challenges of priestly ministry. One of its most important provisions is the restoration of a measure of local and national authority to bishops in seminary matters through the formulation of each country's own seminary program. For the United States, the bishops' Program of Priestly Formation guides Catholic seminary education. The American diocesan seminaries have also responded to modern standards of professional schools and have obtained accreditation with the Association of Theological Schools, thereby reversing the tradition of isolation from the larger educational world. Finally, the seminary has been touched by profound changes in Catholic thought and life in the wake of Vatican Council II that have brought about a reconsideration of every aspect of seminary education.

Acknowledgments

The diocesan seminary is a prominent institution on the Catholic organizational landscape, yet interest in studying the seminary has been very limited within Catholic circles. The lack of historical scholarship related to the seminary has been a significant omission in American Catholic historiography and has left those responsible for contemporary seminary education without the means of understanding the background of the issues that they face. To advance the historical understanding of Protestant and Catholic seminary traditions, the religion division of the Lilly Endowment, Inc., of Indianapolis has supported major research projects related to theological education in the past decade. I thank the Endowment for generously supporting the research and writing of this book. My gratitude extends to the Endowment's vice president for religion, Robert W. Lynn, and his colleague, Frederick Hofheinz, for their lively interest and personal encouragement.

The Charles and Margaret Hall Cushwa Center for the Study of American Catholicism at the University of Notre Dame was the home for the Catholic seminary history project. Under its founding director, Jay P. Dolan, the Center provides a stimulating environment of ongoing exchanges among scholars in American church history that was an ideal setting for research and writing. I thank him for years of close personal interest and encouragement of this work, and I am grateful to the center's secretary, Delores Dant Fain, for her gracious assistance.

An advisory committee which assisted the seminary history project was chaired by Jay P. Dolan and consisted of Philip Gleason, Edmund Hussey, Christopher J. Kauffman, Christa R. Klein, Thomas F. O'Meara, O.P., and Stafford Poole, C.M. These scholars plied me with stimulating questions at regular meetings and offered valuable suggestions and criticisms to successive drafts, for which I am grateful.

By a happy coincidence, Christopher J. Kauffman was writing the history of the United States province of the Society of St. Sulpice as my work began. I thank him for sharing sources and providing me with many

xiii

ideas related to seminary history and the culture of the priesthood. The Sulpician Archives Baltimore was the richest single repository for the study, not only useful for the history of the Society of St. Sulpice in the United States but also valuable for the history of American Catholic seminaries. I am grateful for the cheerful assistance and hospitality of the archivist, John W. Bowen, S.S., during my visits to Baltimore.

I am indebted to archivists at several institutions for their unfailing assistance: Anthony Zito and Ann Crowley, S.N.D., at the Department of Archives and Manuscripts of the Catholic University of America; the staff of the University of Notre Dame Archives headed by Wendy Schlereth; and Kelly Fitzpatrick of the Department of Special Collections of Mount St. Mary's College at Emmitsburg, Maryland.

Thanks are due to John Rybolt, C.M., and John M. Young, C.M., for the benefit of their archival and historical work in Vincentian history respectively at St. Mary's Seminary, Perryville, Missouri, and St. John's University, Jamaica, New York; and to Cyprian Davis, O.S.B., Omer Kline, O.S.B., and Vincent Tegeder, O.S.B., for introducing me to the sources of American Benedictine history at St. Meinrad Archabbey and Seminary, St. Meinrad, Indiana; St. Vincent's Archabbey and Seminary, Latrobe, Pennsylvania; and St. John's Abbey and University, Collegeville, Minnesota.

I thank H. Warren Willis for his assistance at the Archives of the United States Catholic Conference, Washington, D.C., and Robert J. Wister for sharing material from his extensive research in Roman repositories.

The archives of the archdiocese of Baltimore is the most valuable of American diocesan repositories. I thank the archivist, M. Felicitas Powers, R.S.M., for gracious assistance during my visits there. In contrast, the archivists of two historic archdioceses refused to receive me for research and a third declined to respond to communications. Though diocesan archives have improved markedly in the past decade, the policies of some diocesan officials serve as reminders of how recent is a sense of responsibility for making historical records available for research. I am happy to record my thanks to the officials and archivists who received me at the diocesan archives of Boston, Cincinnati, Cleveland, Denver, Los Angeles, Milwaukee, Newark, New Orleans, Omaha, Rochester, San Diego, and San Francisco.

Many records related to diocesan seminaries are held in the seminaries themselves. I thank officials, faculty, and staff for welcoming me as researcher at the diocesan seminaries of Boston, Cincinnati, Cleveland, Denver, Milwaukee, Newark, New Orleans, New York, Rockville Center, St. Louis, and St. Paul, and at the Pontifical College Josephinum at Columbus.

I thank Ann Rice of the University of Notre Dame Press for invaluable assistance in preparation of the final manuscript.

I owe more than I can say to my parents for their love and encouragement throughout my life and their support through the years of work on this study. In gratitude I dedicate this volume to the memory of my father, Denis F. White, and to my mother, Helen Wernsing White.

Prologue: The Rise of Seminaries

The Council of Trent established in 1563 the concept of a seminary in each diocese for training priests under the direction of the local bishop. The antecedents of the seminary idea are numerous but diffuse. When the history of the seminary is considered, it has been a commonplace to designate the twelve apostles whom Jesus called and taught as the first seminary. Another antecedent is St. Augustine's practice of gathering his clergy to live a community life of prayer and study. Other precedents from the early Middle Ages onward are monastic and cathedral schools that kept ecclesiastical learning alive. By the High Middle Ages, the great medieval universities were the leading centers of theological and philosophical thought.[1] Though these important institutions related to ecclesiastical learning, their sole aim was not directed to professional training of diocesan priests.

The scholarly interest in the theology of ministry in the last quarter century has greatly advanced the understanding of how priesthood developed through successive contexts.[2] But the relationship between the development of ordained ministry and clerical training has not come into sharp focus. However, it is clear that before the Council of Trent there was no set of universal practices for training diocesan priests. The Tridentine seminary decree marks an important step in applying to the whole church the concept that preceding ordination to the priesthood there should be professional and moral training for the tasks of ministry.

The state of the clergy provides the proximate context for the concept of the seminary. Through the Middle Ages idealists regularly called for church reform. Among the church's many failings, the diocesan clergy presented an uneven picture of learning and holiness. There were great differences in the condition of the diocesan clergy, from beneficed priests and clerical servants in the households of the great, to poorly compensated parish priests, to priests unattached to a permanent position who said Mass for a stipend. In the Western church there was in effect no uniformity in the practices associated with the diocesan priesthood. Some

1

priests received an excellent education at cathedral schools or universities, while others were barely literate and prepared for holy orders as apprentices to parish clergy.

When reforms were proposed for diocesan clergy, monastic behavior was set forth as an ideal. Movements for reform prescribed the standards of behavior for diocesan priests in the enactments of church councils in the late Middle Ages. Three ecumenical councils met in the Lateran Cathedral in Rome between 1123 and 1215 to enact such reforms. The ideal of celibacy was imposed at the Second Lateran Council of 1138. However, reform decrees including those related to clerical celibacy were unevenly observed and enforced.

The great figures of the Protestant Reformation challenged the status quo in the church, including the sorry moral condition of the clergy. Their challenge went beyond protesting abuses, extending to the body of traditional teachings on the sacraments and priesthood. They sought a return to the freshness and vigor of the New Testament models of church and ministry before the development of concepts of the Eucharist as a sacrifice or ministers with sacramental characters that set them apart from the ordained. They proposed the priesthood of all believers, recognized only baptism and the Eucharist as sacraments, and stressed the authority of Scripture and the ministry of preaching.

The Council of Trent, opening in 1545, began the Catholic church's gradual and belated response to the reformers by strongly affirming the traditions of the sacraments, including holy orders, as they were understood in Catholic theology of the sixteenth century. In 1551, the council affirmed the sacrament of the Eucharist in which was contained "truly, really and substantially the body and blood together with the soul and divinity of Our Lord Jesus Christ and consequently the whole Christ."[3] The current teachings of the sacraments of penance and extreme unction were likewise restated in 1551. The twenty-second session decreed on September 17, 1562, that there was "no perfection" of the Levitical priesthood of the Old Testament and that God intended another priesthood. Accordingly, so that "His priesthood might not come to an end with His death," Jesus at the Last Supper instituted the priesthood of the New Testament. He thereby intended to leave the Mass as "a visible sacrifice, such as the nature of man requires, whereby that bloody sacrifice once to be accomplished on the cross might be represented, the memory thereof remain even to the end of the world, and its salutary effect applied to the remission of those sins which we daily commit. . . ."[4]

In the twenty-third session in 1563 the council addressed the priest in the decree on order declaring that ordination to the priesthood is truly a sacrament and properly one of the seven sacraments of the church. The effect of ordination was to imprint a character on the priest. The wording of the canon did not yield to the ideas of the reformers:

> If anyone says that there is not in the New Testament a visible and external priesthood, or that there is no power of consecrating and offering the true body and blood of the Lord and of forgiving and retaining sins, but only the office and bare ministry of preaching the Gospel; or that those who do not preach are not priests at all, let him be anathema.[5]

Other passages of the same decree reinforce the medieval worldview of hierarchical arrangements by affirming the existence of various orders of ministers "who by virtue of their office should minister to the priesthood."[6] These orders, which were once functional, were reduced to steps on the way to ordination. It assigns the order of subdeacon to the category of major orders (with priest and deacon), and lists the minor orders in descending order of acolyte, exorcist, lector, and porter. The decree affirmed the bishop as successor of the apostles to rule over the church, to supervise priests, and to administer the sacrament of orders as stated in the following canon:

> If anyone says that bishops are not superior to priests, or that they have not the power to confirm and ordain, or that the power which they have is common to them and to priests, or that order conferred by them without the consent or call of the people or of the secular power are invalid, or that those who have been neither rightly ordained nor sent by ecclesiastical and canonical authority, but come from elsewhere are lawful ministers of the word and of the sacraments, let him be anathema.[7]

The reformers had challenged the clerical celibacy that had been imperfectly observed. In addressing marriage in its twenty-fourth session in 1563, the fathers of Trent expressed a decisive preference for celibacy. The relevant canon stated: "If anyone says that the married state excels the state of virginity or celibacy, and that it is better and happier to be united in matrimony than to remain in virginity or celibacy, let him be anathema."[8]

The body of official teaching on the sacraments, especially of holy orders, was set in place for the next four centuries. The priest was distinguished from the unordained by the character of orders, called to a superior life by reason of celibacy. In an ontological, moral, and even social sense the priest's status was superior. The ministry of sacraments was the ordinary sphere of his activity. These teachings provided the framework for the future development of the seminary's aims and methods.

In twenty years of sessions the Council of Trent gradually responded to the idea of training for priests. In the fifth session in 1546, the fathers of Trent decreed that at cathedral, metropolitan, and collegiate churches which had an endowment to support a prebend for public lectures, the bishop was to assure that a qualified official carried out this duty to expound Scripture to the clergy. When such an endowment did not exist, the bishop could assign a benefice for the support of a qualified person to perform this task. At some churches, where income was modest and clergy few, then at least a teacher of grammar should be secured to teach clerics and other poor scholars. The decree was modest in scope and merely clarified and extended a known practice.[9]

After the decree of 1546, several developments served to crystalize interest in clerical training. The historian of the Council of Trent, Hubert Jedin, proposed several influences on the eventual seminary decree.[10] The first dates from the fifteenth century at Verona where the reforming bishop Gianmatteo Giberti converted his cathedral school into one exclusively for clerical training and took a personal interest in supervising the students at what became known as his "Acolyte School." Later, the early members of the Society of Jesus, formed in 1540, took an interest in training diocesan priests. Claude Jay, an early Jesuit, traveled widely in the German states as a participant in various diets, public controversies with Protestants, and local synods. As a critic of the German diocesan clergy, Jay proposed the formation of a college in each diocese to prepare ten or twelve poor boys for the priesthood. He intended these colleges to be attached to universities and circulated his ideas among German bishops with an interest in reform. The papal nuncio in the Holy Roman Empire, Cardinal Giovanni Morone, who was familiar with Jay's ideas, took up the cause of improving German diocesan clergy with the idea of a college for Germans, not in each diocese, but in Rome. With the collaboration of Ignatius Loyola, the founder of the Jesuits, Morone's initiative led to the formation of the Collegium Germanicum in 1552. The Germanicum was planned as a residential college operated by Jesuits with the students attending the Jesuit Collegium Romanum (later the Gregorian University).[11] The ordained alumni of the Germanicum were to serve in German dioceses.

The idea of residential colleges for clerical students who took formal studies elsewhere was taken up by others. In 1540 Friedrich Nausea, Bishop of Vienna, proposed the formation of residential colleges at the German universities still under Catholic influence, at Ingolstadt, Cologne, and Vienna. Augsburg's Cardinal Otto Truchsess von Waldburg had a similar idea in the 1540s but had no university in his diocese. In 1554 he obtained a pontifical charter for a university at Dillingen in order to develop a university for theological studies.

The immediate antecedent of the seminary legislation of 1563 was the plan of Cardinal Reginald Pole (1500–1558), who undertook the restoration of Catholicism in England during the brief reign of Queen Mary Tudor (1553–1559). Pole, a cousin of King Henry VIII, had been educated in Italy and had returned there after the king's break with the papacy. Created cardinal in 1536, Pole had taken part in the early sessions of the Council of Trent. Later, as papal legate and Archbishop of Canterbury, Pole presided at the synod in England in 1555 and 1556 that aimed to introduce the Catholic reform in England.

To develop the diocesan clergy, the English synod took the tradition of the cathedral school and applied it to a program of training priests. The synod's draft decree intended that each diocese gather boys at the cathedral church in proportion to the diocese's size and income to prepare them for the priesthood. The program was called a *seminarium* (seed bed), and was to admit boys at least eleven who could read and write. Preference was to be given to poor boys. The students were to be divided in classes according to age. Younger boys were to be taught grammar while the older ones were instructed in doctrine and church discipline. All were to receive the clerical tonsure, wear ecclesiastical garb, and to assist at liturgical services at the cathedral. After ordination to the priesthood, the new ordinands were to be assigned to duties at the cathedral until the appropriate benefice was found. It was permitted to admit boys who did not intend to be priests, but they were to wear the same garb and submit to the same discipline as the priesthood candidates. The synod's legislation was not completed or implemented before the deaths of Cardinal Pole and Queen Mary.[12]

The Council of Trent's commission of bishops which drafted the seminary decree initially presented a text that was nearly identical to that of Pole's synod. The final version, approved on July 15, 1563, often referred to by its Latin title, *Cum adolescentium aetas*, strongly reflects its English antecedents:

> Since the age of youth, unless rightly trained, is inclined to follow after the pleasure of the world, and unless educated from its tender years in piety and religion before the habits of vice take possession of the whole man, will never perfectly and without the greatest and well-nigh extraordinary help of Almighty God persevere in ecclesiastical discipline, the holy council decrees that all cathedral and metropolitan churches and churches greater than these shall be bound, each according to its means and the extent of its diocese, to provide for, to educate in religion, and to train in ecclesiastical discipline, a certain number of boys of their city and diocese, or, if they

are not found there, of their province, in a college located near the said churches or in some other suitable place to be chosen by the bishop.

The seminary was established at the cathedral as in the English model though exceptions were allowed. The college was to receive boys, "the sons of the poor be given preference," though the sons of the well-to-do were permitted to attend if they paid their own expenses. Students were to be of legitimate birth, at least twelve years of age, capable of reading and writing, and "whose character and inclination justify the hope that they will dedicate themselves forever to the ecclesiastical ministry." The internal life of the seminary was sketched only in very general terms but places the bishop at the heart of the undertaking:

> These youths the bishop shall divide into as many classes as he may deem proper, according to their number, age, and progress in ecclesiastical discipline, and shall, when it appears to him opportune, assign some of them to the ministry of the churches, the others he shall keep; in the college to be instructed, and he shall replace by others those who have been withdrawn, so that the college may be a perpetual seminary of ministers of God. And that they may be the better trained in the aforesaid ecclesiastical discipline, they shall forthwith and always wear the tonsure and the clerical garb; they shall study grammar, singing, ecclesiastical computation, and other useful arts; shall be instructed in Sacred Scripture, ecclesiastical books, the homilies of the saints, the manner of administering the sacraments, especially those things that seem adapted to the hearing of confessions, and the rites and ceremonies. The bishop shall see to it that they are present every day at the sacrifice of the mass, confess their sins at least once a month, receive the body of our Lord Jesus Christ in accordance with the directions of their confessor, and on festival days serve in the cathedral and other churches of the locality. All these and other things beneficial and needful for this purpose each bishop shall prescribe with the advice of two of the senior and more reputable canons chosen by himself as the Holy Ghost shall suggest, and they shall make it their duty by frequent visitation to see to it that they are always observed. [13]

The remaining two-thirds of the decree treats the methods of financing the seminary. The bishop was empowered to redirect revenues of benefices, of the cathedral chapter, or of endowed lectureships. He could also tax other endowments and privileged bodies to provide alternate means of supporting the seminary. The bishop was provided with the option, if his diocese was poor, of cooperating with a neighboring bishop or with the metropolitan in conducting a seminary. The bishop of a populous diocese could establish an additional seminary in another part of the diocese if deemed desirable.

The location for clerical formation corresponded to the institutional arrangements already in place. The seminary was added to the existing activities taking place at the cathedral, where the bishop could participate directly in its operation, the canons of the cathedral chapter could oversee it, and the students could participate in its liturgical life. There are echoes of the residential seminary along the lines of the Germanicum with provision that the diocesan seminary could be located away from the cathedral. The commitment of the fathers of Trent to the seminary is rendered somewhat limited by not making the seminary the required path for all candidates for the diocesan priesthood. It was intended for poor youth. The sons of the wellborn and the wealthy had the option of the universities.

The bishop as leader of the local church was the central figure in conducting the seminary. He was responsible for devising the content of training. His paramount role precluded development of general canonical legislation on the seminary until the early twentieth century. The bishop's role was even more important because, as Hubert Jedin states, the council did not provide an ideal model of the diocesan priest as a basis for clerical training.[14] It might, however, be stated that the council left elements for creating an ideal model of the priest in chapters and canons appearing throughout the body of Tridentine legislation that provided for faithful Catholics to receive the sacraments regularly made available by the priest's faithful ministrations.

Pope Pius IV brought the Council of Trent to a close in January 1564 and confirmed its legislation. Then began the long story of the formal implementation of Catholic reform, including the formation of seminaries. The pope set an example for implementing the seminary decree by announcing his intention to open seminaries in the Papal States at Rome and Bologna. The Roman Seminary opened on February 1, 1565, under the direction of Jesuits.

The most famous early seminary founder was the pope's nephew, Cardinal Charles Borromeo, Archbishop of Milan, who has long been regarded as the model bishop of the Tridentine reform. He began to reform his large ecclesiastical province by holding a provincial council in 1565 to legislate local reforms. The Milan council obliged each diocese of the province to open a seminary. In his own archdiocese of Milan, Borromeo opened not one seminary but several. The first, St. Charles Seminary, was intended to bring together priests who were not suited for ministry because of their lack of training or personal conduct. The second, St. John the Baptist Seminary, offered philosophical and theological studies to those who had completed classical studies. The third, the Canonica, was intended for less gifted candidates who were to study cases of conscience as preparation for hearing confession, the catechism of the Council of Trent in lieu of theology, and Scripture. Additional preparatory seminaries were formed to provide students for one of the advanced seminaries. The reform decrees of Charles Borromeo's successive provincial councils and archdiocesan synods touched on all aspects of church life, including his seminaries. Published in 1582, the *Acta Ecclesiae Mediolanensis* disseminated models of Catholic reform including the rules of governing the community life of a diocesan seminary.[15] The example of the populous and wealthy Milan archdiocese and its suffragan dioceses was followed in due course by hundreds of Italian dioceses, many very small, which formed their own diocesan seminaries.

In the German states composing the Holy Roman Empire, dioceses were larger and less numerous than in Italy. But German cathedral chapters were powerful in the politics of local ecclesiastical life and hindered the alteration of financial arrangements that would have made the formation of diocesan seminaries possible. Some of the early seminaries were pontifical establishments such as those of Fulda and Dillingen. Eventually the influence of the Collegium Germanicum in introducing the Catholic reform was felt as its graduates took their places among the German clergy and bishops. Some early diocesan seminaries were those founded in the dioceses of Eichstätt in 1564, Breslau in 1565, Würzburg in 1570, Salzburg in 1577, Basel in 1606, and Augsburg in 1614. However, seminaries had an uneven success in the century after Trent, as many of them closed because of upheaval of the Thirty Years War (1618–1648).[16]

In France, the seminary movement was slow to start. The first seminaries were outside the sixteenth-century boundaries of the kingdom. Lorraine's Duke Charles I de Guise, Cardinal and Archbishop of Rheims, started the first seminary in 1567. Located near the University of Rheims, the advanced students attended the faculty of theology and the younger students pursued a classical course. The next seminary owes its founding to Duke Charles III of Lorraine, who obtained a pontifical charter for the university at Pont-à-Mousson in 1575. Local bishops established residences for their clerical students at Rheims to attend the university faculties of theology. At Avignon, still a papal territory, the bishop formed a residential seminary and sent the students to the local Jesuit college. Within France, at Bordeaux the local bishop converted a small existing endowed college for poor boys into a clerical seminary. Other French bishops of several dioceses formed small seminaries; several operated in affiliation with the new Jesuit colleges that were being formed for lay students, but the French

seminaries were few in number and had small enrollments. Their foundations did not constitute a general trend, so that by the early 1600s, a half
century after the Council of Trent, there were only about five or six seminaries in France. [17]

The Tridentine seminary decree provided the institutional arrangements for the seminary and not the model of the priesthood to inform
the content of training. But the Tridentine reform in France, though slow,
produced the seminal figures whose religious thought established a compelling explanation of the Catholic priesthood. Through the experience
of developing an attractive spirituality for priests and seminarians, these
figures launched the movement for founding diocesan seminaries in France.

France was deeply divided between Catholics and Protestants, and
the lack of religious unity precluded the state's imposing the Tridentine
decrees as public law. Instead, the Catholic reform was introduced gradually through the media of diocesan synods, provincial councils, and national assemblies of clergy. This process required the leadership of clergy
who were activists for reformed Catholicism and capable of stimulating
religious enthusiasm.

Pierre de Bérulle was a leading figure in bringing the new spirit of
the Catholic reform to France. [18] Born in 1575 to an aristocratic family
prominent in legal circles, Bérulle attended the Jesuit College at Clermont,
where he was introduced to Ignatian spirituality before studying theology
at the Sorbonne. His devotion to mystical thought brought him in contact
with the Paris Carthusians through whom he was introduced to German
mystical literature. He also associated with the Paris Capuchins at whose
friary he made his retreat prior to ordination in 1599. He shared with his
pious family a concern to curb the spread of Protestantism and to introduce reformed Catholicism to France. As a diocesan priest of independent
means and well positioned in the elite of French society, he was able to
devote himself to the spread of the Catholic reform. His enthusiasm for
St. Teresa of Avila and her reformed Carmelites led him to sponsor the
founding of the first reformed Carmelite convent in France in 1604.

After showing interest in several movements within Catholicism, he
chose a path combining the mystical with the active that characterized
several of the figures of the Catholic reform. He was attracted to the model
of secular priests living a community life without vows. He admired the
Italian Counter-Reformation figure Philip Neri, who founded this flexible
model of religious life under the name of the Congregation of the Oratory. Bérulle introduced the oratory in France in 1611 and led the movement until his death in 1629. By then there were forty-five such communities
of priests or "oratories" in France. Among their principal works was the

giving of parish missions to promote among the laity the Tridentine ideal of regular attendance at Mass and sacramental observance. Bérulle and his followers were also interested in the reform of the French clergy and made efforts to provide spiritual preparation for ordination candidates, especially at the old Paris abbey of St. Magloire, which the Oratorians acquired as a benefice. But this new work did not yet attract the support of bishops. The Oratorians were better known in the 1620s for conducting colleges for boys.

Bérulle also demonstrated his political interests by his frequent service to the state. He served King Louis XIII and his chief minister, Cardinal Richelieu, in several diplomatic missions. The king rewarded his service to the state by having him promoted to the cardinalate in 1627. These public activities were an extension of religious activity, for Bérulle idealized the French monarchy and lived in the hope of seeing heresy extirpated and Catholic unity restored in France.

Bérulle's religious thought had a powerful impact on a generation of Catholic reformers. His devotional thought was synthesized from a variety of religious influences. With the help of his friend, Jean Duvergier, abbot of St. Cyran, he published his *Discours de l'état et des grandeurs de Jésus* in 1622. Here he compares his particular insight to the central idea of the astronomer Copernicus:

> An excellent mind of this century wishes to hold that the sun is at the center of the world and not the earth; that it is immovable, and that the earth, in proportion to its round shape moves in reference to the sun. . . . This new opinion, scarcely followed in the science of the stars is useful and ought to be followed in the science of salvation. Because Jesus is the sun, immovable in his grandeur and moving all things. . . . Jesus is the true center of the world and the world ought to be in continual movement toward him.[19]

Bérulle 's "Copernican" view of the centrality of Christ is carried forward by his specific insight on the Son of God as the Incarnate Word. Bérulle developed an approach to Christ's sharing human life and the believer's partaking in Christ's life. He employs a concept of the *état* in designating the events and "mysteries" of Christ's life. The word *state*, according to Henri Brémond, appears on nearly every page of Bérulle's writings. Bérulle states:

> In Jesus Christ there are *states* and *actions,* both worthy of especial honour and of all the attention and affection of our hearts. But particularly His *states* are to be dwelt upon, as much because they contain divers movements and actions, as because by themselves,

and by their quality of states of Jesus, they render to God an infinite homage, and to men are of greatest utility.[20]

The states of Jesus' life, such as the state of his infancy, or his childhood, his teaching, his suffering, his death, and so forth, are not just transitory historical events but permanent qualities of Jesus avilable for contemplation. Bérulle finds, for example, that Christ the Word was born "in order that he should have a divine Infancy, a deified Infancy which should honour God with a supreme honour." All the states of Jesus or mysteries of his life persist as timeless objects of contemplation. as Bérulle explains:

> The spirit of God, by which this mystery has been effected, the *interior state of the exterior mystery*, the efficacy and virtue that render this mystery quick and operative in ourselves, this state and virtuous disposition, this merit by which He has gained us for the Father . . . even the *ever present tasting*, the *lively disposition*, by which Jesus has effected this mystery, is *everquick, actual and present* in Jesus. . . . By this we are constrained to treat of the matters and mysteries of Jesus, not as passed away and extinct, but as matters quick and present, and even eternal, of which we must also gather present and eternal fruits.[21]

Exploring the "interior state of the exterior mystery" is the key concept. The complexity of the mysteries of Jesus leads the devout Bérullian to single out one state or a few states of Jesus that seem appropriate for that individual:

> Thus He gives Himself to His children, rendering them participants of the spirit and grace of His mysteries, appropriating to some His Life, and to others His Death, to one His Infancy, to another His might, to one His Hidden Life, to another His Public Life, to one His Interior Life, to another His Exterior Life. . . . His it is to adapt us as He wills to the states and mysteries of His Divine Person, and ours to cling to and appropriate them.[22]

Following Bérulle the implications of the idea of the states were soon taken up by several figures in developing the devotions characteristic of baroque Catholicism. For instance, Marguerite de Beaune, a French Carmelite nun, had a series of mystical experiences centering on Jesus as an infant that resulted in the popular organized devotion of the infancy and childhood of Jesus. A member of the Oratory, Jean Eudes, focused on the heart of Jesus as embodying Christ's forgiveness and mercy and developed the formal devotion to the Sacred Heart of Jesus. He extended the heart image to the sinlessness of Mary in organizing the devotion to the Immaculate Heart of Mary.[23] Eudes left the Oratory to found his own community of priests, the Company of Jesus and Mary (Eudists).

Bérullian ideas thereby had an impact in developing new and popular devotions that widened interest in the Catholic reform. The other figures whom Bérulle influenced — that is, the "French School" — applied aspects of his thought to the renewal of the diocesan priesthood. After Bérulle's death in 1629, this task took on a great urgency in proportion to the great need to develop a holy and zealous clergy to take the place of the often ignorant, immoral, and itinerant priests who prevailed among the French clergy.

Another influential clergyman, Adrien Bourdoise, though not under Bérulle's influence, developed a practical approach for priestly training. If a novitiate was required for joining a religious order, then it seemed to him appropriate that a diocesan priest should have spiritual and practical training in a parish. In 1612 Bourdoise formed a group of candidates for the priesthood who lived in a community at the parish of St. Nicolas du Chardonnet in Paris. The seminarians were under Bourdoise's rather severe personal direction for training in personal holiness and, for the practical aspects of ministry, under the general authority of the curé of the parish. Bourdoise formed similar groups in several other cities, but he did not intend to form a religious organization. Each group was autonomous, with the common characteristic of personal and pastoral formation in a parish. This practical model would influence subsequent figures.[24]

Among the most important figures under Bérulle's influence was Vincent de Paul.[25] Unlike several major figures of the Catholic reform in France, Vincent de Paul's origins were humble. Born around 1581 to a peasant family at the small village of Pouy in Gascony in southwestern France, Vincent aspired to the priesthood as a worthy career. A patron sponsored him at a nearby college and at the University of Toulouse for theological studies. Vincent was ordained in 1600, during his twentieth year. In the manner of clerics of his time, he wandered around Marseille, Rome, and Paris attached to several patrons. While in Paris, Vincent came under Bérulle's influence and probably made a retreat under his direction in 1611. Thereafter Vincent took an interest in the advancement of Catholic reform. At Bérulle's request, he took on periods of pastoral activity in country parishes, where he preached, taught catechism, heard confessions, and administered the sacraments among ordinary people. Also by Bérulle's arrangement, Vincent was appointed tutor in the household of the powerful Catholic Philippe-Emmanuel de Gondi. This appointment is characteristic of the emerging pattern of Vincent's life of movement to and from the rich and powerful and the poor and humble. The periodic work among the poor left Vincent with a concern for alleviating human want that made him the model of Catholic concern for practical works of charity. His related interest was the spiritual destitution of the rural poor, who lacked access to pastoral care that the urban poor had. In pursuing ministry to the rural poor, Vincent de Paul developed a homiletic approach called his "Little Method" of simple, direct, and practical preaching suitable for the uneducated, thus rejecting the influential styles of polished pulpit oratory of the period which had the effect of emphasizing style over substance.

With the patronage of the Gondi family, in 1625 Vincent formed a company of priests called "the priests of the mission," devoted to giving parish missions to the rural poor. He acquired the priory of St. Lazare, Paris, as a headquarters; hence the members were called Lazarists. In 1633 the Holy See approved his group under the name Congregation of the Mission.

Beginning in 1628 several bishops invited Vincent to give retreats to their candidates for ordination. These candidates had already received formal theological training. In 1631, François de Gondi, Archbishop of Paris, ordered all his clerics preparing for orders to participate in a fifteen-day retreat before receiving major orders. The retreats conducted at St. Lazare for ordinands consisted of exercises of piety, meditation, and theological conferences on some aspect of ministry, such as the theology of penance, and instructions on how to say Mass, administer the sacraments, and perform other ceremonies. But the retreats for ordinands did not seem altogether enough to evangelize clerics. Tuesday conferences were introduced to provide a weekly gathering of local clergy at St. Lazare, and in 1633 annual retreats for clergy were instituted.

In 1636 Vincent opened a seminary for boys in Paris called the Seminary of Bons Enfants to develop worthy clergy from an early age. In doing so, he was probably responding to a request of a high churchman. The seminary for boys represented a literal compliance with Trent's seminary decree. The boys studying at Bons Enfants did not stay with the program long enough to begin their theological studies however. The program failed, and Vincent de Paul regarded the idea of seminaries for boys as unworkable. Unlike some figures of the Catholic reform, Vincent did not have a taste for the theoretical. He looked at the practical side and considered the Tridentine seminary decree worthy of respect "as coming from the Holy Spirit" but maintained that seminaries for boys could not operate successfully.[26]

In 1642, at the behest of Cardinal Richelieu, the chief minister of France, Vincent de Paul opened at Bons Enfants a seminary for ordinands, that is, for those who were in orders or about to receive them. There, they received formation in piety, and instruction in the administration of sacraments, catechetics, preaching, and guidance for solving cases of conscience in confession. The course was to last two years and opened with an enrollment of twelve candidates. The two-year course was seen as a great improvement over a mere fifteen-day retreat, even presuming prior university instruction in theology. The 1642 founding of the seminary at Bons Enfants became a model for future French seminary foundings.

In developing another tradition of training priests, the collaboration of two figures, Charles de Condren and Jean Jacques Olier, advanced Bérullian ideas for the spiritual training of clerics. Jean Jacques Olier de Verneuil was born at Paris in 1608 to an ambitious aristocratic family.[27] Young Olier was destined for a church career to correspond to his brothers' careers in public affairs. He was given clerical tonsure at age eight and received several ecclesiastical benefices through adolescence. After attending the Jesuit college at Lyons, he pursued theological studies at the Sorbonne. His aspirations to study Hebrew led him to Rome in 1630, at which time his eyesight began to fail. After unsuccessful medical treatment, Olier made a pilgrimage on foot to the Marian shrine at Loretto, Italy. There, he was cured of his eye condition and also converted from spiritual apathy. He returned to Paris in 1631 and began to lead a life of service to the poor. He placed himself under the direction of Vincent de Paul for the retreat preceding his ordination in 1633. In the manner of his mentor, Vincent, Olier began his priestly career giving rural missions and was invited to conduct retreats for candidates for orders.

In 1634 Olier came under the influence of Charles de Condren, Cardinal de Bérulle's successor as leader of the Oratory in France. Born in 1588, Condren also came from an aristocratic background.[28] He studied theology at the Sorbonne, where he obtained the doctorate of theology and was ordained a priest in 1614. He joined Bérulle's Oratory and carried on pastoral and educational work at several cities in France. He returned to the Paris headquarters of the Oratory in 1628 where he exercised unique influence as a confidant and counsellor to ecclesiastics and lay people associated with the Catholic reform.

Condren developed a view of Christ and the priesthood that Olier extended and practiced in the work of forming priests. Condren viewed the highest of Christ's states as that of his eternal victimhood. This victimhood, in effect, was synonymous with his other states, all of which involved Christ's surrendering himself to human form. Victimhood had a particular relevance to Christ's state as a priest. As the perfect victim his sacrifice on the cross was the act of priestly mediation that made redemption possible. The resurrected Christ in heaven is the eternal victim and priest and therefore the source of grace. The ordained priest reproduces Christ and provides the means of grace to believers through the Mass and the sacraments. The modern Sulpician scholar Eugene Walsh summarizes the French School's identification of Christ with the priest:

The character of Holy Orders confers, as it were, a new nature, a new personality upon the priest. He is drawn by ordination into the personality of Christ, and with Him becomes by state, by an ontological reality, an official person. . . .

According to the essential economy of sanctification the spirit of Jesus is given to the priest by the character of Sacred Orders to continue the life of Jesus, head and sanctifier of His mystical body. It is the priest in whom Jesus lives in order to communicate the spirit of His grace and power to each member of the Church. By this state of headship in which Holy Orders establishes him the priest is obliged to do on earth all [that] Christ does in heaven. He gives Christ's body to the Church to nourish it. He gives the Spirit of Jesus to the Church to sanctify it. He gives the sacrifice of Jesus to His Church for its own. The relations that the priest has to the Church by reason of Holy Orders is in every respect a created copy of the relation that Christ has to His mystical body, as head of that body.[29]

The figures of the French School had thereby extended the themes of the character of the priest and his separateness from the unordained. They undertook to prepare the candidate for holy orders with a spirituality of close identification with the victimhood and priesthood of Christ and a lifestyle of self-denial. The ordinand was then disposed to receive the sacrament of orders and take on the supernatural work of imparting grace through the sacraments.

Through the 1630s, Olier responded to this sublime conception of the priest. Despite pressures from his ambitious family, he declined nominations to the episcopate. Instead, after a period of spiritual and mental trials and at Condren's urging, Olier devoted himself to the work of forming diocesan clergy. This was a natural extension of the work of parish missions that would have lasting results only with the raising of the spirituality and behavior of the parish clergy from its low state.

Invited to Chartres by the local bishop in 1641, Olier began to give retreats for ordinands. This work was soon moved to Vaugirard, a small village near Paris, late in 1641. A better location and wider stage for seminary work soon developed in the parish of St. Sulpice, located in the rapidly growing Faubourg St. Germain section of Paris. St. Sulpice, the largest parish in Paris and possibly the largest in France, was under the jurisdiction of the abbey of St. Germain, which was a benefice of Henri de Bourbon, a bastard son of King Henry IV. With the latter's approval, the incumbent curé ceded the parish to Olier, who became curé or pastor in August 1642. He installed a community of priests and seminarians at the parish.

The parish priests lived at the parochial house at St. Sulpice, while the clerical students sent by their bishops lived in a separate house with priest directors. The young clerical students assisted at church services on Sundays and feast days and shared in the huge task of religious instruction for thousands of parish children. The seminarians, if they had not already pursued formal studies, took them with the theological faculty of the Sorbonne, supplementing the academic program at their residence at St. Sulpice with the spiritual conferences and practical training in ceremonies, administering sacraments, solving cases of conscience, and teaching catechism. The clerical students, therefore, functioned in several contexts: the university, the parish church, and the house discipline, where they received individual spiritual direction and participated in religious exercises. There was no set period of time for the seminary course since students joined the community at various stages of their preparation. A student might stay for weeks or months prior to ordination.

The keystone of the spiritual preparation of the ordinands consisted of the method of mental prayer developed by figures of the French School.[30] In the spirit of Bérulle's appropriation of the states and actions of Jesus, the method stressed union with Christ the Incarnate Word. Its essential elements were: first, adoration, in which the person praying takes some state, action, or attribute of Jesus and renders adoration, admiration, praise, thanksgiving, or love to Christ or to God for that quality; second, communion, in which the person is drawn into the virtue or perfection adored; and third, cooperation, in which a resolution is made to practice the quality under consideration. The identity with the states and attributes of Christ could be appropriated in a method of prayer practiced as a seminarian and later as a priest. The self-abnegation of seminary life, with its enforced silences, simplicity of living arrangements, and discipline of community exercises approximated the emptying of self. Olier's summary of the purpose of the seminary in his brief guide to seminarians, the *Pietas Seminarii*, was based on Bérullian spirituality:

> The first and ultimate end of this institute is to live supremely for God, in Christ Jesus our Lord, in order that the interior disposition of His Son may so penetrate the very depths of our heart, that each may say what St. Paul confidently affirmed of himself. . . . "I live, but it is not I who live but it is Christ who liveth in me!" Such shall be the sole hope of all, their sole meditation, their sole exercise, to live the life of Christ interiorly, and to manifest it exteriorly in their mortal body.[31]

Olier's program of training candidates for orders prospered at St. Sulpice, and the parish work expanded. A new, baroque parish church and seminary building were constructed to house the growing number of seminarians from many dioceses. St. Sulpice was thereby firmly on the way to becoming the most famous diocesan seminary in France. Olier, who originally had no thought of directing a seminary other than the one of St. Sulpice, received invitations from bishops to conduct seminaries in their dioceses. By the time of his death in 1657, Olier had sent priests of the Society of St. Sulpice to conduct new diocesan seminaries at Nantes, Viviers, Puy, and Clermont.[32] Though the Society expanded its activities to several places, it remained an organization of diocesan priests and not a religious community bound by vows.

At the same time, Vincent de Paul's congregation of the Mission accepted the invitations of bishops and conducted new diocesan seminaries of Annecy, Alet, Cahors, Le Mans, Saint Meen, Marseille, Treguier, Agen, Périgueux, Montauban, Narbonne, and Saintes in the years before his death in 1660.[33] In a similar fashion, Jean Eudes accepted the direction of seminaries in Normandy for his priests of the Company of Jesus and Mary.

Thus, by the 1660s, a century after the Council of Trent, the French seminaries were well under way. Bishops established them and staffed them with communities of clerics who focused on the conclusion of the seminarian's training. The French bishops did not comply with the literal wording of the seminary decree by taking poor boys from age twelve to study grammar and other subjects of a general education before progressing to theological studies at the cathedral under the care of the local diocesan clergy.

The paramount interest of the new French seminaries was the spiritual disposition of the candidate for ordination. Whether the ordinands had a brief retreat or a longer program of training, they were drawn to a realization of the loftiness of the priesthood through a spirituality of close identification with Christ. The ordinands also were trained in practical matters such as administration of the sacraments, the solving of cases of conscience as preparation for hearing confession, catechetics, and preaching to carry on the activities of the new Tridentine Catholicism. But it was the power of the spirituality that paved the way for developing a highly motivated and well-behaved parish clergy that the authors of the Tridentine seminary decree desired but did not articulate.

The network of French seminaries expanded through the late seventeenth century as interest in reform of the clergy spread among French bishops. Local situations played a role in the opening of seminaries as a bishop desiring to found a seminary had to come to terms with the canons of his cathedral chapter and their willingness to redirect endowed revenues for its support. During his pious old age Louis XIV gave official support in a decree of 1698 ordering the opening of seminaries in dioceses that had none. The growth of French seminaries expanded the influence of the Sulpicians and Vincentians who were invited to staff them.[34]

Louis Tronson, superior of St. Sulpice from 1676 to 1700, was the codifier and organizer of the Sulpician way. He edited Olier's *Treatise on Holy Orders* (1676), a systematic exposition of the founder's views on the priesthood. Tronson's *Forma Cleri* was his own contribution to the theology of priesthood and his *Examen Particulier* provided an influential manual for the seminarian's and the priest's ongoing self-scrutiny along the road to a lifetime of holiness.[35]

Vincent de Paul's Congregation of the Mission continued the work of parish missions to the country poor, from whom the congregation naturally drew its rapidly growing membership. Its large though humble membership contrasted with St. Sulpice's small membership drawn from the rich and noble. Vincent de Paul's followers spread his work and name throughout Europe, principally in Spain, Italy, and Poland. The Vincentians eventually engaged in missionary activities in Asia and Africa. Thus staffing seminaries was but one aspect of Vincentian activity.[36]

The expansion of seminaries had consequences for the manner in which they were conducted. French seminaries were initially intended to offer spiritual formation and pastoral education, not theology. Vincent de Paul, Olier, and their collaborators had received theological education at universities. But as diocesan seminaries opened in small cathedral towns where there was no university and few university graduates, they began to offer theological instruction to aspirants to the priesthood. The introduction of formal theology had the effect of lengthening the course from a few weeks or months to a period of six months to one or two years, according to the qualifications of the students or the desires and resources of the local bishop.[37]

The lengthening course of studies in seminaries created the need for pedagogical literature. The 1680s, according to Yves Congar, was the time for the emergence of a body of theological literature appropriate for seminary use. Its purpose was to present a concise and comprehensive body of Catholic doctrine, thereby pushing most current theological controversies to the margin.[38] These works are the starting point of the tradition of textbook or manual theology that became the hallmark of seminary instruction for the following two and a half centuries.

Despite the comprehensive nature of its presentation, a bishop's choice of manual for his seminary was often dictated by its position on current theological issues. The influence of St. Augustine's thought in the age of reform gave rise to a rigorous approach to questions of grace. For instance, Cornelius Jansen, Bishop of Ypres, expounded in his *Augustinus* a restrictive view of God's grace. The practical manifestation of a concern for rigor lay in the approach to the sacrament of penance. The Council of Trent required Catholics to confess their sins once a year, and thus moral questions took on great importance in seminary learning. The new rigor challenged the older moral theology of probabilism which allowed, when there was a difference of interpretation among moral opinions, the less probable — that is, the more liberal of several opinions. In the seventeenth century, however, Jansenist moralists challenged probabilism as too lax. The successive condemnation of Jansenist propositions by several popes, culminating in the condemnation of 101 propositions in Quesnal's *Reflexions morales* by Pope Clement XI in his decree *Unigenitus Dei Filius* of 1713, did not dampen the attractions of rigor. In 1700, France's assembly of clergy endorsed a stern moral system called probabiliorism that was Jansenist in tone. According to this system, when there was a difference of canonical opinion on a moral question, the opinion in favor of the law was to be adopted as more probable (*probabilior*) than the opinion in favor of liberty.[39] The confessor thus had more cause for denying absolution to penitents.

Moreover, absolution from mortal sin was in itself not regarded as sufficient grounds for permitting the reception of Holy Communion. A tendency to fall into venial sin was regarded as a sound reason to forbid communion to avoid an unworthy reception of the sacrament. The decision for communion was the basis for an onging dialogue between confessor and penitent over the latter's interior dispositions. The net effect was to restrict communion and to regard it as a reward for rigorous virtue, which remained a common Catholic approach to the issue well into the nineteenth century.

Another major issue was ecclesiology. The French church, that is, the Gallican church under the absolute monarch Louis XIV, regarded itself as free from the direction of the Holy See except in carefully defined areas. A general council of the church, not the pope, was regarded as infallible. The French state enacted and the national church accepted the Four Articles of 1682 to confirm the Gallican church's historic liberties, and this "Gallicanism" became the normative approach to the nature of the church in French seminary instruction.

The texts used for seminary instruction in France were adopted within the context of these theological currents.[40] In the seventeenth century, the Vincentians relied on the *Medulla theologica* of Louis Abelly (1603–1691), doctor of theology, friend of Vincent de Paul. In keeping with the nonintellectual approach of Vincent de Paul, who emphasized the vanity of learning, Abelly's two-volume manual, one each in dogma and moral theology, emphasized practical, concise treatment of basic theological questions with speculative matters excluded. Since it was brief, its use could easily be adjusted to the varying course lengths in the numerous seminaries that the Vincentians conducted. On moral questions Abelly's approach was probabilist, thereby assuring opposition from rigorists.

The Sulpicians, though not offering formal theology at St. Sulpice, taught theology at their other seminaries. They relied on Abelly or the work of Raymond Bonal (b. 1600). Bonal, doctor of theology and diocesan priest, published eight editions of his *Cours de theologie morale*. It was a popular moral textbook — probably because it was published in French, which was highly unusual, but it eventually was translated into Latin.

With the coming of the eighteenth century, shorter manuals gave way to longer ones with emphasis on dogma to accommodate more seminaries that had a longer course, usually about two years. After enactment of the Gallican Four Articles of 1682, ecclesiology was not a controverted issue in seminary instruction, and probabiliorism was generally adopted in the manuals of the eighteenth century. Of fourteen manual authors whose works were in use in French seminaries from the 1690s to 1789, the most widely used were the theology of Poitiers and the manuals of Honoré Tournely and Pierre Collet.[41]

The bishop of Poitiers ordered professors of his seminary to compile a textbook for seminary use. It appeared in four volumes in 1708 and grew in size with successive editions through the century. With successive editions its ecclesiology developed from a favorable regard for papal authority toward a more Gallican approach. The manual was forthrightly probabiliorist in moral questions. The theology of Poitiers continued to appear in revised editions in the nineteenth century under the common name of the theology of Toulouse.

Honoré Tournely (1658–1729), theology professor at Douai and the Sorbonne, was an active opponent of Jansenism in numerous exchanges of pamphlets. In 1725–29 he published for use in seminaries his *Praelectiones theologicae*, which had many editions before his death in 1739. However, he did not publish a moral theology to challenge the probabiliorists. After his death, Pierre Collet (1693–1770), a Vincentian who taught at St. Lazare in Paris, was charged by the archbishop of Paris with editing and expanding Tournely's work. Collet incorporated a probabiliorist moral theology and added many volumes to those of Tournely. An abridged edition for more convenient use in seminaries appeared in 1767.

By the late eighteenth century, French seminaries generally had adopted textbooks that were rigorist in moral theology and Gallican in ecclesiology. On the eve of the French Revolution, such seminary instruction was carried on throughout France's 130 dioceses. Though some small dioceses had not succeeded in sustaining a seminary, the country still had about 130 diocesan seminaries, as several large sees had more than one. Of these, the Vincentians staffed fifty-six, and Sulpicians conducted fifteen, while other communities conducted most of those remaining.[42] Less than thirty seminaries were entrusted to diocesan priests. The French church, as the wealthiest and most influential in Europe, had for all practical purposes successfully fulfilled the Tridentine ideal of each diocese sponsoring a seminary and was thus supplied with the best trained clergy in Europe.

In other parts of Europe, the success of seminary foundings varied, and seminary life reflected different local contexts.

In Italy, hundreds of small and poor dioceses attempted seminaries. From Trent to 1600, 128 diocesan seminaries were opened — seventy during the seventeenth century, and forty during the eighteenth century.[43] In many Italian cities, the cathedral with flanking episcopal residence and diocesan seminary expressed the Tridentine ideal of the seminary operating in close proximity to the bishop's court and the urban cathedral. The quality of the many seminaries varied drastically with the size and resources of each diocese. Many had so few students that a division of them by age and classes was not possible. Several were exceptional, such as the lavishly financed seminary of Padua renowned in the seventeenth century for the quality of learning demanded by its bishop, Gregorio Barbarigo.

Through the eighteenth century plans were advanced for the reform or redirection of Italian seminaries. In 1725 the Dominican Pope Benedict XIII established the Congregation of Seminaries to promote the founding of seminaries, to enforce new canonical legislation that permitted bishops to direct diocesan and clerical revenues to sustain seminaries, and to settle disputes between the bishop and clergy or religious orders who conducted seminaries. Because state control of church life was pervasive in Europe during the eighteenth century, the effect of this Roman initiative was largely confined to the Papal States. It did not so much advance the Holy See's control of the seminaries but reinforced the bishop's ability to develop the seminary as provided under the Tridentine seminary decree.[44]

As was the case in the French School, in Italy too the importance of an influential individual often exceeded the impact of church legislation. In eighteenth-century Italy, St. Alphonsus Liguori (1696–1787) was such a figure.[45] After his ordination in 1726, Liguori zealously conducted rural parish missions, at first in the Kingdom of Naples and then with his followers in other parts of Italy, in order to return Catholics to the sacraments. In 1732, he founded a community of priests, the Congregation of the Most Holy Redeemer (Redemptorists), to carry on this task. Liguori's writings on preaching parish missions and spreading popular devotions informed his instructional materials for the priest. His *Dignity and Duties of the Priest; or Selva*, with its traditional exalting of the priesthood, offers instructions on the priest's spiritual life emphasizing mental prayer and regular devotional practices (especially devotion to the Virgin Mary), self-denial, and zeal for pastoral activity. It became one of the influential works for priests in the following centuries.

As a practitioner of the parish mission, Liguori was concerned to make the sacrament of penance available to ordinary people. A former lawyer, Liguori devised a more workable theory of moral theology, called equiprobabilism, to oppose the excessive rigor of the probabiliorists while still avoiding laxity. Equiprobabilism pursued a middle ground between law and liberty, had the effect of reducing the pretexts for denying penitents absolution, and made confession and thereafter communion more accessible to ordinary Catholics. Liguori challenged the probabiliorist status quo and set moral theology on a less rigorous path. His approach became normative in Catholicism in the nineteenth century.

In the states of the Holy Roman Empire, the seminary developed slowly following the Thirty Years War. In 1660, Bartholomäus Holzhauser formed a community of diocesan priests to conduct the Mainz seminary and in 1679 that of Würzburg. Holzhauser's institute conducted others for short periods of time but did not enjoy the continuous institutional successes experienced by the French communities of clerics.[46] German diocesan seminaries, often disrupted by war and politics, began to develop more steadily during the early eighteenth century.

By the late eighteenth century, the Enlightenment and the absolutist governments throughout Europe were having an impact on diocesan seminaries. In Spain enlightened governments aimed to reform seminaries along the lines of broader learning and uniform standards by prescribing studies in liberal arts and sciences, requiring the staff to reside in the seminary, and by making the studies subject to government inspection. The suppression of the Jesuits in Spain in 1767 left property and resources available to create new diocesan seminaries. Accordingly, in the three decades after 1759 ten new diocesan seminaries were formed in Spain, several in former Jesuit buildings.[47]

In the Habsburg dominions, official reforms were directed to eliminating small seminaries and creating larger ones, where a well-trained faculty could teach more students. In the 1780s, the Enlightened Emperor Joseph II planned six regional diocesan seminaries in the Habsburg crown lands for the Low Countries, northern Italy, and central Europe. The rationality and efficiency of the plan challenged the more personal tradition of the Tridentine seminary that brought bishop, local clergy, and seminarians together. As with the Emperor's other reforms, the seminary plan was not popular and was only partially implemented.

The internal life of seminaries was also subject to the Emperor's reforms. This task was entrusted to the Bohemian Benedictine abbot Franz Stephan Rautenstrauch (1734–1886), who directed the seminary reform and devised a "Plan for the Direction of Theological Schools."[48] Rautenstrauch's reform stressed bibilical studies in their original languages, patristics, church history, and a minimum of dogmatic and moral theology. The language of instruction was the vernacular, not Latin. Three years were devoted to the subject of "pastoral theology," a new term but not a new concept, that embraced instruction in the sacramental, liturgical, and practical aspects of pastoral activity. A noteworthy figure in developing pastoral theology of the Enlightenment was Matthäus Fingerlos, a Salzburg priest who became director of the seminary there, which was under the dominion of the Prince-Archbishop of Salzburg. Fingerlos's highly rational approach to ministry minimized the dogmatic and supernatural aspects of Catholicism and emphasized the social and practical.[49]

In other German states, the international suppression of the Society of Jesus in 1773 released resources and buildings for the opening of a new round of diocesan seminaries. These appeared at Trier in 1773, Münster in 1776, Paderborn in 1777, and Hildesheim in 1780; several seminaries such as Trier's became noted for their quality of learning.[50]

By the close of the eighteenth century, over two hundred years had elapsed since the formulation of Trent's seminary decree. During that period, compliance with the decree had been uneven and varied. Specific provisions, though stated in general terms to accommodate various interpretations, had not always been observed. Authors of the decree could not have foreseen the rise of the great seventeenth-century figures associated with the French School, who exercised such a powerful influence on the modes and spirituality of the priesthood. Likewise the importance of textbooks in seminary learning had not been foreseen at the time of Trent. Despite the influence of Enlightenment thinking in German-speaking Europe, traditional emphasis in the seminaries remained on the high dignity of the priesthood and the corresponding need for moral and spiritual training. At the end of the century, the great upheaval of the French Revolution and subsequent years of European warfare closed diocesan seminaries in France and other parts of Europe. As Europe's patterns of seminary life came to a temporary halt, the Catholic community in the United States was beginning its formal organizational life, including the founding of seminaries which relied on French models of training.

PART I

Forming Traditions, 1780s to 1884

The century from the 1780s to 1884 spans a period that begins with the formal organization of the Catholic Church in the United States and ends with the Third Plenary Council of Baltimore. During the century, immigrants from Catholic Europe swelled the American Catholic community from thirty thousand members and about thirty priests scattered in Maryland and Pennsylvania to a body of over six million members served by 6,000 priests in dioceses extending across the country.

Through this century of growth, the Catholic community developed ecclesiastical institutions in many local settings. For the development of a diocesan clergy, bishops depended heavily on priests and seminarians recruited from Europe. At the same time, bishops and other church leaders founded seminaries in the expectation of providing a clergy trained in the United States. Neither the American bishops collectively nor Roman authorities imposed some grand design for building a network of diocesan seminaries. Instead, church leaders established seminaries in response to local needs and interests at locations across the country. Though the local bishop had authority over the seminary operating in his diocese, as was consistent with the Tridentine seminary decree, church leaders did not apply the decree's wording literally to determine the seminary's institutional format, location, or personnel. The record of founding and early development of seminaries differed from place to place.

In the first diocese, Baltimore, several seminaries developed following differing institutional models. Baltimore's record contrasts with the founding and then closing of numerous local seminaries as new dioceses were formed. The local seminary gave way to the development of the free-standing seminary at a few important dioceses. Several religious orders took responsibility for training diocesan priests and established their own diocesan seminaries in affiliation with lay colleges and other activities. The attraction of clerical training in Europe resulted in the opening of American colleges at Rome and Louvain affiliated with local universities.

The demand for priests as ministers of sacraments to a rapidly growing immigrant church required that they be trained quickly. The absence of specific church legislation governing the content of seminary learning and the length of its course of studies allowed for a brief course of only a few years of theological study. By the 1870s, the limited status and professional qualities of Catholic priests in the United States were openly discussed. These issues were among the pressing problems leading to the convocation of the Third Plenary Council of Baltimore in 1884. At the council, the American bishops addressed the problems of the clergy in a series of decrees on clergy rights, seminary studies, and graduate education that set new standards for strengthening the internal life of the diocesan seminary.

1. Baltimore and Emmitsburg

E nglish Catholics landed at St. Clement's Island in the Potomac estuary on March 25, 1634, to settle the proprietary colony that King Charles I had granted to the Catholic Cecil Calvert, second Lord Baltimore. As a proprietary colony, Maryland, named in honor of King Charles's Catholic queen, Henrietta Marie, was a commercial venture, but it was also intended to provide a refuge for Lord Baltimore's co-religionists from English penal laws. The founding colonists were mostly Protestants, and they continued to outnumber Catholics in the colony's subsequent history. However, Maryland is distinctive as the cradle of Catholicism in the English colonies that became the United States. From Maryland's rural communities of Catholics, the Catholic church began its formal organization in the United States after the American Revolution. In 1789 the seat of the first Catholic diocese in the United States was established at Baltimore, Maryland's largest city, where the country's first Catholic seminary was soon opened. The archbishops of Baltimore functioned as the spiritual leaders of American Catholics into the early twentieth century. The seminaries formed within the Baltimore jurisdiction, made an archdiocese in 1808, remained influential nationally even as dioceses and seminaries multiplied across the United States in the nineteenth century.

From Maryland's founding, English members of the Society of Jesus ministered to its Catholics. The Jesuits received their seminary training in Europe and were subject to the authority of their English superior until 1773 when Pope Clement XIV suppressed the Society of Jesus. The former Jesuits continued to minister to Catholics scattered in rural estates and towns in Maryland and Pennsylvania through the era of the American Revolution.

Such was the state of affairs when John Carroll, priest and former Jesuit, arrived in his native Maryland in the late spring of 1774, twenty-six years after leaving as a boy of twelve. In those intervening years he had pursued his education at the Jesuit college at St. Omer in French Flanders, entered the Society of Jesus, was ordained priest in 1761, and pursued a teaching career at Liège, Bologna, and Bruges. After the painful experience of seeing the order to which he had vowed his life suppressed, Carroll returned home to live with his mother at her estate at Rock Creek, Montgomery County, Maryland. From there he engaged in a round of ministerial visitations to Catholics scattered in Maryland and northern Virginia.[1]

Maryland's Catholic community had not changed greatly since Carroll left in 1748. Its priests were now former Jesuits, but they continued their rounds to minister to Catholics in Maryland and in Pennsylvania. The priests continued to derive financial support from the estates that they owned as Jesuits. Since the suppression of the Society of Jesus, spiritual jurisdiction had changed. The Maryland missions and priests came under the jurisdiction of the vicar apostolic of the London district, one of the four missionary bishops residing in Great Britain. Distance rendered this connection between Maryland and London tenuous, and the rebellion of the colonies between 1775 and 1781 rendered it nonexistent in practical terms.

The state of the Catholic community forced Carroll to consider its future in the newly independent nation. The priests were aging, and occasionally one of them died, raising the fear that eventually all would die and leave Catholics without priests. With the separation of American Catholics from ties to ecclesiastical authority in Great Britain, Carroll proposed on his own a "Plan of Organization" in 1782 for the administration of the clerical property in Maryland to support the former Jesuit priests and to provide for the governance of the Catholic missions in Maryland and Pennsylvania. In a series of meetings in 1783 and 1784 at Whitemarsh plantation, Maryland, the former Jesuit priests formed a Constitution of the Clergy to govern their temporal affairs, although nominally they remained under the spiritual jurisdiction of the vicar apostolic in London.

Carroll believed that the Catholic community, present in Maryland for a century and a half, constituted a church, and since national independence had been achieved, it was the equivalent of the national churches in Catholic countries. It should not be considered a "mission" nor subject to the church's missionary arm, the Sacred Congregation of Propaganda Fide (hereafter referred to as Propaganda), which administered church affairs in missionary countries in Asia and Africa or in Great Britain. His views on a number of issues flowed from his idea of the character of the American church. For instance, he was annoyed when Propaganda appointed him "Superior of the Mission" in the United States in 1784 and therefore subject to its grant of faculties. This appointment was the act of a foreign tribunal likely to be resented in the newly independent United States. Carroll accepted the appointment but preferred the formation of a diocese headed by a bishop with normal rights.[2]

Carroll's views on the autonomy of the national church included a concern for the local development of a clergy "to perpetuate a succession of labourers in this vineyard."[3] He professed that "the object nearest my heart is to establish a college on this continent for the education of youth, which might at the same time be a seminary for future clergymen."[4] Throughout the 1780s he pursued the establishment of a college through the priest's official organization, the Select Body of the Clergy, raising funds, selecting the location, and overseeing the construction of a building. The result was Georgetown Academy, which opened in the Maryland town of that name in 1791 under the direction of the former Jesuit priests.[5] It was to be, as Carroll envisioned, the "main sheet anchor for Religion" in the formation of the clergy of the American Catholic church.[6]

In due course, the objectionable form of church governance under a "superior of the mission" came to an end. In 1788 the American priests petitioned the Holy See for the formation of a diocese headed by an ordinary bishop for the United States, rather than establish the system of vicars apostolic as existed in England. Thus, when the need for a bishop residing in the United States was made clear to Roman authorities, Pope Pius VI established the diocese of Baltimore in 1789, though subject to Propaganda's administration. The American priests for this one time were permitted to nominate their first bishop. They chose John Carroll.

In June 1790, Carroll sailed to England for a visit that had two major results. The intended purpose of the visit was to receive episcopal ordination from Bishop Charles Walmesley, vicar apostolic for the London district, at Lulworth Castle, Dorset. The rite took place on August 15, 1790. A second and unintended outcome was a plan for the first diocesan seminary in the United States.

The first American diocese was established in 1789 as the early stages of the French Revolution were in progress. In the summer of 1790, Jacques André Emery, ninth superior of the Society of St. Sulpice, assessed the current dangers for his society. The revolutionary government posed a major threat to the Society with the requirement that clergy take the oath to the Civil Constitution of the Clergy, which would subordinate the clergy to the state. Emery opposed the oath though he foresaw as a consequence of refusing it the destruction of the Society of St. Sulpice. Emery conceived the idea of making a Sulpician establishment in the New World to continue the work of forming priests. He presented his idea to the papal nuncio to France, Archbishop Antoine Dugnani, who told him that the diocese of Baltimore had just been erected and that its first bishop was then in England for his episcopal ordination.[7]

Emery obtained the approval of the consultors of the Society to propose to Bishop Carroll the opening of a Sulpician seminary in his diocese.

The superior wrote to Carroll in London to make the offer. Knowing that the new diocese could not fund the project, Emery promised that Sulpicians would fund the undertaking. Carroll was interested but expressed doubts about the success of a seminary since there were as yet no candidates for the priesthood who had completed classical studies at Georgetown College. He believed the Sulpicians might for some time be underemployed. Carroll had only about thirty-five priests in his new diocese; he proposed that several Sulpicians engage in missionary work among "the flourishing congregations on the banks of the Ouabache [Wabash]" in what was then the western part of the United States, where French-speaking Catholics lived.[8] The bishop of Quebec no longer had jurisdiction over these areas, but there were no French priests available to minister there. To discuss these issues, Emery sent François Charles Nagot, a vice president of the Seminary of St. Sulpice, to visit Carroll in London. Undeterred by the problems that Carroll raised, the Sulpicians agreed to come to America. The new bishop directed that they be located at Baltimore, the seat of the new diocese.

The Sulpician founders sailed from France on April 8, 1791, landing at Baltimore on July 10. The group consisted of four priests — François Charles Nagot, the superior; Jean Tessier, Antoine Garnier, and Michel Levadoux — plus five seminarians: two Englishmen, one Canadian, one American, and one Frenchman. A week after their arrival they acquired a house known as the "One Mile Tavern" about a mile from Baltimore harbor. Here they set up their household, having brought the necessary furnishings, liturgical wares, and books from France. And in this place they inaugurated the first diocesan seminary in the United States.

Bishop Carroll had a fully staffed seminary for his new diocese. He also had a greatly augmented local clergy to add dignity to the liturgical services at his modest and temporary St. Peter's Pro-cathedral in Baltimore. He referred to the Sulpicians as the "clergy of my cathedral" in expressing his satisfaction to the Prefect of the Sacred Congregation of Propaganda Fide, Cardinal Antonelli:

> All our hopes are founded on the Seminary of Baltimore. Since the arrival of the priests of St. Sulpice, the celebration of the offices of the Church and the dignity of divine worship have made a great impression, so that, though the church of Baltimore is hardly worthy of the name of cathedral, if we consider its style and its size, it may be looked upon as an episcopal church in view of the number of its clergy.[9]

In 1792 more Sulpician priests with seminarians arrived from France, including several who would be influential leaders in the American church:

Jean Baptiste David, Benedict Flaget, Ambrose Maréchal, Gabriel Richard, and the seminarian Stephen Badin. They began the tradition of Sulpicians arriving from France that would last till the end of the nineteenth century. Several early Sulpicians, as Carroll had proposed, were destined for the missions of the "Ouabache" and other places in the west, where they played a crucial role in establishing the Catholic church in that region.

The Seminary of St. Sulpice at Baltimore, as it was then called, produced its first priest in 1792 when Bishop Carroll ordained Stephen Badin. Badin had taken most of his training at the seminary of Orléans, France. The occasion was the first time Carroll ordained. However, ordinations were few in the early years. Only one student came to the seminary from Georgetown College, regarded as the school that would supply a steady flow of seminarians trained in the classics. The seminary enrolled only sixteen students in its first dozen years. On the other hand, students had been withdrawn from the seminary to teach at struggling Georgetown College. Two Sulpicians, William DuBourg and Benedict Flaget, served as president and vice president of Georgetown.

William DuBourg, a flamboyant personality prone to large plans and big expenditures, left Georgetown's presidency in 1798 after differences with the diocesan clergy there. A native of Saint-Domingue in the West Indies, DuBourg had an interest in the French refugees of revolution residing in Baltimore and in Havana as well, where the Sulpicians Pierre Babad and Benedict Flaget had gone to work among them. DuBourg followed them to Havana in 1799, full of ideas of establishing a college that would supply graduates to attend the seminary in Baltimore. When the Spanish authorities delayed permission for such a venture, DuBourg returned to Baltimore, bringing along three Cuban boys to be taught in his proposed college for lay students. With the persuasiveness that was one of his characteristics, DuBourg quickly secured permission of Nagot and Bishop Carroll to permit the opening of a lay college at the seminary. His "French school" began with the three Cuban and three local French boys in late August 1799. It was soon known as St. Mary's College and gave an additional work to the Sulpicians, who enrolled only one seminarian in the year the college opened.[10] In this hurried fashion, the Sulpicians had opened a school which directly competed with Georgetown for lay students.

DuBourg, as president, ambitiously expanded the college. At first, St. Mary's College received only French and Spanish boys, but by 1803 American students were numbered among its students. In 1805 the Maryland legislature incorporated St. Mary's College and empowered it to grant degrees. A new building was completed in 1804 to accommodate the growing enrollment of Catholic and Protestant boys. And Baltimore's leading architect, Maximilian Godefroy, was engaged to design a graceful chapel that was completed in 1808 to serve the seminary, college, and local Catholics.

The diocesan clergy in charge of Georgetown naturally resented the competition of the Baltimore institution. In 1800 they retained their recent graduates who intended to be clerics by offering them a philosophy course so they could teach part-time and in this manner prevented them from going to the seminary at Baltimore. Such an expression of resentment aimed at the Sulpicians seemed beyond the powers of Bishop Carroll to control.

Georgetown's action left the Baltimore seminary without seminarians. From Paris, Jacques Emery threatened to withdraw the Sulpicians if Carroll could not supply the seminary with candidates for the priesthood. The bishop was naturally alarmed at the prospect of losing the Sulpicians. He begged Emery not to withdraw them. At the same time Emery protested to DuBourg that the conduct of St. Mary's College was a radical departure from the Sulpician vocation to train priests. While DuBourg expanded the potential enrollment by taking in American Catholics and even Protestants to keep the college going, he was testing the superior general's patience. In 1803, the Sulpicians Maréchal, Levadoux, and Garnier returned to France in response to Emery's recall.

When Pope Pius VII came to Paris in 1804 for Napoleon's coronation, Emery reported to him on the work of the Society of St. Sulpice, including its work in the United States. The superior told the pope of the expected recall of more Sulpicians from Baltimore to staff seminaries that were currently being reopened in France. The pope responded with remarks that prevented the closing of the Baltimore seminary: "My son, let it remain; yes, let that seminary exist; for it will bear its fruit in time. Recalling the directors to employ them at other houses in France would be to rob Peter to pay Paul."[11]

As the closing of the Baltimore seminary was averted, its enrollment improved slightly during the first decade of the nineteenth century so that its future seemed secure. The effort to form a minor or *petit* seminary for boys who would graduate to the major or *grande* seminary of Baltimore continued. It was clear that Georgetown could not function as a "feeder" school for the seminary as Bishop Carroll had hoped. Eventually the restoration of the Society of Jesus in 1815 afforded the opportunity for the older former Jesuits at Georgetown to rejoin the Society and thus determined the future direction of the school as a Jesuit institution for laymen.[12] It was obvious also that St. Mary's College was developing a Catholic and Protestant body of students who did not aspire to the priesthood. Jacques Emery was of the mind that the Baltimore seminary would succeed only if there were one or more minor seminaries supplying it with students. The later attempts of Sulpician missionaries, Benedict Flaget in Kentucky and

Gabriel Richard in Michigan, to start schools in part reflected Emery's wishes.

The opportunity to form a minor seminary arose in 1806 when a French emigré, Joseph Harent, offered to hand over his farm near Conewago, Adams County, Pennsylvania, about forty-five miles north of Baltimore, to the Sulpicians for their use during his planned visit to France. François Nagot gladly accepted the offer and settled a Sulpician priest, Jean Dilhet, and two seminarians from Baltimore on the property, called Pigeon Hill, where a seminary was opened in August 1806. The school's twelve initial students were sons of the local ethnic German farmers and, being poor, were not charged for their schooling. When Joseph Harent unexpectedly returned from France in 1808, another place had to be secured for the students.[13]

William DuBourg introduced at this point another French priest, Jean Dubois, into early seminary history.[14] A native of Paris and a graduate of the Jesuit College Louis-le-Grand and ordained after studies at the Oratorian Seminary there, Dubois became a curate of St. Sulpice parish, even though he was not a member of the Society. In 1791, when he came to the diocese of Baltimore, Carroll appointed him to work at Frederick, Maryland, and in surrounding areas. Dubois acquired a seventeen-acre tract of land at nearby Emmitsburg, Maryland, where he planned to build a retirement retreat for himself and other priests. At the same time, he considered becoming a Sulpician.

DuBourg, acquainted with Dubois as were the other Baltimore Sulpicians, visited the priest's property in 1805 and conceived the idea of establishing a Sulpician minor seminary there. As was often the case, the persuasive DuBourg's proposal was carried out. In 1807 Dubois was admitted to the Society, and he deeded his property to the Society so that a minor seminary could be established in a new log building on site. DuBourg rashly acquired adjacent farm property from an elderly Catholic couple in return for an annuity during their lifetime, thereby creating a heavy financial obligation from the school's beginning. With these arrangements in place, Mount St. Mary's College opened at Emmitsburg in April 1809 under Dubois's direction. The first students were transferred from the Pigeon Hill seminary. In addition three new students arrived from Baltimore.[15]

DuBourg had created a heavy financial burden and was unable to supply the promised additional funds from Baltimore to cover the expenses of the new seminary. He departed from Baltimore in 1812, when Archbishop Carroll appointed him apostolic administrator of the Louisiana diocese. At Emmitsburg Jean Dubois was left to his own limited resources to sustain Mount St. Mary's. The school at the "Mountain," as it was called, soon became a complex enterprise with a farm, bakery, garden, hired servants, and a few slaves. There was a parish at the Mountain and one in Emmitsburg that required pastoral care. Mrs. Elizabeth Seton had settled in the town in 1809 with her initial followers, then called the Sisters of St. Joseph. Carroll appointed Dubois their superior. This role included their spiritual direction and the overseeing of the sisters' property as well as the debts revolving around their academy.

Just as DuBourg had redirected Sulpician aims at Baltimore by opening of St. Mary's college for lay students, Dubois altered the purpose of the seminary at Emmitsburg as early as 1811 by enrolling boys who did not intend to be priests in order to bring in needed revenue to pay debts. Dubois justified this move to his Sulpician superiors:

> It is evident that I have no other answer than the boarding school of the college part, for the seminary is composed almost entirely of poor young boys whose own expenses must be provided for, it is certainly not they who will aid me in bearing these other expenses.[16]

Although the Baltimore Sulpicians could not supply funds for Mount St. Mary's, they did provide the services of several priests. In 1815 they sent back the Mountain's first priest alumnus, John Hickey, to assist in conducting the school. In 1818 Simon Bruté abruptly left the presidency of St. Mary's College to help Dubois by becoming chaplain to Mother Seton and the sisters and to teach theology. Augmenting the personnel did nothing to solve the financial problems, however; Dubois needed a surplus of $3,000 per year to service the debts arising from the annuity and the construction costs of an additional building.

Since schooling for lay students at Emmitsburg was not consistent with plans for a minor seminary there, the Baltimore Sulpicians, without recourse to their superior in Paris, resolved in 1818 to suppress one of the two seminaries, stating to Dubois and his colleagues: "As to determining which of the two houses is to remain, we have not yet pronounced the decision. But it is very clear that the opinion will be likewise unanimous here that the house of Baltimore must be continued."[17] The Emmitsburg members, Dubois, Hickey, and Bruté, naturally were opposed to closing their school without raising the matter with the Sulpician superior in Paris. Dubois argued that if Mount St. Mary's were closed there would not be a supply of students for the Baltimore seminary, ignoring the fact that the Mountain had yet to succeed as a feeder school. Perhaps more compelling, Dubois pointed out that the school's closing would make the Sulpicians liable for all its considerable debts.[18]

Late in 1818, the Sulpician superior general, Antoine Duclaux, asked the new archbishop of Baltimore, the Sulpician Ambrose Maréchal, to negotiate a resolution of the difficulties. Maréchal attempted over the following years to arrange a settlement that would bring about one major seminary in his archdiocese.[19] At his suggestion the financial responsibility for Mount St. Mary's was separated from the Society and the property was returned to Jean Dubois, though the Mountain continued as a Sulpician institution whose internal life was subject to visitation by the superior at Baltimore. In the same year, Maréchal permitted instruction in philosophy and theology (under Bruté) at Mount St. Mary's for the several seminarians who taught boys. Without the donated services of seminarians, the school could not operate.

In 1821 Maréchal ordered an end to theology instruction at Emmitsburg, a decree that elicited anguished letters from Dubois. He pointed out that ending theology instruction would put an end to the school, accusing the archbishop of lacking "any embarrassment at the downfall of the seminary" and adding that "there is not a single one of those who compose the theology class this year who by right belong to your diocese."[20] To the future superior general Garnier, Dubois complained about the practices of the archbishop and the "Baltimore Gentlemen" in shoring up the Baltimore seminary. "They want to take in those who will pay, but not any of those who will not pay; Americans, but not the Irish, those who belong to the Baltimore diocese and not any of those who belong to other dioceses."[21] When faced with Dubois's determination to keep Mount St. Mary's open, the archbishop did not then insist on ending theology, but the conflict was far from over.

Maréchal visited the superior general in Paris in 1821, where he stated again his view that there should be but one major seminary in the diocese but expressed his willingness that the Baltimore seminary should take in students who could not afford to pay, giving preference to seminarians of the archdiocese of Baltimore, the Americans affiliated with other dioceses, and that Emmitsburg could accept paying students.[22] In the many exchanges on these issues, Dubois complained that these provisions would be harmful since he would have to sacrifice the services of the Baltimore students who had received free schooling in the humanities just at the time they could be useful to the school by teaching part-time while studying theology. They would have to go to Baltimore. The supply of student teachers was limited at Mount St. Mary's because Dubois did not permit recently immigrated Irish seminarians to teach. The latter were virtually all that the bishops of New York and Philadelphia enrolled at Emmitsburg. These students had not had their classical training at the Mountain so that they were "not suitable for instruction and government, not being accustomed to the discipline of our house rule."[23] The prospect of withdrawing Baltimore students then seemed all the more threatening. The exchanges be-

tween Dubois and the Sulpicians came to an end early in 1826 when Antoine Garnier, the recently elected Sulpician superior general, withdrew
Sulpician jurisdiction over Mount St. Mary's. The priests at Emmitsburg
ceased to be members of the Society of St. Sulpice. The school's future
would thereafter be settled by Dubois and his successors and by Maréchal
and his successors.

After the separation of the Emmitsburg priests, the Sulpicians enjoyed the influence arising from their proximity to the archbishops of Baltimore. In 1822 Archbishop Maréchal obtained from Propaganda the
charter of a pontifical university for the Baltimore seminary that empowered
the granting of pontifical degrees. At a public ceremony in the new Baltimore cathedral in 1824, the pontifical decree was read and the archbishop,
as "grand chancellor" of the pontifical university, conferred doctoral degrees on Louis Deluol, the director of the seminary, Edward Damphoux,
president of St. Mary's College, and James Whitfield, the vicar general
of the archdiocese.[24] For the remainder of the century, the pontifical doctorate was in fact an honorary degree conferred on the faculty or selected
priests of distinction. Maréchal's successor, Archbishop James Whitfield
sought to enhance the seminary's status even more at the First Provincial
Council of Baltimore in 1829 by proposing to the American bishops to
make it the "central seminary" of the country. Whitfield's episcopal brethren did not adopt the proposal, and the archbishop remarked: "They complain of want of money. . . ."[25]

The Sulpicians' attempts to limit their work to conducting seminaries
and to avoid other works not consistent with their calling dated from
Emery's policies. Dubois had been reproached for accepting lay students
at Emmitsburg, it is thus ironic that the Baltimore Sulpicians continued
to find it impossible to avoid several kinds of activities not related to the
seminary. By the late 1820s their activities created internal strains among
the nine Sulpicians at Baltimore. At their request the superior general Garnier sent Joseph Carrière, director of the Seminary of St. Sulpice, from
Paris in 1829 to conduct an official visitation "in order to bring peace to
the house, or to correct any abuse which could have crept in."[26] The visitation records reveal the extent of Sulpician activities beyond the seminary.

The Sulpicians were responsible for the direction of Mother Seton's
Sisters of Charity, nominally under Tessier as "protector," but their direction was actively carried on by the theology instructor Louis Deluol, as
"superior general," who frequently visited the sisters at Emmitsburg to fulfill his duties of spiritual direction.

The Sulpicians ministered to Baltimore's Haitian community at the
graceful seminary chapel. Sulpician Jacques Joubert did this work. He had
seen the need for schooling and religious instruction for the Haitian chil-

dren and formed a group of black women led by Elizabeth Lange, a Cuban, to look after them. After a year of novitiate under Joubert's direction, Lange and three followers professed vows in the crypt of St. Mary's Chapel in 1829, thereby marking the beginning of the Oblates of Providence, the first black sisterhood in the United States.

In addition to Joubert, each Sulpician had some favored outside activity; one was chaplain of the Visitation sisters, another conducted a sodality for laymen, another gave instructions at the orphan asylum, still another was hospital chaplain, and virtually all heard confessions of lay penitents outside the seminary and college community.[27]

Their predominant activity was the direction of St. Mary's College, which engaged seven of the nine Baltimore Sulpicians. From 1812 to 1829 the college enrolled some nine hundred students, largely Protestant, and granted eighty bachelor's and twenty-six master's degrees.[28] The college brought the Sulpicians into contact with local society and was the source of much prestige.

Seminary instruction mainly engaged one priest, Louis Deluol. Seminary enrollment in the 1820s was less than a dozen at any time. The lack of seminarians did not cause the low enrollment. When Carrière asked why there were so few seminarians, the reply was straightforward:

> The Gentlemen answered that the number of seminarians would be as large as one could wish, if they accepted all those subjects who applied; formerly, there was a larger number of seminarians because a large number of Irishmen were admitted; experience proved that those subjects, in general, proved unsatisfactory, that many thought of the Seminary only as a stopping off place, and they left us soon as they found something to do in town; others misbehaved; so it was decided that they would admit subjects of that nation only with discretion and with fitting precaution.[29]

There was a decided preference for seminarians of a more refined background in the lament: "As for the small number of subjects actually in the Seminary, the main reason is that the mentality of the country, especially in the upper classes of society, is hardly favorable to the ecclesiastical state." The faculty admitted that they could not afford the costs of supporting a large number of seminarians who were unable to pay. There seemed no immediate solution to the problem of low seminary enrollment. There was no hope that well-prepared candidates for the seminary would be coming from Mount St. Mary's and the only immediate prospect was to draw seminarians from the Catholic lay students of the college, where they tried "to promote piety."

The recommendations resulting from the visitation exhorted the Sulpician community to renewed attention to the spiritual life and away from exterior activities. In Carrière's words: "We must not be so busy with outside ministry that we might lose the idea that those outside occupations are only secondary: the principal and necessary thing, that we will have to render an account to God for, are occupations proper to our vocation."[30] The spiritual exercises, especially mental prayer, the particular examen, the annual retreat, and community exercises, all marks of the faithful cleric, were special objects of exhortation. The emphasis on the need for permission, in large issues from the Sulpician authorities in Paris, in small matters from the local superior, suggests a reining in of the varied activities.

The visitation was the occasion for the resignation of the aged Jean Tessier and the appointment of Louis Deluol as local superior. Despite exhortations to the contrary, the two decades of Deluol's administration, from 1829 to 1849, saw a continuation of the diverse activities that already characterized the Baltimore Sulpicians. Like his predecessors, Deluol was appointed vicar general of the archdiocese of Baltimore under archbishops Whitfield and the Sulpician Samuel Eccleston. Deluol and other Sulpicians served as officials at the seven national councils of the American bishops which took place at Baltimore between 1829 and 1849, thus reinforcing their closeness to the seat of power in Baltimore and providing a cause for some resentment of French influence in church affairs among the American clergy.

The Sulpicians' most important new undertaking under Deluol was firmly in the Sulpician tradition. It was the effort to realize the longstanding hope of founding a minor seminary to supply students for the major seminary at Baltimore. The Sulpicians enlisted the interest of the country's most distinguished Catholic layman, Charles Carroll of Carrollton. Beginning with Ambrose Maréchal, one of the Sulpicians had visited Carroll's estate at Doughoregan regularly to celebrate Mass. In gratitude the aging statesman deeded to the Sulpicians a tract of land adjacent to his estate west of Baltimore near Ellicott City in 1830 as a site for a minor seminary. On July 11, 1831, the cornerstone was laid for the seminary, named St. Charles College, in the presence of Charles Carroll, then ninety-four years old.[31]

Over the following seventeen years, the Sulpicians slowly raised funds to build the seminary. Archbishop Eccleston participated in these efforts locally and in seeking financial assistance in Europe. In appealing to the Society for the Propagation of the Faith in 1843, he advanced the reason that: "One of the things that I desire most, is the formation of a national clergy accustomed from infancy to the manners and language of the country, and at the same time pious, instructed, and sufficiently numerous."[32] Though the Sulpicians owned the college site, the archbishop, on his own initiative, ordered its opening in 1848 and made a vigorous effort for funds to buy the furnishings that enabled St. Charles College to begin operating in November of that year. The college enrolled seventeen students in its first year; the enrollment grew to forty-six by 1860 and continued a successful existence in supplying the seminary in Baltimore and other seminaries with properly prepared students for theological studies.

In 1849 the Sulpician superior general, Louis de Courson, renewed the effort to restrict the American Sulpicians to seminary work and sent two members of his council to Baltimore to conduct a visitation. While the visitation was in progress for a year, Louis Deluol was abruptly removed as superior and left Baltimore for Paris on December 7, 1849. His twenty years of leadership had not ended the objectionable external activities. The visitation resulted in detailed regulations on the external life of the seminary and the college to assure adherence to the spiritual exercises and the vocation of forming priests.[33]

François Lhomme, who had been assigned to St. Mary's College since 1827, was appointed superior. He dismantled the external activities such as the spiritual direction of the Visitation and Carmelite sisters. The direction of the Sisters of Charity ended when Deluol departed and was not resumed by another Sulpician, thereby ending a relationship that began in 1808. These measures were carried out despite the protests of Archbishop Eccleston, who did not have priests available to replace the Sulpicians.[34] Finally St. Mary's College was brought to a close in 1852, when arrangements were completed for the Jesuits to open a college for lay students in Baltimore.

The closing of St. Mary's College coincided with a growing seminary enrollment. Though there had been only twenty-two seminarians enrolled as recently as 1849, their numbers grew to an annual average of at least forty during the 1850s in the wake of the massive Catholic immigration cresting in that decade. The seminary had trained only 110 ordinands from 1793 until 1848, while eight-eight were ordained between 1850 and 1860.[35] The enlarged seminary community moved into the remodeled college buildings in 1855 and thereafter the seminary took on the name of St. Mary's Seminary. The ending of the college as a means of supporting the seminary marks the emergence of St. Mary's Seminary as a free-standing seminary, that is, one that now had an adequate enrollment and sufficient income that it no longer required the support that an affiliated college provided. The Sulpicians, who were never numerous, also declined to accept invitations from the bishops of Cincinnati in 1849 and New York in 1862 to staff their seminaries, preferring to maintain a strong presence at their Baltimore seminary.[36]

After Lhomme's death in 1860, Joseph Dubreul, who joined the faculty in 1850, was appointed superior. Dubreul continued the policy of exclusive devotion to clerical formation and adherence to French traditions of spirituality as the visitation of 1849–1850 had prescribed.

The appointment of Bishop Martin Spalding of Louisville as seventh archbishop of Baltimore in 1864 began a period of tension for the Sulpicians. Spalding, a Kentucky native, was a frequent critic of foreign clergy and religious orders who clung to European ways in their work in the United States.[37] He regarded the French Sulpicians as "old fogies" and sought to change their foreign ways.[38] He objected to Dubreul's direction and complained to the Sulpician superior general about the Society's overall approach:

> To work well and prominently in this vast country, your Society ought, it seems to me, to adapt itself to the circumstances and the nationalities of those with whom it finds itself engaged. The Fathers, especially the Superiors, ought to remember that they are no longer in France. . . . [39]

Spalding and the Sulpicians exchanged views on improving the seminarians' diet, exercise, and studies, in which the former achieved some mitigations of rigid French traditions. The archbishop was unable to secure two major demands, seminary instructors whose native language was English and the replacement of Dubreul with someone better adapted to the ways of American ecclesiastical life. Given the Society's French membership, it was naturally not possible to supply native English speakers to the faculty, a fact that was reflected in the Sulpicians' limited success in attracting Americans to join.

Spalding also altered the financial relationship between the Sulpicians and the archdiocese. Baltimore seminarians had formerly defrayed their expenses by teaching in St. Mary's College. After St. Charles College opened and St. Mary's College closed, the archdiocese had to help the Sulpicians meet the expenses of these freestanding seminaries with annual collections. After a series of misunderstandings in which the Sulpicians believed that Spalding was intruding into their internal affairs, the archbishop obtained an accounting of how the money from the annual collections for the benefit of the seminaries was spent. In response to Dubreul's demands that tuition be paid for the archdiocese's increasing number of students, the archbishop at first refused but later let the Sulpicians adjust the number of archdiocesan students enrolled in relation to the proceeds from the annual collection.[40]

Despite the Baltimore Sulpicians' French ways, many bishops sent their seminarians to St. Mary's, thereby enlarging its enrollment from seventy at the end of the Civil War to ninety at the time of Dubreul's death in 1878. By the latter date, the Baltimore Sulpicians numbered about sixteen, with seven assigned to St. Mary's Seminary and nine at St. Charles College.[41] The growth of the St. Mary's Seminary community required the construction of a new building in 1875, at the same site the seminary had occupied since 1791: in the heart of Baltimore only a few blocks away from the Cathedral of the Assumption, where faculty and seminarians could continue to participate regularly in the church's liturgical life. Alphonse Magnien, appointed superior of the Baltimore seminary in 1878, would lead St. Mary's Seminary and the Sulpicians into the twentieth century.

After separating from the Sulpicians, Mount St. Mary's continued to operate as a college and seminary. Archbishop Maréchal had insisted that Mount St. Mary's be regarded as a preparatory or *petit* seminary, but he reluctantly permitted seminarians of his archdiocese to remain there for theology study if they were required for teaching. He demanded that those not needed for teaching be sent to the Sulpician seminary. He authorized theology instruction at the Mountain for only five additional years after which the school would presumably be solvent enough to do without them.[42] He further required his seminarians to spend an indefinite time at the Baltimore seminary before ordination, as though they had been poorly instructed at Emmitsburg.

The agreement between Dubois and Maréchal went into effect in September 1826 and assured Mount St. Mary's existence for the near future. Dubois left Emmitsburg in October to become, at age sixty-two, third bishop of New York. He had achieved success in keeping his school going through many difficulties with higher authorities for eighteen years. As recently as 1824 he had overcome the challenge of a fire which destroyed part of the school buildings. Before leaving, Dubois deeded the property to two clerical alumni, Michael Egan and John F. McGerry. Dubois retained an interest in the school by making it the seminary of his diocese for a period of five years and by agreeing not to withdraw any of his New York students, "whether they have finished their theological studies or not," without the consent of the new directors if "such removal would prove too great an inconvenience to the Seminary."[43]

Dubois did not leave behind a stable enterprise to his young successors at Mount St. Mary's. In 1826, Michael Egan, age twenty-four, became president, and John F. McGerry, age thirty, vice president. Bruté, the senior priest at forty-seven, continued to direct the seminarians and, perhaps in view of his personal qualities that made him counselor to all, was given the title "superior." But personnel turned over rapidly due to reasons of health and the attraction of other pursuits. In 1830 John B. Purcell, an Irish-born alumnus who had been sent to St. Sulpice for theology studies at Bruté's expense, became the president, assisted by Francis Jamison as vice president.

Purcell's presidency from 1830 to 1833 began a process of placing the college on a firm legal basis. In 1832, the state legislature enacted "An Act for founding a College near Emmitsburg in Frederick County" with John B. Purcell and Francis Jamison as "principals" under the name of "Mount St. Mary's College." The college was empowered to grant degrees, including the doctorate, though not of medicine, "in any of the faculties, arts and sciences, and liberal professions to which persons are usually admitted in other colleges or universities in America."[44] The state granted successive charters in 1832, 1833, and finally 1836. The faculty then devised "rules and laws for our own good government." These provided for governance by a corporate body or council of diocesan priests from which the college officers were drawn.[45] In the years ahead many but not all priests of the faculty were invited to join the corporation. None of the lay faculty were invited.

Archbishop Maréchal's permission to offer theology expired in 1831; his successor, Archbishop Whitfield, extended the permission in 1832 for an additional two years. By the time Samuel Eccleston became archbishop in 1834, Maréchal's old sense of urgency to prevent Mount St. Mary's becoming a major seminary was a thing of the past. The teaching of theology was recognized as essential to the institution's survival and ceased to be an issue.

Personnel problems continued. In 1833 Purcell became second bishop of Cincinnati, and Jamison became president of the Mount. In 1834, Bruté left to become first bishop of Vincennes. Thereupon the clerical faculty, numbering five, except President Jamison lost confidence in their ability to operate the school and asked Archbishop Whitfield have Mount St. Mary's returned to the Sulpicians. They believed it was better for a "society" with clear lines of authority to govern the school.[46] Whitfield, with the Sulpicians Louis Deluol and Alexius Elder, came to Emmitsburg to discuss the offer, though it was unlikely that the Sulpician superior general would permit the return of Mount St. Mary's to Sulpician direction. The archbishop and his advisors listened to the wrangling of the priest faculty over leadership and debts. Jamison resigned, and Thomas Butler became president and affirmed the school's governing arrangements: "our government, like that of our country is republican."[47] Deacon John McCaffrey was appointed vice president.

Butler's appointment did not lift what a concerned alumnus, John Hughes, called " the perpetual mist" clouding the school's affairs.[48] Both in theory and practice collegial government seemed an untenable way of conducting a Catholic institution and did not command much loyalty. Archbishop Eccleston suggested offering the college to the Jesuits.[49] In 1837 Bishop Dubois, who was seeking a faculty of priests for his proposed seminary in New York, hoped to attract Redemptorists to both Emmitsburg and his own seminary.[50] They did not take up the offers, however, and, in 1842 Eccleston offered the college and seminary to the Vincentians, who also declined.[51]

Meanwhile, President Butler struggled with debts and formed the "Mount St. Mary's Theological Seminary Fund Association" on whose behalf he and vice president McCaffrey embarked on fund-raising tours.[52] The inherent tensions between executive action and collegial government continued. Butler was at odds with the rest of the faculty. McCaffrey, who had been a deacon since 1831, resigned and left with his younger brother Thomas to attend the seminary at Baltimore to prepare for ordination. Early in 1838 Butler resigned. McCaffrey then accepted the college council's invitation to be president in the week following his ordination to the priesthood in March 1838.[53]

Born in Emmitsburg in 1806, John McCaffrey's life revolved around the college until his departure for Baltimore in 1837. He returned as president at age thrity-two, an energetic, self-assured man who dominated the life of the college for the next thirty-four years. A series of loyal associates assisted him through the following decades. These included John McCloskey, ordained in 1840 and appointed vice president and treasurer in 1842; and the president's brother, Thomas McCaffrey, ordained in 1838 and placed in charge of the parish with other duties. Another protégé, William Henry Elder, also born in Emmitsburg, was sent to Rome as a deacon in 1843 for theological studies and returned a priest and doctor of theology in 1846 to direct the seminarians until 1857. This small core group of loyal priests serving indefinitely assured stability and continuity after an era of instability, though McCaffrey attributed the solution to Providence, as he told Orestes Brownson:

> Secular priests are with difficulty brought and held together for the purpose of carrying on educational institutions. Monastic societies alone can supply the want. Mount Saint Mary's is the only institution which now remains under the control of secular priests. I see clearly the advantages, which the religious orders have over us and look upon it as a special providence that has sustained our institution amid all difficulties.[54]

McCaffrey might have added that as the years passed he and his treasurer, John McCloskey, acquired the age and seniority that made challenges to their authority unlikely among the clerical alumni invited to join the faculty.

Mount St. Mary's steadily prospered under McCaffrey, at least until the Civil War. Its unvarying institutional formula consisted of a small faculty of priests with a few laymen. A group of seminarians studied theology part-time and taught boys part-time. The largest volume of activity was related to boys. There were 118 in 1838, rising to a peak enrollment of 204 in 1858. They ranged from grade-school age to their early twenties.[55] Their instruction, discipline, religious ministrations, and organized activities dominated the routine of the institution's life and came under McCaffrey's pessimistic approach to human capabilities, as he told Brownson:

> Engaged in the task of educating American boys, I find that very few indeed have been taught by their parents to obey and sacrifice selfwill to duty. Parents generally tell me, that their boys are honorable and will not lie. I find that about one in a hundred never lies. I find that in three cases out of four the children rule the parents and ultimately study what they please, leave school when they please and at home do what they please.[56]

Corporal punishment and expulsions were the routine means of discipline. Even in an age of firm discipline, Bishop Spalding of Louisville expressed surprise in 1858 when learning that sixty of the older boys left the college as a body after McCaffrey "threw into the fire without reading a petition they had sent him through a committee."[57] It was to boys that McCaffrey devoted his personal attention through catechism instruction, an interest that resulted in his publication of a catechism in 1865.[58]

Whereas the Baltimore seminary faculty was regularly augmented by Sulpicians sent from France, McCaffrey struggled to keep a faculty together. He preferred seminarians who had virtually grown up at Mount St. Mary's. He was reluctant to admit new seminarians late in their training because they had not internalized the school's values. One such had to be let go, because, according to McCaffrey: "He has put it out of his power to be of any service as a teacher, having forfeited the respect of the boys by allowing them to violate rules and humbug him in various ways."[59] In the turnover of teaching seminarians, McCaffrey even tried to slow down the progress to priesthood of a prized instructor or retain him after ordination. He asked an alumnus bishop to permit two of his seminarians to delay their ordinations: "If they remain here," McCaffrey stated, "they will be the more efficient and useful, when they do go on the mission."[60] Remaining at Mount St. Mary's could improve their chances of later success, as he told Purcell concerning a favored seminarian: "I recommend to you to give him time yet to mature his powers. He is always improving and a twelvemonth hence may take the Professorial chair you offer him with much less risk of failing in it."[61] Purcell sent the young man to Rome.

Another of Purcell's promising students, McCaffrey thought, would have a better chance of being a bishop if kept on the faculty.[62]

Despite the strictness of his regime, McCaffrey did not regard the fact that seminarians were teaching lay students as a distraction in their preparation for the priesthood. Teaching gave each seminarian a personal share of reponsibility for the institution and undoubtedly helped to "mature his powers" in a way that seminarians elsewhere could not have.

The promotion of faculty priests to the episcopacy also posed a problem. McCaffrey himself was repeatedly mentioned as a candidate for the episcopacy in the 1850s when the number of dioceses was growing. "Do prevail on your Most & Rt. Rev. Brethren," he told Purcell, "to let us alone. We will have a college and seminary as we ought to have, if the men who are needed here are not taken away."[63] Shortly thereafter, in 1857, William H. Elder accepted the see of Natchez, leaving McCaffrey searching for a director of the seminary. In 1858 the bulls of appointment were issued for McCaffrey to be ordained bishop of Charleston, but McCaffrey declined, professing to have "no vocation to the episcopacy. . . ."[64]

Mount St. Mary's had to adjust to changing circumstances as seminaries were formed at Philadelphia, New York, and Cincinnati, which ended established relationships with these dioceses. The growing enrollment in the 1850s of the Baltimore seminary, which served many dioceses, only increased the challenges. Competition with St. Mary's Seminary sharpened ethnic feeling, for the Sulpicians had earlier shown antipathy to the Irish. Emmitsburg's seminarians were therefore predominantly Irish. As late as the 1860s, when McCaffrey sought a theology professor for the seminary, he specified no "censorious Frenchman."[65] Mount St. Mary's position within the Baltimore archdiocese was not always certain. McCaffrey received little encouragement during Francis Kenrick's years as archbishop of Baltimore (1851 to 1863), afterwards saying of the deceased prelate's attitude toward the Mountain: "He did not encourage it; it seemed as though he would let it go to wreck."[66] McCaffrey was referring to the fact that the archbishop did not support Baltimore seminarians at Emmitsburg; instead McCaffrey had to provide for them, and the archbishop had offered to hand over Mount St. Mary's to the Vincentians in 1862.[67]

Martin Spalding's appointment as archbishop of Baltimore in 1864 cheered McCaffrey. The new archbishop was willing to support students of the archdiocese at Mount St. Mary's, though in fact few Baltimore students attended at that time. The old president was also pleased that in the planning for the Second Plenary Council of Baltimore of 1866, Archbishop Spalding's proposal to sponsor a national Catholic university recommended its location at Mount St. Mary's.[68] However, the American bishops were not yet prepared to establish a university there or elsewhere. When John

McCaffrey retired as president in 1872, the college enrolled 141 lay students and 32 seminarians, a figure that was similar to enrollments of the 1850s.[69] The institution could claim favorable consideration in church circles with twenty-six alumni appointed as bishops by 1880, though they were not in any direct sense responsible for Mount St. Mary's.

During the Civil War, Mount St. Mary's finances were weakened as the school was cut off from its once substantial southern constituency. Enrollment declined for several years, causing a loss of revenue to service debts. The financial situation grew worse during the depression of the 1870s and debts mounted. McCaffrey, living in retirement at the college, arranged in 1880 for the appointment of William Hill, an alumnus and priest of the Brooklyn diocese, to be college president. Hill resigned in 1881 after his efforts to restore finances failed, and the school went into receivership. Though the archdiocese of Baltimore did not own the college and was not responsible for its finances or administration, Baltimore's Archbishop James Gibbons led an effort to raise money to save the college. Several alumni bishops assisted Gibbons in the effort, so that Mount St. Mary's was out of receivership by 1882.[70]

After consultations among alumni bishops, William Byrne, an alumnus and Boston priest, accepted the board's offer of the presidency in 1882. Prior to the Third Plenary Council of Baltimore in 1884, Byrne and his council petitioned the American bishops to form a board to assume ownership of Mount St. Mary's and conduct there a "Missionary Seminary" for the "education of priests for the more destitute missions of this country." The bishops did not take up the offer, which was designed, it appears, to secure the institution's financial stability and, as the petitioners stated, to obtain a status "more in harmony with ecclesiastical law and discipline."[71] Nevertheless, Mount St. Mary's emerged from the years of financial crisis stable enough to continue its unique governing arrangement outside the direct responsibility of a particular diocese. It continued to serve many dioceses under the control of an independent corporation of diocesan priests.

In the century after John Carroll's proposal of 1782 for the Select Body of the Clergy to sponsor a college to train candidates for the priesthood, the archdiocese of Baltimore, the country's premier ecclesiastical jurisdiction and one whose ordinary was the spiritual leader of American Catholics, developed a set of institutions for clerical formation that do not have a parallel in the dioceses formed after Baltimore. The coming of the Sulpicians in 1791 displaced the diocese's direct responsibility for training priests at Georgetown Academy and instead started a chain of events leading to the formation of several institutions: the Sulpician seminary that became known as St. Mary's Seminary, St. Mary's College for lay students at Baltimore until 1852, Mount St. Mary's College and Seminary at Emmitsburg, and St. Charles College near Ellicott City. The archbishops of Baltimore in a manner inconsistent with the standard of the Tridentine seminary decree did not directly administer or finance these institutions though they sanctioned their operation and occasionally intervened in their activities when requested or when they thought the interests of the church required it. The institutions could not have continued if the archbishops had opposed their existence. These seminaries served the Baltimore archdiocese, but they had a significance beyond its immediate jurisdiction. St. Mary's Seminary and St. Charles College of the Sulpicians and Mount St. Mary's College and Seminary served many dioceses, thereby becoming in effect national seminaries, each developing constituencies of episcopal alumni that insured supplies of seminarians from beyond the Baltimore archdiocese. Though unique among the many seminaries that developed through the period in terms of their national significance, the institutions provide examples of seminary models of freestanding institutions, in the case of St. Mary's Seminary and St. Charles College, and mixed, that is, combining a seminary with lay college, in the case of Mount St. Mary's. As such, they anticipate the institutional models that developed in seminaries founded throughout the country.

2. Local Diocesan Seminaries

The American Catholic community grew from approximately 35,000 in 1790 to over 100,000 by 1810 as immigration attracted European Catholics to growing cities on the eastern seaboard.[1] Immigrant and native Catholics likewise began the settlement of the West. Catholic growth called attention to the issue of creating new dioceses. After Bishop John Carroll and Propaganda officials exchanged views on the subject, Pope Pius VII sanctioned in 1808 the formation of new dioceses at New York, Boston, Philadelphia, and Bardstown, Kentucky. At the same time, Baltimore was raised to the status of an archdiocese, and John Carroll became first archbishop. The Louisiana Purchase of 1803 brought a vast territory west of the Missisippi into the United States. This acquisition joined the diocese of New Orleans, dating from 1793, to the American church. Thereafter the division of existing dioceses and the creation of new ones became a familiar pattern of church life as Catholics settled across the United States.

Once a new see was established, its bishop began to build the basic institutions appropriate for a diocese. His first duty was to form a body of clergy for the local church. A missionary bishop's characteristic means of developing clergy was to recruit European priests and seminarians and to form a diocesan seminary. American bishops avidly engaged in seminary foundings as new dioceses were established. These local foundings and their related problems were major aspects of seminary development until the middle of the nineteenth century.

After the opening of the Maryland seminaries, the next diocesan seminary was founded in the Transappalachian West. The Sulpician Benedict Flaget, experienced in education and in the missions of the West, was appointed first bishop of Bardstown. After receiving episcopal ordination in 1810 at Baltimore, he left for his frontier diocese in 1811 with a party of priests and seminarians, mostly French, who observed a seminary life on the boat trip from Pittsburgh to Louisville, as portrayed by one of the party, Jean Baptist David:

48

The boat on which we descended the Ohio became the cradle of our seminary, and of the church of Kentucky. Our cabin was, at the same time, chapel, dormitory, study room and refectory. An altar was erected on the boxes and ornamented as far as circumstances would allow. The Bishop prescribed a regulation which fixed all the exercises, and in which each had its proper time.[2]

Upon arriving in Bardstown among the English-stock Catholics transplanted from Maryland and beholding the "sad dearth of missionaries," as Flaget's biographer noted, "he naturally turned his eyes to his infant seminary, the future hope of the diocese."[3] Entrusted to his fellow Sulpician, Jean David, the seminary started with three students in November 1811 at a site three miles south of Bardstown at a farm donated by a pious Catholic, Thomas Howard. It was named St. Thomas Seminary to honor the donor's patron saint. In the rural setting the seminary's director devised a routine of spiritual exercises, study, and farm work. As the number of seminarians grew to fifteen, the construction of enlarged quarters required that building tasks be added to the work routine. Flaget frequently stayed at the seminary during respites from his circuit of travels around his vast diocese, which embraced most of the American West, and he became personally acquainted with his seminarians.[4]

Faithful to Catholic tradition, Flaget turned his attention to building a worthy cathedral as the seat of the diocese. He raised funds for St. Joseph's Cathedral, built between 1816 and 1819, in Bardstown. Its completion signaled the transfer of sixteen seminarians studying theology from St. Thomas Seminary to the residence at the cathedral. The students of classics and philosophy stayed behind at St. Thomas. The major seminarians at Bardstown could then assist in cathedral liturgies, thereby practicing the public worship of the church, and could be seen by the people. A visiting French priest described the services at the cathedral, at which seminarians assisted:

> The ceremonies, all performed with great exactness according to the Roman rite; the chant at once grave and touching; the attendant clergy pious and modest; everything impressed me so strongly, that I almost believed myself in the midst of one of the finest churches of Rome.[5]

On the Kentucky frontier, slightly more than a decade after the founding of the diocese, Bishop Flaget had literally fulfilled the ideals of the Tridentine decree, gathering at his cathedral candidates preparing for the priesthood. The presence of the seminarians at Bardstown also afforded them the opportunity to take part in conducting nearby St. Joseph College.

Bardstown's diocesan seminary operated with difficulty. Flaget hoped to have his Sulpician confreres assume direction of the seminary to assist Jean David and to assure a qualified faculty for the future. His appeals to the Sulpician authorities in Paris were not heeded because of the varied activities at St. Thomas, such as farm work unknown to the aristocratic Sulpician tradition.[6] Flaget then directed his appeals to the cardinal prefect of Propaganda for a priest trained at the Urban College of the Propaganda to teach at the Bardstown seminary. In 1821 a young Irish-born graduate, Francis P. Kenrick, was assigned to Flaget as a seminary instructor. In 1830 Flaget sent two talented Kentuckians, Martin J. Spalding and John M. Lancaster, to the Urban College in Rome for a better training than they could obtain in Kentucky. The acquisition of Kenrick and the sending of Spalding and Lancaster to Rome gave rise to Flaget's fanciful hope during the 1830s of establishing in his diocese a "Propaganda College of the West" under Roman sanction to train priests for the region.[7] However, the course of the Bardstown seminary's history was not smooth as the diocese struggled with finances, to maintain a staff of instructors, and to attract students. The major seminarians were sent back to St. Thomas Seminary by the 1830s, and the seminary was entrusted to the Vincentians briefly in the 1840s. Later it became a minor seminary until closing in 1871.

Another diocesan seminary arose in the West at a location in the upper Louisiana territory. After appointment as bishop of New Orleans in 1815, Bishop William DuBourg decided to administer his vast diocese from St. Louis. He recruited Vincentian priests from Rome to conduct a seminary. They established themselves in Perry County, Missouri, eighty miles south of St. Louis, where they opened St. Mary's Seminary in 1819. The complex history of the Vincentians' seminary efforts in the diocese of New Orleans and, after its founding in 1826, with the diocese of St. Louis properly belongs with the history of Vincentian seminary activities in chapter 5 of this volume.[8]

The Tridentine model of cathedral and seminary is repeated in the diocese of Charleston. John England of Cork, Ireland, was appointed in 1820 bishop of the new diocese of Charleston, which included the Carolinas and Georgia. In 1822 he opened the "Philosophical and Classical Seminary" of Charleston. After locating in temporary quarters, the school moved into a new building adjoining Charleston's cathedral of St. John the Baptist in 1825. Beginning with a staff consisting of the bishop, two priests, one seminarian, and two laymen, the school at first attracted thirty lay students (boys) from leading Charleston families, most not Catholic. The school's format was designed to permit seminarians to teach boys part-time. However, the sectarian spirit of the times eventually prevented the school from developing a large enrollment of paying students from the local Protestant population. Nonclerical students were instructed until 1836, when that program was discontinued. England's annual collection for diocesan expenses was directed mainly to supporting the seminary. After England's death in 1842, his successor, Bishop Ignatius Reynolds, was able to keep the seminary open only until 1851. It had trained about sixty priests in all.[9]

Bishop England, a prolific writer and apologist, wrote and spoke more on the subject of seminary education than any other American Catholic bishop of his time. As did other bishops of the era, he depended on attracting priests from abroad to his diocese, but he proclaimed the importance of developing a native clergy. Of his addresses at twenty-six conventions of the clergy and laity of his diocese, all but one mention the importance of supporting a diocesan seminary for this purpose. According to his views, the seminary, of course, was intended to impart the ordinary ecclesiastical learning and to insure the holiness expected of seminarians under the watchful care of the bishop. What was noteworthy was the forcefulness of his views on training priests who were "natives of these southern states."[10] They were to be accustomed to the climate as well as the customs and dispositions of the people of the diocese. He stressed

> the knowledge of American laws, intimacy with the American people, the attachment to the American constitution, the habit of American discipline, the zeal for American improvement, and the devotion to American rights, together with the adaptation of the great principles of faith, of morality, and of science to American circumstances.[11]

The development of a native clergy was one aspect of England's overall views on the American church. Throughout the 1820s he agitated for convening the long-postponed provincial council of the American bishops to legislate on the common problems of American Catholics. Archbishops Maréchal and Whitfield had long opposed a provincial council because of the opportunity that such a meeting would have in giving England a platform for his views. Because of England's insistent appeals to Propaganda, a provincial council was at long last convened in 1829 under the presidency of Archbishop Whitfield.[12] In preparation for the council, bishops submitted topics to be discussed. Among England's suggestions were:

> The best mode of proceeding and educating candidates for the ministry. This would involve several topics. Such as the propriety of calling on the laity for their aid, and the mode of so procuring it as to guard against too great and mischievous an interference on their parts.

The propriety and practicability of having a common College, beside our Diocesan Seminaries. The modes of guarding against the admission of unworthy subjects either in orders or candidates, as those who go from Diocess to Diocess, the course of studies best adapted to our Provinces, and a great number of lesser details.[13]

The minutes of the First Provincial Council of Baltimore of 1829 have not survived, but, as mentioned in chapter 1, Archbishop Whitfield promoted without success the idea of making the Sulpician Seminary at Baltimore a national seminary. It can be assumed that the forceful bishop of Charleston promoted his views on a "common college," which would either supplement or supplant local seminaries. However, the council decrees do not mention seminaries.

The Second Provincial Council of Baltimore, as mandated at the first council, was to take place three years later, in 1832; however Archbishop Whitfield, who thought another council unnecessary, did not convene one. Again Bishop England half-openly agitated for one in 1833 in articles under the pseudonym "Philo-Canon," which appeared in the Philadelphia *Catholic Herald* and were reprinted in England's own organ, the *United States Catholic Miscellany*. These articles kept attention on the issue and reminded readers of the long tradition of church councils as beneficial to the life of the church. England's representations to Propaganda again had the desired effect, so that Whitfield convened the Second Provincial Council of Baltimore late in 1833.[14]

Preceding the council's opening, articles appeared in the *Catholic Herald* of Philadelphia under the pseudonym "Providus," calling attention to the need to build up an American clergy—"men accustomed from infancy to the institutions, manners and feelings of our country"[15]—and to the weaknesses of American seminaries:

> While the demand for additional missionaries and the zeal of our bishops to supply vacancies is necessarily so great and increasing, and, on the other hand, the resources of our Seminaries are so contracted and precarious, the education given in them is proportionably rapid, and far from being so profound, extensive, and varied, as it should be, and in older countries generally is.[16]

Providus proposed that three or four large seminaries be established, instead of sustaining many weak ones, pursuant to a plan that the bishops might devise at the forthcoming provincial council. "For it is plain that unless some plan of action be adopted, some system pursued, little effectual and permanent good will be achieved."[17] It is likely that these articles were written by England or at least closely represented his views.

Several years later he stated that he had proposed at the council the idea of forming "an extensive and respectable provincial college," in which:

> under the joint superintendence of our whole hierarchy, the great body of our candidates for the ministry, at far less expense and under more favorable circumstances, would have better opportunities for pursuing a more extended course of studies, and for observing more exact religious discipline than can be at present afforded by any of those seminaries which we are endeavoring to uphold.[18]

England did not see this national institution as completely supplanting the local diocesan seminary, which "for a variety of weighty reasons" should be sustained in the vicinity of the cathedral. He is not altogether clear in balancing the competing claims of a national seminary and a local one, assigning a role to each. It is likely that England's concern for collective episcopal control was directed against the Sulpicians' influential seminary at Baltimore. He had often spoken openly of his objections to the French priests and their seminary as not suited for the American church. "The French," he stated in 1835, "never can become American. Their language, manners, love of *la belle France*, their dress, air, carriage, notions, and mode of speaking of their religion, all, all are foreign."[19]

England's episcopal colleagues, who, he said, admitted in principle the desirability of a national seminary at the second provincial council, nevertheless decreed otherwise. They framed a decree reminding themselves that the Council of Trent's decree requiring the erection of seminaries should be obeyed.[20] This decree and the bishops' pattern of behavior through the period demonstrate repeatedly the episcopal adherence to the Tridentine tradition of the bishop supervising clerical formation locally.

The founding of many local diocesan seminaries coincided with the first impact of the European mission societies whose donations permitted the development of Catholic institutions, especially seminaries, during the 1830s. Their formation in part resulted from a series of initiatives emanating from the United States.

The most important mission society originated in Lyons, France, and was founded by two remarkable women. The one, who has come to be known as Madame Petit or the Widow Petit, gathered a group of lay and clerical friends to collect money for the missions. She was a family friend of Bishop William DuBourg, and his diocese benefitted from their efforts. At the same time, a pious young woman of Lyons, Marie Pauline Jaricot, became interested in Catholic missionary activity through the Seminary for Foreign Missions. She formed the idea of raising funds for missionary activity by an organization divided into groups of ten members who gave a fixed amount for the missions each week. Her organization came into being in 1820. The groups started by Madame Petit and Marie Pauline Jaricot came together on May 3, 1822, at Lyons and formed the Society for the Propagation of the Faith. Jaricot's idea of collecting alms among a small group of ten was adopted with the practice of each member reciting daily the Pater Noster, Ave, and invocation to St. Francis Xavier, the society's patron, for the missions. Leadership of the society remained under lay direction until the twentieth century, when it was placed under church authority. Pope Pius VII approved the society in 1823. It attracted widespread support in France, and in its first decade, 1822 to 1831, disbursed $149,633 to bishops in the United States. From 1831 to 1861 the society distributed $2,789,927 in the United States, mainly to bishops, and provided crucial early support in buying land and in building churches and religious institutions.[21]

A second mission society resulted from the European fund-raising tour of Frederic Rese, a priest of the diocese of Cincinnati, a native of the kingdom of Hanover, and a graduate of the Urban College of the Propaganda. Rese, on behalf of Bishop Edward Fenwick of Cincinnati, visited the Society of the Propagation of the Faith in Lyons in 1828. Afterward, while in Vienna, he sought to interest leading Catholics there in the formation of a mission society affiliated with the one in Lyons. He found that the Emperor Francis I and the Cardinal Archbishop of Vienna, Leopold Firmian, were favorably inclined and approved the foundation of a society. The Austrian society was named for the emperor's recently deceased daughter, Leopoldine, consort of Emperor Pedro I of Brazil. Hence it was called the Leopoldinen Stiftung or Leopoldine Foundation. It had a structure similar to the Lyons society in which members were organized into small groups, gave small donations on a regular basis, and were to pray daily for the missions the Pater, Ave, and an invocation to St. Leopold. The organization at the top was not under lay direction but was administered by the Cardinal Archbishop of Vienna, who approved disbursements. Because of Rese's interest, the foundation was intended especially to support Catholic activities in the diocese of Cincinnati. However, as the number of American dioceses increased, the foundation spread its benefactions to the new dioceses. The foundation was sensitive to ethnic tensions existing among Catholics of differing national backgrounds in the United States and sought to insure proper attention to German immigrants from their Irish and French bishops. Its first payments reached the United States in 1830; from that year until 1861, it sent $436,176.08 to the United States.[22]

A third mission society, the Ludwig-Missionsverein, was formed in Munich in 1838 as an affiliate of the Lyons society after a visit of Frederic Rese, who was by then bishop of Detroit. This society had close ties to the Bavarian court and the personal interests of King Ludwig I in aiding

Germans exclusively. Accordingly, the Ludwig-Missionsverein eventually discontinued its affiliation with the Lyons society. It sent about $364,000 to the United States by 1861.[23]

Mission society donations soon began to have an impact on the development of seminaries. For instance, Bishop Michael Portier, born near Lyons, was appointed first bishop of the new diocese of Mobile, Alabama, in 1829. During a long visit in Europe in 1829, Portier collected funds from the Sacred Congregation of the Propaganda and the Society for the Propagation of the Faith as well as priests and seminarians. The funds made possible his first diocesan project in 1830, the purchase of land and the construction of Spring Hill College, a mixed academy for boys with seminary, located seven miles east of Mobile on a height overlooking Mobile Bay. Matthias Loras, a priest from Lyons, was named president and was aided by a group of six French seminarians who initially taught about thirty boys. The first group of seminarians were ordained by 1832 and were replaced as teachers by additional seminarians from France. For the next few years the college also required the services of four or five diocesan priests.

By 1840 Portier sought a community of priests to conduct the college in order to free his diocesan priests for missionary activity. He secured the services of the Fathers of Mercy of Lyons in 1841. When the approval for their coming was being arranged with officials of Propaganda, Portier obtained the pontifical charter of a university from the Holy See to grant doctorates. But in fact Portier's boys school did not develop as a pontifical university. The French Fathers of Mercy, known for their unbending discipline, could not successfully conduct a school for Americans and had to withdraw. Priests of the Congregation of Jesus and Mary (Eudists) staffed the college briefly. In 1846 Portier secured priests from the Lyons province of the Society of Jesus who successfully conducted the college for lay students. Clerical formation went on sporadically for a few seminarians through this unstable period, at least until the 1850s, but a permanent seminary did not emerge.[24]

The diocese of Cincinnati, formed from the diocese of Bardstown, in 1821, had as its first bishop the American-born Dominican, Edward Fenwick. After obtaining grants from the Society for the Propagation of the Faith, Fenwick completed his modest St. Peter's Cathedral in 1826 on Sycamore Street in Cincinnati. In an old frame structure next to the cathedral the bishop opened St. Francis Xavier Seminary for four students in May 1829. He explained that Cincinnati would need a seminary, since the number of European priests who came to his diocese would not be enough: "With a seminary, I do not lose those that come from Europe while at the same time I form a native clergy, bred to the customs of the country, accustomed to the hardships and well acquainted with the language, etc."[25] With aid from the European mission societies, he completed a substantial building next to the cathedral where in 1831 he opened Athenaeum College for laymen along with St. Francis Xavier Seminary, both under the direction of diocesan priests. The mixed institution of seminary and lay college struggled through the 1830s, leaving much to desired, according to John B. Purcell, who was appointed Cincinnati's second bishop in 1833. In 1840 Purcell obtained Jesuits to take over the college portion of the program and gave them the property of the cathedral and college for the school they renamed St. Francis Xavier College.[26]

After handing over a college to the Jesuits, Purcell devoted Cincinnati's funds from mission societies to building a more imposing cathedral at a new site. The bishop tried several formats for local clerical formation. He briefly had seminarians living in the episcopal residence, where diocesan priests taught them. In 1842 on a donated farm in Brown County, Ohio, about forty miles from Cincinnati he started a seminary to be conducted by a group of Vincentian priests. When this arrangement ended in 1845, he brought the seminarians back to Cincinnati where they were housed at the episcopal residence and tutored by a Jesuit priest.[27] These temporary expedients testify to his determination to have local training and would be succeeded by his more ambitious seminary venture later.

At Boston, the first bishop of the diocese, Jean Cheverus, boarded his first seminarian in his house before ordaining him in 1817. Cheverus ordained several more imported seminarians in the next few years. After Cheverus resigned his see in 1823, his successor, the American-born Benedict Fenwick, continued to receive a small number of seminarians in his house.[28]

Bishop Fenwick hoped to establish a seminary, as he told the Society for the Propagation of the Faith in 1831: "Oh, if I had the means to build a seminary able to house only twelve good students! What an infinite good would be promised by this beginning!"[29] Fenwick was particularly concerned that local boys who would be inclined to become priests had no way of developing this inclination because they had to take up a trade or go into business at a relatively early age. Bishop Fenwick expected that once a seminary was built he could find the means to support as many seminarians as the diocese could produce. With support from the mission societies he enlarged his residence at the Cathedral of the Holy Cross in Boston, where he hoped to keep twenty-five to thirty boarding seminarians and an equal number of local day students.[30] Fenwick's few seminarians taught boys at the cathedral while pursuing theological studies part-time. As early as 1828 he had requested Sulpicians to staff his proposed seminary but was refused. Since he could not obtain a seminary faculty, Fenwick resorted to sending the most advanced students to the Sulpicians at Montreal. Later seminary ideas, such as a school in Maine, then a part of the Boston diocese, or an arrangement with the Jesuits at Worcester or Boston did not get beyond the planning stage.[31]

At New York, Bishop Jean Dubois, the founder of Mount St. Mary's College and Seminary at Emmitsburg, took up his duties as bishop in 1826. He relied on the Emmitsburg seminary to train his students until he could form his own diocesan seminary. In 1829 and 1830 he visited Europe to obtain funds principally for a seminary. As Dubois explained to the Society for the Propagation of the Faith, the ordinary place to obtain English-speaking priests was Ireland but the supply was uneven. (He did not add that he had already had many unpleasant experiences with Irish priests.) It was therefore a necessity to establish a seminary "where we would be able to form a national clergy."[32] With his mission society funds he purchased land on the Hudson River at Nyack about thirty miles north of New York City in 1832 and started to build a spacious three-story building. In a temporary location nearby he had already settled two priests, John McGerry, Emmitsburg's former president, and John McCloskey, a recent Emmitsburg alumnus, with five seminarians. Unfortunately, the nearly completed but uninsured building was completely destroyed by fire in 1834. The bishop had no funds to rebuild it.[33]

Bishop Dubois then accepted from John LaFarge the offer of a manor house located in the Thousand Islands area of northern New York. In the fall of 1838 three priests, three lay instructors, and eight students inaugurated St. Vincent de Paul Seminary there at LaFargeville. However, its enormous distance from New York City or any populated area was a drawback, since the seminary was operated as a mixed seminary and lay college. The school lasted only one year.

Dubois lived until 1842 in declining health, but the administration of the diocese passed in 1838 to his energetic coadjutor and successor, Bishop John Hughes. Hughes also intended to form a seminary. As he told the Leopoldine Foundation, because of his dependence on foreign priests "he was forced to send workers into the vineyard of the Lord whom he did not know." Until he had a seminary, "the Diocese of New York is deprived of the living spiritual resources on which—next to the help of God—its progress depends."[34] Hughes bought an estate named "Rose Hill" in the Bronx where he opened St. Joseph Seminary in 1840 with fourteen seminarians. He also established in the same place St. John's College for lay students. Hughes obtained a staff of Vincentians to conduct only the seminary in 1842. The Vincentians objected to the duties that seminarians were required to perform in the college and withdrew from the diocese's service in 1844. By 1846, Hughes acquired the services of the Jesuits under

August Thebaud, S. J., for both seminary and St. John's College. This arrangement continued until 1856, when Hughes, after a series of conflicts with the Jesuits, dismissed them from the seminary. Hughes staffed the seminary with diocesan priests until it closed in 1860.[35]

At Philadelphia, Francis Patrick Kenrick, the talented instructor of Bardstown's seminary, was appointed coadjutor bishop in 1830 to administer the diocese for the erratic octogenarian Bishop Henry Conwell until the latter's death in 1842, when Kenrick became bishop in his own name. As a former seminary professor, Kenrick's first thoughts on becoming bishop were of forming clergy. While still in Bardstown, he had told the cardinal prefect of Propaganda that he planned to establish a diocesan seminary in Philadelphia. However, he apparently had second thoughts and considered the idea of making Mount St. Mary's at Emmitsburg the Philadelphia diocesan seminary. It seemed a sensible idea since it was located a few miles from the Pennsylvania border and about 120 miles from Philadelphia. The new bishop proposed to Mount St. Mary's then president, John Purcell, that in view of the lack of support for the school from "the ruling powers of Baltimore," it should be made "Mount Saint Mary's Seminary and College for the Diocese of Philadelphia in perpetuum." The plan would assure the college's existence and relieve Kenrick of the "solicitude and hazard" of erecting a seminary in Philadelphia.[36] The idea was seconded by the then Philadelphia pastor and Emmitsburg alumnus, John Hughes, who even favored moving the school to Philadelphia. However, no concrete steps were taken to carry out the idea.

When the Leopoldine Foundation provided $4,803 for the diocese in 1832, Bishop Kenrick started a seminary in Philadelphia at his residence on South Fifth Street. On June 26, 1832, he took in his first seminarian, Patrick Bradley, recently arrived from Ireland, and he had acquired three more Irish seminarians by September. The pastor of the local German parish, Francis Guth, and the coadjutor bishop himself shared the teaching duties until 1833, when the bishop's recently ordained younger brother, Peter Kenrick, arrived from Ireland to teach seminarians who were mostly recent immigrants from Ireland well advanced in their training. The seminary was relocated in 1837 to a house adjoining St. Mary's Church, whose pastor, a recently arrived Irish-born Propaganda College graduate, Edward Barron, was also rector of the seminary. Bishop Kenrick used nearly all of about $15,000 in allotments from the Leopoldine Foundation before 1846 for the seminary.

Kenrick sought to place his seminary on a more secure financial basis by proposing in his Lenten pastoral letter of 1835 the formation of a Seminary Fund Society. Membership in the society was to cost one dollar per year, to be collected by groups of solicitors in each parish. The bishop's seminary pastoral letter of 1838 impressed on Philadelphia Catholics the importance of the seminary above other diocesan projects. He ranked the seminary above support for the multiplying Catholic churches in the city: "In vain has the number of our churches doubled within the last eight years, if there be not a proportionate increase of priests to minister to them." And he placed the seminary above the orphanage: "The asylums for the destitute orphans are calculated to enlist greater sympathy, but a Diocesan seminary has stronger claims on your munificence, because it is to diffuse more widely, blessings of a higher order." For Kenrick, it was time to develop a "respectable" seminary to create a clergy for the diocese "that our youth may be stimulated to enter it, and that they may be educated under the direction of the bishop, whose judgement is to determine their fitness for the holy ministry."[37] The first collection in 1835 brought in $1,451; between 1838 and 1858 the collection averaged between $3,000 and $5,000 annually.[38]

Kenrick secured legal incorporation from the Pennsylvania legislature for the "Philadelphia Theological Seminary of St. Charles Borromeo," in 1838. The incorporated St. Charles Borromeo Seminary opened in a new building at Eighteenth and Race Streets which had been purchased for $5,000 while still incomplete because the previous owners realized their planned building would be too large for their business needs. The new seminary opened in January 1839 to ten students under the direction of Michael O'Connor, an Irish-born graduate of the Urban College. In 1842 the seminary was entrusted to the Vincentians, who supplied a continuous faculty until they withdrew in 1852.[39] In 1845 the bishop obtained the charter of a pontifical university, including the power to grant doctorates. During his Philadelphia years Kenrick succeeded in developing, for his rapidly growing diocese, a seminary that was not affiliated with an academy for lay students, and he had devised a mechanism for financing it. Its location in an urban setting brought the seminary into contact with the nearby cathedral, and the ministerial activities of the faculty assured an awareness of the church beyond the seminary.[40]

At New Orleans, Antoine Blanc, was appointed fourth bishop of the diocese in 1835. With funds from the mission societies, he built, in 1838, the Ecclesiastical Seminary of St. Vincent de Paul at Plattenville in Assumption Parish, about fifty miles from New Orleans. Blanc secured a faculty of three Vincentian priests, to whom he deeded the property. As in Philadelphia, the seminary at Plattenville was exclusively for seminarians and did not have an affiliated academy. Bishop Blanc viewed the seminary as a "necessity" and believed that the destiny of the diocese largely depended on its advancement. Forty-seven priests were ordained for the diocese from the seminary before it was destroyed by fire on February 27, 1855.[41]

The building was not insured, and there were no diocesan funds available to rebuild it. The seminarians were moved to the Vincentians' St. Stephen's parish in New Orleans where small groups continued to receive training until 1867.

The diocese of Detroit was formed in 1832 from territory from the Cincinnati diocese. Its first bishop, Frederic Rese, as noted, had been instrumental in founding the mission societies of Vienna and Munich. When he arrived in Detroit as bishop he brought several priests and seminarians recruited from abroad. The seminarians lived in the bishop's house until their ordination. By 1836 Rese had built a large residence near the cathedral for his household of priests and seminarians. He also arranged for two Oratorian priests to open a boys' academy nearby and the seminarians taught there part-time. This arrangement was probably still in effect in 1837, when Rese retired from the diocese because of his failing mental health, and it may have continued into the administration of coadjutor Bishop Peter Paul Lefevere, who arrived in Detroit in 1841.[42] In the same year Bishop Lefevere related to the Leopoldine Foundation that while it was "necessary" to form a seminary, circumstances prevented it.[43] His inherited household seminary took a more substantial form by 1846, when it was named St. Thomas Seminary and received seminarians from the bishop's native Belgium. It lasted until the 1850s.

The diocese of Vincennes was formed in 1834, and Mount St. Mary's longtime director of seminarians, Simon Bruté, was appointed bishop. He arrived in his Indiana diocese with a seminarian whom he instructed and soon ordained. After a European tour to solicit funds and personnel in 1835 and 1836, he returned to Vincennes with some twenty priests and seminarians. The seminarians resided with the bishop near St. Francis Xavier Cathedral at Vincennes. After Bruté's death in 1839, his successors, Celestine de la Hailandière, until 1847, and Jean Bazin, until 1848, continued the seminary, which consisted mostly of French natives. Bazin briefly joined it to the local boys' college. In 1848, Bishop Maurice de St. Palais transferred the seminarians to a farm outside Vincennes where priesthood candidates continued to be trained intermittently until the late 1850s.[44]

By the late 1830s all the dioceses in the United States except the very youngest had attempted to form a program of training diocesan priests locally. Several dioceses had relatively longstanding seminaries such as Baltimore, New Orleans (when its center of operation was St. Louis), Bardstown, and Charleston. By 1830 the funds from Europe began to have an effect so that bishops of the remaining dioceses undertook seminary programs during the 1830s. At the Fourth Provincial Council of Baltimore in 1840 the generosity of the societies of Lyons and Vienna was publicly acknowledged in the bishops' pastoral letter. The letter noted the impact of aid in the areas of church building, travel expenses of missionaries coming to America, and the support of seminaries.[45]

The American bishops meeting in 1837 in the Third Provincial Council of Baltimore petitioned Propaganda to create new dioceses at Dubuque, Nashville, and Natchez and nominated episcopal candidates for each. Pope Gregory XVI thereupon formally erected the new sees as requested. Meeting for the Fifth Provincial Council of Baltimore in 1843, the American bishops petitioned for new dioceses at Pittsburgh, Hartford, Chicago, Milwaukee, Little Rock, and for a vicariate apostolic in Oregon, then jointly held by the United States and Great Britain. Later that year the Holy See established dioceses at all these places and named as bishops those whom the council had nominated.[46] The new dioceses created in 1837 and 1843 increased the number of American ecclesiastical jurisdictions to twenty-one. With the creation of new dioceses and the continued availability of mission society funds, a new round of seminary foundings took place in the 1840s.

At Dubuque, Matthias Loras, the former president of Spring Hill College in Mobile, was appointed bishop of the new diocese in 1837. After a recruiting trip to Europe, he arrived in Dubuque in 1839. He kept seminarians recruited late in their training at his household in Dubuque in the months preceding their ordination. He told the Leopoldine Foundation in 1841 that he was building a seminary where he hoped "to educate missionaries for the conversion of Indians."[47] However, his hope of founding a seminary that operated separately from his household was postponed until 1850, when Mount St. Bernard's Seminary was built near Dubuque. It opened in 1851 but was closed by 1855.[48]

At Nashville, the American-born Dominican, Richard Pius Miles, became bishop of the new diocese in 1837. He was the sole priest in Tennessee until 1839, when he acquired a second priest and received an allotment from the Society for the Propagation of the Faith. He spent the money on a large house in Nashville in which he lived and welcomed a few seminarians, in the initial years, who conducted a school in the house. After recruiting more funds and seminarians in Europe, the program was strengthened to the extent that the enterprise was named St. Athanasius Seminary by 1844. It closed in 1848 when the supply of seminarians faltered. In 1859 and 1860 it was only briefly reopened.[49]

The diocese of Richmond was formed in 1820, but owing to the lack of means and the small size of the Catholic population, a resident bishop remained only until 1822. The diocese was then administered by the archbishops of Baltimore until 1841, when it was considered populous enough to support a bishop. A Baltimore priest, Richard Whelan, was appointed second bishop of Richmond. Despite the proximity of the seminaries of Baltimore and Emmitsburg, Whelan spent the money he obtained from Lyons and Vienna to buy a farm about a mile from Richmond. Here the bishop gathered ten Irish seminarians and opened St. Vincent's Seminary and College. The bishop was personally in charge of the enterprise. However, the college was too far from the city for the convenience of lay students. The seminary and college closed by 1843.[50]

At Pittsburgh, Michael O'Connor, the rector of St. Charles Seminary in Philadelphia, in 1843 was appointed bishop of the new diocese, embracing the western part of Pennsylvania. With funds from Vienna and ten seminarians from Ireland, O'Connor arrived in Pittsburgh for the first time as bishop. The seminarians lived with O'Connor until 1846, when St. Michael's Seminary was founded (without an affiliated academy) in the Birmingham section of Pittsburgh. The seminary increased its enrollment gradually until 1851, when it closed for financial reasons.[51]

At Little Rock, Andrew Byrne, an alumnus of England's Charleston seminary, was appointed first bishop in 1843. The bishop initially accommodated seminarians in his own household. By 1847 Byrne's household seminary developed into a seminary with boys academy, conducted by two priests and a handful of seminarians. In 1849 the bishop moved the seminary to a site near Fayetteville, Arkansas, where Catholics were more numerous, and named it St. Andrew's College. The school continued to educate local boys and provided a training place for immigrant seminarians until 1861 when it was closed because of a lack of priests to conduct it.[52]

The diocese of Hartford began its existence in 1843 comprising the states of Connecticut and Rhode Island. The second bishop of the diocese, Bernard O'Reilly, arrived in 1850 and followed the example of his predecessor, William Tyler, by residing in Providence, Rhode Island. There he opened St. Mary's Theological Seminary to ten seminarians in his residence. The seminarians also taught in the cathedral parish. By 1855 the bishop abandoned the effort and placed his students in seminaries outside the diocese.[53]

The dioceses of Chicago and Milwaukee were both established in 1843 and quickly started efforts to train clerics. Bishop John Martin Henni carried on clerical training in his household and later in a rectory in Milwaukee soon after arriving there in 1844. Bishop William Quarter of Chicago soon began a seminary in his residence, where he instructed sixteen seminarians himself. He explained that the seminary was necessary because the diocese "did not get sufficient priests from Europe as are needed in these extended Missions."[54] In 1846 the more elaborate University of St. Mary of the Lake, a mixed seminary and college, opened in Chicago built with aid from the European mission aid societies and from local contributions. The beginnings of clerical training in these two dioceses with large Catholic populations concentrated in growing cities gave promise of success in the years ahead.[55]

The bishops of the dioceses formed in the first half-century of the American church demonstrated a close adherence to the Tridentine ideal of each bishop sponsoring a seminary, as the bishops decreed at the Second Provincial Council of Baltimore of 1833. Of the twenty-one dioceses established up to 1843, all except the diocese of Natchez would at least attempt to sponsor diocesan training locally unless clerical formation was already undertaken by other groups, such as the Sulpicians of Baltimore or the Vincentians of St. Louis. The extensive report of Canon Josef Salzbacher, an official of the Leopoldine Foundation who toured the United States in 1842, reported the bishops' expressed intention of forming a national clergy and recruitment of native Americans for the priesthood. Accordingly, Salzbacher noted, it was "one of the first and most pressing concerns" of a newly named bishop to erect a seminary as soon as possible.[56] Even if the beginning was small and the means inadequate, the canon remarked, outside help could be expected from the European mission societies. There was a hint of his disapproval of this practice, as Salzbacher supported the idea of larger seminaries, especially a national one as proposed for training German priests. However, the American bishops in their pastoral letter of 1840, issued after the Fourth Provincial Council of Baltimore, restated their belief in the "necessity and the obligation of providing for the succession of the ministry as well as for its extension, by erecting and supporting seminaries for the education of those who aspire to serve at the altar." The bishops rejoiced "to find that since our last council [1837] much has been done to secure this object,—America must gradually become independent of foreign churches for the perpetuation of her priesthood."[57]

Bishops did not often explain at length the merits of having so many local diocesan seminaries. Bishop Michael O'Connor of Pittsburgh was one who left extended views on the subject, as he did in 1845 in justifying the need for a seminary to officials of the Society of the Propagation of the Faith:

> I did not think that I could possibly defer the erection of a seminary. I may, by exertions, obtain a supply of priests from Europe, but it is under every point of view far more desirable that the wants of the diocese in that respect be supplied by persons educated in this country. Besides, no matter what number of priests I may procure from Europe at present, the growing population, and growing wants of that population will require new supplies, and this will be met far

better by seminarians educated here. Indeed, it is not advisable to send many of those who come from Europe immediately on the missions. A seminary where they could reside for some time would be necessary, if nothing else required it. All these and other considerations made me decide on commencing a seminary last year. . . .[58]

The bishop responded defensively about European "theorists" when his younger brother James, a student at the Urban College of the Propaganda, reported adverse comments in Rome about the numerous American seminaries. The bishop reacted: "Our most practical men are all in favour of diocesan seminaries in most dioceses. It is hard to explain that reason to those who do not feel the practical bearing of things." Not wishing to advance all the arguments in favor of seminaries for his brother, he stated:

> I will merely say that a roving spirit is one of the greatest curses of our priest[s], and that these general seminaries would make it infinitely worse than it is. The effect of having a seminary in its advantages for making vocations and getting students is a point of view that you could no more get one of these theorists to understand than you could get a Roman to understand the tactics of an election.[59]

The practical advantages that the American bishops saw in having their own seminaries did not require much adjustment of the inherited institutional form of the seminary. The numerous local seminaries were remarkably, even literally, consistent with the Tridentine ideal. In many dioceses where the bishop sponsored the seminary, it was located at his modest cathedral and residence. The seminarians could assist at the liturgical services at the cathedral, lending greater dignity to occasions at which the bishop officiated. It thereby mirrored the arrangements presupposed in the Tridentine decree, locating the seminary at the cathedral. Seminarians often taught in a school at or near the cathedral and came under the personal observation of the bishop and his immediate circle of priests. The seminary was at the center of the incipient Catholic institutional life of a new diocese.

The seminarians were usually Europeans recruited in the late stages of their training. Their supply was not necessarily continuous and their number usually small. Accordingly, Canon Salzbacher reported twenty-two seminaries in existence in 1842, collectively enrolling 277 seminarians, or about thirteen per seminary.[60] Since Kenrick's successful Philadelphia seminary enrolled thirty-three and the Emmitsburg and Baltimore seminaries each had about twenty or more seminarians, the average enrollment at the local diocesan seminaries was probably about ten. Despite the seminary's size, it was a convenience to form immigrant seminarians locally for the short period before their ordination. Furthermore, the expense of supporting them at an estalished seminary such as Emmitsburg or Baltimore was avoided. The seminary also held out the hope that local Catholic youth would be attracted to the priesthood in order to form a national clergy, as some bishops mentioned, to be trained locally.

By the 1830s the donations of the missionary aid societies were of crucial importance in the opening of virtually all new seminaries. These societies honored the ideal of the local diocesan seminary by acceding to the requests for funds of the many American bishops who advanced an appeal that a seminary was the future hope of diocesan development. Once seminaries were started, the societies could not possibly subsidize them on an ongoing basis, so that many closed for lack of funding. The difficulty of raising funds for seminaries locally precluded their ongoing development. As early as 1838, Stephen Dubuisson, a Jesuit priest in St. Louis, reported to the Leopoldine Foundation how difficult it was to raise funds for a seminary because of the inability to appeal for the support of non-Catholics, as was done in the case of charitable institutions. It was easier to appeal for support for a present need, but the results of a seminary were too distant and vague to compel the generosity of Catholics.[61]

The supply of seminarians through the period was small and uneven, making it difficult to maintain a seminary even if the financial problems were mastered. England, Fenwick, Kenrick, and O'Connor looked to the diocesan seminary to attract local youth to the priesthood, but few youth among the American-born Catholic population aspired to be priests and the sons of immigrants apparently did not as yet form a large enough pool of seminarians, except in larger communities such as Philadelphia. If financial difficulties did not close the seminary, the lack of students surely would.

As the late 1840s approached, local seminaries began to close, starting a trend that would continue into the 1850s, though a few seminaries such as those of Hartford and Dubuque would not be started until the 1850s. By mid-century the pressures of Catholic population growth forced the creation of new dioceses. Of the twenty-three dioceses formed between 1847 and 1857, only four — Wheeling, Newark, Natchitoches, and Cleveland — attempted seminaries, and of these only two, Newark and Cleveland, survived beyond the 1870s. After the lapse of a decade, 1857 to 1868, when no dioceses were formed, the Holy See, in the latter year, pursuant to the recommendations of the Second Plenary Council of Baltimore of 1866, established twelve new ecclesiastical jurisdictions. Of these twelve, only the new diocese of Columbus briefly supported a seminary, and none of the seven jurisdictions formed in the 1870s attempted seminaries during the period before 1880.

Through the 1840s, the practical advantages coincided with the Tridentine ideal of each bishop sponsoring a seminary. In other words, the bishops combined an inherited ideal with the practical wisdom of training immigrant seminarians for the short period before their ordination, thereby avoiding the expense of sending them to an existing seminary and assuring themselves that they knew the candidates before ordination. However, American bishops in their missionary dioceses did not function in a context similar to that of the episcopate of the Council of Trent. Most dioceses of the sixteenth century would normally have a population entirely Catholic and thereby capable of supplying a large number of poor youth who aspired to the priesthood. In all American dioceses of the time, Catholics were not numerous enough to supply an adequate number of candidates for the priesthood. Unlike the European church of the Council of Trent, the American church had no revenues from endowments and benefices to support the operation of a seminary. Mission society funds would continue to flow to America in the 1850s in larger amounts, but the total sum did not match the expanding volume of Catholic activity. Consequently, these funds were having less impact, and certainly no diocese received the level of funding great enough to launch a large seminary solely on the basis of mission society contributions. By the 1850s a new pattern of seminary foundings under bishops' sponsorship began to emerge.

3. Freestanding Seminaries

Through the middle of the nineteenth century, massive immigration enlarged the American Catholic community. An organizational response to the resulting increase of Catholic activity was the creation of new Catholic dioceses and archdioceses across the country. As the pace of building more churches and institutions increased, the number of local seminaries under the direct sponsorship of the individual bishops decreased. Instead, several large seminaries served a number of dioceses in their region. The shift from local to larger seminaries, called freestanding seminaries, is a major characteristic of American seminary development after 1850.

The severe agricultural crisis in western Europe stimulated a massive movement of people between 1846 and 1854 when some 1,250,000 Irish and nearly 1,000,000 Germans entered the United States. Nearly all the Irish and a majority of Germans were Catholics. The Catholic community in the United States that had grown steadily from 100,000 in 1810 to 600,000 by 1840 rose to 3,100,000 in 1860.[1]

For the better organization of Catholic life among this increased population, the American bishops proposed and Propaganda established twenty new dioceses and three vicariates apostolic (that soon became dioceses) between 1847 and 1857. The wave of new dioceses nearly doubled the number of American ecclesiastical jurisdictions from twenty-four in 1846 to forty-six in 1857. The multiplication of dioceses pointed to the need to divide the ecclesiastical province of Baltimore, coextensive with the United States, into several provinces. In 1846, Propaganda officials raised Oregon City (now Portland) in Oregon, then jointly controlled by the United States and Great Britain, to the rank of an archdiocese. Propaganda assigned several dioceses in Oregon and western Canada as suffragans to form the Oregon City ecclesiastical province. Bishop Peter Kenrick of St. Louis, who regarded the Oregon territory as part of his jurisdiction, protested Propaganda's action of creating an ecclesiastical province within his diocese. The Holy See in 1847 then promoted St. Louis to the rank of an arch-diocese but left the decision of which dioceses would compose the St. Louis province to a council of American bishops. The bishops met in 1849 for the Seventh Provincial Council of Baltimore and proposed to the Holy See the creation of four new dioceses with episcopal nominees, the erec-tion of three archiepiscopal sees at New York, Cincinnati, and New Orleans, and the assignment of suffragan sees to these archdioceses and to St. Louis and Baltimore in order to form five ecclesiastical provinces. Since Balti-more would no longer be the sole archiepiscopal see, the bishops proposed making the archbishop of Baltimore primate of the United States as a fitting dignity for the presiding prelate at future national councils of bishops. The Holy See, as requested, created the new dioceses and archdioceses in 1850 but declined to promote the archbishop of Baltimore to the dignity of a primate.[2]

The creation of new ecclesiastical provinces headed by archbishops around the country was an important step in the jurisdictional develop-ment of the American church and created a sense of regional identity with the province. Heretofore, Baltimore and its archbishops had been the focal point of national leadership through seven provincial councils held from 1829 to 1849. While the tradition of national councils continued with the plenary councils of the American bishops meeting in 1852, 1866, and 1884, the ecclesiastical province headed by its archbishop acquired a share of jurisdictional authority that had once been Baltimore's. At the First Ple-nary Council of Baltimore of 1852, the bishops recommended that in ac-cordance with the Tridentine legislation on provincial councils the bishops of each province hold a council every three years. Accordingly, provincial councils were held in 1855 and 1858 at St. Louis, in 1854, 1860, and 1861 at New York, in 1855, 1858, and 1861 at Cincinnati, in 1856 and 1860 at New Orleans, and in 1855, 1858, and 1870 at the greatly diminished prov-ince of Baltimore.[3]

The development of provincial loyalties touched on ideas about semi-nary foundings. Archbishop Purcell's plans for a seminary at Cincinnati, opening in 1851 in the year following the diocese's promotion to the rank of an archdiocese, stimulated the interest of Bishop Michael O'Connor in making it a regional seminary for the west.[4] O'Connor, formerly such a strong partisan of diocesan seminaries, had closed his Pittsburgh semi-nary in 1851 and expressed the hope that the new Cincinnati seminary would become a general seminary. O'Connor shared his proposal with Archbishop Peter Kenrick of St. Louis, who was attracted to the idea because of the money it would save him in operating his own seminary. His brother, Fran-cis P. Kenrick, who was appointed archbishop of Baltimore in 1851, dis-agreed, urging a seminary for St. Louis because a metropolitan see "needs such a support to which other sees may come."[5] O'Connor continued to pursue the idea, even proposing to Purcell that the Cincinnati seminary might be incorporated and have a board of trustees with each diocese represented by a priest and a layman. Archbishop Purcell's specific reactions to O'Connor's views cannot be found, but in 1851 he submitted a proposal for the planning of the First Plenary Council of Baltimore in 1852 stating: "Is it expedient & practicable to found a Catholic University? And if not, how shall we otherwise efficiently provide for the education of such a clergy as the peculiar circumstances of this country require?"[6] When the bishops met for the First Plenary Council of Baltimore in 1852, they framed a seminary decree that reflected a development in their thinking since the second provincial council of 1833. They urged the founding of diocesan seminaries, but if this was not possible, then the bishops of the province should cooperate to form a provincial seminary.[7] The conciliar discussions on this issue were not recorded. However, Archbishop Peter Kenrick's views stated in 1853 might be taken as reflection of the developing attitude on the subject. He told Purcell:

> I regard it as a matter of highest moment that the principle of Provincial Seminaries should be carried out. The only way to secure this is to make the Provincial Seminary worthy of the name, especially by the number and capabilities of its Professors. With but very few exceptions Diocesan Seminaries cannot have the same advantages as Provincial Seminaries properly conducted possess, and sooner or later will disappear.[8]

The bishops' subsequent collective behavior related to seminaries for the following decades indicates an interest in provincial seminaries or at least those formed on a firmer basis than the numerous local efforts up to the 1840s. At the Second Plenary Council of Baltimore of 1866 the bishops restated the Tridentine ideal of each diocese supporting a seminary but also the desirability of provincial seminaries where diocesan ones were not feasible.[9]

The first of several provincial seminaries to be planned arose at Cincinnati. There, Archbishop Purcell presided over a populous archdiocese that embraced the southern two-thirds of Ohio, and the see city, Cincinnati, was the largest in the West during the 1840s and 1850s. Its Catholics had developed a rich institutional life. After successfully cultivating the mission aid societies and wealthy local donors, Purcell built the elegant neoclassical St. Peter-in-Chains Cathedral, completed in 1845, that proclaimed the substantial Catholic presence in the city.[10] Purcell then turned his attention to establishing the faltering diocesan seminary on a firmer basis.

The outgoing Purcell, who often seemed to have persons of means to draw upon, accepted in 1847 from Michael and Patrick Considine, two Irish brothers, a five-acre plot of land for a seminary on Price Hill, one of the summits overlooking the Cincinnati basin from the west. Two other well-to-do Irish brothers, John and James Slevin, began construction in the same year at their own expense an imposing four-story building on the site, costing $22,116, to which additions were later made. While the construction was in progress, Purcell held a diocesan synod at which, among other issues, the clergy were consulted on a method of financing a seminary. Purcell then announced in a pastoral letter of January 1849 the inauguration of an annual seminary collection in each parish of the diocese. This fund-raising effort was accompanied by explanations of the importance of the seminary in the Catholic newspaper, which listed the parishes and their donations in subsequent years.[11]

Meanwhile, Purcell sought unsuccessfully to obtain a faculty of priests of the Society of St. Sulpice for the proposed seminary. He even traveled to Paris to lobby with the superior general, Joseph Carrière, his close friend from seminary days, but the Sulpicians lacked the needed personnel.[12] Instead, Purcell managed to recruit an Irish-born student at St. Sulpice, Michael Mary Hallinan, who came to Cincinnati after his ordination in 1851 to become seminary rector. A Moravian-born priest, Francis Joseph Pabisch, who held a doctorate in theology from the University of Vienna, was recruited for the faculty and later became rector; and a Cincinnati seminarian, Sylvester Rosecrans, joined the seminary staff after ordination in Rome in 1852. With faculty at hand, Purcell opened his new seminary, named Mount St. Mary's Seminary of the West, on October 2, 1851. The institution's name echoed the Mount St. Mary's of Emmitsburg, of which Purcell had been president eighteen years before.

The bishops of the Cincinnati province held their first provincial council in 1855 when they formally designated Mount St. Mary's of the West the provincial seminary, to which each bishop promised to send at least two students. To enhance the stature of the seminary, the bishops petitioned Propaganda to grant a charter to the seminary empowering it to confer pontifical degrees. The bishops were also asked at the council to consider the pope's proposal to the American bishops to support an American college for seminarians in Rome. The college meant, of course, that the American bishops would be responsible for financing the Roman venture. Purcell and the bishops did not favor an American college in Rome, because it would divert funds needed to build up American seminaries and Roman-trained clerics might be resented in the United States, then rife with nativism. The bishops were frank in expressing their views to Roman officials; the pope himself wrote to Purcell, turning down the request for pontifical degrees on the grounds that Americans pursuing degrees should be sent to the proposed American college in Rome.[13]

Despite setbacks, the Cincinnati seminary generally prospered through the 1850s. Financing the seminary was an ongoing challenge, as, for instance, when the *Catholic Telegraph* announced in April 1855 that the seminary funds were exhausted and appealed for money. In the spring of 1856 an unnamed donor made possible the construction of a new wing with chapel to house a college for lay students opening the same year at the seminary. In 1855 Purcell had obtained incorporation from the state of Ohio enabling Mount St. Mary's of the West to grant degrees. There were no clearly stated reasons for opening a lay college, since the Jesuits already conducted one in Cincinnati. Perhaps it was considered desirable to have a larger collegiate program, since there was already a classical course for seminarians. Perhaps Purcell's anxiety about financing a freestanding seminary caused him to open the college, in which, as in the other seminary colleges, the seminarians were tutors to the younger students. The lay college closed in 1862 because of the Civil War and was not reopened.

Mount St. Mary's of the West enjoyed steady growth. From the twenty-three seminarians of 1854, enrollment grew to ninety seminarians and lay students by 1858. The physical plant was quickly repaired following a fire in 1863, and after the Civil War a new wing was added costing $50,000, paid for in part by wealthy donors. The seminary's faculty was periodically augmented by Cincinnati priests trained in Rome, such as the short-lived young rector William J. Barry, and Henry Richter and Thomas Byrne, who became bishops. By 1877 the seminary enrolled ninety-seven seminarians, of whom twenty-two were theologians, fifteen philosophers, and sixty "preparatorians" or minor seminarians.[14] Though the seminary had enjoyed a period of financial stability based on support of the parishes of the archdiocese and a substantial enrollment of seminarians drawn mainly from the archdiocese, Mount St. Mary's of the West was closed in 1879 because of the bankruptcy of the archdiocese of Cincinnati and the subsequent obligation to repay its creditors. The seminary reopened in 1887.

The provincial character of Mount St. Mary's Seminary of the West was largely symbolic. The province's bishops had promised to support it in 1855 and even formed a board of five trustee-bishops to oversee its operations, but it is not likely that the board met after the First Provincial Council of Cincinnati. The bishops of the Cincinnati ecclesiastical province always knew that the seminary was available as a place to send seminarians, though several bishops already had small seminaries in operation by the time of its opening.

For instance, the bishop of Vincennes, Maurice de St. Palais, continued a small seminary until the early 1860s, where he received emigré seminarians. St. Palais professed not to have funds available to support seminarians at Cincinnati when pressed to support the provincial seminary by Purcell and by the prefect of Propaganda.[15] When the Benedictines opened St. Meinrad Seminary in southern Indiana in 1861, St. Palais had a seminary within his jurisdiction where some of the diocese's seminarians studied. Not always on good terms with the Benedictines, he opened a seminary under his direct control at St. Joseph parish in Indianapolis that lasted through 1874 and 1875.[16]

In Cleveland, Bishop Louis Amadeus Rappe had opened a household seminary in the city in 1848, a year after the establishment of the diocese. By 1850, Rappe had bought the old Spring Cottage and Bathing Establishment east of the downtown area on Lake Erie to house his seminarians. At that location the seminary occasionally operated a boys school in the 1850s and 1860s. The enrollment of seminarians did not exceed thirty by the 1870s, since the modest size of the building could not accommodate more students. For the remainder of the century, successive bishops of Cleveland lacked the means to develop a larger seminary and sent many of their students to other seminaries.[17]

The bishop of Louisville, Martin J. Spalding, was closely associated with Purcell as co-architect of the legislation of the provincial councils of Cincinnati. Spalding was responsible for the province's official minor seminary, St. Thomas, near Bardstown. Purcell conducted his own classical course for seminarians at Mount St. Mary's of the West, in effect competing with St. Thomas Seminary. Bishop Spalding likewise did not feel obliged to send his seminarians to Cincinnati. Spalding's successor, William G. McCloskey, a former rector of the American College in Rome, opened his own modest seminary at an estate, Preston Park, in Louisville in 1871, where most of the diocese's seminarians received their training until the seminary closed in 1888.[18]

The relationship of Bishop Sylvester Rosecrans of Columbus provided a different example of difficulties of provincial support for the seminary. Rosecrans served Mount St. Mary's of the West as theology professor and president of the lay college. A faithful protégé of Purcell, Rosecrans was made auxiliary bishop of Cincinnati in 1863, and when the diocese of Columbus was established in 1868 from territory of the archdiocese of Cincinnati he was appointed bishop. The creation of the new diocese placed great strains on the relationship between Rosecrans and Purcell. The archbishop claimed all the Cincinnati seminarians for the archdiocese, not even conceding to Rosecrans those who came from parishes within the new diocese of Columbus. As Rosecrans grappled with the financial problems of setting up a new diocese, Purcell was rather sharp in demanding payment of tuition for the Columbus seminarians sent to Mount St. Mary's of the West. The sarcastic letters exchanged between Purcell and Rosecrans marked an end of their father-son relationship. Rosecrans vowed to open his own seminary, founding St. Aloysius Seminary in Columbus in 1871 and closing it in 1876, for financial reasons, shortly before his death. His successors did not attempt to start another major seminary.[19]

The Cincinnati seminary enjoyed the support of successive bishops of Fort Wayne, John Luers and Joseph Dwenger, both protégés of Purcell. From outside the Cincinnati province, Bishop Michael O'Connor of Pittsburgh sent several students during the 1850s, as did Purcell's closest episcopal friend, Archbishop Antoine Blanc of New Orleans.

New Orleans already had a functioning seminary when it was made an archdiocese in 1850. The destruction of St. Vincent de Paul Seminary in Assumption Parish by fire in 1855 ended the possibility of its development as a provincial seminary. The subsequent transfer of the seminarians to the New Orleans parish church of St. Stephen was not intended to last, though the program continued until 1867. Archbishop Napoleon Perché opened a seminary in 1870 at his chancery and residence in New Orleans. It remained open until 1881 and educated a handful of seminarians, but local ordinations did not supplant the archdiocese's dependence on imported French clergy. The seminary closed because of the heavy debt of the archdiocese. Though enjoying the status of an archdiocese, New Orleans was unable to sustain a diocesan seminary until the twentieth century.[20] Nearby, when the new diocese of Natchitoches was formed in northern Louisiana in 1853, Bishop Auguste Martin briefly attempted there a household and then mixed seminary after the burning of St. Vincent de Paul Seminary.[21]

At the time of the elevation of St. Louis to an archdiocese in 1847, the Vincentians were conducting the diocese's seminary near their St. Louis parish. Through the same period Archbishop Kenrick had been pondering the future of seminary education for his archdiocese. A reserved and sensitive man, Kenrick did not easily weather the normal differences of opinion that developed between a bishop and communities of priests working in his diocese, such as the Vincentians. Kenrick came to the conclusion that "the Seminary ought to be a distinct establishment and that it ought to belong to the bishop."[22] In 1848 he purchased a plot of land with a two-story brick house in the St. Louis suburb of Carondelet near the convent of the Sisters of St. Joseph and a local parish. He moved his twelve seminarians there, placing them under the direction of a diocesan priest, James Duggan, age twenty-three, a native of Ireland, who had been trained by the Vincentians in St. Louis.[23] The new seminary put an end to the Vincentians' seminary in the city.

The opening of the seminary tested Archbishop Kenrick's skills in financial matters. When Kenrick came to St. Louis in 1841, he found that Bishop Joseph Rosati had completed a cathedral in 1835, though it had a debt. Kenrick received funds from the European mission societies, but he was not among their most frequent supplicants and the debt remained. Kenrick apparently did not like raising money and expressed himself to Purcell as opposed to "peregrinations" around Europe for that purpose, as was the practice of most American bishops.[24] Kenrick stayed in his diocese and received some grants from Europe until 1853, when they were discontinued. He also attempted to sustain the seminary with a series of local fund-raising efforts. In a pastoral letter of 1849 he called for an annual seminary contribution of one dollar from adult Catholics, which, he believed, "would enable us to meet all the expenses we shall have to incur in this work of Christian charity and zeal."[25] From 1850 to 1852, he published the names of donors in the diocesan newspaper in the hope of stimulating donations. These efforts raised only an average of eighty-seven dollars per month. By 1853, he formed the "Roman Catholic Association of St. Louis" as a general fund-raising organization to support the seminary, the Catholic orphanage, and "the education and Christian training of the Catholic youth of this city."[26] Unlike his brother's seminary society in Philadelphia or Purcell's efforts in Cincinnati, Kenrick did not emphasize the distinctive necessity of a seminary. Despite the publicity given to the association in the diocesan newspaper, it soon passed from view. Unlike the outgoing Purcell, Kenrick had not cultivated a number of wealthy donors who could be relied on for large benefactions.

The St. Louis Seminary at Carondelet maintained an enrollment of at least twenty in its initial years. In 1855 the bishops of the St. Louis province met for their first provincial council and recommended that each diocese in the province sponsor a minor seminary and that there should be a provincial major seminary. However, no plan was proposed for interdiocesan support of Kenrick's seminary.[27] In 1856 Kenrick opened a minor seminary program to develop local candidates for major seminary studies. This move enlarged the enrollment to over thirty. Through the 1850s the faculty turned over quickly as its members were promoted to the episcopate, thereby forfeiting the advantages of continuous leadership. John Duggan was soon succeeded as rector by Anthony O'Regan, Patrick Feehan, and John Hennessy, all promoted to the episcopate.

The archdiocese lacked the funds and the personnel to conduct a seminary, so that Kenrick called on the Vincentians to conduct the seminary in the 1858–1859 school year. Shortly thereafter when the archbishop and bishops of the St. Louis province met for their second provincial council in 1858, they petitioned the Vincentians to provide seminary training for the province. They responded by converting their own St. Vincent's College at Cape Girardeau, Missouri, initially to a seminary and later a seminary and lay college to which many bishops of the region sent seminarians until the closing of the seminary portion in 1896. Kenrick showed his ambivalence to the institution by sending most of his students to other seminaries in the ensuing decades.[28]

After the Civil War, Kenrick again planned to have his own seminary in St. Louis and incorporated the "St. Louis Roman Catholic Theological Seminary" in 1869 to be built at the Annunciation Parish in St. Louis. Kenrick went to Rome the following year and gained international attention as one of the leading opponents of papal infallibility at the First Vatican Council. His opposition to the pope, his departure from Rome before the end of the council, his long travels in Europe, the protracted negotiations with Roman authorities over an acceptable submission to the council's decrees, and his virtual retirement from public activities following the appointment of Coadjutor Archbishop Patrick J. Ryan in 1872 diverted his interest from developing a seminary.[29] It appeared that the archdiocese of St. Louis would not have a seminary during his lifetime.

Kenrick did not succeed in developing a successful seminary for his archdiocese and province, but one of his suffragans, John Martin Henni, had a much better record as a seminary founder. In 1843, Henni, a Swiss-born Cincinnati pastor, was appointed bishop of the new diocese of Milwaukee, whose Catholic population was largely German. In the custom of the time Bishop Henni soon sponsored a household seminary in Milwaukee for seminarians recruited from German-speaking Europe or from Ireland who were ordained shortly after their arrival.[30]

Henni devoted the early years of his episcopate to the construction of a cathedral with the assistance of local Catholics and the German missionary aid societies. St. John's Cathedral was completed in 1851 in a simple neoclassical style. The edifice was free of debt and proudly asserted the Catholic presence in Milwaukee. The elaborate ceremonies of its consecration in 1853 brought together Archbishops Kenrick of St. Louis, Hughes of New York, and Purcell of Cincinnati as well as the papal diplomat, Archbishop Gaetano Bedini, and the bishops of the region. The consecration also brought the clergy of the diocese together for a retreat in separate German and Irish sections. The proposal to build a seminary was made among the German priests, who pledged $3,145 toward its construction. The English-speaking priests promised to give at a later date.[31]

In planning the seminary, Henni enjoyed the services of two priests capable of executing a large-scale project. The first, Michael Heiss, a young Bavarian priest who had served in Cincinnati with Henni, joined the new diocese when Henni became bishop. An alumnus of the University of Munich, Heiss was designated the first rector of the proposed seminary.[32] The other priest, Joseph Salzmann, a young Austrian who came to Milwaukee in 1847, had been assigned to pastoral activity in Milwaukee before being assigned by Bishop Henni to start the Catholic newspaper *Der Seebote* in 1852. This publication was intended to offset the aggressive anti-Catholic agitation of the German freethinking press in Wisconsin. Salzmann, energetic, determined, and articulate, sustained an aggressive fund-raising effort for the next twenty years on behalf of the seminary. The atmosphere of spirited sectarian controversy played a part in creating a sense of urgency to build a seminary. In appealing for funds, Salzmann portrayed the dire consequences for the future of the faith without a sufficient number of priests and especially German priests. German immigrants, it was feared, could be lost forever to the church. The challenge of outspoken freethinkers in Wisconsin required the training of not only numerous but well-educated and articulate priests.[33]

Salzmann started a fund-raising organization, the Salesian Society, named for the proposed St. Francis de Sales Seminary. The annual membership fee was one dollar. Salzmann traveled to parishes throughout Wisconsin establishing units of the society. He also embarked on extensive fund-raising tours, visiting German Catholic communities in the Middle West. His first extensive tour outside Wisconsin in the spring and summer of 1854 brought $4,000 to the seminary fund. Over two decades, until his death in 1874, Salzmann raised about $100,000 for the seminary and spread the word about the seminary's importance to the German Catholic population generally.

St. Francis de Sales Seminary was built on a spacious fifty-two acre site about four miles south of Milwaukee on the Lake Michigan shore. The Milwaukee German architect Victor Schulte planned a large five-story, vaguely classical building surmounted with a cupola. It was formally opened on January 29, 1856. Salzmann reported that the intitial cost of the completed building was $24,000. With the completion of the handsome chapel in 1861 and the construction of a substantial addition in 1875–1876 to create a wing for the theology students, separating them from the minor seminarians, most of the funds that Salzmann was able to raise must have been devoted to capital expenses. Given the lack of wealthy donors, the seminary's founding and successful operation from its initial years bespoke the skills of its founders and the generosity of German immigrants.

The opening of St. Francis Seminary was attended by some theoretical questions concerning the seminary's purpose. The preponderance of Germans among the clergy and people to whom the fund-raising efforts had been directed naturally created the impression that the purpose of the seminary was to create German priests for German Catholics. In the address at the cornerstone laying, Michael Heiss, speaking in German, reminded the Germans present that the greatest gift to their children would be their religious faith. The success of the seminary assured success in handing on the faith first brought to them through the apostle of the Germans, St. Boniface. Heiss's discourse spoke to the particularist feeling of Germans even if it did not exclude other nationalities. George Riordan, a Milwaukee priest, also addressed the assembled crowd in English, emphasizing that the seminary was intended for all nationalities.[34] Heiss, on another occasion, explained the Irish-German problem as related to the seminary in this way: the seminary was built on the basis of appeals to the Germans, and after its success had been demonstrated, the Irish and other nationalities would be asked for their support. Whatever the ethnic tensions surrounding the opening of the seminary, there were, in fact, Irish seminarians from Wisconsin at St. Francis Seminary from the earliest years.

St. Francis de Sales Seminary enjoyed immediate success in attracting a substantial enrollment, which reached 265 minor and major seminarians by 1877. By 1880, 505 priests had completed their studies at the seminary.[35] The faculty was composed mainly of German priests for the remainder of the century, thereby reinforcing its reputation as a German seminary. Bishops of dioceses in the upper Mississippi valley filled the institution with seminarians drawn from the substantial German communities in the region. The archdiocese of St. Louis and the diocese of Chicago were heavily represented in the student body. Thus St. Francis Seminary became the *de facto* provincial seminary of the St. Louis ecclesiastical province. When Milwaukee was promoted to the status of an archdiocese in 1875, it already had a flourishing seminary for the new province.

The success of the Milwaukee seminary differed from the experience of clerical formation in Chicago, another suffragan see of the St. Louis province. Bishop William Quarter's promising University of St. Mary of the Lake, a mixed seminary and lay college that opened in downtown Chicago in 1845, soon became a source of conflict between bishop and clergy.[36] Bishop Quarter died unexpectedly in 1848, only four years after arriving in Chicago. He personally owned much of the diocese's ecclesiastical property, which he willed to the University of St. Mary of the Lake. Quarter's successor, Bishop James Van de Velde, S. J., a former president of St. Louis University, in due course obtained the ecclesiastical property from the university trustees, who were all diocesan priests. However, this process established the pattern of the university's clerical trustees viewing the rest of the Chicago church from the vantage of their imposing institution, and the bishop viewing the university as a center of clerical opposition to his authority. The bishop sought without success to obtain a community of priests to conduct the university, which was consistent with the tradition of religious orders conducting schools to release the diocesan priests for parish ministry. However, this effort could be interpreted by the university priests as a hostile move. Rather than pursue conflict with the university priests, Van de Velde arranged with the Holy See in 1853 to resign the see of Chicago, becoming instead second bishop of Natchez.

Archbishop Kenrick arranged for the rector of his seminary, Anthony O'Regan, to become third bishop of Chicago in 1854. O'Regan quickly tired of challenges to episcopal authority posed by the trustees over the conduct of the university and over construction of a university church that was also intended to be a local parish church. He dismissed the four priests on the university faculty and engaged the services of priests of the Congregation of the Holy Cross from Notre Dame to staff the university. At this point, a few seminarians were separated from St. Mary of the Lake and taken into the bishop's residence, where they were trained. Tiring of the strained relationship with the Chicago clergy, Bishop O'Regan resigned the see in 1858.

Archbishop Kenrick arranged for the promotion of still another St. Louis priest, James Duggan, his former seminary rector, to become fourth bishop of Chicago in 1859. Bishop Duggan ended the Congregation of the Holy Cross's direction of the university and returned it to the diocese. It opened in the fall of 1861 under the direction of diocesan priests, and in 1863 the seminary portion was reopened with a faculty of four Chicago priests. The institution flourished, moving into an expensive new building in 1864, but in January 1866, after some relatively minor financial difficulties, Bishop Duggan suddenly closed the University of St. Mary of the Lake. The seminary continued to exist as a separate institution until Bishop Duggan closed it peremptorily in 1868. There is no available reason to account for the bishop's behavior other than to attribute it to the insanity which led to his forced removal in 1869. There was no attempt to restart the seminary after Duggan's departure. The Chicago fire of 1871 destroyed the buildings of the university and the energies of the diocese under Duggan's successors were absorbed in rebuilding churches. The proximity of the successful seminary of Milwaukee, where many Chicago seminarians were trained in the late nineteenth century, diminished interest in forming a seminary for the Chicago diocese. In 1880 Chicago was made an archdiocese but had no seminary to serve the new ecclesiastical province.

By the 1850s the archdiocese of New York became the largest Catholic community in the country. Its St. Joseph's Seminary, operating near St. John's College at Fordham, had been conducted by Jesuits since the departure of the Vincentians in 1846. New York's Archbishop John Hughes eventually feuded with the Jesuits over a range of local issues including property, debts, educational activities, and the promise of having a Jesuit parish in New York. The archbishop sold the seminary building at Fordham to the Jesuits for $20,000 in 1856 but retained its use as a seminary staffed by diocesan priests until 1861, when he closed the seminary. During the period of its existence from 1841 to 1861, the seminary at Fordham had produced 107 priests.[37]

Before closing the seminary Hughes committed the archdiocese to a more costly project than a seminary. In 1858, he laid the cornerstone for the new St. Patrick's Cathedral on Fifth Avenue. This project took up the energies and funds of New York Catholics, costing $1,900,000 by the time of its opening in 1879.[38] The cathedral project had not diverted Hughes's interest in a seminary. In 1862, a priest in Albany, New York, told the archbishop of the availability of a bankrupt Methodist college at nearby Troy. This large college building of 200 rooms had been built a dozen years before on a thirty-seven acre site called Mount Ida near the center of Troy at a reported cost of $197,000. Hughes acted quickly to purchase it, paying $60,000 for the land and building, including furniture, organ, laboratory equipment, a museum, and a library. Hughes naturally felt that he had come across a bargain. Though Troy was located in the diocese of Albany, Hughes announced to the bishops of the province that he would be responsible for purchasing the buildings for a provincial seminary. Hughes found its location attractive since "it is the central point of my ecclesiastical province, there being a railway from the home of each of my suffragans as well as from my own to that central point."[39]

Once he acquired the property for a seminary, Hughes hoped to open a minor and major seminary and attract the Sulpicians to conduct it "almost on any terms."[40] He was even willing to deed the property to them. He asked Boston's Bishop Fitzpatrick while in Europe to appeal to the Sulpicians, and he sent Bishop John McCloskey of Albany to Paris in 1863 to ask them again without success. Hughes next turned to the Belgian primate, Cardinal Engelbert Sterckx, for assistance in securing a faculty. On the cardinal's recommendation Bishop Louis Delebecque of Ghent was able to supply a faculty of priests from his diocese. Four priests, all alumni of the University of Louvain, along with three members of the Brothers of Good Works to manage domestic arrangements, arrived to open St. Joseph's Provincial Seminary at Troy in October 1864.

Archbishop Hughes did not live to see the opening of St. Joseph Seminary because he died in January 1864. The opening of the seminary was the responsibility of Hughes's successor, John McCloskey. The new archbishop planned to share the expenses and responsibility for the seminary with the other bishops of the province. The bishops of Boston, Hartford, Burlington, Portland, and Albany joined the archbishop of New York to support the seminary, while the bishops of Buffalo, Newark and Brooklyn declined. Most of the $30,000 needed to remodel the seminary was donated by the four richest dioceses, New York, Albany, Boston, and Hartford, whose bishops were for many years the seminary's principal supporters. Although Hughes had left the impression that he intended to pay for the building, Archbishop McCloskey set New York's share at $30,000, and the other dioceses, principally Boston, Albany, and Hartford, paid the remaining $30,000.[41] St. Joseph's Seminary then became a provincial seminary in which the interested bishops of the province truly shared financial responsibility and met periodically to formulate policies regarding the seminary. As new dioceses were formed in the New York province, such as Rochester, Springfield, Ogdensburg, Providence, and Syracuse, their bishops joined in sharing responsibility for the seminary.

St. Joseph's opened as a major seminary, initially offering three years of theology and one of philosophy to a student body of seventy students from the various dioceses of the province. Through the 1870s the seminary had an annual enrollment between one hundred and one-hundred and thirty students, and annual ordinations between a low of twenty in 1879 and a high of thirty-eight in 1880.[42] It had the largest enrollment of major seminarians among the diocesan seminaries in the country during the 1870s. The principal figures on the faculty where Ghent diocesan priests who were periodically replaced. Their most notable figure was the longtime rector, Henry Gabriels, who served from 1871 to 1892, when he was appointed second bishop of Ogdensburg. American priests served on the faculty from its opening, when Alexander Sherwood Healy, of a well-known black family in the Boston diocese, was appointed professor of moral theology. The faculty of five or six priests usually included at least two Americans in the following years.

The founding of the provincial seminary at Troy did not supplant other efforts for training diocesan priests within the province. The diocese of Buffalo was formed in 1847, with former Vincentian provincial superior John Timon as bishop. He formed a modest seminary in his household to accommodate immigrant seminarians. By the late 1850s Timon attracted his own Vincentians to the diocese to form a mixed college and seminary at Niagara Falls, New York. Likewise, Italian Franciscans were invited to western New York in 1862; they settled at Allegany near the Pennsylvania border, where they formed St. Bonaventure College and an affiliated seminary that trained diocesan priests.[43]

When the new provincial seminary at Troy was established, the diocese of Newark, formed in 1853 for Catholics in the state of New Jersey, was already training its own priests. Newark's first bishop, James Roosevelt Bayley, opened a boys academy in 1856 at a farm near Madison, New Jersey. The school, named Seton Hall in honor of the bishop's aunt, Mother

Elizabeth Seton, was conducted by Bernard McQuaid, the pastor of St. Patrick's Cathedral in Newark. However, the distance from populous Newark to Madison, about fifteen miles, was soon deemed too far for daily commuting. In 1860, Bayley purchased for $35,000 a sixty-six acre estate with a handsome villa at South Orange. He built another building on the property and the school was relocated from Madison, as Bayley explained in a pastoral letter:

> The object I have in view is to enlarge the present institution — to unite to it, as soon as possible, a theological school similar to that connected with Mt. St. Mary's near Emmitsburg — and by bringing it nearer the episcopal city, to increase its usefulness and to render it more accessible to the clergy of the diocese, for retreats, conferences and other ecclesiastical purposes.[44]

Seton Hall College opened in the fall of 1860 with fifty students, was incorporated by the State of New Jersey and empowered to grant degrees. Theological instruction for seminarians was begun during the 1861–1862 school year, with the first ordinations taking place in 1863. The seminarians were assigned to duties as prefects and tutors for the boys of the college. Hence the Seminary of the Immaculate Conception came into existence. It was the only Catholic diocesan mixed seminary and lay college formed in the nineteenth century that survived the generation of its founding. Its enrollment was modest, remaining between twenty and thirty seminarians until the 1890s.

Within the Baltimore ecclesiastical province, the growth and influence of the Sulpicians' St. Mary's Seminary at Baltimore and Mount St. Mary's Seminary at Emmitsburg, which served many dioceses of the Baltimore province but were not designated provincial seminaries, did not supplant the efforts of the dioceses of Pittsburgh, Wheeling, and Philadelphia to sponsor seminaries.

At Pittsburgh, Bishop Michael O'Connor completed the building of St. Paul's Cathedral in 1855. Despite his previous interest in a general seminary, he next turned his attention to a diocesan seminary. After briefly sponsoring a seminary in rural Cambria County, the bishop reopened in 1857 his St. Michael's Seminary (closed in 1851) at a converted boardinghouse in the Glenwood section of Pittsburgh, reappointing his younger brother rector.[45] The seminary was a continuous financial burden to the diocese and was closed in 1877 when the bishop of the short-lived diocese of Allegheny withdrew his seminarians in a dispute with the then bishop of Pittsburgh.[46]

At Wheeling, Bishop Richard Whelan, who had been bishop of Richmond until 1850, opened a household seminary attached to his residence in Wheeling. St. Vincent's School for Boys was started nearby in the 1850s and the seminarians taught there part-time. This modest mixed academy and seminary, about which little is known, was closed in 1875.[47]

By the 1850s Philadelphia had about 250,000 Catholics, which made it the most populous diocese in the Baltimore province. Its St. Charles Borromeo Seminary prospered because of its successful system of annual collections and large enrollment. Before Bishop Francis Kenrick left the diocese in 1851 to become sixth Archbishop of Baltimore, he completed an expansion of the buildings at Eighteenth and Race Streets in downtown Philadelphia. Its enrollment was large through the 1850s, having about forty students and two or three priests on the faculty.[48]

The timing of subsequent developments awaited the completion of the other major diocesan project. In 1846 Kenrick announced plans to raise funds for a cathedral named for St. Peter and St. Paul in Philadelphia.[49] The bishop emphasized the responsibility of all Catholics to support the construction of the mother church of their diocese. The cathedral was expected to open in five years, but the construction and fund-raising stretched out through the peak years of Irish immigration and was finally completed in 1859. With its completion not yet in sight, Kenrick's successor, John Neumann, issued a pastoral letter in 1855 expressing the need for a native clergy. He cited the fact that of the 175 priests in the diocese only forty-seven were born in the United States. The bishop expected that with the leveling off of immigration, foreign sources of clergy would likewise decline. He hoped to raise up a native diocesan clergy by means of a minor seminary, which he opened at Glen Riddle in September 1859 to twenty-eight students and a group of clerical and lay faculty.[50]

Before Bishop Neumann's death in 1860, James Frederick Wood was appointed coadjutor bishop of Philadelphia in 1857 and succeeded to the see when Neumann died. Wood, a native Philadelphian of Unitarian background, had grown up in Cincinnati, where he started a career in banking. He met Bishop Purcell and was converted to Catholicism, was ordained a priest after studies in Rome, and was appointed pastor of a Cincinnati parish Purcell had formed for the Irish.[51] Wood was appointed to Philadelphia largely on the strength of his reputation as a financier. He was to take hold of the complicated financial administration of one of the largest dioceses in the country, while Bishop Neumann, noted for his piety, would devote himself to spiritual and pastoral duties.

After completing the cathedral Wood turned his attention to St. Charles Seminary at the end of the Civil War. In December 1865 he announced the purchase of a 124-acre estate at Overbrook, west of Philadelphia, as the site of a new diocesan seminary.[52] From 1865 to 1871, Bishop Wood, despite a postwar recession, solicited funds in his diocese to build a spacious, modern seminary. The annual seminary collection rose from $11,000 in 1859 to about $28,000 to $30,000 annually from 1865 to 1875.[53] According to Wood's seminary rector, James O'Connor (Bishop Michael O'Connor's brother and himself a future bishop), Bishop Wood manifested a style of "absolutism" in governing the diocese. His control of the seminary project was consistent with his overall approach. The bishop ignored O'Connor's early role in planning the seminary and personally oversaw the project, in due course offending the unconsulted architect, dismissing construction superintendents, and incurring enormous expenses.[54]

The new St. Charles Seminary that Wood completed in 1871 consisted of an imposing main seminary building designed with a frontage of 400 feet and surmounted by a dome 180 feet high. Its reported cost at its opening was $484,665, an extraordinary amount for a seminary for an immigrant flock and considerably more than the cost of the other seminaries built during the period.[55] Wood also applied similar zeal and expense to collecting books for the seminary library. A seminary visitor, Canon Peter Benoit, president of Mill Hill College near London, England, described the new St. Charles Seminary in 1875 as "probably the neatest and most complete in material arrangement in the world." He elaborated further:

> The corridors, chapel, refectory, kitchen, etc. are patterns of cleanliness, & the interior is heated by steam, there is everywhere a feeling of comfort wh. is seldom or never to be found in establishments of this sort. The rooms of the professors have also, to one who has been brought up in simpler and poor habits, too much of the apartment of a rich gentleman and not enough of the Apostle. . . .[56]

Indeed, by the standards of the time, the new St. Charles Seminary was a remarkable building, a reflection of Bishop Wood, the financier, who tolerated cost overruns in its interest. His background as a Cincinnati priest close to a great seminary founder, his mentor Archbishop Purcell, may in part explain his interest. His upbringing as a middle-class Protestant from a family of professionals speaks through the seminary's excellent physical arrangements and professional life-style that these arrangements encouraged. It is hard to imagine Wood's ascetic predecessor, Bishop John Neumann, conceiving and executing such a project.

With the opening of the new St. Charles Seminary, the preparatory seminary at Glen Riddle was closed and its students were brought to the new building. The seminary enrolled between 95 and 100 minor and major seminarians annually through the 1870s and produced 104 ordinands from 1871 to 1880.[57] Unlike the seminaries of Cincinnati, Milwaukee, and New York, the Philadelphia seminary related exclusively to the diocese of Philadelphia and did not seek the patronage of the dioceses of the region—even, it appears, after Philadelphia was promoted to the archiepiscopal status in 1875.

The opening of St. Charles Seminary at Overbrook, after the successful foundation of the seminaries of Cincinnati, Milwaukee, and New York under episcopal sponsorship and the development of the Sulpicians' St. Mary's Seminary as an exclusively clerical seminary, completes the emergence of five freestanding seminaries at major sees during the period. These seminaries commanded the kind of financial support and an adequate enrollment that freed them from dependence on a lay college or location in a bishop's residence. Through the same era the ending of seminary efforts by the dioceses of New Orleans, St. Louis, Chicago, Pittsburgh, Wheeling, Columbus, Vincennes, and Natchitoches contrasts with the successful modest seminaries of Cleveland, Louisville, and Newark to demonstrate the financial and personnel difficulties of sustaining a seminary, even at large dioceses, such as New Orleans, St. Louis, and Chicago.

The establishment of freestanding seminaries at major sees points to the move away from what had been the assumed function of the bishop since the Council of Trent and operative among the American bishops up to the 1840s, of each bishop overseeing clerical formation locally. By 1880 there were sixty dioceses in the United States, of which only a few conducted diocesan seminaries. By then most bishops would have their students receive formal training at seminaries beyond their immediate control, either at large freestanding seminaries, at mixed seminaries conducted by communities of priests, or at seminaries abroad.

The large freestanding seminary also represented a move away from the model of the Tridentine seminary decree that assumed that clerical formation would take place within the context of an existing institution, the cathedral, with its many allied activities of which the training of seminarians was to be a part. This model operated in several of the local diocesan seminaries up to the late 1840s. The large enrollments of the freestanding seminaries of a hundred or more contrasted with the handful of students in the early diocesan seminaries at the bishop's residence or at a seminary combined with a local boys school. The size of the seminary communities at Cincinnati, Milwaukee, and Philadelphia was augmented by the presence of a large number of minor seminarians who were candidates for the major seminary. The seminaries thus required a more detailed and rational organization to supervise the activities, spiritual formation, and formal instruction of such a large group of seminarians. It also required a larger number of priest faculty than the two or three instructors of the early diocesan seminaries.

The freestanding seminary created an environment in which seminarians and faculty priests lived a community life separated from other activities. Except at Baltimore's St. Mary's, this separation was reinforced by a physical setting away from an urban neighborhood. The seminaries of Cincinnati, Milwaukee, and Philadelphia were in suburban neighborhoods accessible to the city, while the New York province's seminary at Troy was in a small city. The last four were on ample tracts of land that were buffers to the lay culture beyond the seminary.

The attributes of the freestanding seminary parallel changes in arrangements for secular social institutions of the period. The nineteenth century saw the emergence of what social historians have called the "total institution," such as prisons and asylums for orphans and the insane.[58] The new social theory advocated removing, say, the care of prisoners, orphans, or the insane, from local and often familial settings, as had been practiced up to the nineteenth century, and placing them in large institutions devoted totally to providing for large numbers. The freestanding diocesan seminary was such a total institution. This model of the seminary was not the only one; many church leaders of the period thought in terms of education in Europe, and some religious orders took up the training of diocesan priests as part of their varied activities. But in the decades after the middle of the nineteenth century the freestanding seminary became an influential model for future development of diocesan seminaries in the United States.

4. Seminaries Abroad

The numerous diocesan seminary foundings did not supplant a parallel interest in training future priests for ministry in the United States at seminaries in Europe. Advocates of such institutes proposed either seminaries for training Europeans for missionary activities in the United States or seminaries for training Americans abroad. From the varied proposals considered during the period, two permanent establishments emerged, the American College at Rome and the American College at Louvain, Belgium, and became leading seminaries for American diocesan priests.

The idea of seminary training abroad was raised at the very beginning of the formal establishment of the Catholic church in the United States. The letter of Cardinal Leonardo Antonelli, Prefect of the Sacred Congregation of the Propaganda, dated June 9, 1784, which announced the appointment of John Carroll as superior of the Catholic church in the United States, also announced that two scholarships were now available to "two youths from the States of Maryland and Pennsylvania, to educate them at the expense of the Sacred Congregation in the Urban College; they will afterwards, on returning to their country, be substitutes in the mission." The cardinal invited Carroll to select youths between the ages of twelve and fifteen of "promising talents and a good constitution."[1]

The Urban College was founded in Rome by Pope Urban VIII in 1627 as a seminary for missionaries in countries where the church was under the direction of the Sacred Congregation of Propaganda Fide. Propaganda required an oath of those admitted to its college promising obedience to the rules of the college, which included a prohibition against entering a religious order after leaving the college without the permission of the Holy See and required a detailed report of personal activities every two years.

John Carroll, as always in dealing with officials of Propaganda, was wary. He upheld the ideal of the church in the United States as responsible for its own development, selecting its own bishops, and forming a clergy locally, not as an appendage to Propaganda. He feared the repercussions of the Urban College's oath in the United States and sought reassurances from Antonelli concerning Propaganda's subsequent control of ordained graduates. "For, every caution must be used," Carroll wrote, "in order that as far as possible the Catholic priests and laity understand that it is only in necessary spiritual things that a foreign power has control of them."[2] Antonelli assured Carroll that any objections to the oath could be addressed when the time came for any American students to take it. Thus reassured, Carroll sent in the summer of 1787 the first American students, Ralph Smith of Maryland, age fourteen, and Felix Dougherty of Philadelphia, age thirteen, to attend the Urban College. The inauguration of training Americans for the diocesan priesthood abroad, then, preceded by several years the opening of Georgetown and of the Sulpician seminary of Baltimore.

Smith and Dougherty pursued studies in the humanities until 1791, when they were ready to enter the seminary course and the question of taking the Propaganda oath arose. It was proposed to them without forewarning, and they refused to take it despite the pressures on them. In due course, after Carroll's agent in Rome, the English priest John Thorpe, had calmly reassured them, they took the oath to the Sacred Congregation's satisfaction. There was apparently no attempt to amend the wording of the oath as Carroll had been assured in 1787. In due course, the first Americans eventually gave up the intention of becoming priests and returned to America. Carroll did not send any more Americans to Rome during his lifetime. At the time of the return of Smith and Dougherty, Carroll expressed his attitude toward the Urban College to his confidant Charles Plowden: "But I find, what others said, & I always suspected, that the atmosphere of the Propag[an]da, was not favourable to the studies or principles of those who are destined to the ministry here."[3]

The relationship of the American church with the Urban College was resumed in the 1820s and maintained thereafter. Several noteworthy American churchmen not born in America but trained at the Urban College and sent to the United States after ordination became bishops, such as Francis P. Kenrick, Frederic Rese, Michael O'Connor, and James O'Connor. Likewise Americans sent to the Urban College, such as Martin J. Spalding, William Henry Elder, James F. Wood, and Sylvester Rosecrans, became bishops.

The presence of the Sulpicians at Baltimore assured a connection with the Seminary of St. Sulpice. Future bishops Samuel Eccleston, John B. Purcell, John J. Williams, Louis de Goesbriand, James A. Healy, and Richard V. Whelan completed their studies at this famous seminary. The Sulpicians at the Grand Seminaire at Montreal trained many priests for dioceses in the United States, especially those in New England.

In some dioceses with predominantly German populations, seminarians were sent to the Jesuit theological faculty at Innsbruck, Austria.

As dependence on recruiting European priests for the American church and the bishops' annoyance with the behavior of unfit immigrant priests became realities of church life, proposals were periodically made for programs that would supply priests trained abroad specifically for the American church.

Bishop John England had a proposal in mind when he visited Ireland in 1832 and arranged with the episcopal board of trustees of Ireland's national seminary, the Royal College of St. Patrick's at Maynooth, and the presidents of St. Patrick's and, his own alma mater, Carlow College, that they constitute a board to evaluate and approve applications of Irish seminarians who wished to pursue a missionary career in an American diocese. This procedure was expected to eliminate the unfit before they had an opportunity to come to the United States. The Irish churchmen were willing to perform this service for American bishops, and Bishop England proposed it to Archbishop Whitfield and other American bishops. They apparently did not respond and the matter was dropped. It seems unlikely that Archbishop Whitfield and other bishops not of Irish background would desire a system to bring more Irish clergy to the United States.[4]

Shortly thereafter England raised an alarm in Catholic circles with an essay that appeared in the *Annals* published by the Society for the Propagation of the Faith in 1838 in which he stated that in the previous fifty years millions of immigrants in America had been lost to the Catholic faith. He believed that the Catholic population of the United States should have been five million, but he estimated it at a million and a quarter. England's figures have long been regarded as highly inflated. But at the time of the essay's publication, they deeply impressed those concerned with Catholic missionary activities. England attributed the great loss to: "The absence of a clergy sufficiently numerous and properly qualified for the missions of the United States."[5]

England's essay was published in Ireland in 1839. Its apearance there may have helped to stimulate interest in missionary activity, especially that of John Hand, an Irish diocesan priest who was concerned about the religious faith of the Irish diaspora. In 1842 Hand opened the Missionary College of All Hallows in Dublin to train Irish seminarians for the diocesan priesthood throughout the English-speaking world. Because Ireland produced more priests than could be used locally, the college would also provide a means of placing the many Irish candidates for orders where they were needed. Hand advertised the services of his college to bishops throughout the English-speaking world. All Hallows was to cover about half of the expenses of its students through its own fund-raising efforts.

Sponsoring bishops were to defray the remaining costs for the students adopted for their dioceses. The bishops' annual fee was set at ten pounds per student. The ordained student would then be sent to the diocese of the sponsoring bishop.[6]

Despite the need for priests in America, relatively few American bishops of the 1840s were willing to adopt Irish seminarians and pay for their education in Ireland. Many did not have the funds to pay even the modest student fees. Only the bishops of Boston, where Irish immigrants were numerous, and Richmond availed themselves regularly of the services of All Hallows up to 1860.[7] Other bishops expressed a decided preference for seminarians who would receive at least the final part of their training in the United States. Such an arrangement was not what Hand had in mind for All Hallows. Bishop Celestine de la Hailandière of Vincennes, who had been in the United States less than ten years by the time of his exchange of letters with Hand, stated why he was hesitant to accept newly ordained Irish priests from All Hallows:

> The habits, customs and manner of the people in this country are so much at variance with those of Europe, that they necessarily suppose in the exercise of the Holy Ministry, views, habits and discretion, which young men have not, and scarcely can possess, who have been brought up in the various colleges of the old country, however well conducted they be.

Hailandière believed that Irish priests would need two years "studying the moral habits of the people, before going on any mission."[8] Hand eventually accepted these conditions and sent four students to Vincennes where they finished their studies before ordination.

It appears that few other bishops followed Hailandière's example by insisting on supervising the conclusion of the Irish seminarians' training, though some shared his misgivings. By 1865 103 All Hallows alumni had been placed in American dioceses, though their presence was not universally appreciated. In 1860, Jeremiah Cummings, New York City pastor and an American-born alumnus of the Urban College, published an article objecting to the importation of Irish priests, especially those from All Hallows. This plan, Cummings found, "does injustice to our country and to the young men who are sent here. They are pious and devoted to their holy calling, but they have not been drilled to the habits of rapid thought and bold resolve, without which a man is unfit for American life."[9] Instead he looked to the formation of minor seminaries to develop an American clergy by starting the training of boys for the priesthood before they could be attracted to other occupations. Despite such expressions of lack of interest in All Hallows alumni, the college succeeded in its mission of exporting Irish priests throughout the British Empire and the United States in the nineteenth and twentieth centuries.

During the 1830s the officials of the Society for the Propagation of the Faith of Lyons briefly considered the idea of a seminary for training European priests for American dioceses. The successful Seminary for Foreign Missions, serving dioceses in the French colonial empire, was located at Paris. A seminary for American dioceses, which the society was already committed to supporting, seemed a reasonable idea. Bishop Michael Portier of Mobile, a native of the Lyons area and close to the officials of the society, proposed to the Holy See in 1840 the formation of an American seminary at Lyons which would be dependent on the society for funds and would train European seminarians for American dioceses. Lyons was proposed as a site because it was accessible from northern and southern Europe, and the area was already producing more priests than it could use locally. Local aspirants to the priesthood could be directed to the missions. But Portier's proposal was not pursued. [10]

The growing immigration of German Catholics and the issue of how to care for them produced proposals for seminaries for Germans. Canon Josef Salzbacher's American tour of 1842 and subsequent published report on Catholic life for the Ludwig-Missionsverein drew the attention of Catholic leaders in German-speaking Europe to the needs of the German Catholics in America. Salzbacher reported that only about fifty German priests cared for an estimated 300,000 German Catholics in America. He described the proposals that had been made to develop a German-speaking clergy in America, such as Bishop John Purcell's idea of starting a national seminary for Germans, which he aired at the Fourth Provincial Council of Baltimore of 1840. The committee of theologians formed to consider the matter, headed by Louis Deluol and consisting of three German priests, reported that it was not opportune to form such a seminary. This lack of support did not alter the plans of the then Cincinnati pastor John Martin Henni for a national seminary for Germans for which he had bought a house in Covington, Kentucky, near Cincinnati in 1842. [11] Henni's appointment as first bishop of Milwaukee in 1843 ended the prospects of a German seminary in the vicinity of Cincinnati.

King Ludwig I of Bavaria, the major patron of the Ludwig-Missionsverein, took up the issue in 1845 and proposed the formation of a seminary to train priests for German Catholics in America. His idea was to entrust the project to members of the Congregation of the Most Holy Redeemer (Redemptorists) from Austria, who had been engaged in ministry among Germans in several American cities. He suggested that the Redemptorist house at Altötting in eastern Bavaria, the site of a noted Marian shrine, be enlarged to accommodate a mission seminary. However, the superior of the American Redemptorists, Friedrich von Held, effectively opposed the idea of a special seminary when existing ones were sufficient. Held instead proposed that the Ludwig-Missionsverein donate its funds to support church building among Germans in America.[12]

The next major initiative for an American seminary abroad emanated from the interest of the Holy See in issues related to the Catholic church in the United States, of which clerical formation was but one. After the First Plenary Council of Baltimore in 1852, the Holy See delayed confirming its decrees apparently out of concern about the state of the church in the United States. In 1853 the secretary of Propaganda announced to the American bishops that the nuncio to Brazil, Archbishop Gaetano Bedini, would visit the United States, but the purpose of the visit was left vague.[13] One historian of Bedini's American tour found that Bedini's private instructions from Propaganda reflected a lengthy letter recently sent by Thomas Heyden, a priest in Bedford, Pennsylvania, complaining about "serious abuses" in the church, especially the frequency of national church councils and the way that they were conducted. Heyden objected to a party atmosphere with dinners and receptions and the presence of many priests serving as personal theologians to the bishops. These priests, he asserted, were often nominated for the episcopacy at these national councils. Heyden recommended fewer councils and the appointment of an "Apostolic Nuncio so that we might speak more often with the Holy Father."[14] Heyden also commented unfavorably on the large number of American seminaries. Bedini was instructed to look for abuses, tactfully call them to the attention of the bishops, and to report on the conditions that he found. It was clear also that Bedini was to sound out the possibility of establishing diplomatic relations with the United States.

The American bishops had not been consulted about the advisability of the Bedini visit before it was announced. They were uneasy during the months of Bedini's travels throughout the country, from July 1853 to February 1854. The United States had experienced an inundation of Catholic immigrants in the previous five years, and anti-Catholic feeling was running high. Antipapal incidents marred Bedini's appearances in Pittsburgh and Wheeling. In Cincinnati a Christmas night demonstration was directed at Archbishop Purcell's residence, where Bedini was staying, and included the burning of a Bedini effigy. In the melee with the police near Purcell's home, one protester was killed, two policemen and fourteen protesters were injured, and over sixty were arrested, thus drawing national attention to Bedini's visit.[15] In such an antipapal atmosphere the Pierce administration was not in a position to consider establishing diplomatic relations with the Holy See.

Bedini left the country in February 1854 annoyed that the United

States government had not taken better care of an accredited ambassador, albeit to another country, and hurt that the American bishops had not publicly supported and defended the visit. The entire Bedini affair was a classic case of Roman misunderstanding of American affairs. It was, according to Archbishop Peter Kenrick, "a blunder in every point of view."[16] The visit was symptomatic of and reinforced the Roman view that the church in the United States was too independent.

Bedini's lengthy report with recommendations submitted to Roman authorities remains one of the most interesting and extended contemporary views of the American church. The first major recommendation was the establishment of diplomatic relations with the United States, a matter that was not likely to be pursued. The second major recommendation related to the education of clergy. Bedini described the clergy in terms of their national groups, pointing out the obvious fact that: "For the most part they are European and not American, and each one has the customs and prejudices of his own nation." He did not conclude from the situation that there was a need to develop an American clergy or to strengthen American seminaries for that purpose. He was not impressed with the seminaries he visited: "They are well managed, but all of them labor under the burden of their vast dioceses." Instead, he recommended as the solution to clerical problems of the American church: "The single most important thing, that would satisfy every desire, achieve every purpose and would give the greatest enthusiasm to America would be the erection of an American College in Rome." Bedini foresaw many advantages in a college: (1) "Roman Catholic spirit would be assured among priests and people," citing the record of other national colleges in Rome as proof. (2) The college would "facilitate and encourage vocations to the priesthood" because the number of American seminaries was not sufficient and the seminarians attending them returned to their homes during the summer, a practice "sometimes fatal" to their perseverance in the seminary. A Roman college would eliminate such a danger and would educate students at a lower cost than American seminaries. (3) The college could provide "a wider, more complete and more solid education to the American clergy." Bedini cited the unsatisfactory scholastic exercises that he witnessed at the American seminaries during his visit. (4) The college would be the logical place to prepare "successors" of the many bishops that were in the United States, because American seminaries left much to be desired as places for the education of future bishops. The only answer was education in Rome "where the means, the resources, the occasions for perfecting oneself in learning, in spirit and zeal abound." Since the Urban College of the Propaganda already had a large number of Americans, it was time to form them into a separate college. And as if the foregoing reason was not strong enough he reiterated (5) that "By means of this College, the Holy See will be able to know the American Clergy better in its representatives, and thus can make its selection with greater confidence."

Bedini cited several less cogent reasons. He was concerned that the visit of the "first Pontifical Nuncio" to America be vindicated by some result more important than "the ashes of effigies which were burnt to mock him." He hoped for either the establishment of diplomatic relations or the establishment of the American college. He rather inaccurately claimed that the bishops already desired an American college in Europe and that Rome should take the initiative now. "What an embarrassment it will be for Rome, if by its silence, this College rises at some other place." He exaggerated the interest not only of bishops and Catholics but of the "majority of Americans," regardless of religion, who would be made proud of having an American college in Rome.[17]

In recommending the formation of an American college in Rome, Bedini was advancing an idea that was already a policy of Pope Pius IX to encourage the formation of national colleges to reduce particularist feelings among the national clergies and to reinforce Roman loyalties. The policy resulted in the formation of the French, Irish, Latin American, and Polish colleges during his pontificate.[18] The Bedini visit and report seem to be more of an occasion than a cause for initiating an American college. The issue was apparently not raised during the course of Bedini's visit, since it seems unlikely that a canvassing of episcopal opinion would have resulted in expressions of support for the idea.

Pope Pius IX first expressed his desire for the formation of an American college to a delegation of American bishops visiting Rome in 1854 to attend the solemn definition of the doctrine of the Immaculate Conception. The bishops present at the time were Archbishops Francis P. Kenrick and John Hughes, and Bishops Michael O'Connor and John Timon. Kenrick, who had recently demonstrated his independence of mind by criticizing the drafts of the decree defining the doctrine of the Immaculate Conception, immediately favored such a national college. He viewed such an institution as a means of developing a native clergy.[19] Bishops Michael O'Connor and John Timon both favored a national college, the former enthusiastically. Archbishop Hughes, on the other hand, immediately expressed himself against the project. The issue was pursued in a letter of January 1, 1855, from the pope to Archbishop Hughes. It contained the approbation of the Holy See to the decrees of the First Provincial Council of New York of 1854. The pope expressed again the desirability of an American college in Rome to train priests:

In this way young men chosen by you and sent here in pious hope, will thrive like trees in a nursery. Imbued in Rome with devotion and good habits, drinking deep of pure doctrine from the very fountainhead, instructed in the sacred rites and ceremonies according to the laws and customs of the Church, Mother and Teacher of all men, and thoroughly trained in the best mental disciplines, they will be able, when they return home, competently to fulfill the offices of pastor, preacher, or teacher.[20]

The pope's interview with the American bishops in 1854 and the letter to Hughes were all the gestures of consultation that preceded the decision to establish the American college. In February 1855, the Prefect of Propaganda, Cardinal Giacomo Fransoni, wrote to the American archbishops stating that the pope had "reached the conclusion that the project should be recommended; and he was willed by this letter of the Sacred Congregation to urge Your Grace to enter into consultation with the other bishops for the erection of the proposed college."[21] The letter promised that the Sacred Congregation would furnish all the assistance to the bishops necessary to establish the college.

The American bishops placed the question of the American college on the agendas of their provincial councils held in 1855. The proposal elicited mixed reactions. The bishops of the Baltimore province — where Archbishop Kenrick and Bishop O'Connor, both alumni of the Urban College, were avid supporters of the college — endorsed the idea and even proposed a detailed fund-raising and organizational plan for its operation under the direction of the American bishops. The bishops in the other provinces did not seem to recognize that the founding of the college was already decided upon and that they were expected to endorse it. The bishops of the Cincinnati province expressed opposition to forming an American college in Rome when funds were needed for seminaries and colleges in the United States. For them, a seminary abroad would provide nativists with proof of the foreign character of Catholicism. At the same council, the Cincinnati bishops designated the new Mount St. Mary's Seminary of the West as the official seminary of the province and petitioned the Sacred Congregation for a pontifical charter. The bishops of the St. Louis province, in a more politic fashion than their Cincinnati colleagues, expressed approval of an American college, but they declared that it was too early to establish one, because American Catholics did not have the means to support it.[22] Archbishop Peter Kenrick of St. Louis privately expressed opposition to the project, maintaining that the funds thought necessary for the college "would be better and more profitably applied" to one in America.[23] Likewise the bishops of the New Orleans province expressed appreciation for the pope's solicitude in proposing a national college in Rome, but they declared that they did not have the means to contribute to its support. New Orleans Archbishop Blanc believed that the college would be of no use in fulfilling his need for priests fluent in French and English.[24]

The bishops of the New York province, having met in their provincial council in 1854, did not have the opportunity to record their views. The influential Archbishop Hughes changed his original opposition and approved of the American college once he saw that the pope was so much in favor of it. His earlier opposition was based on his belief that Roman training was not suited for priests planning careers in the United States. He changed his mind when he realized the college would be under the management of American priests, who would direct the students and could prepare them for "the peculiarly novel condition of the Catholic people among whom they are to labor afterwards in the United States."[25] It was understood that the students' formal studies were to be taken at the Urban College. After consulting the eight bishops of his province for their views, Hughes promised Roman authorities that he and his suffragans were willing to put up $5,000 toward the furnishing of the building and would collectively furnish twenty-five seminarians at a tuition of $150 each per year.

On his own initiative, Hughes polled the archbishops of the country and reported: "Not one is able to give immediate or direct practical encouragement in the way of supplying funds or students."[26] The mixed reactions of the bishops surely reached the officials of Propaganda, as did the report of Louis Binsse, the Consul General of the Papal States in New York, who stated:

> It has been remarked that there is no particular excellence among those who have studied at Rome over those educated here, and the result of the comparison, on the contrary, is that there is to be found a superiority in the students of the Sulpicians, whose system tends to give a truly ecclesiastical spirit well adapted and very necessary in the present circumstances of this country.[27]

Undeterred by the limited support of American bishops, Roman officials moved forward with the project in 1856. Archbishop Gaetano Bedini was appointed to the influential post of secretary of Propaganda that year. He was in a position to advance his pet project and had the support of Bishop Michael O'Connor as representative of the American bishops. Propaganda purchased the former convent of the Visitation Sisters in the Via dell'Umilta to house the college. The American bishops collected $47,879 in 1858 and 1859, mostly from the archdioceses of Baltimore and New York, to renovate and furnish the building. Though bishops were slow to select students and nominate a rector, Archbishop Bedini formally opened the American College on December 8, 1859 with only twelve students on hand from eight American dioceses. The college was intended only for citizens born in the United States sent from American dioceses; hence it was not a missionary college.[28]

As rector, the American bishops selected and Propaganda appointed William G. McCloskey, age thirty-seven, who arrived in Rome in March 1860. McCloskey had been educated at Mount St. Mary's at Emmitsburg and ordained for the archdiocese of New York in 1852. He did parish ministry briefly in New York before returning to Emmitsburg to teach moral theology and Scripture and in 1857 became director of the seminary. At the American College, he was known for his cold, rigid, and authoritarian manner. In 1863, he arranged for the appointment of a vice rector, Francis Chatard, a Baltimore aristocrat and Emmitsburg alumnus who had been a physician before entering the Urban College in 1857 to study for the priesthood. After his ordination in 1863, Chatard took up his duties as vice rector. In 1868 William McCloskey was appointed bishop of Louisville. Chatard succeeded him as rector and maintained the rigid forms of his predecessor until his own appointment in 1878 as bishop of Vincennes.

McCloskey and Chatard shared the authoritarian outlook of Emmitsburg's president, John McCaffrey, under whose regime they passed their formative years. Accordingly, life in the American College was one of discipline and strict attention to clerical propriety. There were occasions for the students to enjoy the "fine and inoffensive customs with which they grew up," which Bedini foresaw in planning the college, such as Washington's birthday and Fourth of July celebrations.[29] But neither rector manifested concern about preparing students for ministry in the American context. McCloskey had limited experience in an American parish, and Chatard had none. The spiritual director appointed for the college was an Italian, Ubaldo Ubaldi, professor of Scripture at the Roman Seminary and the Urban College. He remained at his post until his death in 1884. The students were immersed in the clerical culture of Rome, attending pontifical functions and welcoming high ecclesiastics to the college. They spent summers in a villa outside Rome, where the routine and discipline of seminary life could be continued. There was no hint that seminarians were being trained in the ways of ministry in America that had led Archbishop Hughes to endorse the founding of the college. The Roman spirit corresponded to the expectations of some of the college's supporters. For instance, Orestes Brownson lent his influence to endorse the college when it opened, because it would be "educating our clergy to be neither German nor Irish, neither French nor American, but Roman Catholic: for in the Roman education there is no exclusive or distinguishing nationalism at all."[30]

Rome's intellectual life to which the students were exposed left much to be desired through the period. Contemporary observers such as John Henry Newman and Wilfrid Ward were sharply critical of Roman learning. Newman found little theology and philosophy during his stay in the 1840s.[31] In the 1870s Wilfrid Ward found the powers of reason disparaged in philosophical studies there: "We were taught the various philosophical positions as the 'right view' and if any of us did not find those positions convincing we were accounted heterodox. Thus philosophy . . . was not really enforced by reason but by authority."[32] The Irish Canon William Barry found the dogma lectures of the 1870s devoid of history: "All, I might say, was idea, was *a priori*, deductive and legal, in the teaching of doctrine, despite an admirable knowledge of Aristotelian methods. But the inductive, experimental spirit of Aristotle must be sought elsewhere." The great Jesuit dogmatist Giovanni Franzelin was found to ignore bibilical criticism and was "completely unaffected by any modern influence, I may say that for this pure unworldly spirit time stood still."[33] In summary, Roman academic life did not provide American students with training that prepared them to deal with contemporary thought or ministry in the United States.

The American bishops, who would not have founded a Roman college on their own, extended limited financial support once the American College was in operation. There was no endowment. The student fees paid by sponsoring bishops did not cover expenses. The American Civil War and the unstable political situation in Italy during the 1860s did not encourage bishops to send students to Rome. Enrollment declined to twenty-eight students by 1866. Unable to cover deficits with student fees and the bishops' periodic donations, William McCloskey toured the United States in the latter half of 1865 to raise funds. McCloskey found in his travels "great prejudice existing against 'Roman Doctors,' as they [Roman alumni] are called, and part of my mission to the West was to remove, in some degree, if possible, this prejudice." He found a similar prejudice in the East.[34] Even an advocate of the college, Archbishop Hughes, had not been inspired to support it based on the example of Roman alumni, as he told his Roman agent, the English Benedictine priest Bernard Smith, before its opening: "American youth who receive their education in Rome, with few exceptions, have not corresponded with their better opportunities, and are by no means looked upon as models of what is to be looked for from the American College proper."[35]

The best means of sustaining the American College was to raise an endowment. Without one, the Sacred Congregation would not transfer ownership and direction to the American bishops by providing for its canonical establishment. In 1868 Archbishop Spalding and Bishop Wood circulated a special appeal directed to wealthy Catholics to establish an endowment of $250,000 to $300,000, without which the college with its growing annual deficits might have to be closed. Their circular to the wealthy stated: "It would be one thing never to have had a college, but it is another thing altogether to have had it and lose it."[36] In this back-handed way the bishops cited the fear that, at the forthcoming Vatican Council, it would be an international embarrassment if the Roman college of the Americans would have just been closed.

Spalding sent George Hobart Doane, chancellor of the diocese of Newark, around the country to collect pledges among wealthy Catholics. He found the most support from Catholics in New York, Baltimore, Philadephia, and St. Louis. The campaign brought in more money than previous efforts. But many pledges were burses to support students; unrestricted gifts were preferred. The campaign raised under $200,000 in pledges. Spalding thought the sum inadequate and complained about the lack of support of many bishops. Doane's bishop, James R. Bayley of Newark, attributed the lack of bishops' interest to two causes: "One difficulty is that we do not own the College. The other is that it is conducted as a mere appendage to the Propaganda."[37]

Nevertheless, the pledge campaign saved the American College, and its enrollment rose to fifty in 1869, thereby showing a renewed interest in Roman training. But Propaganda kept the college, because the endowment did not reach expectations. In the 1870s, the economic depression in the United States caused a rapid decline in enrollment as few bishops could afford to send students to Rome. Enrollment reached a low of twenty-three students in 1877 before it started to rise as economic conditions improved. Despite these difficulties the college produced 135 ordinands by 1880.[38]

In a report on the general condition of the Catholic Church in the United States as of 1883, Cardinal Giovanni Franzelin, a member of the Sacred Congregation of the Propaganda, reviewed the American bishops' record of support for their Roman college over the previous quarter century. When Franzelin asked American bishops why they did not send more seminarians to Rome, they advanced two reasons: the cost of travel and student expenses were too great and the seminarians were not educated there in a manner suitable for work in the American mission. Franzelin recorded additional objections to the college from informants: the priests educated in Rome were too proud when they returned home or Roman alumni told unflattering stories about the Roman curia. Cardinal Franzelin considered the bishops' reasons for not sending students mere excuses. He believed the cost of an American student's voyage to Rome and personal expenses to be modest. He stated that the real reason for the American bishops' lack of interest was their indifference to all things coming from

Rome. He cited as evidence that the richest dioceses, that is, Baltimore, Chicago, and Milwaukee, had not been sending students to the college.[39]

Cardinal Franzelin's views had a basis in fact. The bishops' attitudes reflected a lack of genuine interest in the college. Its founding had not proceeded from a careful consideration of the interests of building an American clergy. The bishops were scarcely consulted in what was a Roman initiative, yet they and American Catholics were pressured into giving substantial sums of money to a college that produced a relatively modest number of ordinands in its initial years. It is unlikely that American bishops would have thought of forming a national college on their own because the presence of Americans in the Urban College seemed a sufficient tribute to the idea of clerical formation in Rome.

The Americans' record in supporting the college with funds and students furnished more reasons for Roman suspicions of a lack of loyalty. The American bishops' frequent provincial councils and the opposition of leading bishops to the declaration of papal infallibility at the Vatican Council in 1870 strongly suggested that they were indeed indifferent to all things coming from Rome.[40]

The American College finally achieved its delayed canonical establishment in 1884, despite the lack of an endowment. The event had been preceded by the attempt of the Italian government to confiscate the college in the ongoing conflict between Italy and the Holy See. The college was still the property of Propaganda and thus liable for confiscation. On behalf of the American bishops, the United States government pressured the Italian government not to take the college that had been sustained by the donations of American Catholics. Shortly thereafter, Pope Leo XIII issued the brief, *Ubi Primum*, that transferred the college to the American bishops in October 1884.[41] Henceforth a board of American bishops was actively engaged in financing and administering the college and directing the policies of the rector.

As the sequence of events leading to the opening of the American College in Rome was unfolding, a plan for clerical formation in Belgium was underway. The idea of forming an American college there originated during the European tour of Bishop Martin J. Spalding of Louisville in 1852–1853 to solicit funds and personnel for his diocese. When he visited Belgium, he was impressed by the Catholic development of the country, which had been independent only since 1830. While visiting Cardinal Engelbert Sterckx, Archbishop of Mechlin and Primate of Belgium, Spalding proposed the idea of a missionary college at the Catholic University of Louvain, Belgium. Cardinal Sterckx, a moving force behind the vitality of Catholic life in Belgium, heartily endorsed the project. Spalding had in mind a residential college for the priestly training of Europeans who would serve as missionaries to America. It would be related to the University of Louvain, where the students would receive their academic training. He wrote at once from Belgium to Archbishop Francis Kenrick to describe his proposal:

> The discipline of the college will be under the direction of an American missionary, who will teach English, and exert himself to procure the necessary funds for keeping up the establishment, which, the Cardinal thinks, can be easily realized in Belgium; and this is the opinion of all of those clergymen with whom I have conversed on the subject. Students will not be wanting, for in this diocese particularly the number of candidates for the ministry far exceeds the demand for clergymen.[42]

Spalding's proposal would supposedly not cost the American bishops anything; it raised hopes of bringing to America foreign-born priests at a time of a high level of immigration, and promised association with the University of Louvain, which Cardinal Sterckx had been instrumental in reopening in 1834. Spalding arrived in Italy still full of enthusiasm. He wrote to Kenrick again, this time pointing out: "Our studies in America are woefully below the European standard, and a few good missionaries educated in Belgium scattered through our various Dioceses would leaven the whole mass."[43] Spalding also mentioned the desirability of sending American students to Louvain. Archbishop Francis Kenrick opposed the project as did his brother, Peter Kenrick, who upheld the ideal of the education of a native clergy in America. The matter was not pursued until 1854, when Bishop Michael O'Connor visited Belgium to meet Cardinal Sterckx and the question again arose. After returning home, O'Connor contacted Bishop Spalding and other bishops, but nothing concrete was undertaken. It did not seem wise to pursue the idea when the pope was urging the opening of the American College in Rome.

In 1856 the delicate problem of proposing a college at Louvain when the pope wanted one in Rome was easily overcome. Peter Kindekens, a native of Belgium and vicar general of the diocese of Detroit, whose bishop, Peter Paul Lefevere, was also a Belgian, visited Rome on diocesan business and also on behalf of Archbishop Francis Kenrick to assist in finding a site for the American College there. Kindekens brought up the idea of an American college at Louvain in separate discussions with the pope and the prefect of Propaganda. Both warmly endorsed the idea as they found no conflict between a missionary college for Europeans at Louvain and a college for Americans at Rome. When Kindekens reached Belgium, he found that "an earnest wish prevailed with persons of distinction," to offer financial support for the college.[44]

In 1856 Kindekens addressed a circular letter on the subject to the American bishops. It elicited mixed reactions. Archbishop Francis Kenrick was not interested in it but did not use his influence to oppose the college idea. Archbishop Peter Kenrick again opposed the idea of a foreign college. Archbishop Purcell preferred seminary training in American seminaries and expressed the hope for the opening of a theological university in the United States. Other bishops favored a college at Louvain but would not be able to offer financial support. The principal proponents of the college were Spalding, Lefevere, O'Connor, and Bishop John McCloskey of Albany.[45]

Spalding and Lefevere took the initiative to start the college. They decided that Peter Kindekens, as an experienced American missionary and a Belgian, should be the founding rector. To gather additional support, Spalding and Lefevere sent out a circular letter to the bishops in February 1857, asking that those favoring the college become patrons and so notify the bishop of Detroit as early as possible, "as the Rector [Kindekens] proposes to leave for Europe early in March, and it will be highly important to his success that he should have the sanction of as many American prelates as possible." They welcomed contributions, but they did not press for them urgently.

In the lengthy prospectus accompanying the letter, the two bishops described the advantage of its location in Catholic Belgium, which had supplied "most efficient" missionaries and had a famous university. They emphasized the proposed college's "facility" to obtain "suitable German missionaries, thereby supplying a great want." Louvain's "contingency to the Provinces of Lower Germany will naturally draw many German candidates for the Holy Ministry to the American College." They also saw no clash between the college at Rome and the one at Louvain "for the obvious reason that the former would be chiefly for young men sent from America — wherein the latter, at least in the beginning, would be filled principally with young men from Belgium, Holland, France, and Germany." To meet the objection that the formation of the Louvain college detracted from support needed for American seminaries, the bishops did not foresee that it would interfere with institutions "for the Higher Ecclesiastical Studies" in the United States, and in fact related it to the improvement of American seminaries:

> Many of the young men educated at Louvain may hereafter be very usefully employed as Professors in our Seminaries, and thus they

will rather aid than impede the early development of a taste for such studies in our own Country, where it is highly important that the standard of Ecclesiastical education should be elevated as speedily as possible.[46]

Kindekens opened the American College of the Immaculate Conception on March 19, 1857, the feast of St. Joseph, though the rector did not purchase a small building for it until April and the first students did not appear until the summer. The college was under the direction of the archbishop of Mechlin, to whom the rector was responsible. Belgian benefactors paid the initial expenses. Eventually, American benefactions were added, and much support came from the Ludwig-Missionsverein because of the college's large enrollment of Germans.

The early enrollment consisted largely of Europeans, as expected. Late in 1857 Bishop Spalding sent the first American seminarian, David Russell, who was joined in 1859 by another Louisville student and the bishop's own nephew, John Lancaster Spalding. However, most of the 593 priests trained there by 1898 were Germans and Belgians.[47]

The advantages of proximity to the university did not preclude the interest in an abbreviated theological course. Bishops Lefevere and Spalding requested that the university offer a shortened course for future missionaries. When this request was declined, John DeNeve, the second rector, began to assemble a part-time, nonresident faculty who gave the desired shortened theology course at the college during the 1860s. Forming an ad hoc faculty seemed contrary to the aims of the episcopal founders to "leaven the mass" of American clergy with university-trained priests. Some students, such as John Lancaster Spalding, were free to pursue university studies and degrees. Throughout the founding era there was much stress on mastering English before leaving the college. German was also offered, since Flemish ordinands would often be sent to German communities in America.[48]

The opportunities for Germans to study at the American College at Louvain did not end the interest in forming a seminary in Germany for missionaries in America. Joseph Ehring, a priest of the diocese of Münster, had long had an interest in mission work among the German diaspora, but poor health prevented him from leaving Germany. In 1865, with the blessing of the bishop of Münster, Ehring formed a mission aid society with several other like-minded diocesan priests to sustain a missionary seminary. The priest gathered a group of seminarians interested in American work and formed a small college, first located at the rectory of a Münster church and then at a villa outside the city. The seminary was sustained by contributions collected locally and from a few American sources. The students took their theological studies at the University of Münster and learned English at the college. The seminary supplied some thirty-three German priests for American dioceses from 1867 until its closing in 1874 during the *Kulturkampf*.[49]

With the demise of the modest college at Münster, the American Colleges at Rome and Louvain remained the institutions to emerge successfully from the proposals and efforts of the previous decades to train priests at a specifically American college abroad. The colleges at Rome and Louvain, formed in the context of issues facing the American Catholic church in the 1850s, are permanent legacies from this era. Roman concern about conforming the American church to the new ultramontane trends was paramount in the founding of the American College at Rome. Its role in extending Romanizing influences to the Catholic church in the United States would be fully realized in the twentieth century, when its graduates became leaders of the American hierarchy. The need for well-trained European missionaries brought about the founding of the American College at Louvain. Its role in training American-born seminarians would be realized in the twentieth century. The foundings of the American colleges reflected in different ways a concern for priests better trained than the existing clergy in the United States. The discussions taking place at the time reveal a concern about the importance of developing strong seminaries in the United States where priests would be trained in the context of their future ministry, thus pursuing an idea that would receive more attention at the end of the century.

5. Religious Communities and Diocesan Seminaries

The American bishops pursued their traditional duty of developing a diocesan clergy by sponsoring clerical formation locally or by recruiting from abroad. Communities of priests shared in the responsibility of forming diocesan clergy. Priests of the Society of St. Sulpice confined their seminary activities to their influential seminaries in the archdiocese of Baltimore during the period. Several religious orders of priests engaged in the work of forming diocesan priests at a few seminaries for limited periods, such as the Jesuits at New York's seminary from 1845 to 1856. Franciscans founded a successful seminary for diocesan clergy in the diocese of Buffalo. But the Congregation of the Mission, that is, Vincentians, and the Order of St. Benedict, or Benedictines, were the foremost religious orders to engage in the work of training diocesan priests.

The sequence of events that brought the Vincentians to seminary work in American dioceses began when the United States purchased the vast Louisiana Territory in 1803 and thereby brought into the American Catholic church the diocese of New Orleans.[1] The diocese had been without a bishop since 1801. Once the area belonged to the United States, Pope Pius VII appointed Bishop John Carroll administrator of the diocese. In 1804 Carroll appointed a New Orleans priest as his vicar general, and, in 1812, Propaganda authorized him to send an apostolic administrator. Carroll sent the president of St. Mary's College of Baltimore, the Sulpician William DuBourg. After encountering opposition to his authority from some New Orleans clergy and their lay supporters, DuBourg visited Rome in 1815 to report on the diocese and to obtain priests. While there, DuBourg accepted appointment as bishop of New Orleans and received episcopal ordination.

During his Roman stay Bishop DuBourg resided at the Vincentian house at Monte Citorio, where he became acquainted with Felix DeAndreis,

104

who taught theology to Vincentian seminarians preparing for the foreign missions. DuBourg was deeply impressed by the conferences on the duties of the priesthood that DeAndreis gave to the Roman clergy, an activity the Vincentians undertook at the pope's request. The new bishop asked DeAndreis to come to New Orleans to conduct his proposed diocesan seminary. DeAndreis was attracted to the idea, but the reluctant Vincentian superiors agreed to part with him only after DuBourg had enlisted the aid of Pope Pius VII and his Secretary of State, Cardinal Consalvi, in obtaining that permission. DeAndreis chose as his companions two Vincentian priests, Giovanni Acquaroni and Joseph Rosati. DuBourg also secured seminarians and diocesan priests to join the party.

The Vincentian group crossed the Atlantic in the summer of 1816 and landed at Baltimore before traveling to Bardstown. They remained at the seat of the diocese of the West as guests of Bishop Flaget from November 1816 to October 1818 while Bishop DuBourg remained in Europe gathering priests and funds. Meanwhile the Vincentians joined the seminary community at St. Thomas Seminary near Bardstown, where they instructed the seminarians they had brought as well as the ones already there. The Italians also took the opportunity to learn English and practice the French that was necessary in the diocese of New Orleans. The ordained members of the party shared in the tasks of pastoral ministry in the parishes and missions around central Kentucky.

Bishop DuBourg finally arrived at Baltimore in 1817 but decided against proceeding immediately to New Orleans. At his request, Flaget visited St. Louis to determine if the Catholics there would welcome the bishop residing among them and if there was a suitably prepared place for a bishop to reside. Flaget was satisfied that St. Louis Catholics would welcome the bishop and arranged for repairs on the dilapidated church and rectory. DuBourg then decided to reside in St. Louis in the central part of the diocese rather than in the environment of opposition to church authority that he had known in New Orleans.

DuBourg left Baltimore with a large party of priests and seminarians for Bardstown, where he was united with the Vincentians and their seminarians. From there, the party moved to St. Louis, arriving there on January 6, 1818, nearly three years after DuBourg had left the diocese. Felix DeAndreis, who had gone ahead, was on hand to welcome him. From then on the Congregation of the Mission would play a prominent role in Catholic life in the St. Louis area.

Even before DuBourg arrived, a delegation from the Catholics of English stock who had come from Maryland and settled at the "Barrens" at Perryville, Perry County, Missouri, eighty miles south of St. Louis, called on Bishop Flaget and offered him land for a college next to their little mission church. A priest visited them only four times a year since 1813, and their hope was to have a Catholic college so that their settlement would always have resident priests. In March 1818 DuBourg came to Perryville to inspect the site. As a former president of Georgetown College, founder of St. Mary's College at Baltimore, and a founder of Mount St. Mary's Seminary at Emmitsburg, DuBourg was predisposed to developing colleges. Though the site was on the frontier rather far from St. Louis and twenty-three miles from the Mississippi River, he accepted the local Catholics' offer of 640 acres. He made arrangements with them for costs of constructing a building that would become the property of the bishop. Before the building was completed, Rosati and the seminarians arrived from Bardstown in October 1818 and temporarily took up residence in private homes in Perryville. Their arrival signaled the opening of St. Mary's of the Barrens Seminary of the diocese of New Orleans.

Felix DeAndreis, greatly esteemed for his holiness, became indispensable to DuBourg as vicar general of the diocese and pastor of the only church in St. Louis. He remained superior of the Vincentians although his confreres were established at the Barrens, where Rosati was in actual charge of operating the seminary. On October 15, 1820, DeAndreis, never in robust health, died at St. Louis, leaving Rosati as superior of the Vincentians. The latter also took part in the administration of the diocese when, in 1823, DuBourg arranged for his appointment as coadjutor bishop. DuBourg intended that Rosati reside at the Barrens and look after the seminary and the northern part of the diocese, while DuBourg, who found more support for his authority in New Orleans than he expected, decided to move there and even contemplated opening a seminary there. However, the accumulation of difficulties in lower Louisiana in the form of clerical opposition, trustee conflicts, and financial troubles strained DuBourg's capacities. He left for Rome in 1826 and resigned the see and so passes out of the history of the American Catholic church. He found more agreeable work as bishop of Montauban and later as archbishop of Besançon.

For a while Rosati administered the entire diocese, until it was divided in 1826 and the diocese of St. Louis was erected. Rosati chose to be the first bishop of St. Louis, and recommended his Vincentian confrere and seminary president, Leo DeNeckere, to be bishop of New Orleans.

Meanwhile the seminary at Perryville soon required the support that only the operation of a school with paying students could provide. In 1822, the Vincentians opened a boys' academy affiliated with the seminary, which was training both diocesan and Vincentian candidates for the priesthood. On this occasion the Vincentians obtained incorporation of St. Mary's Seminary, marking the first time the new state government of Missouri issued a college charter. Thus the seminary was the state's first college.

Bishop Rosati remained superior of the Vincentians until 1830, when the Italian province, to which the growing number of Vincentian priests from Europe and locally trained ones belonged, appointed John Tornatore superior. The latter's inept direction of his confreres who were engaged in missionary work throughout the Mississippi valley and the harsh regime imposed on the Vincentian community at the Barrens led to the departure of many Vincentian candidates. Turmoil prevailed while Tornatore remained in office.

The sexennial assembly of the Congregation of the Mission met in Paris in 1835 and addressed these difficulties by creating an American province of the congregation. The American-born John Timon was appointed provincial superior or, in Vincentian parlance, "visitor" of the new province. Timon had served on the faculty of St. Mary's Seminary since 1823 and had recently been president of the seminary-college. His efforts to collect longstanding debts owed to the college considerably improved its financial condition.

Like the Sulpicians, the Vincentians struggled with the issue of conducting a college for lay students. The work was foreign to their traditions and disrupted the house discipline expected in a Vincentian community. Accordingly, the same Vincentian assembly of 1835, acting on the recommendation of Jean Marie Odin, the Barrens' representative, ordered the lay college at Perryville closed. To offset the loss of revenues Bishop Rosati was to be charged $120 per year for each seminarian of his diocese. Rosati's views on this issue had not been sought, and he understandably resented the order. He was in no position to pay cash for the education of his seminarians. The bishop protested the decision to the Cardinal Prefect of Propaganda, who persuaded the Vincentian superior general to withdraw the order.[2]

The restoration of good relations between the Vincentians and Rosati did not prevent the latter from planning a seminary in St. Louis. As did other bishops of the period, Rosati wanted a seminary related to the cathedral, as he stated in his pastoral letter of 1839:

> We, also, feel that this city, in which our Episcopal residence is fixed, is without one of its natural ornaments and appendages, whilst it remains without a seminary. Here young Clergymen would find a holy and most useful apprenticeship of zeal, in teaching Catechism to the very numerous Catholic youth of the city; and, whilst adding to the dignity and beauty of divine worship in our Cathedral, or in other future Churches, they would form themselves to a due accuracy in the holy chaunts [sic] and in the sacred ceremonies of the Church.[3]

Rosati also believed that the combined college and seminary was undesirable because the lay students influenced the clerical students to lose interest in becoming priests.

Bishop Rosati's plans for a seminary in St. Louis depended on the means available to provide one. In 1838 Rosati accepted the donation of a city block of land on the south side from a prominent Catholic widow, Julie Soulard, as the site for a church. Rosati also bought property next to the donated block on which he built a row of modest houses, the rent from which was to support his seminary program to be built at the proposed church. In 1839, Rosati began construction of Holy Trinity Church on the donated block on which the seminary was to be located. However, only the church's foundation was completed before the financial panic of 1840 halted construction.

A change of leaders redirected the course of St. Louis seminary plans. In 1843 Bishop Rosati died unexpectedly while on a visit to his native Italy. Before his departure he had arranged for the appointment of Peter Richard Kenrick as coadjutor bishop. Kenrick then became second bishop of St. Louis. Rather than build a seminary at the church site, Bishop Kenrick decided to locate the seminary in the yet unfinished row houses that had been intended as rental property. After repairs had been made to the structures, the St. Louis seminarians took up residence in the houses under the direction of Vincentian priests. The diocesan seminary program at St. Mary's of the Barrens came to an end.

The crudely made row houses proved to be inadequate, so that John Timon bought the Soulard mansion in the next block at the Vincentians' expense in 1844. The decaying foundation work on Holy Trinity church was abandoned; the Vincentians instead built the Church of St. Vincent de Paul on the mansion property. Thus what began as a diocesan venture to start a seminary in St. Louis owed its realization to the efforts of John Timon and the Vincentians.[4]

In 1848, Kenrick, by then an archbishop, opened a freestanding seminary at the St. Louis suburb of Carondelet. It was staffed by his own diocesan priests as the intended provincial seminary, but it closed in 1859 because of inadequate funding, as described in chapter 3.

The Vincentians complied with the request of the bishops of the St. Louis province in their council of 1858 to conduct a provincial seminary. The Vincentians converted their St. Vincent's College for lay students, founded in 1838 at Cape Girardeau on the Mississippi River, 110 miles south of St. Louis, to a freestanding major seminary for the diocesan seminarians of the ecclesiastical province.[5] The new seminary reached a substantial enrollment of sixty by 1861. However, the seminary's success was complicated by the outbreak of the Civil War, so that the enrollment soon dropped by half in 1862. The federal occupation of Cape Girardeau isolated the seminary from southern dioceses. Ethnic tensions were aroused when the Irish-surnamed Vincentian personnel in their zeal to fight lax discipline expelled many students, especially the German students sent by Archbishop Kenrick from the substantial German community of St. Louis. Kenrick thereafter sent his German students to the Milwaukee seminary and distributed his other seminarians among several seminaries.

Without support from St. Louis, the enrollment of St. Vincent's declined, imperiling its financial stability. A fire at the Vincentians' lay college at the Barrens led to an alteration of St. Vincent's institutional arrangements. In 1866 the Vincentians moved their lay students from the Barrens to St. Vincent's, thereby converting it to a seminary with a classical college and a commercial course for lay students. The enrollment of lay students averaged 80 to 100 by the 1870s, but the seminary did not attract substantial numbers, enrolling 25 in 1871 and declining steadily to a low of four in 1878, as Kenrick continued to ignore the seminary and the other bishops of the region either followed his example or were unable to support seminarians because of the lingering economic effects of the Civil War and the depression of the 1870s. Gradually, in the 1880s the enrollment of seminarians recovered.

The Vincentians, as mentioned in chapter 2, had continued their relationship with the diocese of New Orleans by conducting the seminary in Assumption Parish, Louisiana, until its destruction by fire in 1855 and then at St. Stephen's parish in New Orleans until it was closed in 1867. The Vincentians thereby maintained the seminary commitments to the dioceses of St. Louis and New Orleans, thus fulfilling the purpose for which they had been invited to the Mississippi valley.

The rise of many local seminaries by the 1840s engaged the Vincentians in clerical training in other parts of the country. The bishops' esteem for John Timon attracted attention to the Congregation of the Mission. Augmented by Vincentians recruited from France, Spain, and Ireland, the congregation was able to accept several invitations to staff diocesan seminaries.[6]

Bishop Francis Kenrick obtained the Vincentians to staff St. Charles Borromeo Seminary in Philadelphia in 1840. They found this seminary to their liking because there was no lay college attached to it. A three-priest faculty was maintained through the 1840s, which served as something of a standard among seminaries staffed by Vincentians. Conducting the seminary did not preclude interest of the priest faculty in pastoral activity beyond its walls. Kenrick took an interest in the workings of the seminary that occasionally caused resentment, but the relationship of bishop and faculty did not break. By 1852, Thaddeus Amat, the seminary rector, reported that the enrollment was the "most numerous" among seminaries in the United States with forty-three seminarians of whom twenty-two were studying theology, the others were studying philosophy. He considered St. Charles the "premier" seminary in the United States because of its reputation for discipline. At the time of the change of bishops in Philadelphia in 1852 from Francis Kenrick to John N. Neumann, the Vincentians were experiencing a shortage of personnel to fulfill their obligations in several areas.[7] In 1853 they withdrew from Philadelphia, ending thirteen years of one of their most stable relationships with a diocese of the period.

After accepting the direction of the Philadelphia seminary in 1840, the Vincentians received an extraordinary number of invitations to staff seminaries. As Timon wrote to the superior general of the Congregation of the Mission in 1842, "God is calling us to the direction of all the seminaries in this country except two." And as he repeated shortly thereafter, "The Bishops of this country, as if by a preconcerted move, are offering us their seminaries."[8] Though not a preconcerted move, the early 1840s, as mentioned earlier, was the high tide of local seminary activity, and episcopal founders had urgent need to find seminary faculties. In 1842 alone, Timon reported offers from Bishops John Hughes of New York, Benedict Flaget of Bardstown, Richard Whelan of Richmond, Michael O'Connor of Pittsburgh, John Purcell of Cincinnati, Celestine de la Hailandière of Vincennes, and Archbishop Eccleston of Baltimore, who wanted the Vincentians to staff Mount St. Mary's Seminary at Emmitsburg. In 1843 Bishops Richard Miles of Nashville and Michael Portier of Mobile also wanted Vincentians for their seminaries.[9] These numerous invitations could not be accepted. The fact that several seminaries such as Mount St. Mary's of Emmitsburg were conducted with colleges for lay students made them objectionable. Only those of New York, Cincinnati, and Bardstown were accepted.

In 1842 the Vincentians came to New York to staff Bishop Hughes' St. Joseph's Seminary at Fordham on the condition that they conduct the seminary only and not the lay college. Hughes agreed to the idea of separating seminary and college in theory, but it was difficult to implement in practice because the nonpaying seminarians had duties in the college which took them away from the seminary. Lacking control of the seminarians, the Vincentians withdrew from the seminary in 1846.

A similar issue arose at Bardstown. Bishop Flaget, whose see was transferred from Bardstown to Louisville in 1841, acquired the Vincentians to staff his seminary at Bardstown in 1842. When the bishop wanted the seminarians to teach at the nearby St. Mary's College for lay students in Lebanon, the Vincentians withdrew from the diocese of Louisville in 1845.

In 1842 Bishop John Purcell of Cincinnati engaged the Vincentians to staff his seminary, which he moved that year from Cincinnati to a donated farm near Fayetteville, Brown County, about thirty miles east of Cincinnati. Purcell took an interest to the point of interference in the work of the seminary to the Vincentians' annoyance. In 1845 Purcell suddenly moved the seminary back to Cincinnati without consulting the faculty. As a veteran of struggles with local Dominicans and Jesuits, Purcell was inclined to treat religious orders in an abrupt manner. Tiring of such treatment, the Vincentians withdrew from the seminary in 1845.[10]

The Vincentian record of conducting seminaries for bishops through the period indicated the difficulties of achieving a stable formula for the successful conduct of a seminary. By 1855 when the New Orleans diocesan seminary burned, it appeared that the Vincentians' historic work of conducting diocesan seminaries might come to an end. But a promising seminary effort began with the appointment of John Timon as bishop of the new diocese of Buffalo in 1847. As bishop, Timon first attempted a seminary in his household, then a seminary program affiliated with an academy for lay students conducted by the French Oblates of Mary Immaculate. In 1856 he obtained the services of his own Vincentian confreres to begin a seminary. Under Vincentian John Lynch, a seminary was opened in a former orphanage near Buffalo in 1856 before a 300-acre farm on "Mount-Eagle Ridge" about twenty miles north of Buffalo on the Niagara River was purchased in 1857. A seminary opened in the farmhouse on the property. The school was incorporated in 1863 as the Seminary of Our Lady of the Angels, a seminary with lay college. Lynch was appointed coadjutor bishop of Toronto in 1859, and the leadership of the institution passed to others, most notably Robert E. V. Rice, who took charge in 1863 before being formally appointed president at age twenty-eight in 1865. A substantial building for the school was completed in 1864 and was destroyed by fire in the same year and quickly reconstructed. Despite poor health, Rice vigorously led the school, which by 1875 attracted an enrollment of sixty-five seminarians from dioceses of the region and 200 lay students.[11]

By the 1870s, the Vincentians conducted St. Vincent's College at Cape Girardeau, Missouri and the Seminary of Our Lady of the Angels at Niagara, New York as seminaries for diocesan candidates with an affiliated college for lay students. The Vincentians were no longer contracted to dioceses to staff seminaries as had been their experience in France and in several dioceses in the United States, where the number of local diocesan seminaries had been in decline since the 1840s. Instead circumstances had forced them to overcome their opposition to conducting lay colleges in order to sustain their traditional activity of engaging in clerical formation. By the 1870s, the Vincentians had come full circle through the previous half century back to the institutional model of a combined seminary and lay college that they had known at St. Mary's Seminary at the Barrens in the 1820s.

The activities of Benedictine monks on behalf of diocesan seminary training provide a study in contrasts with the Vincentians. Broadly speaking, Benedictine activity arises from the context of missionary activity among Germans. The monastic and missionary vision of a remarkable Bavarian, Boniface Wimmer, provides the specific starting point for Benedictine activity in the United States. Born in 1809 to the family of a tavern keeper at Thalmassing near Regensburg in eastern Bavaria, Sebastian Wimmer, as he was named at birth, entered a world undergoing religious changes that would inform his religious calling.[12]

At the time of Wimmer's birth, German-speaking Europe was in the process of profound political and religious change. Napoleon's conquest of continental Europe brought an end to the historic political arrangements of the Holy Roman Empire. Under Napoleonic hegemony, the map of central Europe was redrawn. The head of the house of Habsburg transformed himself from Holy Roman Emperor to the Emperor of Austria. Small principalities were combined with larger states, such as Wimmer's Bavaria, which emerged as a modern nation and its ruler, Elector Maximilian, became a king. In religious matters, the German princes met in 1803 at the Diet of Regensburg and agreed to secularize, that is, to appropriate for their governments the substantial tax-exempt property holdings of Catholic religious orders and dioceses. The assumption of the age of the Enlightenment held that such property could be put to better use than sustaining a dying religion. In Bavaria, King Maximilian and his enlightened minister, Count Montgelas, sought to make Bavaria a modern state and to subordinate and regulate religious activity.

After Napoleon's defeat in 1815 and the concurrent rise of romanticism, the reaction against the Enlightenment gained ground. The romantic reaction developed rapidly in Bavaria after the accession of King Ludwig I in 1825.[13] The king's policies ranged from turning Munich into a northern Florence following classical, medieval, and baroque themes in art and architecture, to moving the country's university from rural Landshut to Munich and bringing together a brilliant faculty of leading thinkers associated with romantic idealism, Friedrich Schelling, Friedrich Schlegel, Josef Görres, Franz von Baader, and Ignaz von Döllinger. Interpenetrating these developments was the reassertion of Bavaria's Catholic heritage that had been suppressed in the previous generation.

In the year of King Ludwig's accession, Wimmer completed gymnasium studies in Regensburg, from which he entered the diocesan seminary in the same city. His aptitude for study led to his reassignment to the University of Munich to seek a degree in theology. While there, he entered more fully into the Catholic revival. In 1831 he was ordained a priest of the diocese of Regensburg and was at first assigned to a parish in the nearby diocese of Passau, where there was a shortage of priests.

As part of the general policy of reviving Bavarian Catholicism, King Ludwig pursued the restoration of monastic life, which had been obliterated by secularization earlier in the century. He was attracted to the Order of St. Benedict because the monastic life integrated faith, learning, and art. The king sponsored the establishment of the new St. Boniface Abbey in Munich, and, in 1830, he reestablished the ancient Abbey of Metten, which had been in existence from the eighth century until 1803. The two surviving monks from the pre-1803 period returned to the abbey to restart monastic observance. The most influential Bavarian churchman, Bishop Josef Michael Sailer of Regensburg, invited priests of his diocese to join the abbey. Wimmer accepted the invitation and joined Metten in 1832 with four other diocesan priests. After a year of novitiate, he professed vows and took the name Boniface and was sent out to minister in parishes attached to the abbey and later to the Benedictine college at the restored St. Stephen's Abbey in Augsburg and the Benedictine Ludwigs-Gymnasium in Munich.

During this period of revival of Catholic life in Bavaria, the religious condition of the growing number of German-speaking immigrants in the United States engaged the attention of Catholic circles in Bavaria. In 1838 the Ludwig-Missionsverein was formed as a branch of the French Society of the Propagation of the Faith. The Bavarians' desire to assist German immigrants exclusively led to its separation from the French society in 1844. In the same year Canon Josef Salzbacher's journal of American travels with its account of the spiritual plight of German Catholics in America became known. Accordingly, the king proposed founding a German missionary seminary at Altötting, Bavaria. Wimmer was attracted to this issue and proposed to the abbot of Metten that their abbey establish a mission house in Munich for the training of priests for the German diaspora. He intended that student missionaries take formal studies at the Ludwigs-Gymnasium and the University of Munich. Since the abbey was in the early stages of its own restoration, the proposal was not acted upon.

In 1845 a German priest, Peter Lemke, of the recently formed diocese of Pittsburgh, visited Munich to seek funds and priests for missionary activities in western Pennsylvania. Wimmer met Lemke and was attracted to the idea of going to America. Lemke offered to sell Wimmer his property at Carrolltown, Cambria County, Pennsylvania as the site of a monastery. But Wimmer's initial attempts to secure permission and support for a Benedictine mission in America were rebuffed.

Wimmer wrote an unsigned article that appeared in the *Augsburger Postzeitung* on November 8, 1845, in which he developed his ideas about the missionary possibilities of monasticism. He began by taking issue with the idea of Canon Josef Salzbacher of having traveling German diocesan priests seeking out the many Germans scattered in the United States. Instead he believed that German missionaries needed the support that a home provided; thus he looked to monks to care for Germans:

> It is apparent, therefore, that religious are better adapted for missionary work than secular priests. In a community the experiences of the individual become common property; all have a common interest, stand together and have the same object in view. A vacancy caused by death or otherwise can be filled more readily, and having fewer temporal cares, they can devote themselves more exclusively to the spiritual interest of themselves and others.[14]

Wimmer proposed implementing his idea by forming a monastery in the interior of the United States that would be sustained by farming. The founding monastic community would consist of two or three priests and fifteen lay brothers. The lay brothers would operate the farm and assist in instructing children. In due course, a school for boys would be formed at the monastery, drawing its students from the German families nearby. From the school, candidates for the diocesan clergy and the monastery would be forthcoming. The monastery would train them both, thereby assuring an increase of monks to conduct the seminary and college and of diocesan clergy for the local parishes. As the original monastery grew in members, satellite monasteries would be formed to repeat the process. In outlining this plan of monastic missionary work, Wimmer appealed to the historic Benedictine tradition of missionary activity in the first millennium of Christianity that resulted in the spread of Christianity in England, Germany, and Scandinavia.

King Ludwig read the article and summoned its author to an audience. Devoted to the interests of German Catholics in America, the monarch offered Wimmer financial assistance to carry out the project. With such powerful backing Wimmer again sought permission of the abbot and monastic chapter of Metten Abbey to launch a Benedictine monastery in America. During their deliberations, Wimmer absorbed some stiff criticism as a dreamer and a troublemaker with his romantic ideas of monasteries in America, but the necessary permission was secured.

In July 1846 Wimmer left Munich with eighteen followers consisting of four seminarians and fourteen lay brother candidates. The group arrived at Lemke's farm at Carrolltown, Pennsylvania on September 30, 1846, and refitted the farmhouse to accommodate community life. Wimmer was soon disappointed with the site because the ground was too stony for farming. The bishop of Pittsburgh, Michael O'Connor, who welcomed the Benedictines to the diocese, offered Wimmer the care of St. Vincent parish and adjoining property in Westmoreland County, sixty miles east of Pittsburgh. The land there was suitable for farming and grazing, though the Catholics in the area were largely Irish and not German.

Wimmer accepted Bishop O'Connor's offer, though the original aim of assisting Germans had to be reconsidered. Wimmer thus had to grapple at once with the problem of ethnic diversity among American Catholics. Bavarians supporting Wimmer's project did so in the expectation that Germans in America would be assisted. Wimmer explained to Archbishop Karl von Reisach of Munich, president of the Ludwig-Missionsverein, the need to relate Benedictine activities to non-Germans:

> To devote this help exclusively to the Germans could not be my intention. Had it been, then closer insight into the native circumstances would have had to convince me that this would not be feasible, or at least not out in the country where in my opinion Benedictine monasteries are chiefly intended to be. Besides, there is hardly a larger congregation which would be completely unmixed. . . . Usually Germans and Irish, or anglicized Germans, live mixed with one another, and usually the Germans are in the minority.[15]

Wimmer braved the resentment of the Germans of Carrolltown and moved the monastic community to St. Vincent's parish in Westmoreland County. The Bavarians moved into the parish rectory and began building a permanent monastery. The lay brother candidates and the seminarians were invested with the Benedictine habit and the routine of monastic observance began. The seminarians, as choir monks, chanted the Latin liturgy of the hours in common, studied theology together under Wimmer, and engaged in some manual labor, while the lay brothers recited the Little Office of the Blessed Virgin in German and worked on the farm and construction projects. In a year the first of the seminarian monks was ordained to the priesthood. Bishop O'Connor sent the first diocesan seminarian to St. Vincent's within a year to inaugurate the monastery's long history of training diocesan priests.

Wimmer's monastery became firmly established as more monks, candidates for the lay brotherhood, and seminarians arrived from Bavaria to augment the original group. In 1851 the monastery was canonically erected as a priory, and in 1855 the priory became the canonical Abbey of St. Vincent de Paul, the first monastic community in the New World to achieve the abbatial status, with Wimmer elected abbot. From St. Vincent's Wimmer succeeded in founding a network of Benedictine monasteries in the United States by the time of his death in 1887.

Once St. Vincent's was established, Wimmer received invitations from bishops around the United States to establish a Benedictine monastery in their dioceses usually in conjunction with the pastoral care of German immigrants. Wimmer accepted the invitation of Bishop Joseph Cretin of St. Paul, Minnesota to form a monastery in his diocese.[16] In 1856, he sent a veteran missionary, Demetrius di Marogna, a Florentine nobleman who had been a diocesan priest in the Midwest before joining St. Vincent's monastery, as superior with a group of monk-seminarians and lay brothers to form a monastery. The group planned to establish a monastery in central Minnesota, where Germans were arriving in large numbers. The Benedictines first settled at a site on the Mississippi River near the village of St. Cloud, where they dedicated a chapel on June 24, 1856, the feast of St. John the Baptist; hence they called the school they established St. John's. Later the same year, they claimed land four miles west of St. Cloud that was more suitable for farming and grazing than the river bank site and also had woodland and a body of water, Lake Sagatagan. On the new site overlooking the lake, a monastery and a seminary were established. The Benedictine pioneers weathered the challenges of grasshopper plagues, the financial panic of 1857, and differences of opinion among themselves that caused several changes in superior. The monastery, nevertheless, became a canonical priory and was promoted to the status of an abbey in 1867 under the title of the Abbey of St. Louis of the Lake in recognition of the benefactions of King Ludwig (Louis) I to the Benedictines in America. Rupert Seidenbusch, a native of Munich, was elected the first abbot.

At Wimmer's two abbeys, the training of diocesan priests developed within the context of other educational activities.

At St. Vincent's about twelve diocesan priests had been ordained by 1856. The earliest enrollment figures are those of 1865–1866, when there were eleven diocesan and seven monastic seminarians pursuing the three-year seminary course. Seminary enrollment increased to forty-two diocesan and twenty-eight monastic seminarians by 1880. The seminary produced from ten to sixteen diocesan priests annually during the 1870s for dioceses in the Middle Atlantic states. For boys who did not intend to be priests St. Vincent's offered a six-year "classical" course corresponding to a German gymnasium, a three-year commercial course, and an elementary school. These educational activities were incorporated as St. Vincent College in 1870 by the Pennsylvania legislature, which empowered the school to grant degrees.[17]

Similar arrangements developed at St. John's, which was incorporated in 1857 by the Minnesota Territorial Legislature. The school was rather informally conducted in its initial decade. Most of the young priest monks had received all or most of their schooling at St. Vincent's. After the monastery achieved the abbatial status in 1867, Abbot Rupert Seidenbusch set about organizing the schools in a more formal fashion. In 1868 the training of diocesan seminarians began with five students, of whom two were Irish-Americans. They joined seven German monastic seminarians for the three-year course. In 1869 St. John's obtained an amended charter from the Minnesota legislature, empowering the granting of degrees. The school at that time offered the six-year classical gymnasium course for lay students, and, starting in 1872, a three-year commercial course. The institution also obtained in 1878 the status of a pontifical faculty from the Holy See, enabling St. John's to award the doctorate in theology, philosophy, and canon law. As was customary at the time, the degree-granting power was used to confer doctoral honors on members of the seminary faculty. This exalted status did not alter the academic character of the struggling seminary on the Minnesota frontier, whose annual enrollment ranged from fifteen to thirty during the 1870s.[18]

As the Bavarian Benedictines, under the vigorous leadership of the practical visionary Boniface Wimmer, developed monasteries, seminaries, and colleges in Pennsylvania and Minnesota, Swiss Benedictines were attracted to a similar activity. Their story begins with the Croatian-born priest, Joseph Kundek, who came to the diocese of Vincennes in 1838 to minister to the Germans settling in the area around Jasper, Dubois County, Indiana. Kundek worked to maintain the German character of the area and to attract German Catholic immigrants to southern Indiana, where they could maintain their faith and language by forming settlements. With funds from the Leopoldinen Stiftung, Kundek bought land to resell to immigrants. They came in substantial numbers to Dubois, Perry, and Spencer counties, where German Catholic farming communities sprang up, each with a church. The sole German-speaking diocesan priest in the area, Kundek hoped to attract a community of German priests for the local parishes. After German Redemptorists from Baltimore declined his invitation to come to Indiana, Kundek set out for Europe in 1851 to raise funds and find a community of priests. While visiting Vienna, Kundek learned that monks of the Benedictine Abbey of Maria Einsiedeln, Canton Schwyz, in central Switzerland were interested in making an American foundation. Kundek visited the abbey in June 1852 and presented his case for establishing a Benedictine house in Indiana. The abbots and monks looked favorably on his proposal but made no commitments.[19]

The Abbey of Einsiedeln had been founded in 934 at the site of the hermitage or *Einsiedeln* of the Benedictine monk-hermit, St. Meinrad, who was killed by robbers at the site in 861. The abbey became a place of pilgrimage at which the relics of St. Meinrad and a miraculous Black Madonna were venerated. The principal activities of the monastic community were a school and the care of pilgrims. The abbey's long history of monastic observance was interrupted during the period of French hegemony from 1798 to 1802. The community grew gradually through the first half of the nineteenth century, and when, in 1852, the cantonal government of Ticino closed the monks' school at Bellinzona, there was a surplus of monks. The Einsiedeln monks were thus in a position to make an establishment in America.

Abbot Henry IV Schmid von Baar of Einsiedeln decided to send two monks to America to explore the possibilities of establishing a mission but not a monastery and not necessarily in Indiana. They were to report their findings to Einsiedeln. After Kundek's departure, the abbot sent one of his monks to Rome to secure the authorization from Propaganda to make a foundation in America. Though Einsiedeln did not have an articulate theorist such as Wimmer, nevertheless, the abbot's memorial presenting the case for permission included the intention of engaging in clerical formation and indicates the extent to which the Einsiedeln community was touched by the general interest in missionary activity among Germans:

> Men endowed with both learning and authority have for many years unceasingly urged that in view of the needs of the times we devote ourselves also to the sacred task of the foreign missions, and, in particular, that our monastery establish in North America a so-called daughter house, connected with it and dependent on it, and for that very reason dependent on the Holy See; in which house young men are to be educated for the sacred ministry by the religious of our monastery and, having completed the course of studies, are to be placed at the disposal of the Bishops of that country, so that from that institute ever new laborers can be presented to the Church.[20]

After the necessary permission was secured, the abbot appointed two priests, Ulrich Christen, age thirty-eight, a Swiss native, as the senior, and Bede O'Connor, age twenty-six, son of a poor Irish family from London, who spoke English. The pair arrived in New York on January 31, 1853. They investigated the possibility of a mission in the diocese of Albany and visited Bishop John Neumann of Philadelphia and Wimmer at St. Vincent's before making their way to Indiana. Ulrich Christen rather precipitously committed the Benedictines to Indiana, taking a liking to the state because he had heard it disparaged elsewhere. While the monks spent much of their time in parish ministry at the German communities in the diocese of Vincennes, they looked for a site for a monastery and agreed in 1854 to purchase a farm in northern Spencer County.

Abbot Henry Schmid was annoyed by such independent action without authorization from Einsiedeln, but he reluctantly approved and sent additional monks to Indiana. A mission house was established on the property on March 14, 1854, and was named, on Abbot Henry Schmid's orders, St. Meinrad. Personnel difficulties plagued the establishment in its initial years. Christen and O'Connor had become absorbed in parish ministry in the diocese and the responsibility of leadership fell to a succession of monks sent from Switzerland. Expenses and debts mounted with building plans and the attempts to start a school.

St. Meinrad's fortunes took a turn for the better in 1860, when the Abbot of Einsiedeln sent out a thirty-six-year-old monk, Martin Marty, as troubleshooter.[21] Marty took hold of affairs at the struggling mission. He divided its property in order to sell lots for a town named St. Meinrad, thereby raising money and paying debts. He persuaded the Abbot of Einsiedeln to permit him to admit novices to the community to augment the monastery's personnel, and he opened a seminary for clerical students in 1861 — at first for students intending to become monks and then for diocesan students. A commercial course for lay students was introduced. The bishop of Vincennes sent his students to the new seminary in 1866, though within a few years differences between Marty and Bishop St. Palais over financial issues caused a temporary withdrawal of the Vincennes students. But eventually St. Meinrad became identified as the seminary of the diocese of Vincennes and also served neighboring dioceses.

Marty's appointment to St. Meinrad was initially intended to be only temporary and he was not to displace the existing personnel. However, his stay was lengthened, and in 1865 he was appointed prior. When St. Meinrad was raised to the status of an abbey in 1870, he was elected abbot. As St. Meinrad grew stable, Marty, who was smitten with the desire to pursue missionary activity, became increasingly absorbed by his work among the Sioux in the Dakotas. He resigned as abbot when he was appointed vicar apostolic of the Dakotas in 1879, but he left behind a set of stable institutional arrangements. After the institution's buildings burned to the ground in 1887, the commercial course for lay students was reopened at nearby Jasper in 1889. The fire and reorganization of the schools were the occasion for obtaining incorporation from the state of Indiana in 1890. Thus the monastic community at St. Meinrad, unlike Wimmer's monasteries, devoted its educational work exclusively to clerical training. This work complemented the care of German-speaking parishes in the surrounding area.

Other communities of priests were engaged by dioceses for limited periods to staff seminaries for diocesan priests. Despite their prominence in education, the Society of Jesus was not engaged to conduct diocesan seminaries after they ended their direction of St. Joseph's Seminary at Fordham, New York, in 1856. In the 1870s Bishop James O'Connor sought to have the Jesuits assume direction of St. Charles Seminary in Philadelphia. He proposed that Jesuit seminarians receive formal instruction with diocesan students, but they would reside in separate communities. The American Jesuits were initially receptive to the proposal but the matter was not pursued.[22]

Franciscans were engaged in training diocesan seminarians. In the 1860s, Bishop Henry Juncker of Alton, Illinois persuaded German Franciscans to start a diocesan seminary at their friary at Teutopolis, Illinois. They trained diocesan seminarians there from 1862 to 1865 until they gave up the effort because of a lack of suitable personnel.[23]

Italian Franciscans in western New York imitated the institutional model already adopted by the Vincentians and Benedictines. Their coming to the United States originated with the Roman visit of Buffalo's Bishop John Timon in 1854 for the solemn definition of the dogma of the Immaculate Conception.[24] Acting on the prompting of Nicholas Devereux, a Catholic land speculator, railroad promoter, and banker who desired a community of Franciscan priests to serve Catholics in western New York, where he had business interests, Timon persuaded the minister general of the Order of Friars Minor, Venantius a Celano, to send three Franciscan priests and a lay brother to Timon's diocese. The Franciscans traveled to the United States at Devereux's expense and after several changes of location were settled at Allegany in Cattaraugus County, New York near the Pennsylvania border. Devereux died later in 1855, but members of his family and Bishop Timon carried out his wishes of providing the Franciscan colony with land and a building. A friary, chapel, and college building was erected and was opened under the name of St. Bonaventure College in 1859. The college offered a six-year classical gymnasium and a three-year commercial course for lay students and a seminary program for Franciscan candidates for the priesthood. The first diocesan seminarians, who were affiliated with the diocese of Buffalo, were ordained to the priesthood by Bishop Timon in 1863.

No single figure dominated the development of St. Bonaventure's. The first Franciscan superior or *custos*, Pamphilus da Magliano, was recalled to Italy in 1867, also the year of Bishop Timon's death. Diomede Falconio, future archbishop and apostolic delegate in the United States, was president of the college and seminary from 1867 to 1870. The frequent rotation of personnel did not prevent the orderly development of the institution, which was chartered as a college by the Regents of the University of the State of New York in 1875, a measure made permanent in 1883. St. Bonaventure College and Seminary continued to provide training for candidates for dioceses of the region into the twentieth century.

From the 1850s through the 1870s as freestanding seminaries at major dioceses were emerging and the American colleges abroad were taking shape, six diocesan seminaries owned and staffed by religious communities of priests developed to serve the dioceses of their regions. These six were: St. Vincent's at Latrobe, Pennsylvania; St. John's, Stearns County, Minnesota; St. Meinrad, Spencer County, Indiana; St. Vincent College, Cape Girardeau, Missouri; Seminary of Our Lady of the Angels, near Buffalo, New York; and St. Bonaventure College and Seminary, Cattaraugus County, New York. Though they were sponsored by religious orders with different charisms, organizational models, and ethnic identities, they developed similar institutions, combining a college for lay students and a seminary — the Vincentians by default and the others by design. The mixed character assured the financial stability of the institution, making seminary education possible in the absence of ongoing financial support from dioceses except for the cost of tuition and lodging for students. The union of a seminary with a lay college provided the seminarians with the opportunity to live and learn in a larger community among those who did not intend to be clerics. There was a rural isolation to the seminaries, though St. Vincent's at Cape Girardeau was located within a small city and the Seminary of Our Lady of Angels was within twenty miles of Buffalo. The others were located in rural areas far removed from major centers of population. The agricultural activities conducted by unordained members of the religious communities were necessary elements in the stability of the institutions. Despite the physical seclusion, the sponsoring communities were deeply involved in pastoral activities in the local diocese.

The six seminaries represent a variation on the inherited institutional model. The Tridentine seminary decrees did not envision religious orders conducting seminaries on their own property and in the context of educational pursuits for laymen. The mixed institutional model is an adaptation to the needs of a missionary church. Though religious communities required the sanction of the local bishop to carry on their activities of training priests, and diocesan seminarians had to be affiliated with a diocese, the religious communities were in effect financially and educationally responsible for their seminaries. Like most freestanding seminaries, the mixed seminaries were normally patronized by bishops from dioceses in their area. The latter practice was not consistent with the assumptions of the Tridentine decree of each bishop forming his own clergy. The six seminaries were an adaptation to the conditions of the American missionary church. All were to survive the generation of their founding. St. Vincent's College at Cape Girardeau discontinued its seminary program in 1893 because the seminary was supplanted by the new freestanding one in St. Louis. The others continued to flourish and serve the church in the twentieth century.

6. Formation and Learning

The formation and learning provided in the nineteenth-century American Catholic seminary aimed to prepare priests for pastoral work as it was practiced through the period. Tridentine Catholicism, whether in the United States or elsewhere, stressed the importance of the faithful Catholic regularly receiving the sacraments, the ordinary means of salvation. The priest's ministry was thus directed to sanctification of souls through the ministry of sacraments, especially baptism, confession, Holy Eucharist, matrimony, and extreme unction. The priest's success in ministry depended on his devotion to these routine tasks. His seminary training was to prepare him morally and professionally for the faithful performance of these duties.

The role of the American priest developed according to social changes within the Catholic community and changes in religious practices through the period. The missionary priest of the early nineteenth century engaged in a demanding routine of travel to reach scattered Catholics. The Jesuit priest John Grassi described the typical duties of a priest active in Maryland or Pennsylvania in 1818:

> On Saturday, the missionary leaves his residence, and goes to take up his lodging with some Catholic living near the church. Having arrived at the house, he puts the Blessed Sacrament in some decent place, and also the Holy Oils, without which he never sets out on a journey. On the following morning he rides to the church, and ties his horse to a bush. The whole morning is spent in hearing confessions: meantime, the people from distances of four, six, ten miles, and even more, are coming in on horseback, so that often the church is entirely surrounded with horses. Mass begins towards noon; during the celebration, those who can read make use of prayer books, and pious hymns, for the most part in English, are sung by a choir of men and women. The sermon comes after the Gospel, and it is

122

preceded by the Gospel read in the vernacular. The preacher either reads or delivers his sermon, according to his inclination, and sometimes it is deferred until after Mass, to enable the priest to take some refreshment, which the faithful never fail to supply. There is no necessity to recommend attention, because they display the greatest eagerness to listen to the word of God. Vespers are not said, as the people live so far off and are so scattered; and so, when Mass is over, the children recite the catechism, infants are baptized, or the ceremonies are supplied in the case of those already baptized in danger, prayers for the dead are recited or the funeral services are performed over those who have been buried in the churchyard during the absence of the priest. Finally, one must attend to those who ask for instruction in order to join the Church, or who wish to be united in the bonds of Holy Matrimony.[1]

Through the middle of the century, Catholic immigrants swelled America's cities, where complex Catholic cultures began to develop. In urban communities resident priests, of course, engaged in the routine of ministering sacraments to large congregations with regularity.

Throughout the century, church authority actively promoted movements to bind Catholics more closely to the routine ministrations of the church. A characteristic means of encouraging the regular observance of church practice was the parish mission. The mission consisted of a week-long series of sermons, devotions, and liturgies given in the parish church by priests who specialized in this activity. The mission's aim was to renew the devotion of regular churchgoers and to return to the church those who had fallen away. The forgiveness of sins in the sacrament of penance and the reception of Holy Communion were the immediate goals of the mission. To carry on the rhythm of religious practices, church authority promoted extraliturgical devotions such as to the Virgin Mary, the Sacred Heart of Jesus, the Blessed Sacrament, or a particular saint. Devotions were often organized in associations, called sodalities or confraternities, which committed members to private and corporate prayers. The groups were organized on a parish basis and periodically met there. Indulgences were attached to the associations' prayers and devotions, subject to the usual conditions of regular confession and communion. The routine of devotions and reception of sacraments available at the parish church at which the clergy presided increased the prominence of the priest's position in Catholic life.[2]

To make priests available to the ever-growing Catholic population, bishops and seminary educators were willing to have priests trained quickly. In the absence of church legislation on the subject, they were free to ad-

just the length of the seminary course. Rapid training outweighed concerns for a long and thorough seminary course. Bishop John Carroll, writing to John Grassi, then president of Georgetown, in 1813, gave his views
on training Jesuit candidates for the priesthood. He expressed his "most
earnest desire":

> for your active and uniform concurrence in preparing, as quietly as
> possible for holy orders, as many as can be trusted to receive them,
> tho they may not have studied all the Treatises of Divinity, provided
> they know the obvious and general principles of moral Theology. . . .
> In exigencies, such as ours, less time should be allotted to the finish-
> ing of theological tracts. . . .[3]

Bishop John England, who argued eloquently for thorough clerical learning on several occasions, made adjustments in his own seminary by ordaining priests urgently needed for missionary activity in his vast diocese
before the completion of "half" their usual studies. Of these he said, "They
have generally acted well & are well disposed, but I am obliged to keep
perpetually changing their places, so as to try & give them in turn an opportunity of coming hither [to Charleston] to supply their deficiency of
knowledge, — & they are too few."[4] Even as late as 1861, Cincinnati's young
seminary rector, William J. Barry, remarked: "We have known cases of persons having been ordained after their first year's theology; and some have
graduated in ecclesiastical science, after an extensive course of six months."[5]

While bishops accepted the necessity of rapid seminary training, contemporary problems of clerical behavior informed a concern for well-
behaved priests. From the late eighteenth century, American bishops had
to cope with errant priests or a "medley of clerical characters" as John
Carroll called them.[6] Unable to adapt to the routine of church life in Europe, such priests could easily obtain positions in America, where priests
were needed. They soon manifested their instability, either of intemperance,
contentiousness, or greed. They often moved from diocese to diocese,
thereby enlarging their reputation for irregular behavior.

The roving spirit was not confined to poorly behaved priests, but was
also to be found among those in good standing. Immigrant priests, having
no local loyalties, moved from diocese to diocese looking for the situation
that suited them. Bishop England reported in 1839 that after nineteen years
as bishop of Charleston fifty-one priests had served his diocese. Of these
seven had died, but twenty-six had left "at various times and for different
causes"; of those departing "three [left] for just and sufficient reasons, three
on account of infirmity, four whose departure was not regretted by either
me or their people, and sixteen, most of whom are now engaged in other
missions, very few of whom were by any means justified, as I believe, in

their departure."[7] American bishops addressed the problem of roving priests in the legislation of their provincial councils by requiring priests to accept the assignments given them by the bishop and to stay in the diocese and not leave it without permission. Priests coming into American dioceses from abroad were not to be received without proper credentials.[8]

Good clerical behavior was regarded as essential because, once ordained, priests were more or less on their own in the missionary conditions of the American church. Archbishop Bedini reported the contemporary situation for newly ordained priests as it was described to him in the 1850s:

> No sooner are they ordained than the Bishops must send them to different churches and missions, sometimes the most remote. There they are in the flower of their youth, far from watchful authority, alone, without another priest who can assist them in their ministry and give constant witness to their behavior, forced to exercise the full and delicate adminstration of a parish; and they must do this among Catholics who are most devoted to their priests, and among Protestants who are trying their best to seduce them and corrupt them.[9]

Priests in good standing, in addition to their roving spirit, often left much to be desired for other reasons. Archbishop Bedini reported that Irish Catholics were greatly attached to their Irish priests, but "if intemperance and selfishness did not at times tempt the Irish priest, he would be the best in the world." He learned during his visit that Irish priests "liked to accumulate wealth" and that the Irish were regularly taking up collections for priests. He found fault with German priests as "too zealously nationalistic" by encouraging "national feeling as much as possible in a land where there are more Irishmen than Germans."[10] Cincinnati's seminary rector, William J. Barry, the son of Irish immigrants, shared his unfavorable views on Irish seminarians and priests with Orestes Brownson, finding that "They aspire to the priesthood because of its powers and wealth."[11]

John Carroll issued an early plea for training priests to good behavior in the same letter to Grassi quoted above: "their Superiors will, it is hoped, never relax in vigilance over their morals, or be inattentive to their dispositions, temper, religious principles, and subordination."[12] Francis Kenrick, shortly after becoming coadjutor bishop of Philadelphia, reminded his contemporary, John B. Purcell, then president at Emmitsburg, "I need not tell you how much you should inculcate humility, *disinterestedness*, obedience, docility, *temperance,* and *purity,* with zeal, charity, patience and all the train of virtues. On your exertions it depends in a great measure to redeem the character of the Priesthood which some unworthy men continue to degrade."[13]

The pastoral letters of the First Provincial Council of Baltimore, issued October 17, 1829 — one addressed to the laity and one to the clergy — set the official standards of behavior expected of both groups. Bishop John England composed the letters, which were signed by all the bishops. In the letter to the clergy, priests were reminded of their high calling and described as the "light of the world" and the "salt of the earth," to which ideal they should be faithful. They were reminded "that the faults which are trivial in a layman are crimes in the priest: and that, as your place is higher, so are the virtues which a God of justice demands from you of a far superior grade to those required from a layman." But the influence of the priest was augmented by the example of his life. A high standard of priestly behavior consisted of more than avoiding major failings. England was concerned with the "want of that influence which is naturally created by the presence of a man whose correct demeanour proclaims that he is a priest of God." This concern for behavior was so great that England, who stressed clerical learning on other occasions, could express the overriding importance of behavior, stating "that the example of a pious and zealous clergyman though of limited attainments is a richer treasure to the Church, than talents and learning and eloquence combined."[14]

The Catholic seminaries set out to develop good behavior of future priests by enforcing a highly controlled routine of life to form the habits of self-discipline to serve the priest through life. The priest's behavior related to the very meaning of the priesthood as a representation of Christ and the Church, as explained by the French seminary tradition since the seventeenth century. The secluded and recondite nature of seminary training was seldom explained to the English-speaking Catholic public. A nineteenth-century Irish alumnus of St. Sulpice provided a rare contemporary explanation in English of the characteristics of the Sulpicians' often repeated purpose of imparting *esprit ecclésiastique*, a term that is usually translated as "ecclesiastical spirit" but might be accurately rendered as the spirit of an *ecclésiastique*, or an ecclesiastical person, hence in English a "clerical spirit":

> It is understood to be effected by a system of training thoroughly clerical, and, as such, so affecting the ideas, the feelings, the knowledge, and even the tastes of the individual, that the *man* is, as far as possible, transformed into the *priest* — will think and feel, and will, therefore, also speak and write, only as a priest would be expected to do; so that not only in his official capacity, but in the details of his private life, the priest shall be unmistakeably stamped on all he says and does.[15]

This spirit was not confined to Sulpician seminaries, for Emmitsburg's John McCaffrey told his seminarians to be always "mindful of the
sublimity of the Sacred Priesthood to which they aspire." The seminary
rule, written in his own hand, explained how this personal transformation
came about in practice: "Each one must study so to correct & form his
whole deportment as to avoid . . . the affectations of worldlings. . . ."[16]

The seminary rule was the key to maintaining the routine of discipline considered appropriate for training seminarians. The Sulpicians had
a detailed house discipline followed by the priest directors and the seminarians. It was periodically read to the seminary community. The Vincentians were in theory guided by the *directoire* for the conduct of seminaries,
as approved by the Vincentian superior general. The *directoire* was a "how
to" manual that outlined the internal life of a seminary, spiritual exercises,
studies, and the duties of superior, faculty, and students with thorough-
ness and clarity, so that Vincentian seminaries everywhere would have "a
uniformity as perfect as possible."[17] The regimen of community exercises,
classes, and spiritual direction is only slightly different from the Sulpician
routine.

The provisions of written rules could not always be carried out as
literally as they were intended. For instance, until the 1850s the Baltimore
Sulpicians were unable to exclude the "external" activities that compromised some aspects of a strict observance of the house rule for seminarians
and priests. The Sulpicians Flaget and David tried to maintain Sulpician
standards at St. Thomas Seminary in Kentucky, but necessity required the
seminarians to spend part of the day in manual labor, usually farm work.
Farming was clearly not a part of the tradition of St. Sulpice. Likewise,
the Vincentians could not literally comply with the seminary aspect of their
rule when concurrently conducting colleges for lay students. The ideal was
nevertheless the regular execution of the rule in everyday life, so that the
life of prayer and recollection could be pursued. The sameness prompted
the Vincentian rector of the Philadelphia seminary to write to his superior that there was nothing new to report: "you know the monotony of
a seminary."[18]

The rule of St. Joseph's Provincial Seminary, Troy, New York, approved by the bishops of the New York ecclesiastical province in 1871 and
printed in Latin, is one of the most thorough seminary codes dating from
the period. Its provisions spell out the controls on seminarians that are
common for seminaries before and afterward. As a freestanding seminary
without the distractions of a lay college, St. Joseph's provided the seclusion for developing the spirituality of the priest's life. The seminary's internal rule enforced isolation from people in ordinary walks of life, laity
and especially women. The rule explicitly forbade "above all" as "most

dangerous" a familiarity with persons of "the other sex." The rule also forbade students visiting each other in their rooms. Permissions, probably seldom given, were necessary to leave the seminary premises, visit the kitchen, and to talk to the servants. Drinking alcohol and smoking were prohibited. Likewise, bringing food or drink of any kind into the seminary was forbidden. Silence prevailed through most of the day, except for the short interval after breakfast and afternoon recreation. The New Testament or devotional literature was read aloud during meals. Students were expected to go to their rooms for quiet study at intervals between classes. The aim of the house rule was to build an abstemious man who was not dependent on social contacts with women or, to a degree, even his peers in the seminary.[19]

The seminary year began with the annual retreat. At St. Mary's in Baltimore, the seminarians began the school year in September with an eight-day retreat that reintroduced the seminarians to the routine of spiritual exercises in an atmosphere of solitude and recollection, preparing them for the forthcoming year. In addition to the normal seminary routine of exercises, the retreat, according to Henri Icard, permitted them to "examine the state of their consciences" in the light provided by the reading of Scripture and the *Imitation of Christ* by Thomas à Kempis, visits to the reserved Sacrament, and consultation with their confessors.[20]

Once the school year was under way, the weekday schedule began with rising, usually at five o'clock; a half hour later the seminary community (the faculty or "directors," as they were called, with the seminarians) met in the prayer hall for short morning "vocal" prayers as a prelude to meditation or mental prayer according to the method of St. Sulpice. The latter exercise was supposed to last an hour, according to French usages. At the visitation of the Baltimore seminary in 1829, meditation was held for thirty-seven minutes. Every two weeks one of the directors explained the method of meditation. From meditation the seminarians went to the chapel for Mass, at which they received Communion according to the advice of their confessors, usually no more than once a week. Breakfast followed, consisting in 1829 of a piece of bread with a hot beverage. Until the close of St. Mary's lay college in 1852, the day proceeded with a single class of dogma or moral theology and, twice a week, a class in Sacred Scripture. The remainder of the day was taken up with teaching and prefecting duties for the college students.

At midday, the seminary community assembled in the prayer hall for *examen particulier*, an exercise consisting of a short reading from the New Testament followed by a reading on a specific virtue and then personal reflection on the role of that particular virtue in the individual's life.

After the midday meal the afternoon schedule of classes and assigned duties continued. Late in the afternoon the rosary was recited in unison before the evening meal. In the evening, night prayers were conducted with the general examination of conscience. In contrast to the particular examination on one specific virtue, at the evening examination the seminarian reviewed and evaluated his personal actions during the day in the light of a life of virtue. Spiritual reading was also held for a half hour, usually a public reading of a pious work or a discourse of the rector.

Other spiritual exercises of seminary life took place during the week. Each seminarian chose a confessor from the directors to whom he made his confession of sins and received absolution at least once a week. The confessor was also available for counsel and advice. The relationship of the confessor to the penitent introduced an element of a personal relationship in the seminary that the strict adherence of the formal schedule of religious activities did not provide. By means of the confessor-penitent relationship, individual faculty members could have a deep impact on the life of a seminarian. At Baltimore the close relationship of faculty with students would develop only with time, because of the cultural distance separating French priests from Irish and American seminarians. As the minutes of the 1829 visitation record: "It is painful to have to say that few of them [alumni] keep any affection for the Seminary and come back willingly."[21]

In the course of the school year, the seminarians were called to receive the minor or major orders of the church which culminated in ordination to the priesthood. At faculty meetings the directors voted on seminarians as each was summoned to the various steps to the priesthood. The minor orders of porter, lector, exorcist, and acolyte were often conferred together in the nineteenth century, and the three major orders of ministry, subdeacon, deacon, and priest, were taken in succession. On these occasions the directors conferred privately and only the results of the deliberations on individuals were recorded. The directors could consider only the candidates' external conduct and formal learning based on their own observations. The individual's confessor was not permitted to take part in the discussion of one of his penitents so as not to breech the confidentiality of their relationship. Once the directors decided to call a candidate to one of the orders, his bishop was notified that one of his "subjects" was approved and the bishop in turn issued an authorization for him to be ordained to the order to which he had been called. Minor orders and major orders up to the priesthood were usually conferred at the Baltimore cathedral. Ordinations for the priesthood were often conducted at the candidate's home diocese by his own bishop.

The call to orders was not always such a well-ordered procedure. A bishop could not be held to follow a recommendation not to ordain one of his students, or a bishop could, and many bishops did, withdraw a student from the seminary toward the end of his course in order to ordain him because of the urgent need for priests. In this case the formality of a call to orders was meaningless. At the visitation of the Sulpician seminary in 1850, the faculty agreed that in such cases the bishop was to be informed that he assumed sole responsibility for the ordination.[22]

If good behavior for priests was the hallmark of seminary training, a broader articulation of qualities the priest should cultivate for ministry in the United States seldom arose during the period. Archbishop Bedini found the clergy "European and not American, and each one has the customs and prejudices of his own nation."[23] So too the seminarians were immigrants or the sons of immigrants; they were destined to serve an immigrant Catholic community. Archbishop Spalding provides a rare manifestation of the desire to promote an explicitly "American" style in his attempt to eliminate some of the French traits of the Baltimore Sulpicians as described in chapter 1. The absence of an articulation of ministry for Americans was matched by the lack of literature in English directed to the spiritual life or ministry of the priest. The seminarian had to rely on traditional literature translated into English that was suitable for the pious laity or vowed religious such as the *Imitation of Christ* of Thomas à Kempis, Richard Challoner's eighteenth-century classic *Garden of the Soul*, or the nineteenth-century works of Frederick Faber, but nothing dealing specifically with the priesthood. The importance of spreading the continental model of priestly spirituality was apparently one of the reasons for having European priests teaching in seminaries. For this reason Archbishop John Hughes sought the Sulpicians to staff his provincial seminary, as he told Bishop John McCloskey:

> And one great advantage [of having Sulpicians] would be that in the preparatory seminary it should be required that the students should learn French, inasmuch as theological works in English are very rare and imperfect. The standard works, of course, in Latin, will be on hand. But a knowledge of French is almost essential in this country to a candidate for the priesthood.[24]

It was only in 1878 that Louis Tronson's volume of *Conferences,* which imparts the French School of spirituality, was translated into English. In 1871 the English priest Frederick Oakley published his volume *The Priest on the Mission*, which outlines the pastoral activities of the priest from the contemporary British perspective, but no comparable work was published in the United States to address American parish life.[25]

The seminary was a school for formal learning in theology and professional skills for ministry, though this essential aspect presupposed an attainment of an acceptable level of personal holiness and good clerical behavior. The unevenness and brevity of the course at many seminaries rendered formal learning even more secondary. Most seminaries before the middle of the century did not have a set number of years of study for such subjects as philosophy and theology. This flexibility seems appropriate, since many local diocesan seminaries were little more than finishing schools for immigrant seminarians well advanced in their training. A short period of study gave them an opportunity to practice English and learn the practical aspects of ministry prior to ordination. In such cases the character and habits that they would have as priests were already formed and their basic theological learning had taken place in Europe.

Flexibility and study at the student's individual pace apparently prevailed at some seminaries. At the Vincentians' St. Louis seminary during the 1840s, one student, Irish-born John O'Hanlon, left a detailed memoir of life there. He leaves the impression of school life in which students taught each other: "We had hours assigned for the study of Greek and Latin classics, which were ably taught us by a fellow-student and an Irishman; while we had lessons in French, German, and Italian by those of our community." Vincentian priests taught the theological subjects. Bishop Peter Kenrick examined the students himself prior to the conferral of orders. "So far as I could form an opinion," O'Hanlon found, "our very learned prelate was not greatly disappointed with the result of his searching examinations in Philosophy, Theology, Ecclesiastical History and Hermeneutics."[26]

In contrast, St. Michael's Seminary of Pittsburgh offered philosophy and theology courses under the direction of two priests, Thomas McCullagh as disciplinarian and instructor in philosophy and John Mosetizh, a Slovenian emigré, as instructor in theology. The seminary had fourteen students in its first year, seven learned philosophy and seven theology. In their small building one professor conducted class in the parlor and the other in a study room. The two priests shared a partitioned bedroom while the fourteen students shared two other bedrooms. There were no younger students for older students to teach, so that Mosetizh could offer as much as four hours of dogmatic and moral theology daily in addition to four hours of Scripture per week.[27]

Seminary teaching was often the responsibility of a very small faculty. The seminaries of the first half of the century, with their small enrollments, required a faculty of no more than one or two. As Providus (John England) complained in 1832: "As our theological schools are at present constituted, the duties of several distinct professorships are necessarily devolved on one individual."[28] The sole theology professor was the case for a long time at the Baltimore seminary where Louis Deluol taught theology from 1819 to 1849; at Emmitsburg with Simon Bruté from 1817 to 1834 and William Henry Elder from 1846 to 1857; in Bardstown with Francis Kenrick in the 1820s, and at any number of local diocesan seminaries where there was a brisk turnover of seminary personnel. The Vincentians normally assigned two and sometimes three priests to staff the seminaries of dioceses in the 1840s.

Reliance on theological textbooks was such that classroom instruction did not demand much preparation. At St. Charles Seminary in Philadelphia, the two priests who succeeded the Vincentians in the 1850s had not decided how to divide the subjects between themselves shortly before the opening of the school year.[29] With the emergence of the freestanding seminaries in the 1850s, seminaries developed larger faculties with a specialization of subjects.

Interest in the professional preparation for seminary faculties advanced gradually through the period. Roman-trained European priests coming to America were often assigned to seminaries, as was Francis Kenrick in Kentucky; and American priests sent to Rome returned to teach in seminaries, as did William Henry Elder of Emmitsburg and James Madison Lancaster at Bardstown. The Roman doctors had not had a course of studies longer than the ordinary seminary course. The Sulpicians with their thorough training at St. Sulpice did not ordinarily have postordination studies until the late 1870s, when the Society established a residence in Rome to enable their members to pursue studies there. The Vincentians officially forbade their members to earn degrees until the 1880s because of St. Vincent's views on the vanity of learning. On the other hand, Boniface Wimmer began to send monks from America to Rome as early as the 1860s for advanced studies. Several freestanding seminaries enjoyed the services of university graduates, such as Michael Heiss and Joseph Salzmann at Milwaukee, the Louvain-educated Belgians at St. Joseph's Seminary at Troy, the Roman-trained American priests at Philadelphia by the 1860s, and the Roman and Paris-trained diocesan priests at the Cincinnati seminary.

The freestanding seminaries and the Benedictine places by the 1870s had standard courses of at least three years of theology, usually preceded by one or two years of philosophy. If the seminary had not taught the seminarian the humanities, as was possible at Emmitsburg, Baltimore, Cincinnati, Milwaukee, Philadelphia, and the Benedictine places, then the candidates for orders would not have had a prior training in clerical culture and spirituality.

The seminary course culminated in ordination, so that there was a limited interest in earning degrees. The Holy See granted pontifical charters to St. Mary's Seminary at Baltimore, Spring Hill College in Mobile, St. Charles Seminary in Philadelphia, and St. John's Abbey and Seminary in Minnesota, thereby enabling them to grant doctorates. These powers were seldom used and then usually to honor faculty members and a select few priests outside the seminary. There was apparently no provision for granting the lesser pontifical degrees after the ordinary seminary course. Emmitsburg, Seton Hall, the Benedictines' St. Vincent's and St. John's and others conferred bachelor degrees on lay students and seminarians for the collegiate course. Cincinnati's seminary did not confer bachelor degrees on seminarians after the short-lived lay college closed. The charter of St. Charles Seminary in Philadelphia permitted the conferral of degrees, but these powers were not used during the nineteenth century. Milwaukee's seminary had a state charter that did not include the power to grant degrees. Unless a lay college was attached, interest in baccalaureate degrees was slight.

Despite the lack of interest in degrees, public examinations and exercises commanded some interest. At the seminaries affiliated with lay colleges, the system of honors for students in various disciplines usually included the seminary. Public examinations were practiced at several free-standing seminaries. At Cincinnati the local Catholic newspaper announced the dates for semiannual public examinations at Mount St. Mary's of the West and included theses that seminarians would be defending. The announcement was sufficiently early to allow time for seminarians to prepare for the examination and the visiting local clergy to prepare objections to pose to the seminarians.[30] Archbishop Purcell often presided at these examinations, and the practice was in keeping with his ambitions to develop a theological university at Cincinnati. Public exercises were apparently used elsewhere. Bedini visited the seminaries of Cincinnati, New York, and Baltimore, where he attended "some examinations and scholastic exercises, or concursus" and found himself "not at all satisfied with the results."[31] Public examinations were an attempt to introduce some aspects of European university traditions to the seminary.

Boniface Wimmer, with his roots in the Bavarian Catholic revival, offered an aesthetic dimension to the preparation for ministry that was not found elsewhere and which supplemented accepted aspects of spiritual formation and formal learning. For Wimmer, art had an importance of its own, as he informed his Bavarian benefactors:

> In a country like America where Protestant services are so devoid of everything that elevates the mind and heart, religion and art must go hand in hand to give to religious services outward splendor, dignity, and loftiness.

Art makes religion "more highly esteemed by the earthly-minded man who finds it difficult to enter into her inner spirit and who thus feels himself less attracted toward her." Monasteries provided a means of diffusing the arts throughout the country. "I am absolutely persuaded," he stated, "that a monastic school which does not give just as much attention to art as to knowledge and religion is a very imperfect one and that a deficiency in scholarship at the beginning can be more readily excused than a neglect of art." He assigned a proselytizing purpose to art:

> Heretics have seldom been converted by learned treatises, but almost always found their way to the true faith through the beauties of Catholic worship, the holiness of its ministers, the fervor of the people, and prayers. It will hardly be different in America.[32]

Wimmer took care to provide instruction in drawing and painting at St. Vincent's. Bavarian donors provided more than three hundred oil paintings for St. Vincent's in its early decades to hang on the walls of the college and seminary. Wimmer took similar care with musical instruction, including an orchestra. The daily conventual Mass and the public celebration of the liturgy of the hours provided a daily exercise in liturgical music. No member of the extended community of a Benedictine abbey, college, and seminary would be untouched by the pervasiveness of visual and musical arts.

Whatever the variations in seminary education in terms of time, place, size of the seminary community, the approach toward learning or length of the course, American seminaries adhered to the tradition of reliance on theological manuals to impart a measure of theoretical and practical knowledge in those aspects of theology considered appropriate for ministry.

The choice of manuals corresponded to changing trends in Catholic theology during the period. A central issue was the location of ecclesiastical authority. Most churchmen who led the American church in the first half of the nineteenth century inherited to some degree the Gallican ecclesiology. For instance, John Carroll as an eighteenth-century churchman viewed the pope's powers as rather limited. Likewise, Bishop John England, whose seminary training had been conducted by French priests at Carlow College in Ireland, viewed the pope as subject to the canons of the church and to a general council. Carroll and England were not partisans of papal infallibility.[33]

By the beginning of the nineteenth century Gallicanism itself was undergoing modifications. The context of a strong Catholic monarch of *ancien régime* France that informed the Gallican Four Articles of 1682 was no longer present. The concept of the state's role in the church had altered since the French Revolution, especially after the experience of Napoleon's attempts to subordinate the pope completely. Instead the Gallicanism of the nineteenth century was modified and stressed the collegiality of the episcopate and not the role of the state. Hence, a moderate or episcopal Gallicanism emerged, in which the pope enjoyed the primacy of honor, exercised jurisdiction in discipline, and spoke for the church, but in matters of doctrine his decisions required ratification by the bishops. A general council of the church was infallible, not the pope.[34]

In the United States a strong tradition of episcopal collegiality was operative through the national and provincial councils of bishops throughout the nineteenth century. The exercise of the bishops' authority through councils was consistent with French influences in the American church as represented by the number of French immigrant priests and especially French seminary personnel.

The theology manual in widest use in France during the early nineteenth century and among the Sulpicians in Baltimore at the same time, and probably also at Emmitsburg and Bardstown during the early years, was the resoundingly Gallican textbook *Theologia dogmatica et moralis* by Louis Bailly, professor of theology at the seminary of Dijon. It was first published in 1789, shortly before the French Revolution closed the country's seminaries, and was reissued in a series of editions in the early nineteenth century. The Gallican Abbé Regnier's *Tractatus de Ecclesia Christi* (1780) was also used in France. At Baltimore, Louis Deluol's handwritten syllabus and his notes listing authors which he used in class presentation indicate that in his treatment of the church he relied on Bailly and included references to other Gallicans, including Regnier and Tournely.[35]

The reign of Pope Gregory XVI (1830–1846) marks the beginning of the assertion of Roman control over the Catholic church in Europe. The appointment of Fornari as papal nuncio to France in 1843 signaled Rome's active encouragement of those elements in the French church that were sympathetic to Rome, that is, the ultramontanists, and was meant to reduce the influence of the old elements in France, the bishops and clergy trained in the older traditions of Gallicanism.

Pope Pius IX, who was elected in 1846, began a long reign that greatly advanced the influence of the Holy See in doctrinal matters. In August 1852, Pius IX learned in the course of a conversation with a visiting seminary educator from Ireland that the theological manual of Louis Bailly was in use in seminaries throughout Europe. The pope, as bishop of Spoleto, had Bailly's manual removed from the syllabus of his diocesan seminary. He ordered the papal nuncio to France, Archbishop Garibaldi, to investigate the use of Bailly in French seminaries. Garibaldi reported its use along with other texts and recommended that no action be taken on the matter. In fact, successive editions had diluted the Gallican and antipapal tone of the eighteenth-century edition. Pius IX did not see the matter in those terms, and Bailly was placed on the Index of Forbidden Books on December 7, 1852. The condemnation created a shock in French ecclesiastical circles, because the textbook with which priests had been trained in the previous half-century was now judged heretical. The pope's action created consternation in French seminaries, for they were scarcely able to change textbooks in the middle of the school year. On Janaury 19, 1853, the pope backed down to the extent that seminaries could use the heretical textbook for the remainder of the year. But the pope's condemnation effectively ended Bailly's influence.[36]

The Sulpicians' adherence to moderate Gallicanism continued with the adoption at St. Sulpice and other seminaries in France of Jean-Baptiste Bouvier's manual, *Institutiones theologicae*. Bouvier (1783–1854), bishop of Mans, had demonstrated his opposition to ultramontanism in conflicts with Dom Prosper Gueranger, a leader of the liturgical revival, over the introduction of a standard Roman liturgy in France. Bouvier's manual, which had first appeared in 1834 and endorsed the inherited Gallican ecclesiology, had gone through eight editions by 1853. Bouvier escaped condemnation by revising his manual to conform to the new anti-Gallican requirements of Roman authorities, and the work enjoyed an additional seven editions. It seems likely that the text was immediately introduced at Baltimore, in view of the deference that Lhomme and Dubreul always paid to the authorities in Paris. The visiting Canon Peter Benoit found that Bouvier's manual was in use at Baltimore during his visit in 1875.[37]

By the middle of the century, American seminaries other than Baltimore's came under the influence of Giovanni Perrone (1794–1876), probably the most widely known theologian in the Catholic world. Perrone, a Jesuit, joined the faculty of the Collegio Romano (the Pontifical Gregorian University) when Pope Leo XII entrusted it to the Jesuits in 1824. In the early nineteenth century Roman authorities condemned the semi-rationalist theology of Georg Hermes and Anton Günther, who held that all the truths of Christianity could be arrived at by human reason, and the fideism of Louis Bautain and Louis de Bonald, who impugned the powers of human reason. Perrone emerged as a spokesman for the Roman point of view by the 1830s with his balancing of the claims of reason and revelation. Perrone was a Scholastic theologian by tradition, but, as Gerald McCool states, he did not look on scholasticism as a "tightly organized, intrinsically articulated theological system structured by one coherent philosophy of knowledge, man, and being."[38] Instead, he was a "positive" theologian lacking an interest in speculation. Perrone was capable of mastering and organizing a large amount of theological literature. He was well read in contemporary theology, including Protestant authors. He participated in the formulation of the doctrine of the Immaculate Conception and in the preparations of the First Vatican Council. His influence extended beyond Rome through the publication of the nine-volume *Praelectiones theologicae* between 1835 and 1842, which eventually had thirty-four editions. He subsequently offered a five-volume abridged *Compendium* in 1845 suitable for use in seminaries. The latter work went through forty-two editions, a fact which attests to its wide use in Catholic seminaries.

Perrone's manual was probably first used in an American seminary in 1846. In that year the newly ordained William Henry Elder returned from Rome to teach seminarians at Mount St. Mary's in Emmitsburg and adopted the manual he had undoubtedly known in Rome.[39] It was adopted at the seminaries of Milwaukee and Cincinnati as well as the three Benedictine seminaries by the 1870s and possibly at other seminaries that left no record of textbooks.[40]

An analysis of the treatment of each major theological issue by each manual writer of the period properly belongs to the field of historical theology. However, Perrone, as the era's most influential manualist, deserves some attention here as the practitioner of a then typical method of presenting theological issues to seminarians. Perrone's treatment of *De Ordine* provides an example and one related to the seminarians' understanding of the sacrament of holy orders. Perrone presents a detailed presentation of church belief and practice concerning holy orders in a lengthy treatise of ninety-three pages. The subject is divided into several headings and one or more propositions are the starting point of each subdivision. These initial propositions on the nature of the sacrament are:

> Orders or sacred ordination is truly and properly a sacrament instituted by Christ the Lord.
>
> There is in the New Testament a visible and external priesthood instituted by Christ the Lord, that is not common to all, but characteristic of the apostles, propagated through an external rite whose substance is a true sacrament.
>
> Besides priesthood, there are other minor and major orders in the Catholic church, through which one advances to the priesthood by steps.
>
> Bishops are superior to priests by divine law.
>
> Bishops have the power of ordaining that is not common to priests.[41]

In discussing the foregoing propositions over fifty-four pages, Perrone begins his brief explanation of each one by stating that it is *"de fide,"* that is, defined by a general council and therefore a part of the faith. He quotes the relevant passage from the Tridentine decrees, along with the "anathema" attached to the contrary opinion. Therefore the starting point of each proposition is that the authority of the Council of Trent is behind the proposition before a positive explanation is developed. A section of *Difficultates* follows in which he lists objections to the proposition, often by Protestant authors, and answers the objections point by point with quotations from Scripture, the church fathers, or church councils, accompanied by a brief explanation.

The propositions *de fide* are followed by a presentation of thirty-nine pages devoted to the "law of continence," which is not *de fide*. The discussions begin with the following propositions:

> The law of continence imposed on sacred ministers is most certainly based on the most ancient tradition of the church.
> The law of continence imposed on sacred ministers is the most fitting condition for clerics.
> The law of continence is neither contrary to divine or natural law.
> The law of continence imposed on sacred ministers is not adverse to the good of society but rather wonderfully promotes it.[42]

Here the same method of presentation, objections, and answers to objections with an amassing of quotations is pursued to indicate the desirability of celibacy and to justify the church's law on the subject.

The method of dividing up a complex issue into small propositions and paragraphs has the pedagogical value of making it easy to study and facilitates examinations. The assumption behind the presentation is that the doctrine and the practices of priesthood are the same as they had been in every age, with the exception of celibacy, which was obviously more recent. In other words, concepts had not undergone change and development over time. In concluding his tract Perrone asserts that the Catholic priesthood is "truly universal," existing "in every age and region of the earth."[43]

The influence of manualists from Rome and France was not effectively challenged by the dogmatic work of the theological luminary of the American Catholic community, Francis Patrick Kenrick. A professor at the Bardstown seminary and Catholic apologist in theological controversies in Kentucky, Kenrick entered the ranks of the manualists in 1840 with the publication of his *Theologica Dogmatica*, intended for seminarians and missionary priests in America. Kenrick was the American figure closest to being a disciple of the theological impulses emerging from Germany. In his explanation of tradition Kenrick relied on Johann Adam Möhler, the leading figure of the University of Tübingen school, and his *Symbolik*. Through Möhler, Kenrick introduced theological students in America to the idea that history was the starting point in theology and that the church is an organic, developing community of believers. In dealing with the standard topics of his dogmatic theology, Kenrick relied on the church fathers for explanations of Scripture and doctrine, ignoring Scholastic authors. The consensus of the fathers was then the basis of the church teaching. Noted church historian Gerald Fogarty also finds in Kenrick's ideas of development and community a basis for the collegiality that operated among the American bishops of the nineteenth century.[44]

Kenrick's textbook on dogma probably had limited influence in American seminaries. It was presumably in use at his own Philadelphia seminary and that of his brother in St. Louis in the 1850s, but the evidence is not clear. By the time of the appearance of early printed seminary catalogs in the 1860s and 1870s Kenrick's volumes are not mentioned.

A major concern related to clerical formation was the preparation of the future priest to administer the sacrament of penance. The study of moral theology had in recent centuries become increasingly related to this function of the priest, and it is likely that the subject was regarded as the most important in the seminary curriculum. As Archbishop Samuel Eccleston wrote to President John McCaffrey in 1845: "I could not ordain Mr. B. until he has gone through a good course of Moral Theology. . . . If either must be postponed, let it be Dogmatic Theology. . . . Hence give, I entreat you, a decided preference to Moral Theology. . . ."[45]

The choice of moral textbook was the main factor in teaching moral theology. The French tradition in moral theology inherited from the eighteenth century was one of Augustinian rigor in reaction to the supposed laxity of the Jesuit moralists. The Sulpicians and Vincentians were not identified with the extreme rigor of Jansenism, but the net effect of the controversies in moral theology was that the mainstream tended toward rigor. The eighteenth-century Italian, St. Alphonsus Liguori (1697–1787), a lawyer before becoming a priest, was a pivotal figure in turning moral theology away from these controversies. Liguori mastered the canonical literature on moral questions. He then articulated a practical approach between laxity and rigor based on individual judgment of cases rather than a mechanical adherence to law. In the opinion of the time, this approach, called equiprobabilism, was considered lenient. Though his approach was not influential in his lifetime, Liguori's views gradually achieved pre-eminence in Catholic moral theology in the nineteenth century. Official favor was conferred when he was elevated to sainthood in 1839 and then proclaimed a doctor of the church in 1871.[46]

Rigor in moral theology was still pervasive in the French ecclesiastical world in the early nineteenth century. The influential Bailly, Gallican in ecclesiology, was a rigorist in moral questions. Deloul, for instance, considered Liguori "too sweet."[47] Despite the fact that Gallicanism usually was associated with rigor in moral questions and ultramontanism with the Liguorian approach, the Gallican Jean-Baptiste Bouvier adopted the Liguorian approach in his moral theology, assisting its spread in France and at places under French influence in the United States.

Just as the Jesuit Perrone became the most influential dogma manualist after the middle of the nineteenth century, the Jesuit Jean Pierre Gury (1801–1865) became the most influential author of moral textbooks. Gury, born in France and professor of moral theology at the Jesuit seminary at Vals, advanced the influence of the Liguorian approach to moral theology with the publication of *Compendium Theologiae moralis* in 1850. This work had seventeen editions during its author's life and many additional editions in other countries and after his death.[48] It was in use at Cincinnati, Milwaukee, the Benedictine seminaries, and possibly others by the 1870s. Thus American seminaries were following the general trends toward the consensus around Liguori's moral theology.[49]

The content of Gury's textbook bears some consideration in view of its extraordinary influence and the importance of moral theology as a preparation for ministry. The first volume contains the standard offering of tracts or topics on human acts, conscience, law, sin, virtues, the Decalogue, precepts of the church, justice and law, and contracts. The second volume is the more practical for ministry, offering tracts on particular states of life in which the obligations of the clerical state are developed, the sacraments in general, and then each of the seven sacraments. The sacraments of penance and matrimony are several times longer than the others; in fact these two tracts combined comprise one fourth of the two volumes (246 of 990 pages).

The matrimony tract was more than a treastise on the nature of the sacrament and provided much practical information for the priest by listing positive law concerning marriage banns, the range of legal impediments to marriage, conditions for validating marriages, and the treatment of various sexual sins.[50]

Gury's wide acceptance in American seminaries was not compromised by Francis Kenrick's moral manual, published in 1843, in which he also adopted the Liguorian approach to moral questions. Kenrick, who spent his initial American years in Kentucky and his later years in Maryland, both slaveholding states, had dealt with the moral life of the Catholic slaveholder. He elaborated the idea that if the slaveholder had not personally reduced a free person to slavery but had inherited slaves then it was permissible to keep slaves to avoid the supposed ill effects of liberating them.[51] The ending of slavery in the United States rendered discussion of this issue obsolete and perhaps embarrassing. It is possible that the lack of influence of his moral manual was related to this issue.

Scripture was taught in separate courses in many seminaries, such as at Baltimore two periods per week on Thursday and Sunday. There and elsewhere Scripture studies did not equal the attention given to dogma and moral courses. The latter courses touched on Scripture in the sense that biblical quotations were given as proofs in the various tracts. The introductory texts or biblical commentaries were not generally listed in the few printed catalogs of course offerings. The most noted Catholic devoted to biblical scholarship was Francis Kenrick, who spent years on an English translation of the Bible; however, this phase of his work did not take place in the context of a seminary. Michael Heiss of Milwaukee's St. Francis Seminary produced a commentary, *The Four Gospels*, in 1863. James A. Corcoran, faculty member of St. Charles Seminary in Philadelphia and an alumnus of the Urban College of the Propaganda, was learned in Semitic languages and taught Scripture to seminarians, but his literary work lay with the *American Catholic Quarterly Review*, which he founded in 1876.[52]

Church history commanded slight interest. Though the Baltimore seminary reported instruction in the subject in the 1850s, Canon Benoit found that there was no instruction in the subject there in 1875. Interest in church history was sufficient to bring about a manual on the subject in English appropriate for use in seminaries. Francis J. Pabisch and Thomas S. Byrne of Mount St. Mary's of the West in Cincinnati produced a translation of Johann Alzog's church history, one of the most widely used volumes of church history in Catholic Europe. The Pabisch and Byrne translation appeared in 1874 in three volumes of over 700 pages each, with the express purpose of providing a modern church history in English for seminarians, priests, and the interested layman. Alzog's volumes placed emphasis on the institutional development of the church, though issues of doctrine, sacraments, and worship were treated. Canon Benoit noted with disapproval that at the Louisville seminary Alzog was used, but the professor skipped the "dogmatical" parts and "simply lectures on history." The canon noted that Pabisch himself only taught two periods per week of church history at the Cincinnati seminary.[53]

Other subjects received little or no attention during the period. Canon law was little regarded in a country where the laws of the church were not in full force because of its mission status. Archbishop Maréchal advised young Samuel Eccleston, who was studying at St. Sulpice and desired to learn some church law: "I regard its study as a thing only secondary and ornamental."[54] In 1858 Archbishop Hughes explained to Roman officials that since there was no connection of the church to the state in the United States there was no need for a priest to have a grasp of legal matters. There was only the need for a little canon law pertaining to the "simple duties of the Ministry."[55]

The American church was as yet untouched by the beginnings of the liturgical movement in France and Germany; extraliturgical devotions commanded growing interest at the parish level and the strong influence of the Irish, whose church life in Ireland was rudimentary, did not lay the ground for interest in liturgical life. Liturgy courses in American seminaries related to formal instruction in offering Mass and administering the sacraments, not to the theology of worship. Such instruction usually took place in the final stages of seminary training, as immediate preparation for ordination.

The concepts of preaching closely followed European models. The Sulpician André Jean Marie Hamon published *Traité de la prédication* in France in 1844, which carries on the tradition of seventeenth-century France and Vincent de Paul's *Little Method*. Hamon's work was subsequently passed on to the English-speaking clerical world through the works of Thomas J. Potter. The latter was born in Great Britain in 1828, converted to Catholicism as a young adult, and was ordained a priest after studies at All Hallows in 1857. After obtaining Hamon's permission, Potter produced *The Pastor and His People* in 1869. In this and a subsequent work in 1872, titled *The Spoken Word*, Potter adapted Hamon's ideas for English-speaking priests. As rare examples of contemporary Catholic pastoral thought in English, Hamon's works were the most influential on Catholic preaching in the United States. He continues the tradition that preaching should move the hearer to a definite resolution as its ultimate aim, and its intermediate aims are to teach, to please, and to move. He outlines the kinds of preaching, such as holiday preaching, the familiar instruction, or the Sunday sermon, and provides detailed preparation for each type.[56]

The actual time that was allowed for preaching in seminaries is difficult to ascertain. Instruction in preaching was, of course, conducted in some practical way, with the seminarians giving practice sermons before their colleagues at least once a year. The importance of preaching in the American church was regularly proclaimed, but a general discussion of how to develop good preaching does not come into view.

Clerical formation and the content of learning taking place in seminaries continued the traditions of Tridentine Catholicism from Europe. The methods of learning, especially the reliance on dogma and moral manuals, continued general church practices. The trend toward a papalist ecclesiology in dogma and a Liguorian moral theology is at work in the consensus forming in favor of the respective manuals of Perrone and Gury. By the 1870s, patterns of imitation among seminaries are appearing, as is evident in the adoption of three years of theology in most seminaries.

From the internal evidence of seminaries, the impact of spiritual training and formal learning on seminarians seldom comes into view before the 1870s. Discussions of delinquent seminarians can be found in correspondence between seminary officials and sponsoring bishops, but not the general performance of those in good standing. The minutes of the official visitation conducted by Sulpician officials at St. Mary's Seminary in Baltimore in October 1874 record a rare evaluation of a body of seminarians. In response to the inquiry of the visitors, the faculty described the students as well-behaved and regular in their observance of the rule and in attendance at community exercises, but beyond these positive observations the faculty found much fault with the students. The faculty believed the students observed the rules out of fear of being caught and as the price of remaining in the seminary and awaiting the call for orders. The Sulpicians believed that the house rules should be willingly observed as a means of developing ecclesiastical spirit. They found genuine piety among the students as manifested by good behavior in exercises. But it was found that few seminarians entered with much knowledge of or practice of the interior life based on "abnegation and mortification." They manifested the "cold, positive, and too practical character of Americans." The faculty said it was not "too rare" to find that seminarians had already made the determination to become priests, therefore "attaching little importance to the sentiment of their directors." The seminarians' view of the ministry focused "too exclusively" on "exterior works" such as "preaching, construction of churches and schools, and put in second place the life of prayer, discipline, and study." The performance in studies was weak because many had inadequate or "rushed" instruction before coming to the seminary, and most had not had sufficient Latin. Furthermore, the "spirit of the country" did not dispose them to the love of study and the desire for knowledge. "They attached importance to what they thought to be immediately useful in the ministry." The French Sulpicians recognized the cultural distance separating them from their predominantly Irish-surnamed seminarians. The Sulpicians admitted that the "rapport" between faculty and students was cordial but formal and lacked "confidence and openness of heart." The students were prejudiced against the instructions and counsels of the faculty because they had heard from American priests that the seminary's practices and French manners were not appropriate for the American clergy. The faculty found these attitudes a "great obstacle" in building mutual confidence between faculty and students and believed that their influence on the seminarians was compromised.[57]

The practical spirit that the Sulpicians saw in their students perhaps emanated from the obvious requirements of the American church at that time. Though an occasional critic of seminaries expressed the desire for more learning among priests, what was ordinarily expected of priests was zeal for the ministry of sacraments. Archbishop Hughes of New York composed a detailed report in 1858 for Roman officials to review the progress of Catholicism in his diocese since his appointment as coadjutor in 1838. He expressed a rather harsh realism in describing his clergy, a portion of whom had been trained at the diocesan seminary at Fordham. What Hughes valued in the clergy of New York was probably similar to the qualities other bishops esteemed in their priests in good standing and what aspirants to the priesthood expected after ordination:

> If any one looks for extraordinary eloquence in the pulpit, or immense erudition, or able writers among the Clergy of New York, he may be prepared for much disappointment. They are in the Holy Ministry laborious and working priests; The duties which cannot be postboned [*sic*] leave them scarcely time for the ordinary rest which nature absolutely demands; and if there be a few, who are capable of eloquence in the pulpit, or able to write in defence of religion, they neglect their capacity, and, on the other hand, are but little distinguished for their zeal, or laboriousness in the duties of the Ministry.

Hughes admitted the desirability of having a better educated clergy, but he hoped that Roman officials would understand that the American bishops had been unable to provide better training:

> There is too much work to be done, and too few priests for its accomplishment. It is only where the supply of the Clergy is greater than the wants of the mission that these desirable and important studies can be prosecuted to a point of eminence, which it has not been possible for the Bishops of America to aim at with success.[58]

7. The Third Plenary Council of Baltimore

On November 9, 1884, a solemn procession of eleven archbishops and coadjutor archbishops, fifty-eight bishops, six abbots, thirty-one superiors of religious orders, eleven seminary rectors, eighty-one theologians, and twelve other clerical officials entered the Cathedral of the Assumption in Baltimore. The press reported that several thousand spectators lined the streets to view the colorful spectacle preceding the formal opening of the Third Plenary Council of Baltimore under the presidency of Archbishop James Gibbons.[1] Though not noted at the time, the bishops assembled just a century minus seventeen days after John Carroll received official notification (on November 26, 1784) of his appointment as "superior of the mission" of the Catholic community in the United States. The council thus closes the first century of Catholic organizational life in the United States. Though it could not have been known at the time, it was the last time the bishops assembled for a national council to frame church legislation. Thus the council of 1884 brought to an end the conciliar traditions of the American bishops. But at their tenth and perhaps most important national council, the bishops gave unprecedented attention to issues of clerical life, seminary training, and higher education for priests.

In addition to issues related to the priesthood, the council addressed a range of contemporary problems of American Catholics, including schools, secret societies, mixed marriages, and tenure of church property, all of which lie beyond the scope of the present study. Gerald Fogarty has proposed five reasons to account for the council's convocation. First, the Catholic population's rapid growth to over six million, doubling since 1860, had enlarged the problems of the Catholic community. Second, the challenge of religious pluralism raised questions of how American Catholics should relate to secret societies, labor unions, and the public schools. Third, the relations between bishops and the country's six thousand priests had

145

reached a high level of tension during the 1870s. A fourth reason may have been Roman officials' recognition that the American bishops were divided on the issue of a council and such a division of opinion would postpone dealing with pressing matters. And a fifth reason, the factor that Fogarty finds possibly "determinative" was that Roman authority "wished to test the loyalty of the American bishops, since many had opposed the definition of papal infallibility. This it would do by bringing the American Church more directly under Roman supervision."[2] Thus, unlike the previous councils that were initiated by the American bishops, Roman authority ordered the American bishops to convene a plenary council.

A major problem leading to the council's convocation, and in turn informing the attitude toward seminary training, was the relationship between bishops and priests, which had become increasingly tense since the 1860s. In the United States there were no canonically established parishes except one in New Orleans that dated from French ecclesiastical administration. The numerous Catholic congregations throughout the country were only missions to which bishops appointed priests and transferred them at will. The career of the outspoken priests' rights advocate Eugene O'Callaghan, a priest of the Cleveland diocese, demonstrates the frequency and manner in which priests were transferred. As in O'Callaghan's case, a priest could be appointed to start a mission, work hard to erect buildings among a poor flock, often not drawing a salary, achieve a level of success at the mission, then find himself abruptly changed and ordered to start the process again. There were also few provisions for sick or aged priests.[3] American dioceses did not have cathedral chapters of canons, as in Europe, consisting of the senior clergy of the diocese, who had specified rights and duties in diocesan administration. The American bishop was virtually a law unto himself, while the full force of canon law was not in effect in the United States. Bishops, for their part, believed that they had to be free to transfer priests at will because of the complex clerical problems arising from the rapidly growing numbers of Catholics and priests. There was a need to match priests with the appropriate ethnic congregations, and, because of the uneven quality of priests of various nationalities, levels of training, and personal behavior, there was often a need to change their appointments.

Shortly after the decrees of the Second Plenary Council of Baltimore were published in 1868, James A. McMaster, publisher of the nationally circulating, *New York Freeman's Journal and Catholic Register,* launched a campaign for priests' rights. A Scottish-born convert from the Presbyterian and Episcopal churches, McMaster was a zealous ultramontane Catholic and frequent critic of bishops. He began by raising the canonical question: "*Why* have we Dioceses, and Dioceses multiplying, and *not one*

Parish, in all these States?" The erection of canonical parishes would naturally bring about canonical rights to pastors. His editorial elicited favorable responses from aggrieved priests from across the country whose cases McMaster publicized in his journal.[4] Prominent among these was Eugene O'Callaghan, who wrote a series of articles for McMaster under the pseudonyms "Ecclesiasticus" and "Jus" in which he argued for the full implementation of canon law in the United States. A pamphlet literature flourished during the period with such publications as *Notes on the Second Plenary Council of Baltimore* by a Newark priest, Sebastian Smith, in 1874 and Richard L. Burtsell's *The Canonical Status of Priests in the United States.*

Propaganda officials were concerned by the agitation and the rising number of Roman appeals of suspended priests. Propaganda sent the apostolic delegate to Canada, Bishop George Conroy, to the United States in 1877 to investigate, and, in 1878, Propaganda officials issued an *Instructio* to American bishops ordering them to hold diocesan synods at which a permanent investigating committee was to be established in each diocese, consisting of three to five priests, to investigate clerical grievances. It was unclear what power these commissions would have. After the lobbying of Bishop Bernard McQuaid, Propaganda issued a clarification that rendered the commission's powers largely advisory, much to the bishops' satisfaction.[5]

The highly audible question of priests' rights received much attention during the 1860s and 1870s, but it was not directly related to seminary training, which typically was seldom accorded public attention. A rare case of open discussion of seminaries had occurred from 1859 to 1861, when Orestes Brownson published articles of Jeremiah Cummings and William J. Barry in his quarterly review. Cummings, as mentioned, disapproved of the importation of foreign priests and sought to promote a native clergy by establishing minor seminaries to start boys on the path to the priesthood before they could be attracted to other pursuits. Barry's ideal was a minor and major seminary in each diocese, a provincial major seminary, a national seminary in the United States, and the American college in Rome. He employed a hierarchical model to justify this system: "Nothing so promotes a spirit of noble emulation in any society or service as several grades of standing, rising regularly in importance and dignity."[6] Barry, a youthful idealist, privately expressed very harsh views on the American clergy, finding that they "as a body, lack depth & height — depth of thought, & height of love. Education is only skin-deep on the brain and spirituality — at least among the secular clergy — only skin deep in the heart. . . . The necessary consequence is that while Catholicity spreads, it scarcely takes deep root."[7] The American bishops at the Second Plenary Council of Baltimore (1866) promoted some of these ideas by endorsing minor seminaries, provincial seminaries, and expressing the hope that someday a national Catholic university would be established. [8]

The question of a national university was an idea that attracted increasing attention before the Third Plenary Council of Baltimore. The idea was not new. In 1821, the Jesuit priest Maximilian Rantzau proposed to Archbishop Maréchal the formation of a national Catholic university to be located in Washington, D.C., where it would attract national attention. [9] As noted previously, Bishop England promoted a national seminary in the 1830s under episcopal direction. Archbishop Purcell suggested a university for consideration at the First Plenary Council of Baltimore in 1852 and attempted to secure graduate degrees for his provincial seminary to make it, in effect, a pontifical university. The idea of a Catholic university was discussed at the Second Plenary Council of Baltimore, probably by Archbishop Spalding, who had privately proposed Mount St. Mary's at Emmitsburg as the site. The council's decree suggested a university for future consideration as an institution "where all the letters and sciences, both sacred and profane, could be taught."[10]

Others took up the university idea in the 1870s. The American religious order the Congregation of St. Paul sponsored *Catholic World*, in which unsigned articles appeared in 1868 and 1871, probably written by Isaac Hecker, endorsing a Catholic university. The daring 1871 article urged that philosophy be studied in English rather than in the usual Catholic manner of instruction in Latin. In 1876 Bishop Thomas A. Becker of Wilmington published articles in the *American Catholic Quarterly Review* calling for a Catholic university that envisioned a more thorough and complete program of instruction than the contemporary colleges were offering, but he ignored the idea of formal graduate training that was gaining ground in American university life. [11]

The leading spokesman for university level education under Catholic auspices through these years was John Lancaster Spalding. His first public expression on the subject was an unsigned article in Louisville's *Catholic Advocate* in 1871, when he was secretary to the bishop of Louisville. He lamented then: "There is in the church of this country a deplorable dearth of intellectual men." He found that there were fewer able Catholic writers capable of defending Catholicism in 1871 than there had been twenty years before. He found the "chief defect" in this state of affairs the fact that "We have no university—no central seat of learning encircled by the halo of great names, to which the eyes of Catholics from every part of the land might turn with pride and reverence."[12] He was optimistic about finding the means to establish a university in a land as wealthy as the United States, and with an obvious reference to efforts to raise money for the American College in Rome, he stated that it would be easier to raise two million dollars for a Catholic university in the United States than a half million dollars for an American college abroad. He imbedded a plea for a university in his 1873 biography of his late uncle, Archbishop Spalding.[13]

In 1877, Spalding, at age thirty-six, was appointed bishop of the new diocese of Peoria, Illinois. As a bishop, Spalding was in a more advantageous position to promote the university idea. He took the opportunity arising from the bankruptcy of the archdiocese of Cincinnati to propose to Cincinnati's coadjutor bishop Elder, in 1880, the founding of a Catholic university at the archdiocese's Mount St. Mary's Seminary of the West. Spalding hoped to persuade the American bishops to buy the seminary buildings, thereby helping to ease Elder's financial problems and at the same time acquiring an existing set of buildings at a reasonable price. Elder was willing to sell the closed seminary for $125,000, but Spalding did not obtain the support of Cardinal McCloskey of New York and Archbishop Gibbons of Baltimore, and the idea was dropped.[14]

By the time of his overtures to Elder in 1880, Spalding had changed his idea from the university of 1871 to that of a "high school," in the German sense of *Hochschule* or graduate school, exclusively for priests. He described the concept to Elder as:

> a Theological High School for the best students who have already made the three years course of theology in the different seminaries of the country. In this high school they would go through what is called the profound course of theology. I see no other way by which we can hope to raise the standard of Clerical Education and you know better than I how difficult it is to find priests who have the learning which bishops ought to have; and as our dioceses are becoming so numerous it seems to me to be necessary to set about doing something in earnest by which we may raise up a class of men in the priesthood who will be the ornament of our holy faith.[15]

Spalding repeated the high school idea at a public forum in an address at St. Francis Seminary in Milwaukee on June 30, 1881, to commemorate its silver anniversary. He spoke at length on the "Catholic Priesthood" and used the occasion to urge more attention to clerical learning. He addressed the tension existing between holiness and learning for the priest:

> If sin is the universal negative of Christianity, a sinful priest is Antichrist. And since man's life is more than his knowledge, and character is better than culture, and to be holy is more desirable in every way than to be learned, if it were possible that we should be compelled to choose between a virtuous but ignorant priesthood and a priesthood which with high mental cultivation would lack righteous-

ness and the spiritual mind, the choice ought not to be difficult. But, in point of fact, this dilemma can never be anything else than a mere hypothesis. A virtuous priesthood cannot remain ignorant, and an ignorant priesthood cannot remain virtuous. "Without knowledge," says St. Augustine, the profoundest of Christian doctors, "it is not possible to have the virtues which make life holy."

Spalding then attributed to the church the aim "to create a priesthood which to the highest culture of mind will unite the most perfect discipline of life." By this time he was so attached to the idea of graduate training for priests that he had no interest in seminary reform, stating that "Our theological seminaries are at present, if I may express an opinion, not in any essential point inferior to those of Europe. . . . They are elementary schools of theology, and to deprive them of this character would not only be a departure from the end for which they were instituted, but would render them useless. . . . They give the education which the common run of students are capable of receiving."[16]

Spalding's first *ad limina* visit to Rome as bishop of Peoria in late 1882 and early 1883 gave him the opportunity to promote his views on clerical education there. He told Propaganda officials of the desirability of an institution where a "certain number" of priests could receive advanced education. These educated priests were needed to fill episcopal sees, and they were needed for the pulpits of churches in large cities "where men of all shades of opinion are ready to receive the Catholic faith." Such priests were necessary to take part as writers and speakers in the social and religious questions of the day. "There is no other country wherein wise and educated priests are able to perform such great services to the cause of the Church."[17]

As the question of priests' rights was being agitated and Spalding's proposal for advanced training of priests at a university was circulating, Propaganda ordered the convocation of a plenary council. In an action unprecedented through the American bishops' previous councils, the prefect of Propaganda invited the archbishops of the United States to Rome for a preliminary meeting to devise an agenda for a national council.

Before meeting with the American prelates in November 1883, the cardinals of Propaganda considered the state of the American church as described in a massive *ponenza*, or memorandum, with allied documents prepared by one of the cardinals of the Sacred Congregation of Propaganda, Giovanni Franzelin, the noted Jesuit dogmatist and concurrently prefect of the Sacred Congregation of Rites.

Franzelin's document describes the condition of American Catholic affairs based on the information gathered through the years as filtered through the author's Roman mentality. In its lengthy preface, the author identifies the two major difficulties of the American church as discipline and debts. The problem of discipline pertains to the behavior of clerics. It was found to have worsened since issuance of the *Instructio* of 1878, because of the growing number of appeals to Propaganda from suspended priests. These cases, it was feared, generally stirred a local controversy wherever they took place, or, in Franzelin's mind, a scandal because of newspaper publicity—"to the great joy of the enemies of Catholicism." The problem of debts, which was related to the rapid institutional expansion of the church, apparently had less to do with the availability of funds than it did with the means of raising them. Fund-raising methods of lotteries, fairs, and picnics offended Roman sensibilities, particularly since these were activities in which parish priests were engaged.

The Franzelin document begins with an extended treatment of clerical discipline. A major concern was the quality of episcopal candidates. It was noted that few bishops chosen during the 1870s were highly regarded for learning or piety. They were promoted to the episcopate because of their administrative talents. And among candidates for the episcopate, it was feared, there was too much "prejudice" against Roman ideas, which was regarded as a "great impediment to harmony between the episcopate and the Holy See."

In discussing American priests, Franzelin observes that they were trained in the United States but also in Belgium, Germany, and France. He designates the more "noted" American seminaries as the Sulpician Seminary of Baltimore, St. Charles Borromeo Seminary at Philadelphia, St. Francis de Sales Seminary in Milwaukee, and the New York provincial seminary at Troy. The seminaries pointed out were the diocesan freestanding ones, except Cincinnati's, which was temporarily closed. Emmitsburg was mentioned in the context that it had recently suffered a financial disaster that might close it. The six seminaries with lay colleges conducted by religious communities were not mentioned. Franzelin noted that few dioceses had their own seminaries, thereby not adhering to the prescriptions of the Council of Trent, though many dioceses had colleges—that is, secondary schools for boys conducted by religious at which lay students studied with aspirants to the priesthood, "with how much ecclesiastical spirit God only knows." These institutions were far from providing a native clergy. The priests schooled in them left much to be desired in the areas of discipline and learning. Though these priests were not bad, they were found to be more inclined to "business affairs, to mix in the whirlwind of secular life, than to live in the quiet of the sanctuary." There was little in these seminaries of the proper attention to liturgy, ceremonies, and rites. The recent letter of an unnamed Urban College alumnus who had taught at Emmitsburg was summarized in the text (rather than included in the appendix with other such documents) to support the view that American seminaries were neglected. The correspondent complained that if American bishops thought less of building grand cathedrals at each small diocese and more about seminaries, then the faith would spread faster; and if more attention were given to seminarians there would not be so much difficulty governing them later as priests.

Franzelin concluded that two principal causes of the defects of American seminary training were: the brevity of the seminary course and the departure of seminarians for summer vacations. He objected to the lack of preparatory training and the course of three or four years of philosophical and theological studies, as well as the American attitude that a good missionary did not need much learning. Moreover, he greatly disapproved of the way seminarians passed summer vacations. Candidates for the priesthood returned to their families "in which case nothing does more harm." Franzelin makes sweeping generalizations about American seminarians' vacations:

> The young seminarian having returned to his family, indulged by all, passes the vacation in visits to relatives, making continual journeys on horseback, going hunting, and, what is worse, to beach resorts, dressed entirely as laymen, and there, so much in contact with the spirited company of friends, among petty politicians and other such types, that they are made to lose the love of study that they had and all idea of ecclesiastical spirit.

The safeguards that the bishops recommended of commending seminarians to their pastors over the summer was alleged not to work because of the distance of seminarians' homes from the parish church and the active life of the parish priests.

Franzelin pointed out that the bishops had failed to follow the prescriptions of the Second Plenary Council of Baltimore of 1866 (repeated from the First Plenary Council in 1852) that each ecclesiastical province should have a major seminary and each diocese a minor seminary. It was noted that many populous provinces were without major seminaries, such as Chicago, San Francisco, and St. Louis, as well as archdioceses less able to sustain one, such as Santa Fe, Oregon City, and New Orleans. At this point Franzelin returned to the theme of the many priests educated abroad, by the Sulpicians at Paris or Montreal, or at the American College at Louvain, and, as mentioned in chapter 4, the bishops' neglect of the American College in Rome. Their neglect caused Franzelin to allege that the American bishops were indifferent to all things Roman. The issue of a Catholic university was raised by merely noting the interest taken by the young Bishop of Peoria, John Lancaster Spalding, to promote the idea, while the Bishop of Rochester, Bernard McQuaid, opposed it because of a lack of qualified priests capable of profiting from advanced studies.

The state of the American clergy that was next considered in the *ponenza* continues the unfavorable estimation of American priests. The latter were found for the most part to have been born, raised, and trained in Europe and followed their countrymen to America. Many were former religious who had left the discipline of their orders. "To govern a diocese with such priests of diverse nationalities, studies, training, habits, and motives, as in America, where all want to think and act on their own, ought not to be very easy for bishops." It was hoped that a "precise and clear" law outlining the rights and obligations of bishop and priests could end the conflicts between bishops and priests. In outlining the problems of bishops and priests, unfavorable animadversions were made about American priests that reflect the Roman concern about the clear boundaries of clerical culture. There was, it seemed, too much freedom of movement and too much familiarity with lay people. Priests often handled large sums of money, and they had large amounts of personal money. Drunkenness was not rare, especially among Irish priests. In short, there was too much free activity without control.

Franzelin's document continues with discussions of other issues to provide the most systematic Roman view on the Catholic community in the United States since Bedini's report on his visit to the United States in 1853. It provides a rare treatment of the status of the clergy and the state of seminaries in the years immediately preceding the Third Plenary Council of Baltimore. It concludes with a series of fifteen "dubbi" or questions regarding the American church. Two of these pertained to seminaries: first, whether to urge the bishops to found provincial and diocesan seminaries and how to reform the content of clerical training in them, and, second, whether to promote Spalding's project for a Catholic university.[18]

The perspective of the Franzelin document was fresh in the minds of the Propaganda officials who met in Rome on November 13, 1883, for their first conference with the delegation of American bishops. Each ecclesiastical province was to be represented, many by its archbishop, such as Gibbons of Baltimore, Seghers of Oregon City, Feehan of Chicago, Heiss of Milwaukee, and Williams of Boston; others were represented by coadjutor archbishops, such as Michael Corrigan of New York and Patrick Ryan of St. Louis (soon to be transferred to Philadelphia); or by suffragan bishops, such as William O'Hara of Scranton (for Philadelphia), Francis Chatard of Vincennes (for Cincinnati), Edward Fitzgerald of Little Rock (for New Orleans), and John Salpointe of Arizona (for Santa Fe). San Francisco was not represented. The Roman cardinals were the Prefect of Propaganda Giovanni Simeoni, Giovanni Franzelin, and Lodovico Jacobini, then Secretary of State.

Upon their arrival in Rome the American delegation had been given an agenda for a national council that was not to their liking. The conferences with the cardinals of Propaganda gave the American bishops a chance to express their views on the seminary and other issues. The fact that the seminary was the first issue on the agenda indicates the importance Roman officials attached to it. The Americans at once took issue with the proposal that major seminaries should have villas so that seminarians would not be sent home during summer vacations. Archbishop Gibbons stated that villas should not be mentioned in the council's documents but should be left to the discretion of individual bishops. He added that the vocation of seminarians would be tested if they were given liberty during the summer. Archbishop Ryan took the lead in explaining that villas were contrary to the customs of the United States and that poor dioceses would be incapable of establishing them. The cardinals did not accept this explanation and insisted that villas be established to protect the vocations of seminarians during the summer. They did not accept the argument of poverty of dioceses, since they proposed villas for major seminaries for the present. The American delegation agreed that establishing villas was to be recommended at the forthcoming council, and in the absence of villas, rules governing seminarians' conduct and dress were to be drawn up for the summer vacation.

The bishops concurred with the agenda on other seminary issues: that the major seminary course was to include two years of philosophy and four of theology; faculties in the major seminaries were to be properly organized, especially in regard to philosophy and theology; textbooks were to be used that contained the entire course of theology, lacking nothing but a supplementary explanation from the professor; and qualified instructors were to be appointed. The bishops were also to appoint clerical deputies to oversee the seminary's temporal and spiritual matters.

The bishops agreed to adopt again the idea from the Second Plenary Council of Baltimore of 1866 to recommend that each province have a seminary under the control of the archbishop to which the bishops of the province could send their students. At a later conference Bishop William O'Hara of Scranton, who was probably speaking from his experience of dealing with Archbishop Wood and the Philadelphia seminary, raised the problem of suffragan bishops in an ecclesiastical province who sent their seminarians to the provincial seminary but had no say in the seminary's academic, administrative, or disciplinary policies. The cardinals recognized the difficulties involved but admitted that if the archbishop owned the archdiocesan seminary it was his to operate without right of interference from other bishops of the province. On the other hand, suffragans would have some rights if they founded the seminary with the archbishop and shared the responsibility for maintaining it. [19]

The American bishops had additional opportunities to discuss seminaries after their delegation returned from Rome. The bishops of each province were assigned one of the chapters of the council's proposed agenda. They were to meet and discuss the assigned chapter and report their findings to the archbishop of Baltimore. The bishops of the Baltimore province were assigned the chapter on seminaries; however, the bishops of the Milwaukee province reported on several chapters, including the one on seminaries. The Milwaukee bishops endorsed the major and minor seminary courses of six years each for diocesan seminaries, even urging that seminaries conducted by religious communities be required to subscribe to the same lengths in order to bring about uniformity in seminaries. The Baltimore bishops formally recommended the establishment of villas for seminarians who did not have the permission of their bishop to stay home, while the Milwaukee bishops stated that villas would be harmful to religion because of the expense of building them, that parents would discourage vocations to the priesthood if their sons were to be sent away for six years, and that seminarians needed some limited experience outside the seminary during summer vacations. [20]

The reports from the bishops of each province preceded the drafting of a *schema* of council decrees at Baltimore before the council's opening. The schema contained the chapter "De Clericorum Educatione et Instructione," consisting of sections on minor and major seminaries, a principal seminary, junior clergy examinations, and theological conferences.

The minor seminary schema, which was eventually adopted with minor revisions, cited the need for developing qualities for the priesthood from boyhood. It quotes the opening line of the Tridentine decree, "Since the age of youth, unless rightly trained, is inclined to follow after the pleasure of the world. . . . " The bishops urged the founding of minor seminaries in each diocese and thus simply repeated the policy of the previous plenary council. The minor seminary section provided for a course of studies of not less than six years. The curriculum was outlined, assigning first importance to the study of Christian doctrine. Language instruction stressed English and Latin, including the ability to write and speak in that language, but a reading knowledge of Greek was sufficient. Modern languages were stressed for the tasks of ministry appropriate for the ethnic groups of particular dioceses. Other subjects were listed: sacred and profane history, geography, mathematics, natural sciences, and plain chant, music, and ecclesiastical bookkeeping. The minor seminary was to be governed by a set of rules approved by the bishop, and these were to be strictly observed. The seminary outlined in the decree was a freestanding one, but a mixed seminary with lay students was allowed if the former was not feasible.

In the course of the council discussions on the minor seminary, Bishops Spalding and McQuaid objected to what they considered too much emphasis on Latin and preferred more emphasis on English, the language in which priests would have to express themselves to their people. Their objections were not shared by their colleagues, such as Ryan of Philadelphia, Gross of Savannah, and Dwenger of Fort Wayne, who stressed the importance of Latin in the priest's lifelong studies of theological literature. Spalding's and McQuaid's proposed changes were not agreed to when put to a vote. Artistic studies did not fare well. Bishop Hendricken of Providence narrowly won acceptance of a course in drawing because of its practical relation to architecture, about which future bricks-and-mortar priests should have some knowledge. Bishop Richard Gilmour of Cleveland proposed required instruction in music, which Ireland of St. Paul opposed on the grounds that neither exhortation nor command could force boys to study music. A general exhortation for music study and practice in plain chant passed by one vote.

The bishops expressed different views on the admission of candidates to the major seminary who had not attended a minor seminary. Since not all candidates for the major seminary would have attended minor seminaries, Corrigan of New York proposed seminary boards of examiners to screen candidates for the major seminary. Ireland added the provision that the entrance examination be based on the curriculum of the minor seminary decree, otherwise the spirit of the decree would be avoided. Spalding objected that the decree did not contain a program of studies but only broad objectives, and that Ireland's proposal was aimed at colleges conducted by religious, where few diocesan seminarians were trained anyway. Corrigan's proposal for examination boards was approved without Ireland's idea of tying the board to the subjects of the minor seminary decree. Bishop James O'Connor of Omaha then proposed that a committee of bishops be appointed to meet after the council to devise a program of seminary studies and a plan of examinations to bring about some uniformity. The bishops approved the motion, and Archbishop Gibbons appointed a committee consisting of Heiss of Milwaukee, O'Connor, Stephen V. Ryan of Buffalo, Winand Wigger of Newark, and John Moore of St. Augustine.

The major seminary schema and final draft contained a recommendation for establishing a major seminary in each province, thereby continuing the precedent of the first and second plenary councils that in effect acknowledged that the Tridentine ideal of each diocese having a seminary could not be implemented in the United States.

As Roman officials required, the major seminary course was to consist of six years of study devoted to philosophy and theology. The philosophy course was to include the study of logic, metaphysics, and ethics with natural law, and continuation of natural science from the minor seminary course. The theology course was to consist of dogmatic-scholastic theology, moral theology, biblical exegesis, church history, canon law, theoretical and practical aspects of liturgy, and sacred eloquence. The spiritual director was to impart theoretical and practical aspects of ascetical theology. The decree called for adherence to the thought of St. Thomas Aquinas in philosophy instruction, as prescribed in Pope Leo XIII's recent encyclical *Aeterni Patris* of 1879. Instruction throughout the major seminary program was to be based on textbooks that treated the subject matter of the entire course.

San Francisco Archbishop Joseph Alemany and his coadjutor, Patrick Riordan, objected to the required length of six years for the major seminary course. In the West, priests were urgently needed, and they considered six years too long. Ryan pointed out that a general law was being discussed and that necessity was a valid excuse from the law. Alemany and O'Connor endorsed wording in the decree that would exempt bishops from observing the six-year major seminary course if necessity compelled them to ordain seminarians earlier. The bishops agreed to flexible wording on the issue.

The bishops considered the insertion of a course of ascetical theology in the seminary curriculum, which some of the consulting theologians urged be dropped because there were no textbooks in English in the subject. Elder of Cincinnati, Watterson of Columbus, and O'Connor insisted that there was literature enough on this subject, even though not arranged in a textbook form. Watterson and Kain of Wheeling proposed that ascetical theology be retained in the curriculum. The bishops approved the study of ascetical theology.

Chatard of Vincennes proposed that professors of exegesis be urged to teach their subject in Latin. Healy of Portland reminded his colleagues that Trent's decree requiring the use of the Vulgate in public remained in force. Ryan of Philadelphia found the study of Scripture more useful in English, since it would have to be quoted in English in sermons. Gibbons believed it was a matter for the professor to decide. Chatard's proposal was soundly defeated.

The bishops had agreed in Rome to a general recommendation that summer villas be established. But at the council no bishop expressed support for establishing them. Ryan of Philadelphia perhaps came closest to favoring some kind of villa program by endorsing the idea of retaining the deacons at the seminary during the summer for more extensive preparation for ordination. Spalding and McQuaid were the most vocal opponents of villas, because they valued seminarians experiencing freedom during the summer. McQuaid added that the behavior of European clerics who had spent their seminary summers in villas did not furnish a good argument in their favor. Dwenger and O'Connor objected to the money that would have to be spent on villas. Healy proposed that there be no recommendation of villas, and his colleagues agreed. Instead, seminary officials were to instruct seminarians carefully on their duties during the summer, and pastors were to issue reports on the conduct of seminarians during vacation. [21]

With the exception of the villas, the bishops generally endorsed the seminary reforms that Propaganda officials proposed, with minor clarifications. The issue of establishing a school of higher studies had not arisen in discussions with Roman officials but evolved out of the decree on clerical education. The theologians drafting the schema had not been able to agree on a formula for an institution of higher learning.

At the council Bishop John Lancaster Spalding prepared the ground for the founding of a such an institution. He arranged for the Louisville heiress Mary Gwendoline Caldwell to be present at its public opening. A convert to Catholicism and a longtime friend of Spalding, Caldwell made known to Archbishop Gibbons her willingness to donate $300,000 for the founding of a graduate institution for philosophical and theological studies. A complete university was to develop from this graduate school.

Spalding arranged with Gibbons to give one of the public lectures during the council. The bishop of Peoria gave the most important address of his career on Sunday evening, November 16, 1884, in the Cathedral of the Assumption. He spoke on "University Education Considered in its Bearings on the Higher Education of Priests," wherein his ideas on the subject were given their most elegant and complete expression. He shared with his hearers the common concern among believers for the advancement of unbelief: "Never has the defense of religion required so many and such excellent qualities of intellect as in the present day." He delineated the kind of learning needed for priests:

> Ah! let us learn to see things as they are. In face of the modern world, that which the Catholic priest most needs, after virtue, is the best cultivation of mind, which issues in comprehensiveness of view, in exactness of perception, in the clear discernment of the relations of truths and of the limitations of scientific knowledge, in fairness and flexibility of thought, in ease and grace of expression, in candour, in reasonableness; the intellectual culture which brings the mind into form, gives it the control of its faculties, creates the

habit of attention and develops firmness of grasp. The education of which I speak is expansion and discipline of the mind rather than learning; and its tendency is not so much to form profound dogmatists, or erudite canonists, or acute casuists, as to cultivate a habit of mind, which, for want of a better word may be called philosophical, to enlarge the intellect, to strengthen and supple its faculties, to enable it to take connected views of things and their relations, and to see clear amid the mazes of human error and through the mists of human passion.

Spalding borrowed from John Henry Newman to describe the perfection of the intellect as "the clear, calm, accurate vision and comprehension of all things as far as the finite mind can embrace them, each in its place and with its own characteristics upon it." Spalding again was not interested in the issue of improving the seminary, whose purpose he defined as "to prepare young men for the worthy exercise of the general functions of the priestly office." Beyond this purpose it had no other function:

> But the ecclesiastical seminary is not a school of intellectual culture, either here in America or elsewhere, and to imagine that it can become the instrument of intellectual culture is to cherish a delusion. It must impart a certain amount of professional knowledge, fit its students to become more or less expert catechists, rubricists, and casuists, and its aim is to do this, and whatever mental improvement, if any, thence results, is accidental. Hence its methods are not such as one would choose who desires to open the mind, to give it breadth, flexibility, strength, refinement and grace. Its text-books are written often in a barbarous style, the subjects are discussed in a dry and mechanical way, and the professor wholly intent upon giving instruction, is frequently indifferent as to the manner in which it is imparted, or else not possessing himself a really cultivated intellect, he holds in slight esteem expansion and refinement of mind, looking upon it as at best a mere ornament.

Spalding did not intend his remarks on the seminary as a criticism but merely as a realistic appraisal. He believed that lengthening the seminary course "to five, to six, to eight, to ten years" would improve students' professional training but would not result "in more really cultivated minds."

Once enough priests have attained the cultivation of intellect "then will Catholic theology again come forth from its isolation in the modern world; then will Catholic truth again irradiate and perfume the thoughts and opinions of men." Spalding looked to the founding of a "true university" to begin, as did the University of Paris in the twelfth century and the reopening of the University of Louvain in 1834, with a national school of philosophy and theology, around which other faculties would in due course be added.[22]

The issue of an institution of higher learning came up for council discussion ten days after Spalding's address. It encountered opposition. The council minutes at this point do not record the views of specific bishops. One can assume that Spalding spoke again in its favor, and most likely Bishop McQuaid, who was its chief opponent in the years ahead, spoke against it. After hearing enough of the discussion, Bishop Tobias Mullen of Erie moved that the entire matter be dropped from the schema or at least referred to the next plenary council. Kenrick seconded the motion, which was defeated by only three votes, thereby showing that a broad consensus had clearly not been formed around the idea. Gibbons then referred the matter to a committee of bishops consisting of Alemany, Kenrick, Corrigan, Ryan, and Spalding, who were to report on the matter. This they did on December 2, recommending:

> 1. A Seminary is to be erected like the Dunboyne in Ireland or Louvain in Belgium, from which as from a seed the University is to grow. 2. It is to be erected near a large and populous city. 3. A very respectable lady has promised that she will give $300,000 for the erection and endowment of the Seminary. 4. A commission is to be formed of five or seven prelates and some laymen to whom is to be given the care of erecting and administering the Seminary.[23]

The views of Healy of Portland and Hennessy of Dubuque suggesting respectively that priests be admitted to the commission and that the number of bishop members exceed the number of priests and laymen combined were adopted. On December 6, the day before the close of the council, the letter of Spalding's friend Miss Mary Gwendoline Caldwell was read, offering $300,000 for the founding of the university and containing the names of the committee of bishops and others who were to be responsible for executing the founding of the institution in the following years. The bishops were Gibbons, Corrigan, Spalding, Ireland, Ryan, Williams, and Heiss. The bishops accepted the offer of funds, and the nominees to the committee provided that others could be added later. The project to establish the university was then under way.[24]

The American bishops also legislated in the area of clergy rights. Though Roman officials had favored the creation of cathedral chapters of canons to extend to the American church an institution existing in canon law, the bishops resisted. As a compromise, the bishops enacted a system of boards of diocesan consultors, consisting of four to six diocesan clergy, half chosen by the bishop and half by the clergy. Consultors had specified rights in diocesan administration and episcopal nominations. A system of "irremovable rectors" provided that ten percent of the pastors in the diocese be irremovable. Another decree provided for the establishment of a diocesan fund for sick and aged priests. These provisions were designed to meet some of the demands of the priests' rights advocates. Other provisions were designed to improve the professional standing of clergy, such as examinations for junior clergy and for candidates for irremovable rectorships. In other areas of clerical life, previous conciliar decrees were repeated and extended. Priests were enjoined to lead holy lives, make a retreat every two years, and spend some time in daily study. Clerical decorum was to be maintained by avoiding the scandal of attending theaters or visiting racetracks, and the clerical collar was made obligatory.[25]

The Third Plenary Council of Baltimore had thereby acted in several areas bearing on clerical life. The bishops gave detailed attention to clergy rights, duties, and expectations. But these issues had often been the subject of legislation of previous national and provincial councils. The council of 1884 did not provide all the answers to these problems. However, the council gave unprecedented attention to issues of clerical formation. It lengthened the course of studies for the major and minor seminaries in response to the urging of Propaganda officials and established a comitee to devise a model curriculum. It laid the foundation of a graduate school for priests as the start of a national Catholic university for the United States. These enactments responded to the problems that had developed in the decades of growth of the American Catholic community, and they set an agenda for the future. In the following years, bishops and seminary educators were to provide a record of how well the conciliar decrees on these subjects were implemented. The bishops' pastoral letter after the council communicated to the American Catholic community the importance of their new departure in the area of clerical training:

> One of our first cares has been to provide for the more perfect education of aspirants to the holy Priesthood. . . . In every age it is and shall be the duty of God's priests to proclaim the salutary truths which our Heavenly Father has given to the world through His Divine Son; to present them to each generation in the way that will move their minds and hearts to embrace and love them; to defend them, when necessary, against every attack of error. From this it is obvious that the priest should have a wide acquaintance with every department of learning that has a bearing on religious truth. Hence in our age, when so many misleading theories are put forth on every side, when every department of natural truth and fact is actively explored for objections against revealed religion, it is evident how extensive

and thorough should be the knowledge of the minister of the Divine Word, that he may be able to show forth worthily the beauty, the superiority, the necessity of the Christian religion, and to prove that there is nothing in all that God has made to contradict anything that God has taught.

Hence the priest who has the noble ambition of attaining to the high level of his holy office, may well consider himself a student all his life. . . . And hence, too, the evident duty devolving on us, to see that the course of education in our ecclesiastical colleges and seminaries be as perfect as it can be made. During the century of extraordinary growth now closing, the care of the Church in this country has been to send forth as rapidly as possible holy, zealous, hard-working priests, to supply the needs of the multitudes calling for the ministrations of religion. She has not on that account neglected to prepare them for their divine work by a suitable education, as her numerous and admirable seminaries testify; but the course of study was often more rapid and restricted than she desired. At present our improved circumstances make it practicable both to lengthen and widen the course, and for this the Council has duly provided.[26]

PART II

Americanist Era,
1884 to 1910

The American bishops in the last two decades of the nineteenth century engaged in lively controversies as they sought to formulate Catholic responses to modern problems of public and parochial schools, secret societies, organized labor, ethnic identity, and relations with other faiths. Several leading churchmen, Archbishop John Ireland, Bishop John Keane, and Denis O'Connell—the Americanists—articulated a belief in the providential destiny of the Catholic Church in the United States. As a model for Catholicism, they offered the American ideals of separation of church and state, republican government, social reform, and lay initiative in church activities. Some leading churchmen, Cardinal James Gibbons, Bishop John Lancaster Spalding, and others, shared part of the Americanists' vision, while other conservative churchmen and the substantial German Catholic community resisted the Americanists. These opposing factions clashed in public, and their views and activities have been standard topics in American Catholic historiography.

A new interest in articulating the attributes of the priest appropriate for the United States coincided in a quiet way with the more dramatic public controversies. Churchmen imbued with the Americanist spirit, such as Ireland, Gibbons, Bishop Camillus Maes, John Talbot Smith, and William Stang, left a body of writings that project the model priest as possessing a liberal education and schooled in a range of professional skills. New journals and textbooks of pastoral theology were published to aid the priest's ongoing learning and professional skills. The new model of the priest was not an entirely Americanist enterprise, as a leading conservative prelate, Bishop Bernard McQuaid, articulated similar views and founded a model seminary to implement them.

The growth of the American Catholic community and the hope of providing diocesan priests to serve the community led to the founding of new freestanding seminaries at major dioceses. At several seminaries the ideas of the new model priest informed the programs of seminary life and learning. The bishops' great common undertaking, the Catholic University of America, opened as a graduate school for priests to provide for the cultivation of intellectual life among clergy.

Through the era, the Holy See took an unprecedented interest in areas of intellectual activity through the imposition of the Scholastic philosophy of St. Thomas Aquinas and new direction for biblical studies. Popes Leo XIII and Pius X advanced existing movements of devotional life that informed the spirituality for priests and seminarians. Roman authority brought the era to a close with a forceful condemnation of modernism and imposition of controls on the content of clerical learning that limited the possibilities for further development.

8. New Seminaries

By the late nineteenth century the American Catholic community was over a generation removed from the massive immigration from Catholic Europe which took place in the middle of the century. During the period American Catholics developed a religious subculture around their neighborhoods, parishes, and schools. By the end of the century, Catholics in several parts of the country were capable of extending Catholic institutions to include supporting seminaries and supplying seminarians to fill them. Accordingly, church leaders directed a new round of freestanding seminary foundations at major dioceses. During the 1880s a reprise of German immigration and the arrival of Poles pointed to the need for ethnic seminaries to train priests for these nationalities. The new freestanding and ethnic seminaries augmented the pattern of existing seminaries and gave promise of fulfilling the expectation of developing a native clergy trained in the United States.

The Society of St. Sulpice greatly expanded its activities with the opening of several freestanding seminaries. Its historic St. Mary's Seminary in Baltimore led the others in a remarkable expansion of influence that coincided with the tenure of Alphonse Magnien as superior. Born at Bleymard, diocese of Mende (France), in 1837, Magnien attended the minor seminary at Chirac and the Sulpician major seminary at Orléans, whose bishop, Félix Dupanloup, was the leader of the progressive bishops in the French church and a leading opponent of papal infallibility at the First Vatican Council. Ordained in 1862, he served briefly in parish ministry in the diocese of Orléans before joining the Sulpicians. Magnien was appointed to the faculty of St. Mary's Seminary in Baltimore in 1869 in the wake of Archbishop Spalding's complaints about the Sulpicians' foreign ways.

After his appointment as superior in 1878, Magnien manifested his adaptability to the American temperament, which made him an attractive figure among the Baltimore clergy, St. Mary's seminarians and alumni, and the Americanist bishops. As an admirer of the reform views of Bishop

Dupanloup, Magnien saw in the Americanist bishops the same hope for adaptation of Catholicism to modern life. Accordingly, he became a friend and confidant of Archbishop John Ireland and Bishop John Keane. In 1877, a year before Magnien's appointment as superior, James Gibbons, a Baltimore native and former vicar apostolic of North Carolina and bishop of Richmond, was appointed ninth archbishop of Baltimore. Gibbons and Magnien formed a close relationship reminiscent of the old days of Louis Deloul's relationship with Archbishops Whitfield and Eccleston, so that Magnien became a kind of discreet *éminence grise* of Gibbons's regime as spiritual leader of the American Catholic community. Magnien's national influence widened as the host for the working sessions of the Third Plenary Council of Baltimore of 1884, which took place in St. Mary's Seminary's prayer hall, and it was reinforced by his position as superior of the seminary where dozens of bishops sent seminarians.[1]

Magnien's appreciation of the American church reversed the poor record of his predecessors, Lhomme and Dubreul, of attracting only one American to join the Sulpicians. Before becoming superior Magnien drew three Americans to the Society, Charles Rex, Edward Dyer, and Richard Wakeham, the first Americans to join in years. Rex and Dyer were destined to become important figures in seminary education in the years ahead.

Magnien presided over the booming growth of St. Mary's Seminary. Though a new building was completed in 1876, additions were made in 1881, 1891, and 1894 to accommodate an enrollment that grew from ninety in 1878 to 250 by the time of his death in 1902. During Magnien's years as superior, 1,098 alumni were ordained priests. The faculty grew from six Sulpicians in 1878 to eleven Sulpicians and five diocesan priests in 1902.[2] Despite the beginnings made in recruiting Americans to the society, most Sulpicians serving on the faculty were French, though Magnien insisted that the French members be capable of learning English and adapting to the American mentality.

Magnien shared responsibility for governing this large seminary with Edward R. Dyer, who was appointed the superior of the community of philosophy seminarians in 1885. Born in Washington in 1854, Dyer had attended the Sulpician minor and major seminaries before studying at St. Sulpice, where he was ordained in 1880. He took graduate degrees in Rome before joining St. Mary's faculty. His appointment as superior of the philosophy department marked the beginning of a transition of the Sulpicians to American membership and control. After Magnien's death in 1902, the superior general appointed Dyer superior of St. Mary's Seminary and in 1903 to the new position of vicar general of the American Sulpicians, which included responsibility for the members at the other Sulpician seminaries in the United States.[3]

In addition to the extraordinary growth of St. Mary's Seminary, Sulpician activities expanded as the society was called to staff the new free-standing seminaries of Boston, New York, and San Francisco.

In 1875 the see of Boston was promoted to the status of an archdiocese and the dioceses of New England were detached from the ecclesiastical province of New York and formed the new Boston province. In 1877 and again in 1880 Cardinal Giovanni Simeoni, Prefect of Propaganda, exhorted Boston's Archbishop John Williams to establish a seminary for the new province. Williams in due course complied but first completed building the Cathedral of the Holy Cross and liquidating its debt. In 1880 Williams bought an estate near the center of Brighton, a town of six thousand residents recently annexed to Boston. To secure a seminary faculty, Williams traveled to Paris in 1880 to visit his alma mater, St. Sulpice, and his old confessor from seminary days, Henri Icard, superior general of St. Sulpice. Icard accepted Williams's invitation to the Sulpicians to staff the proposed seminary.[4]

To finance the construction of the seminary, Williams secured pledges of money from the clergy, received gifts from wealthy lay donors, and ordered special collections in the parishes. The funds financed the construction of a large four-story seminary building in Norman chateau style, built with Brighton pudding stone quarried on the property. The main building with temporary chapel cost the archdiocese $149,173 by 1885; an additional wing and permanent chapel were constructed in the following years. The institution was incorporated as the "Boston Ecclesiastical Seminary," though called St. John's Seminary in honor of the archbishop's patron saint, and was empowered by the Commonwealth of Massachusetts to grant degrees in philosophy and theology.

St. John's Seminary opened as a major seminary on September 22, 1884, to a group of thirty-two seminarians of the Boston archdiocese. In the following years seminarians from the other New England dioceses swelled the number of seminarians to an annual average of about one hundred by 1900. Though New England bishops sent students to the Brighton seminary, there is no evidence that the other dioceses shared in the initial capital expenses. Non-Boston students paid a higher tuition than that charged to Boston students. The opening of St. John's Seminary ended the relationship of the New England dioceses with St. Joseph's Provincial Seminary at Troy, New York.

St. John's founding faculty consisted of four Sulpicians from France and the American Sulpician Charles B. Rex. The seminary's opening introduces its remarkable first superior, John Hogan, to the American seminary scene. Hogan was born in County Clare, Ireland, in 1829, and continued the tradition of Irish contact with the French church, when, at the behest of his uncle, a priest of the diocese of Périgueux, he entered the minor seminary at Bordeaux, from which he began his theology studies in 1849 at St. Sulpice. He joined the Society of St. Sulpice and in 1853 was ordained a priest. Because of his brilliant academic record, he was at once appointed to teach dogmatic theology at St. Sulpice and later moral theology. He remained there for the thirty-one years before his appointment to Brighton.

St. Sulpice was located at the crossroads of ecclesiastical life in France. There, Hogan developed a sympathy with the views of leading progressives in the French church, Lacordaire, Montalembert, and Dupanloup. He was influenced by the Sulpician ontologist philosopher, Branchereau, and by the thought of John Henry Newman, whom he visited in England. Hogan developed a reputation as a provocative and stimulating teacher, whose classroom presentations went beyond the boundaries of the theology manual. He soon acquired an admiring group of followers among his students, who, as alumni of St. Sulpice, were marked for leadership in the French church. Hogan brought a lifetime of experience as a leading French seminary educator to the organization of St. John's. He remained superior until 1889, when he was appointed first president of the Divinity College at Catholic University.[5]

Hogan's successor at St. John's, Charles B. Rex, appointed superior at age thirty-three, was the protégé of Alphonse Magnien. Rex was born of Quaker parents in Baltimore in 1856. After converting to Catholicism in his teens, he was educated by the Sulpicians at Baltimore and at St. Sulpice in Paris, where he was ordained in 1880. He then earned doctorates in theology and canon law in Rome. He first taught philosophy, then dogma at Brighton. As rector Rex was preoccupied with creating a model seminary in compliance with the decrees of the Third Plenary Council and in adapting modern American attitudes toward discipline, physical exercise, and extracurricular activities to the inherited Sulpician traditions.[6]

In 1895, when Rex was reassigned, Hogan returned to Brighton as superior after his service at the Catholic University and remained in office until his death in 1901. The seminary enjoyed success in training large numbers of seminarians through the first decade of the twentieth century under Hogan's successors, Daniel Maher and Francis Havey. But Sulpician direction of St. John's ended in the spring of 1911, after a series of protracted personal and ecclesiological conflicts with Boston's Archbishop William H. O'Connell, which will be discussed in chapter 11.

While the Sulpician direction at Boston expanded the society's presence beyond Baltimore, a greater opportunity for enlarging the Society's work arose in New York. The position of the New York province's St. Joseph's Seminary at Troy, New York, was being altered by the 1880s. First, the opening of St. John's Seminary at Brighton drew away the New England students; and then the long-awaited opening of St. Bernard's Seminary at Rochester, New York, in 1893 caused the withdrawal of students from western New York state. The Buffalo, Brooklyn, and Newark dioceses had not participated in the provincial seminary, so that St. Joseph's character as a seminary for the province was greatly diminishing by the 1890s, with only the archdiocese of New York and the smaller dioceses of Syracuse, Albany, and Ogdensburg supporting it. New York's Archbishop Michael A. Corrigan recognized its diminishing function as a truly provincial seminary. He announced at a diocesan synod in 1886 his intention of building a New York archdiocesan seminary nearer to the city. He cited the distance of the Troy seminary for clerical retreats and other functions that imposed an inconvenience for the New York clergy and the fact that Troy was located in the diocese of Albany and therefore outside his jurisdiction.

Corrigan began his seminary by buying a farm at Valentine Hill in the Dunwoodie section of Yonkers, two miles north of the limits of New York City. Here he laid the cornerstone for his seminary in 1891. The fund-raising necessary for the seminary building was conducted over the next several years. Pledges were first obtained from leading laymen, then from pastors and curates, and finally from parishes. To sustain interest in the parish phase of the campaign, a monthly periodical, *The Seminary*, was published between 1893 and 1896 to publicize the need for a seminary and to report the progress of the campaign. New York Catholics contributed about $700,000 for the campaign by the time of the seminary's opening.[7]

The New York clergy were not entirely pleased with Corrigan's new seminary. The new institution would soon put an end to their alma mater at Troy. Corrigan made it known that he intended to have the Sulpicians staff the new seminary, which could be interpreted as an insult to the New York clergy. They were now numerous and a group of priests of the archdiocese was surely capable of staffing the seminary.[8]

Corrigan, through his episcopal career, had a history of difficult relationships with diocesan priests. As bishop of Newark in the 1870s he had among his clergy two of the leading activists for clerical rights, Sebastian Smith and Patrick Corrigan (no relation). When he was promoted to New York, Corrigan became the ordinary of the group of progressive priests forming a circle named the *Accademia*, one of whose members was the articulate priests' rights advocate, Richard L. Burtsell. Corrigan was a principal figure in the most famous bishop-priest conflict of the period in his struggles with the political activist priest, Edward McGlynn. This controversy dominated clerical life in the archdiocese of New York from 1886 to 1892.[9] Accordingly, Corrigan was not well disposed to develop a local group of intelligent and educated priests for the seminary faculty. Instead, he wanted a faculty wholly devoted to the work of clerical formation and uninterested in local clerical politics outside the seminary walls. His choice of the Sulpicians, as their historian, Christopher Kauffman, finds, was "replete with irony," because the leading Sulpicians in the United States led by Magnien were aligned, albeit discreetly, on the side of Cardinal Gibbons, Archbishop Ireland, and other Americanist bishops in the major controversies in which Corrigan and the conservative bishops were engaged. [10]

Archbishop Corrigan's wishes prevailed, and he concluded a contract with the Sulpicians for staffing the seminary in 1894. Brighton's rector, Charles Rex, was designated the first superior or "President." Rex resigned as superior of St. John's in 1895 to become president of St. Charles College at Catonsville, Maryland for the planning phase of the New York seminary. However, Rex was aleady suffering from the tuberculosis, which took his life in 1897 at age forty. In his place Edward R. Dyer was appointed the first superior of St. Joseph's Seminary.

New York's St. Joseph Seminary opened at Dunwoodie as a major seminary in 1896. The massive building was capable of accommodating 260 students and fifteen professors. The seminary was out of debt the following year as the fund campaign reached a million dollars. [11] Dyer was responsible for implementing the kind of model seminary that his colleague and friend, Charles Rex, had done in Brighton. When Dyer returned to Baltimore in 1902, James F. Driscoll, a Scripture scholar who was head of the Sulpicians' small house of studies at Catholic University, succeeded him as president. He continued the tradition of promoting the seminary's academic quality with the opening of the short-lived *New York Review*. The controversy surrounding the *Review*, as discussed in chapter 11, resulted in the withdrawal of Driscoll, with several others, from the Society in 1908.

St. Joseph's prospered as a major seminary, providing 345 priests between 1897 and 1910. Most clerical alumni were affiliated with the archdiocese of New York. Its success as the major seminary was reinforced in the years ahead with the opening of Cathedral College in 1903 on Madison Avenue and 51st Street in New York as a minor seminary for day students of the archdiocese. Cathedral College was intended to supply seminarians for St. Joseph Seminary. [12]

By 1896 the Sulpicians were conducting three important seminaries at major archdioceses along the Atlantic coast. Their attention was first drawn to the Pacific coast in 1879, when Archbishop Joseph Alemany of San Francisco planned to open a major seminary for his archdiocese, the largest diocese on the West Coast, and invited the Sulpicians to staff the proposed seminary. Henri Icard declined the invitation because of the lack of personnel, though he would accept the invitation of Archbishop Williams to conduct the Boston seminary soon thereafter. Alemany instead engaged priests of the Society of Mary (Marists) from France and set about raising funds for a modest institution called St. Thomas Seminary, which opened in 1883 near Mission San José, thirty-six miles south of San Francisco. During the next year, four Marist priests conducted a seminary for a student body that did not exceed five students. The Marists withdrew from these unpromising circumstances and a diocesan priest conducted the seminary for another year, until it was closed in 1885.[13]

In late 1884 Alemany retired and was succeeded by his coadjutor, Archbishop Patrick Riordan, who at age forty-three began an ambitious program of development for the archdiocese. Riordan raised money and built a new Cathedral of St. Mary of the Assumption between 1887 and 1891 at a cost of $350,000. While the cathedral was in progress, Riordan turned his attention to a seminary. He believed that the major seminary of his predecessor had been poorly planned and failed because of the lack of a complete parochial school system and a minor seminary to supply candidates for it. Riordan set about strengthening Catholic parish schools and planned to build a minor seminary.[14]

In 1888, Riordan visited Europe to make his *ad limina* visit to Rome and stopped first in Paris, where he called on Henri Icard to invite the Sulpicians to staff his proposed seminary. Once again Icard declined. While in Rome, Riordan reported to Pope Leo XIII and Cardinal Simeoni his desire to have a seminary and his failure to secure the Sulpicians. The pope promised to intercede for Riordan and directed Simeoni to write to the Sulpicians urging acceptance of the archbishop's invitation. "In a region so vast," Simeoni stated to Icard, "which is growing in importance because of continuous and increasing immigration, attracted by the excellent climate and rich soil, the need of a Seminary is keenly felt."[15] Indeed as of 1888, there was no freestanding diocesan seminary west of the Mississippi River. The time and place seemed appropriate for a new seminary. When Riordan returned to Paris in time to assist at a celebration of the aged Icard's sixty-second anniversary of ordination, the letter of Cardinal Simeoni had been received, and the superior general and his consultors agreed to staff the proposed seminary of San Francisco.

Riordan began fund-raising for his new seminary at first among wealthy donors. Six prominent Catholics contributed $50,000 each to launch the effort. He also received a tract of eighty acres of land from a Catholic lady, Kate Doyle Johnson, at Menlo Park, located thirty-two miles south of San Francisco. The place could be reached by railroad and was about a mile from the new Leland Stanford Junior University. Riordan raised the remaining funds from special collections in the parishes.[16] The archbishop encountered an undercurrent of skepticism about the planned seminary from the San Francisco clergy, most of whom were Irish emigrés drawn from All Hallows College and Carlow College. The clergy regarded the native youth as "soft" as the result of growing up in California's undemanding climate. Some were the offspring of families drawn to California for reasons of health. These youth, it was believed, were unsuitable for the rigors of seminary life and the priesthood. Riordan himself had not always been pleased with his Irish priests and their unbending ways and brogues so thick they could not be easily understood by Americans. It has been suggested that Riordan named the seminary for St. Patrick to attract his Irish clergy's support for the campaign to raise funds.

Riordan had the main wing of the new seminary constructed in a Romanesque style. The major seminary wing was built later. In 1901, Jane Lathrop Stanford, who had given aesthetic direction to the development of the splendid campus of Stanford University, donated $50,000 for the construction of a worthy seminary chapel.

St. Patrick's opened as a minor seminary in August 1898 with a staff of four Sulpicians, headed by Arsenius Vuibert, for thirty-four students. The choice of Vuibert soon proved to be a mistake. The Frenchman lacked the flexibility to deal with the affairs of a new institution and to relate to American colleagues and students. He was replaced in 1904, when the major seminary department opened, with a talented young French native, Henri Amans Ayrinhac, who remained as superior until his death in 1930.

On the morning of April 18, 1906, the great earthquake that destroyed large portions of San Francisco extensively damaged St. Patrick's Seminary. The building's imposing tower over the main entrance and heavy decorative stone work on the upper story fell inward into the roof, destroying much of the building's interior. After simplification of the design of the upper story and repairs costing $200,000, the seminary reopened.[16] By 1910 St. Patrick's enrolled eighty-five minor and major seminarians and had trained twenty-seven ordinands, most of whom were affiliated with the archdiocese of San Francisco.[17]

The highly regarded Sulpicians figured in the founding of the seminary of St. Louis. In 1891, soon after the celebrations of the fiftieth anniversary of his episcopal ordination, Archbishop Peter Kenrick, at age eighty-five, decided that the time had come to start a diocesan seminary. The opportunity arose when the Visitation Sisters decided to sell the decaying buildings of their academy at Nineteenth and Cass Avenue in downtown St. Louis. Kenrick bought the building for $75,000, with the intention of starting a diocesan seminary there.[18]

When it became known that Kenrick had invited the Sulpicians to staff his seminary, Thomas J. Smith, the superior of the Vincentians' western province, decided to take action. He appealed to Archbishop Kenrick to withdraw his invitation to the Sulpicians and allow the Vincentians to conduct the seminary. Smith appealed to Cardinal James Gibbons to enlist his aid to avert the Sulpicians' coming to St. Louis because "to have the Sulpician Fathers come to St. Louis to supersede us as it were in the work in which we have been engaged for fifty years would involve a great disgrace. It would be a kind of condemnation of our past work and be of incalculable injury to us elsewhere as well as in the Diocese."[19] Smith also wrote to Alphonse Magnien to prevent the Sulpicians' acceptance of the seminary. It seems likely that the Sulpicians did not have the personnel to send to St. Louis, even if they were willing to accept another seminary. Magnien assured Smith that the Sulpicians would not accept the St. Louis position, citing the fact that the Vincentians and Sulpicians had always lived in "perfect harmony" and would respect the Vincentians' prior claims in the St. Louis archdiocese.[20]

In 1892 Kenrick agreed to engage the Vincentians for the proposed seminary and a contract was negotiated whereby the Vincentians would own the seminary property and were to be permitted to raise funds in the parishes of the archdiocese for the renovation of the buildings. Typical of his *laissez faire* approach to financial issues, Kenrick did not himself raise funds but in effect delegated the whole matter to the Vincentians. The president of St. Vincent's College at Cape Girardeau, Francis Nugent, was assigned to visit the parishes in St. Louis to solicit funds for the seminary renovation. The Vincentians raised about $30,000 for the seminary renovations costing $40,000. The order had to absorb the deficit.

The Vincentians named their hard-won acquisition Kenrick Seminary. It opened on September 14, 1893, as a major seminary to forty-two students. Its opening ended the major seminary that the Vincentians conducted at St. Vincent's College at Cape Girardeau. Smith appointed Louis Meyer, a German native and superior of the Vincentian parish and academy in Los Angeles, as Kenrick's first rector. Smith apparently appointed one of the few German Vincentians to attract the support of St. Louis's numerous diocesan clergy of German background, who were dismayed by the ending of the archdiocese's longstanding relationship with St. Francis Seminary in Milwaukee.

Kenrick Seminary's opening created serious controversies among the Vincentians of the western province. Its leading members believed that there were not enough qualified priests to conduct a major seminary and hoped to obtain some from Europe or have younger members sent away for advanced studies. Smith had asked the Vincentian superior general to send qualified French members to staff the seminary, but none were available.

His confreres found Smith uninterested in issues of faculty development once the seminary had been acquired for the province. They accused him of adopting the attitude that a priest can do any task assigned to him.

The superior general ordered a special visitation of the St. Louis Vincentians, which was conducted by an Irish Vincentian, Malachy O'Callaghan, in 1894. O'Callaghan relieved Meyer from the office of rector and appointed Peter V. Byrne, who was succeeded by two other priests before the appointment of Michael S. Ryan in 1906. The latter remained rector for the following twenty years. These undistinguished leaders were formed in the era prior to the opening of Kenrick Seminary, when the Vincentians gave little thought to developing personnel for seminaries. Improvement in the quality of the faculty was slow. It was not until 1897 that three young Vincentians were sent to Europe for advanced studies. More members were sent in the following years.[21] After several requests for a qualified French Vincentian, Charles Souvay, an early recipient of a doctorate from the Pontifical Biblical Commission, was appointed to the Kenrick faculty in 1903.

The internal criticism among the Vincentians reveals that they did not equal the Sulpicians in the quality of the faculty that they could provide. But the acquisition of Kenrick Seminary forced them to come to terms with the issue of developing qualified personnel in the following years and laid the groundwork for expanding their seminary activities in the western province. Though several Vincentians expressed fears about the possible loss of Kenrick Seminary because of their lack of academic qualifications, the Vincentians continued to staff it. A minor seminary program was added for day students of the archdiocese in 1900. Kenrick Seminary enrolled one hundred minor and major seminarians by 1910.[22]

At New Orleans, Archbishop Placide Chapelle invited the western Vincentians to reopen a major seminary at their St. Stephen's parish. They accepted the offer and opened St. Louis Seminary at the parish. The enrollment reached a high of seventeen students in 1905, the year of Archbishop Chapelle's death. His successor, Archbishop James Blenk, was not interested in sustaining a seminary and closed it in 1907. A more promising opportunity arose at Denver, where the western Vincentians sought to establish a small seminary for their own members. Bishop Nicholas Matz of Denver permitted them to come if they would also train diocesan seminarians. Under this condition and owning their own building, the Vincentians opened the modest St. Thomas Seminary in Denver in 1907, an undertaking that developed slowly in its initial years.[23]

In the Vincentians' eastern province, the Seminary of Our Lady of Angels continued its affiliation with Niagara College near Buffalo. Their seminary work expanded in 1891 when Bishop John Loughlin of Brooklyn arranged with the Vincentians at St. John's College in Brooklyn to offer seminary instruction as an adjunct to their college. However, the modest program could not accommodate more than a fraction of the diocese's seminarians, most of whom were sent to several other seminaries.[24]

The archbishops of Boston, New York, San Francisco, and St. Louis shared the responsibility for developing their new freestanding seminaries with Sulpicians and Vincentians. Two of the most prominent bishops of the era, Archbishop John Ireland of St. Paul and Bishop Bernard McQuaid of Rochester, leaders respectively of the Americanist and conservative factions of the American hierarchy, developed model seminaries staffed by their own diocesan clergy.

At St. Paul, Bishop Thomas Grace planned and built the modest St. Thomas Aquinas Seminary that opened in 1885 on the west side of St. Paul. The diocese's seminarians were withdrawn from other seminaries to form the initial student body of sixty-six students of both minor and major seminary.[25]

John Ireland succeeded Grace as bishop of St. Paul in 1884 and became archbishop when the archdiocese and province of St. Paul was erected in 1888. Through the period Ireland was well acquainted with the railroad magnate and St. Paul resident James J. Hill, founder of the Great Northern Railroad and a powerful force in the economic development of the region. Hill, son of a Methodist mother and a Baptist father, had a Roman Catholic wife and ten children. Through them, Hill had known and admired for decades the St. Paul priest, Louis Caillet, an old French missionary. On the basis of his regard for his Catholic family and Louis Caillet, Hill announced in 1890 a donation of $500,000 for the construction and endowment of a Catholic theological seminary in St. Paul to supersede the modest St. Thomas Seminary.[26]

James J. Hill, a man with definite ideas about the expenditure of money, was well aware of Archbishop Ireland's carelessness in financial matters. Hill personally supervised the design and construction of the new seminary. He hired the best local architect, Cass Gilbert, designer of the Minnesota state capitol, to provide six red-brick buildings for faculty and student residences, dining hall, classrooms, and a chapel, located near St. Thomas Seminary on a scenic campus overlooking the Mississippi River. After the original buildings were completed in 1894 at the cost of about $250,000, he turned over the complex to Archbishop Ireland and provided an endowment of $250,000 to pay faculty salaries. James J. Hill was rightly designated the founder of the new St. Paul Seminary. Having been criticized for such a substantial gift to the Catholic church, Hill enlarged the justification for his benefaction at the seminary's dedication:

Almost all other denominations have in their various flocks those who are able to help their church work in every material way, but the Catholic church, with its large number of workingmen and women, coming from almost every nation and clime, have little else than their faith in God and the aid of those earnest, pious and devoted men who have been placed in charge of their spiritual welfare. They have to provide places of worship, and while the state provides schools for all, their consciences call upon them to see that the education of their children goes hand in hand with their spiritual training, thus making for them an additional burden.

Having seen the efforts of Archbishop Ireland in behalf of the church of which he is so distinguished a prelate, to spread throughout the country the light of religious truth and divine revelation, I felt called upon to devote a portion of this world's goods with which I had been blessed, to the work of educating for the priesthood men who would be able to preach down the spirit of unbelief, and to stand as shining lights along the pathway that leads to heaven.[27]

Archbishop Ireland sought out a qualified faculty for his major seminary, some of whom were Europeans recruited by Denis O'Connell, rector of the American College in Rome. These figures were prominent in the early years of the seminary, until Minnesota priests had received advanced training in Rome or at the Catholic University of America before joining the seminary faculty.

Ireland was a strong advocate of the new Catholic University at Washington as the great hope for elevating the quality of American priests. St. Paul Seminary was the first seminary beyond Washington to affiliate with the university, so that its students could earn the university's bachelor and licentiate degrees.

The seminary enjoyed a rapid growth after its opening, requiring an additional building and the construction of an elegant permanent chapel by 1911. Its enrollment grew to 200 by 1910, and by 1912, 399 clerical alumni had been ordained for dioceses in Minnesota, the Dakotas, Nebraska, and Illinois.[28]

Another great seminary founder was Bernard McQuaid of Rochester, who became first bishop of his new diocese in 1868. As a New York suffragan, McQuaid sent his seminarians to St. Joseph Provincial Seminary at Troy, but he intended as early as 1875 to build a mixed lay college and seminary along the lines of Seton Hall College, of which he had been president. Instead, he founded St. Andrew's Seminary at his cathedral as a minor seminary for day students in the 1870s. He resolved to form a freestanding major seminary after his Roman visit in 1879, when Pope Leo XIII had asked him if Rochester had a seminary. In McQuaid's pastoral letter of 1881, which announced his intention of beginning a seminary, he stated, "The Seminary will become the central pivot of ecclesiastical work, the nursery of priests, the home of learned professors devoted to theological studies, a sacred place that in time will grow in the affection of priests and people." Though he had supported New York's provincial seminary, he spoke also from the Tridentine tradition of each diocese having a seminary connected to the activities of the cathedral and episcopal curia:

> The diocese of Rochester needs this Seminary; this diocese is able to do its own work without dependence on any other. A bishop feels the need of able and learned professors, whose time and services he can in some degree command. An Episcopal See, all of whose resident priests are laboriously engaged in the active work of the ministry, fails to render its bishop the aid of counsel and wisdom which his necessities demand. The bishop needs this Seminary, and the help it will be to him in various ways. A Cathedral that has to depend on chance assistance whenever a Pontifical function is to be held, is only half equipped.[29]

Through the 1880s McQuaid raised funds slowly for the planned seminary. The seminary collection's printed annual report listed all contributions of one dollar or more by name and contained the bishop's pastoral letter of about 2,500 words impressing on his people the importance of a diocese having its own seminary. McQuaid remembered the modest seminary that he had known in the early 1840s when he was a student at the New York diocesan seminary at Fordham. He spoke harshly of those early seminaries housed in inadequate buildings, poorly ventilated and heated, wherein seminarians were badly fed and from which ordinands left physically broken and ill prepared for the rigors of active ministry. He hoped to break the "old-time consecrated miseries and needless suffering on the part of seminarists" with modern buildings and adequate diets.[30]

Bishop McQuaid intended to have the requisite funds in hand before building a seminary so that debt would not interfere with its operation. In 1891 he obtained pledges of $60,000 from clergy and laity to supplement his seminary building fund. He engaged Rochester's leading architect, Andrew J. Warner, to design an imposing Victorian Gothic building that was built of native stone at a magnificent site overlooking the Genesee Gorge, just north of Rochester. McQuaid's St. Bernard's Seminary was dedicated in 1893 and was initially capable of accommodating sixty-four students of the major seminary level and nine professors.[31] It was a remarkable achievement for a diocese of about 75,000 Catholics.

As early as 1879, McQuaid began sending clerical students to Rome to prepare for seminary teaching, though he was not easily impressed by Roman ways and complained that Roman training leading to the S. T. D. degree was the equivalent of undergraduate training in seminaries elsewhere. Roman institutes offered degrees but no systematic graduate study, so he supplemented the Roman education of several priests intended for the seminary faculty with stays at Jerusalem or Louvain. The attention to the professional needs of the faculty did not end with their training. McQuaid insisted that the basic chairs in the seminary be endowed, so that the professors could be adequately compensated, given sabbatical leave periodically, and have teaching duties of no more than seven or eight hours per week to provide ample time for class preparation. To give the academic program a definite goal, the bishop successfully obtained a charter for St. Bernard's from the Holy See in 1901 to grant pontifical degrees, including the doctorate. Most of the degrees awarded in the following years were baccalaureates in philosophy and theology to a minority of students who sought them.[32]

Since McQuaid seldom left his diocese, he had ample time to devote to the seminary. Though in his seventies, he held the office of rector and lived at St. Bernard's about three-fourths of the time. He reported that he "takes care of the elocution department and preaching," to impart his own vigorous style of communication on his future priests. He described his other duties as "practically the bursar, the preacher of the retreat at the opening of the scholastic year and general lecturer on dress, manners, care of person, health, physical exercises, etc."[33]

McQuaid intended his seminary to be diocesan in scope, but, like the seminaries of major archdioceses, it soon began to serve other dioceses and became in effect a regional one. To accommodate the growing enrollment, he made additions to the seminary, including the separate wings flanking the original main building to house the philosophy students, completed in 1901, and a larger wing for the theology students, completed in 1908. In 1907 he wrote to a friend:

> Fifteen years ago I started . . . to build a Seminary, but a good one—the best I could—for sixty-eight students. Now I have one for one hundred and fifty; and in two years I shall have one for 260, patronized by over forty bishops. It is not what I meant in the beginning, but it has been forced on me.[34]

At the time of his death at age eighty-six in 1909, McQuaid could take pride in the remarkable personal achievement of firmly establishing during the last two decades of his life a model seminary of the era without the assistance of wealthy donors, the resources of a populous archdiocese, or by engaging a ready-made faculty from a community of priests. In 1910

St. Bernard's enrolled 233 students, making it second only to St. Mary's at Baltimore in the enrollment of diocesan major seminarians.[35]

The new freestanding seminaries of major archdioceses and the smaller diocese of Rochester that were to train the new generation of American-born youth aspiring to the diocesan priesthood did not supplant the interests in forming seminaries to serve ethnic constituencies. Two such seminaries, one for Germans and one for Poles, were successfully formed during the 1880s.

Proposals for a national German seminary had been made, as previously mentioned, in the 1840s, when Germans became numerous enough to require a substantial number of German-speaking priests. The need to train German clergy had been met in part with the opening of St. Francis Seminary in Milwaukee, the Benedictine monasteries and seminaries, and the American College at Louvain, all of which had strong German characteristics, though not intended exclusively for Germans.

The rise of a seminary exclusively for Germans owed its foundation to the personal initiative and drive of a German-born priest, Joseph Jessing.[36] Born to a poor family in 1836 at Münster, Westphalia, Jessing did not have the opportunity for education. He entered the Prussian army as a youth and probably intended to be a career soldier, but, as a zealous Catholic, he wanted to join the army of the Papal States. With this in mind, he left the Prussian army in 1860, after one term of enlistment; however, the recruiting policies of the pope's army abruptly changed and he was unable to realize his hope. Instead he served as secretary for several years to a quixotic leader of the *St. Michael Brüderschaft*, a military-religious organization determined to defend the papacy during the Italian *risorgimento*. The St. Michael organization did not gather influence, but his service with it allowed him free time to study standard theology manuals. By now Jessing hoped to become a priest, an idea that seemed impossible to pursue in Germany because of his lack of a secondary education. Accordingly, in 1867 he migrated to Cincinnati and obtained a teaching job at a Catholic parish school in nearby Hamilton, Ohio. From there he entered Mount St. Mary's Seminary of the West in 1868 and was ordained a priest in 1870 for the Columbus diocese. He was appointed pastor of Sacred Heart Church in Pomeroy, Ohio. Jessing was an energetic pastor there and soon started a parochial school, a newspaper to engage in spirited sectarian controversy with German freethinkers and Protestants, and St. Joseph Orphanage for boys. In 1874 he renamed the newspaper *Ohio Waisenfreund* to raise funds throughout Ohio to support the orphans. At the invitation of Bishop Sylvester Rosecrans, he moved the orphanage to Columbus in 1877, expanded its operation, and developed a network of contacts that brought in more orphans from around the country and placed them in German Catholic homes in the Middle West.

Jessing responded to the desire of some of his orphan boys and other German youth to become priests and even paid for the secondary schooling of some who were so inclined. Through his newspaper, he formed a "Clerical Students Aid Society" to solicit funds for their education. Typical of Jessing's sense of initiative, in 1888 he opened his own minor seminary, conducted by clerical and lay teachers, at the orphanage in Columbus. He intended to train German youth for the priesthood free of charge. Jessing owned the buildings of his orphanage, with the attached industrial school, printing establishment, a religious goods factory, and a minor seminary. He now sought a means of securing a permanent status for his complex operation. Attaching the seminary to the local bishop would not assure its future as a German institution.

Through the period, there was a high level of tension between German and English-speaking Catholics in the United States. Some differences were cultural, since most leading Irish-American prelates were active in the total abstinence movement, which annoyed German Catholics for whom alcoholism was not a problem. The Germans cherished parish schools where their language and culture as well as their faith were handed on. The Americanist bishops' liking for the public schools seemed to have imperiled the parochial school.

A series of incidents during the period were flash points of conflict between Germans and Irish Americans. In 1886, Peter Abbelen, a prominent Milwaukee priest, had circulated a petition among German clergy in Milwaukee, St. Louis, and Cincinnati and submitted it to the Holy See, seeking to insure German rights by requiring the appointment of a German vicar general in dioceses with large German populations in cases where the bishop did not speak German. He also sought the requirement that a German ethnic should obtain the permission of the pastor of a national parish before joining the nearby territorial, English-speaking parish. In 1890, the death of Archbishop Michael Heiss signaled a spirited movement among leading Irish-American bishops to secure the appointment of a non-German archbishop in Milwaukee. And in 1891, the memorial submitted to the Holy See by Peter Paul Cahensly, a wealthy German merchant who assisted immigrants, sought the appointment of more Germans to the American hierarchy. These incidents were occasions of open controversy between Germans and the Americanist bishops, who were concerned about reinforcing the foreign qualities of the American Catholic community.[37]

In the course of developing his enterprises at Columbus and defending the German point of view in the pages of the *Ohio Waisenfreund* amid the tension of ethnic hostilities among American Catholics, Jessing had cultivated a number of important contacts in Europe. He had developed friendly relations with Cardinal Paul Melchers, archbishop of Cologne and a fellow native of Münster. In 1891 he entertained a well-placed Roman ecclesiastic, Monsignor Paul Baumgarten, who was visiting the United States to attend the conventions of the German Catholic organizations. During this visit, Jessing and Baumgarten formulated plans to offer the seminary to Propaganda's authority. Their idea was to keep the minor seminary in Columbus and open the major seminary in Rome. Jessing informed Melchers of the efforts to affiliate with Propaganda, which elicited expressions of support from the cardinal. The effort to obtain favorable consideration from Propaganda was probably aided by the appointment early in 1892 of Cardinal Miecislaus Ledochowski, former Archbishop of Gniessen-Posen in the Prussian partition of Poland, as Prefect of Propaganda. After negotiations between Jessing and Roman authorities, the idea of having a major seminary in Rome was dropped, but on December 12, 1892, Propaganda announced that Jessing's St. Joseph's Seminary— henceforth the Pontifical Collegium Josephinum—came under the protection of the Holy See.[38] With the apostolic delegate serving as chancellor, assisted by a self-perpetuating board of trustees subject ultimately to Propaganda, Jessing's seminary would continue as he intended it after his death. This pontifical status reversed the tradition of local episcopal control of diocesan clerical training that is the starting point of the Tridentine seminary decree. The clerical alumni of the Josephinum were intended for dioceses in the United States, yet the policies for their training could be determined elsewhere. The Pontifical Josephinum is the lasting legacy of the vision of a determined individual, working in a period of ethnic tension in the American Catholic community, who gained the Holy See's permanent intervention in the area of diocesan clerical training.

The Josephinum's first ordination class of six completed studies and were ordained on June 29, 1899, by the apostolic delegate, Archbishop Sebastiano Martinelli. Jessing died after a long illness on November 2 of the same year, having witnessed the first ordinations. After his death the Josephinum flourished as a part of a multifaceted enterprise with the orphanage, both sustained by the *Ohio Waisenfreund*'s fund-raising appeals and income from the religious goods works. The Josephinum was staffed by Jessing's loyal priest associates and in the following years by the clerical alumni recruited to remain after ordination.

While Germans had been a major constituency of the American Catholic community for a half century at the time of the founding of the Josephinum, Poles came to the United States in large numbers only in the 1880s, settling in northern industrial cities such as Buffalo, Cleveland, Detroit, Chicago, and Milwaukee as well as a few rural communities in the Middle West.

The key figure in developing a Polish seminary was Joseph Dabrowski, born in a village near Lublin in the Russian partition of Poland in 1842.[39] After local schooling, Dabrowski attended the "Main School," a forerunner of the University of Warsaw, where he studied engineering. As a student he was attracted by the romantic appeal of Polish nationalism and participated in the ill-fated January Insurrection of 1863 against Russian authority. His revolutionary activities compelled him to flee the country, first to Switzerland and then to Rome, where in 1866 he entered the founding class of the Pontifical Polish College. The college's rector, Peter Semenenko, a co-founder of the Congregation of the Resurrection, a community of Polish priests, influenced Dabrowski to react against the romantic movement of Polish messianism, which expected Poles to rise up against political oppression and then become champions against all forms of oppression. After the sad experiences of periodic unsuccessful uprisings in Poland, the antiromantics saw how useless political actions were for the foreseeable future. Instead Polish national identity was to be cultivated through self-education, work, temperance, economic development, and attachment to the Catholic Church. The Resurrectionist priests in their ministry among the Polish diaspora adopted this philosophy, referred to as "organic work," and concurrently struggled again the unholy trinity of socialism, modernism, and materialism.

Dabrowski adopted these antiromantic ideals in his work among Poles. Ordained a priest in Rome in 1869, Dabrowski affiliated with the new diocese of Green Bay, Wisconsin. He was appointed pastor of a rural Polish settlement, Poland Corner, where he started a parochial school and obtained the Felician Sisters from Poland to staff it. The Felician Sisters expanded their activities and decided to relocate their headquarters in a large city with a Polish community. In 1880 they established themselves in Detroit, where they built a motherhouse and normal school across from the Polish church of St. Albertus on St. Aubin Street in the eastern part of the city. As chaplain, Dabrowski followed them to Detroit, taught in their normal school, and began a career as an influential Polish educator.

The idea of providing a national educational institution for Poles had been one of the reasons for the founding in 1873 of the Polish Roman Catholic Union of America (PRCUA). Shortly after its founding, the president of the Union, Leopold Moczygemba, one of the first Polish priests in the United States, promoted the idea of a national Polish college and seminary. Plans were made to locate it at a proposed Polish colony in Nebraska, where land was purchased. However, in the next few years efforts to establish the institution were not successful.

At Detroit, Dabrowski took up the idea of a Polish seminary, which was important to the local community that needed Polish priests. To serve Poles Detroit's Bishop Caspar Borgess had been seeking priests from Poland for service in the city. In 1884, Dabrowski proposed to Borgess that a national seminary for American-trained Polish priests be established in Detroit. The bishop showed immediate interest and gave it his enthusiastic support. The seminary and preparatory college were to be under the canonical jurisdiction of the bishop of Detroit, and the institution was to be an interdiocesan seminary, training priests for many dioceses. Dabrowski had the assistance of Moczygemba, who arranged for the sale of the Nebraska property and turned over its proceeds with other donations in the amount of $8,000. Dabrowski then secured property on the block north of St. Albertus Church that was deeded to the bishop of Detroit. The cornerstone for a four-story building for Saints Cyril and Methodius Seminary was laid on July 25, 1885, with elaborate ceremonies. Bishop Borgess and Bishop Stephen Ryan, ordinary of the Buffalo diocese, which had a substantial Polish population, officiated.

The cornerstone-laying provided an occasion for Dabrowski to elaborate on the purpose of the new seminary:

> I have in view the education of the Polish candidates for the priesthood and the education of others, so that they may be on par with other young men in this country. Heretofore we have been obliged to procure Polish priests from Europe, but they cannot speak English and cannot do what a native American might. We Poles have the right to enjoy complete liberty in this country, but liberty cannot be enjoyed fully by uneducated people. The better a people is educated, the better they enjoy liberty and the better citizens they become of America.[40]

Raising the necessary funds to complete the seminary building was a challenge that was largely met by the Polish-American community beyond Detroit. While Dabrowski and his associates were planning and executing the founding of the Polish seminary, the pastor of St. Albertus Church, Dominik Kolasinski, a charismatic and flamboyant personality, was building the largest Polish church in America a block away. Kolasinski appealed to the aspect of Polish pride that responded to the construction of massive edifices. Dabrowski's self-effacing manner, unremarkable appearance, and his concern for advancing the Polish community through education contrasted sharply with Kolasinski's style. Dabrowski pointedly directed the conclusion of his address at the cornerstone laying to Kolasinski by stating: "I deem the erection of this seminary more necessary than the building of expensive churches. Intelligence only makes men free."[41]

Kolasinski's ambitions and mounting debts by late 1885 involved him in conflict with church authority. Bishop Borgess suspended him from his clerical functions and interdicted the parish. Local Catholics loyal to church authority then attended the services that Dabrowski conducted at the chapel of the Felician Sisters motherhouse until the interdict was lifted. Thus the context for the Polish seminary's founding in 1885 and 1886 was a community deeply divided into warring factions.[42]

Saints Cyril and Methodius Seminary opened in December 1886 in a scaled-down version of the planned four-story building. The seminary offered a two-year philosophy and three-year theology program for seminarians taught by Polish clerics recruited from Poland. The college offered a five-year classical program as in a European gymnasium. Instruction in the college placed emphasis on Polish, English, and Latin. Though the institution was intended to train clergy, Dabrowski, as indicated in his address at the cornerstone laying, recognized that most of the college students would be interested in other pursuits. The college had less of a seminary quality to it since it was largely comprised of day students taught by laymen. In its early years the college and seminary coped with the challenges of raising funds and keeping qualified personnel. Dabrowski presided over the institution and continued to be closely involved with the development of the Felician Sisters until his death in 1903, three weeks after dealing with the stress of a student rebellion in which he expelled most of the seminarians.

Saints Cyril and Methodius Seminary continued to supply American-trained Polish priests for American dioceses from its first two ordinations in 1890. The college normally accounted for three fourths of the enrollment, which reached 326 students and seminarians in 1909, the year the school moved to a new site at rural Orchard Lake, west of Detroit.

The ethnic seminaries, the Pontifical College Josephinum and Saints Cyril and Methodius Seminary, provide a contrast to the several freestanding seminaries formed during the era. The ethnic seminaries existed in the context of related activities, resembling the mixed seminaries conducted by religious communities. Jessing had an orphanage, a publishing business, and a religious goods factory. Dabrowski conducted a seminary with a college for lay students and a printing business in close proximity to the local parish and the Felician Sisters motherhouse and normal school. Both seminaries were dedicated to preserving cultural elements of their respective nationalities and depended on a large ethnic constituency beyond the immediate area for financial support and to provide a student body. Their priest alumni were to be found in dioceses across the country.

The eight new seminaries founded between 1884 and 1898 joined the pattern of existing freestanding and mixed seminaries. With the exception of St. Mary's at Baltimore, the older seminaries continued to develop along the paths set down in the previous period and did not manifest the innovative aspects of the new seminaries.

A noteworthy development among the older seminaries was the reopening of Mount St. Mary's Seminary of the West, which had closed in 1879 in the wake of the financial crisis of the archdiocese of Cincinnati. The future of seminary education in Cincinnati seemed to be in doubt until the death of the archdiocese's long-time benefactor, Reuben R. Springer, in 1885. Springer willed $100,000 to the archdiocese for the education of priests. Archbishop William Elder announced at once that the means were at hand to reopen the seminary. The seminary building on Price Hill had been closed up and suffered the effects of physical decay and vandalism through the years. Springer's bequest covered expenses for extensive repairs to the building and enabled Mount St. Mary's of the West to reopen as a major seminary with seventeen students in 1887. Its enrollment grew rapidly and by 1897 reached 152, consisting of students of the Cincinnati archdiocese and other dioceses of the ecclesiastical province. The seminary appeared to recapture some of its old influence, though there was little sense of the innovation that marked the new seminaries of the era. The rector appointed in 1887 was Thomas Byrne, who left the seminary to become bishop of Nashville in 1894. He was succeeded by a series of conscientious and undistinguished priests.

To prepare candidates for the major seminary, the archdiocese opened St. Gregory's as a preparatory seminary in 1890 on the far east side of Cincinnati. In 1904, Archbishop Elder's successor, Archbishop Henry Moeller, moved the major seminary into the buildings of St. Gregory's Seminary, because the old seminary building was considered too costly to repair.[43] The move did not interrupt the local seminary traditions established when the major seminary reopened.

St. Francis Seminary in Milwaukee continued to enjoy success as an archdiocesan seminary for Milwaukee and a regional seminary for Germans. Its circumstances did not force a redirection of policy. There was a normal succession of younger leaders as the older generation died out. Among the new leaders were the Austrians, Augustine Zeininger and Joseph Rainer, whom the seminary's co-founder, Joseph Salzmann, brought to Milwaukee from Europe after a visit in 1866. Zeininger, an alumnus of the Linz Seminary, taught philosophy and science before becoming seminary rector in 1881. Rainer, an alumnus of the Jesuit theological faculty at Innsbruck, taught classical languages before succeeding Zeininger as rector in 1887 and remained in office until 1920. Rainer was noted for encouraging the devotional life of the students. He wrote several short inspirational works and was the biographer of Joseph Salzmann.[44] Zeininger and Rainer carried on the traditions already established. There was no incentive to adapt to American ways, in view of the seminary's historic German traditions and constituency.

Philadelphia's St. Charles Borromeo Seminary, relocated in suburban Overbrook in 1871, was completing its first decades in its magnificent buildings during the period. Unlike most freestanding seminaries in other archdioceses, St. Charles Seminary did not ordinarily train seminarians for the suffragen dioceses of its ecclesiastical province. Excepting a few seminarians of the Harrisburg diocese, St. Charles Seminary was intended for the growing Philadelphia archdiocese. Its enrollment grew from 104 in 1884 to 171 in 1911.[45] Apparently the large enrollments precluded admitting students of other dioceses. The seminary enjoyed the leadership of rectors who were conscientious but unremarkable figures. The seminary's most widely known figure was the Scripture professor Herman Heuser, who edited the influential *American Ecclesiastical Review*, which he established at the seminary in 1889.

Smaller seminaries formed before 1884 continued to develop along the inherited lines. St. Mary's Seminary in downtown Cleveland functioned in cramped buildings that were incapable of accommodating all the seminarians of the diocese. The Newark diocese's Seminary of the Immaculate Conception continued to share in the institutional life of the Seton Hall College. Both seminaries maintained modest enrollments, rarely exceeding forty and related exclusively to their respective dioceses. The Seminary of Our Lady of the Angels at Niagara University and the seminary at St. Bonaventure College at Allegany, New York, continued their affiliation with lay colleges and served the dioceses of their region.

Historic Mount St. Mary's Seminary at Emmitsburg recovered from the financial crisis of the early 1880s. In 1883 the seminary program was placed under the direction of Rev. Edward F. X. McSweeney. An alumnus of the Urban College of the Propaganda and priest of the New York archdiocese, McSweeney was pastor at Poughkeepsie, New York, for ten years before coming to Emmitsburg as rector. McSweeney was valued as a priest who exerted a strong influence on his students by reason of his personal warmth and strong interest in progressive causes of the day. His social views were demonstrated by the honored place in his room given to a portrait of the abolitionist John Brown. Except for the 1887–1888 school year, when he directed the small seminary in St. Paul at Archbishop Ireland's invitation, McSweeney remained as seminary director at Emmitsburg until resigning in 1899.[46]

The Benedictine seminaries were just emerging from their founding periods at the end of the century. They continued to educate diocesan candidates in the context of a rich liturgical life, local parish ministry, farm work, and (excepting St. Meinrad) an affiliated lay college. The Benedictines' German character continued, though non-Germans were not excluded. The network of Benedictine abbeys grew but newer ones did not always engage in seminary work, though at least two did so in a systematic fashion. The Abbey of Mount Angel in the Willamette Valley of Oregon was founded by the Swiss abbey of Engelberg in 1882. By 1889 the monastery had developed sufficiently to open a college for lay students and a small seminary for monastic and local diocesan seminarians.[47] The Pacific Northwest was still a missionary region heavily dependent on recruited clergy, so that there was need for a diocesan seminary. But Mount Angel Seminary did not attract a large enrollment of diocesan seminarians and could not duplicate the size and strength of firmly established seminaries elsewhere. In the 1870s, Boniface Wimmer established the Abbey of Mary Help of Christians at Belmont in rural North Carolina to bring Catholicism to an area where it was nearly unknown. In 1887 Leo Haid, the abbot of Belmont Abbey (as it was commonly called), was appointed vicar apostolic of North Carolina's tiny Catholic community while retaining the direction of the abbey. One reason for this unusual arrangement was that the abbey's St. Mary's College would be the seminary for the monastery and the vicariate. Accordingly, the abbey trained a small number of diocesan priests in the following years.[48]

In the late nineteenth century, foundations of freestanding minor seminaries developed slowly. The Third Plenary Council of Baltimore assigned new importance to minor seminary training with a decree outlining its curriculum, in the expectation that better minor seminary programs would provide well-behaved and well-schooled candidates for the major seminary. When Archbishop Francesco Satolli was appointed the first apostolic delegate to the United States in 1892, the Prefect of Propaganda, Cardinal Simeoni, instructed him to encourage the development of minor seminaries. Satolli agreed with the idea and even considered minor seminaries more important than parochial schools.[49] However, if Satolli privately encouraged American bishops to establish freestanding minor seminaries, the results were slight. Several seminaries already had minor and major seminary programs within the same institution, such as those of Milwaukee, Philadelphia, San Francisco, and (after 1900) St. Louis. Others had a lay college either affiliated or located nearby that also trained young aspirants for the priesthood. As noted, Archbishop Elder founded St. Gregory Seminary as a minor seminary for Cincinnati in 1890, and Archbishop Corrigan established Cathedral College in New York as a preparatory seminary for day students in 1900. Bishop Michael Tierney founded St. Thomas Minor Seminary at Hartford in 1897 to develop a native clergy among his multiethnic flock. These minor seminary foundations were the beginnings of a trend that would gather momentum in the twentieth century.

The volume of seminary foundations, minor and major, is matched through the period by the growing number of seminarians. The size of the community of seminarians at freestanding institutions became large. St. Mary's at Baltimore and St. Bernard's at Rochester had enrollments of at least 200 major seminarians by the end of the period. Other seminaries often enrolled between 100 and 200. This growth reflects the transition of foreign-born to American-born seminarians taking place at the end of the century. Groundbreaking studies of diocesan clergy by James Hitchcock, Daniel O'Neill, and Dolores Liptak demonstrate the stages of this process at selected areas.[50] For the entire United States, there were a total of 6,835 secular and religious priests for a Catholic population of 6,623,176 in 1884. The numbers grew to 12,274 diocesan priests and 4,276 religious order priests for a Catholic population of 14,347,027 in 1910.[51] The quarter century had been a time of remarkable growth and development in which the seminary had achieved a new importance and visibility in American Catholic life.

9. Catholic University

The American Catholic bishops undertook their most ambitious enterprise to date with the foundation of the Catholic University of America. Their collective responsibility for a university of graduate learning for clergy and laity far exceeded their obligations to the more modest and less expensive American College in Rome. The bishops' university paralleled the pattern of Catholic development in France, where the church had been separated from university life. There, five regional pontifical graduate institutes of theology had been founded in the 1870s at Lille, Lyons, Paris, Angers, and Toulouse.[1] The university's foundation also paralleled the expansion of American diocesan seminaries, and, as a pontifical graduate institute, the university introduced the advanced study of Catholic theology in the United States. The university's foundation took place as American graduate education advanced with its emphasis on research. The era witnessed the foundations of the Johns Hopkins University in 1876 and Clark University in 1889, exclusively for graduate education, and the organization of graduate schools at Harvard, Yale, Columbia, Stanford, Princeton, Chicago, Wisconsin, Pennsylvania, Michigan, and Cornell.[2] The signs of the times favored a bright future for the bishops' university.

The university committee formed at the Third Plenary Council of Baltimore was responsible for bringing the university into existence. Its members held their first formal meeting under Archbishop Gibbons' chairmanship in May 1885, and after the strongest urging of Bishops Ireland and Spalding, voted to designate Washington, D. C., as the site for the university. They favored the Washington location because of its proximity to the public life of the country. It was also known to be the choice of the university's principal donor, Mary Gwendoline Caldwell. But the selection of Washington did not settle the issue and, instead, opened a controversy as to the wisdom of the national capital as the site. Archbishop Corrigan and Bishop McQuaid were among the leading opponents of the university to agitate against the Washington site, which they regarded as

189

too close to the corrupt influences of national politics, a southern city removed from the centers of Catholic activity, and located too close to the Jesuit's Georgetown University, an undergraduate college with some professional schools. Corrigan's opposition to Washington was reinforced by his desire to have the university in New York and staffed by the Jesuits. The opponents could not reopen the question of the university's location, but they continued to complain about the defects of the proposed site.

Another setback for the university occurred when Archbishop Michael Heiss, who shared the German Catholics' lack of enthusiasm for the university, resigned from the committee in 1886. He pleaded the demands of his work in Milwaukee and the inconvenience of traveling to meetings. The resignation of the country's leading German prelate and the opposition of leading conservative prelates reinforced the impression that the university was the work of the Americanist wing of the hierarchy.[3]

It had been expected that Bishop John Lancaster Spalding, the leading proponent of advanced learning for priests, would become the university's first rector, but for unexplained reasons he declined the office. Instead, the committee invited John Keane, bishop of Richmond since 1878, who accepted the office and the responsibility for organizing the university. Keane, born in Ireland in 1839, came to Baltimore with his family as a boy. He was educated by the Sulpicians at St. Charles College and St. Mary's Seminary and was ordained a priest of the archdiocese of Baltimore in 1866. He served as curate of St. Patrick's in Washington until his promotion to Richmond. Keane was deeply influenced by the thought and spirituality of Isaac Hecker, who was a frequent visitor at St. Patrick's. Keane shared the Americanist vision of accommodating the church to the new age and developed a close friendship with John Ireland.[4]

John Keane began his duties as rector of the prospective university in 1886 with a visit to Rome, accompanied by John Ireland, a university committee member, to secure the Holy See's approbation for the university. Their negotiations were complicated by the letters of several American bishops, notably Corrigan and McQuaid, expressing opposition to the university, especially its proposed location. Propaganda officials postponed consideration of the university until Gibbons arrived in Rome, where on March 17, 1887, he received the red hat that completed his installation in the College of Cardinals. In the meantime Keane and Ireland had solicited letters to Propaganda from the American bishops in favor of the university. After Gibbons' arrival Ireland prevailed on the new cardinal, whose support for the university had been perfunctory, to overcome the opposition to the university by writing a strong letter to the pope urging its approbation.[5] The pope granted the requested approval in a brief dated Easter Sunday, April 10, 1887. The pope's letter expressed the concern over the advancement of error in the modern world and looked to the university to counter false ideas. The pope also exhorted the divided American bishops to carry out "with one mind" the establishment of the university that was "destined to provide the Church with worthy ministers for the salvation of souls and the propagation of Religion, and to give to the Republic her best citizens."[6]

The pope's formal approbation of the university and Keane's official designation as rector were announced at the next meeting of the university committee in September 1887. The choice of Washington as the site was again affirmed. Thereupon, Keane traveled around the country to raise funds for the university to add to Mary Gwendoline Caldwell's $300,000 donation. In keeping with the wishes of the council, the university was to be financed by the contributions of wealthy donors so that the Catholic dioceses would not be called upon for general collections for causes beyond their boundaries. Keane was assisted by the other official collectors, Ireland, Spalding, and Bishop Martin Marty. The latter was one of the few German supporters of the university and was to cultivate German support. The work was not promising, as wealthy Catholics were few. Corrigan, who resigned from the university committee late in 1887, compounded the difficulty by forbidding solicitations for the university in New York, which was one of the few large cities where Catholics of means could be found. He cited the priority of paying off the debt on St. Patrick's Cathedral and the planning for St. Joseph's Seminary.[7]

The collected funds, nevertheless, permitted the trustees to take steps to build the university. The trustees incorporated the Catholic University of America in the District of Columbia and purchased a site in northeast Washington. There Cardinal Gibbons laid the cornerstone for the first building, Caldwell Hall, on May 28, 1888, in the presence of President Grover Cleveland, members of his cabinet, and a crowd of prelates, clergy, and laity. In a steady rain the gathering heard Spalding deliver a wide-ranging address in which he touched on many ideas dear to progressive Catholics. Spalding praised the American experience of government: "We have shown in a word that under a popular government, where men are faithful and intelligent, it is as impossible that society should become chaotic as that the planets should dissolve into star dust." And he extolled the Catholic experience in the United States: "The special significance of our American Catholic history . . . lies in the fact that our example proves that the Church can thrive where it is neither protected nor persecuted, but is simply left to itself to manage its own affairs and to do its work."[8] Such ideas were capable of irritating European and Roman sensibilities at a time in which the union of church and state was the Catholic ideal.

Spalding did not relate the new university to improving clerical culture, as he had done in the past, or to the battle against infidelity and error. He spoke instead of the great advances in learning made in the nineteenth century that American Catholics could not ignore. They needed a university that "will teach the best that is known and encourage research; it will be at once a scientific institute, a school of culture and a training ground for the business of life; it will educate the minds that give direction to the age; it will be a nursery of ideas. . . ." He portrayed the learning of the past in unflattering terms that were well calculated to dismay Roman authorities. The official Catholic position since Pope Leo XIII's encyclical of 1879, *Aeterni Patris*, was to reestablish the Scholastic methods of Aristotle and St. Thomas Aquinas in Catholic intellectual life. Spalding came close to open rebellion on this issue:

> Aristotle is a great mind, but his learning is crude and his ideas of Nature are frequently grotesque. Saint Thomas is a powerful intellect; but his point of view in all that concerns natural knowledge has long since vanished from sight. What a poverty of learning does not the early medieval scheme of education reveal; and when in the twelfth century the idea of a university rises in the best minds, how incomplete and vague it is.[9]

After he heard about the address, the Prefect of Propaganda, Cardinal Simeoni, expressed disapproval of Spalding's views to several American prelates and may have made known his displeasure to Spalding himself.[10]

The university took physical shape with the construction of Caldwell Hall during 1888, and Bishop Keane spent the late summer of that year at the University of Notre Dame to plan the organization of the university. He studied the constitutions of several Catholic universities before drafting the university's constitution and statutes. These documents were circulated among the university trustees, as the university committee became after incorporation. They approved an amended draft in November 1888.

Bishop Keane drafted two documents, a constitution for the general governance of the university and the statutes outlining the operation of the divinity program. The constitution assigned to the bishops of the United States as a body the plenary authority for the university. Their authority was normally to be exercised through the bishop trustees, whom they were to choose. Much initiative lay with the university senate, with whom the trustees were to confer. The archbishop of Baltimore was to be *ex officio* chancellor, and executive authority was assigned to the rector, who was to be a priest and a doctor of divinity. The statutes of the divinity program provided graduate instruction in theology for clerics who had completed the ordinary course of seminary studies.[11] Therefore it was assumed that students for the theology program were to be drawn from the seminaries of the country. The university was to cultivate close relations with Catholic colleges and seminaries.

Keane visited Rome late in 1888 to secure approval for the statutes. His dealings with Propaganda officials brought out some of the differences between the American founders and Roman authorities as to the university's purpose. Since the Third Plenary Council of Baltimore, the university supporters had envisioned a strictly graduate school according to the example of contemporary American graduate schools. Thus they would avoid competition with existing seminaries. The conservative Jesuit Cardinal Camillo Mazella, who chaired the Propaganda commission assigned to study the statutes, balked at permitting the university to be exclusively graduate. He insisted that students preparing for the priesthood be permitted to study theology at the university. Keane gave way on this issue and agreed to wording to that effect. Allied with that issue was the program for degrees, which Mazella desired to be identical to that of Roman institutes. Roman practice provided for the granting of the baccalaureate after two years of theological studies, the licentiate at the end of the third year, and the doctorate at the end of the fourth year. Thus the final wording of the statutes outlined minimum requirements according to the Roman model, which presumed that the ordinary seminary course of four years would lead to the doctorate.[12]

Keane's draft of the constitution contained some words on the affiliation of colleges and seminaries. Before Keane left for Rome, Bishop James O'Connor of Omaha traveled to New York to see the rector in order to urge on him the idea of having the university take over supervision of the diocesan seminaries of the country. As noted earlier, O'Connor had hoped to have the institution where he served as rector, St. Charles Seminary in Philadelphia, staffed by Jesuits. Through the years O'Connor had been a harsh critic of the quality of diocesan seminaries. He saw "outside coercion," as Keane remembered, as the only way of elevating them to the desired status. Keane pointed out to O'Connor the political impossibility of implementing such a plan, but promised to do something for seminaries.[13]

Pope Leo XIII gave approval to the constitution and statutes for the Catholic University of America on the feast of St. Thomas Aquinas, March 7, 1889. The pope's brief of that date, entitled *Magni nobis gaudii*, addressed to Cardinal Gibbons and the American bishops, assigned to them the responsibility for the university under the authority of the Holy See. He urged that seminarians be admitted to the course of studies, and exhorted the affiliation of seminaries, colleges, and other institutions to the university in a manner that would not destroy their autonomy.[14] The latter provision, according to Keane, was the result of Bishop O'Connor's lobbying.

Before Keane left for Europe, the university trustees authorized him to secure a faculty for the university while he was abroad. They approved an initial faculty of no more than six regular members, including a professor of English literature. Thus five members were to form the faculty of the divinity school that would be the first part of the university to function. Keane had no easy task, since the most desirable candidates declined to join the new venture. After visiting seminaries and universities in Europe, he assembled a faculty of promising younger scholars: Henri Hyvernat, a Frenchman and professor of Scripture at the Apollinaire in Rome; Joseph Schroeder of the Cologne seminary for dogmatic theology; Thomas Bouquillon, a Belgian and professor of moral theology at the Institut Catholique at Lille; and Joseph Pohle of the Fulda (Germany) seminary, for philosophy. Charles Warren Stoddard, the sole layman of the group, was hired from Notre Dame as professor of English literature.

The trustees later secured John Hogan, rector of the Boston seminary, as president of the Divinity College, a position that included directing the studies and spiritual life of the priest graduate students, and another Sulpician priest, Alexis Orban, as librarian and assistant to Hogan. Since the priests of the Congregation of St. Paul (Paulists) opened a residence near the university for their members attending its classes, two Paulists were engaged part-time for the faculty: Augustine Hewit, their superior general, to lecture in church history, and George Searle, lecturer in astronomy and physics. The original faculty consisted of five priests born in Europe; the administrative officers, Hogan and Orban, were born in Ireland and France respectively; and the three born Americans, Stoddard, Hewit, and Searle, were converts to Catholicism. The original faculty of 1889 had no Americans who were born Catholics. Archbishop Ireland's friend Thomas O'Gorman, a talented American-born priest, joined the faculty in 1890 as professor of church history. O'Gorman had no formal training in history.

Arrangements were made before the university's opening for talented American priests to study abroad in order to join the faculty later. Thomas J. Shahan, a Propaganda alumnus and priest of the diocese of Hartford, studied at the University of Berlin to prepare to teach church history. Edward A. Pace, also a Propaganda graduate and priest of the diocese of St. Augustine, studied psychology with Wilhelm Wundt at the University of Leipzig before joining the philosophy faculty. Sebastian Messmer, a native Swiss and priest of the diocese of Newark, studied canon law in Rome. And Charles Grannan, a New York priest serving on the faculty of Mount St. Mary's Seminary at Emmitsburg, was sent to Rome to advance his studies in Scripture. These priests joined the university faculty in 1890 and 1891.

The promising venture of the Catholic University of America opened on November 13, 1889, amid feelings of self-confidence and self-congratulation accompanying the centennial celebrations of the founding of the American hierarchy that had taken place in Baltimore three days before. Keane had invited Spalding to speak at the dedication ceremonies, but the latter declined, citing his doctor's orders for rest.[15] Cardinal Gibbons, as chancellor, dedicated the university, Bishop Michael O'Farrell of Trenton delivered extemporaneously an unmemorable and unrecorded address at the ceremonies, and President Benjamin Harrison and his cabinet arrived in time for the toasts and short speeches after the banquet in the Caldwell Hall dining room.

On the evening of the dedication, university life began for the entering class of thirty-eight priest graduate students. As in a seminary, the year opened with a retreat of spiritual exercises and conferences under the direction of the rector and John Hogan. The retreat closed four days later with a solemn Mass of the Holy Spirit celebrated by Bishop Keane in Caldwell Hall chapel. After the Mass, the theology faculty made a profession of faith before Bishop Keane and kissed a book of the Gospels as a pledge of orthodoxy.[16] A seminary regimen continued thereafter with daily attendance at meditation, Mass, personal examen, a spiritual conference, and evening prayers. The priest students were permitted to leave the campus only one day per week. John Hogan, as president of the Divinity College, brought to bear his years of experience as a seminary rector to govern student life. Several students and faculty questioned the rigor of the seminary routine. One student, John Belford, priest of the Brooklyn diocese and an alumnus of St. Mary's Seminary, complained to Alphonse Magnien about life at the university:

I hope for the sake of the University that they will make some changes in the rule. It was a disappointment to me in many ways to find there a system of discipline substantially the same as in the seminary. While I admit the necessity of certain regulations in every community, I do not admit the necessity of all the restrictions and limitations set forth in the rule of the University, and most of all do I object to the watching, that thing so distasteful and so disgusting to any one who has even a spark of manhood in him. I assure you that it made my blood boil to see the restless eyes of the President [John Hogan] cast from face to face at all the public exercises. Such a thing as that, though Sulpitians are accused of it, I never saw in Baltimore and when it was laid at their door, I have always stoutly denied it. . . .

Priests who go to the University from the mission mean business. They are not idlers, they are not pleasure-seekers, they are not disgraced, they are not untrustworthy. They are serious men possessing the confidence of their Bishop, fond of study, ready to give up much for the sake of knowledge.[17]

But there was no consideration given to the fact that many priest students had been ordained and on their own for several years and that when they left the university they would again be on their own. Instead, as Bishop Keane stated, "we resolved to stand inflexibly by the principle that the spiritual & priestly life & training of the student was at least as essential as their intellectual development."[18] Likewise, Archbishop Ireland agreed that spiritual exercises should be in common, as he told the rector: "Those who object are those who would not make them in private and those who would not make them in private do not deserve to be in the university." Ireland believed that bishops would lose confidence in the university if the clerical students were left on their own. He went so far as to associate the spiritual development of the students with the purpose of the university: "The object of the University is to form model priests, and in such piety is as much needed as intellect. We do not want to reproduce in America the levity and tepidity of European universities." However, Ireland acknowledged the need to loosen up some aspects of traditional discipline: "I would be disposed to let up a little on usual Sulpitian rigidity" by "frequently" dispensing with public reading at meals. "Fr. Hogan must not assume, if he does, a scolding attitude, rather that of primus unter pares."[19] Thus the issue of the internal ife of the student community was quickly settled in favor of a seminary atmosphere.

The administration and faculty devoted much of the first year to organizing a plan of studies. The theology program assumed that the entering students had a thorough course of at least three years of elementary theology in a seminary. After entering the university, the students were given a general examination in their first semester covering the subjects of the seminary course. The examination consisted of a four-hour written part and a one-hour oral exam. The baccalaureate in theology (S.T.B.) was awarded for passing this examination. The student was then qualified to take the examination for the licentiate (S.T.L.) at the end of the second year of studies.

The theological faculty organized itself in the first year into four branches: biblical sciences, dogmatic and philosophical sciences, moral sciences, and history and patrology. Each student was to pursue courses in two areas. Students pursuing a degree were also to designate a specialty in one area. For the licentiate, the faculty imposed a dissertation requirement a few years after the university opened along with the more traditional examination for a theological degree that consisted of an oral defense of fifty theological theses prepared in advance. For the doctorate (S.T.D.), two years of study beyond the licentiate were required in addition to the public defense of seventy-five theses at three-hour sessions on two consecutive days and a dissertation.

The university's record of success in enrolling and then turning out graduates with degrees was not impressive during the 1890s. From the initial class of thirty-eight students in 1889, only five remained to earn licentiates in the spring of 1891; a sixth licentiate was awarded to a priest of the Society of Mary (Marists), which had a seminary nearby. The students annually enrolled in degree programs numbered in the thirties during the first five years of the university's life; few students returned for a second year to earn the licentiate. The first two doctorates in theology were awarded in 1895 to Edmund DuBlanchy, a Marist, and George Lucas, priest of the diocese of Scranton.[20]

The university trustees regarded the slender enrollment of diocesan priests in graduate theology programs as a matter of grave concern. In the spring of 1891 they resolved to have the chancellor, Cardinal Gibbons, write to the bishops of the country to urge support for the university by sending student priests. Gibbons' circular letter advanced all the reasons for sending students: to fulfill the aims of the Third Plenary Council of Baltimore of having a university, to respond to the wishes of the pope, who endorsed the university, and to realize the success of the university, which "in the eyes of the world, the honor and welfare of the Church in America are so largely bound up." He hoped the university "may reach the degree of reputation and usefulness which is its due."[21] The board also permitted seminarians to enroll after their third year of seminary theology.

Gibbons' appeal and the new enrollment policy did not fulfill the expectation of having at least one student from each of the country's eighty-six dioceses. The rector's third annual report in 1892 recorded the third successive year of declining enrollment from thirty-eight in 1889, thirty-four in 1890, and thirty-three in 1891. He noted "The Bishops almost universally declare that they are anxious to send students to the University, but that they find it to be at present impracticable, owing to the scarcity of priests and the pressing needs of the missions." Keane could only speculate on other causes of the lack of students: the benefits of study were not sufficiently recognized nor that the privations during the course of study would be compensated by benefits during their priestly careers. The rector also touched on the issue of episcopal support: "there may be reason to fear that some of the Bishops overlook the fact that the University belongs to them, and that their proprietorship in it ought to make them eager to cooperate for its success."[22]

While complaints were raised about the low enrollment, the students who enrolled at the university were not well prepared. As Dean Bouquillon recorded in the fourth annual report: "At the same time we must insist that the *quality* is the chief consideration. We want students who possess real ability and are eager to pursue their studies not in a slipshod way, but according to scientific methods."[23] The length of time the students were permitted to stay at the university related to the development of their academic qualities. As Dean O'Gorman stated in the fifth annual report: "One year does not suffice to initiate a young man to scientific methods. . . ."[24] Henri Hyvernat lamented that the lack of quality lowered the standard of teaching, since professors had to teach elementary matter that had not been treated in the seminary. He found that "it further came to pass that the professors gradually desisted from their higher standards and by degrees got reconciled to the idea of giving just about the same courses as seminary professors would have given, treating their subject-matter in fuller detail, to be sure[,] and with a greater array of texts and arguments, but, otherwise, on the very same principles and with the same methods as in a seminary."[25]

The problem of low enrollment of diocesan priests became less conspicuous with the augmentation of the student body from other sources. In the fall of 1895 the School of Philosophy with its departments of philosophy proper, mathematics, physical and biological sciences, and letters, and the School of Social Sciences with departments of sociology, economics, political science, and law opened in the university's new MacMahon Hall. These graduate schools were open to laymen and began the gradual expansion of the university's offerings. Through the 1890s, several religious orders opened seminaries or residential colleges in the neighborhood around the university. Their members could earn degrees in the university's programs, and, if they were seminarians, they pursued a course of studies leading to ordination at their own seminary and audited theology courses at the university. The influx of auditors increased the volume of students attending theology classes but did not enlarge the number of formal matriculates seeking degrees. Hyvernat complained that the auditors came to study elementary matters for the first time and that the superiors of religious seminaries used the university in this fashion in order to save themselves the expense of acquiring their own professors in subjects considered secondary in importance, such as Scripture, Hebrew, and history. Hyvernat lamented that auditors outnumbered the matriculates "thus placing our professors practically under obligation of lowering the standard of their teaching."[26]

A serious hindrance to the ability of the university to win the general confidence of bishops, who in turn would send diocesan priests to the university, was the bishops' deep division over current nationality and school controversies and the participation of the university faculty in those controversies.

The grievances of the German Catholic community had surfaced in the Abbelen memorial of 1886, which sought the appointment of German vicars general for dioceses with substantial German populations, and again in the 1891 Lucerne memorial of Peter Paul Cahensly, who sought the appointment of more German bishops to American dioceses. These efforts stirred progressive American bishops to a spirited reaction against German influence in the United States. At the Catholic University, the German professors, Schroeder and Pohle, were outspoken defenders of Cahensly, which provoked the ongoing resentment of university supporters.

Controversy divided the bishops on the issue of Catholic responses to public education. In 1890 Ireland addressed the convention of the National Education Association, in which he praised the public schools as the "pride and glory" of the country. Such praise was bad enough from the perspective of Germans, who saw in their parochial schools the preservation of faith and culture, and the perspective of Irish conservatives, who saw in the public schools the threat of religious indifferentism. To make matters worse, in the following year Ireland permitted the pastors of Faribault and Stillwater, Minnesota, within his archdiocese to contract with local school boards for the lease of parish schools and the payment of the salaries of Catholic sisters to teach all the children entitled to attend the public school. Religious instructions were to be given to the Catholic children at the schools after regular school hours. To Protestant critics, the plan ceded too much to the church; to Catholic critics, the arrangement gave away the Catholic character of the parish schools. The plan seemed to violate the legislation of the Third Plenary Council of Baltimore that mandated the establishment of parish schools.[27] The Faribault-Stillwater plan became a subject of national controversy dividing the Catholic community between the progressives or Americanists, who favored it, and the conservatives and Germans, who opposed it.

Thomas Bouquillon, the university's professor of moral theology and a partisan of Ireland and the Americanists, published a pamphlet entitled *Education: To Whom Does It Belong?* in which he strongly defended the state's right to provide education. Archbishop Corrigan then asked the Jesuit priest, René Holaind, of Woodstock College in Maryland to respond to Bouquillon. Holaind's pamphlet *The Parent First* denied the right of a non-Christian state, such as the United States, to provide its citizens education. The publicity surrounding the pamphlets widened the controversy and divided the hierarchy. Bouquillon's presence on the university faculty reinforced the hostility of conservative and German bishops to the university. The cardinals of Propaganda in due course issued a ruling in April

1892 that tolerated the arrangements at Faribault and Stillwater, Minnesota, in the given circumstances but did not commend them as an ideal to be adopted elsewhere. Both sides of the controversy thereby felt at least partially vindicated.[28]

The nationality and school controversies had repercussions for the university. Conservative and German bishops did not see their views adequately represented there and were not inclined to support it by sending students or assisting in raising funds. Some bishops hesitated to send students to the university where tensions were known to be running high. The faculty was divided into warring camps yet lived, worshipped, and studied together with their clerical students in Caldwell Hall. Maurice Francis Egan, a layman who joined the faculty in 1894 as professor of English, noted the tense atmosphere and commented on the appropriateness of the organist playing the processional "War March of the Priests" from Mendelssohn's *Athalia* at an academic convocation opening the school year.[29]

The warfare produced casualties. Joseph Pohle resigned from the faculty in 1894, when he obtained an academic position in Germany. Georges Périès, a Frenchman who had succeeded Sebastian Messmer as professor of canon law in 1893, supported the conservative faction. His contract was not renewed in the spring of 1896. Joseph Schroeder, who openly criticized progressives at gatherings of German Catholics around the country, escalated the hostilities by reporting to Roman authorities on the Americanists. In 1895 he told the Cardinal Secretary of State Mariano Rampolla that heresy was rife at the university and that the rector tolerated it. Schroeder specifically objected to the list of theses to be defended for the licentiate examination of William Russell, a Baltimore priest and future bishop of Charleston. Charles Grannan, who had adopted historical and critical methods of Scripture study, had prepared the theses. They appeared to be drawn from the writings of Alfred Loisy, the Scripture scholar dismissed from the Institut Catholique in Paris in 1893. Schroeder held Keane responsible for this instance of heterodoxy.[30] At the same time, Archbishop Francesco Satolli, the apostolic delegate who had lived in Caldwell Hall for a period in 1892 and 1893, reported to Rampolla that Keane should be relieved of the rectorship because of the university's intellectual shortcomings, the lack of student discipline, and continuing financial problems. Satolli had grown increasingly hostile to the Americanists because of their participation in interfaith activities, such as the Parliament of Religions in Chicago in 1892. Keane had addressed the Parliament and had even spoken at Harvard in 1891. Roman authority looked on such activities as leading to indifferentism.[31]

Schroeder's accusations achieved their desired result in September 1896 when Pope Leo XIII asked for the rector's resignation. The pope's letter rather disingenuously cited the custom that holders of pontifical appointments should not hold them in perpetuity. The indefiniteness of the rector's appointment could be presumed, since there was no mention of a set term of the rector's office in the university constitutions. The pope's arbitrary action took no account of the bishops' statutory responsibility for the university. Keane promptly resigned.[32]

In 1897 the university trustees nominated and the Holy See duly appointed Thomas J. Conaty, a priest of the diocese of Springfield, Massachusetts, as second rector of the Catholic University. Conaty, a native of Ireland, had grown up in Massachusetts. After studies at the College of the Holy Cross in Worcester and the Grand Séminaire in Montreal, he was ordained in 1872. From 1880 until his appointment as rector, he was pastor of Sacred Heart Church in Worcester. Conaty became widely known as a temperance activist and served a term as president of the Catholic Total Abstinence Union, which endeared him to such fellow temperance activists as Keane and Ireland. Conaty was active in education through his interest in the Catholic version of Chautauqua, the Catholic Summer School at Cliff Haven near Plattsburg, New York. He served as president of the summer school in the 1890s. As "The People's University," the summer school was a favorite project of Archbishop Corrigan, who admired Conaty. With associations in the progressive and conservative camps of the hierarchy, Conaty appeared to offer less potential for conflict at the university. He was appointed a titular bishop in 1901.[33]

The ill-feeling produced by Keane's dismissal, however, stimulated a movement to punish his enemies. Keane's partisans on the board of trustees (notably Ireland) and faculty members directed an attack against Joseph Schroeder as the cause of the dismissal. Unflattering tales about Schroeder were reported to Roman authorities, especially his visits to taverns. Public drinking easily offended the Americanists, who were all strong advocates of total abstinence. Germans, of course, were largely unmoved by the total abstinence movement. The Holy See eventually agreed to Schroeder's departure but awaited the offer of an academic position for the professor in Germany before permitting him to resign in 1897. The resignation was justified on the basis of securing harmony on the university faculty. The faculty was then free of conservative and German critics.[34]

The reputation of being identified with one faction of the Catholic community in the United States did not in the following years enhance the university's influence and attract a larger enrollment of candidates for degrees. However, in the years of Thomas Conaty's rectorship from 1897 to 1903, the university made efforts to advance one of the announced purposes of the university, that is, to affiliate seminaries. The first seminaries to enter into a relationship with the university were those of religious orders that were attracted to establish themselves in the neighborhood of northeast Washington. The seminaries of the Congregation of St. Paul (Paulists), Society of Mary (Marists), and the Congregation of the Holy Cross were in operation in the 1890s. Students from these seminaries, though ineligible to enroll as candidates for degrees because they were seminarians, often attended university classes as auditors. Some of the students from religious orders enrolled in the university as students after ordination.

The first seminary beyond Washington to affiliate with the university was Archbishop Ireland's St. Paul Seminary in 1894. The affiliation permitted St. Paul's students to earn the university degree of S.T.B. by examination after their four-year seminary course and then enroll at the university and take the S.T.L. examination after only one year of study. Through the 1890s the university negotiated with St. John's Seminary in Boston for affiliation, but, as discussed in chapter 11, the parties had such serious differences about the terms of agreement that the seminary was not affiliated.

Rector Conaty sought to develop closer relations between the university and the seminaries of the country to advance affiliation. At the trustees' meeting in October 1897 the rector raised the matter of the relations of seminaries with the university in regard to the inadequate preparation of students sent to the university. It was hoped that with the addition of affiliated seminaries, the students sent to the university would be better prepared. The trustees authorized the rector to hold a conference with seminary presidents to consider the relations between seminary and university. The theology faculty advised Conaty to remind the seminary officials that the apostolic letter founding the university endorsed affiliation with other institutions while at the same time respecting their autonomy, that the university was not in competition with seminaries, and that the purpose of the seminary was to offer general studies and the university's aim was to specialize. The theology faculty looked to a close relation with seminaries: "There would also be more advantage all around if Presidents of Seminaries made a good choice of young men for the University and if they chose from such young men, once they have made a University course, their future Seminary Professors."[35]

Conaty consulted with several seminary leaders and a conference was arranged on May 25, 1898, at St. Joseph's Seminary, Yonkers, New York. Ten rectors of diocesan seminaries attended, representing the seminaries of Baltimore, Boston, New York, Philadelphia, Brooklyn, Cincinnati, San Francisco, Newark, and the independent seminaries of Our Lady of Angels Seminary, Niagara, New York, and Mount St. Mary's Seminary, Emmitsburg, Maryland. The heads of St. Meinrad Seminary, Indiana; Christ the King Seminary, Allegany, New York; St. Mary's Seminary, Cleveland;

Kenrick Seminary, St. Louis; and St. Paul Seminary, Minnesota, were unable to attend but sent "letters of approval."[36] The Rochester and Milwaukee seminaries, disdaining the university and all its works, were not represented.

Conaty addressed the seminary educators and expressed the desire for the founding of an educational conference, at first among seminaries, and then among colleges. He hoped that a conference of seminary presidents may "give careful consideration to the true relations which should exist between the University and the seminary. . . ."[37] He directed their attention to the outstanding problem of the work of preparing seminary students for the university and the standards that university requirements demand for affiliation. Conaty's address and John Hogan's article on the meeting indicate the good will of the rector and the seminary leaders. However, as John Hogan indicated, the problems surrounding the task of preparing seminary students for university study were considerable. Language study was among the foremost problems. The seminary with its general studies was not always equipped to prepare students in this area. The purpose of the meeting was fulfilled in the general agreement to form an organization, the Educational Conference of Seminary Faculties. The participants agreed to meet the following year at St. Charles Seminary, Philadelphia, in September 1899. But before the meeting could be arranged, the seminary conference lapsed into inactivity for several years.

In 1899 Conaty sponsored a conference of leaders of Catholic colleges that resulted in the formation of the Catholic Colleges Association. This group generated wide support from the colleges and held annual conventions. The rector also brought together the leaders of Catholic schools to form the Parish School Conference in 1902. The leaders of the Catholic college and parish schools conferences decided in 1903 to merge their organizations. Seminary educators who were active in the Catholic College Conference decided that there should also be a seminary component, and several seminary rectors were mobilized to plan a seminary group. Accordingly, the Catholic Educational Association, renamed National Catholic Educational Association in 1927, was launched and held its organizational convention at the St. Louis World's Fair in 1904 as a voluntary organization of Catholic educators with college, parish school, and seminary divisions.[38] Thereafter, the seminary division provided a forum for the exchange of views among seminary educators at annual conventions. The forum did not necessarily aim at a close cooperation between the seminaries and the university in order to raise up seminary standards to prepare seminarians for the university. The sessions usually dealt with pedagogical issues of interest to seminary educators. An affiliation program of diocesan seminaries beyond Washington did not attract much interest until the 1940s.

Conaty's six-year term as rector ended in 1903 and he was appointed bishop of Monterey–Los Angeles. His successor was Denis J. O'Connell, former rector of the American College and then rector of Cardinal Gibbons' titular church in Rome, where he acted as the agent of the progressive American bishops.

As university rector O'Connell soon had to cope with a major financial crisis that had been developing from the university's beginning when the endowment had been entrusted to Thomas Waggaman, a Washington financier of an old Maryland Catholic family. Waggaman guaranteed a return of six percent interest to the university on its investments and used the university money for his own speculations. In 1903 Waggaman's speculations backfired. He was unable to pay the university's six percent and bankruptcy proceedings began. After years of litigation and an out-of-court settlement in 1909, the university recovered about $360,000 of its original investment of $900,000. However, in the intervening years, the university had to be operated. In 1903, after representations were made to the Holy See, Pope Pius X permitted an annual collection to be taken in Catholic churches in the United States for the benefit of the university. The record of support for the collection was uneven. All dioceses, except aloof Rochester, participated, though many poor dioceses of the South and West could give only token amounts and midwestern dioceses with large German populations donated sparingly. Nevertheless, the collection covered a large part of the operational expenses of the university and kept it from closing. The collection became an annual one and reversed the original intention that the university was to be sustained by the donations of the wealthy.[39]

The challenge of survival forced a reconsideration of the university's purpose. Cardinal Francesco Satolli, Prefect of the Sacred Congregation of Studies, strongly recommended to the trustees that the graduate programs in the Schools of Philosophy and the Social Sciences that enrolled laymen be discontinued and that the university be returned to a graduate program in theology exclusively for priests.[40] The trustees, however, looked to an expansion of patronage and revenue for the university and inaugurated an undergraduate program in 1904. This change reversed the university's unique character as an exclusively graduate institution on which it had based its appeals for financial support. It now entered into competition with Catholic colleges to attract undergraduate students.

The exertions of the first decade of the twentieth century to overcome the pressing financial problems and to expand the enrollment yielded modest increases. In 1909, twenty years after the university's opening, 225 students were enrolled, of which ninety-nine were laymen. The remainder were divided between fifty-seven diocesan and sixty-nine religious order clerics. The diocesan priest graduate students comprising the residential community of Caldwell Hall numbered between a low of twenty-three in 1904–1905 and a high of thirty-four in 1909–1910.[41]

The priest graduate students who matriculated at the university to study theology between the 1889 and 1909 school years numbered 476, of these about half or 235 enrolled for a second year. Two years were required to earn the licentiate of theology (S.T.L.), which was awarded to only 153 out of the 476 priests during the twenty-year period, or about seven or eight per year.[42] Doctorates in theology (S.T.D.) were awarded to only nine priests between 1895 and 1909, after which none was awarded until 1918.[43] The statistics suggest some compliance with Spalding's idea of pursuing a desultory study to improve mental culture and not to earn degrees. The lack of a steadily growing enrollment of priests in graduate theology in the university's initial years is more striking in view of the steady growth of American priests from 9,168 in 1890 to 16,550 in 1910.[44]

In the early 1890s when the matriculated students were diocesan priests, there was a concern about their small numbers. After the university was opened to religious orders and lay students, the absence of diocesan priests was not regularly discussed. The seventeenth annual report of the university in 1906 returned to the problem of the diocesan priest students and recorded reasons for low enrollment:

> Among the reasons to assign for the falling off are the assignment of some of last year's students to work on the missions; the loss of salary and the loss of diocesan rank in seniority, which studentship at the University sometimes entail. These conditions, together with the general desire of the junior clergy to incur no further financial obligations after ordination, act as deterrent and keep down the number of those who would otherwise enter the University for their first year of study, as well as those who would return to the University to complete their second year.[45]

Though it was not mentioned, it also seems unlikely that a recently ordained priest would willingly return to the seminary life that the Catholic University required of them.

University officials and trustees did not raise another issue for the written record, that is, the competition for diocesan students that the university faced from the American College in Rome. During Denis O'Connell's term as rector at the American College from 1885 to 1895, the enrollment, which had annually fluctuated between twenty and thirty in the 1860s and 1870s, stabilized between sixty and seventy. After 1895 American College enrollment grew steadily and reached 137 in 1908, on the eve of its fiftieth anniversary. The students took advantage of earning degrees at the Urban College of the Propaganda, where they studied, though it was not a requirement for ordination. From 1861 to 1883, only thirty-four doctorates in theology were earned by American College students. From 1883 to 1908, 123 doctorates of theology were earned, as well as 195 licentiates and 304 bachelors. These degrees were earned according to the Roman plan during the seminary course of four years of theology and after written and oral defenses of theses. The student ordinarily would take the doctoral examination around the time of his ordination. Many American College students also took advantage of the opportunity to earn degrees in philosophy. Between 1882 and 1908 American College alumni earned 85 doctorates in philosophy, 75 licentiates of philosophy, and 107 bachelors of philosophy by the same method of examination.[46] Thus the brightest and most promising diocesan seminarians, most of whom presumably would be capable of pursuing advanced learning, earned ecclesiastical degrees that were more easily obtained in Rome than those available at the Catholic University. There was neither reason nor incentive for a Roman alumnus with one or more degrees afterwards to study theology at Washington. It was assumed, as Herman Heuser noted, that the university was established as "a centripetal force tending to bring together the best elements from our seminaries."[47] However, there was no sure way of doing so, and the pool of potential graduate students among the diocesan clergy was considerably reduced as the most talented and promising were sent to Rome as seminarians.

The founders of the Catholic University had a strong desire for developing a national institution, but they failed to take into consideration the fact that important constituencies within the Catholic Church are not organized along national lines. For instance, religious orders such as the Jesuits and Dominicans, who had the greatest interest in intellectual activity, were international orders with headquarters in Rome, where their own graduate schools were located. Their form of organization did not take cognizance of a national institution such as the Catholic University. Thus the most academically minded religious clergy were cut off from the Catholic University, leaving the smaller orders and congregations to patronize the university. The latter did not usually have strong academic interests.

The founders, too, did not have a clear vision of the academic and intellectual activity that the university was to perform. For instance, John Lancaster Spalding's idealistic addresses did not yield a specific plan of graduate education for diocesan priests. In his address at the Baltimore council, he disdained the traditional subjects of seminary learning and held that even if the course of studies were prolonged, it was mere professional learning anyway. He called instead for training in mental culture. However, Spalding declined to accept the rectorship and the challenge of putting his ideas into practice.

When the university opened, its officials and faculty devised a program based on the accepted apologetical dimension of theological study by holding examinations based on a defense of theses, as was customary in Catholic universities. They acknowledged the modern idea of research by adding a dissertation to the requirement for degrees. But, for many, the university had the straightforward apologetical purpose of defending the Catholic faith. Pope Leo XIII's letter of 1889 viewed the university as a bastion against the errors and heresies of the day. Bishop Camillus Maes, a leading university supporter, also looked upon it as a college for apologetical warfare. He hoped that the university would train priests for various levels of the struggle to meet opponents "in the ponderous quarterly, the learned monthly, the bright magazine; on the public rostrum and in the college chair." For every opponent who would attack the divinity or Christ or the Catholic church, Maes anticipated that "a dozen Catholic priests trained to polemics at the School of Theology and Philosophy of the Catholic University, will rise in the strength of their logic and the bravery of their knowledge and vindicate Christian truth."[48] And New York's auxiliary bishop John Farley looked on the university as "an armory on which we can confidently draw in time of siege from without or dissention from within the church."[49] John Hogan, whose appreciation of recent developments in learning was more refined than that of Maes or Farley, recognized that the university had opportunities in apologetics. Hogan did not state the need for apologetics in terms of refuting error and heresy, but he foresaw that its task was to come to terms with contemporary thought in a broad sense. Once the university had all the departments of learning normally associated with a complete university, Hogan predicted that

> a large body of men of distinguished merit and acknowledged authority . . . will meet within its walls to labor together for the cause of truth, human and divine; each one a master in his special sphere of knowledge, familiar with all its facts, and with all its bearings on revealed religion, ever ready to supply to colleague, pupil, or inquirer the most accurate data of his department, to tell him the true value of the newest speculations, and to enable him to set aside the unwarranted assumptions that so often claim recognition under the name of science.

He saw such an institution as "invaluable for the defense of the faith."[50]

Some expected practical results from university studies. When sending a student priest to the university, Bishop Maes wanted practical training, as he told the rector: "Remember that the man I will send you is destined for the great missionary work I have in view and try to shape his two years course to the best advantage for the aim to be attained."[51] And a young priest, Patrick J. McCormick of New York, destined for study at the university, was told that study there was "of immense advantage as a preparation for the mission."[52]

The clarification of purposes and enlistment of a constituency to support the university with students, especially among the diocesan clergy, for whom the institution was originally intended, were the tasks of leadership. The trustees and officials did not come to terms adequately with these issues. The university was not able to enlist the whole-hearted support of the American bishops, who were deeply divided along ideological and ethnic lines during the period. The university's fortunes were tied closely to the Americanist wing of the church, which lost influence during the period. Moreover, it appears that some serious problems in establishing a constituency were left unstated, such as the effects of competition with the American College in Rome. Other problems did not receive sustained attention, such as the attempt to develop a relationship with the seminaries of the country to advance affiliation with the university. The seminary leaders responded favorably to the idea of a seminary organization, but there was slight demand for affiliation.

It can be concluded that the university was handicapped by uneven leadership and a limited demand for the services that it had to offer in the area of advanced clerical learning. It is likely, too, that in founding a university to raise the quality of the clergy, the founders misstated what was actually needed. The demand for intellectual improvement of the clergy was generally acknowledged, but it was stated within the context of the priest's overall professional training that went beyond the strictly academic aspects of clerical learning and earning degrees. Influential church leaders articulated a model of the diocesan priest for the late nineteenth century that the seminary, not the university, was better equipped to address.

10. Model Priest and Model Seminary

The Third Plenary Council of Baltimore directly addressed the education of the clergy with decrees outlining seminary studies and laid the foundation for the Catholic University to provide advanced learning for a few priests. Annual examinations for newly ordained priests and for clerical promotions and quarterly clerical conferences insured that there was a limited amount of ongoing clerical learning. But, beyond specific acts directed to priests and their training, the council legislated in areas with an indirect impact on clerical life. The decrees on mixed marriages, administration of parish property, secret societies, a national catechism, and the mandate that each parish have a school, in effect, enlarged the responsibilities of the parish priest to include their implementation. Bishop James O'Connor, for instance, quickly recognized the conciliar implications for the work of the diocesan priest: "The late Council having given to the second order of the clergy [priests] a large share in the government of the church in this country, their higher education and better moral training, have, now, become matters of greatest urgency." The bishop feared the "evil" resulting from priests "without greater knowledge, and more enlightened zeal than they have exhibited in the past. . . ."[1] There was a growing interest in broadening the professional qualities of the diocesan priest that led to the delineation of a model of the priest appropriate for the American church. In turn, the new model informed adaptations of seminary life.

A major effort to improve the priest's ongoing professional learning began with the founding of the monthly journal *American Ecclesiastical Review* in 1889. Its founder and editor, Herman Heuser, was a German-born Philadelphia priest who taught Scripture at St. Charles Seminary at Overbrook. He defined the purpose of the *Review* as a "help in carrying out the legislation of our holy Church, and, in particular, the decrees of the Councils of Baltimore. Our next object will be to strive for the promotion of what has been called the higher culture of the clergy." He made the journal's "province" pastoral theology and offered "such information as is calculated to make the priest efficient, whether in church, or school, or the homes of his people, or the assemblies of strangers."[2]

In the following years, Heuser provided American priests with articles on varied topics including homiletics, church music, parish school management, parish societies, total abstinence, canon law, liturgical and rubrical matters, and clerical fiction. Book reviews brought European scholarship to the attention of the American clergy. Articles on the priest's library suggested the basic volumes suitable for ecclesiastical learning. Scholarly articles in dogmatic theology occasionally appeared, and, as an aid to confessors, short articles on moral cases were published. A longer series on the physical aspects of marriage appeared, of course, discreetly printed in Latin. Catholic scholarship was in an early stage of development, so that many authors were Europeans, including the modernists Alfred Loisy and George Tyrell. Contributors from the United States included faculty members from Catholic University and seminary educators.

During the same period John F. Brady, a New York priest, addressed the development of the priest as preacher and catechist with the founding of the *Homiletic Monthly and Catechist* in 1899. Brady was a member of the faculty of St. Joseph Seminary at New York, and the monthly was published from the seminary. He provided clerical readers with articles written by prominent priests that could be used in the preparation of homilies related to the liturgical season, sermons on devotional themes and doctrinal subjects, and information on effective catechetics.[3]

As Heuser and Brady sponsored successful publications that enriched professional learning for priests in the 1890s, influential churchmen considered the expanded duties and responsibilities of the priest, not only as an executor of church legislation, but in terms of the varied ministerial needs of the era. They expressed their views either through published writings or through reforms quietly introduced in seminaries. When taken together, their ideas form a model or ideal type of a diocesan priest for the United States at the end of the nineteenth century. The model priest had functions beyond the ministry of sacraments, to include the professional skills of preaching, teaching, and the varied aspects of parish administration. Unlike John Lancaster Spalding's concern for cultivating habits of mental culture at the university for a few priests, the new model of priesthood related to the professional skills of all diocesan clergy. Articulating the model took place as a renewed emphasis on the supernatural qualities of the priest and the traditional devotional practices were being promoted. The result was a dialogue of ideas relating to the competing claims of the natural and the supernatural in the model of the priest.

A leading figure setting the standards for the priest was James Gibbons, who, as archbishop of Baltimore from 1877 and the country's only cardinal from 1887 to 1911, was the unofficial spiritual leader of American Catholics. Gibbons had set a moderate and sensible tone to Catholicism before the American public with his popular work *Faith of Our Fathers*, published in 1877. His book *The Ambassador of Christ*, which appeared in 1896, consisted of topical essays on the priesthood written in a non-scholarly fashion for priests and seminarians. It is noteworthy as a rare contribution on the subject in English arising from the American experience of the priest's ministry.

Gibbons begins *Ambassador* with a brief summary of the standard Catholic teaching on the priesthood, the concept of vocation as a call from God, and the spirituality of the priest as received from the seventeenth century. The priest's ordinary tasks as minister of sacraments are thereafter simply presumed. Gibbons then devotes twenty-six of the following twenty-eight essays to the external qualities of the priest: personal behavior, education, and professional skills beyond the ministry of sacraments. He employs a consistently practical, even homey, style with stories cited from his own experiences or those of clerical friends and quotations drawn from Scripture, the church fathers, and saints, as well as an array of American generals, jurists, politicians, industrialists, and Indian chiefs.

Gibbons stresses the priest's personal behavior in topics such as "Truth and Sincerity of Character," "Self-Respect and Human Respect," "Humility Specially incumbent on Priests," and "Charity, Politeness, and Cheerfulness." Truth, respect, sincerity, humility, charity, politeness, and cheerfulness, all good in themselves, enable the priest to get along with his fellow priests and "fellow beings." These qualities will thereby permit them to be effective priests. Other chapters treat "Spirit of Poverty" and "Sacerdotal Chastity." The proper spirit of poverty leads the priest to a modest and balanced lifestyle, and chastity is proper to his calling. Gibbons warns that priests who pursue affluence will pay a price in loss of "public estimation," and "there is no vice which people more abhor, which they are less disposed to condone than clerical incontinence."[4]

Gibbons devotes eighteen chapters to the priest's acquisition of religious knowledge and the occasions for imparting that knowledge to others. His approach to seminary learning is largely anecdotal. His main point, directed to seminary educators, is that in American seminaries, a regimen of harsh discipline, surveillance, and distrust is not useful. He quotes Petrarch with approval: "The office of teacher was to inform the mind. He had no power to extinguish the flame of freedom, or break down the noble independence of the soul by the degrading application of the rod."[5] Gibbons commends the idea of the lifelong pursuit of learning in chapters entitled "Ambassador of Christ should be a Learned Man," "Personal Advantages and Blessings of a Studious Life," and "Persevering Labor, the

Key to Knowledge." He considers the priesthood as "pre-eminently one of the learned professions" and that there is "no spectacle more deplorable and humiliating to the Church, than that of an ignorant and torpid clergy."[6] He recommends that the priest devote at least an hour a day to study. First place among these studies is given to the Bible, but other branches of learning are accorded a place: dogmatic and moral theology, canon law, church history, and finally, Greek, Latin, and English classics.

In the essay on "The Study of Men and the Times," Gibbons recommends that after the Bible, "the study of mankind is the most important and instructive pursuit for the ambassador of Christ." His ideal is a "thorough knowledge of man, his springs of action, his yearnings and desires, his passions and emotions, his vices and temptations, and the arguments and motives, as well as the means that are best calculated to promote his spiritual progress." These are the first steps in fulfilling the aim of the priest's ministry "to enlighten and convince, to persuade and convert his fellow being, and to elevate him to a higher plane of moral rectitude." The choice of anecdotes and quotations gives evidence of wide reading in contemporary issues because as "the friend and father of the people" the priest "cannot be indifferent to any of the social, political, and economic questions affecting the interests and happiness of the nation."[7]

The priest as a man of general learning is thereby equipped for the functions of preaching and teaching. Gibbons recommends simple, direct, and undramatic sermons. The remote preparation for sermons "is the work of a whole life" that embraces "every department of knowledge."[8] The priest's function as an educator continues with the direction of the parish school, which he must supervise even though there may be sisters staffing it. The priest is also to engage in the work of instructing parish children. Gibbons commends a mild approach to their instruction, finding it useful in winning interest and affection.

Gibbons' contemporary, John Ireland, had pointed views on the model priest. As John Hogan recorded during a conversation at the Third Plenary Council of Baltimore, Ireland declared "what is needed is men *who know the period, the condition* of people's minds — the prevailing errors and the way to combat them and then good speakers — men . . . of refinement of thoughts and feelings — *gentlemen* that no man of education need to be ashamed to acknowledge as pastor."[9] The archbishop gave public expression to such views in his 1891 preface to Walter Elliot's biography of Isaac Hecker, in which Ireland designated the latter as the "the ornament, the flower of our American priesthood — the type that we wish to see reproduced among us in widest proportions." Ireland found in him "gifts of mind and heart that go to do great work for God and for souls in America at the present time."

Ireland believed in the particular pastoral needs of the United States, which many immigrant priests could not grasp. The latter "remained in heart and mind and mode of action as alien to America as if they had never been removed from the Shannon, the Loire, or the Rhine." Ireland singled out Hecker's stress on "natural and social virtues," which Americans especially esteemed. These virtues were "truthfulness, honesty in business dealings, loyalty to law and social order, temperance, respect for the rights of others." Without first cultivating these virtues, the American church would not be able to win respect for supernatural virtues. "An honest ballot and social decorum," Ireland declared, "will do more for God's glory and the salvation of souls than midnight flagellations or Compostellan pilgrimages."[10]

Ireland elaborated his views in talks to students of St. Paul's Seminary, according to the threefold characteristics of the priest as gentleman, scholar, and saint.

Ireland presumes the priest's duties as minister of sacraments and the explanation of the priest as a configuration of Christ. He endorses the accepted concepts of the priest's spirituality that would lead to personal holiness. He draws practical conclusions from these traditions as the priest manifests Christ by his social qualities, such as truthfulness. "Never for a moment," Ireland says, "think of defending the Church or anybody by a lie." The church is harmed by "equivocation and unfair arguments" because Americans prefer truth and fact. The priest's personal deportment, manners, courtesy, and dress are elements that manifest his identity with Christ. These qualities, good in themselves, have a dimension of pastoral effectiveness: "Remember you must cultivate courtesy if you wish a successful career." A natural courtesy permits the priest to fulfill his functions: "The priest must be able to enter with equal ease and politeness the cottage of the poor and the palace of the prince."[11]

Ireland gives detailed attention to the priest as scholar. His scholarship is that of the liberally educated, not the specialist. As a man of the nineteenth century, Ireland shows his fascination with the general advancement of knowledge and the diffusion of information to the public. "There never was an age in the world's history when intellect was so much admired as it is today, and in no country on the globe is it more appreciated and respected than in the United States." The priest should be conversant with many modern developments including scientific ones. Ireland stresses the importance of reading widely and taking notes on reading as a lifelong pursuit. "I like to see a young man with a passion for books, avaricious for books, who will spend his spare dollar in the purchase of them." There is a ministerial dimension to the pursuit of learning. "By taking in knowledge, he is ready to give it out" to Americans, whom Ireland believes, are impressed by knowledge. The priest, then, needs communications skills. "Good preaching and good writing are essential to draw the people and keep their attention and attendance."[12]

Bishop Bernard McQuaid repeated many themes of Gibbons and Ireland on the model priest through years of annual pastoral letters to raise funds for the seminary. His annual appeal provided the occasion for restating his views on the importance of training priests. On one occasion he stated:

> To meet the difficulties of such an age the church needs that her clergy should be equipped with depth and broadness of knowledge not limited to the ordinary text books of theological lore, but reaching out into the various roads traveled by the secularist and the scientific scholar. . . . We cannot shut our eyes to what is going on in the world, and in preparing our young men for the ministry, it is a duty to prepare them for the world as it is to-day.[13]

McQuaid was prompted to inform his flock on a number of occasions that in regard to priests: "The expectations of the laity are constantly on the rise." Or, the laity "are learning year by year to demand more and more of their priests." The bishop surely formed the laity to expect more from priests. These high expectations led him to state that "There is getting to be less and less room in the ministry for the slow and unintellectual."[14] As with other figures defining the model priest, intellectual qualities were not enough if the priest did not have communication skills: "the young priest should come out of the Seminary with some gift of speech and pleasant delivery. He is not expected to be a Bossuet, but he can be, and he should be, a well-trained speaker in his own vernacular, having clear ideas, orderly arranged and distinctly delivered."[15]

The practical and professional qualities of the model priest find a systematic treatment appropriate for seminary instruction in the two manuals of pastoral theology that appeared in the period. These were the first textbooks on the subject arising from the American experience of ministry. The authors, William Stang and Frederick Schulze, both German-born, were influenced by the rich German tradition of manuals of pastoral theology that had appeared regularly since the late eighteenth century. They cite these works in devoting over half of their books to basic instruction on the administration of sacraments within the context of national customs and American conciliar and synodal legislation. Beyond the sacraments, their treatment touches on the model priest's expanding pastoral activities in the American parish.

The first manual, *Pastoral Theology* by William Stang, appeared in 1896. The author was born in 1854 at Langenbrücken, Baden and received his seminary training at the American College at Louvain. In 1880 he arrived in the United States to take up ministry in the diocese of Providence. Because there were few Germans in Providence, Stang worked hard to master English free of accent and to adopt American ways. He returned to the American College at Louvain in 1895 to serve as vice rector and professor of pastoral theology. His students were mostly Europeans destined to arrive in the United States for the first time as priests ready for parish assignments. Stang produced a textbook for their instruction based on his own years of ministry.[16]

In his text Stang stresses the importance of the model priest as a spokesman for the church in the roles of preacher and teacher. He expects a good grounding in the fields of ecclesiastical learning pursued through life as a qualification for preaching. He describes several kinds of public addresses: sermons, homilies on Scripture texts, panegyrics of saints, and sermon series for Advent and Lent. He singles out "dogmatical sermons" as an "especial necessity" in the American atmosphere of sectarian competition in which Catholics needed to have their faith strengthened by arguments.[17] He is concerned about matters that should not be raised in American pulpits and developed a list of twenty-five propositions each beginning with an emphatic "*NEVER*." Some "nevers" are matters of common sense such as avoiding personal resentments, singling out individuals, and discussing complex theological ideas. Other "nevers" reflect a sensitivity to American conditions. Stang recommends that the priest refrain from: attacking American institutions, expressing preferences for other countries, personal attacks on Protestants, casting aspersions on the public schools, speaking on political candidates or issues, and condemning fashions in dress that continually change anyway. General characteristics were not to be ascribed to specific nationalities, such as "Germans are misers" or "Irish are drunkards."[18]

Stang outlines the priest's role as the official teacher of the parish. The pastor is considered responsible for the direction of the parochial school, even though women religious or lay people may actually staff it. In parishes where there is no school, of course, the priest is required to be the principal catechist of the parish. Stang's recommendations in the field of catechetics continue the moderation that he desired in sermons. Children are to be drawn to religious teaching, as Stang advises the priest catechist: "Often praise, never scold, seldom rebuke." The priest is never to give corporal punishment to children, since it is beneath his dignity.[19]

The second work, *Manual of Pastoral Theology* by Frederick Schulze, appeared in 1899. Schulze was born in 1855 at Paderborn, Prussia. He was educated at the University of Münster and received his seminary training at the American College at Louvain. After ordination in 1877, he was assigned to the diocese of Alton in southern Illinois, where he ministered to rural German Catholics. In 1886 he was appointed professor of moral theology at Milwaukee's St. Francis Seminary.[20] Schulze's experience in ministry and his career as a seminary educator kept him in close contact with the German-American community, its parish life, and its desire to preserve German culture. His students at Milwaukee were largely German Americans. His pastoral theology does not convey Stang's theme of adjusting to American culture. For instance, Schulze's brief and concise treatment of preaching assumes that the priest will most likely be speaking only to his own congregation. There is an absence of the varied and pointed instruction of Stang's model preacher who is a versatile spokesman for the church.

Nevertheless, Stang and Schulze shared a concern for the diverse functions of the priest in the parish. Their model priest has a range of functions as moderator of parish societies, administrator of the parish school, and parish treasurer. His duties occasionally require knowledgeability in banking, dealing with problems related to construction of buildings, and tactful handling of the sisters who staff the parish school. The model priest was also lord of the rectory. His lifestyle was to be dignified without being ostentatious. Dealings with the resident woman housekeeper had an importance for the priest's personal convenience at home and his reputation beyond the rectory. All of these functions beyond the ordinary tasks of ministry reflected the full development of parish life by the end of the century. The priest's professional skills and prudent handling of parish affairs were prerequisites for pastoral success and maintaining the confidence of his flock.

The qualities of the model priest naturally led to a consideration of the model seminary. In the 1890s two churchmen published extended considerations of the seminary. These figures, Bishop Camillus Maes and John Talbot Smith, who were not personally engaged in seminary education, nevertheless sought a seminary appropriate for producing the model priest.

Camillus Maes was born in Belgium in 1846 and was educated at the American College at Louvain. After ordination in 1869, he took up ministry in the diocese of Detroit before appointment as bishop of Covington, Kentucky in 1885. In a series of articles on the seminary appearing in the *American Ecclesiastical Review* in 1896, Maes outlines a model seminary program. He presupposes an active diocesan priest with varied ministerial tasks. Accordingly, the bishop did not want young seminarians to receive their early education in an atmosphere of seclusion from the world, but they should attend a college with nonclerical students.[21] The theological students were, however, to be in a seminary devoted exclusively to training for ministry. Maes's idea for the modern seminary reaffirms the Tridentine ideal of location at the cathedral. He preferred to have the seminary there so that the professors and seminarians could enrich its liturgical life. If the seminary could not be located there, it should be attached to a parish church. Whether at cathedral or parish, proximity to the life of an active congregation would "enable the reverend professors to practice what they teach." Maes, who remembered Belgian seminary professors who had little contact with practical ministry, hoped to provide for the seminary instructors' ongoing learning:

> The professors will have a chance to confer the sacraments to the people in full view of the seminarians; they will preach to a real flock in the presence of the young clerics who are only too anxious to learn how to reach the hearts of the people and how to break to them the word of God. The seminarians will, in turn, have an opportunity of taking their first steps in the work of the ministry under the vigilant eye of their teachers. [22]

Maes expected the model seminary to offer students greater personal liberty to come and go from the seminary. He had in mind the seminarians' preparation "for the life of self-reliance which most of our young priests have to face almost immediately after leaving the seminary." [23] For instance, Maes recommended two afternoons per week spent away from the seminary. One afternoon as well as Sunday mornings were to be devoted to catechetical instructions of children, a function that Maes believed to be an important part of a priest's training. Another afternoon should be spent away from the seminary in some cultural pursuit, such as visiting a museum or library, or even in visiting friends. He valued excursions into the country as a refreshing respite from the city. Maes recognized that freedom might occasionally be abused, but such abuses would soon be found out. He considered it better to learn before ordination if a seminarian could exercise self-restraint and, if necessary, have misbehavior corrected or have an incorrigible student dismissed. After ordination it would be difficult to control the behavior of an irresponsible priest.

John Talbot Smith provided a detailed look at the model priest and the model seminary from a perspective different from that either of a bishop or of a seminary educator. Born in 1855 at Saratoga, New York, Smith attended St. Michael's Seminary in Toronto and was ordained a priest for the diocese of Ogdensburg, New York in 1881. After several years of parish ministry in his diocese, Smith became increasingly absorbed in educational and literary work and by 1889 took up residence in New York City. His varied activities included teaching at the Catholic summer school at Cliff Haven, New York, writing histories of the diocese of Ogdensburg and the archdiocese of New York, producing essays of literary criticism and drama reviews. He was active in the Guild of Catholic Authors and Writers and in Catholic theater activities.[24]

As a seminary critic, Smith drew from his own experiences and observations for his book *Our Seminaries: An Essay on Clerical Training,* published in 1896. He modestly describes it as an inquiry into "means, methods, and standards," but the essay is in fact an extended critique of seminary education of the recent past and a program for reform of seminary education for diocesan priests.[25] Smith was aware of the new seminaries of Boston, New York, Rochester, and St. Paul and believed that old methods of clerical training should not be restarted in the new institutions. In considering the seminary, he first looks to the American context in which the priest practices ministry. He sees that the priest is obliged to be a Catholic spokesman before the non-Catholic public. The priest should have qualities of "spirit, ability, education and refinement" equal to that of the most educated and refined of the non-Catholic public. These qualities "would give him the right to teach, to speak with authority." While the priest is thereby intended for the "entire American nation," he is also sent to the Catholic community, or communities — since American Catholics were composed of a "conglomeration" of the Catholic nations of Europe. The priest is to have the charity, knowledge, and tact to deal with various peoples. Smith provides what he calls the "practical standard" for the diocesan priest in his role as the "immediate leader" of the people. This might be considered a concise definition of the model priest that American seminaries should be able to produce, that is, "an educated gentleman fitted for public life, physically sound, in sympathy with his environment, and imbued with the missionary spirit."[26]

Smith's model priest is effective in duties because of his personal behavior: "The priest who is to enjoy the fullest influence over all classes of citizens must have the manners, habits, and appearance of a gentleman." Producing an educated gentleman is in part the function of college training, but the education that Smith has in mind relates to ministry: "The love of study should be of the practical sort, not the mere love of books." The priest's studies should include the study of his surroundings, his people, the times, and "of the ways and means to reach and help them; and it sends us to our books more for men's sakes than for our own pleasure." The educated gentleman is to be fitted with the professional skills for public life. Smith demands that "he ought to be well trained for his role as a public man; and in this country special care should be used in fitting him for the position, because the demand for his appearance on the public platform and in public movements is certain to increase."[27]

Smith expects the priest to be physically sound. He recalls the unhealthy conditions of seminaries and the bad food of the past. He portrays the old seminary experience by describing a class of healthy, robust, cheerful youth entering the seminary and five years later leaving it "lean or worn" in appearance. He states that "it would be safe to say that fifty per cent of the newly ordained need nursing for months, and sometimes years, after ordination."[28]

Smith's ideal priest, as one "acquainted and in sympathy with his environment," is in part a reaction against immigrant priests who did not adapt to their new country. But he also finds fault with American priests who do not know their country for lack of attention to the subject in the seminary: "In the seminaries it has never been heard of that a particular study is made of the institutions of the nation, of the prejudices of the people, of their likes and dislikes, of their national sentiments and hatreds." He hopes instead for "knowledge of the American nation and intelligent sympathy with it."[29]

Smith defines the "true missionary spirit" as that of the "true disciple of Christ, ready for any sacrifice, any labor, any hardship." He fears the presence of careerists who enter the priesthood for the opportunities for self-advancement it affords, in other words, priests "who can see their own future in the successive degrees of promotion and salary, and plan how they may shorten the road to the top rank."[30]

Smith and Maes enjoyed the liberty of proposing ideas for publication without being responsible for implementing them. Maes's diocese was too small to sponsor a seminary, and his articles did not launch a movement to relocate seminaries at cathedrals. Smith's outline of the model priest corresponded to the views of other churchmen who thought about the seminary. His extensive views on seminary life and clerical learning follow in due course. Smith struck responsive chords among several readers. From Rochester, McQuaid told him: "You and I are so much of the [same] mind that up here the remark is common that in your book you are only putting in print what we have in practice in St. Bernard's." The rector of St. Paul Seminary reported to Smith that the book was read aloud at meals, and the students often commented: "The author must have had St. Paul Seminary in mind when he wrote his book."[31]

The model priest outlined in the views of Gibbons, Ireland, McQuaid, Stang, Schulze, Maes, and Smith is engaged in the practical tasks of ministry in the United States, though the emphasis varies. Gibbons and Ireland stressed the importance of honesty, truthfulness, courtesy, and civility for priests, thereby implying that these qualities had heretofore been lacking. Gibbons, Ireland, McQuaid, and Smith expected broad learning and communications skills. Except for Stang and Schulze, the figures generally presumed the model priest's role as minister of sacraments without much mention of it. But all addressed the varying tasks of a priest's life that require the development of professional skills, especially preaching and teaching. They were concerned about the reaction among Catholics to the quality of the priest's ministerial skills. All urged continuing professional learning.

The American churchmen defined the professional qualities of the model priest at a time when there was great concern over the current challenges to the supernatural premises of Catholicism. Within the English-speaking world, Cardinal Henry Manning, Archbishop of Westminster, was a leading figure in reaffirming and defending all aspects of Catholic tradition. In 1883 Manning published *The Eternal Priesthood*, which circulated widely in American rectories and seminaries. His study, intended as devotional reading for priests and seminarians, is an apologetical exposition of the inherited Tridentine theology of the priesthood as directly instituted by Christ, theologically unchanged through the centuries, and highly supernatural. Manning's model priest achieves a high degree of holiness that leaves him virtually detached from the world. The priest's ministry imparts sanctification to the faithful. The author's exhortations on the practical aspects of ministry have an abstract quality about them; they could be applicable to any time or place and are stated with a few contemporary examples.[32] Manning's influential volume provides a striking contrast to the practical spirit of the American approach to the priesthood.

These delineations of the new model priest correspond to developments in the seminary. Changing emphases were most noticeable at the new seminaries of Boston, New York, Rochester, and St. Paul, where local traditions of clerical formation were just being started. But at first glance the internal life of the diocesan seminary, whether at old or new seminaries, continued inherited practices of personal formation. All American seminaries of the period adhered to the classic purpose of forming priests who were models of holiness. The routine of spiritual exercises and the discipline of community life were directed to that end. The school year opened with a spiritual retreat. Through the rest of the year the daily routine consisted of community exercises of prayer, Mass, meditation, personal examen, visits to the Blessed Sacrament, periods of silence, rosary, and spiritual reading. The weekday schedule or "horarium" of Kenrick Seminary in St. Louis was typical of seminaries of the period:[33]

A.M.   5:00 Rising
        5:20 Morning Prayer and Meditation
        5:50 Mass
        6:25 Study

7:00 Breakfast — Recreation
7:45 Study
9:00 Class
10:00 Study
11:00 Class
11:45 New Testament Reading, Particular Examen
12:00 Lunch — Recreation

P.M. 1:30 Study
3:30 Class
4:30 Recreation
5:00 Visit to the Blessed Sacrament
5:15 Study
5:45 Class
6:25 Spiritual Reading
6:45 Rosary, Examen
7:00 Dinner
8:30 Evening Prayer
9:00 Retire followed by lights out

Classes and study were not scheduled on Wednesday afternoon at Kenrick to provide a block of recreation time in midweek. Most seminaries had one or two free afternoons during the week to provide some free time, since Saturdays were class and study days. The Sunday schedule at Kenrick provided the same times of rising, prayers, and meals, but included solemn High Mass at 9:30 A.M., followed by plain chant class; at 3:00 P.M. sung Vespers and Benediction of the Blessed Sacrament was conducted, followed by an "Academy" meeting at which students presented papers on theological or literary topics. Sundays did not provide a large block of free time. Modifications of the basic schedule were constantly being made at the Sulpician seminaries. Bedtime was delayed, as Alphonse Magnien explained to Sulpician authorities, because Americans seldom retire before 10:00 P.M.[34] Most seminaries served the evening meal earlier than Kenrick to provide an evening study period.

Seminarians were ordinarily expected to confess their sins once a week to their personal confessor, who was available for personal counselling. The seminarians generally received Holy Communion on Sundays and on major feast days, until 1907, when the movement for the frequent reception of Holy Communion altered the older traditions. There was the spiritual retreat of several days at the beginning of the academic year, and another retreat preceded ordination to minor and major orders.

Community living was imposed on all in an environment that excluded ordinary contact with those who were not priests or seminarians. The physical setting of the great freestanding diocesan seminaries on ample property that assured a separation from their surroundings reinforced the exclusiveness of the seminary. The priest faculty lived in the seminary with the students and served as role models of clerical conduct. The seminary was therefore overwhelmingly male in its orientation. However, women other than visiting relatives of priests and seminarians were an important presence at most seminaries. The feminine influence was maintained by hiring a community of sisters to take charge of the seminary kitchen and laundry. Many such sisters were devoted to domestic service of priests as a vocation and were therefore very traditional in their view of women's roles. The regular contact of seminarians with sisters as domestics naturally informed their attitudes toward women.[35]

The occasions for leaving the seminary grounds were carefully chosen. At Sulpician seminaries and several others, seminarians spent the Christmas and Easter holidays at the seminary. Their stay afforded seminarians the opportunity to assist at the lengthy and solemn liturgical ceremonies of these holy days and to participate in the accompanying personal devotional exercises. Staying at the seminary kept them from the secular amusements associated with these holidays, but they were usually allowed a mid-year holiday in January. The separation of the seminary from the life of the cathedral was bridged at several seminaries by having seminarians assist at liturgical exercises there. The St. Paul and Rochester seminaries were on the streetcar line to the city's cathedral. Bishop McQuaid had the sanctuary of the Rochester cathedral enlarged and remodeled to provide seating for seminarians, so that half the student body could participate in High Mass on alternate Sundays.[36] They were available to assist at other solemn functions there. St. Mary's Seminary was within easy walking distance to the Baltimore cathedral, and the seminary community there continued to assist at the major liturgical and ceremonial occasions at which Cardinal Gibbons presided. Thus the tradition of relating the seminary to the cathedral could at times be maintained.

Inside the seminary, clerical decorum prescribed the wearing of the cassock as the ordinary household garment. Periods of silence were observed usually from evening prayers to breakfast. Seminarians were forbidden to visit each other in their rooms. Smoking was banned at most seminaries for ascetic and health reasons. St. Mary's Seminary permitted smoking at limited times outdoors as a compromise to keep it under control. St. Joseph Seminary at Yonkers banned smoking, but, it was admitted, the students found the ban difficult to understand.[37]

Drinking was strictly prohibited at all seminaries. Possessing alcohol or returning to the seminary drunk were grounds for expulsion. Seminary educators and their students were influenced by the high tide of the "Hibernian Crusade" against alcohol carried on by the Catholic Total Abstinence Union during the 1890s. Members of the union pledged not to drink and participated in the organized work of spreading total abstinence. Affiliates of the union were organized in Mount St. Mary's Seminary at Emmitsburg and St. Mary's Seminary at Baltimore as early as 1884. Though Germans generally avoided the movement, the leadership of a German-American priest from Cincinnati, Anthony Siebenfoercher, was the catalyst for developing the union in colleges and seminaries.[38] By 1904, affiliates were established at Kenrick Seminary, St. Mary's Seminary in Cleveland, St. Paul Seminary, Mount St. Mary's of the West, St. Charles, Our Lady of the Angels, and Immaculate Conception in New Jersey.[39]

Seminarians pursued the highly structured routine of the spiritual life, which was not accorded the attention to reform that was given to other aspects of seminary life. As McQuaid stated,

> Little need be said on the spiritual life of the seminary. All bishops, all superiors, are of one mind on this point. The exercises of piety are much the same in all. Exactness in assisting at them is insisted on. They sanctify the day, and habituate the student to devotional practices and duty.[40]

In fact, John Talbot Smith found that in developing a spiritual life too much was "taken for granted" so that in the college or minor seminary careful instruction in methods of mental prayer and ascetical theology was not given. By the time the student came to the major seminary, it was assumed that the fundamentals of spirituality were already known when in fact they were not.[41]

The literature on spirituality was derived from Europe. Smith deplored the lack of attention of American priests to writing spiritual literature for Americans; "we go to England for our English spiritual writers, and eke out their store by translations from the European tongues. How low is the tide of original thought in our seminaries. . . ."[42] Smith was wary of Continental masters. He felt that Rodriguez's *Christian Perfection* could be mentioned with respect "provided that an order be issued against reading him." The *Spiritual Exercises* of St. Ignatius Loyola was to be "kept from students." And Butler's *Lives of the Saints* made sainthood undesirable. Smith recommended recent biographies of Philip Neri, Francis de Sales, Vincent de Paul, and John Vianney, and proposed that spiritual life should begin with the writings of Manning, Wiseman, Newman, Faber, and Hedley.[43] Stang recommended the classics, *The Imitation of Christ* by Thomas à Kempis, *Introduction to the Devout Life* by St.

Francis de Sales, Scupoli's *Spiritual Combat*, and the works of Frederick Faber: *Growth in Holiness, All for Jesus*, and *The Blessed Sacrament*.[44] These works were classics, but they spoke from various times and several approaches. This literature was applicable to vowed religious and pious lay people and did not pertain directly to the priesthood. There was a lack of literature directed to preparing seminarians for the priesthood. In 1900 Francis Nugent, the rector of Kenrick Seminary, was surprised to discover after writing to Vincentian confreres in Paris that there were no published books of conferences, manuals of meditations, or spiritual readings in the Vincentian tradition for seminarians.[45] John Hogan's *Daily Thoughts for Priests*, published in 1899, provided short meditations on the Beatitudes and the virtues.[46]

As the traditions of seminary spirituality were maintained, American seminaries shared in the popular devotional practices that were widespread in the late nineteenth century. The recitation of the rosary had long been the daily minimum requirement for Marian piety in seminaries. This devotion received stronger official endorsement as Pope Leo XIII sought to strengthen Marian piety by issuing eleven encyclicals on the rosary—eight appeared in succeeding years from 1891 to 1898. Rosary confraternities were a favored means of promoting Marian piety, since members earned additional indulgences through the daily rosary and prescribed prayers. Pope Leo issued encyclicals on devotion to St. Joseph in 1889, on the Holy Spirit in 1897, and the Sacred Heart of Jesus in 1899. These exhortations usually provided an organized approach in order to strengthen devotion, such as a confraternity and indulgences. New indulgences were attached to prayers to St. Joseph, to public novenas to the Holy Spirit preceding Pentecost, and for the firmly established Sacred Heart devotion with its characteristic act of consecration. The pope approved a new constitution for the Apostleship of Prayer, the organizational arm of the Sacred Heart devotion, which was directed by the Society of Jesus. Pope Leo consecrated the world to the Sacred Heart in 1900; his successor did the same annually.[47]

American seminarians shared avidly in these devotions. At the visitation of the Boston seminary in 1886, the minutes recorded that the students practiced the devotions that were popular among their pious, Irish-American families. The "principal devotion" was to the Sacred Heart, though the students' approach to the devotion was described as vague and based heavily on sentiment.[48] In the 1896 visitation at Boston, the minutes recorded a seasonal rhythm of Marian devotions with the rosary during May, Sacred Heart in June, St. Joseph in March, and devotions on behalf of the souls in purgatory in November.[49] At the 1904 visitation at St. Joseph Seminary in New York devotions to the Blessed Sacrament and the

Sacred Heart were described as "dear" to the seminarians, with first Friday devotions in honor of the Sacred Heart and exposition of the Blessed Sacrament. Many seminarians also made the "Way of the Cross" as they prepared for their weekly confession.[50] St. Paul Seminary encouraged seminarians to join the seminary units of the Sodality of the Blessed Virgin, the Eucharistic League, and the Propagation of the Faith.[51]

The visits for a short period of mental prayer before the reserved Blessed Sacrament had long been a tradition in seminaries. Eucharistic devotion outside of Mass developed strongly through the period, again with the highest official endorsement. The devotional forms in Europe included public exposition of the Blessed Sacrament for devotions and the convening of diocesan, national, and international Eucharistic congresses. Pope Leo enthusiastically sanctioned this movement in his encyclical *Mirae Caritatis* in 1902, in which he recommended Eucharistic confraternities, devotions before the Blessed Sacrament, processions and congresses, and frequent communion. The greatest successes of the Eucharistic movement came in the first decade of the twentieth century with the endorsement of Pope Pius X, who issued a series of decrees, letters, and exhortations between 1905 and 1907 that resolved the previously controverted issue of the conditions for the reception of communion. The Holy See came down decisively in favor of viewing communion not as a reward for virtue but as an aid to acquiring it. The pope thus endorsed the practice of frequent, even daily, communion, and in his 1910 *motu proprio* decree, *Quam Singulari*, lowered the age for first communion for children.[52] The seminary followed the trend toward frequent communion. At most seminaries, weekly communion had been hitherto encouraged, then communion at daily Mass became the normal practice.

One of the organizational arms of Eucharistic activity was a new community of priests, the Society of the Blessed Sacrament, founded in France by Julien Eymard in 1856. The society emphasized the various devotions to the Eucharist outside of Mass. One of their activities was the Priests' Eucharistic League, sanctioned by the Holy See in 1887, which enlisted diocesan priests to make a private hour of adoration before the Blessed Sacrament once a week. The League sponsored diocesan meetings of members to organize the spread of the devotion and assisted in advancing the convening of Eucharistic congresses. The movement attracted the interest of Bede Maler, a Benedictine priest who taught dogmatic theology at St. Meinrad Seminary. Maler began to organize the League at first in the Midwest in the 1890s and served as its first director general in the United States. Accordingly, St. Meinrad Seminary had the first seminary Eucharistic Association, organized in 1894. The League's leading episcopal supporters were Maes of Covington (who was its longtime episcopal "protector"), Elder of Cincinnati, and John Kain of St. Louis. Seminary associations were soon formed at Mount St. Mary's of the West of Cincinnati, Kenrick Seminary in St. Louis, and St. Francis Seminary in Milwaukee.[53] The seminary members were required to perform the same weekly hour of prayer before the Blessed Sacrament as priest members. The membership lists of the 1890s indicate a large number of seminary faculty members and members of the hierarchy. Following the League's first national convention at Notre Dame in 1894, diocesan conventions of the League were held around the country. These events attracted substantial numbers of bishops and clergy after the 1890s.[54]

A contemporary movement of somewhat limited influence was directed to devotion to the Holy Spirit. Cardinal Henry Manning of Westminster promoted this movement in the English-speaking world. His approach was directed to animating the Catholic faithful to devotion to the Holy Spirit as the means of binding the devout more closely to obedience to the church's leadership. With approval of the Holy See, he founded the Confraternity of the Servants of the Holy Ghost with regular devotional practices and indulgenced prayers. A leading American exponent of devotion to the Holy Spirit, Isaac Hecker, whose mentality was informed by republican political culture, took a different approach. He stressed devotion to the Holy Spirit as a means of personal union with God and to animate all to work for regeneration of church and society.[55]

Hecker's chief follower, Bishop John Keane, formalized devotion to the Holy Spirit with a confraternity in the parishes of his diocese of Richmond. The influence of Hecker and Keane was evident in the decree of the Third Plenary Council of Baltimore that related devotion to the Holy Spirit to the formation of priests:

> Finally, since it would be idle to hope that those who are raised up to the apostolic ministry will be worthy of their holy calling unless they have within themselves, live and are moved by, and work through the ecclesiastical spirit, which is a certain abounding or copious partaking of the spirit of Christ, let devotion to the Holy Ghost be cultivated continually and fervently in the seminaries, so that the Spirit of Christ the High Priest may enter into the clerics, abide in them, and operate in them. For this reason we commend the propagation in the seminaries of the Confraternity of the Servants of the Holy Ghost, which confraternity has already been approved by the Holy See.[56]

The Holy Spirit devotion had been introduced in 1883 at St. Francis Seminary at Milwaukee by its professor of dogmatic theology, Otto Zardetti, who had been strongly influenced by Cardinal Manning's approach.

With the approval of Archbishop Michael Heiss, Zardetti formed a Confraternity of the Servants of the Holy Ghost at the seminary and had it affiliated with Manning's confraternity. Members of the confraternity had prescribed prayers through the year, a monthly votive mass of the Holy Spirit, an annual novena consisting of nine days of devotional prayer preceding the feast of Pentecost, and a program of addresses and declamations on Pentecost Sunday.[57] The confraternity flourished at St. Francis Seminary until 1921. The devotion was established at St. Vincent Seminary at Latrobe, Pennsylvania, where it lasted from 1887 to 1901, but the idea of specific devotional activity on behalf of Holy Spirit to comply with the conciliar decree did not spread to other seminaries during the period.[58]

The seminarian ordinarily received the major orders of subdiaconate and diaconate in the last year or six months before ordination to the priesthood. The reception of major orders imposed the obligation of the daily recitation of the "office" or "breviary," that is, the liturgy of the hours that was recited or chanted in common in monastic orders. The office was recited by seminarians in major orders privately, just as they would normally do as diocesan priests for the remainder of their lives. Parts of the liturgy of the hours were occasionally recited or chanted in common, such as vespers on Sundays and major feast days, and matins and lauds on Christmas and Easter. However, the official and originally public liturgy of the hours was a private devotion for clerics in major orders.

Through the period 1884 to 1910 the spiritual exercises of the seminary expanded in an increasingly diffuse fashion. Some aspects were part of the heritage of the seventeenth century, such as meditation, personal examen, visits to the reserved Sacrament, and the practice of close spiritual direction from a personal confessor. The official liturgy played an essential role with the daily Mass which was attended in common, but the liturgy of the hours had become a private devotion. The private and extraliturgical rosary had long been practiced in seminaries, and, depending on local custom, it was prayed privately or in common. The contemporary trend of popular devotions was intensified. Many of these essentially private devotions were practiced in common. The range of practices did not relate directly to the priesthood. They did not provide a coherent and unified approach to cultivating personal holiness, but this eclectic situation was apparently not questioned.

The record of how well seminarians' spiritual qualities were developed is fragmentary at best. At St. John's Seminary at Boston the faculty reported on the difficulty of personal spiritual direction because the largely Irish-American students of New England were very reticent.[59] The students opened up only under questioning. The same problem was not reported at St. Mary's Seminary at Baltimore, whose student body came from across the country. The minutes of the official visitation of the Baltimore seminary conducted in 1896 by the Sulpician superior general, Artur Captier, provide a general evaluation of a large group:

> The young men consider as important the fundamental habits of devotion common to all the faithful; they take easily to frequenting the sacraments, and seem to have conscientious dispositions towards them. However, rarely do the principles of their faith and their devotional practices bring them all the conclusions and all the fruit which engender the spirit and habits of interior life to the degree which is considered normal in priests. They take seriously their duty properly so-called, their obligation in conscience, but, in general, do not worry too much about what is suggested to them along the lines of counsel and perfection.

The more conscientious seminarians were found to cultivate virtues such as charity, however, even they did not have "a mind open to the fine points of mortification or recollection." As for mental prayer, reflection on practical virtues and prayers of petition were "more accessible" to their minds than "the contemplative and affective acts of devotion." The faculty reported to Captier that the students "attend mental prayer regularly when they are checked on it. Spiritual profit is doubtful for a large number of students." Also for many the recitation of the rosary was outwardly regular, but "there are few signs of real devotion." Captier responded to the evaluation by urging renewed efforts "to develop, along the lines of priestly virtues found in the young men, and the fundamental devotions that they accept whole-heartedly."[60] He recommended the need to develop a method of mental prayer adaptable to the mentality of the seminarians.

The minutes of Sulpician seminaries reflect a synthesis of faculty views. In contrast, Francis Havey, a Sulpician at St. John's Seminary, offered an interpretation of seminary life from his own rigorist perspective in observations made about 1899. He objected to two attitudes prevalent in the seminary: (1) "that the Seminary is not adjusted to the particular needs of the American church and that some of its traditional spiritual exercises are of little utility to the American priest" and (2) that seminarians saw a "manly" character as "the summit of personal perfection." The characteristics of manliness were described as "independence of character, jealously of restraint on personal liberty, and a disposition to follow reason rather than authority, and tends, also, to disparage the Christian, crucifying virtues."[61]

Modest adaptations of seminary life to American values, despite the strictures of Havey and those of similar mind, were in fact implemented at several seminaries. The seminary decree of the Third Plenary Council of Baltimore itself suggested a moderate approach to the traditional seminary regimen:

> Let the discipline of regulating the whole course of life in the seminary be so arranged that it may savor neither of excessive rigor nor indulge pernicious laxity. The vigilance of superiors should be so tempered and moderated in maintaining it that it will not pry too closely into minute details, nor so hamper the minds of youth, as it were with chains, as to impede the normal expansion of their energies.[62]

Several observers saw the value of a positive approach to seminary discipline. They questioned a regimen of harshly applied rules and surveillance that presumed the seminarians would never behave unless watched. McQuaid believed the American seminarian "the most readily amenable to discipline, to a discipline that appeals to his good sense, and which has been reasonably placed before him." He recognized the influence of American culture in informing this approach:

> His [the American seminarian's] schooling in the political thought and methods of the country teaches submission to the law, once it is law. He dislikes coercion, except the coercion of a manly compliance with rule and order. He cannot abide, nor should he, the faintest suspicion of espionage. His best feelings revolt at the thought. It puts him on a par with a convict, or an unprincipled schemer. The honest man chafes under the system, and the dishonest man sets himself to get the better of the watcher.[63]

Likewise, Alphonse Magnien explained to Sulpician authorities in Paris the adaptations of seminary discipline that were necessary in Baltimore when he was faced with suspicions of laxity on the part of the rigorous Sulpicians at Montreal, where unbending French traditions held sway. Magnien stated:

> it would be a wrong method to follow with the young men of the United States if predominance were given to severity in discipline [as was the case in Canada]. A certain element of fear must be present: the seminarians [in the United States] must realize that there are certain limits beyond which they may not go without being punished: their mentality accepts a reasonable firmness, even when it affects them. . . . But once these basic principles are established, there must not be too much repression towards these young men. They have a taste for freedom and are used to it: appealing to their reason, their

conscience and their heart is the means to teach them gradually how
to use that freedom responsibly and to be able to give up some of
it in matters required by our Rules. . . . Kindness toward them is quite
fruitful, and they are sensitive to what we may do to please them.
Finally, treating them with a broad mind and trust, we have the great
advantage of seeing them open to us, and thus letting us know them
as they really are. On the contrary a supervision filled with anxiety
and suspicion would put them on their guard: they might make efforts
to circumvent it, and they would succeed. Once their hearts are closed
to us, we might lose any solitary influence we might have over them.[64]

The minutes of the 1896 visitation reported the feelings of openness that
the students had toward the largely French faculty. The evidence of mutual trust contrasts with the distance between students and faculty reported
in the visitation of 1875 and can be attributed to Magnien's moderation.

The adaptations of the seminary's internal life took cognizance of
the seminarian's health and personal development. Modern buildings at
the new seminaries provided more personal comfort, McQuaid finds, "as
favoring intellectual progress along with physical growth and development."[65] These improvements moved away from the ascetic mentality of
the past that Smith describes as "it was often regarded as a sin against
the spirit to complain of cold rooms, bad food, poor hospital treatment,
long kneeling at prayers, and other violations of the rules of health and
common sense."[66]

A notable concern for physical exercise emerged through the period
as it became apparent that more varied forms of exercise were needed than
the traditional chaperoned walks of the seminary community once a week.
Provisions were made for physical exercise at new seminaries. At St. Paul
Seminary, the gymnasium was described as "fully equipped" and "furnish-
ing the young men with every variety of means for taking healthful exercise" throughout the year.[67] At Rochester, McQuaid relied on the tradition
of the group walk two afternoons per week, when the seminary community hiked six to nine miles to a designated point and back without supervision. For the long winters, he provided a gymnasium of fifteen thousand
square feet with sets of exercise apparatus and two bowling alleys.[68]

Smith proposed that exercise should not be left to individual initiative but that each student should be given a physical examination and the
seminary's "physical instructor" should prescribe a method of exercise appropriate to the students. All should attend classes of exercise: "the
seminarians are to attend the gymnasium as they would a class in dogma."
Lectures in hygiene and personal health should be a part of the gymnasium
class. After exercise courses of five or six years, Smith believed that the

seminarians would then have what a West Point cadet enjoyed: " fine vitality, sound health, a graceful body, and a graceful carriage. . . ."[69]

Charles Rex, who was to die of tuberculosis himself, was concerned about exercise as rector of St. John's. He hired a "gymnastic instructor" who came out to the seminary between December and Easter and "for a good half hour or more puts our young men through a course of exercises."[70] For the rest of the school year Rex modified the Sulpicians' chaperoned walks of the seminary community in the neighborhood. He introduced walks in small groups as a move away from the regimented walk that he regarded as a humiliation to Americans, since it made it appear that they could not be trusted to walk on their own.[71]

The strong desire to have the model priest well informed about contemporary issues through wide reading was evident in providing the means for general reading. The seminary library was presumed to be devoted to books related to theological subjects; a separate "reading room" was introduced at several seminaries, beginning at Baltimore, and merited Smith's endorsement. His idea of a reading room was a

> gracious apartment, lofty, lightsome, quiet, comfortable; on its bookshelves must be found the best books of the month and the year,— selected solely with the view of illustrating the temper and condition of the times,— from the latest novel to the latest essay. . . . Every representative review of Europe and America will have its place on the reading-table, and ten of the best dailies from five leading cities of the land along with them. . . .[72]

Charles Rex established such a reading room at St. John's for his students. It contained the usual range of Catholic periodicals, some of which, he found, "are not good for much." In addition to the newspapers he had a range of secular journals and the "four great English Reviews—Contemporary, Fortnightly, Westminster, & Nineteenth Century."[73]

Such innovations as providing a reading room and varied opportunities for exercise were a departure from the conservative approach of keeping the seminarians' minds fixed on the supernatural. That these reforms were novel was demonstrated by the reaction of Louis Colin, the strait-laced rector of the Sulpician seminary at Montreal, who visited St. John's Seminary in 1892. Rex escorted Colin on a tour of the seminary and made a point of showing off the exercise class in progress. In silence Colin observed the seminarians exercising not wearing their cassock. He overcame his surprise long enough to remark politely: "After all, there's nothing in all that against the natural law." When brought to the reading room, Colin's surprise was even greater as he exclaimed: "But you don't permit them to read newspapers?" Rex replied that he did and swiftly added: "After all, *Monsieur le Superieur*, there's nothing in all that against the natural law."[74] An argument ensued.

The opportunities for developing the professional skills of the future priest took on various other forms. The timeless custom in Catholic monasteries, convents, and seminaries of public reading during meals, while hearers dined in silence, was generally followed in the United States. Many seminary reformers used the table reading to have books of intellectual substance read to the seminarians instead of devotional fare. Works of church history were favored at the Sulpician seminaries. McQuaid deplored this custom even to advance contemporary reading and did not permit table reading at St. Bernard's. He regarded practice in the art of conversation as important to the future priest.[75]

The seminaries sought to provide pastoral experience in various ways. At St. Mary's Seminary a program of visiting hospitals and poor houses for an hour and a half one afternoon per week began in 1894 and were formalized under the name Association of St. Camillus. In these visits seminarians sought "by friendly conversations and kindly acts to acquire over the individual such a strong personal influence as may be exerted for his or her real good and happiness." These were nonsectarian institutions, and seminarians made no attempt to proselytize or to supplant the work of chaplains. Its value lay in teaching the student "how to console, cheer, and judiciously aid the needy; its enkindles within his breast love for the poor and ready sympathy for the afflicted."[76] A St. Camillus Association was also established at St. John's Seminary in Brighton. And at St. Joseph's Seminary at New York an affiliate of the St. Vincent de Paul Society was formed that coordinated a program of visits to charitable institutions with catechetical instruction on Sundays.[77]

The implementation of the reform of the seminary did not take place in isolation from trends in the life of the universal Catholic church. The adaptations of the American church to aspects of contemporary life attracted the interest of progressive Catholics in Europe. In particular, the separation of the church from the state in the United States required the Catholic church to rely solely on the voluntary support of the laity. Union of church and state was the Catholic political ideal that church authority upheld in Europe.

The American priest Isaac Hecker was a figure who attracted the interest of progressive Catholics in Europe. Walter Elliot's biography of Hecker as translated into French by Abbé Felix Klein portrayed Hecker as one who was attuned to modern science and who, in Gerald Fogarty's words, "based his spirituality on the interior direction of the Holy Spirit, and who responded to the active virtues which produced the new saints of the marketplace rather than to the passive virtues which produced monks and hermits."[78]

The publication of Klein's translation of the Hecker biography produced a sharp reaction from the Holy See. In 1898 Pope Leo XIII issued an apostolic letter to the Archbishop of Baltimore with the ironic title *Testem Benevolentiae*, that is, "Testament of Benevolence," in which Hecker's views were summarized and then condemned as the heresy of "Americanism." The pope states his interpretation of the concept:

> The principles of which the new opinions we have mentioned may be reduced to [are] this, that, in order the more easily to bring over to Catholic doctrine those who dissent from it, the Church ought to adapt herself somewhat to our advanced civilization, and, relaxing her ancient rigor, show some indulgence to modern popular theories and methods. Many think that this is to be understood not only with regard to the rule of life, but also to the doctrines in which the *deposit of faith* is contained.[79]

The Roman pontiff finds the approach advocated by those who embrace Americanism "reprehensible." He admits that while the Church constantly maintains the "same doctrine," it occasionally makes adjustments in the rule of life so as not to disregard "the manners and customs of the various nations which it embraces. If required for the salvation of souls, who will doubt that it [the Church] is ready to do so at the present time?" But the supreme authority of the church was to determine the adjustments, not individuals. At the heart of the pope's objections was his admonition "natural virtues [are] not to be extolled above supernatural." The supernatural was to be placed above the active. Thus the interior life of prayer and personal sanctification was superior to the cultivation of qualities for a life of virtuous action. Many progressive American churchmen did not agree with the pope that the ideas condemned under the title "Americanism" actually existed in the United States in a way the pope defined them. They considered "Americanism" a phantom heresy that largely existed in the minds of fearful European churchmen.[80] Nevertheless, it is clear that the American tendency for the pragmatic in church life was under fire.

Pope Leo XIII's *Testem Benevolentiae* did not relate directly to the life of priests or to clerical formation in the United States. But the letter spoke to some widespread fears that supernatural virtues were threatened by the example of American ways. For instance, John Talbot Smith describes the impression that American priests sometimes left: "It may be of interest to American priests to know that their brethren of France and Quebec look upon them as anything but a credit to the sacerdotal order, refer to them as Protestant priests, and take our free manners and fondness for unconventional costume as evidence of low morality."[81] John Ireland delineates the difference between Continental and American priests by relating the story of the "good old priest, who said his beads well and made a desert around his pulpit by miserable preaching." The old priest had criticized Hecker for putting "too much reliance in man, and not enough on God." Ireland declares that the priest had thousands of counterparts in Europe and America who were "more than half willing to see in all outputtings of human energy a lack of confidence in God."[82] Peter Guilday, as a seminarian at the American College at Louvain in 1908, recorded the negative perception of spiritual life in America made by a conservative Jesuit who gave the college's retreat in 1908. The Jesuit made a "violent attack upon America, calling the people to whom we were to preach the word of God, barbarians, pagans, uncivilized, and pigs."[83] Timothy Holland, a young priest of the diocese of Ogdensburg, joined the Society of St. Sulpice in 1904 and made the required year of novitiate or "Solitude" in France. Holland received strong negative impressions of French Catholic life during his year in France. He objected to carrying on the artificiality in religion that he traced to reforms based on the artificiality of the seventeenth century. "The result is an *un*natural religion which they take for a *super*natural one — a piety that tends toward effeminacy and becomes insipid." The priests were "prudish old women." He found fault that they "whined over meditations and examinations of conscience etc. in the sacristy when they should be at work among the people."[84]

When faced with suspicions of French superiors that traditional aspects of seminary life were not sufficiently observed in America, American Sulpicians often had to adopt a defensive stance. Edward R. Dyer said of the Sulpician superior general, Henri Icard: "The old gentleman, I think, has got it pretty well into his mind that there is very little of the esprit surnaturel in the American ecclesiastic."[85] The differences between the traditional French seminary ways, with stress on the supernatural, are not easy to define. The American tendency to stress the practical is not a sufficient answer, since the French, too, had to deal with practical affairs. Charles Rex struggled to come up with an interpretation of how the American approach differed from the French. He described to Dyer his lack of success in interpreting the issue:

> I would willingly enough write down my ideas about the American spirit in our work. But I hardly know where to begin. Indeed, it has always been with me more a matter of instinct . . . than of reflected & reasoned principle, so much so that at the beginning I could not fully understand all that people said about the difference between the French and the American spirit. I suppose my ideas must have been on my mind, but they were not evoluted, not developed

& and made conscious to me. Later on, when I had to deal with cases and situations myself, I did what common sense & good feeling seemed to suggest, and then, upon reflection, I often saw that I had acted more or less otherwise than a Frenchman might have done.[86]

The differences between European and American approaches to seminary life and ministry may be difficult to define. But the differences were regarded as posing a challenge. From the traditionalist viewpoint, the supernatural was under attack in the United States. As the Sulpician Francis Havey believed, "It is very hard to live up to supernatural views of life, seeing that materialism and naturalism are identified with the glory of the country."[87]

By the early twentieth century, the official stress on the supernatural was ascendant, as demonstrated by the emphasis on popular devotional activity. Leo XIII's successor, Pope Pius X, extended these concerns specifically to the spiritual and devotional dimensions of priests. On the occasion of his fiftieth anniversary of ordination in 1908, Pius X issued a lengthy apostolic exhortation on the priesthood entitled *Haerent animo*. The pope did not intend to state anything that had not already been heard, but he aimed to call attention to the priest's obligation of personal sanctification. The importance assigned to supernatural virtues was clear:

> There are some who think, and even declare openly, that the true measure of the merits of a priest is his dedication to the service of others; consequently, with an almost complete disregard for the cultivation of the virtues which lead to the personal sanctification of the priest (these they describe as passive virtues), they assert that all his energies and fervour should be directed to the development and practice of the *active* virtues. One can only be astonished by this gravely erroneous and pernicious teaching.

The pope designates the priest's daily offering of the Mass, the "great sacrifice," as the starting point of holiness, for which "we [priests] have the duty of conforming our minds to that spirit in which he offered himself as an unspotted victim to God on the altar of the Cross."[88] The priest was to develop holiness through daily meditation, mortification, praying the liturgy of the hours, spiritual reading, and examination of conscience. These were essential and could not be dispensed with even under the many burdens of active ministry.

The Holy See thereby ended the period with an authoritative exhortation on the model priest as filled with supernatural virtues. The era had opened in the wake of the Third Plenary Council of Baltimore with the articulation of the model priest possessing the professional skills appropriate for the tasks of ministry in the United States. Through the period 1884 to 1910 the diocesan seminary developed an approach to priestly training which sought to prepare the candidate for expanded functions in the American church while still adhering to the seminary's inherited purpose of forming holiness. In the early twentieth century, the Holy See began the practice of regularly issuing decrees and exhortations to reinforce its model of the priest with emphasis on the supernatural virtues. These decrees had universal application in the Catholic world and did not arise from the American clerical experience but required adherence in the life of American diocesan seminaries for the next half-century.

11. Clerical Learning

From the seminary decrees of the Third Plenary Council of Baltimore, and through the publications and activities of seminary educators, the standards of seminary learning were reconsidered to meet the intellectual demands made of American Catholic diocesan clergy of the late nineteenth century. The major developments consisted of lengthening the course of studies, introducing new textbooks, improving the professional training of the faculty, and an unprecedented interest in offering degrees for seminary studies. The seminaries of the period provide a mixed record of interest in enlarging the boundaries of clerical learning. The Holy See likewise took a new interest in informing the content of seminary learning that culminated with decrees issued by 1910 sharply delimiting development of clerical studies.

The new standards of clerical learning rested on the minor and major seminary decrees of the Third Plenary Council of Baltimore. It was left to a committee of bishops to translate the decrees' mere listing of seminary courses into a specific program of studies of six years each for minor and major seminaries. For this purpose, the committee chaired by Archbishop Michael Heiss with Bishops Stephan V. Ryan of Buffalo and Winand Wigger of Newark met at the cathedral in Buffalo, New York from July 5 to 8, 1885. Two members, Bishops James O'Connor of Omaha and John Moore of St. Augustine, were absent, but a group of seminary educators was on hand to assist, including the Sulpicians Alphonse Magnien and John Hogan.[1]

The committee produced a "Plan of Studies" published in pamphlet form and issued by the archbishop of Baltimore. The document gave detailed attention to the curricula and textbooks of the minor and major seminary courses. The minor seminary program adhered to the European model of the gymnasium or lycée, and was also followed at many Catholic academies in the United States which offered a six-year classical course. This program provided courses in Christian doctrine, Latin, English, and

German (for Germans), and mathematics to be taught in all six years; Greek and German (for non-Germans) were to be taught five years; and courses in history, geography, penmanship, natural history, and natural philosophy were treated in four or fewer years. The six-year major seminary curriculum was divided into two years of philosophy, followed by four years of theological studies. The philosophy program addressed the principal philosophical components: logic, ontology, psychology, cosmology, ethics, and the history of philosophy. Other courses in the two years included Latin, Hebrew, and Greek, biblical archaeology, hermeneutics, exegesis, natural science, and plain chant. Since no textbook was prescribed for the study of philosophy, specific commitment to the thought of St. Thomas is left in doubt. The course of four years of theology placed heavy emphasis on dogmatic and moral theology, as the following table shows. The committee recommended textbooks in major areas, Hurter for dogma and Konings or Lemkuhl, both in the Liguorian tradition, for moral theology. Brück or Birkhaüser were recommended for church history. There were no textbook recommendations in other subjects, many of which then lacked standard texts, such as liturgy, canon law, and ascetical theology. Sacred Scripture, church history, and canon law were given new prominence, and unprecedented though limited time was devoted to catechetics and ascetical theology.

The "Plan of Studies" provided one way the decrees of the Third Baltimore Council could be implemented. It was not a radical break with past practice and continued the traditional stress on dogmatic and moral theology. It offered something new in the variety of secondary courses added to the curriculum. The document had no binding force and its specific provisions were not the focus of a sustained discussion of the seminary curriculum in the following years. The "Plan" marked the end rather than the beginning of official and collective episcopal activity on behalf of the content of seminary learning for the period.

Unofficially, others were prepared to propose seminary standards. Foremost was John Hogan, who provided a comprehensive consideration of the content and purpose of the various branches of seminary learning in a series of articles in the *American Ecclesiastical Review* between 1891 and 1895. The articles were brought together in a book published in 1898 under the title *Clerical Studies*. To elaborate themes of the Baltimore council's seminary decrees, Hogan addresses the volume to seminarians and young priests, all of whom leave the seminary "imperfectly equipped" for their duties but able to make up what is wanting on their own. Hogan aims to show the conscientious cleric how clerical studies "may be pursued with greatest advantage" over a lifetime of learning and to appropriate that learning for use in ministry.[3] By doing so, Hogan provides American cleri-

Plan of Studies[2]

Divisio Scholarum in Cursibus Philos. et Theol.

	Philosophia		Theologia			
	I.	II.	I.	II.	III.	IV.
Philosophia	6	6				
Historia Philosophiae		3				
Disputatio Philosophia		2				
Philosophia Naturalis	2	2				
Hermeneutica		1				
Archaeologia et Geographia	1	1				
Lingua Hebraica	2	2				
Lingua Latina	2					
Lingua Graeca	2					
Cantus Planus	1	1	1	1	1	1
Theologia Dogmatica			6	6	6	3
Disputatio Theologica			1	1	1	
Theologia Moralis			6	6	6	3
Historia Eccleasiastica			3	3		
Exegesis			3	3		
Introductio in Libros S.			1	1		
Ius Canonicum					3	3
Liturgia					2	3
Homiletica					1	2
Theologica Ascetica					1	1
Cathechiteca						1
	16	18	21	21	21	16

cal readers with his extensive understanding of Catholic intellectual developments during his career (dating from 1853) as a seminary instructor. Through four decades of contact with leading Catholic thinkers in Europe, Hogan was in touch with what he called the "unparalleled intellectual activity of the nineteenth century, spreading out almost in every conceivable direction." Two principal realms of the new knowledge were: "Nature and History—the physical sciences and the past of the human race."[4] Advances in these areas posed a challenge to seminary learning and were having a permanent impact on modes of Catholic intellectual activity. "In the ages of faith," according to Hogan, "authority reigned supreme; later on, abstract principles and logical deductions were predominant; in our day facts and inductions are everything,—the facts and inductions of science on one side, the facts and inductions of history on the other."[5]

Natural science, then, is the first issue Hogan addresses. He points out that science had now been prescribed as part of the seminary curriculum, and henceforth, though it had not been a part of liberal learning in the past, it is to be a part of the culture of the educated. It is to take its place among clerical studies. Science not only provides training in mental discipline, but the priest in his role as defender of the Christian faith should have a grasp of the "bearings of science on faith, their points of contact, few or many, real or imaginary." The priest could not expect to master the details of scientific learning, but at least he could have a general acquaintance with "their main lines, their fundamental laws or principles, their processes and methods."[6]

Philosophy is a main point of contact with the challenges posed by modern thought. Hogan explains its importance as a means of culture and influence and, for the cleric, as a prerequisite for the study of theology, which was built on the assumption of a personal God and belief in the soul. In considering what philosophy is best suited to Catholicism he reviews the relation of several philosophies used in the past. He definitely leaves the impression that Catholicism could get along without Scholasticism. He presents the main points of Pope Leo XIII's *Aeterni Patris* without endorsing the desirability of having St. Thomas's methods as the only philosophy. In fact, he finds that the encyclical allows liberty in the choice of philosophical method and recommends the study of Duns Scotus.[7] As to its actual study, Hogan, in what amounts to a pedagogical heresy for a Catholic seminary educator, questions the method of teaching philosophy in Latin, which results in little more than the memorization of formulas. He believes that if students are to appropriate philosophy for use, it should be taught in the vernacular and that if philosophical ideas are to gain influence, they must be written in an attractive style.[8]

The importance of apologetics is greater than ever, as Hogan finds, "There is no denying, we have entered a period of exceptionally deep and widespread unbelief."[9] The problem of apologetics is great, since the current age no longer responds to the apologetical appeals of the past. New scientific, philosophical, and historical knowledge requires the Christian apologist to come to terms with a wider range of information and new ways of using that knowledge. The inherited Scholastic approaches no longer compel attention.

The study of dogmatic theology, as Hogan surveys the discipline, still rests on the traditional supports or proofs used from the Bible, the Fathers, philosophy "as taught by Aristotle and developed by the schools," and deduction, which "was to the scholastic mind, not only a method of demonstration, but the principal means of discovery in every sphere of knowledge."[10] He calls attention to the limitations of these supports: in regard to Scripture, "it becomes more and more difficult, as we advance in the intelligence of the Bible, to say just when and where its statements should be taken literally"; and in regard to the Fathers, "the closer and more critical study to which they have been subjected during the last two centuries has long since put an end to the indiscriminate trust given them in older times." And he calls deduction into question, stating that "the *a priori* method is never entirely reliable, and can do solid service only on condition of its results being verified by direct observation." Instead, he stresses the Bible over the Scholastic method: "It is the book itself, reverently yet critically examined, no *a priori* argument, that will best tell us with what measure of perfection or imperfection God has vouchsafed to use the medium of writing to convey to mankind His truth and His will."[11]

After presenting these "principles by which Catholic theology is being renovated," he concludes that theology is not to be studied "once for all, but something to be kept habitually before the mind through life, and returned to faithfully . . . ; secondly, that as much as possible this study should not only lead backward to what has begun to fade from the memory, but onward too, in the various directions opened up to it by research, ancient and modern."[12] He brings out the historical element in urging that theological issues be traced historically to give Christian doctrine "a grasp of its full sense and bearings, such as no other method can give, but it [history] shows far better than any other form of exposition the grounds upon which it rests."[13]

Hogan's belief in the importance of history, of course, extended to the formal church history course. He believes that the priest who hopes to be influential should "lay hold of so formidable power [as history] and learn to wield it. The more he is prepared to appeal to history on any subject, the surer he is to get a hearing."[14] Hogan recognizes the difficulty of planning survey courses in church history and the arbitrariness of its main divisions, but he recommends "An outline of the main facts and features of the Church's life in the past; her doctrinal and disciplinary developments, with the circumstances which gave rise to them; her relations, friendly or unfriendly, with the temporal power; her great men."[15]

Addressing the importance of biblical studies, he again marvels how in the nineteenth century the boundaries of knowledge had "indefinitely enlarged" and most prominently in the study of the Bible. "That Book, which might be thought long since to have yielded up all its secrets, so closely had it been questioned by the brightest minds, age after age, seems to have reserved for our time the revelation of some of its most interesting contents."[16] He demonstrates the importance of the study of Greek and Semitic languages and of archeology for undertaking serious biblical studies. For the purposes of the seminary, a course of introduction to the Bible was essential: "It is among the questions of introduction that are to be found most of the Biblical problems of the day—the origin, the true character, the date, inspiration, textual value, etc., of the various books."

He proposes that the introductory course offer the seminarian "a general conception, clear and accurate, though limited, of the work that has been and is being done on and around the Bible; of the principal views that have been held in succession regarding it, and especially of those that are presently in the ascendant."[17]

Hogan includes discussions of the remaining subjects of the seminary program: moral theology, liturgy, pastoral theology, homiletics, and canon law. His remarks often correspond to accepted contemporary attitudes. His views of moral theology pertain almost exclusively to personal morality, though he allows that new questions were being raised by the expansion of political, juridical, and social sciences. In other areas, he shares the view of the expanded functions of the model priest of the period. He recognizes the increasing importance of preaching and, as the basis of good preaching, continuous "growth in religious knowledge, speculative and practical."[18] Pastoral theology was to instruct the cleric in the duties of ministry in a systematic fashion. He recommends the recent volumes of Gibbons and Stang in this area. A general knowledge of canon law was useful in the task of ministry. Hogan endorses a historical approach to its study as a prerequisite for thorough understanding. Canons would thereby be studied from the point of view of the circumstances that brought them into existence and their transformations through history. Hogan apparently intends to oppose a mentality of legalism in canonical studies.[19]

As John Hogan brought the perspective of years of contact with European intellectual life, John Talbot Smith approaches seminary learning from the experience of a diocesan priest working in the American church. Smith includes extensive and very unorthodox recommendations for reorganizing the seminary curriculum in *Our Seminaries*. He sharply criticizes the attention given to moral theology as "holding first place in the curriculum, and in the mind of the student."[20] He challenges this preeminent rank and proposes a rearrangement of seminary studies in their order of importance. Smith believes that the seminarian's principal study should be Jesus Christ, from which he concludes that biblical studies deserve first place. He places philosophy second; "Christ is first, and man second. Therefore if we give Scripture first place in intellectual training, philosophy would have the second, because it is as near to man as the Scriptures are to Christ."[21] He places exclusive emphasis on philosophy as a study of man without assigning it a role in justifying belief in the existence of God or the soul. He ignores the official endorsement of the thought of St. Thomas as the method for philosophy and theology.

Third place in his scheme is assigned to dogmatic theology and fourth place to literature, which he finds as noble a study as philosophy or theology. While philosophy and theology have the scientific expressions appropriate to their disciplines, "literature is the artistic expression of every force, religious, political, racial, social, which has affected man's nature and career." He allows fifth place to moral theology, which he sees as "in one sense simply a method of applying certain principles to human conditions. . . . It ranks only with law."[23] For sixth place, he believes that the "social upheavals" of the nineteenth century gave urgency to the study of moral philosophy, which a later age might call "social ethics."

Seventh place is given to the physical sciences, because "the whole round of physical science in our day has been turned into a weapon against religion." The priest requires at least a general grasp of modern scientific developments to answer convincingly "eager questions about the age of the world, the testimony of the rocks against Moses, the likeness of ancient religions to Christianity, and a score of such matters."[24] He gives eighth place to the study of canon law. Smith does not assign a place to the study of history, not because he intends to neglect it, but "it ought to be the very atmosphere in which the studies breathe. It should precede, accompany, follow each individual branch of learning like the astrologers of ancient days accompanied their kings."[25]

Smith and Hogan thought deeply about seminary studies in their separate ways. Both recognized the growth of knowledge in their times. Both attached unprecedented importance to biblical studies and history. Both lacked interest in promoting the thought of St. Thomas as the point of reference in Catholic intellectual activity. Both stressed the need for continuous learning. Hogan, of course, was a prominent seminary educator in a position to practice his views and to influence others in seminary education. He did not propose a general rearrangement of the seminary curriculum but only a modern spirit in conducting its courses. Smith, on the other hand, was not in a position to implement his views, and his proposed reorganization of the seminary curriculum was too great a reversal of current practice to command realistic interest.

The themes that Hogan and Smith developed were at least in part shared by others in the practice of seminary education. For instance, Archbishop Ireland's eloquent address at the dedication of St. Paul Seminary in 1895 proclaims the importance of the branches of learning for the priest as progressive figures such as Hogan and Smith understood them: "The education of the clergy to the fullest share of knowledge proper to their calling and to the fullest realization of their responsibilities is the master work in the education of the whole people." Ireland expected to place the study of modern sciences "side by side" with theology in seminary studies. He desires the study of political economy and sociology "so akin to moral theology that I should bring them into closest quarters with it." The study of religion in the seminary was to benefit from the serious study of English literature, so that it would "robe itself in the worthiest garb of literature when presenting itself to the children of men."[26] There is no mention of reviving the thought of St. Thomas Aquinas as the basis for the priest's intellectual training. As Hogan recorded after a conversation with Ireland at the Third Plenary Council of Baltimore, the latter "fails to see the good of Leo XIII['s] letter on Philosophy."[27]

Interest in articulating new standards of seminary learning extended to active seminary educators through the period. The *American Ecclesiastical Review* and the Conference of Seminary Presidents, which later merged with the Catholic Educational Association, provided opportunities for a public discussion of seminary issues. These were modest beginnings, but the articles and printed addresses of conferences disseminated new ideas concerning the organization of seminary life and learning. However, such groups as the Catholic Educational Association had no official standing in the actual direction of seminaries. Organization of seminary studies was left to the individual bishops and seminary administrators acting in their own seminaries.

Seminaries of the period provide a record of interest in and capabilities for introducing new ideas of seminary learning. The ideals of reform, as always, came to terms with the contingencies of church life, one of which was the need to train priests quickly to fill up the ranks of the clergy. The conciliar decrees were specific in establishing a course of six years of study each for the minor and major seminary, but the record of compliance with the six-year major seminary program was mixed. For the major seminary, the two-year course of philosophy with humanities and sciences found general compliance, but four years of theology was not uniformly adopted. East coast seminaries such as St. Joseph's Seminary at Troy, New York, St. Charles Seminary in Philadelphia, and Immaculate Conception Seminary at South Orange, New Jersey, adopted four years of theology. The new seminaries of St. Bernard's at Rochester, St. Paul at St. Paul, and St. Joseph's Seminary at Yonkers, New York — where strong episcopal leadership was present — complied with the four-year requirement from their foundings.

Except for New York, however, the Sulpicians had difficulty adhering to the decree, since client bishops, long accustomed to three years of theology, withdrew their students for ordination before the end of the course. At St. Mary's Seminary the Sulpician's first implemented, then abandoned, a four-year course of theology to adjust to the expectations of some forty client bishops across the country. At St. John's at Boston, the Sulpicians abandoned the four-year course of theology in 1892, as Archbishop Williams did not exert influence with the bishops of his province to keep their students at the seminary long enough for a full course.[28] The Sulpicians at Boston and Baltimore offered a course of three years and three months. In other words, the seminarians who advanced to the priesthood, completed their studies and were ordained at Christmas of the fourth year of the theology course. At Mount St. Mary's at Emmitsburg, a four-year course of theology was in effect, but the seminarians had duties of teaching and prefecting in the college which made their seminary studies part-time.[29]

In the seminaries west of Rochester, except St. Paul Seminary, the six-year major seminary course was not implemented. At the Seminary of Our Lady of Angels at Niagara, New York, a course of three and a half years of theology was offered. Benedictine seminaries, which were patronized by many rural dioceses in the Middle West and West and were largely isolated from the discussion of ideas of seminary training, offered three years of theology. Archbishop Ireland's apostolic visitation of St. John's Abbey in 1889 raised the question of the brevity of the seminary course there. But the economic state of the monastery and need for more priests in the vast rural dioceses of the region precluded formal compliance on this issue. Even firmly estalished St. Francis Seminary in Milwaukee, which served many dioceses in the region, continued three years of theology, and Kenrick Seminary offered three years of theology from its opening in 1893.[30]

The curriculum offered at St. Mary's in Baltimore, as the country's largest Catholic seminary, patronized by many dioceses and offering a theology program that was neither as long as four years nor as short as three, serves as a useful example of the organization of seminary learning for the period. Its first printed catalog appeared for the school year 1894–1895.

The two-year philosophy course offered five hours per week of instruction in philosophical subjects. The first year covered logic, ontology, and cosmology; the second treated anthropology, natural theology, and ethics. Natural sciences were offered in four hours of class instruction per week for two years. Physics and chemistry were treated in the first year, general biology the second. The students received two hours per week of historical introduction to Sacred Scripture: Old Testament the first year, New Testament the second. The lowest priority was church history, which was taught one hour per week in a two-year cycle covering the period from 64 A.D. to 1870.

The basic program of the Department of Theology was covered in three and a half years and reflected the continuity with past learning in its emphasis on dogmatic and moral theologies.

The first year of moral theology introduced the student to "human acts" and then "conscience and laws" from theological and philosophical perspectives. The Catholic moral position was set forth with special reference to competing moral systems with a view to "refuting the anti-Christian and materialist or evolutionist theories." The second part of the year dealt with sin and the first three commandments of the Decalogue. In the second and third years of moral theology topics were treated in alternate years. One year was given to the fourth, fifth, and eighth commandments of the Decalogue, the obligations of the various "states of life," and a tract on "justice and rights" and contracts. The other year was devoted to the sacraments of penance and matrimony. The seminarian thereby received "full directions" concerning one of the priest's principal duties: the "wise and fruitful administration of the Sacrament of Penance." However, the catalog stated an interest in the "vital questions of the day" treated in "their moral and social bearing,—monopolies, trusts, strikes,—the indissolubility of the marriage life."[31]

Instruction in dogmatic theology began with a first-year course devoted to basic apologetical questions: introduction to theology, natural religion, supernatural religion, the evidences of Christianity, proofs of Christ's divine mission, and institution of the church. The nature of the church, particularly in contrast to Protestant views, and other ecclesiological questions, such as the hierarchical structure of the church, the function of church councils, and church-state questions. The second- and third-year dogmatic subjects were presented in alternate years. One year was given to faith, God, creation, the elevation of man to a supernatural state, and the Incarnation. The other year was given to grace, merit, the sacraments, and eschatology. The course description gave prominence to the presentation of the Catholic position as opposed to the Protestant and the rationalist positions.

The study of Sacred Scripture advanced markedly from the previous era of neglect. Three hours per week were offered for three and a half years. The first semester was given to outlining the historical development of the canons of the Old and New Testament, original texts of both canons, principal versions of the Bible, and exegesis and higher criticism. The second semester treated contemporary problems of the authorship, inspiration, and the synoptical problem of the Gospels. Unlike the approach in dogma and moral theology, the students were given "dissertations" to write each semester, one on an assigned topic, the other of the student's own choice. The remaining two and a half years were given to selective exegesis of the Bible, one year devoted to the Gospels, another year to the epistles, and a half year to the Old Testament. The approach was described as accurate and comprehensive with "critical attention to details, and broad lines of investigation; hence the necessity of historical and textual criticism, of studies in geography, political conditions, etc." All this was done "in that reverent spirit characteristic of all Catholic investigation."[32]

Church history and canon law were required one hour per week each for three years. A single class of church history was presented each year so that the series of chronological issues was covered in a three-year cycle. Canon law was also studied for one hour per week for three years; the decrees of the Third Plenary Council of Baltimore formed the basis of instruction.

A course of one hour per week in plain chant was required.

Homiletics was treated outside the classroom, as all students were required to prepare a sermon over the summer for delivery before the seminary community. The seminary faculty then evaluated the sermon.

The foregoing was the course of studies required of all. Hebrew was the sole elective course in the theology curriculum, with two hours of instruction offered per week for those who desired it.

After three years of course work, a final semester in the fall was intended to prepare candidates for ordination. They were offered four hours instruction per week in pastoral theology, in which the rubrics of the Mass and the ritual for sacraments and other ceremonies were explained. The five weekly periods of moral theology consisted of a review especially of sexual and marital matters as an immediate preparation for hearing confessions. A final section of the course in exegesis was offered as noted above.

At St. Mary's and most other seminaries, the textbook or manual of dogmatic and moral theology remained the characteristic medium of seminary learning. There was only slight questioning of this method despite the harsh public strictures of Bishop John Lancaster Spalding of its "barbarous" style.[33] A defender of the textbook, Herman Heuser, nevertheless frankly described the "gaunt outlines" of the theology manual as "a long series of tracts, sections, chapters, articles, theses, conciliar definitions, Scriptural and Patristic excerpts, with a few analogies, discovered by reason, and sundry objections stated and solved." All this was "dry, unfleshed, unvitalized bones." But Heuser dissented when Cardinal Satolli, Prefect of the Sacred Congregation of Studies, issued a letter to the Spanish bishops in 1898 calling for the use of St. Thomas's *Summa* as the dogmatic textbook. Heuser believed that the manual with its concise explanations and references to modern problems was surely preferable to St. Thomas alone.[34] Indeed the manual provided a general textbook geared to imparting the basic theology necessary for the priest's pastoral activity and on a level accessible to the average seminarian. Its use provided students and professors a guide for classroom explanation and recitation.

Though manuals were heavily footnoted, collateral reading or independent study was unlikely in a weekly schedule of at least fifteen hours of formal classes. Even a progressive seminary educator, Charles Rex, found class the most useful time for the students and would have been "glad to see the number of classes increased; not to lengthen the matter to be seen, but to discuss and explain and impress it more perfectly."[35] A rare spirit, John Hogan, jettisoned the textbook, instead using the socratic method that, in the words of one former student, filled the student's mind with the "unrest of inquiry." "Often he would seem to go to the very limits of daring in the vigor with which he plied us with objections, annihilated all our arguments, and then walked off without vouchsafing an answer to our difficulties."[36] On the other hand, the textbook was intended to meet all objections. Despite the challenges of new learning, the textbook was in fact entering its heyday.

The textbook was supreme in the study of moral theology. This discipline was seemingly unchallenged by any hint of reform during the period. The Liguorian approach of equiprobabilism, as presented in chapter 6, governed the moral manuals that were in use throughout the Catholic world into the twentieth century. The moral texts of the Jesuit Jean Gury had gained general influence in the previous period. His work was succeeded by that of his fellow Jesuit Augustin Lehmkuhl, a German and longtime moralist at the Gregorian University. In his *Theologia moralis*, published in 1883 and enjoying many editions, Lehmkuhl continued the ascendant trend of reliance on Alphonsus Liguori and joined with it the weight of St. Thomas. The moral textbook of the Dutch Redemptorist Anthony Konings (1821–1884) was another choice. Konings, as a member of the Redemptorist order, was a faithful disciple of St. Alphonsus Liguori. The Jesuit tradition was augmented after Lehmkuhl by the moral texts of Luigi Sabetti (1839–1898), who taught moral theology at the Jesuit's Woodstock College from 1871. In 1884 his *Compendium Theologiae Moralis* appeared and had thirteen editions by 1898.[37] It was adopted at St. Meinrad, St. Vincent, St. Bernard, Kenrick, and elsewhere during the period.

In the study of dogmatic theology, the long influence of Perrone gave way to that of another Jesuit, Hugo Hurter. Born at Schaffhausen, Switzerland, in 1832, he converted to Catholicism at the age of twelve when his father, the church historian and Protestant pastor Friedrich Emmanuel von Hurter, converted. Hurter attended the Germanicum in Rome before ordination and then joined the Society of Jesus. Thereafter he spent his entire career as professor of dogmatic theology at the University of Innsbruck. His *Medulla theologiae dogmaticae* appeared in 1870 and went through eleven editions by 1903. His more concise *Theologiae dogmaticae compendium* appeared in 1878 and had seven editions by 1902.[38] It was used at St. Paul, Rochester, St. Meinrad, and Collegeville at various times in the 1880s and 1890s.

Hurter's influence was eventually supplanted in American seminaries with the introduction of the dogmatic manuals of Adolphe Alfred Tanquerey. The latter was born at Blainville, Manche, France in 1854. He attended the minor seminary of St. Lô and major seminary at Coutances and St. Sulpice, from which he was sent to the newly opened Sulpician residence or "Procure" in Rome, where he pursued studies at the Dominicans' Minerva and at the Apollinaire. He obtained doctorates in theology and canon law in 1878, the year of his ordination. After entering the Society of St. Sulpice in 1879, he was appointed to teach dogma, first at the seminary of Rodez and then, in 1887, at Baltimore. At St. Mary's the experience of teaching mostly second-generation Irish Americans shaped his pedagogical texts. The dogma manual of Bonal was in use when he arrived, but he found the textbook inadequate and increasingly relied on his own lecture notes. Tanquerey was soon appreciated as a teacher capable of explaining complex matters in an understandable manner and drawing out practical applications. His students collaborated in taking down a complete version of his notes to be mineographed. Tanquerey even lent them his prepared notes to assist in the task. He, too, realized the need for a published version of his volume of dogmatic theology, which appeared in 1894 entitled *Synopsis theologiae dogmaticae specialis,* followed by *Synopsis theologiae dogmaticae fundamentalis* in 1896. The textbook was immediately successful in the United States and was soon in use, of course, at the Sulpician seminaries of Baltimore, Boston, New York, and San Francisco. In the decade following publication it was adopted at the three Benedictine seminaries, St. Paul Seminary, Immaculate Conception Seminary at South Orange, New Jersey, and Mount St. Mary's at Emmitsburg. It began the extraordinary influence that it would have in American and European seminaries until the middle of the twentieth century. Tanquerey was appointed to teach moral theology at St. Mary's in 1895, and continued until 1902 when he returned to France. From his teaching he published a moral theology manual that appeared in France in 1904, but it did not supplant the more popular moral textbooks already enjoying wide influence.[39]

The attraction of Tanquerey's volumes was their readable, compact treatment of theological issues and their attention to modern Protestant and rationalist thought. He adhered to the classic apologetical approach of the other manualists. Catholic teaching was presented as fixed, normally by the formulations of the Council of Trent, and the opposing views of Protestants and rationalists were presented and refuted with proofs drawn from Scripture, the church fathers, and church decrees. Tanquerey's dogma volumes were particularly appealing in the United States because of the simplicity of the Latin text. The tradition of textbooks published in Latin was firmly established, though the instructor may have in fact used more of the vernacular in the classroom than was thought desirable. Tanquerey's Latin style was well adapted to the reading abilities of English-speakers by reason of its uncomplicated word order and vocabulary. It was therefore accessible to those possessing only a fair command of Latin.

Through the period Hogan and Smith had advocated the importance of a historical approach to the various branches of ecclesiastical learning. It is difficult to see that historical thinking renovated the pedagogical approaches to moral and dogmatic theology in view of the apologetical approach of seminary textbooks. Moreover, the formal course of church history did not expand greatly in the curriculum, as was evident in the weekly hour devoted to the subject at St. Mary's. The history textbooks in use continued the emphasis on the external and institutional developments of church history and avoided doctrinal and ecclesiological development. The most influential manual used in the United States was Jodok Adolph Birkhaeuser's *History of the Church from Its First Establishment*, which appeared in 1887. Birkhaeuser was born in Germany in 1841, grew up in Wisconsin, and was in the first class to have his entire training at St. Francis Seminary in Milwaukee. He joined the faculty after ordination in 1864 and taught mostly philosophy. He adapted the church history of the noted German Jesuit Cardinal Hergenrother and borrowed from other European textbooks to produce a seminary textbook in English that outlined general church history. His practical and concise manual had seven editions by 1903.[40] The alternate history manual in use was the *History of the Catholic Church* by Heinrich Brück (1831–1903), professor of church history at the seminary of Mainz, Germany. Brück's manual also relied on the work of Cardinal Hergenrother and appeared in an English translation in 1884.[41]

Biblical studies advanced markedly in the seminary curriculum during the period. The Sulpicians, beginning with John Hogan, were especially preoccupied with relating the advances in this area to the seminary curriculum. The Holy See addressed the challenges of the expansion of biblical learning in the era with Pope Leo XIII's encyclical *Providentissimus Deus* of 1893, in which the pope exhorted the teaching of courses of Sacred Scripture in seminaries and the special training of clerical professors to teach the discipline. The encyclical was a forceful statement of the importance of biblical studies. However, the pope greatly restricted the scope of critical study with his views on inspiration and inerrancy. He believed that Scripture had been dictated by the Holy Spirit to the sacred writers, which made the text free of error, notwithstanding the myriad textual problems pointed out by modern biblical scholarship.[42]

Sulpicians were in the forefront of advanced training in biblical studies. Among these was James F. Driscoll, a native of Vermont who joined the Society after attending the seminary at Montreal. Driscoll took his graduate training in Semitic languages with Henri Hyvernat at the Apollinaire in Rome. He joined the faculty at St. Joseph's Seminary in

1896. The French-born Sulpician Francis Gigot attended the Institut Catholique in Paris, where he received the S.T.L. in 1884. There he studied under Paulin Martin, Fulcran Vigoroux, and Alfred Loisy. He thus absorbed both conservative and progressive approaches to Scripture studies. Gigot joined the faculty of St. John's Seminary at Brighton in 1885 to teach Scripture before his appointment to St. Joseph Seminary in 1896. His publications resulted from his teaching and were intended for seminary use: *General Introduction to the Study of the Holy Scriptures* in 1898, *Outlines of New Testament History* in 1898, and *Special Introduction to the Study of the Old Testament* in 1900. Gigot cautiously attributed the method used in the textbooks to Richard Simon, a seventeenth-century French Oratorian, describing it as "historico-critical." The volumes' purpose was "to give as genuine facts, or as valid inferences from facts, only those which, in the light of historical knowledge and sound criticism, are entitled to be considered as such."[43] The volumes were regarded as rather cautious in areas that might cause controversy. They were adopted in American seminaries in the following decades. Gigot's role in controversies during the period will be taken up in due course. A third Sulpician, Joseph Bruneau, a native of Lyons, France, received the S.T.L. at the Institut Catholique in 1889. Bruneau joined the faculty of St. Mary's Seminary in 1894 and then the opening faculty at St. Joseph's Seminary in 1896. He was an enthusiast for spreading the higher criticism of the Bible in the classroom, in published translations, and in bibliographic essays in the *American Ecclesiastical Review*. His single book was *Harmony of the Gospels*, a standard arrangement of Gospel texts related to similar topics.[44]

The Vincentian Charles Leon Souvay was another noteworthy Scripture scholar. The French-born Souvay joined the faculty of Kenrick Seminary in 1903 after studies in Rome. He later returned to Rome to take the examination and submit his dissertation for the doctorate from the Pontifical Biblical Commission in 1910. Souvay was in every way a man of very conservative dispositions and did not raise any critical problems in his scholarly work.[45]

Expanded instruction in Scripture posed challenges for the organization of the seminary curriculum. The recognition of its importance did not supplant the amount of time given to dogma and moral theology, which were needed to impart the general knowledge required for the tasks of ministry. Both subjects were generally offered five or six periods per week. Scripture was offered four periods per week at St. Paul Seminary and three periods per week at Baltimore and even at St. Joseph's Seminary at New York where it was the subject of greatest concern among the faculty. It was natural that competing views arose concerning how much and in what manner Scripture studies should be pursued in the seminary. A thoughtful conservative, Herman Heuser, argued in favor of imparting a working knowledge of the Bible for the threefold tasks of developing the priest's spiritual life, sustaining Catholic doctrine, and as a defense of Christianity as the standard of morality against contemporary errors. He explicitly rejected the need for bringing up all the contemporary problems related to biblical studies, since they were not apt to arise in the course of the priest's pastoral activities.[46] On the other hand, Driscoll and Gigot, while recognizing the limitations placed by time and the competing claims of other disciplines in the curriculum, argued for a solid and scientific introduction to Scripture that included attention to problems raised by higher criticism. Both held that it was essential for the priest to be familiar with contemporary issues.[47] Gigot found it "inadmissible" for the priest in his role as defender of the faith to be in ignorance of the Bible. Driscoll described "as mistaken and shortsighted" the "policy to bring up our candidates for the priesthood in ignorance of the critical problems and issues of the day or to train them to look upon the labors of critical scholars generally as the work of an enemy."[48] The priest would only be embarrassed later, Gigot believed, on discovering that he did not know about these problems when they arose in the course of his ministry. The priest should have the knowledge at least to know what to read to come to terms with these problems. The issues raised by Heuser and Driscoll and Gigot were not, of course, capable of easy resolution.

Recognition of the need for expanded clerical learning was often related to how the priest's functions in the pulpit, in religious instruction, and in public activities were perceived. It is not clear that the attention given to formal instruction in preaching met the expectation of forming articulate priests. Seminary catalogs are normally vague about instruction and textbooks in homiletics. But the standard practice in major seminaries was the preparation of a practice sermon over summer vacation to be delivered during the school year. Sometimes the sermon was given during a meal, in place of the normal table reading. This custom was followed at St. Mary's Seminary and St. John's Seminary at Boston, where, in their last semester, members of the ordination class gave two sermons to the students and faculty. At St. Paul, a weekly homiletics class was offered for two years in which theory was combined with practice. Practice sermons were given before assemblies of faculty and students. At Rochester, Bishop McQuaid, who taught homiletics, expected more. Each student gave two practice sermons per year and the deacon class gave four sermons per year in the main lecture hall before the assembled students, faculty, and bishop. McQuaid personally corrected the sermon manuscript and privately counseled the student preachers.[49]

The homiletic textbooks of Thomas J. Potter, *Sacred Eloquence* and

The Pastor and His People, achieved widespread influence as the standard works in the field for English-speaking Catholic priests. In seminaries under German influence, German homiletic manuals circulated. The influential manual of Ignaz Schüch was translated into English by Boniface Luebbermann of the Cincinnati seminary as *The Priest in the Pulpit: A Manual of Homiletics and Catechetics* in 1894. Thus, homiletic instruction continued its ties with European textbooks.[50]

Additional opportunities for practicing communication skills were available through the literary and debating societies that are described in the catalogs of most seminaries. These gave outlets for presenting papers, sponsoring debates, and organizing dramas. Peter Johnson has described the especially rich history of literary societies at St. Francis Seminary, where major ethnic groups sustained German, English, and Polish societies, and, for short periods, Czech and French clubs. Their activities provided opportunities for practice in the languages their members would use in ministry. These groups often geared their activities to celebrating the national and religious holidays of the particular group. In seminaries of less ethnic diversity, at least one literary society operated. Even the clerical graduate students at Catholic University started a literary society.[51]

The priest's principal functions, of course, related closely to liturgical and devotional leadership. The formal study of liturgy was aimed to impart the proper method of saying the liturgy of the hours, the ceremonies of the Mass, and the rites of administering the sacraments. Larger issues of the history and theology of the church's liturgical life were peripheral to that task. This is reflected in the principal textbook for liturgy, Innocenz Wapelhorst's *Sacrae Liturgiae Compendium*, which emanated from the American seminary experience.[52] Wapelhorst, a priest of the St. Louis archdiocese, joined the faculty of St. Francis Seminary in Milwaukee in 1865 to teach dogmatic theology and liturgy and served as rector from 1873 to 1879. He then joined the Franciscan order. The first edition (1887) of his liturgy manual was adopted in virtually all American diocesan seminaries in the period. With its many editions it continued as a standard textbook on the subject into the twentieth century.

Pastoral theology was offered in the final year or semester before ordination in all seminaries and consisted of the instructions in practical pastoral functions not covered in the liturgy or homiletics classes. It was most often the prerogative of the seminary rector to conduct the class. William Stang's *Pastoral Theology* was in use at most seminaries during the period, though some seminaries also recommended Schulze's manual.

The students trained under the seminary regimen of the era elicited appraisals similar to those of the previous period. The seminary, of course, drew candidates for the priesthood whose intellectual capacities ranged from poor to excellent. All students were sponsored by their bishops, and it was recognized that intelligence and capacity for learning were not the only qualities to be considered in evaluating fitness for orders. As Edward Dyer reminded a meeting of seminary educators, "we all know well that some of our most worthy and successful priests are men whose scientific acquirements do not go beyond the *scientia competens*. No one acquainted with their work would dream of discouraging such men from aspiring to the sacred ministry."[53] Therefore, while it was not possible to erect high standards of admission to exclude the less gifted, there remained the problem of those less well prepared for clerical learning. The strengthening of the minor seminary course was decades in the making. The students who came to the major seminary, it was complained, were still poorly prepared. During extensive travels through the United States in 1896, Archbishop Francesco Satolli recorded what he heard about the uneven classical training of candidates for the seminary. He complained about the brevity of classical studies that resulted in a lack of knowledge of Latin, literary tastes, and an interest in study. After these cursory studies, the theological course did not last beyond three years.[54]

Sulpician Francis Havey, the son of Irish immigrants, acknowledged the deficiency and unevenness of preliminary studies in accounting for the level of seminary learning but added harsh strictures for Irish Americans. From his experiences he found "particularly true of the Irish-American character" a "dislike of mental discipline and steady application. . . ."[55] The minutes of the 1904 visitation of St. Mary's Seminary at Baltimore acknowledged a few gifted students but described the great majority as making serious application only for those things "clearly practically useful for the needs of the ministry." The students were said to lack intellectual curiosity in general.[56]

Thus the task of challenging seminarians to excel in studies was great. Ordination was the final goal of the seminary course, not academic degrees, which were unavailable at most seminaries. Devising a suitable system of examinations was an ongoing issue in the faculty minutes of Sulpician seminaries. They weighed the merits of weekly tests, alternately oral or written, monthly examinations, and the scope of semester examinations. Most seminaries had a system of annual prizes of various grades for performance in each subject. Several seminaries, such as Rochester and St. Paul, had semester examinations at which the bishop and leading clergy presided.

The most ambitious and unprecedented proposal for strengthening emulation in the seminary was aimed at awarding degrees for the theology course. St. Mary's Seminary was already in a position to do so since it had a pontifical faculty since 1822 and had awarded doctorates to its own Sulpician faculty and to a few outsiders into the early twentieth century. The seminary also held the degree-granting charter given by the Maryland legislature to the old St. Mary's College in 1805. At the end of the century lower degrees in philosophy and theology began to be awarded to seminarians in course. St. Mary's first printed catalog for the 1894–1895 school year stated the requirements: "In the Philosophical department the degree of Bachelor of Arts is conferred upon those who have received the note of 7 out of 10 for Philosophy and 6 out of 10 for the other branches in the examinations of two consecutive terms; . . . . The degree of Bachelor of Theology is conferred upon such of the students as have secured an average note of 7 out of 10 for the examinations of four consecutive terms. . . ." Licentiates and doctorates in "Sacred Sciences" were conferred after special examinations.[57] By the early twentieth century a small group of St. Mary's students earned bachelor and licentiate degrees annually.

Other seminaries did not have an old pontifical charter and sought degree-granting authority. At St. John's, Charles Rex sought to obtain degrees for theology, at first on the basis of affiliation with St. Mary's Seminary. The Baltimore Sulpicians favored this arrangement, but the Sulpician superior general disapproved, in part because of the appearance of competition with the new Catholic University. Rex then began a series of protracted negotiations with the Catholic University for affiliation. These were continued when John Hogan returned to the rectorship of St. John's in 1894. However, an affiliation agreement could not be reached because of differences concerning the university's examination of St. John's degree candidates. The university's faculty senate refused Hogan's request to waive examinations in Hebrew and canon law. Hogan's position was that the seminary's introductory courses in those subjects were not sufficient preparation for the university's examination. So the attempt for university affiliation ended.[58] Instead, Hogan, with the endorsement of Archbishop Williams, petitioned Cardinal Ledochowski, Prefect of Propaganda, for the granting of a pontifical faculty to St. John's Seminary in order to grant degrees. In his petition Hogan cited the fact that in the United States secular institutions granted degrees; Americans thereby expected institutions of learning to grant degrees. He believed that Catholic clergy in New England would command more respect if their leading members earned degrees. He added that the Catholic University would be assisted if St. John's students destined for the university would already have their bachelor of theology degree. Cardinal Ledochowski denied the request in 1895 on the grounds that, if granted, other seminaries would seek the privilege.[59]

Archbishop John Ireland's interest in degrees was demonstrated by affiliating with the Catholic University of America in 1894. St. Paul Seminary was the first seminary beyond Washington to affiliate, though the program was not in actual operation for a number of years.[60]

Bishop McQuaid, who was no friend of the Catholic University, obtained a pontifical charter for St. Bernard Seminary in 1901. The charter permitted the Roman practice of awarding the bachelor's degree after two years of study, the licentiate after the third, and the doctorate after the fourth. McQuaid did not intend to make things so easy in Rochester. The bachelor of theology degree (S.T.B.) was to be awarded after the four-year course, the licentiate (S.T.L.) and doctorate (S.T.D.) after the fifth and sixth years, respectively. The examination for the bachelor's degree was available only to those who had an average of 85 percent in their course work. Then the candidate had to pass a defense of theses. Few of St. Bernard's hundreds of students earned degrees. In the years 1902 to 1908, the S.T.B. was awarded nine times, the S.T.L. four times, and the S.T.D. twice. St. Bernard's could also award philosophy degrees, of which twenty bachelor degrees and one doctorate were awarded.[61]

The new interest in degrees for theological studies was confined to a few seminaries. Where degrees could be earned, they were intended as demonstrations of high achievement for the few gifted students and not as a goal for a program pursued by all. Degrees were not required for any pastoral function, and they were not a prerequisite for seminary teaching, which makes interest in them remarkable. Other opportunities for developing the talents of the gifted were available at two Sulpician seminaries, St. Joseph's and St. Mary's. During the 1890s a few gifted students from St. Mary's began to attend selected classes, usually in Semitic languages, at the nonsectarian Johns Hopkins University in Baltimore. Owing to the sensitivity of this unorthodox practice, the Sulpicians soon declined to take responsibility for letting the seminarians attend the university. Instead, the students required the permission of their bishops before seminary officials permitted them to attend. Before Edward R. Dyer left the rectorship of St. Joseph's Seminary in 1902, arrangements were made for seminarians to attend selected courses at Columbia University. Only a few students at these seminaries took advantage of these courses, and the practice ceased after the condemnation of modernism.[62]

Advanced training leading to degrees took on a new importance for the development of seminary faculties through the period. The expansion of enrollment at the American College in Rome and the growing number of its alumni who received doctorates enlarged the number of degreed priests available for seminary faculties. The inadequacy of Roman degrees was recognized so that Roman doctors often took further study in preparation for teaching positions. For example, Edward J. Hanna of Rochester, who was destined to join the faculty of Bishop McQuaid's new seminary, stayed in Rome for several years after earning his doctorate. Likewise, future Catholic University professors Edward Pace and Thomas Shahan attended European universities before returning to join the faculty.

Among Sulpicians the practice of advanced training culminating in degrees was recent. Their house of residence or "Procure" opened in Rome only in 1875 and Adolph Tanquerey was in the first group to live there and study at Roman institutes. In 1878 Charles Rex, Edward Dyer, and Richard Wakeham were the first of many American Sulpicians sent to Rome for studies in the renewed interest in pontifical degrees. The Sulpicians also patronized the Institut Catholique in Paris, which opened in 1875 as a pontifical theology faculty and where biblical studies stirred ongoing controversy.

Boniface Wimmer was ahead of his time by opening a Roman residence in 1867 for monks sent from America for studies. Wimmer lobbied for the revival of the international college for Benedictines that had been suppressed in the wake of the French Revolution. In 1887 Pope Leo XIII reestablished the Collegio Sant' Anselmo as an international center for Benedictines, thereby strengthening the tradition of American Benedictines sent to Rome for studies.[63]

The Vincentians had a long tradition of regarding academic degrees as a manifestation of vanity. To conform to the new emphasis on learning, however, in 1882 the superior general, Antoine Fiat, urged Vincentian provinces to send young priests to Rome for higher studies as preparation for teaching in the many seminaries conducted by the congregation. He assured his confreres that the scholars' "humility will not suffer any harm and that the memory of Saint Vincent will always keep them in the modesty that suits his disciples." It was not until 1897, under the pressures of improving Kenrick Seminary's faculty, that the American provincial superior, Thomas Smith, sent the first Vincentian priests from the United States to Rome for studies.[64]

The interest in advanced training for the seminary faculty gave new importance to academic degrees. Though specialization in various fields would develop slowly, the ideal of postordination training and degrees as a prerequisite for priests in seminary teaching became established during the period. The central direction of Catholic intellectual life from Rome reinforced the importance of Roman training, though, as noted previously, the Catholic University was available for pontifical degrees. However, it could not attract widespread interest for advanced degrees in theology.

Limitations placed on significant changes in the patterns of clerical learning marked the later years of Pope Leo XIII. The encyclical *Providentissimus Deus* had earlier limited the scope of Catholic biblical studies with restrictive approaches in the areas of inspiration and inerrancy. In 1902 Pope Leo issued *motu proprio* the decree *Vigilantiae* that created the Pontifical Biblical Commission to promote biblical interpretation according to the pope's 1893 encyclical and guard against future unorthodox interpretations. The commission was to grant doctorates in biblical studies preceded by exacting language study and an examination that was designed to confirm the candidate's orthodoxy. The commission alone could award degrees in biblical studies to Catholic priests.

The trend restricting the areas of Scripture studies continued after Pope Leo XIII. In 1906 Pope Pius X issued the apostolic letter *Quoniam in Re Biblica*, which prescribes that Scripture studies were to be taught in seminaries and that they should be distributed over the entire seminary course. Professors were to adhere closely to the official teachings of the church and avoid innovations. In 1906 the commission began to issue the decrees that were in opposition to many ordinary findings of modern biblical criticism. Against learned evidence to the contrary, Roman authority, for instance, declared firmly for the Mosaic authorship of the Pentateuch and for the single authorship of Isaiah. In the United States the case most closely associated with a ruling of the Biblical Commission was that of the Dutch scholar Henry Poels, associate professor of Scripture at Catholic University. Poels could not agree to the single authorship of the Pentateuch and was dismissed from the faculty in 1910.[65]

Within the Society of St. Sulpice, the new climate of orthodoxy was reflected in the election of Jules Lebas as superior general in 1901. Lebas began his tenure by professing the strongest possible allegiance to the neo-Scholastic revival. At the same time a commission on seminary studies issued lengthy recommendations prescribing the manner in which various subjects were to be taught in Sulpician seminaries. A major point was directed to Scripture studies, in which, it was found, that, under the pretext of dealing with the history of the various books, traditional belief was too easily rejected in favor of modern scholars, who were most often "nonbelievers or rationalists." In theology instruction, the commission expressed fears of the weakening of traditional proofs of Christianity and not caring for the actual practice of the church. Historical methods had been abused by confusing evolution of dogma with alteration of teaching and overemphasizing the differences between various authorities of the past. The report recommended the "common teaching of the Church" as the basis of instruction, not a variety of opinions, because priests were to transmit official teachings to Catholics.[66] Therefore, the provisions of *Aeterni Patris* and *Providentissimus Deus* were to be followed. Above all, the manual approved for the seminary was to be the basis for seminarians' study and recitation, and professors were to abstain from giving lectures. To what extent there was a general compliance with such rigid directives that dealt a blow to personal pedagogical initiative is unknown, but it was a powerful statement that instructors could not be relied upon to convey orthodox teaching. The rulings of the study commission also protected the leadership of the Society from charges of neglecting their duty to defend orthodoxy.

The intransigent direction of the Lebas administration was keenly felt at St. Joseph's Seminary in New York. Lebas had withheld approval for publication of the second volume of Francis Gigot's *General Introduction to the Old Testament*. Lebas's course of action planted the seeds of disillusionment in the minds of Gigot and the other Sulpicians at the New York seminary, Driscoll, Richard Wakeham, John Mahoney, Timothy Holland, and Joseph Bruneau. They believed that Lebas's policies would discourage young American priests from entering the Society and thereby prevent the expected transition of its membership in the United States from French to American priests.[67]

In 1905 St. Joseph's rector, James F. Driscoll, notified Edward R. Dyer that two non-Sulpician priests belonging to the faculty, Francis Duffy and John Brady, were about to launch a serious theological review entitled the *New York Review* with the approval of Archbishop John Farley. Driscoll represented this undertaking as the work of the archdiocese and its seminary, not of the Sulpician faculty. By adopting this position, Driscoll sought to evade the requirement imposed on Sulpicians of obtaining permission from the superior general for publication. The *Review* proceeded to be published as a work of the archdiocese. Dyer, who thought a serious theological journal desirable, was notified of its beginning on rather short notice and was not in a position to object.[68]

The publication of the *New York Review* between 1905 and 1908 represented the high point of intellectual vitality among the American clergy. The articles appearing in the *Review* challenged the official trend favoring the *a priori* methods of the neo-Scholastic revival. The founders looked to Cardinal Newman and his developmental approach as appropriate to the development of modern apologetics. Francis Gigot in his own series of articles on the higher criticism of the Bible and through articles of other Scripture scholars explained the importance of modern scientific methods of biblical study. Francis Duffy, as a student of the history of Scholastic thought, pointed out the diversity of thought within the Scholastic tradition. He and other authors demonstrated the importance of Duns Scotus as a Scholastic alternative to St. Thomas Aquinas. Edward J. Hanna, of the Rochester seminary, published several articles, including one on the human knowledge of Christ, delineating the idea that Christ had a developing sense of his own divine mission. In general, then, readers of the *Review* were introduced to the current theological concerns from a non-Scholastic historical perspective, the problems and findings of modern biblical scholarship, and the consequences of the new scholarship in developing modern apologetics. [69]

In January 1906 four of the five Sulpicians on the faculty of St. Joseph's Seminary left the Society. These were James F. Driscoll, Richard Wakeham, Timothy Holland, and Francis Gigot. Only Joseph Bruneau remained a Sulpician and was reassigned to St. John's at Boston. The four erstwhile Sulpicians announced that they had accepted the invitation of Archbishop John Farley to continue to staff the seminary under the direct authority of the archdiocese. Though no specific crisis had led to the break, the four had grown progressively disillusioned with the controls that the superior general in Paris imposed on the American Sulpicians. They shared the hope that only a measure of autonomy for the American Sulpicians could insure the attraction of American candidates to the Society, thereby insuring its future development in the United States. Dyer, by then vicar general of the Sulpicians in the United States and an advocate of autonomy for American Sulpicians, viewed the resignation of the four as an act of treason. The Society had a contract with the archdiocese to staff the seminary. The defection of the four had in effect rendered the contract invalid. Archbishop Farley had no qualms about the matter because he viewed the seminary as belonging to his archdiocese. He believed in his own responsibility for determining the staff to teach in it. [70]

At the time of the New York Sulpicians' departure from the Society, the pressures building in Rome on behalf of the narrowest conception of orthodoxy culminated in the decree of the Sacred Congregation of the Holy Office entitled *Lamentabili*, issued on July 3, 1907. The decree condemned sixty-five theological propositions labeled "modernism." The propositions were inadequately summarized from the writings of Tyrell and Alfred Loisy. On September 8, 1907, Pope Pius X issued the encyclical *Pascendi Dominici Gregis*, in which the condemnations were explained in greater detail. The encyclical restated the insistence that "scholastic philosophy shall be the foundation of the sacred sciences." This command was further clarified: "When we prescribe scholastic philosophy, we mean principally—and this is a point of capital importance—the philosophy which has been bequeathed to us by St. Thomas Aquinas." It is from the philosophy of St. Thomas that "the edifice of theology should be carefully built." On November 18, 1907, the pope issued another decree, *motu proprio*, entitled *Praestantia*, directed to seminaries, which stated "bishops shall refuse to ordain to the priesthood young men who give the slightest reason for thinking that they are attached to condemned doctrines and dangerous novelties." [71]

In the United States the *New York Review* came under suspicion of modernism. Two condemned figures, Alfred Loisy and George Tyrell, had published articles in the journal, and several American priests had published on sensitive issues of higher criticism of the Bible and non-Scholastic methods in theology. When the Apostolic Delegate, Archbishop Diomede Falconio, attacked the *Review* and those associated with it, Archbishop Farley eloquently defended it. However, Farley could see that the new climate of orthodoxy from Rome was not favorable to serious theological thought, and he ordered the journal to cease publication with the issue of May 1908. The reason cited for ending publication was limited interest in the serious theological thought. Later that year Driscoll was appointed a pastor in New York, and his successor as rector of St. Joseph's Seminary, John P. Chidwick, had previously been chaplain of the New York police department and possessed no academic qualifications. Francis P. Duffy also left the faculty for a pastoral assignment, and the era of scholarship at St. Joseph's Seminary or "Dunwoodie" came to an end.[72]

The new Roman trend forced important changes in Boston, where the Sulpicians had always enjoyed the confidence of Archbishop John Williams. In 1904 the aging Williams sought the appointment of a coadjutor archbishop who would in due course succeed him. The standard procedures then in effect were followed: the securing of separate *ternae* or lists of three nominees for coadjutor, one from the Boston diocesan consultors, the other from the bishops of the Boston ecclesiastical province. The name heading both lists was that of Bishop Matthew Harkins of Providence, an alumnus of St. Sulpice. At this point Bishop William Henry O'Connell of Portland, Maine, an alumnus and former rector of the American College in Rome, mounted a vigorous lobbying effort in Rome in which he alleged the anti-Roman biases of Harkins and his supporters. As a protégé of Pope Pius X's powerful Secretary of State, Cardinal Rafael Merry del Val, one of the architects of the anti-modernist crusade, O'Connell's views were well received in Rome. After several delays in acting on the Boston appointment, the Holy See set aside Harkins's nomination and announced in January 1906 the appointment of O'Connell as coadjutor archbishop. As the historian of Vatican relations with the American hierarchy notes, the appointment was a "gross violation" of the existing procedures and a reversal of the policy in effect since 1866 of seeking episcopal nominations from bishops and diocesan consultors. O'Connell succeeded as archbishop of Boston upon the death of Williams on August 30, 1907.[73]

O'Connell's accession as archbishop marked the beginning of a virtual persecution of the Sulpicians on the faculty of St. John's Seminary. O'Connell, with all his Roman biases, regarded the Sulpicians as harboring the historic Gallican independence of the Holy See. He also nurtured resentments against them dating from his student days at St. Charles College at Catonsville. While a student there, O'Connell had supposedly been the object of ridicule from fellow students. He felt that college officials had not done enough to protect him, and he left the school. As archbishop he demonstrated contempt for the Sulpicians by removing them, including the rector, Francis Havey, from the board that approved candidates for ordination. He excused the non-Sulpician diocesan priests on the faculty from participating in the common exercises of the seminary community. He objected to the presence of several Sulpicians on the faculty and demanded their reassignment, and he appointed diocesan priests to the faculty without consulting Havey. He forbade overnight priest guests, Sulpician or otherwise, to stay at the seminary without his permission. He questioned the Sulpician system of the faculty's sharing responsibility for the spiritual direction of the seminarians though that system had been approved by the Holy See.[74] These were all acts of harassment that damaged the morale of the faculty and served no positive benefit.

O'Connell posed as a champion of orthodoxy by ordering Joseph Bruneau removed from the faculty in 1909. The Sulpicians reassigned him to the faculty of St. Mary's Seminary at Baltimore, but O'Connell continued to hound Bruneau by reporting his heresies to the Holy See. The pretext was Bruneau's French translation of H. N. Oxenham's *The Catholic Doctrine of the Atonement*, a work circulating since 1865. After all these years, Oxenham's book was suddenly found to be heterodox and was attacked in *Civiltà Cattolica*, the influential Roman journal. Cardinal Merry del Val ordered the Apostolic Delegate, Archbishop Diomede Falconio, to bring Bruneau's alleged heterodoxy to the attention of Cardinal Gibbons. After studying the many favorable reviews of Bruneau's translation of Oxenham's work that had appeared in leading Catholic journals in Europe and hearing Bruneau's professions of orthodoxy, Gibbons wrote to Merry del Val to assure him of Bruneau's orthodoxy and to declare general support for the Sulpicians.[75] Neither Merry del Val nor others pursued the matter further. Bruneau continued to teach at St. Mary's until his death in 1933. This bizarre affair ended without a real heretic being caught and punished.

The Sulpician superior general, Henri Garriguet, visited North America in 1910 and had a strained interview with O'Connell on September 29. The archbishop asked Garriguet for the removal of St. John's long-suffering rector, Francis Havey, which was agreed to. O'Connell gave assurances that if he desired the removal of Sulpicians from the seminary he would give two or three years notice. However, in the following month O'Connell notified Garriguet by mail that the Sulpicians were to leave the seminary at the end of the 1910–1911 school year, which was accordingly accomplished. O'Connell was thereafter able to pursue his own version of a Roman seminary.[76]

The decrees condemning modernism were applied to the diocesan seminary when Pope Pius X issued, *motu proprio*, the decree *Sacrorum Antistitum,* on September 1, 1910. This document summarized the major provisions of the encyclical *Pascendi.* It elaborated the theme that the seminary is a place of piety and study. Directors of seminaries were enjoined to inquire closely into the students' personal fitness for the priesthood in terms of the "appropriate degree of sanctity." "Holiness of life and sound doctrine, therefore, are the two conditions which must be regarded as essential for the promotion of clerics." The pope presented the role of learning in the life of the seminary:

> The very conditions of the present age, which exalts above all the enlightenment and progress of humanity, reveal to us something of the labour which must be devoted to the acquisition of learning in its many and varied departments. A cleric who wishes to exercise his ministry in a manner appropriate to the present time, so as to fruitfully "exhort with sound doctrine and refute opponents," and to apply his intellectual resources for the benefit of the Church, must strive to acquire a standard of learning which is above the ordinary and practically on the level of the expert. He must engage in conflict with skillful opponents, the elegance of whose studies is combined with a learning which is often fallacious; their specious and rolling phrases are uttered with such flow and thunder that one might think some great novelty is about to burst upon the world. . . .

After such a tribute to the importance of formal learning, especially in its apologetical functions, and a sarcastic portrayal of recent learning, the pope appeared to shift ground to delimit learning. He did so in a tone that was contrary to the approach of leading American seminary educators who had stressed the importance of wide learning as necessary for the priest in the modern world. In contrast the pope stated:

> As a fact, however, man's life is confined within such narrow limits that he can barely sip from the rich sources of knowledge which lie before him: it is proper, therefore, that enthusiasm for learning should be kept under control and that the words of St. Paul be kept in mind: "Let no one esteem himself more than he ought, but let him esteem himself according to moderation." Clerics already are obliged to undertake the study of many weighty subjects, sacred Scripture, the doctrines of faith, moral theology, ascetical theology (the science of piety and of duties), Church history, canon law, sacred eloquence; lest the young students should waste their time on other questions and be distracted from their principal study, we absolutely forbid them to read newspapers and reviews, however excellent these may

be, and we make it a matter of conscience for superiors who fail to take precautions to prevent such reading.[77]

The document requires a profession of faith and an oath against modernism of all seminary instructors. With these unprecedented provisions, the Holy See made a decisive advance in exerting control over the seminary and by doing so reversed the Tridentine tradition that assigned the ordinary responsibility for determining the content of clerical training to bishops. Henceforth, Roman authority would exert a powerful influence in determining the content of seminary life.

The provisions of *Lamentabili, Pascendi,* and *Sacrorum Antistitum* applied to the entire Catholic world. The Holy See directed its attention specifically to seminaries in the United States in the spring of 1906, when Cardinal Girolamo Gotti, Prefect of Propaganda, wrote to Cardinal Gibbons to call attention to the bishops' duty to assure four full years of theology in seminaries. Gibbons had Gotti's letter read at the annual meeting of archbishops at Washington on April 26. The archbishops immediately agreed to enforce the course of four years of theology in diocesan seminaries. The archbishops requested that in his reply Gibbons call the Cardinal Prefect's attention to the lack of compliance to the ideal of four years of theology among the seminaries conducted by religious orders that trained diocesan clergy. At the annual meeting of archbishops in 1907 another letter of Cardinal Gotti was read in which information on seminaries of religious orders that trained diocesan clergy was requested.[78] The exchanges between Gibbons and Gotti resulted in the rapid introduction of the four-year course of theology as outlined by all the printed seminary catalogs in the next few years.

By 1910, the diocesan major seminary in the United States achieved the form, in terms of the length of its course of studies, that it would retain for the next half-century. During the period of transition in the development of the seminary from 1884 to 1910, the Holy See began to have an impact in directing the intellectual content of the seminary curriculum. It placed such severe restrictions on theological inquiry that the seminary could scarcely become the venue for intellectual activity. Instead, the seminary was primarily a place of professional learning. American seminary educators adopted a curriculum that was designed to impart a general knowledge useful in the varied tasks of ministry. This curriculum and the era's new textbooks would carry forward the vision of the priest of the 1890s into the decades ahead.

PART III

Roman Direction, 1910 to 1962

From the early twentieth century, the Holy See maintained its strong stance against current intellectual life with the oath against modernism for church officials including seminary personnel and by prescribing neoscholastic thought as the basis of Catholic intellectual activity. In the decades before the Vatican Council's opening in 1962, popes and Roman officials aimed to shield Catholics against the influences of unapproved ideas by frequently articulating the content of the Catholic tradition with a growing number of encyclicals and decrees. A major aspect of this process of Roman centralization was the Code of Canon Law, which took effect in 1918, to provide a legal framework insuring uniform church life. Roman authority controlled the code's interpretation and supplemented its provisions with numerous decrees touching all areas of church life. For the diocesan seminary, the code outlined an institutional structure which the Tridentine seminary decree had not done. Since the Council of Trent, the bishop had been the key figure in determining the values governing the diocesan seminary, but from 1910 to 1962 Roman authority through the Sacred Congregation of Seminaries and Universities increasingly prescribed the contents of seminary life. In the seminary, as in other areas of Catholic life, authoritative direction yields the impression that seminaries, regardless of location, were local manifestations of a universal ideal.

In the United States, universal ideals met the realities of local applications, Through the period, major realities included the steady growth of seminaries across the country, especially of minor seminaries, and the numerical growth of priests and seminarians as the general Catholic population grew. The efforts to improve advanced theological studies at the Catholic University of America exemplify the ironies of maintaining a pontifical university in the United States during a period of preference for Roman graduate training for clerics.

By the 1940s Roman endorsement of new trends in biblical studies, ecclesiology, social thought, and liturgy gave rise to American movements and organizations that touch on seminary life and learning. New professional organizations, enlisting the support of seminary educators, reconsidered approaches to pastoral activity, academic life, and the seminary curriculum. This interaction began a gradual process of overcoming the isolation of seminaries and seminary personnel and resulted in efforts to relate the seminary to standards of contemporary education. Despite the authoritative and unchanging formal structures that Roman authority affirmed with a mindset of certainty and timelessness, the diocesan seminary was adapting to new circumstances so that the period can be viewed as a starting point for subsequent changes.

12. The Roman Way

The Holy See's direction of the internal life of local churches advanced steadily in the decades after Vatican Council I. Its dogmatic constitution on the church, *Pastor Aeternus*, issued in 1870, declared the Roman pontiff infallible, but only in matters of faith and morals when speaking *ex cathedra*. The same decree declared, in virtually unqualified wording, the pope's "immediate" power over all other churches:

> This power obligates shepherds and faithful of every rite and dignity, both individually and collectively, to hierarchical subordination and true obedience, not only in matters pertaining to faith and morals, but also in those pertaining to the discipline and government of the Church throughout the world; so that by maintaining with the Roman Pontiff unity of communion and unity in the profession of the same faith, the Church of Christ may be one flock under one supreme shepherd. This is the teaching of Catholic truth. No one can deviate from it without danger to faith and salvation.[1]

This conception of universal jurisdiction had far-reaching consequences for the role of bishops in governing Catholic life in their dioceses. For the United States, one consequence of enlarging papal powers over local churches was the ending of the flourishing tradition of episcopal collegiality as practiced in ten national councils of bishops between 1829 and 1884, that is, the seven provincial and three plenary councils of Baltimore. For the universal church of the late nineteenth century, Pope Leo XIII issued landmark encyclicals to direct the content of clerical learning: *Aeterni Patris* of 1879, imposing the Scholastic thought of St. Thomas Aquinas on Catholic intellectual activity, and *Providentissimus Deus* of 1893, responding to the advancement of biblical studies with authoritative guidance for Catholic scholarship. Pope Pius X's profoundly anti-intellectual mentality, demonstrated in the crusade against modernism, was extended indefinitely by means of the oath against modernism required of seminary instructors. Leo XIII and Pius X used the powers of their office to strengthen devotional activities by means of encyclicals and other decrees on Marian piety, Sacred Heart devotion, Eucharistic activities outside the liturgy, and devotion to saints. Seminarians and priests shared these practices with the laity, and priests shared in the promotion of devotional life as part of their pastoral ministry. Furthermore, Pius X's policy of promoting frequent communion was a major initiative in developing popular religious life. The patterns of Roman direction and exhortation, continued in the subsequent reigns of Benedict XV (1914–1922), Pius XI (1922–1939), Pius XII (1939–1958), and John XXIII (1958–1963) through authoritative statements that informed the content of seminary learning, reinforced inherited forms of devotional life and articulated the Tridentine concept of priesthood and ministry.

At the turn of the century, the Holy See began to take an interest in the internal organization of seminary life, at first somewhat locally — that is, in the city of Rome and in Italy. For instance, Roman authority called into question the historic French method of seminary spiritual direction, in which the rector and the resident priest faculty shared in spiritual direction and confessions of the seminarians. On July 5, 1899, the Supreme Sacred Roman and Universal Inquisition forbade superiors of the many residences of seminarians within Rome to hear confessions of their seminarians. The French Seminary in Rome obtained an exemption from this provision, but the decree left an impression that the French system of direction was under attack.[2]

Pope Leo XIII took an interest in seminary life in the 1890s with encyclicals, to the bishops of Hungary, France, and South America, in which he urged careful attention to spiritual direction. After the turn of the century the Holy See began to reform the chaotic seminary network in Italy, where the tradition of many small dioceses sponsoring weak seminaries had gone unchallenged. In 1908 this process began to close many local diocesan seminaries and to create fifteen regional seminaries under the direct control of the Holy See. Such reforms appear inconsistent with the Tridentine ideal of local episcopal control but demonstrated a modern concern for efficiency and centralization. The ideal of pontifical regional seminaries would later be applied to missionary countries such as China and India. The precedent of Roman centralization in seminary administration was thus established.[3]

The early twentieth century was marked by a process of juridical reorganization to insure uniformity and centralized direction of all aspects of Catholic life. The administrative status of the Catholic church in the United States was altered within the context of several changes in the Roman curia outlined in the apostolic constitution *Sapienti Consilio* of 1908, among which was the removal of the Catholic church in the United States from the jurisdiction of the Sacred Congregation of Propaganda. The American Catholic church thereby ended its formal status as a missionary country. Thereafter, issues arising from the Catholic church in the United States would be treated in the same manner as those from other nonmissionary countries, that is, the apostolic delegate channeled American business to the relevant Roman congregation instead of Propaganda handling them all.

The more wide-ranging juridical reform began under Pius X with the motu proprio *Arduum sane munus*, issued on March 19, 1904, which started the vast undertaking of codifying church law. In the following years Cardinal Pietro Gasparri directed this task, which reshaped disparate church legislation into a unified code. Contradictory and obsolete laws were eliminated, and issues without prior treatment, such as seminaries, were given a legal framework. Pius X died in August 1914, and the work of codification continued under his successor, Cardinal Giacomo della Chiesa, former archbishop of Bologna, who took the name Benedict XV. The latter issued the apostolic constitution *Providentissima Mater Ecclesia*, which promulgated the new Code of Canon Law (*Corpus Juris Canonici*) on Pentecost Sunday, May 27, 1917. The code went into effect on Pentecost Sunday, May 19, 1918.[4] In the following years, the ordinary channel of jurisdiction in seminary affairs was the Sacred Congregation of Seminaries and Universities, which was created on the feast of St. Charles Borromeo, November 4, 1915, by the motu proprio *Seminaria Clericorum*. The new congregation superseded the old Congregation of Studies, which related to pontifical universities, and absorbed the Consistorial Congregation's formerly limited jurisdiction in seminaries.[5] Cardinal Gaetano Bisleti was appointed prefect of the new congregation and remained in office until his death in 1937.

The Tridentine ideal of the priest was legislated in various canons scattered throughout the code. The priest was obliged "to lead a more saintly interior and exterior life than the laity, and to give them example by excelling in virtue and righteous conduct" (canon 124). The bishop was obliged to see that priests confessed their sins regularly and that they daily fulfilled the spiritual exercises of mental prayer, visits to the Blessed Sacrament, recitation of the rosary in honor of the Virgin Mary, and the examination of conscience (canon 125). Priests were obliged to have a spiritual retreat annually (canon 126) and to recite the canonical hours daily (canon 135). In other words, the elements of seventeenth-century spirituality became normative. Other canons prescribed behavior that reinforced the differences between priests and the laity, such as requirements of ecclesiastical dress and prohibitions against engaging in business, politics, or military service (canons 137–140). Many canons outlined the pastoral ideal of the priest, appropriately trained and zealous, as minister of sacraments, preacher, and active in catechetical instruction.[6]

The code addressed the seminary in canons 1352 to 1383, which went far beyond the simple provisions of the Council of Trent's seminary decree, to outline basic characteristics of the seminary as it had evolved since the sixteenth century. The canons reflected many situations that had arisen in Europe. For instance, the first seminary canon (1352) insisted on the church's right to educate Catholic clergy free of interference from the state. Thus the Church upheld its rights against state claims to regulate seminaries, as happened in Austria in the eighteenth century under Emperor Joseph II or in Prussia under the *Kulturkampf* during the 1870s. Canon 1353 treated the necessity of a vocation or call from God as a condition for ordination. One measure for discerning ecclesiastical vocation was an estimation of the intentions and personal gifts of candidates for the priesthood, such as an aptitude for learning that gives promise of success in the priesthood.

The subsequent canons (1354 to 1361) treated the seminary as an institution. Every diocese was to have a seminary at a suitable place, determined by the bishop. In other words, it was no longer necessarily within the context of the cathedral as in Trent's decree. Large dioceses were to have a minor seminary for the training of boys in the classics and a major seminary for philosophical and theological studies. A diocese which found it impossible to have its own seminary was allowed to send seminarians to the seminary of another diocese, or to an interdiocesan or regional seminary. The bishop of the diocese was responsible for the seminary's administration and internal rules, within the framework of legislation from the Holy See. The bishop was urged to visit the seminary frequently and to be familiar with all the aspects of the seminary and its students. The seminary officials were enumerated as rector, vice-rector, économe (or treasurer), and spiritual director.[7]

The earlier prescriptions on the issue of spiritual direction of seminarians were made universal. The seminary was to have the separate office of spiritual director. He was ordinarily not to have other duties so as to be freely accessible to the students. The seminary was to have two ordinary confessors who were to be available to the students for confession. The spiritual director and the confessors were not to take part in the decision to call seminarians to holy orders in order to protect the confidentiality of their relationship with penitents. For the same reason, the rector of the seminary was not to engage in spiritual direction of seminarians or hear their confessions unless he was requested to do so by individuals.[8]

The exercises of piety were prescribed in a general sense and reflected the growth of practices and devotional forms arising since Trent. The students were to have morning and evening prayers in common, have a designated time for mental prayer, confess their sins at least once a week, receive communion frequently, make an annual retreat of spiritual exercises at least once a year, and hear a spiritual instruction once a week.

Canons 1364 and 1366 treated academic issues in the seminary. For the minor seminary, the instructions were stated in very general terms to be equivalent to the education offered in local secular institutions, but religious instruction and Latin were emphasized. For the major seminary, the requirements were more specific but fell short of providing a detailed curriculum. The major seminary was to cover six years. Two years were to be devoted to philosophy in its various branches accompanied by study of the vernacular language, Latin, Greek, history, natural sciences, and mathematics. Then four years were prescribed for dogmatic theology, and moral theology, Sacred Scripture, church history, canon law, liturgy, homiletics, and sacred music. A course of pastoral theology was to include hearing confessions, teaching catechetics, visiting the sick, and attending to the dying.[9]

Developing church legislation based on the code and elaborating themes on the spirit and purpose of seminary life was the subsequent task of the pope and other Roman officials. Pope Benedict XV's motu proprio *Cum novum juris* of August 7, 1917, prescribed the teaching of the new code in seminaries.[10] On more general issues touching on the priesthood, he issued the encyclical *Humani Generis*, on June 15, 1917, on preaching, in which he expressed in an authoritative fashion themes he had pursued in a number of addresses. He insisted on the importance of the priest's role and skills as preacher in the modern world.[11] His encyclical *Spiritus Paraclitus*—issued September 15, 1920, on the occasion of the 1,500th anniversary of the death of St. Jerome—was a plea for Bible reading among all Catholics, and to priests he urged that Sacred Scripture be the foundation of personal spiritual life and the basis for preaching. The latter encyclical does not deal with problems of biblical scholarship found in the decrees of the Biblical Commission earlier in the century but, with the 1917 encylical on preaching, is concerned with applications of biblical learning, especially in preaching.[12]

Benedict XV died unexpectedly at a rather youthful sixty-seven on January 22, 1922. As his successor, the College of Cardinals elected the Archbishop of Milan, Cardinal Achille Ratti, on February 6, 1922. He took the name Pius XI. Born in a small village near Milan in 1857, the new pope studied for the priesthood in Milan and was ordained in 1879 before pursuing studies in Rome in which he successfully took the standard examinations and obtained doctorates in theology, philosophy, and canon law in 1882. He returned to Milan to teach homiletics at the seminary before joining the staff of Milan's renowned research institute, the Ambrosian Library, in 1888. Ratti developed an understanding of scholarly activity as librarian at a research library, which scholars from across Europe visited, as editor of published volumes of Milanese church history, and as a regular participant in historical conferences in various cities of Europe. He became director of the Ambrosian Library in 1907 and then prefect of the Vatican Library in 1914. His thirty years of scholarly activity ended in 1918, when he was unexpectedly appointed the Holy See's representative in Poland before his brief appointment to the see of Milan in 1921. Throughout his reign Pius XI maintained a deep interest in the Vatican Library and museums and in issues related to education.[13] He pursued the clarification and elaboration of provisions of the code in all areas of church life, with particular attention to seminaries and clerical life.

In the first year of the pontificate Pius XI issued the apostolic letter *Officiorum Omnium* on August 1, 1922, on the subject of the recruitment and training of priests.[14] The immediate context was the problem of the church in Europe following World War I. He expressed the great shift away from the Tridentine presumption of clerical formation as the responsibility of bishops when he stated that among the sacred duties of the "supreme pontificate" there was "none more important or of more far-reaching significance than the responsibility of ensuring that the Church has a sufficient number of worthy ministers to enable her to discharge her divine mission." He called attention to the duty of parish priests, already stated in the code, "to preserve from the contagion of the world boys who showed signs of an ecclesiastical vocation" and to encourage their piety and learning. The pope emphasized the study of Latin because the church that "allows no share in government to the simple faithful" needs a language that is "universal, unchanging and not vernacular." Priests were to be thoroughly knowledgeable in Latin for these aforementioned reasons and for the opportunity it afforded to study the church fathers (but apparently not the Greek fathers). Latin's unifying effect seems to be the paramount concern in his exhortation to priests to defend it "inasmuch as they know how bitterly it has been attacked by those opponents of catholic doctrine who in the sixteenth century destroyed the unity of faith in Europe."[15] The pope called also for philosophical and theological studies according to St. Thomas Aquinas and thorough studies of pastoral theology.

Pius XI reaffirmed the importance of studying the thought of St. Thomas Aquinas at length in the encylical *Studiorum Ducem*, issued June 29, 1923, on the occasion of the 600th anniversary of the saint's canonization. The pope recommends the study of theology and philosophy according to the method of the "Angelic Doctor." He extends the praise to the example of his life, in which learning and piety were joined.[16]

Through the 1920s several Roman instructions prescribed more specifically what the code treated in general terms. In the motu proprio *Bibliorum scientiam* of April 24, 1924, the pope required professors of Scripture in major seminaries to have degrees from the Pontifical Biblical Institute or the Pontifical Biblical Commission in Rome.[17] He thereby reinforced the Roman monopoly on biblical studies. The Sacred Congregation of Seminaries and Universities issued the letter *Ad Regnum* on September 8, 1926, requiring the introduction of a course in catechetics in the seminary.[18] The letter declared that the seminarian's knowledge of church teachings was not sufficient qualification for catechetical instruction, but it was necessary to have a course in pedagogy accompanied by practical exercises. On August 28, 1929, the Sacred Congregation issued a general instruction that attention be given to oriental theology, history, and liturgy in seminaries and encouraged bishops to send priest graduate students to the Pontifical Oriental Institute in Rome for advanced studies.[19]

Of immediate impact on all seminaries, the Sacred Congregation of Seminaries and Universities issued the decree *Quo Uberiore*, February 2, 1924, requiring all bishops to submit triennial reports on seminaries within their dioceses. Seminary officials were obliged to complete a printed questionnaire that asked for such information as enrollment figures, course offerings, the faculty and their qualifications, textbooks in use, and extracurricular activities of seminarians. The decree set the initial timetable for submission of reports by continents. The first triennnial reports from the United States were due in 1927.[20] The bishops returned the completed questionnaires to the apostolic delegate in the United States, Archbishop Pietro Fumasoni-Biondi, who composed a report on American seminaries based on his five years of observations. Questionnaires and report were submitted to the Sacred Congregation of Seminaries and Universities. After the first submissions of the triennial report from the United States, the Cardinals of the congregation issued a general report on American seminaries expressing their reactions and making recommendations in the form of a letter issued May 26, 1928, under the signature of Archbishop Pietro Fumasoni-Biondi. The letter was published in the *American Ecclesiastical Review*.

The letter's first observation was the obligation of priests to encourage vocations to the priesthood among boys of their parishes. It recommended that vocation activity be formally organized along the lines of Italy's Society for Developing Priestly Vocations. A second major consideration was the format of the preparatory seminary in a number of cities such as New York, Chicago, Cleveland, and Rochester, which operated as day schools whose students either lived with their parents or, if they came from outside the city, lived with approved families. These seminaries were to be converted to boarding schools so that the students "so easily led away by the bad example of others" might have their vocation "safeguarded more adequately." They were to be "day and night under the watchful care of responsible Superiors."[21]

A major concern was spiritual training. The starting point was to insure compliance with the canon requiring that the seminary have a spiritual director with functions separate from those of other officials of the seminary. The spiritual director's role was that of teaching a deep spirituality, and he was to explain the method of mental prayer. The spiritual director was to be noted for his personal qualities and his experience in giving spiritual direction.

The letter contained additional exhortations on the study of Latin as the preeminently "Catholic language." Its study was vigorously enjoined as the church's official language, and it was to be the language of lectures, recitations, and examinations in classes of philosophy, theology, and canon law. "Ignorance of Latin," the letter concluded, "can only be regarded as a sign of languishing love for the Church itself."[22]

The study of canon law was expected to be given a more important place in the curriculum than it had been heretofore. The bishops were reminded that a professor with advanced training in the subject was to be assigned to teach the subject. The bishops were urged to provide suitable salaries for priest professors to enable them to live in dignity and save for retirement. Accordingly, bishops were to ensure greater respect for the seminary faculty among the diocesan clergy and the laity.

A series of observations on seminary athletics and bathing arrangements were most likely a result of Archbishop Fumasoni-Biondi's observations of seminary life rather than the product of the questionnaire. The cardinals of the congregation found fault with seminarians' developing athletic skills beyond the requirements of normal physical exercise and disapproved of public viewing of athletic events in which seminarians participated. In the same paragraph, the cardinals' exhortation on the need to ensure modesty in bathing arrangements apparently refers to unenclosed showers in seminaries.

Reactions of American bishops and seminary leaders to the letter were not circulated. Apparently the Catholic press did not carry expressions of opinion on the topic nor was there any forming of a consensus of opinion to endorse it, just a silent acceptance. There were, however, localized reactions to specific issues.

For instance, one American archbishop, Cardinal O'Connell of Boston, engaged in spirited exchanges with Monsignor Ernesto Ruffini, the secretary of the Sacred Congregation of Seminaries and Universities, over the issue of the absence of a diocesan minor seminary for Boston. A substantial number of Boston seminarians received preseminary training at the Jesuits' Boston College, located near St. John's Seminary. The Jesuit institution operated as a lay college, but many of its alumni entered the seminary and became diocesan priests. The Cardinal of Boston, who had risen to prominence on the basis of uncompromising adherence to Rome and was himself an alumnus of Boston College, was satisfied with the existing arrangement and placed himself in the ironic position of resisting directions of a Roman congregation. O'Connell's resentment of Ruffini was so great that the cardinal twice treated the trustees of the Catholic University to a denunciation of the monsignor by name.[23]

The triennial report of 1927 raised the problem of noncompliance with the provisions of canon law at Mount St. Mary's Seminary at Emmitsburg. The seminary was required to appoint a spiritual director separate from other activities and the priest president of the college was to be a separate position from that of the seminary rector in order to comply with provisions of the code.[24]

Certain provisions of the code, instructions of the Sacred Congregation of Seminaries and Universities, and the apostolic delegate's letter of 1928 dealt directly with the seminary. In other acts and encyclicals Pius XI treated such issues as the ministry of priests and their spiritual formation. He reinforced with exhortations the aspects of devotional activity stressed by his recent predecessors and enjoined upon all, laity and priests. As appointed leaders, priests were to promote and lead these devotional activities in the Catholic community.

Pius XI took as the motto of his reign "Peace of Christ in the Kingdom of Christ," as expressed in his first encyclical, *Ubi Arcano*, of December 23, 1922, and expanded in the encyclical *Quas Primas*, issued December 11, 1925, to commemorate the 1,600th anniversary of the Council of Niceae. In the latter encyclical he sought to reintegrate Christ into "lives, families, and public life."[25] The pope gave liturgical expression to the theme by instituting the feast of Our Lord Jesus Christ, the King, on the last Sunday of October. He tied devotion to the Sacred Heart of Jesus to the feast of Christ the King by designating it as the appropriate day for the annual consecration of the world to the Sacred Heart, which had been inaugurated by Pius X. The devotion was further emphasized in the encyclical *Miserentissimus Redemptor* of May 8, 1928, which brought the devotion closer to the official liturgy by raising the feast of the Sacred Heart to the highest liturgical rank.[26] And the encyclical, *Caritate Christi compulsi*, of May 3, 1932, related devotion to the Sacred Heart to the worldwide economic crisis.[27] The two Sacred Heart encyclicals stress the necessity of atonement for sin through the exercises of the devotion, especially the communion of reparation that ties the devotion to the regular reception of the sacraments. In another act related to the Sacred Heart devotion Pius XI canonized John Eudes a saint on Pentecost, May 31, 1925. Eudes was acknowledged as the formal author of the Sacred Heart devotion.

Marian devotion was not lacking in official endorsement through the period. The encyclical *Lux Veritatis* was issued on December 25, 1931, for the 1,500th anniversary of the Council of Ephesus, in which the human and divine natures of Christ and Mary's designation as the Mother of God were defined.[28] To commemorate the anniversary, the pope instituted the feast of the Divine Maternity of Mary. Pius XI's last encyclical, *Ingravescentibus Malis,* issued September 29, 1937, on the rosary, recalls the many encyclicals of Leo XIII on the same subject, that is, relating the recitation of the rosary to combating contemporary evils.[29]

The Holy See promoted John Mary Vianney as the universal model of priestly behavior for modern times. Vianney was born in a small village near Lyons, France, in 1786. As a youth, he aspired to the priesthood and studied Latin privately with a village priest but showed little aptitude for language study. Moreover, military service in Napoleon's army and an illness that prevented him from staying with his unit, thereby making him a deserter, delayed studies. After an interlude of hiding from the law, an amnesty permitted him to resume his studies. However, the Lyons seminary dismissed him because of his lack of aptitude for learning. After private instruction and private examination from the local bishop, Vianney was ordained a priest in 1815. He was appointed to a small village parish at Ars, where he won over a hostile congregation and became famous as a confessor because of his reputed ability to read hearts. Troubled souls from across France were attracted to confess their sins to the "Curé of Ars." His pastoral life became virtually tied to the confessional until his death in 1859. The message of Vianney's life was that an academic underachiever could become an effective and holy parish priest. Pope Pius X beatified him in 1905 and designated him patron of parish priests in France. Pope Pius XI canonized him a saint on May 31, 1925, in the same ceremony with St. John Eudes. In 1929 Pius XI made St. John Vianney the patron saint of parish priests everywhere.[30] Throughout the era, he was regarded as the universal model for priests by reason of his personal holiness and tireless devotion to the ministry of sacraments. Among struggling seminarians his difficult pursuit of ordination was a source of consolation.

The spiritual exercises were the subject of the encyclical, *Mens Nostra*, issued on December 20, 1929, on the occasion of the pope's own fiftieth anniversary of ordination.[31] The encyclical recalls the similar document, *Haerent animo*, issued on Pius X's anniversary in 1908. Pius XI's 1929 encyclical stressed the importance of regular spiritual exercises for both laity and priests. For priests, the pope took the occasion to endorse the

approved methods as a means of character training, for personal sanctification, and as training for pastoral activity.

The Sacred Congregation of the Sacraments raised a number of issues
related to the reception of holy orders in a general instruction to all bishops
titled *Quam ingens Ecclesiae*, dated December 27, 1930.[32] The instruction
was designed to protect the freedom of the candidates for orders. The candidate for minor or major orders was required to write out in his own hand
a petition for the reception of orders. If individual cases warranted, the
bishop could direct the rector to conduct an examination of the candidates
to determine if they sought ordination of their own free will and if they
had a true calling to the priesthood. These precautions were taken to eliminate the pressures and even coercion that parents or relatives were occasionally known to exert on a son or relative who during his candidacy had
decided not to become a priest. The instruction was to be read in seminaries once a year. Shortly after its issuance, Archbishop Fumasoni-Biondi
wrote a circular letter to the American bishops to remind them of the contents of the letter. He exhorted bishops to have seminary rectors bring the
instruction to the attention of seminarians, to hold conferences of seminary officials and professors to discuss the instruction's provisions, and
to have sermons in seminaries on the instruction.[33]

Internal dispositions of seminarians for frequent communion was
the subject of another confidential instruction of the Sacred Congregation
of the Sacraments, issued December 8, 1938, by the Prefect, Cardinal Domenico Jorio.[34] The letter addressed the problems arising from the practice of frequent communion in seminaries, houses of religious orders, and
colleges where residents attended Mass in a body. Because of the inherent
pressures of conformity in such communities, it was difficult for those who
did not desire to receive communion to abstain without attracting attention. The letter advised that all were to be reminded that frequent communion was optional and not obligatory, and that they were free not to
receive communion. It was also urged that in such communities a priest
be routinely available for confession at the time of community Masses,
so that members of the community could confess their sins so as to receive
communion worthily.

The most important and far-reaching juridical act in the area of
clerical learning during Pius XI's pontificate was the apostolic constitution *Deus Scientiarum Dominus*, issued on May 24, 1931.[35] The constitution provided a charter for the Sacred Congregation of Seminaries and
Universities in its direction of pontifical faculties. The provision for graduate degrees represents Pius XI at his most modern as he imposes uniform
standards on pontifical faculties for advanced studies in philosophy, theology, and canon law. When the constitution was completely implemented,

it ended the quick doctorates of theology and canon law conferred by Roman universities after written and oral examinations at the end of the ordinary seminary course. Henceforth, pontifical faculties at Rome and elsewhere had to meet minimum standards of course work and seminars. In theology, a minimum of four years of study was required for the licentiate and a fifth year for the doctorate, but the latter would ordinarily take longer, because a dissertation was now required. In canon law, a priest who had already taken the ordinary theology course was to take at least two years of study for the licentiate and a third year for the doctorate with a dissertation required. The pope thereby implemented elements of northern European academic practice to the Roman world. The dissertation alone introduced the idea of research into theological study, with far-reaching consequences for bringing critical and historical methods into Catholic theology. The provisions of the constitution would have their impact in the training of theological faculties for seminaries. In the United States the implementation of the constitution would largely focus on the country's pontifical university, the Catholic University of America, discussed in chapter 14.

Several American diocesan seminaries, however, had pontifical faculties to grant graduate degrees, including the doctorate, and therefore the provisions of the new constitution pertained to them. Such institutions were required to draft new constitutions to conform to the provisions and submit them to the Sacred Congregation of Seminaries and Universities for approval. The pontifical faculty granted in 1929 to Chicago's new St. Mary of the Lake Seminary, which had been founded by the influential Cardinal George Mundelein, had no difficulty being renewed in 1934. Others were not so fortunate. For instance, St. Vincent's Archabbey in Latrobe, Pennsylvania, had obtained a charter to grant pontifical decrees as recently as 1914, but interest in obtaining pontifical degrees at Latrobe was slight and few were earned. Likewise St. Bernard's Seminary at Rochester had a pontifical charter, which had meant so much to Bishop McQuaid. A few bachelor and licentiate degrees were awarded there annually during the 1920s. However, with the increased requirements of the apostolic constitution, the Latrobe and Rochester seminaries could not meet the new standards and lost their pontifical faculties.[36] The result of the Roman policy was clearly to make pontifical degrees less readily available at ordinary seminaries.

Baltimore's St. Mary's Seminary provided a different case. Since obtaining a pontifical charter in 1822, St. Mary's had used the privilege sparingly to award doctoral degrees to its own faculty and a few distinguished churchmen until bachelor and licentiate degrees became available to seminarians in the late nineteenth century. A Roman inquiry in 1924 raised the question of St. Mary's use of its pontifical faculty, and the Sulpicians and Archbishop Curley sent rather defensive letters to Rome explaining the seminary's practices.[37] In 1931 the Sulpicians drafted a constitution for St. Mary's to conform to the apostolic constitution, but the Sacred Congregation promptly rejected it, thereby ending the pontifical faculty. This act drew the ire of Archbishop Curley, who reproached Cardinal Bisleti for depriving St. Mary's "in one short and hurtful sentence" of its historic privilege.[38] Curley contrasted the inadequate guidance on drafting a constitution for St. Mary's with the numerous exchanges with Monsignor Ruffini on drafting a new constitution for the Catholic University of America, which was in progress at the same time. The Sacred Congregation showed patience with Catholic University but none with St. Mary's. Nevertheless, Curley's protests secured a reconsideration, and St. Mary's had its constitutions approved in 1933. By the late 1930s St. Mary's activated a small doctoral program, patronized mostly by its own young Sulpician priests. At the time, Sulpician superior John Fenlon was unhappy with the disarray at the Roman universities, no doubt caused by the difficult transition to the provisions of the apostolic constitution. He kept several Sulpician graduate students at St. Mary's rather than send them to Rome.

In the 1930s the Sacred Congregation raised the issue of controlling seminarians' activities during summer vacation. For instance, in response to the triennial report of St. Mary's Seminary in 1933, the Congregation praised the Sulpicians for providing a summer villa — Camp St. Mary's, in upstate New York — for seminarians' vacations, during which a modified seminary routine could be maintained. Attendance at the camp, which operated for six weeks during the summer, was optional because students were subject to the policies of their own bishops, who would have to support them during a stay at the camp. The Congregation urged the Sulpicians to enlarge the camp to house all St. Mary's students during vacation. In reply, Archbishop Curley pointed out to Roman officials the impossibility of expecting all the seminary's client bishops, whose resources varied, to support all their seminarians at the summer camp and the vanity of suggesting construction for such a project during the Depression.[39]

In 1934 the apostolic delegate, Archbishop Amleto Cicognani, informed Curley that the Sacred Congregation was considering issuing a general prohibition of seminarians holding paying jobs during the summer. Cicognani, who realized the necessity of many American seminarians' holding summer jobs to earn money for school expenses, was soliciting additional observations to forward to Rome. Though Curley's views cannot be found, it is likely that he favored the status quo. Curley shared Cicognani's inquiry with John Fenlon, who offered candid opinions of the Sacred Congregation's ideas of seminary training:

> Their chief idea of [clerical] education seems to be to surround clerics with all sorts of safeguards and to keep the candidates for the priesthood, from childhood almost up to ordination, away from contact with their family and with the world. Perhaps that is the only way in which Italian boys can be turned into good priests, but that is certainly not true in our country. I think such a system of education has very decided defects. Men so trained can hardly have the manliness that is necessary for the priesthood. When they are released from the training, there is almost an inevitable reaction. Priests with such training do not know how to work among the people. I do not wonder that there is an estrangement between the Italian people and the Italian clergy and that Italian men have not much esteem for the clergy. . . .
>
> If our American clerical students are to be subjected to the same hothouse system of development, the results will be still more disastrous because of the greater freedom which American priests have, and I cannot help dreading the results if the Sacred Congregation of Seminaries imposes Italian ideals more and more upon American seminaries.[40]

In whatever manner Cicognani interpreted the American reaction to Rome, the Sacred Congregation did not forbid seminarians to hold summer jobs but reaffirmed existing practices for seminarians to report to their pastors during the summer vacation. At the Third Plenary Council of Baltimore, the American bishops had vigorously opposed Roman suggestions of keeping seminarians in summer villas. Nevertheless, Roman ideas had sufficiently influenced a number of leading American prelates that several seminary villas were established in the United States. Cardinal O'Connell maintained a summer villa in New Hampshire for his seminarians; Cardinal Mundelein of Chicago had a summer camp for his students in northern Wisconsin; Cardinal Hayes had a villa at Suffern, New York; Bishop Thomas Walsh of Newark kept his seminarians for a period during the summer at their new rural seminary opened at Mahwah, New Jersey, in 1927; and Brooklyn seminarians had a summer villa at Water Mill, New York.

In his continuing concern for all aspects of the priesthood, Pope Pius XI issued what he came to regard as the most important encyclical of his pontificate, *Ad Catholicii Sacerdotii*, on December 20, 1935, the fifty-sixth anniversary of his ordination.[41] He regarded it as the culmination of his interest in raising the level of clerical culture, which he had manifested in

Officiorum Omnium, Menti Nostrae, and *Deus Scientiarum Dominus.* The encyclical essentially contained nothing new, but was, according to Cicognani, "a veritable 'Summa' of all that has been said and written on the priesthood, its dignity and duties, and on the preparation for the priesthood."[42] In it Pius XI endorsed practices of personal sanctification as superior to and a prerequisite for external works. Such a concept, of course, was already firmly established in the Catholic tradition. However, the pope was also concerned about adequate learning for the tasks of ministry. It might be noted that the encyclical points to a more corporate approach to the priesthood. The priest is not entirely the sanctified "loner" of some traditional literature but a participant in the larger action of Christ in the church. Archbishop Cicognani, in a circular letter to the American bishops, requested that the encyclical be read in public in "your seminary or studentate," that discourses be addressed to seminarians on its contents, and that students be provided with personal copies.[43]

In August 1937 Cardinal Gaetano Bisleti died, and instead of appointing a successor, Pius XI, who turned eighty that year, assumed the office of Prefect himself for the remaining seventeen months of his life. The pope's most noteworthy action as Prefect was to order an apostolic visitation of the world's Catholic seminaries to take place in 1938 and 1939. In the United States Archbishop Cicognani announced the visitation in a letter to the American bishops and that he had been appointed "Apostolic Visitator." With the approval of the Sacred Congregation, Cicognani stated that seven American bishops had been appointed "Associate Visitators."[44] There was apparently no public announcement of the visitation or stories and comment on the visitation in the Catholic press of the period. Consistent with the mentality of the times, it was an internal and completely confidential church affair.

While detailed reasons for the visitation were not given, it seems likely that the pope, a demanding administrator who often found Roman dilatoriness insufferable, was checking up on the results of his years of activity on behalf of clerical education. John Fenlon had developed his own views on the forthcoming visitation. As Fenlon had been told, a recent visitation of Canadian seminaries conducted by the apostolic delegate there was not taken seriously because of the inept manner in which it was conducted. Fenlon knew that Cicognani would conduct the visitation more thoroughly and predicted that he would find fault with seminaries because Latin was not used enough. But Fenlon found "the same situation obtains in France and other continental countries and in England; he will find it prevailing in nearly every American seminary, unless the professors put on a show for his visit."[45] Fenlon was able to assure Archbishop John Mitty of San Francisco that Cicognani adopted the "policy of not reporting very much to Rome, for fear that Monsignor Ruffini might take some radical action. This is just between you and me. . . ."[46] Assessing the Roman approach to the American seminary issue, Fenlon stated "The Congregation has a small opinion of the wisdom of hierarchies; all wisdom seems to be concentrated in the head of Monsignor Ruffini, whose mind seems, (to himself at least) to mirror the eternal wisdom."[47]

The visitations were preceded by the sending of a questionnaire requesting basic statistical information for each institution. The actual stay of one of the visitators usually lasted only a day or two. The series of visits took longer than the one academic year originally allotted and stretched throughout 1939. Archbishop Cicognani personally conducted the visitations in the Archdiocese of Baltimore, which included three of the most important seminaries in the country, St. Mary's Seminary at Baltimore, the Sulpician Seminary at Catholic University, and St. Charles College at Catonsville, Maryland, all conducted by the Sulpicians. Cicognani visited Mount St. Mary's Seminary at Emmitsburg, Maryland, also within the Baltimore archdiocese. The visitator had high praise for the Sulpician seminaries, though, as Fenlon predicted, he urged more Latin and Greek, "particularly Latin."[48] Cicognani's reaction to the Emmitsburg seminary contrasted sharply with his favorable attitude toward the Sulpicians. Mount St. Mary's was found inadequate in many ways and serves as a case study of what was regarded as a weak seminary.

Immediately following his visitation Cicognani brought the problems of Mount St. Mary's to the attention of Archbishop Curley for remedy. He did so before any report of its condition was made to Rome, apparently believing that an immediate correction would render an unfavorable report to the Sacred Congregation unnecessary. At the head of the series of complaints was the lack of designated confessors for seminarians; instead they were heard by the ordinary confessors who also heard the college students. Homiletics, moral theology, Scripture, and church history were taught by professors either too elderly or too eccentric to impart an adequate course for the students. The seminarians' complaints were directed to the quality and quantity of food and alleged unsanitary conditions in the seminary building. These conditions were attributed to the stringent economies of the college treasurer. Archbishop Curley exacted from the president and seminary director the promise of reform of the system of confessions and the retirement of several older members of the faculty. The president promised to improve the quality of the seminarians' diet and assured the archbishop that a large-scale remodeling that was already planned would soon improve the living conditions in the seminary. With these assurances, Cicognani apparently did not issue an unfavorable report to the Sacred Congregation concerning Mount St. Mary's.[49]

The Sacred Congregation of Seminaries and Universities promoted an international and universal vision to the seminary with its two major publications of the period. The first, appearing in 1934, was the *Elenchus Seminariorum,* an international directory of seminaries listed by dioceses. But more important was the collection of seminary-related documents of the popes and Roman congregations titled *Enchiridion Clericorum,* which was published in 1938.[50] The bishop or seminary educator now had a convenient reference work of official statements, from which the reader could readily see that most of the Roman documents on seminary subjects appeared since Leo XIII. The *Enchiridion* and the apostolic visitation conducted during 1938 and 1939 placed a period on the extensive seminary initiatives of Pope Pius XI, who died on February 10, 1939. The passing of Pius XI caused John Fenlon to wonder what would now happen to Monsignor Ruffini and all the rules of the Sacred Congregation.[51] It appears that they were all firmly in place as a guide for the future.

Eugenio Pacelli, the Roman-born career papal diplomat and Secretary of State, was elected supreme pontiff on his sixty-third birthday, March 2, 1939. He chose the name Pius XII, in honor of his predecessor and patron. His previous career and subsequent reign were marked by an absorption in diplomatic activities, heightened by the start of World War II in September 1939. In the area of seminaries, he did not continue his predecessor's role as Prefect of the Sacred Congregation of Seminaries and Universities and appointed Cardinal Giuseppe Pizzardo prefect, a post he would hold until 1967. (Monsignor Ruffini was appointed archbishop of Palermo in 1945.) The machinery of routine supervision of seminaries and universities was by then firmly in place. There appeared to be less scope for new initiatives. Though the internal history of the Sacred Congregation's activities are closed to historical research, apparently the results of the international apostolic visitation of seminaries did not warrant additional exhortations or regulations, except to particular seminaries. No letter was issued to the American bishops on the condition of their seminaries, as had been done in 1928 after the first triennial reports.

Despite the preoccupations of war and its aftermath, the first decade of the new reign was marked by major encyclicals of doctrinal significance that touch indirectly either on the idea of the priesthood or the content of seminary learning. The first of these was the encyclical *Mystici Corporis,* issued June 29, 1943, which, despite the divisions of the current war, affirmed the unity of Christians united in the body of Christ. Pius XII recognized the deepening attachment to the "unsearchable riches of Christ" that had been manifested in the Catholic world in recent decades by the progress of the liturgical movement, the practice of frequent communion, and the devotion to the Sacred Heart of Jesus. The pope stressed the organic unity of the members of the church as the body of Christ "linked together in such a way as to help one another."[52] Yet, the encyclical did not fail to stress the importance of the ordained ministry and the hierarchical structure of the visible church. The renewed emphasis on the church as Christ's mystical body entailed the endorsement of a closer interaction of the ordained ministry with the laity.

Pope Pius XII issued, on September 30, 1943, the encyclical *Divino Afflante Spiritu,* on biblical studies, to commemorate the fiftieth anniversary of Leo XIII's encyclical *Providentissimus Deus.* The pope naturally endorsed the warnings of previous Roman directives, yet he placed modern historical and critical approaches to biblical studies in a more positive light and is credited with ending some of the excesses of previous restrictions.[53] The Pontifical Biblical Commission elaborated on the themes of seminary pedagogy with an instruction titled *Sanctissimus,* issued May 13, 1950. The instruction restated the need for Scripture professors to have an advanced degree from the Pontifical Biblical Institute and asserted that teaching Scripture should be their only academic duty. But the document's main emphasis was directed to practical purposes in seminary training so that priests would make use of the Bible as "their principal cultural resource and intellectual occupation, and the consolation and joy of their hearts."[54] The Bible was to be taught so that it later formed the basis of daily study, devotional reading, and preaching.

Pope Pius XII issued an encyclical on the liturgy entitled *Mediator Dei* on November 20, 1947, in which he strongly endorsed the revival of liturgical studies, which had gradually gained influence since the nineteenth century. He mentioned the "zealous and persistent labor" of the Benedictine order in promoting liturgical prayer as "the fountainhead of genuine Christian devotion."[55] The pope emphasized the Mass as public worship of the community and the importance of the participation of the laity. This was meant to counteract the widespread habit of merely passive participation at Mass or making Mass attendance an occasion for private devotions, divorced from the actions of the priest. The essential role of the ordained priest in the Mass was not neglected, but the encyclical reinforced the themes of *Mystici Corporis* regarding the corporate life and action of the Christian community.

The nature of the sacrament of holy orders was directly addressed in the apostolic constitution *Sacramentum Ordinis,* issued November 30, 1947, which clarified the matter and form of the sacrament.[56] Previously it had not been clear what precise action conferred orders. Henceforth, the imposition of hands was defined as the essential form of the sacrament.

The encyclical *Humani Generis,* issued August 12, 1950, reaffirmed church authority in doctrinal matters.[57] It was apparently occasioned by the rise of the "New Theology" in France that was based on biblical and patristic sources. Pope Pius XII took the occasion to affirm the church's magisterium as the source and guide of church doctrine and to reaffirm the importance of the thought of St. Thomas Aquinas in the intellectual formation of priests, but he still hoped to encourage theological scholarship in biblical and patristic sources.

The foregoing papal statements had the theological significance of restating what was already well defined yet permitting development in a number of areas, such as elaborating the implications of the ordained ministry and the functions of the laity in the mystical body and in the acts of the church's public worship. The reaffirmation of doctrinal warnings of previous popes in the areas of biblical studies and theological methods did not at the same time foreclose new theological developments.

Several directives of the Sacred Congregation of Seminaries and Universities dealt with seminary learning. In 1944 a new instruction was issued to strengthen catechetics in the seminary curriculum. It was to be taught in the six years of the major seminary. General educational and pedagogical theory was to be offered in the two years of philosophy at least one period per week, and catechetics was to be taught in the four years of theology and was to be at least half of the content in the pastoral theology course.[58]

Church music was the subject of the Sacred Congregation's general instruction of August 15, 1949, which called attention to the uneven record of musical education in seminaries. Some seminaries had good programs, but most were hindered by a lack of qualified instructors. Bishops were exhorted to approve the program of music in their seminaries and to see to it that lectures and practice in music were given almost daily by qualified instructors.[59] The theme was taken up again at a more authoritative level and in a broader treatment with the encyclical *Musicae Sacrae Disciplina,* issued December 25, 1955. Bishops were enjoined to see to the cultivation of sacred music in seminaries and encouraged to send clerics with musical talent to the Pontifical Institute of Sacred Music in Rome for advanced training.[60]

Pope Pius XII had given new emphasis to the church's official worship in his encyclicals on the liturgy and church music. But he continued the recent papal tradition of reinforcing devotional activities lying outside the liturgy. The devotion to the Sacred Heart of Jesus was again endorsed in the encyclical *Haurietis Aquas,* issued on May 15, 1956.[61] Here, the pope related this baroque devotion more closely to sources from the church fathers and the New Testament, apparently to counteract criticisms that had been raised against it for an inadequate theological foundation. The stress on Marian devotion reached a crescendo under Pius XII with four encyclicals: *Deiparae* in 1946, raising the possibility of defining Mary's Assumption; *Ingruentium Malorum* in 1951 on the rosary; *Fulgens Corona* proclaiming the Marian year of 1954; and *Ad Caeli Reginam* in 1954, proclaiming the queenship of Mary. The most significant act was the dogmatic constitution *Munificentissimus Deus* of 1950, defining the dogma of the bodily assumption of Mary into heaven.[62] Through this period the traditions of extraliturgical devotion thoroughly permeated Catholic life, including the lives of priests and seminarians.

The spiritual life of clerics was again taken up in the lengthy apostolic exhortation *Menti Nostrae*, addressed to the clergy of the Catholic world on September 23, 1950. This document was issued a year after the pope's fiftieth anniversary of ordination, and its title is a reminder of Pius XI's encyclical *Mens Nostra,* on spiritual exercises, issued for the latter's anniversary of ordination in 1929. *Menti Nostrae* is a parallel document to Pius X's *Haerent Animo* and Pius XI's *Ad Catholicii Sacerdotii* in that the pope affirms virtually every apsect of the Catholic tradition of the priesthood: the superior holiness, the spiritual exercises of meditation and personal examen, the importance of the daily recitation of the office, the perfect chastity, the immolation of the self with Christ, and zeal for the tasks of ministry without the "heresy of action" that would drive out the supernatural dimension of ministry. The pope calls attention to the need for discerning vocations to the priesthood among youth and recruiting them. Pope Pius XII goes beyond some of the themes of his predecessors. He gave pointed directions for training in the minor seminary, where boys were to receive a training "as near as possible to the normal life of all boys." He apparently reacted against unnecessarily harsh and restrictive programs by demanding that training was to take place "in broad, spacious surroundings that are conducive to health and peace of mind."[63] He set down the objectives of intellectual training of seminarians in words that were often quoted by American seminary leaders in the 1950s: "In this matter, it is our most earnest wish that, in literary and scientific studies, future priests should at least be in no way inferior to lay students who follow corresponding courses."[64] Another relatively new approach was to promote the idea of diocesan priests living in small communities, especially for the instruction and moral support recently ordained priests could gain by living with and learning from experienced priests. He cited the College of St. Eugene in Rome as such an informal institution and endorsed the opening of similar residences elsewhere.

A model for the zealous priest was set forth with the raising of Pope Pius X to sainthood in 1954. Pius X's zeal for the ministry of sacraments as a longtime parish priest and activist bishop were recounted and praised. As pope, his zeal for the spiritual life of the faithful, especially through the promotion of frequent communion and lowering the age of first communion, were regarded as milestones in the development of modern Catholic devotional life. The state of theological thinking was such within the Catholic world that Pope Pius X's policy of restricting intellectual activity in the church, especially by the manner in which the crusade against modernism was carried on, did not then harm his reputation.

Clerical celibacy was taken up in the encyclical on virginity, *Sacra Virginitas,* issued on March 25, 1954. It appears to be the first encyclical devoted entirely to this subject and clearly reacts to contemporary developments in sexual morality. The encyclical reviewed the tradition of the excellence of virginity and the Catholic tradition of stressing its superiority over married life. For priests, celibacy was explained and defended. Its value in the freedom for ministry was raised, but it was not the paramount reason:

> Consider again that sacred ministers do not renounce marriage solely on account of their apostolic ministry, but also by reason of their service at the altar. For, if even the priests of the Old Testament had to abstain from the use of marriage during the period of their service in the Temple, for fear of being declared impure by Law just as other men, is it not much more fitting that the ministers of Jesus Christ, who offer every day the Eucharistic Sacrifice possess perfect chastity?[65]

The pope had to acknowledge the traditions of the eastern churches with its married clergy, but their worthiness as priests appears to be open to question because of their lack of "perfect chastity" for celebrating the Eucharist.

The concern for the proper dispositions of candidates for orders was the occasion for an instruction circulated to all bishops from the Sacred Congregation of the Sacraments under the signature of Cardinal Aloisio Masella on December 27, 1955. Its issuance was timed for the twenty-fifth anniversary of the previous instruction on the scrutiny for holy orders of 1930. The document is confidential and did not appear in the published *Acta* of the Holy See. The bishops' attention was again drawn to the importance of investigating the intentions of candidates for orders. The Sacred Congregation informed the bishops that some priests had been appealing for a release from the obligations of the priesthood. The letter described the problem and the Sacred Congregation's reaction:

> It is almost impossible to describe the keen anguish and the bitter torments which those miserable priests suffer, as the days pass after the beginning of their sacred ministry, who without any divine

call have rashly presumed to be marked with the sacred priesthood. Their plight can be clearly conjectured, however, from the petitions we receive imploring a declaration of nullity of sacred ordination or of the obligations attaching thereto. And when these men meet with a refusal, either because of the absence of a canonical reason for nullity or because the reason has not been juridically demonstrated in the case, they are obliged to be content with a simple reduction to the lay state but without any lessening of their obligation to preserve sacred celibacy. But this burden, too, they cannot refrain from trying to shake off by making almost infinite appeals to be freed from it. In order to have this discipline continue whole and inviolate in all its vigor, it is necessary to put aside mercy and to render ineffectual the attempts of these priests to contravene a law which has come down intact to our times from a venerable and ancient tradition and which has been incorporated in the Code of Canon Law.

For the common good, which this law was established to protect, must prevail over the personal convenience of individuals: otherwise attempts would be made, if only to mitigate the discipline, which would put an end to it and would bring, with the passage of time, consequences of such magnitude as no one perhaps can now measure.[66]

Cardinal Masella then makes the bishops aware of many problems arising from a lack of attention to the provisions of the 1930 instruction. The letter states that many clerics who appealed to the Sacred Congregation never heard of the instruction of 1930 and therefore had not been subject to a close scrutiny before ordination. Once ordained, those seeking release were offering as reasons various pressures placed on them to be ordained. For instance, some were poor boys sent to the seminary at an early age and simply did what was expected of them in following the path to ordination. Others wanted to leave the seminary because of doubts and anxieties about their vocation but were told by spiritual directors that God would provide the grace for them to be good priests once they were ordained. Undue pressures from relatives were also cited. Parents or close relatives saw economic advantage and social prestige in having a priest in the family and pressured and even threatened a son or relative to be ordained. Some seminarians feared abandonment and lack of means of support if they left the seminary or did not take holy orders. But the greatest number of appeals for release were on sexual grounds. Such applicants "depict themselves as invincibly and constitutionally prone to inordinate passion."[67] For them, extraordinary spiritual remedies such as frequent confession, communion, penances, and mortifications had not had the desired effect.

In response, the Sacred Congregation urged bishops to insure a closer scrutiny into the intentions of candidates for orders. Seminarians were to be asked if they were under pressures and threats to seek ordination. If this was the case, they were not to be ordained against their will, and the bishop or seminary officials were to assist them in resisting the pressures. More detailed instructions were offered on the scrutiny of candidates with a family history of mental and sexual problems or those candidates who had experienced difficulty with chastity, including the habits of solitary vice. The expectation was that those with prior problems in these areas would probably have them in the future. The Sacred Congregation gave no indication that the grounds for release from the priesthood would be mitigated in the future. Their remedy was to reaffirm the current practices. This document, nevertheless, appears to acknowledge that a rising though undisclosed number of petitions for "reduction" to the lay state was a matter of official concern by the middle 1950s.

Pius XII died on October 9, 1958, and nineteen days later the College of Cardinals elected as his successor the seventy-seven-year-old Patriarch of Venice, Cardinal Angelo Roncalli, who took the name John XXIII. Three months after his election, on January 25, 1959, he announced his intention to hold a general council of the church and a diocesan synod for Rome. This surprising act belied the initial expectation that John XXIII would be a caretaker pope because of his advanced age. However, after such a bold move and with the exception of launching the bureaucratic organization to plan for the council that was to open in 1962, the Holy See's central administration settled down to maintain business as usual before the opening of the council.

The Holy See's inherited ideas were apparently congenial to John XXIII, who was a product of the inherited traditions of clerical life and spirituality. At his age there was no need to reconsider the mental and spiritual habits of his years as a priest. His hortatory addresses to gatherings of priests and seminarians on the priesthood reflect the values that had been normative during his lifetime. His position was demonstrated during the observances of the centennial of the death of St. John Vianney in 1959, which was the occasion for a number of addresses throughout the year. The most authoritative of the statements on Vianney was the encyclical *Sacerdotii Nostri Primordia* of August 1, 1959, which is John XXIII's contribution to the tradition of encyclicals on the priesthood.[68] The encyclical quotes freely from the priesthood statements of Pius X, Pius XI, and Pius XII in the course of extolling St. John Vianney as the ideal priest in his faithfulness to personal holiness and zeal for ministry of the sacraments, especially confession.

The continuity of traditions related to the priesthood was again indicated by the direction of the synod of Rome, which took place in January 1960. Its legislation was noteworthy for a firm and even harsh emphasis on restricting the personal freedom of the local Roman clergy with rules governing dress and lifestyle, without a corresponding interest for innovative pastoral initiatives.

Cardinal Pizzardo, Prefect of the Sacred Congregation of Seminaries and Universities, took the occasion of the observance of the third centenary of the death of St. Vincent de Paul to issue a letter to the Catholic bishops of the world on selected problems of ecclesiastical formation. The letter, dated September 27, 1960, naturally extolled the contributions of St. Vincent de Paul. However, it aimed to warn bishops of the dangers of ordaining priests who lacked the requisite natural and supernatural qualities. This situation had arisen recently because of the pressing need to ordain more priests to serve the increasing number of Catholics. Accordingly, the cardinal called for a closer scrutiny of seminarians. He also deplored the loosening of discipline for seminarians and urged "that they must be made to accept subjection to rule and to realize the force of law." Without strict attention to rule and discipline in seminaries, the cardinal believed that seminarians could not develop self-control. He lamented the "naturalism" and "externalism under the guise of charity" that had penetrated some seminaries and the search for "up-to-date" methods of priestly training. Calling instead for a renewed emphasis on the supernatural, he designated the "true foundations" of clerical formation: "prayer, intimate union with God, a spirit of mortification, humility, obedience, withdrawal and separation from the world."[69]

The Sacred Congregation was likewise concerned about changes in the academic aspects of the seminary by the late 1950s. On October 27, 1957, less than a year before Pius XII's death, Cardinal Pizzardo issued a letter to all Catholic bishops on the study of Latin in seminaries. He informed them that it was common knowledge that the general culture of priests had declined. He lamented in particular that some recently ordained priests were not only unable to speak and write Latin but could not even read it. He did not name specific countries in a general indictment of the linguistic attainments of the clergy, but he based the assessment on reports from visitors to seminaries. He repeated the belief that unless priests know Latin, the sources of the Catholic tradition are inaccesible to them. The cardinal prefect urged greater attention to the study of Latin and, after evaluating current pedagogical techniques, recommended an approach that balanced grammatical instruction with the reading of literature.[70]

Official concern for Latin did not end with Pizzardo's letter but reached its highest juridical expression in a half-century of regular exhortations with the issuance of the apostolic constitution *Veterum Sapientia*, on promotion of the study of Latin. John XXIII, who as pope was regularly drilled in Latin conversation and pronunciation with a tutor, signed the document in an elaborate public ceremony in St. Peter's Basilica on February 22, 1962, eight months before the opening of Vatican Council II. The constitution restated the themes of previous exhortations by extolling the importance of Latin and Greek "in which wisdom itself is cloaked, as it were, in a vesture of gold." Latin is judged essential for all priests because they may be able "to acquaint themselves with the mind of the Holy See on any matter, and communicate the more easily with Rome and with one another."[71] After universality, Latin's value is said to adhere in its immutability, which was lacking in modern languages.

The constitution outlined a series of steps to defend Latin. Bishops and superiors of religious orders were to see that seminarians be well trained in Latin; they were to "be on their guard" and presumably take action against anyone within their jurisdiction "eager for revolutionary changes, [who] writes against the use of Latin in the teaching of the higher studies or in the liturgy, or through prejudice makes light of the Holy See's will in this regard or interprets it falsely." Latin instruction in minor seminaries was not to be compromised to meet state requirements for courses in other subjects. Otherwise heavier course work in Latin would have to be added or the length of studies extended to accommodate it. To protect the priesthood, the constitution demanded that seminarians who had not mastered Latin could not proceed to study theology which, of course, must be taught in Latin. Professors who would not speak Latin or use Latin textbooks in theological subjects were to be replaced by those "who are suited to this task." The Sacred Congregation of Seminaries and Universities was to establish a "Latin Academy" staffed by an international body of Latin and Greek experts "to superintend the proper development of Latin," that is, to develop additional Latin vocabulary to express modern concepts.[72] Finally, the same Sacred Congregation was charged with devising a syllabus for Latin instruction.

Veterum Sapientia is a remarkable document that reflects a Roman defensiveness on a range of issues. Roman officials recognized that theological discourse had shifted to modern languages and that pressures were developing for liturgy in the vernacular. Their response was to recommend the suppression of those advocating the removal of Latin in the liturgy or in theological learning. Latin instruction was more strictly enjoined, even to the point of disrupting the rest of the curriculum. Ironically, Latin was extolled for its immutability, while the Latin Academy was formed to enlarge its vocabulary to match the larger and richer vocabularies of modern languages that made them more appropriate for contemporary academic activity. The apostolic constitution attempted too much and was issued too late to stem the changes that were only a few years in the future. Its rigorous provisions were incapable of commanding realistic compliance, and the constitution soon became a dead letter.

Over a half-century, Roman statements rather consistently reaffirmed familiar official views on the priesthood and the seminary. Longer papal statements, *Ad Catholici Sacerdotii, Menti Nostrae,* and *Sacerdotii Nostri Primordia,* treated a range of issues related to the ideal priest and his preparation. Other decrees of Roman Congregations were directed to separate issues related to seminary studies, thereby limiting attention to some topics. When taken together, the decrees do not add up to a uniform curriculum for seminaries throughout the world. Still, those responsible for conducting seminaries knew that Roman officials articulated the ideals of priesthood and the seminary. The seminary's regular report to the Sacred Congregation of Seminaries and Universities reminded bishops and seminary educators that seminaries were subject to Roman scrutiny. By the end of the era before Vatican Council II the evidence of change in seminaries had come to the attention of Roman authorities who tried to stem it by issuing increasingly defensive statements.

13. Seminary Expansion

During the half-century from 1910 to 1962 the network of seminaries expanded and seminary enrollments grew as the American Catholic population increased. Seminaries in existence at the beginning of the century continued to prosper, and virtually all either enlarged their facilities or relocated in new buildings to accommodate expanding enrollments. New freestanding diocesan seminaries opened, epecially in the West and South where substantial Catholic communities emerged to sustain them. Though church canons outlined the internal structure of seminary administration, official legislation was limited on the subject of institutional governance. Thus, founding bishops developed governing arrangements that reflected local circumstances and personal preferences. Increasingly, bishops shared responsibility for conducting the new seminaries with communities of priests. The expansion augmented the influence of the Sulpicians and the Vincentians, but Marists, Dominicans, and Jesuits were also represented at new diocesan-owned seminaries. The Order of St. Benedict expanded its tradition of diocesan seminary training, adding new seminaries at several monasteries that were beyond direct episcopal responsibility. By 1962 the seminary network enjoyed an enormous success in numbers and influence.

During the first decade of the century American Sulpicians suffered blows to their morale with the successive losses of administration of St. Joseph's Seminary of New York in 1906 and St. John's Seminary of Boston in 1910. Another blow was the fire that completly destroyed historic St. Charles College near Ellicott City, Maryland, on March 11, 1911, without loss of lives. The Sulpicians relocated the college closer to Baltimore, on a property called "Cap Cloud," at Catonsville. The new St. Charles College was built and dedicated in 1913 and continued to serve as a minor seminary for many dioceses, particularly those of the East Coast.

The future of St. Mary's Seminary was a cause for concern among American Sulpicians during the early twentieth century. They believed its development was intertwined with the issue of providing a diocesan seminary for Catholic University. The expectation of a university seminary was stated in Pope Leo XIII's letter of approbation in 1887, and in negotiations for approving the university's constitution and statutes Roman officials desired the preparation of seminarians for the priesthood at the university. With the expansion of the university's offerings to include graduate and undergraduate divisions for laity and religious, the seminary idea came under consideration. In 1904 university Rector Denis J. O'Connell proposed to Edward Dyer the opening of a university seminary under Sulpician direction. In 1916 O'Connell's successor, Bishop Thomas J. Shahan, believed that the time had come to open a university seminary.[1] Shahan had in mind that the university would own the seminary and provide the academic training for the students while the Sulpicians would be responsible for the seminarians' discipline and spiritual direction. Such a program approximated the existing arrangement of the Sulpician direction of the priest graduate students at Caldwell Hall, which had been in effect since 1889.

The Sulpicians did not respond favorably to this proposal. In 1916 Edward Dyer and his council addressed a lengthy memorial to Cardinal Gibbons in which they expressed fears as to how the Shahan proposal might affect Sulpician interests and the future of St. Mary's Seminary.[2] The Sulpicians took into account that the diocesan seminaries founded in the 1890s were in successful operation and were likely to grow and attract the patronage of dioceses that currently sent students to Baltimore. It was also known that the founding of several seminaries was under consideration, especially those for Chicago, Dubuque, and Cleveland and the expansion of the seminary at St. Louis. It appeared that with the proliferation of seminaries and increases in their enrollment St. Mary's would face the loss of its national enrollment and be increasingly limited to students of the archdiocese of Baltimore and neighboring dioceses. It was feared too that if Bishop Shahan established a university seminary it would soon become a national seminary attracting the brightest students of many dioceses and the position of St. Mary's at Baltimore would be even more isolated. But, in the immediate future, St. Mary's was burdened by large enrollments that strained the capacity of its buildings, which were crammed into a small downtown property where further expansion was impossible. The issues that the Sulpicians faced were whether to relocate St. Mary's, how to maintain a position of leadership in seminary education, and how to come to terms with the Catholic University.

In fact the Sulpicians solved what was perceived as a challenge to them from the university by building on a current practice. In 1910, with the approval of the university rector, six gifted St. Mary's students enrolled in their fourth year of theology at the university. The six were ordained to the priesthood before taking up residence at Caldwell Hall for their year at the university. The practice of sending fourth-year students continued in the following years. Also in 1910 Dyer purchased a tract of land across from the university as the site for a future seminary. With the encouragement of Cardinal Gibbons, who was always very loyal to the Sulpicians, and with the approval of Sulpician officials in Paris, Dyer began the actual development of a seminary at the university. In 1917 some forty fourth-year St. Mary's students were brought to the university to reside in Caldwell Hall or in the Paulist community's St. Paul College as a kind of extension of St. Mary's Seminary. They were under the direction of three Sulpicians and one Paulist priest. In the meantime, the Sulpicians constructed a building on their property opposite the university, and it was opened in 1919 to accommodate the selected group of St. Mary's students from various classes, not only the fourth-year students. The program was regarded as an extension of St. Mary's until 1924, when it became known as Sulpician Seminary. The latter was entirely a Sulpician enterprise in finances and administration though it became affiliated with the university and some of its students concurrently attended university courses in nontheological disciplines and earned degrees according to university requirements.[3]

As the Sulpicians were planning their Washington seminary, a wealthy New York businessman, Theodore B. Basselin, who died in 1914, left his estate to the university to develop a program in homiletics for future priests. Rector Shahan and university officials, after years of consideration, decided to place the seminarians supported by the Basselin Foundation under the supervision of the Sulpicians for their spiritual formation and philosophy courses, while all other pre-theology courses were be to taken at the university. The Basselin College opened in 1923 to a select group of students who were to complete a bachelor's degree and then a master's degree before beginning theological studies.

Planning for a new St. Mary's Seminary went on during the 1920s. The earlier fears that St. Mary's enrollment would decline in the face of increasing competition from other seminaries and even the new Sulpician Seminary in Washington proved to be unfounded. St. Mary's annual enrollment exceeded 300 during the 1920s. It was opportune to plan a new St. Mary's Seminary at a new site. With the warm support of Archbishop Michael J. Curley, who succeeded Cardinal Gibbons as tenth archbishop of Baltimore in 1922, fund-raising was started in the parishes of the Baltimore archdiocese in 1923 and among seminary alumni. The goal was to raise one million dollars to build a new seminary in Baltimore.

Edward Dyer presided over the early planning for the new seminary, for which a tract of eighty acres was purchased in Roland Park, a wealthy Baltimore suburb, in 1925. Dyer died in November 1925 after a period of declining health. John F. Fenlon succeeded him as superior of the United States Sulpicians' province and continued the planning for the new seminary. Born in Chicago in 1873, Fenlon had attended St. Mary's Seminary and was ordained a priest of the archdiocese of Chicago in 1896 before joining the Sulpicians in 1900. Under his direction the Catholic architectural firm of Maginnis and Walsh of Boston was chosen to design the new seminary. The architects planned a large building of great dignity in a modified baroque style that echoes seventeenth-century France and makes a statement of solidity and authority. Its stateliness was also aimed to appease the uneasiness of Roland Park's affluent and largely non-Catholic residents about the presence of a Catholic seminary in their neighborhood. The great seminary was dedicated on November 5, 1929, by Archbishop Curley with the apostolic delegate, some fifty bishops, clerical alumni, and the governor of Maryland and mayor of Baltimore in attendance. Incomplete at its opening, the new St. Mary's absorbed the enrollment of theology students from the old seminary in stages. By 1933 the 305 theology students were housed in the new seminary. However, the new building was not large enough to house the philosophy students. They remained at the old St. Mary's on Paca Street, which could not be closed until 1969.[4]

During the interwar years several opportunities to staff new seminaries presented themselves to the American Sulpicians. As early as 1905 Archbishop Alexander Christie of Oregon City had approached the Sulpicians about opening a seminary in Oregon. However, Archbishop Riordan of San Francisco opposed the idea because the West was still mission country producing few candidates for the priesthood. Riordan's St. Patrick's Seminary, which served the West Coast dioceses, would have suffered. Christie, an alumnus of the Sulpicians' Montreal seminary, renewed the idea in 1910 during Superior General Garriguet's American tour. And in 1917 the bishops of the province of Oregon City wrote a joint letter to Edward Dyer proposing the formation of a provincial seminary under Sulpician direction. The Sulpicians were not then in a position to make a promise of personnel for a seminary that had yet to be built.

Meanwhile, a bishop of the Oregon City ecclesiastical province, Edward O'Dea of Seattle, expressed interest in building a seminary and had contacted the Sulpician Superior General Garriguet as early as 1922. O'Dea already had a rural site near Seattle and had been collecting money for a building. Though O'Dea originally wanted only a minor seminary, Fenlon proposed that the Sulpicians conduct a minor and major seminary. After experiencing the Sulpicians' losses of the Boston and New York seminaries, Fenlon was so concerned for security of tenure that he persuaded

O'Dea to deed the property to the Sulpicians, who would build and own the seminary. O'Dea also agreed to give them $200,000 toward construction. The building eventually cost $600,000, with the balance paid by the Sulpicians. The new St. Edward's Seminary, named for O'Dea's patron saint, was dedicated on October 31, 1931. Cardinal Denis Dougherty, archbishop of Philadelphia, officiated. St. Edward's operated as a minor seminary until 1935, when the first major seminary class started. After O'Dea's death in 1932, the new bishop of Seattle, Gerald Shaughnessy, raised questions about seminary ownership and finances that strained relations with the Sulpicians. The bishop was eventually made to realize that the Sulpicians had spent over $350,000 of their own money for the seminary that served the dioceses of the province.[5] St. Edward's Seminary once again became exclusively a minor seminary in 1957, when the new St. Thomas Seminary was built on a separate campus on the same property to house the major seminary program.

With seminary activities firmly established on the East and West Coasts, the Sulpicians agreed to staff seminaries in other parts of the country during the interwar years. Dubuque, which had been an archdiocese since 1893, had been considered the likely spot for a provincial seminary. In response to lobbying from the apostolic delegate in 1927, Archbishop James Keane decided to start a seminary and asked the Sulpicians to staff it. Fenlon was eager to staff a seminary in the Middle West and was of the opinion that Iowa had many "manly, religious-minded young men" who might join the Sulpicians.[6] However, the archdiocese did not have the requisite funds to build a seminary before the depression and the project was postponed. In 1931 the Sulpicians agreed to accept the invitation of Bishop John Floersh of Louisville to staff a minor seminary that was expected to grow into a major one someday. However, the Louisville project did not get under way before the depression.[7]

The first of the triennial seminary reports in 1927 brought St. Mary's position as an interdiocesan seminary under closer scrutiny by the Holy See. Officials of the Sacred Congregation of Seminaries and Universities misinterpreted St. Mary's small enrollments of seminarians from the suffragan sees of the Baltimore province, that is, dioceses in the states of Delaware, Virginia, West Virginia, the Carolinas, Georgia, and Florida, where the Catholic population was slight, to mean that the seminary restricted their enrollment. Roman officials wanted to see more students from these dioceses at St. Mary's and fewer from New England. John Fenlon replied that southern dioceses produced few seminarians and that St. Mary's enrollment would be considerably diminished if a policy of excluding students of the New England dioceses were adopted. It appears that some thought was given in Rome and in New England to establishing an interdiocesan major seminary for the New England dioceses in the 1920s. The idea was raised because Cardinal O'Connell of Boston excluded students of other dioceses from St. John's Seminary at Brighton. However, the idea was not pursued and many New England dioceses continued the tradition of sending students to Baltimore.[8]

Instead of New England, Detroit was the next major seminary that the Sulpicians staffed. Bishop Michael Gallagher of Detroit had opened Sacred Heart College, a minor seminary, at Detroit in 1919 under the direction of diocesan priests. The diocese's seminarians normally pursued their theological studies at Mount St. Mary's Seminary of the West in Cincinnati. The promotion of Detroit to an archdiocese in 1937 and continuous growth of the Catholic population in Michigan pointed to the need for a diocesan seminary. As World War II was nearing an end, Archbishop Edward J. Mooney, appointed to Detroit in 1937 and made a cardinal in 1946, began the planning for an interdiocesan seminary. Mooney was an alumnus of St. Charles College and invited the Sulpicians to staff the new seminary, which they accepted.[9]

Cardinal Mooney's plans for a diocesan seminary presented a novel aspect. He planned the seminary as a joint project of the bishops of the Michigan province, which, in addition to the archdiocese of Detroit, then included the dioceses of Grand Rapids, Lansing, Saginaw, and Marquette. The province's archbishop and bishops formed a board to own and operate the seminary and were collectively responsible for approving its policies of administration and formation. The new seminary would not have the kind of governing arrangement that prevailed in most archdiocesan seminaries whereby the archbishop was the final authority and the bishops of other dioceses, who patronized the seminary, had no say in seminary policies.

In 1947 the Michigan bishops entered into a contract with the Society of St. Sulpice for the operation of the new St. John's Seminary. Its operation presented another novel aspect in that it would be a four-year school of theology. The archdiocese of Detroit continued its Sacred Heart College for pre-theology seminarians, and the diocese of Grand Rapids also had a minor seminary. The Sulpicians needed only to supply a staff of theology professors. The new St. John's Seminary was built at Plymouth, Michigan, west of Detroit, with funds raised in all the Michigan dioceses. The seminary was built in a modified Italian Renaissance style characteristic of the Assisi area. It had a central building from which six wings radiated. The complex — minus chapel, gymnasium, and auditorium wings, which were to be completed later — opened in the fall of 1949 to a student body in the first three years of theology.

The expanding work of the Sulpicians was further augmented by staffing freestanding minor seminaries: St. Stephen's Seminary in Honolulu opened in 1946 and St. Thomas Seminary in Louisville opened in 1952.[10] The division of the Seattle seminary to form separate major and minor seminaries has already been noted. A similar splitting had occurred at St. Patrick's Seminary at Menlo Park, California, when the archdiocese of San Francisco opened a minor seminary, St. Joseph Seminary, at San Jose in 1924. The Sulpicians staffed St. Joseph's. A major reverse for the Sulpicians occurred when the Catholic University took over the Sulpician Seminary in Washington, as described in chapter 14. Nevertheless, the Sulpicians' commitment to minor and major seminaries grew as their American membership reached 159 by 1967.[11]

The expansion of the seminary activities of the western province of the Congregation of the Mission advanced rapidly with the growth of major dioceses in the West. The most important of the western Vincentians' seminaries was Kenrick Seminary in St. Louis. After his appointment as archbishop in 1903, John Glennon of St. Louis launched a program of construction activities. His most ambitious undertaking was the new and vast Cathedral of St. Louis, begun in 1907 and under construction for the following decades. Glennon also turned attention to the archdiocesan seminary. In 1911 he announced plans to build a new seminary to replace the old one housed in the decaying buildings that Archbishop Kenrick had deeded to the Vincentians. Glennon acquired property of some 370 acres in St. Louis County southeast of the city. Here in 1913 he began construction of an imposing seminary building in a stately English collegiate Gothic style to house 168 students. It conformed to the ideal of the other freestanding seminaries of the era, being located in a suburban site yet close to the city. The archbishop had already collected about $1,700,000 from St. Louis Catholics for the cathedral project in the preceding years and so he did not launch a seminary fund drive. He financed the seminary construction in part by collecting an initial pledge from the St. Louis clergy and by using proceeds from the sale of several suburban properties, but he borrowed more than half the $600,000 estimated for cost of construction.

The new Kenrick Seminary opened to students in the fall of 1915 and was solemnly dedicated on April 27, 1916, with elaborate ceremonies and the participation of the apostolic delegate and visiting bishops and clergy.[12] The Vincentians staffed the seminary but the archdiocese was responsible for operating expenses. Kenrick Seminary developed as the most important of the Vincentian seminaries. Because it was located at the metropolitan see of a large ecclesiastical province, the seminary attracted the patronage of the Missouri dioceses and those in neighboring states. Vincentian support for the St. Louis archdiocese was enlarged with the staffing of the archdiocesan minor seminary, Cardinal Glennon College, which opened adjacent to Kenrick Seminary in 1957.

The new Kenrick Seminary was the start of an expanding network of Vincentian seminary activity in the West. The seminary at Denver had been started on a modest scale in 1906 under Vincentian ownership and operated with a small enrollment from Denver and neighboring dioceses of the West. During the 1920s Bishop J. Henry Tihen of Denver sought to strengthen the seminary, though he did not wish to buy it from the Vincentians. In 1925 he announced a statewide campaign to raise funds for seminary expansion. Between 1925 and 1931 Colorado Catholics raised $450,000. These funds, combined with Vincentian contributions, paid for the construction of a substantial seminary building and a chapel with an imposing 128-foot bell tower on the seminary's suburban site. St. Thomas Seminary obtained incorporation from the State of Colorado and was empowered to grant degrees. The new buildings were dedicated on October 17, 1926, by Cardinal Patrick Hayes, archbishop of New York. Hundreds of bishops and clergy, and thousands of laity attended.[13] The greatly strengthened seminary served the growing Denver diocese as well as numerous dioceses of the western states.

The Vincentians were also active in southern California, where they had opened an academy, St. Vincent College, in 1865. The Catholic population in California through the end of the nineteenth century was concentrated in the San Francisco area. Southern California Catholics were within the sprawling diocese of Monterey-Los Angeles which, until 1910, extended from just below San Francisco to the Mexican border. Then the more compact diocese of Los Angeles was erected. Anticipating growth in Catholic population, Los Angeles Bishop John J. Cantwell sought to build a minor seminary to begin developing a native clergy and to end dependence on priests imported from Ireland. In January 1926 he issued a pastoral letter announcing his plans for a seminary fund. After a campaign of three months, assisted by the Catholic oil magnate Edward L. Doheny, the diocese raised the requisite funds for the new minor seminary, Los Angeles College, located on Detroit Street in Los Angeles and formally dedicated on March 27, 1927. The Vincentians ended their old academy for lay students and took on the direction of the minor seminary.

At the time of the seminary's dedication Bishop Cantwell announced the donation of a tract of land in Camarillo County northwest of Los Angeles as the site of a theological seminary. The donors were the Camarillo family, who had owned land there since the seventeenth century. Cantwell intended to build a major seminary there within a few years, but the years of economic depression postponed the project. In 1936 Los Angeles was raised to the status of an archdiocese with Cantwell as first archbishop.

The new archbishop took the occasion of Los Angeles's new status to express the need for a seminary: "What better monument to record the creation of the Archbishopric of Los Angeles than the erection of a Major Seminary—A School of Philosophy and Theology that would bring to completion the work begun when the Junior Seminary was founded?"[14] He again raised the ideal that Los Angeles Catholics should be self-sustaining in the development of priests. Another fund drive was begun in 1938 and resulted in the construction of a beautiful seminary in a Spanish mission style at a magnificent hilltop site in rural Camarillo County, fifty miles from Los Angeles. Archbishop Cantwell engaged the western Vincentians to staff his new major seminary, which was dedicated on October 14, 1940. The seminary complex was enhanced by the construction of the Edward L. Doheny Library, a memorial to the deceased millionaire, which housed art treasures and rare books and manuscripts in addition to the seminary library.[15]

The Vincentians were invited to take direction of the seminary at San Antonio that had already been in existence. John Shaw, an Irish émigré, became coadjutor bishop of San Antonio in 1910 and succeeded to the see the following year. In his first pastoral letter of 1910, Bishop Shaw promoted the idea of developing a native clergy to overcome the missionary status of the diocese, which depended on outside clergy. In October 1915, with the assistance of an English-born priest, William Hume, Shaw opened a minor seminary in the chancery building in San Antonio with an enrollment of seventeen young men. Hume served as rector, and other faculty members in the early years were émigré Irish or Mexican priests.

Bishop Shaw was appointed archbishop of New Orleans in 1918. His successor at San Antonio, Bishop Arthur Drossaerts, a native of the Netherlands and formerly a priest of the archdiocese of New Orleans, retained a keen interest in developing a seminary. In the few years after its opening, the minor seminary moved to a second location, and in 1919 Bishop Drossaerts organized a campaign to raise funds for a permanent location. The new St. John's Seminary was begun on the grounds of Mission Concepcion and though still incomplete, was occupied and dedicated, in the fall of 1920. After encountering difficulty placing graduates of the minor seminary in such crowded major seminaries as Kenrick and St. Meinrad, Drossaerts opened a major seminary program in the fall of 1928 and withdrew his students from various major seminaries to form the student body. San Antonio had been raised to the status of an archdiocese in 1926, and it seemed fitting that the new ecclesiastical province should have a seminary for the Texas dioceses. St. John's produced its first group of ordinands in 1930.[16]

Archbishop Drossaerts died on September 8, 1940, and was succeeded in January 1941 by Bishop Robert Emmet Lucey of Amarillo. Bishop Lucey was a native of Los Angeles and, after studies at the American College in Rome, was ordained a priest of that diocese. Lucey had attended the Vincentians' St. Vincent's College in Los Angeles when Marshall Winne, the provincial superior of the western province of the Vincentians, had also been a student there. Immediately after his installation ceremonies as archbishop on March 27, 1941, Lucey approached Winne about the possibility of having the Vincentians staff St. John's Seminary. It appears that Lucey regarded the quality of the seminary staff as weak. The seminary's shortcomings may also have been brought to his attention by the apostolic delegate. In any case, there appeared to be some urgency. Lucey asked Winne to provide a rector and a few faculty members by September. With the approval of the western province's council on June 30, 1941, the Vincentians accepted direction of the seminary. The public announcement of the transfer of direction was made on August 3, 1941. The speed of the action surely came as a surprise to the diocesan priests who served on the seminary faculty and who would be reassigned. Winne provided St. John's Seminary with a faculty of ten priests at the opening of the school year on September 15, 1941. Out of consideration for the limited resources of the archdiocese of San Antonio, Winne required stipends for only seven of the faculty.[17]

In the 1950s, Archbishop Lucey reorganized the San Antonio seminary. In 1951 he purchased the campus of Trinity University, a Presbyterian institution, built an additional building, and moved the archdiocesan major seminary to the campus. The new establishment was named Assumption Seminary. St. John's Seminary reverted to its former status as a minor seminary. The western Vincentians staffed both institutions.[18]

The western Vincentians also figured in the development of a seminary for the diocese of Galveston (later Galveston-Houston). Bishop Nicholas Gallagher had established St. Mary's Seminary in an old hotel at LaPorte, Texas, in 1901 with a small staff of priests of the Congregation of St. Basil from Toronto, who remained until 1911. Thereafter Bishop Gallagher and his successor, Bishop Christopher E. Byrne, supplied a staff of diocesan priests for St. Mary's Seminary for the following forty years. Bishop Byrne raised money over the years to build a permanent seminary building. His successor, Bishop Wendelin Nold, sought to assure the seminary a regular supply of faculty personnel and entrusted St. Mary's Seminary to the western Vincentians in 1951. He also fulfilled the long-delayed plans for better facilities by relocating St. Mary's Seminary in a new complex of buildings in Houston in 1954.[19] Apparently, no thought was given in the diocese of Galveston-Houston to assisting in the development of the archdiocese of San Antonio's seminaries only 200 miles away.

To provide Vincentian priests with advanced studies for seminary faculties, Winne sought to develop a residence or house of studies of the kind established by other orders at Catholic University. The Papal Countess Estelle Doheny, widow of Edward L. Doheny, funded the building of a Vincentian residence at the university as a memorial to her husband. The residence, located near the center of the university campus, was completed and dedicated in 1941.[20] In the following years young Vincentian priests could pursue graduate studies at the university during the school year or during the summer session. Vincentians who taught the major subjects in theology, however, generally went on to obtain their doctorates at the Dominican's Angelicum in Rome.

In addition to the Vincentians' seminary activities at St. Louis, Denver, Los Angeles, San Antonio, and Houston, they staffed new freestanding minor seminaries of St. John's in Kansas City (Missouri) in 1928, St. Francis in Bethany, Oklahoma, for the diocese of Oklahoma City–Tulsa in 1946, and Regina Cleri for the Tucson diocese in 1956. This record contrasts with the limited seminary opportunities available to the eastern Vincentians, whose important seminary commitment was the Seminary of Our Lady of Angels at Niagara University. By 1960 the western Vincentians had 139 priests on seminary staffs, and the strain of developing trained personnel for all their institutions was beginning to show.[21] When James A. Fischer became superior of the western province in 1962, he announced to his confreres that, because of the shortfall of ordinations for the province, over the next five years only about half of the needed personnel would be available to meet the many seminary commitments taken on during the 1940s and 1950s. He predicted trying years in the future.[22]

Diocesan seminaries in the western United States advanced markedly from the interwar years onward. The bishops who were responsible for founding new western seminaries did not have the time or resources to develop seminary faculties among their own diocesan clergy, or they were unwilling to do so. Instead, bishops shared responsibility for conducting seminaries with communities of priests. Of the freestanding diocesan major seminaries west of the Mississippi River, those of the larger urban Catholic communities at San Francisco, Seattle, St. Louis, Denver, Los Angeles, San Antonio, and Houston were conducted by Sulpicians or Vincentians by the 1950s. Only the smaller major seminaries founded during the period, at Little Rock and San Diego, were staffed by diocesan priests. The Catholic communities of the West developed sufficiently that they were able to supply the funds and the students to sustain seminaries. However, in the case of seminary staffing they depended on communities of priests from the older Catholic areas of the Middle West and East.

Benedictine seminaries continued to train diocesan candidates for the priesthood along with their own monastic candidates throughout the period, in the context of each abbey's particular educational, pastoral, and institutional enterprises. The seminary of St. Vincent Archabbey at Latrobe, Pennsylvania, drew diocesan students from the populous diocese of Pittsburgh (which sent many but not all of its seminarians there) and from other Pennsylvania and Ohio dioceses. The monastic community of St. Meinrad prospered and was elevated to the honorific status of an archabbey as the leading American Benedictine monastery of the Swiss tradition at the time of its centennial in 1954. St. Meinrad was patronized largely by the Indianapolis diocese (created an archdiocese in 1944) and other dioceses in Indiana, Illinois, and Kentucky.

St. John's Abbey in Collegeville, Minnesota, achieved great distinction for American leadership in the liturgical movement through the liturgical activist Virgil Michel, the publication of the periodical *Worship* (earlier called *Orate Fratres*), and publications of its Liturgical Press.[23] These activities provided a countertradition to the often extreme manifestations of extraliturgical devotion that had often overshadowed the position of the official liturgy in Catholic life. Emphasis on understanding of and participation in the liturgy, always great in Benedictine monasteries, was particularly strong at St. John's Abbey and permeated the life of its lay college and seminary.

The seminary at St. John's Abbey continued to serve dioceses of the region, especially the diocese of St. Cloud, where it was located. In 1947 Bishop Peter Bartholome of St. Cloud purchased a small tract of land from the abbey located near the monastery buildings. He built there, at diocesan expense, St. Cloud Seminary, a residence for the students of his diocese and those of other dioceses. The residence opened in 1949. The bishop appointed diocesan priests as rector and spiritual director. The diocesan seminarians continued to take their academic courses at the abbey's seminary.[24] The policy of the bishop of St. Cloud is the only case among the Benedictine seminaries of the local bishop assuming direction of the spiritual and pastoral formation of diocesan seminarians.

The major seminaries at St. Vincent and St. Meinrad archabbeys were substantial undertakings with annual enrollments of about two hundred monastic and diocesan seminarians by the late 1930s. Their enrollment paralleled many of the freestanding diocesan seminaries of the East and Middle West. The major seminary at St. John's Abbey in Minnesota began to achieve annual enrollments of over one hundred by the late 1930s. Thus St. Vincent, St. Meinrad, and St. John's were the three large and influential Benedictine seminaries. Other Benedictine abbeys developed seminaries enjoying generally more modest influence during the period.

Mount Angel Abbey at St. Benedict, Oregon, continued to train a small number of seminarians sent from dioceses in the region. The abbey's old buildings were destroyed by fire in 1926 and the rebuilt complex, which opened in 1927, included a seminary wing that provided better accommodations for diocesan seminarians.[25] However, with the founding of St. Edward's Seminary in Seattle, the number of diocesan seminarians available in the region did not permit the enrollment to rise above one hundred major seminarians.

St. Benedict's Abbey in Atchison, Kansas, a monastery founded from St. Vincent's Archabbey, also trained diocesan seminarians along with its own during the period, but the major work continued to be a liberal arts college for men. Fifty miles from Atchison, the monks of Conception Abbey, in rural northwestern Missouri, had sponsored a lay academy and college with limited success. In 1940 they decided to discontinue work in education for laymen because the abbey was poorly located to attract an adequate enrollment. Instead they turned their attention to opening an interdiocesan major seminary as more suitable to their monastery's spirit and location. Subsequently they developed Immaculate Conception Seminary with minor and major departments to serve dioceses in the region.[26]

By the 1940s St. Bede Abby at Peru, Illinois, founded from St. Vincent's in the 1890s, had developed a college for laymen and opened its monastic seminary to include a modest enrollment of diocesan seminarians from the region. By the late 1950s St. Mary's Abbey in Morristown, New Jersey, St. Gregory's Abbey in Shawnee, Oklahoma, and Assumption Abbey in Richardton, North Dakota, also took in a few diocesan students for training with monastic seminarians. St. Bernard's Abbey in Cullman, Alabama, another establishment of St. Vincent's, which also operated a lay college, opened a diocesan seminary in 1952 to serve southern dioceses. St. Maur's Priory at South Union, Kentucky, was founded in 1947 from St. John's Abbey as an interracial monastery. It too opened a diocesan seminary in the 1950s.[27]

The Benedictines ordinarily settled in rural areas in order to develop large farming enterprises. In 1885 Boniface Wimmer made an exception to this pattern by sending three of his monks of Czech nationality to staff the Czech parish of St. Procopius in Chicago. The monks established a priory at the parish that was raised to the status of an abbey in 1894; they also sponsored a college for laymen. The abbey and college of St. Procopius was moved to a more spacious location in suburban Lisle, Illinois, in 1900. The monastic community and its college maintained a strong Czech identity. The St. Procopius monks also founded a major seminary in 1914 that was open to diocesan seminarians of Czech origin sponsored by their bishops.[28]

The volume of Sulpician, Vincentian, and Benedictine activities in diocesan seminary education was not matched by the activities of other communities of priests. However, the Order of Friars Minor, the main branch of the Franciscan order, continued to operate its diocesan seminary, which came to be called Christ the King Seminary, at St. Bonaventure University in Olean, New York, through the period. Another branch of the Franciscans, the Third Order Regular, developed St. Francis College for laymen at Loretto in western Pennsylvania early in the century.[29] The order opened a seminary there in 1912 for its own candidates and for seminarians of local dioceses. Eventually it was named Our Lady of Loretto Seminary. The interdiocesan seminary at Loretto is located about fifty miles from the Benedictine seminary at Latrobe. The seminaries of western Pennsylvania are located within two hundred miles of the western New York diocesan seminaries at St. Bonaventure University and Niagara University. The region provided a number of seminary options for the patronage of bishops.

Several religious orders that had not previously figured in staffing diocesan seminaries became active in the field — for example, the Marists in New Orleans, the Jesuits in Chicago, and the Dominicans in Dubuque.

The Society of Mary (Marists) shared in the development of the diocesan clergy in Louisiana during the period. The seminary experience of the New Orleans archdiocese had been uneven in the nineteenth century. The previous Vincentian effort at St. Stephen's parish in New Orleans lasted only from 1900 to 1907. The diocese continued to depend on the importation of French clergy, so that by 1914 three-fourths of the 175 priests of the archdiocese of New Orleans were émigrés, mostly from France. Only eighteen priests had been born in the United Sates. Louisiana Catholicism with its French background was marked by a Jansenist tendency toward infrequent contact with the sacraments and a high proportion of nominal Catholics. These characteristics were not conducive to attracting young men to become priests. In the early twentieth century the growth of devotional practices and the new trend toward frequent communion began to alter the older patterns of religious behavior.[30]

While his predecessors had been unable to sustain a seminary, Archbishop John Shaw, who had previously founded the San Antonio seminary, was determined to establish a major seminary after becoming archbishop of New Orleans in 1918. In August 1919 he gathered a group of 200 prominent laymen to establish the "Diocesan Seminary Fund Crusade" with elaborate publicity plans with literature, lectures, and solicitations. The seminary effort was launched on January 8, 1921, with a public parade culminating in solemn Benediction of the Blessed Sacrament in Jackson Square. The "crusade" closed on January 20 after 50,000 subscribers had pledged $1,170,115. Construction of the seminary building was begun in a residential neighborhood in New Orleans in February 1922 and was completed on September 1, 1923. The new Notre Dame Seminary was designed as a graceful combination of French and Spanish colonial architecture and was large enough to house ninety-six students and six faculty. Archbishop Shaw engaged the services of the Washington, D. C., province of the Society of Mary (Marists) to provide a faculty. The seminary opened in 1923 to a first-year class of twenty-five major seminary students representing the three Louisiana dioceses, Alexandria, Lafayette, and New Orleans.[31] The successful seminary founding was a turning point in the long history of Catholicism in Louisiana. Thereafter the Louisiana dioceses became less dependent on foreign clergy.

Of the new seminaries founded during the 1920s Chicago's was the largest and grandest and brought the Society of Jesus into the work of conducting a diocesan major seminary.[32] Chicago's turbulent ecclesiastical history during the 1850s and 1860s did not allow for the stability to sustain a seminary. When Archbishop James Quigley arrived in Chicago from the see of Buffalo in 1902, he recognized that a seminary was long overdue and intended to build one. In 1905 he bought a building in downtown Chicago where he started Cathedral College as a preparatory seminary for day students. He intended to establish a major seminary in due course. In the meantime Chicago's numerous major seminarians continued to be trained at various seminaries according to ethnic background. Germans and Poles attended St. Francis in Milwaukee, other Poles attended Sts. Cyril and Methodius in Detroit. Irish Americans enrolled at St. Mary's in Baltimore or Kenrick in St. Louis. There was no lack of students for the priesthood; the only thing Chicago lacked was its own seminary. But Quigley, whose health had been poor for years, died in 1915 without building a seminary.

Quigley's successor was George William Mundelein, the dynamic auxiliary bishop of Brooklyn, who, unlike many German American priests of the era, was thoroughly American and at age forty-three in 1916 had the energy and the years to carry out major projects. Installed as archbishop of Chicago in February 1916, Mundelein began his administration with a flurry of projects. Among the first to be announced was the plan to build a worthy minor seminary as a memorial to Archbishop Quigley. According to his biographer, Mundelein was accustomed to "going first class." He hired his New York architect, Gustav Steinback, to design a seminary complex in a graceful French Gothic style with an elegant chapel that copied Sainte Chapelle in Paris. The Quigley Preparatory Seminary was built on Rush Street between Pearson and Chestnut streets and opened in 1918.

Mundelein's plans for a major seminary soon followed. In 1918 he bought up parcels of land that included a lake in Lake County, about forty miles north of downtown Chicago. The public announcement to build a seminary was made in April 1920. The new seminary was to be called St. Mary of the Lake Seminary, thereby continuing the name of the ill-fated nineteenth-century university and seminary. Mundelein acquired the services of a young Chicago architect, Joseph W. McCarthy, who was commissioned to give shape to the archbishop's ideas of a seminary complex unlike any other in the United States. McCarthy planned a campus of separate buildings laid out in a cross arrangement in front of a lake. The buildings were of a modified Georgian or colonial style that was resoundingly American. The Chapel of the Immaculate Conception echoed the Congregational church in Old Lyme, Connecticut, that Mundelein admired during family vacations as a boy. The archbishop had a residence built on the property that was a copy of Washington's home at Mount Vernon. The resemblance to things American usually stopped at the door. Inside the mentality was Roman and Catholic. The seminary library echoes Thomas Jefferson's University of Virginia, but is interior replicates the Barberini Palace in Rome. In other words, "American on the outside," as Mundelein's biographer points out, "but Roman to the core. . . ."[33]

The magnificence was sustained by the archbishop's skills as a financier. He had some wealthy donors to draw on at the start of the project, such as Edward Hines, the lumber magnate, who initially donated $500,000, followed by smaller donations, but such donors were few. Mundelein consigned a gift of $256,000 from Chicago priests for his twenty-fifth anniversary of ordination in 1920 to the seminary. But there was no fund drive with announced goals. Chicago's large parishes were simply taxed over the years to pay ongoing costs of constructing some fourteen buildings, of which the last major one, the auditorium, was completed in 1934. In the absence of announced figures, Edward Kantowicz has estimated from the existing evidence that the buildings of St. Mary of the Lake Seminary cost about $12,500,000, a figure that far exceeded the costs of other American diocesan seminaries during the era.

St. Mary of the Lake Seminary opened to its first class of philosophy students in the fall of 1921 and a class was added each year (and as new buildings were finished) until the first ordination class completed studies in 1926. Mundelein's initial grand idea was to sponsor a great Catholic university at the site, surrounded with affiliated residential colleges of religious orders. Such an idea was already in operation at the Catholic University in Washington and was not likely to attract support. However, some elements of his university aspirations survived. For instance, he succeeded in engaging the Jesuits to form the seminary teaching faculty. The

Society of Jesus was the premier teaching order in the Catholic church. Having Jesuit professors meant having the best or "going first class." However, the seminary rector, J. Gerald Kealy, and his staff were diocesan priests. A strict separation was maintained between the Jesuit faculty and the students outside of class hours so that the seminarians would not be attracted to become Jesuits. In 1929 Mundelein also acquired a charter from the Holy See to grant pontifical degrees in theology, including the doctorate. This formidable political achievement was accomplished at a time when such pontifical charters were being withdrawn elsewhere. The first doctorate was granted in 1930. He also opened a residence in Rome, Santa Maria del Lago, as a kind of finishing school for the most promising of St. Mary of the Lake's ordained alumni. In such a style and scale, Mundelein created a first-class seminary in which he molded a unified Chicago clergy despite diverse ethnic backgrounds.

In the 1920s, Archbishop James Keane of Dubuque considered founding a major seminary for his archdiocese and province, and he secured the agreement of the Society of St. Sulpice to staff it. However, economic depression and World War II indefinitely postponed his seminary plans. Subsequently Archbishop Francis Beckman welcomed the Dominican priests of the Province of St. Albert to Dubuque in the 1940s. In 1951 they moved their province's theologate from River Forest, Illinois, to Dubuque. In the same year Dubuque's Archbishop Henry Rohlman and the Iowa bishops announced their intention to open a provincial seminary and that the Dominicans agreed to provide an academic staff. A modest seminary program was begun that fall in temporary quarters. The Iowa bishops launched a fund campaign that raised $2,500,000 to build a worthy seminary building. The successful campaign financed the construction of Mount St. Bernard Seminary, which was completed in 1954 at Dubuque. It was planned to serve the province, consisting of the archdiocese of Dubuque and the dioceses of Davenport, Des Moines, and Sioux City. The bishops of the province shared responsibility for the seminary in an arrangement similar to that of the Michigan bishops' governance of their provincial seminary.[34]

Diocesan clergy dependent solely on the authority of the local bishop staffed only a few new seminaries formed during the era, as in the case of the ones at such diverse places as Little Rock, Brooklyn, and San Diego.

The South, excepting Louisiana, characteristically was not known for large-scale Catholic activity and seminary training was rare in the region. Bishop John B. Morris of Little Rock, Arkansas, entertained that old expectation among bishops of missionary dioceses to develop clergy locally. In 1911 Bishop Morris opened St. John's Home Missions Seminary under the direction of diocesan priests and affiliated with the diocesan-owned Little Rock College for lay students. The arrangement brings to mind the older idea of the mixed seminary and lay college of the nineteenth century. In 1916 the college and seminary moved to a new campus at Pulaski Heights, several miles from the city, but the seminary soon moved back to the city in 1918. Little Rock College closed in 1930 and St. John's Home Missions Seminary moved back to Pulaski Heights and continued as a freestanding seminary. The seminary enrollment was limited as Little Rock and neighoring dioceses did not produce large numbers of seminarians. However, St. John's progressed and boasted 400 ordained alumni at the time of its fiftieth anniversary in 1961. The seminary program emphasized home missions work and catechetics.[35]

In the diocese of Brooklyn a portion of the clergy had been trained at the Vincentians' St. John's College, but most of the diocese's seminarians had to be sent outside the diocese for training. By the 1920s Bishop Thomas Molloy of Brooklyn hoped to discontinue sending seminarians away and planned a seminary to train all the priests of the diocese. In 1924 the bishop purchased a 200-acre estate with mansion for $300,000 in the town of Huntington, on the northern shore of Long Island. He started the "Diocesan Institute of Philosophy" in the mansion, that is, the first two years of major seminary, with a first-year class of twenty-five seminarians. After their two years of study the students were sent to other seminaries for theology.

Bishop Molloy launched a fund campaign to build a six-year major seminary, named the Seminary of the Immaculate Conception, to be built on the Huntington property. He placed quotas on the parishes of the diocese to be paid over a three-year period. The bishop began construction of an imposing seminary building in an eclectic style combining Spanish and Mediterranean elements. Its major requirement was the requisite size to accommodate the diocese's students. The building was finished and dedicated on September 27, 1930, the month of its opening. The seminary fund drive had been successful so that the building's entire cost of $2,645,000 was paid by the day of dedication. The seminary opened with eighty-five students. Both philosophy and the first year of theology were taught by priests of the Brooklyn diocese, whom the bishop had been preparing for some years. The first class to complete studies was ordained in 1934.[36]

As shown in the case of the Brooklyn diocese, the heritage of the bishop providing a faculty of diocesan priests for a new seminary did not entirely die out. The same was true in San Diego. Charles Buddy, appointed bishop of San Diego when the diocese was created in 1937, at first honored the idea of the provincial seminary by sending San Diego seminarians to

St. John's Seminary at Camarillo. For his own diocese he planned St. Francis Minor Seminary, which opened in temporary quarters in San Diego before being relocated in a converted ranch at El Cajon in 1944. He constructed additional buildings on the El Cajon property and opened a major seminary, Immaculate Heart Seminary, under the direction of diocesan priests in the fall of 1947. Previously Buddy had stopped patronizing St. John's Seminary at Camarillo because the canon law professor there had successfully defended a San Diego diocesan priest in an ecclesiastical process against the bishop.

The minor and major seminaries figured in Bishop Buddy's ambitious educational plans whose scale of grandeur Cardinal Mundelein would have envied. Buddy began work in the 1950s to build the diocesan-owned University of San Diego, located at Alcala Park, a beautiful hilltop area north of San Diego with a commanding view in all directions. He built his chancery and residence at the site. The first of the university components was the San Diego College for Women, completed in 1952 and conducted by the Religious of the Sacred Heart. It was followed by the construction of a complex of buildings in a modified Spanish Renaissance style that included a large church, library, law school, College for Men, and university high school. The bishop began construction of a building at Alcala Park to house St. Francis Minor Seminary and Immaculate Heart Seminary at an estimated cost of $2,000,000. The seminary building was occupied in January 1957.[37] The seminaries were institutional constituents of the University of San Diego, though the academic and formation programs for seminarians kept them at the expected distance from other components of the university. Nevertheless, the institutional arrangement of the seminaries at the university is reminiscent of the mixed lay colleges and seminaries.

The relocation of St. Mary's Seminary in Baltimore and Kenrick Seminary in St. Louis was paralleled by the relocation of the three Ohio seminaries. Cincinnati's Mount St. Mary's of the West had been located since 1904 in the buildings of the old minor seminary in the Mount Washington section of Cincinnati. As early as 1906 Archbishop Henry Moeller planned to locate a new cathedral, episcopal residence, and seminary on acreage purchased in the Cincinnati suburb of Norwood. The idea of building a cathedral on the site was dropped, the episcopal residence was constructed in 1908, and plans for a seminary were not acted on until after World War I. In 1921 Archbishop Moeller began constructing a new seminary at Norwood in an imposing neoclassical style. The building could accommodate 180 students and cost the archbishop $750,000 to construct and $250,000 for furnishings. The new Mount St. Mary's of the West was dedicated on October 23, 1923. The archdiocese could then reopen the St. Gregory Minor Seminary in the building previously occupied by the major seminary. Archbishop John T. McNicholas, appointed to Cincinnati in 1925, reorganized the seminaries and Catholic colleges in Cincinnati under the larger organizational umbrella called the Athenaeum of Ohio. The Athenaeum offered degrees at the seminaries along with the constituent colleges for lay students.[38]

Cleveland's St. Mary's Seminary had continued its operation in a downtown neighborhood on Lakeside Avenue. For decades plans had been postponed to move from the crowded location and inadequate buildings that could not accommodate all the diocese's seminarians. Joseph Schrembs, the German-born bishop of Toledo, was appointed bishop of Cleveland in 1921 and at once started plans for a new seminary. He closed the old seminary in 1922 and sent the seminarians to the new Cincinnati seminary. Funds had been collected over the years for a new seminary, and these were augmented by new funds collected during an extensive fund campaign in October 1922. With the view of convenient commuting for day students of the minor seminary, Bishop Schrembs acquired a site on Ansel Road centrally located within the city and bordering Rockefeller Park. Construction began in the spring of 1924 for a three-story major-minor seminary in a modified Spanish mission design—an "adobe Hacienda"—as it has been called. The building was designed to house 155 boarding students. By the fall of 1924 it was sufficiently completed to be opened to major seminary philosophy students. With the completion of the chapel the seminary was dedicated on October 28, 1925. In 1925 the minor seminary opened to day students. However, after 1928 the new St. Mary's Seminary was a boarding major seminary and the minor seminarians were sent to other locations until the founding of the college seminary, St. Charles Borromeo College, in 1954.[39]

The Pontifical College Josephinum continued its programs at its location in downtown Columbus through the 1920s while its officials laid plans for a move to a less crowded location. A national constituency of German Americans continued to support the seminary through the efforts of the periodicals *Josephinum Weekly* and the *Ohio Waisenfreund.* Construction for the new seminary began in 1929 at a semirural site near Worthington, north of Columbus. Donors had contributed $609,000 by the opening of the buildings in November 1931.[40]

The diocese of Newark continued to rely on its Immaculate Conception Seminary, affiliated with Seton Hall College. The seminary's annual enrollment had never exceeded sixty into the 1920s. After World War I, Bishop John O'Connor and the Seton Hall College trustees considered building a larger seminary at the campus in South Orange. But these plans were dropped. Instead, in 1926 the bishop bought an estate of 1,100 acres with a magnificent thirty-room mansion and other buildings located at Darlington near Mahwah, Bergen County, in rural northern New Jersey near the New York border. The seminary community of forty-five theology students moved into the mansion on April 21, 1927; later the philosophy students were placed in another building on the new campus. The enrollment grew and a new seminary building on the campus at Darlington was planned as early as 1931, but construction was postponed during the depression. It was left to O'Connor's successor, Bishop Thomas J. Walsh, to direct the seminary expansion. Walsh announced an intensive seminary fund drive that took place in November 1936 and resulted in raising $1,679,348. Completed by the fall of 1938, the new seminary building was capable of accommodating 300 students and contained dining, recreational, and classroom facilities and a connected Gothic chapel. With the move to northern New Jersey, Immaculate Conception Seminary severed its relationship with Seton Hall University and was separately incorporated.[41]

In 1937 Newark was raised to the status of an archdiocese, with the New Jersey dioceses of Trenton, Camden, and Paterson as suffragan sees. With the new Immaculate Conception Seminary, the New Jersey dioceses had a seminary capable of accommodating the seminarians of the ecclesiastical province.

A number of diocesan seminaries were planned and went into operation in the late 1950s and early 1960s.

The diocese of Steubenville was formed in 1944 for thirteen counties in southeastern Ohio. Its first bishop, John King Mussio, soon established St. John Vianney Minor Seminary under the direction of diocesan priests, at first in Steubenville and then in a new set of buildings at nearby Bloomingdale. By the middle 1950s a major seminary program was under way and the first alumnus was ordained in 1957.[42] The major seminary closed in the 1960s.

The diocese of Scranton, Pennsylvania, dated from 1868. Its fifth bishop, Jerome Daniel Hannan, appointed in 1954, had been longtime dean of the School of Canon Law of the Catholic University of America. From the day of his installation he planned to fulfill the Tridentine and canon law ideal of having a diocesan seminary and began to send priests to graduate school to form a faculty for its expected opening. He acquired an estate at nearby Dalton, where he constructed a complete major and minor seminary at an announced cost of $1,500,000. The new institution, St. Pius X Seminary, opened in the fall of 1962 to twenty-four students. Bishop Hannan died in 1965 and his successor, Bishop J. Carroll McCormick, closed the seminary in 1968.[43]

In the diocese of Buffalo, the historic diocesan seminaries conducted by the Franciscans at St. Bonaventure University and by the Vincentians of the eastern province at Our Lady of the Angels at Niagara University had for many years trained priests for Buffalo and neighboring dioceses. In the 1950s Bishop John Burke of Buffalo determined to have a major seminary under diocesan ownership and administration. He acquired land near the town of East Aurora, New York, and built St. John Vianney Seminary, which opened in 1959. It was conducted by diocesan priests, assisted by several priests of religious orders. By the late 1960s the diocese of Buffalo faced difficulties staffing the seminary. In 1971 the Franciscans of Holy Name Province, which conducted Christ the King Seminary at St. Bonaventure University, entered into an agreement with the diocese to lease the seminary buildings. St. John Vianney Seminary came to an end and the Franciscans moved in their Christ the King Seminary from St. Bonaventure. The seminary continued to be staffed largely by Franciscans and served the dioceses of the region.[44]

When the Buffalo diocese no longer used the Vincentian seminary, the eastern province Vincentians accepted the invitation of the diocese of Albany, New York, to staff a seminary. The diocese built a major seminary complex at Albany and the Vincentians moved their Seminary of Our Lady of the Angels from Niagara University in 1961. The seminary remained an academic unit of Niagara University and conferred its degrees. These arrangements were not destined to last, however. With the decline in the number of seminarians, the diocese of Albany could no longer sustain a seminary and Our Lady of the Angels closed in 1969.[45]

While it may seem eccentric that the bishops of Buffalo, Albany, and Scranton sought to found their own new seminaries in a region with a number of firmly established interdiocesan seminaries, the founding of a seminary in an area of booming growth seems less so. From 1868 to 1958 the entire state of Florida was under the jurisdiction of the diocese of St. Augustine. In 1958 the diocese of Miami was created for south Florida. Its first bishop, Coleman Carroll, was the model builder bishop of the kind suitable for Miami's booming growth from the fifties onward. The diocese was dependent on clergy from the North and from Ireland during the period, but Bishop Carroll hoped to start a tradition of native clergy by establishing in 1959 a minor seminary, St. John Vianney Seminary, located in Miami and staffed by priests of the eastern province of the Vincentians. Bishop Carroll next announced the construction of a diocesan major seminary. It too would be conducted by the Vincentians, to whom he deeded property at Boynton Beach for St. Vincent de Paul Seminary. After a diocesan fund-raising campaign, St. Vincent de Paul Seminary opened on September 24, 1965; it was a rare outpost of Catholic seminary education for the region.[46] The seminaries of the Washington and Baltimore area were the nearest ones to the north and Notre Dame Seminary at New Orleans the nearest diocesan seminary to the west.

The patterns of expansion during the era brought the major seminary into all parts of the country. The close relationship of major seminaries with minor ones was a consistent pattern throughout the era: the founding of several major seminaries was preceded or accompanied by the formation of minor seminary programs. The idea that a successful major seminary program should be preceded by a strong minor seminary was thereby widely honored as the proper means of developing clergy. In a related fashion, many smaller dioceses that had no expectation of opening a major seminary nevertheless sponsored minor seminaries to cultivate seminarians locally who would in due course be sent to an interdiocesan major seminary outside the diocese. The following dioceses developed freestanding minor seminaries during the period: Albany, Alexandria, Amarillo, Belleville, Buffalo, Columbus, Covington, Dallas, El Paso, Erie, Fargo, Fort Wayne–South Bend, Grand Rapids, Green Bay, Hartford, Honolulu, Kansas City–St. Joseph, Jefferson City, LaCrosse, Lafayette, Louisville, Ogdensburg, Oklahoma City–Tulsa, Providence, Richmond, Rockville Centre, Sacramento, Saginaw, Spokane, Springfield (Illinois), Tucson, and Yakima. A few others developed high school or college residences for seminarians who attended a neighboring Catholic high school or college for lay students, such as in the dioceses of Davenport, Dubuque, Helena, and Winona.

The major and minor diocesan seminaries had grown rapidly during the period. In 1910 there were 6,969 students in 82 diocesan and religious seminaries. At the time 17,084 priests (12,650 diocesan and 4,434 religious) served a Catholic population of 14,618,761.[47] In 1962 the total number of all seminarians, major and minor, diocesan and religious, was 45,616 in 409 seminaries, novitiates, and scholasticates. Of these 26,892 were diocesan major and minor seminaries. Priests numbered 56,540 (34,465 diocesan and 22,075 religious) for a Catholic population of 43,851,538. The Department of Education of the National Catholic Welfare Conference (NCWC) recorded 102 diocesan seminaries in 1963, of these 30 were identified as major, 63 as minor, and nine combined major and minor.[48] The following table is adapted from the NCWC's listing of major seminaries, but their programs are not all equivalent to each other. Most have a six-year program, but several have a four-year program of theology, eight-year college and theology programs, and a few are twelve-year combined minor-major seminary programs. Several have combined enrollments of diocesan and religious seminarians. The number of students is given to indicate the relative size of the institutions at the end of an era of enormous institutional and numerical growth.

MAJOR SEMINARIES FOR DIOCESAN STUDENTS,
1962–1963[49]

A. Diocesan Seminaries with Diocesan Staffs   **Students**

The Athenaeum of Ohio (Mount St. Mary's of the West), Cincinnati, Ohio	299
Immaculate Conception Seminary, Huntington, N.Y.	214
Immaculate Conception Seminary, Mahwah, N.J.	n.a.
Immaculate Heart Seminary, San Diego	79
Mount St. Mary's Major Seminary, Emmitsburg, Md.	132
Pontifical College Josephinum, Worthington, Ohio (theology and college)	185
St. Bernard Seminary, Rochester, N.Y.	241
St. Charles Borromeo Seminary, Philadelphia	417
Sts. Cyril and Methodius, Orchard Lake, Mich.	73
St. Francis de Sales Seminary, Milwaukee	323
St. John's Home Missions Seminary, Little Rock	154
St. John's Seminary, Brighton, Mass.	391
St. John Vianney Seminary, East Aurora, N.Y.	160
St. John Vianney Seminary, Bloomingdale, Ohio	38
St. Joseph's Seminary, (Dunwoodie), Yonkers, N.Y.	224
St. Mary's Seminary, Cleveland	79
St. Paul's Seminary, St. Paul	270

B. Diocesan Seminaries Staffed by Communities of Priests

Assumption Seminary, San Antonio	391
Kenrick Seminary and Cardinal Glennon College, St. Louis	404
Mount St. Bernard's Seminary, Dubuque, Iowa	107
Notre Dame Seminary, New Orleans	138
Our Lady of the Angels, Albany, N.Y.	88
St. John's Provincial Seminary, Plymouth, Mich. (theology)	215
St. John's Seminary, Camarillo, Calif. (college and theology)	357
St. Mary of the Lake Seminary, Mundelein, Ill.	361
St. Mary's Seminary, Baltimore	624
St. Mary's Seminary, Houston	125
St. Patrick's Seminary, Menlo Park, Calif.	158
St. Thomas the Apostle Seminary, Kenmore, Wash.	142
St. Thomas Seminary, Denver (college and theology)	246

C. Seminaries of Religious Communities Admitting Diocesan Seminarians

Christ the King Seminary, St. Bonaventure, N.Y.	228
Immaculate Conception Seminary, Conception, Mo.	360

Mount Angel Seminary, St. Benedict, Oreg. (minor and major)   229
Our Lady of Loretto Seminary, Loretto, Pa.   83
St. Benedict Seminary, Atchison, Kans.   16
St. Bernard Seminary, Cullman, Ala. (minor and major)   90
St. John's Seminary, Collegeville, Minn.   83
St. Maur's Seminary, South Union, Ky.   42
St. Meinrad Seminary, St. Meinrad, Ind. (college and theology)   391
St. Procopius Seminary, Lisle, Ill.   57
St. Vincent Seminary, Latrobe, Pa.   221

D. University Seminary

Theological College, Catholic University of America   136

14. Catholic University Reform and Influence

As the country's pontifical university the Catholic University of America remained the most important educational institution in the United States under the direct sanction of the Holy See. The American bishops through the board of trustees continued to own the university. The chancellors (the archbishop of Baltimore until 1947, when the archbishop of the new see of Washington inherited the position *ex officio*) and successive rectors served in their highly visible offices. However, the roles of trustees, chancellors, and rectors were increasingly reduced to routine functions as interventions of the Holy See through the Sacred Congregation of Seminaries and Universities determined the university's direction. Roman authority launched a process of reorganization to strengthen graduate programs in theology, thereby recovering some of the university's original aim of providing advanced theological studies for priests. The reorganization resulted in the acquisition of a diocesan seminary in the 1930s and the establishment of an affiliation program for the country's seminaries. And to inform the model of priesthood in the United States, university faculty members set the tone of unbending orthodoxy in theological and pastoral studies through their influential publications.

In the second decade of the twentieth century the founding generation of episcopal leaders, who had carried the weight of moral and financial support for the university, passed from the scene. John Lancaster Spalding died in 1916. John Ireland and John Keane died in 1918. And the first chancellor, Cardinal James Gibbons, died in 1921. The university advanced slowly through their years of leadership, but was perhaps most noteworthy as the academic home of a number of influential individuals in American Catholic life, such as John A. Ryan in moral theology, William J. Kerby in sociology, and Edward A. Pace in philosophy. But the administrative efficiency, financial condition, and prospects of future de-

318

velopment were poorly regarded. In 1917 the apostolic delegate, Archbishop Giovanni Bonzano, asked Henri Hyvernat, professor of Semitic languages and a founding member of the faculty, to draft a memoir analyzing the problems of the university. Hyvernat's massive document, submitted to Bonzano and presumably passed on to Rome around 1921, was a scathing critique of the university's difficulties, such as the problems of sponsoring graduate education for students having inadequate preparation, the chronic lack of funds that forced the lay faculty to take part-time positions elsewhere to supplement their salaries, and above all the lack of serious interest and financial support of most American bishops and the ignorance of academic matters among the few interested bishops.[1]

It is possible that Hyvernat's memoir had an impact in Roman quarters, where concern for clerical education was growing. Shortly after its submission Pius XI issued, on April 25, 1922, the apostolic letter *Quandoquidem probe novimus* to the American bishops on the subject of the Catholic University. The letter echoes a repeated theme of Hyvernat's memoir, that is, the bishop's common ownership should be translated into a greater sense of common responsibility for the university, which had clearly been lacking. The pope's letter states that all the bishops were to take an interest in the university. They were urged to take counsel together to study and adopt a definite plan for its development, which was to be presented to the Sacred Congregation of Seminaries and Universities.[2] The chancellor, Archbishop Curley, directed the subsequent study of the university in which the faculty expressed its grievances, especially the low salaries and the need for reorganization and clarification of the university structure. The Holy See too advised university officials that the pope desired the establishment of a school of canon law at the university. The results of the process of study and reform were few. The university constitution was revised but did not provide for a reorganization of the numerous university schools along American lines that several faculty had requested.[3]

The formation of the separate School of Canon Law in 1923 was the enduring achievement of the inquiry. Monsignor Fillippo Bernardini, nephew of Cardinal Pietro Gasparri, was appointed the first dean. The school was a great success from the start. In the following years it absorbed a large portion of the American clergy available for graduate study because dioceses and religious orders needed trained canonists to function properly according to the provisions of the new code. The school granted 416 doctorates in canon law (J.C.D.) up to 1962 (as enumerated in its published canon law series) and hundreds more licentiate (J.C.L.) and bachelor (J.C.B.) degrees during the same period.

The absence of additional reform might be attributed to the lack of leadership. The rector since 1909, Bishop Thomas Shahan, was in the final phase of his administration and was greatly absorbed in building a university church, the National Shrine of the Immaculate Conception, and the university library. Administrative reform did not hold his sustained interest. The larger issue of the American bishops' interest and support for the university was not adequately addressed. While a high degree of interest on the part of each bishop was perhaps unrealistic to expect, there were no members of the hierarchy during the 1920s who took a lead in university issues. The leadership of the American Catholic bishops, once the role of the archbishop of Baltimore, was divided up after the death of Cardinal Gibbons. The historic see of Baltimore had long been surpassed as a center of Catholic population and wealth by other archdioceses. Baltimore was in effect reduced in rank as Gibbons's successor, Michael J. Curley, was not given the cardinal's hat. Instead, the most visible figures in the hierarchy were the four cardinals at major archdioceses during the interwar years. As archbishops they were members of the board of trustees. Their limited interest in the university and lack of initiative in its affairs were indicative of the general absence of episcopal understanding of and support for the university.

The foremost figure was Cardinal William O'Connell of Boston, who, after Gibbons's death, was the senior American bishop and as such was chairman of the board of trustees until his death in 1944. He faithfully came to preside at trustees' meetings until his declining years. He sent no priest students to the university for graduate theology and his financial support was consistent but perfunctory.

Cardinal Patrick Hayes of New York, known as the "Cardinal of Charity" because of his charity causes had no intellectual interests, sent no priest students for theology, and avoided trustees' meetings. His financial support through the annual collection was unremarkable for the size of his archdiocese.

Cardinal Denis Dougherty of Philadelphia sent the fourth-year theology students of St. Charles Seminary to the Catholic University from 1926 to 1928 because of overcrowding at St. Charles. When his new seminary building was completed the practice stopped. Dougherty was chairman of the Basselin Foundation, which sponsored the scholarship program at the Sulpician Seminary. He took an interest in building the National Shrine of the Immaculate Conception on the university grounds, but he stopped attending trustees' meetings around 1930, after Cardinal O'Connell attacked the Philadelphia priest who was director of the National Shrine during a trustees' meeting. Philadelphia's financial support paralleled that of New York and Boston.[4]

Cardinal George Mundelein of Chicago stopped attending trustees' meetings in 1927, after his motion to have the university moved to Chicago failed. There was no need for him to send priest students to the university while he was developing his grand archdiocesan seminary and a Roman residence for Chicago priest students. He sent the token amount of only $8,000 per year to the university before the depression, a figure well below that of Boston, New York, and Philadelphia.[5]

When called to articulate ideas about the university, bishops revealed slight understanding of the modern academic life. A rare expression of bishops' views can be found in the national radio addresses given by leading bishops on behalf of university fund-raising in 1932 and 1933. The addresses reveal slight knowledge of higher education as the bishops tended to repeat standard warnings of the dangers of secular education. Their idea of advanced research seemed largely confined to the sciences, which they endorsed, because they appeared eager to profess that there was no real conflict between religion and science. However, the role of advanced learning for priests, the idea on which the university was founded, was simply ignored.[6] The rest of the American episcopate apparently seldom thought of their university. Archbishop Michael Curley remarked in 1942 that through more than twenty years of attending annual meetings of the hierarchy, he never heard the university discussed. A search of the indexed minutes of bishops' meetings in the interwar years yielded a few passing references to the university but no deliberations focusing on its welfare or long-term interests.[7] The American bishops simply had little interest in their university and none cared to articulate a body of ideas about it. The field was wide open for continual interventions of the Holy See without a corresponding body of views from the episcopate.

Nevertheless, the most positive development during the interwar years was the election of James Hugh Ryan as fifth rector of the university in 1928. Ryan was born in Indianapolis in 1886 and, after Roman training, was ordained a priest of his home diocese. He had taught philosophy at the university since 1922 and had been the National Catholic Welfare Conference's chief spokesman on education. Forty-two years old at the time of his election, the rector had the energy and years to develop the university.[8] He was ordained a titular bishop at the beginning of his second five-year term in 1933.

Ryan presided over an extensive reorganization of the university along American lines to provide distinct graduate and undergraduate schools in arts and sciences. He placed great emphasis on research as one of the university's aims, a novel concept in Catholic higher education at that time and one that would expose him to attacks in the following years for attempting to secularize the university. Ryan effected positive developments to improve the university's financial base. He reorganized the university's annual collection in the parishes by activating bishops and clergy through regional fund-raising meetings, designating specific days for the collection, and organizing publicity such as the radio addresses. Ryan nearly doubled its proceeds from $218,000 in 1928 to $410,000 in 1932. He also organized the "Friends of the Catholic University" to develop large donations. The new publicity expanded university enrollment from 892 in 1928 to 1,415 in 1932. And to build the university endowment from a modest $3 million, the rector persuaded the trustees in 1931 to set the goal of raising it to $20 million for the university's fiftieth anniversary in 1939-1940.[9]

The issuance of the apostolic constitution *Deus Scientiarum Dominus* was the start of a new revision of the university constitution and brought attention to the sorry record of the university's School of Sacred Sciences and the need for reform of theological studies. From 1931 to 1934 the rector, a trustees' committee, and canon lawyers carried on the revision of the university constitution with consultations with Monsignor Ruffini and Cardinal Bisleti of the Sacred Congregation. The constitution was given Roman approval in 1934, but with the expectation of revising the statutes governing theological studies, the Sacred Congregation of Seminaries and Universities added a "Visiting Committee" for the ecclesiastical schools. The new committee was inaugurated and its members chosen without recourse to the board of trustees, the chancellor, or rector. The committee was chaired by Archbishop John T. McNicholas of Cincinnati and consisted of Archbishop Samuel Stritch of Milwaukee and bishops Edward Mooney of Rochester, John Peterson of Manchester, and Gerald P. O'Hara, auxiliary of Philadelphia. The committee's function was "to revise the programs of sacred studies, to draw up or complete the programs where necessary, and to look to their faithful observance" according to the new constitution and other "prescriptions of the Holy See."[10]

The establishment of the visiting committee introduced Archbishop John T. McNicholas (1877-1950) as a major figure in university affairs in the following years. The Irish-born McNicholas grew up in Philadelphia, joined the Dominican order, and was ordained a priest in 1899. He was sent to Rome for a period of studies at the Dominicans' Angelicum. After several years teaching at the Dominicans' house of studies at Catholic University and periods of travel to spread the Dominicans' Holy Name Societies in parishes, he returned to Rome to the office of the Master General of the Dominican order. He became a protégé of the Dominican Cardinal Tomaso Boggiani, prefect of the Consistorial Congregation which appointed bishops, and of Pope Benedict XV. The pope, who referred to the short-statured McNicholas as the "Dominicanetto," periodically called on him for advice in American affairs. In 1917, under the new arrangements of direct Roman appointment of bishops, McNicholas was appointed bishop of Duluth and in 1925 was promoted to archbishop of Cincinnati.[11] Mc-

Nicholas took a very active interest in the university as a trustee. He served as chairman of an ad hoc trustees' committee appointed by the chancellor in 1931 to investigate the differences between the faculty of theology and the rector. He then served as co-chairman of the national fund-raising campaign with Archbishop John Gregory Murray of St. Paul.

McNicholas's "Visiting Committee" began its work by investigating the condition of the School of Sacred Sciences, which had been in decline for years. During the 1920s, annual enrollment scarcely exceeded twenty, and an average of one or two doctorates and four to seven licentiates were awarded annually. In order to attract greater interest in the theology program, to realize a longstanding university aim, and to give the theology faculty something to do, the university inaugurated in 1927 an undergraduate seminary patronized by the seminarians of the smaller religious orders that had houses of studies in the neighborhood. The situation did not improve in the 1930s and enrollment in graduate theology reached a low of eight students in 1932. The next year John A. Ryan, the dean of the School of Sacred Sciences, appealed to the bishops for more students and offered some observations on the state of higher theological studies:

> For several years the great majority of our priest students have pursued courses in Canon Law, Education, the languages or the social sciences. Apparently they have preferred the immediate practical subjects. To be sure, the theological degrees have also a practical aspect. Their possessors are qualified to teach in theological seminaries, according to the requirements of Canon Law. Nevertheless, the number of our graduates that have obtained such assignments is small, both absolutely and relatively. Moreover, the great majority of the registrants in the School of Sacred Sciences for the last few years have been members of religious congregations. Last year the diocesan priests therein registered numbered only two.
>
> It is clear, then, that the increased enrollment which is so badly needed will have to be provided by priests who seek theological culture for its own sake, or who appreciate the relations between advanced theological training and a more efficient performance of the manifold duties of their great office. At the present time many American dioceses have a surplus of priests, while practically all have a sufficiency. In these conditions it seems not unreasonable to assume that every year forty or fifty young priests would desire to pursue advanced theological studies. As a matter of fact, the attitude of the younger clergy in this matter seems to have grown worse instead of better. In my student years at the University (1898–1902) the number of young priests in attendance never exceeded thirty-five, but the great

majority of them were enrolled in the School of the Sacred Sciences, and very few were expecting to turn their studies to professional account as teachers. For the most part they sought higher theological culture as a broader equipment for the duties and opportunities of the mission.[12]

Archbishop McNicholas and his committee conducted interviews with the faculty of ecclesiastical studies at the university in December 1934. The situation in canon law and philosophy was promising, but the theology faculty was indeed unimpressive. In 1931 the Holy See had dismissed two German-born Scripture professors, Franz Cöln and Henry Schumacher, because of their highly publicized opposition to the rector. Cöln, who had been dean, and Schumacher held to the belief that the rector had no executive authority over the affairs of the School of Sacred Sciences. Their departure left no tenured Scripture professors. The subject was covered by two part-time outsiders, Edward Donze, S.M., from the nearby Marist Seminary, and Edward Arbez, S.S., from the Sulpician Seminary. There was no full professor of dogmatic theology, normally regarded as the most important subject. Another nondiocesan priest, Edward Fitzgerald, O.P., associate professor, taught dogma, though his specialty was sacramental theology. Full professors Patrick J. Healy and Hugh Henry, both elderly, taught church history and homiletics respectively. Joseph Barron was associate professor of apologetics.

The professors generally agreed that the faculty should be enlarged because essential areas were not adequately covered. The problem of the lack of students was not directly addressed. There was much criticism of the rector for expenditures on collegiate athletics and his emphasis on research.[13] Professors outside the School of Sacred Sciences were also asked for their views. The apologetics professor in the College of Arts and Sciences, Fulton J. Sheen, offered the visiting committee a detailed lecture on the purpose of the university. He found research acceptable in the natural sciences, but not in the speculative sciences where deduction was required. Sheen strongly emphasized the "primacy of the spiritual" and feared the dangers of the university becoming a copy of American universities.[14]

The church historian Peter Guilday, not a member of the School of Sacred Sciences but invited to give his views, addressed the problems of graduate theology. He found that a major difficulty dating from the twenties was the widespread expectation that just as the Holy See monopolized Catholic biblical studies with the creation of the Pontifical Biblical Institute, a similar action would concentrate Catholic theological studies in Rome. In such an event American priests would have to be sent to Rome for graduate training in theology. Guilday cited the brevity of the course leading to the Roman doctorate as a major cause for the absence of interest in a prolonged program of graduate theology at Catholic University. And among the additional reasons for the failure of graduate theology, he cited the few incentives for priests to study at Washington, such as a lack of financial support, uncertainty that a diocesan priest with an advanced degree would be hired for seminary teaching, and the hiring practices in some seminaries which would discourage candidates. For instance, he noted that at his alma mater, St. Charles Seminary in Philadelphia, a priest joining the faculty might serve a long apprenticeship teaching several minor seminary courses before advancing to major seminary courses, perhaps culminating his career by teaching dogmatic or moral theology. [15]

The visiting committee was not capable of addressing some of the problems raised in the interviews, such as how to attract graduate students or how to provide suitable employment for those earning advanced degrees in theology. The committee, under McNicholas's influence, formulated recommendations to the Sacred Congregation on the organization of the graduate program and forwarded views on a subject outside its responsibility, namely, the role of the rector.

Among the faculty members interviewed, several had been sharply critical of Bishop Ryan for his interest in creating a modern research university. McNicholas's letters to committee members reveal that he came to share a strong fear of the rector's "secular" tendencies. According to McNicholas, the rector's idea of the university "seems to be to make it a little Harvard, a little Yale or Princeton." The archbishop's own ideas were clear: "One would think that a Rector in his position would realize more than any prelate in the country that the purpose of the Catholic University is to serve to the greatest extent the Church, Bishops, priests and laymen who are to speak for the Church." He found the rector "an almost impossible impediment in restoring the university" and even stated that the rector's "*mens* is *aliena* from that of the Church." McNicholas's aim was to restore the "Pontifical character of our university."[16] He also objected to the emphasis given to research. In personal correspondence McNicholas mused about the possibility of creating separate faculties of teachers and research scholars. But closer to his true feelings was probably his outburst: "I am thoroughly fed up on this 'research.' Good teaching seems to count for nothing."[17]

McNicholas declared to Bishop Gerald P. O'Hara that "it is absolutely our duty" to tell the apostolic delegate and the Holy See "that practically nothing can be done to strengthen the Pontifical character of the University while the present Rector is in office."[18] McNicholas apparently shared his views with the apostolic delegate in the late spring of 1935. The course of events that followed at the Apostolic Delegation and in Rome is not recorded. In any case, on July 23, 1935, Bishop Ryan was summoned to the Apostolic Delegation in Washington, where Archbishop Amleto Cicognani informed him that the Holy See was offering him the vacant see of Omaha. Ryan had known that he was under attack in Rome and protested that an appointment to Omaha would be looked upon as a demotion by irate bishops and that a transfer a year later might look better. His protests were in vain, and he reluctantly accepted the appointment.

Ryan's removal so soon after his reappointment to a second term mocked the bishops' rights in governing the university. The incident provoked Archbishop Curley to observe that the American bishops "have been treated very much as children for a very long time." Curley, who as chancellor was in a position to know, attributed Ryan's "elimination" to the "hatred of a little man," an obvious reference to the dimunitive Mc-Nicholas. To a close friend in the papal diplomatic service Curley designated the "main agent" behind the dismissal the "juvenile Savanarola [sic] of Cincinnati."[19]

The process of choosing a new rector was marked by the intervention of the apostolic delegate, who wrote to Curley to request that in his capacity as chancellor he solicit nominations for the rectorship among the bishops by mail prior to the trustees' meeting of November 1935. Cicognani expected that the names would be ready for presentation. Cicognani's approach was certainly out of order because he was not a member of the board, the request violated the procedures of election of the rector, and the move was quickly recognized as an attempt to exclude the lay members of the board from the nomination process. Curley duly solicited the views of the bishops and received a number of replies. As a friend and supporter of the dismissed rector, Curley was happy to pass on the views of the respondents to Cicognani, since many bishops expressed resentment of Ryan's dismissal. Curley reported to the apostolic delegate that the name of Archbishop McNicholas's candidate, Joseph M. Corrigan, was the name already conceded by many bishops as the next rector.[20]

The trustees' meeting of November 12, 1935, was noteworthy for a wrathful address of Cardinal O'Connell, chairman of the board, who expressed the common resentment by lashing out: "We have traitors in our midst. We have those who are writing to Rome, who are interfering with us in the government of this University."[21] O'Connell rejected Curley's report on nominees for rector. As the statutes prescribed, the cardinal permitted nominations from the trustees. The trustees then voted to send three nominees for rector to the Sacred Congregation. Their leading candidate with fifteen votes was Robert H. Lord, a convert and priest of the archdiocese of Boston. Lord had a Ph.D. in history from Harvard, where he had been professor and chairman of the history department, and was currently a professor at St. John's Seminary at Boston. Corrigan received eight votes, and Monsignor Francis Thill of Cincinnati, president of the Catholic Students Mission Crusade, received three. Despite the favorable vote for Lord and to no one's surprise, the Holy See appointed Corrigan the sixth rector of the Catholic University.[22]

Joseph Moran Corrigan was born in Philadelphia in 1879, was trained and ordained in Rome, and rose in the Philadelphia church to be rector of the archdiocesan seminary. His name had been mentioned for the rectorship of the North American College in Rome in the 1930s. He was a friend of McNicholas since student days in Rome. Corrigan was affable and spoke well. McNicholas saw his "good nature" and "common sense judgment" as important in winning the support of bishops for the university.[23] Poor Corrigan was also obese and narcoleptic. His administrative talents were slight and did not improve as his health declined throughout his tenure. He had no knowledge or experience of modern university life. Corrigan once told Roy J. DeFerrari, the graduate school dean, that before he became rector of the university he had not known that a doctor of philosophy degree could be earned in disciplines other than philosophy.[24] The Catholic University, accordingly, lost the most dynamic and farsighted rector of its series of bishop rectors since John Keane and received its least able and least energetic.

As McNicholas was lobbying for Bishop Ryan's dismissal, the visiting committee formulated its official recommendations for submission to the Sacred Congregation in August 1935. The committee recommended the hiring of additional faculty members in order to facilitate the operation of the graduate program and to promote confidence on the part of the bishops to sponsor priest students. However, the committee was "unable to take responsibility of proposing the immediate establishment of the full degree course in the University School of Theology"—that is, a complete and continuous course of undergraduate and graduate study culminating in the doctorate—unless the Holy See recommended its establishment to the American bishops.[25] What the committee was reluctant to do was to attempt to resolve the problem arising from the undergraduate program of the university's new and poorly regarded seminary for students of religious orders and the absence of one for diocesan students. The committee could not propose the opening of a university seminary for diocesan students to be trained with the seminarians of religious orders because the autonomous Sulpician Seminary was already training diocesan students. McNicholas, bold in advancing his views on Bishop Ryan, was too timid to propose a solution to a knotty problem involving overlapping interests and many political complications.

The issue of the undergraduate theology programs remained unresolved through 1936, Corrigan's first year as rector. During the winter of 1937, Corrigan made a long visit to Rome during which Cardinal Gaetano Bisleti informed the rector that McNicholas, as head of the visiting committee, should approach the Sulpicians to resolve the issue of the competing seminary programs. Bisleti felt that McNicholas's representations had the "weight of authority" because of his appointment by the Holy See. Corrigan in turn told McNicholas that the Cardinal wanted a definite solution proposed rather than advice or a series of alternative proposals. In response, McNicholas and his committee were "unanimous in concluding that as a visiting body of Bishops appointed by the Holy See it must not exercise the duties of an Executive Committee."[26]

McNicholas frankly admitted that for the committee to propose a definite solution would arouse the opposition of the board of trustees and the chancellor of the university. He declined to approach the Sulpicians himself, because he knew from Corrigan's informal approaches to their American superior, John Fenlon, that they were opposed to a university takeover of the Sulpician Seminary. Bisleti next proposed sending Corrigan to Paris to approach the Sulpician superior general, Cardinal Jean Verdier, who was also archbishop of Paris. Corrigan quickly declined this suggestion, fearing that just the news of such a visit might arouse the hostility of the Sulpicians and their friends in the American hierarchy. Bisleti then personally presented the whole matter to Pope Pius XI, who directed that a letter be sent to Cardinal Verdier stating that the Sulpician Seminary was to be placed at the disposal of the Catholic University, thereby ending the impasse.[27]

The Catholic University negotiated an arrangement with the Sulpicians in which they would be in charge of the discipline and spiritual formation of seminarians in the Sulpician Seminary building. The university then would not be buying the building, which it could not afford, but it would provide the academic faculty. Initially the Sulpicians continued to teach the upper classmen while the university provided instruction for the first-year theology students entering the seminary in the fall of 1937 and added a class each year. In 1940 the transition of the former Sulpician Seminary to the university was completed. The Sacred Congregation of Seminaries and Universities ratified the contract made between the Sulpicians and the university on July 1, 1940.[28] Thereafter, the seminary became the Theological College of the Catholic University. To the Sulpicians, the new arrangement was regarded as a loss of an institution that they had started and financed. It was a blow to their morale that revived the unhappy memories of the loss of the administration of the seminaries of New York and Boston decades earlier.

During his 1937 visit in Rome, Corrigan negotiated, with the assistance of one of Catholic University's canon law professors, the Italian-born Francesco Lardone, new arrangements with the Sacred Congregation for a program of affiliation of seminaries with the university. In the course of the previous activities of the visiting committee and in the records of the School of Sacred Sciences, there is no mention of reviving the nearly moribund program of affiliation with seminaries. Bishops and seminary leaders had not expressed interest in developing such a program, and their views were not solicited. However, the idea rather suddenly reappears and forms a noteworthy activity in the years ahead.[29]

With the absorption of the Sulpician Seminary and a program of affiliation devised, the university's statutes for the ecclesiastical faculties could be completed according to the apostolic constitution. In the new statutes of 1937, the McNicholas committee was given a permanence under the new name, Pontifical Commission for Ecclesiastical Studies, which was to conduct visitations of the ecclesiastical schools. There seemed to be no question that McNicholas would continue to chair the commission and report to the Sacred Congregation. In 1940 an additional revision was made providing for the office of Director of Ecclesiastical Schools, a kind of superior dean coordinating the activities of the Schools of Theology (changed from Sacred Sciences), Canon Law, and Philosophy as well as the affiliation program with seminaries. The energetic canon law professor Monsignor Francesco Lardone was appointed director.[30] By 1940 a revised curriculum for undergraduate and graduate theology was in place and virtually a new theology faculty was in the process of being hired in the late 1930s and early 1940s.

The reorganization of theological studies during the 1930s was a high point of Roman intervention in the affairs of the Catholic University. Reform was accomplished with minimal recourse to the ordinary channels of university governance. Instead, a committee, appointed directly by the Holy See and chaired by an American archbishop whose views were compatible with official positions, played a crucial role. Yet, the committee was not consistent in accomplishing its assigned task. Its greatest success was lobbying for the removal of the rector. On the crucial issue of reorganizing the undergraduate theology programs, the committee evaded responsibility to recommend a course of action and deferred to the Holy See. The pope himself made the crucial decision that determined the organization of theological studies for diocesan students at the Catholic University.

The success of these new arrangements ordinarily would have been tested against the competition the university had always faced from the North American College in Rome for undergraduate seminarians or from Roman and European universities for priest graduate students. But the start of World War II in 1939 foreclosed the possibility for American seminarians and priests to study there. Suddenly the Catholic University enjoyed a monopoly on higher ecclesiastical studies for American priests. Enrollment in the ecclesiastical schools soared from the handful of students and skeleton faculty of the middle 1930s to 280 graduate and undergraduate students by 1943; 55 doctorates in theology were awarded between 1943 and 1948, and about 40 to 50 licentiates were granted annually during the 1940s.[31] The McNicholas commission conducted a visitation in 1944 in which it received reports, conducted interviews, asked questions, and made recommendations that resulted in adjustments of the graduate program. McNicholas described the findings of the visitation a "consolation" after the sorry state of affairs during the 1930s.[32] The Pontifical Commission's role subsequently consisted of receiving routine reports and making relatively minor recommendations. McNicholas died in 1950 and was succeeded as commission chairman by Cardinal Edward Mooney of Detroit.

The new success of graduate theology, ironically, paralleled a disastrous administration for rector Corrigan, who was promoted to titular bishop in 1940. He did not have the energy to undo Ryan's secularizing structures, such as the graduate and undergraduate schools and the athletic program, or the vision to impose ideas of his own. He, nevertheless, had the indolence to permit the fund-raising activities to collapse. Organization and publicity for the annual collection was neglected, the endowment campaign was forgotten, and by 1941 the university was in a financial crisis because there was no leadership to control rising expenses or to raise money. Archbishop Curley, whose role as chancellor had been greatly diminished in recent years by the interventions of the apostolic delegate and the McNicholas commission, stepped in and made vigorous efforts to save the university. Bishop Corrigan, whose health had been in decline, died on June 9, 1942, thus bringing to an end the weakest administration of the university's nine bishop rectors. It is difficult to find any positive aspects to Corrigan's administration or to understand why McNicholas, who was blind to the rector's shortcomings, considered him a desirable candidate for rector.[33] Corrigan was succeeded by a series of three colorless but dutiful bishop rectors through the 1960s.

The weaknesses of the rectors did not detract from the fortunes of graduate theology. Understandably, the number of theology doctorates tapered off after the war as opportunities for graduate studies in Rome and elsewhere in Europe again became available. However, the university's theology programs continued to attract interest so that a total of 176 S.T.D. degrees were granted between 1938 and 1958 to diocesan and religious priests.[34] The Theological College attracted a large number of diocesan seminarians, and nearby houses of religious orders supplied a steady number of seminarians, many of whom earned bachelor and licentiate degrees.

The organization of the system of studies and theology degree programs remained essentially unchanged until the 1960s.

The affiliation program developed gradually during the 1940s under Lardone's direction. McNicholas initially involved himself in promoting the program by writing to selected members of the hierarchy who conducted seminaries, such as the archbishops of Philadelphia, New York, San Francisco, and others. If the bishop was interested, Lardone would follow up with a personal visit to the seminary and begin the negotiation of an affiliation agreement. The agreement was then subject to ratification by the Sacred Congregation of Seminaries and Universities. After McNicholas assisted with the early affiliations, Lardone carried on the activity alone. The first affiliate was the Immaculate Conception Seminary, Mahwah, New Jersey, in 1939 and was soon followed by other diocesan seminaries. St. John's Seminary, Camarillo, California affiliated in 1942. In 1943 McNicholas's own Mount St. Mary's of the West, as well as St. Meinrad and the Seminary of the Immaculate Conception, Huntington, New York affiliated. St. Thomas Seminary, Denver, and St. John's Provincial Seminary, Plymouth, Michigan, affiliated in 1946 and 1954 respectively. The later diocesan seminaries to join the program were St. John Vianney Seminary, Bloomingdale, Ohio, in 1960, St. Mary's Seminary, Cleveland, in 1962, Pontifical College Josephinum, Columbus, in 1963, and St. Francis Seminary, Loretto, Pennsylvania, in 1963. Religious order seminaries also joined the program so that by 1963 there were twelve diocesan and eleven religious seminaries affiliated with the university.[35] The program attracted several large seminaries such as those of Cincinnati, Cleveland, Detroit, and Los Angeles, but many of the largest remained aloof. The seminaries of Chicago and Baltimore had their own pontifical degrees. Seminaries of the great cardinalitial sees of New York, Boston, and Philadelphia apparently did not need affiliation, and their example was followed by smaller seminaries. The program did not attract widespread interest, perhaps because it had a limited usefulness.

At the program's inception, the affiliated seminary had to meet certain basic requirements, such as a qualified professor with a doctorate in each of the major disciplines, the prescribed number of years and courses, and an adequate theological library. None of these minimum requirements seemed to pose a problem with the affiliates. Once affiliated, the seminary was entitled to transfer seminarians to the university, which was usually done at the end of the third year of theology for the superior students, who would take their fourth year at the university to earn the licentiate of theology (S.T.L.) at the end of the fourth year. As with the interest in degrees during the 1890s, the theological degree was intended to reward the few talented seminarians and was not intended for all. Only a handful of students of each seminary would normally be interested in pursuing degrees, and sometimes an affiliated seminary would have no candidates for degrees for several years. The university awarded only 110 S.T.L.s to students of the affiliated seminaries between 1939 and 1953. The most consistent supporter of the affiliation program was Immaculate Conception Seminary, Mahwah, New Jersey, which sent seventy-eight students to Washington between 1942 and 1958 for the S.T.L.[36]

The Sacred Congregation of Seminaries and Universities abolished the S.T.L. program in 1958 and substituted a new program to permit students of affiliated seminaries to earn the bachelor of theology degree (S.T.B.). The S.T.B. program permitted seminarians to take the entire four-year theology course at their own seminaries and then take the university's examination for the bachelor's degree administered by their own seminary.[37] Success in the examination resulted in the conferral of the S.T.B. There were advantages to the new program in that the expense of moving to Washington was avoided. The implementation of the new program did not expand interest in the program. And, as with other initiatives of the Holy See, bishops and seminary educators were not involved in planning the new affiliation program. It was simply announced to them. Throughout the history of the affiliation program, which the university ended in 1970, there was no serious consideration given to soliciting the views of faculty or administrators of affiliated seminaries or to evaluating the entire program.

Beyond the formal programs of studies, the university's influence advanced in theological and pastoral areas through its faculty's publications. The most prominent vehicle for faculty publications was the *American Ecclesiastical Review,* whose founder, the remarkable Herman Heuser, retired in 1927 and transferred his publication to the university. Thereafter the university's faculty gained prominence in disseminating theological and pastoral learning for American priests. William J. Kerby, professor of sociology, edited the monthly from 1927 until his death in 1936. After several editors, the *Review* began in the 1940s to reflect the influence of the new generation of theology faculty who were hired in the period of expansion. Their contributions, of course, pertain to their particular fields. However, the *Review* became their house organ for the regular publication of articles, columns, and book reviews.

The *Review*'s most prominent figure was Joseph C. Fenton, who served as editor from 1944 to 1963. Fenton, born in 1906, was a priest of the diocese of Springfield, Massachusetts. After studies at the Grand Seminaire in Montreal and doctoral studies at the Angelicum in Rome, he taught at several seminaries before joining the Catholic University faculty to teach dogmatic theology in 1938. He served as dean of the School of

Theology from 1944 to 1949, but his influence as editor was the more prominent aspect of his career. His approach to theology was to sustain the church's official teaching, as expressed in his article "The Church and the State of Siege" and his book *The Concept of Sacred Theology.*[38] He was the *Review*'s most frequent contributor, with 189 signed articles appearing during the years of his editorship. He also contributed book reviews and articles to other publications. Many articles were expositions of official church teaching or polemics against his theological opponents inside and outside the Catholic church. His most important public controversy was with the Jesuit theologian John Courtney Murray over the latter's unorthodox interpretation of church teaching on church-state relations.[39] Murray's dissenting position was adopted in the Declaration of Religious Freedom at Vatican Council II in 1964, and Fenton's positions have been eclipsed. Though now almost a forgotten figure, Fenton was the spokesman for the official position on a wide range of theological matters during his active years. However, for all his forceful orthodoxy, Fenton brokered for his American clerical readers some highly original contemporary European ideas on the diocesan priesthood (see chapter 15 below).

Fenton's close colleague through the period was Francis J. Connell. Born in Boston in 1888, Connell joined the Redemptorist order, studied in his order's seminaries in the United States and in Rome, and taught in Redemptorist seminaries before joining the university faculty in 1940. He served as dean of the School of Theology from 1949 to 1957. As a moral theologian, he initiated the exchanges with John Courtney Murray in 1943 before Fenton entered the discussion. Connell's academic reputation was developed as a teacher of moral theology and director of dissertations. But he became widely known beyond the university as the theologian whom journalists called on for a Catholic reaction when contemporary moral questions arose. He was well known among the Catholic clergy as a prolific writer of articles and columns. Up to the time of his formal retirement from the university faculty in 1958, he had published 641 signed pieces in the *Review,* of which 515 were lengthy answers in his "Question Box" column, which he continued until his death in 1967.[40] Parish priests from across the country submitted questions to Connell dealing with problems ranging across the theological, canonical, and rubrical spectrum. His answers reflected unwavering orthodoxy. Fenton described Connell's approach to his role as columnist:

> He has always manifested a masterly knowledge of and a joyous confidence in the workings of the ecclesiastical *magisterium*. He realized that the pronouncements of the Roman Pontiff always demand a true and sincere inward religious assent from the faithful and

from the Church's theologians, even when those statements are not manifestly covered by the Holy Father's charism of infallibility.[41]

Indeed Connell always left the impression of an authoritative interpretation of a matter the church had already considered and defined at some time.

By the 1950s the Catholic University had achieved a position in American Catholic life as an official and authoritative organ of the Holy See in formal studies and in the thought of its faculty. As the era ended and Vatican Council II was underway, the university became more defensive about theological issues. For instance, in the spring of 1963 three leading American Catholic theologians, Godfrey Diekman, Gustave Weigel, and John Courtney Murray, along with the Swiss-born Hans Küng were barred from speaking in a series of Lenten lectures at the university sponsored by a committee of graduate students. None of the figures was under any form of ecclesiastical censure at the time, but the university rector, Bishop William J. MacDonald, had taken the action at the behest of the apostolic delegate, Archbishop Egidio Vagnozzi. It was apparently assumed that the rector's action would remain a routine administrative matter within the Catholic University and would be known only to a few. The student newspaper printed the story, which *Time* magazine then picked up. The university was soon the subject of unfavorable national publicity that lasted for weeks. Monsignor John Tracy Ellis, professor of American church history and one of the university's most influential figures, stated openly in an interview at the time that similar instances of suppressing diverse views had been going on for a decade. Ellis left the university later in the year.[42] The intervention of Archbishop Vagnozzi in university affairs and the resulting controversy presaged conflicts lying ahead on the issue of academic freedom at Catholic University.

The story of the Catholic University throughout the period presents a mixed record of successes and failures in the areas of clerical learning, especially for diocesan priests. The success of the School of Canon Law in attracting clerical students compared favorably with the Graduate School's successes in attracting lay, religious, and clerical students, but the School of Canon Law was the only graduate school in the United States offering that subject. For graduate theology, in which the university competed with other universities, it did not fare as well. The competition from European, especially Roman universities, was strong. During the era of Roman hegemony in church life, it was unlikely that Catholic University, despite its pontifical status, could compete with the attractions of Roman training. The university could not realize the expectations of its founders as a national seat of Catholic theological learning or become the graduate institution where the faculties of major seminaries were trained. Its relations with seminaries was closest through the affiliation program, which even during the years of its greatest patronage, the 1940s and 1950s, enlisted only a small fraction of the country's seminaries. The university had a greater impact in seminary education through its own programs for seminarians of religious orders and diocesan students at the Theological College. The larger issue of locating responsibility for the university was never adequately dealt with. The university depended on the financial support of a body of bishops whose interest in the university and knowledge of academic life were limited. The claims of the Holy See to direct theological activity and its repeated interventions in the life of the university did not encourage the bishops to assume a greater responsibility and to create an academic institution of national distinction.

15. New Directions for Priesthood and Seminary

R oman authority regularly stressed the primacy of supernatural virtues for priests in acquiring personal holiness and directed seminary training to cultivate those virtues. For the American context, Bernard Feeney and William J. Kerby carried forward Americanist ideas of
seminary and priesthood into the twentieth century without reference to
Roman direction. In the actual practice of clerical formation the Roman
spirit had several expressions as reflected in the diocesan seminaries that
leading archbishops such as Cardinals Hayes, O'Connell, and Mundelein
sponsored. In addition to legislation addressing issues related to priesthood and seminary, Roman initiatives in other areas of Catholic thought
and life, such as the theology of the Mystical Body of Christ, Catholic
Action, social teachings, and liturgical movement, began by the 1930s to
influence the model of the priest and the life of the seminary. New movements activated the interest of seminary leaders and seminarians in catechetics, social thought, liturgy, and Catholic Action. European ideas related
to the nature of the priesthood and the practice of ministry began to cir-
culate in the United States by the 1950s that raised questions about the
role of the priest. Accordingly, by 1962 new ideas were redirecting the seminary away from an exclusive preoccupation with cultivating personal holiness in isolation from the world and toward preparation for the professional roles that priests face in actual ministry.

In the early part of the century the perennial theme of personal holiness advanced with a growing body of literature that became the staple
of reading for priests and seminarians during the following decades. Millet's *Jesus Living in the Priest* appeared in translation from the French
in 1901. Books from the British Isles also circulated: Bishop John Cuthbert Hedley's *Lex Levitarum* in 1906 and *A Spiritual Retreat for Priests*
in 1918 continued the emphasis on the supernatural virtues of the priest.

E. J. Mahoney's *The Secular Priesthood,* which appeared in 1930, reviewed the traditional aspects of the priest's vocation, training, and duties. Cardinal Francis Bourne, Archbishop of Westminster and a former seminary rector, published in 1927 the treatise *Ecclesiastical Training,* which dealt exclusively with seminarians' spiritual training. Bourne admired the Sulpician approach to clerical spirituality. The Irish experience was reflected in Canon James Keatinge's *The Priest, His Character and Work,* appearing in 1903, and the rector of All Hallows College in Dublin, Vincentian Thomas O'Donnell, produced *The Priest of Today, His Ideals and Duties* in 1910. Adolphe Tanquerey's concise manual *Spiritual Life,* appearing in 1930, summarized the major aspects of Catholic spirituality and its various schools, though Tanquerey preferred the methods of the French School.[1]

The literature on priests' spirituality appropriate for seminary use was drawn from several countries and approaches. For the American environment, the themes on the priesthood and seminary that Gibbons, Smith, Ireland, McQuaid, Maes, Stang, and Schulze had developed during the Americanist era continued to find spokesmen. Through the early years of Romanization, the most prominent figures to sketch an American vision of the priest were Bernard Feeney and William J. Kerby, whose views first appeared in the *American Ecclesiastical Review.*

Bernard Feeney outlined the model priest and seminary for the period in a series of 1911 *Review* articles. Born in Ireland in 1867 and a graduate of St. Patrick's College at Maynooth, Feeney served on the faculty of Mt. Angel Seminary in Oregon, Mount St. Mary's of the West, and finally from 1902 to 1917 at St. Paul Seminary. He had addressed the American requirements for ministry in a series of short works on catechetics and preaching.

For the American seminary, Feeney offered the distinction between teaching and training. Teaching was directed to the formal learning of the seminary curriculum, for which he urged a practical approach to such courses as Scripture, dogma, and church history. His views on training were more original. While admitting that he knew of no instance in which his ideas were in practice, Feeney proposed that the seminary have a model parish attached to it, in which the seminarians could take an active part. The deacons were to preach. The other seminarians were to give religious instructions to the parish children. After proper instruction seminarians were to take part in pastoral visitations in the parishioners' homes. Feeney stressed the importance of the pastor visiting the homes of his people "not as censor or preacher, but as a kind, anxious father, sympathizing with those in trouble, cheering the despondent, comforting the sick, winning the confidence of poor sinners, and especially making friends of the children."[2] He advised the seminarian on the tactful accomplishment of such visits so that those visited might find the experience pleasant.

Feeney insisted that the ordinary seminarian's life of piety and observance of seminary rules gave no indication of fitness for the work of parish ministry. Actual practice, he believed, is essential. He stressed the seminarians' personal qualities as the key to future success in the priesthood. He assigned a high place to trustworthiness as an essential quality, even ranking it above learning and ascetics. The trustworthy priest does not merely fulfill the minimum requirements of ecclesiastical law but exhibits the charity, conscientiousness, and prudence that will make him a worthy priest in the parish. Within the context of traditional seminary life, trustworthy qualities were to be developed through the faithful accomplishment of numerous small assigned tasks, such as sacristan, bell-ringer, librarian, and so forth. However, Feeney says these may not be enough and concludes that the "artificial, quasi-monastic system of seminary life has to be modified considerably, but with great prudence, to make it merge and vanish insensibly into the future life of the mission."[3]

There is no evidence that Feeney's views enjoyed any influence in actual practice in the early twentieth century. After his death in 1919, a colleague edited his articles for the volume *The Ideal Seminary* (1923). But the signs of the times did not favor his innovative proposals, which would have modified existing institutional arrangements and given seminarians unheard of freedom of movement outside seminary walls.

Through the early decades of Roman legislation, William J. Kerby undertook the most extensive portrayal of the qualities of the American priest.[4] Born in Lawler, Iowa, in 1870 to Irish immigrant parents, Kerby attended St. Francis Seminary in Milwaukee and was ordained priest of the archdiocese of Dubuque in 1892. He was then sent to the Catholic University of America for the two-year licentiate course. There, during the university's controversial founding years, he came under the influence of Bishop John Keane and John Hogan and took as mentor Thomas Bouquillon, the moral theologian engaged in grappling with contemporary moral questions. Kerby was then sent to Louvain for further study and obtained the doctorate in social sciences in 1897. He joined the Catholic University faculty as its first professor of sociology in 1898. His career thereafter revolved around the university and national Catholic activities. His promotion of the idea of organized charity work led to the founding of the National Conference of Catholic Charities, and he served as director of Catholic University's National School of Social Service. His ideals are perpetuated in the organizations that he was instrumental in founding and for which his thought is developed in his volume *The Social Mission of Charity*.

The other major aspect of his activities consisted of some forty-five articles on the priest in the *American Ecclesiastical Review* from 1916 to 1936. He served as editor of the *Review* from 1927 until his death in 1936. These articles were intended as preliminary studies for a systematic treatise on temperament and character in the priest. Though Kerby never got around to developing a large study, twenty-seven of his essays were published in two volumes, *Prophets of the Better Hope* in 1922 and *The Considerate Priest,* posthumously, in 1938.

Kerby does not state an intention to address in particular the diocesan priesthood in the United States, but he takes up issues that pertain only to priests in parish ministry and refers only to the American scene. Though the articles appeared in the 1920s and 1930s, when Roman direction was at its zenith, his essays seem curiously out of place for the times. He does not refer to the priest's dependence on authority. The supervision of bishop or pope is virtually absent in his writings. Despite occasional references to the relations of young priests to older ones, Kerby's model priest, like the model priest articulated in the 1890s, is virtually alone in the cultivation of personal qualities and in the performance of his duties. The laity, of course, are present as the objects of ministry.

Kerby endorses the inherited model of the Tridentine priest, who is "primarily a citizen of the supernatural." Ordination separates the priest from the laity: "elevation is separation." "No priest," Kerby states, "enhances his prestige or increases his effectiveness by laying aside his distinctive point of view and merging in to the laity as almost one of them."[5] He pays more attention to the interior spiritual life of the priest than the Americanist figures of the 1890s, but, like them, he stresses the priest's exterior qualities. These qualities relate to the priest's activities beyond administering sacraments or leading worship. The priest's personal influence depends on the cultivation of these qualities. While previous Americanist figures had stressed that the times required more skills of priests because a better educated laity demanded more, Kerby notes that roles of leadership were passing away from the clergy to other leaders in society, such as the politician, the journalist, businessmen, and civic leaders. The priest urgently requires the highest qualities to maintain leadership. Kerby outlines attributes necessary for developing personal influence: unselfishness, human sympathy, sense of humor, and common sense, which are external and natural virtues, and the cultivation of the supernatural virtues that reflect the traditions of the priest's spirituality.[6]

Kerby does not elaborate on these qualities in a very systematic fashion. Though writing during the age of official neoscholastic thought marked by deductive reasoning and application of principle, he consistently points to an inductive approach to the priest's self-development. For instance, in an essay on priestly temperament, he stresses what he calls the "habit of interpretation." As Providence directs the everyday life in small things as well as great, the priest should learn from the myriad patterns of life. Kerby finds that "all things should teach a priest" and "experience cannot teach unless it is interpreted."[7] In other words, the priest is shaped by the many circumstances of his life and must be alert to the ways of interpreting them.

In another essay Kerby takes up the desired trait of "clerical docility," a term that suggests a cheerful dependence on authority, and redefines it in a novel fashion. Here again he turns the priest away from applying directions from a juridical code or a priori concepts, in which he finds many young priests. "Knowledge of principles," Kerby finds, "is extremely satisfying to a mind that is remote from the tyrannies of life and has not yet developed respect for facts and ability to see and judge them." Instead he desires a priest who is cultured and thereby prepared to become informed about contemporary issues through precise information. This process develops "docility" in which the priest "will be disposed to take advice, to change his mind, to admit error, correct injustice and follow the impersonal ways of prudence."[8] Kerby's ideal priest will be happy to find truth "anywhere" and welcome it.

An essay on "clerical shyness" is directed to overcoming the isolation of the priest from the surrounding world. Kerby notes that priests are often ill at ease with different types of men and women because they "lack the poise, self-confidence, and the easy manner which accompany ripened culture." He laments a growth of what he calls shyness among priests as they increasingly decline to take part in public activities and social movements that need strong moral direction. Priests, too, are seldom to be found in gatherings of scholars because seminary training has given them only a taste for "corroborative erudition" which defends defined teachings.[9] Despite his often carefully qualified, judicious style, Kerby's views grow more pointed as he finds:[10] "there are certain large facts concerning the priesthood which demand explanation. The clergy's lack of interest in the world outside the Church is one. Their lack of contact with the general scholarship of the country is another. Their failure to take commanding positions in the social movements that are inspired by a passion for justice, their preference to shrink their social contacts to their own circle, are others." Kerby rather modestly ascribes this problem to personal shyness among priests without exploring the climate of intellectual life within the church or treating the ways of clerical learning that contribute to the lack of intellectual curiosity. Still, he raises the notion that the status quo was not satisfactory.

Kerby's other points relate to personal behavior and the safeguards against the priest's secure position of "power, security, privilege, and deference."[11] Because the priest's role was often unchallenged in the parish, constant care was required not to abuse his position in the exercise of his duties. In other contexts, security within the routine of church life could lead to a mere formalism in the execution of daily official activities. Doctrinal certainty could make the priest indifferent to the need for learning and cultural development on an ongoing basis.

Throughout the body of his writings there is a concern for ongoing learning and a cultivation of the personal qualities of thoughtful discernment necessary for successful relations with people or, in other words, the attributes of the "considerate" priest. Kerby's views do not contradict aspects of official Roman direction; they in fact reinforce recommendations for holiness and personal development. However, Kerby stresses the importance of the constant adjustments to environment that a discerning priest will make. Kerby's ideal priest is not driven by a relentless application of defined principles but instead is accustomed to flexible responses to many situations. It is in the latter area that Kerby is most at odds with then official expectations of the priest.

The influence of Kerby's ideas on his contemporaries is difficult to assess in the view of more traditional ideas on the priest current during his time. He was not a seminary educator who had direct influence on a group of future priests. William J. Kerby was able to command influence only by reason of his positions as editor and activist.

Philip Murnion's recent examination of priests trained at St. Joseph's Seminary at Dunwoodie during the 1920s provides an overview of seminary training and its relation to the problems of the contemporary priesthood. Dunwoodie's seminarians, of course, followed the classic routine of seminary life. In addition to classes, there was daily meditation and prayers, liturgical functions, and frequent confession and counsel with a spiritual director. The cycle of nonliturgical devotional practices centered on the Sacred Heart of Jesus, the Way of the Cross, and the rosary in honor of the Virgin Mary. The seminarians lived a rigidly disciplined community life in a seminary removed from ordinary contact with the world beyond it. For most of the day's activities they wore the cassock as an external sign of their clerical status.

Once ordained, the New York priest of Murnion's study could ordinarily expect to spend years as a curate in an urban parish to minister sacraments and to participate in other aspects of parish life. The young curate was under the rule of a pastor who was entitled to lay down numerous controls governing parish liturgical practices, rules of rectory living, including curfews, deducting petty expenses from the curate's salary, and other restrictions. The life of a curate with an eccentric or demanding pastor could be difficult beyond description. In such cases, it required a great deal of personal flexibility to cope with the rigidity and eccentricities of others.[12]

From questionnaires and interviews, the Dunwoodie alumni indicated that the aspects of the priesthood given great stress in the seminary did not correspond to the realities of their activities in the parish. For instance, the priests whom Murnion interviewed faithfully conformed to the basic requirements of the priest's spirituality throughout their careers: saying daily Mass, reciting the divine office, and praying the rosary. However, they were seriously at odds with the contemporary exhortations in favor of daily meditation for priests. All but two interviewees stopped the practice of daily meditation after their seminary training. The priest's cultic functions of saying Mass, hearing confessions, and leading the parish in devotional activities was also a primary focus of seminary training. However, the interviewees did not rank these official aspects of ministry as their most important and satisfying activities. Instead, when queried, they most often mentioned activities that required the development of personal skills, such as attending the sick (in which the administration of sacraments often played a part) and working with school children and young people. Murnion concluded how "curious" it was that "celebrating Mass and hearing confessions were not more highly placed among priorities and got such moderate consideration when it came to gratification." He found that activities regarded as most important related to "care for those in need," such as the sick, bereaved, penitent, the young, and all who sought teaching, as manifested in preaching and instructing converts.[13] In effect there was a congruence between satisfactions that Dunwoodie alumni cited and Kerby's external qualities that extended the priest's personal influence. The activities that were most satisfying corresponded to those that were marked by personal initiative and often required thoughtful and flexible responses to varying situations.

At the beginning of the era, seminary methods appear to have been designed to isolate seminarians as much as possible from contact with the external and practical aspects of the priest's activities. Two institutions, St. Joseph's Seminary at Dunwoodie and St. John's Seminary in Boston, were outstanding in the 1890s for their intellectual dimensions and the efforts to relate seminarians to contemporary activities. These seminaries had experienced decisive changes of direction in the early decades of the century after changes in their leadership. They provide examples of the seminary in its most isolated phase.

The manner in which St. Joseph's Seminary at Dunwoodie was conducted responded to the antimodernist spirit. After dismissing the biblical scholar James Driscoll from the rectorship in 1909, Cardinal Farley appointed John Chidwick. A chaplain on the battleship U.S.S. Maine before the opening of the Spanish-American war, Chidwick later served as a chaplain of the New York Police Department. He had the reputation of being a powerful speaker and his manner was usually described as "virile," but he had no academic background or inclinations. He provided the model of a pragmatic and effective priest for New York seminarians. Farley's successor, Cardinal Patrick J. Hayes, replaced Chidwick in 1923 with James McIntire, a New York pastor who had been a parish priest for the thirty-eight years since his ordination. McIntire was a kind, fatherly figure and presented an alternate model of a practical, pastoral priest. McIntire continued the nonintellectual interests of his predecessor.[14]

Cardinal Hayes, who had no academic interests, was not concerned about the quality of intellectual life at the seminary and showed no inclination to develop innovative programs. He pursued the policy of isolating the seminary and its students. He opened a summer villa in Suffern, New York, for third- and fourth-year seminarians in 1923 but discontinued the unpopular program within a few years. Possibly the expense of the villa led to its closure, because, as the historian of the New York archdiocese finds, Hayes's "chief concerns were that the students abstain from smoking and that the Seminary be run as cheaply as possible."[15] Hayes appointed a seminary procurator with the mandate to keep expenses down. Through the Hayes years, economies were legendary, life was spartan, and expenses beyond the basic necessities were regarded as frills. Hayes showed the depth of his interest in the seminary by not visiting it for years. Consequently, Hayes did not follow the example of those bishops who articulated a vision of the priesthood for the local church through the values promoted in the diocesan seminary. The appointment of Francis Spellman in 1939 as archbishop of New York following Hayes's death was an important milestone in the life of the seminary. In the following years Spellman spent lavishly to improve its physical facilities, including a new library, and took care to develop a qualified faculty.

Unlike Hayes, Cardinal William Henry O'Connell in Boston had Roman training and the experience of five years as rector of the American College in Rome to inform his policies at St. John's Seminary. After the Sulpicians left in 1911, his initial approach was to permit the internal life of the seminary to continue much as before. He appointed the church history professor John Peterson to the rectorship. Peterson had had all his seminary training with the Sulpicians at St. John's and only a period of two years of graduate training in Europe. His background was Sulpician in outlook; he maintained their traditions and even personally gave the nightly spiritual reading as a Sulpician rector might do.

Several of O'Connell's early initiatives lay in the direction of isolating his seminary, such as excluding students from other dioceses. He ordered the resident faculty of Boston priests to live "absolutely in harmony as one family" and to seek friendships among themselves and to remain aloof from the diocesan clergy. He did not want "information pertaining to the Seminary and its inner workings to become a matter of public knowledge, even amongst the priests."[16] Another isolating practice was to keep students at the seminary for a period during the summer. In 1918 this summer "villeggiatura" was moved to an estate that had been acquired on Lake Winnepesaukee near Center Harbor, New Hampshire. In the following years the seminarians spent about half of the summer vacation at the villa.

O'Connell took a closer interest in the internal life of the seminary in the late 1920s. After Peterson was made an auxiliary bishop in 1926, O'Connell appointed the Roman-trained Charles Finn to the rectorship. In 1927 Cardinal O'Connell moved to a stately mansion built on the seminary grounds. Thereafter he ran the seminary in a real sense, for the rector and seminary treasurer regularly reported directly to him.

O'Connell determined to limit the horizons of seminary life and follow only Roman methods. Indicative of his continued contempt for French Sulpicians, he had the remains of several Sulpicians removed from the small cemetery on the seminary grounds and eliminated extracurricular activities dating from their administration. For instance, he ended the monthly meetings and in-house publication of the Mission Academia that cultivated an awareness of the church's missionary activities. He abolished the St. Camillus Society, thereby ending the practice of student visitations to hospitals and catechetical work. He introduced the *camerata* system, as in Roman colleges, under which the whole student body was divided into groups of ten to twelve students, each subject to a student prefect or "beadle," who in turn reported to one of the house prefects, a priest faculty member. Accordingly, as the seminary historians record, "the whole student body moved like companies of a regiment to all its various activities."[17] Making the *camerata* the student's point of reference insured personal isolation even within an already isolated community. O'Connell also standardized the style of cassock to be worn and, instead of allowing personal choices of outerwear, prescribed the Roman over-cape. All these measures created a standardized, uniform, regimented, and certainly isolated seminary world that conformed to O'Connell's idea of what was Roman. St. John's historians, Sexton and Riley, who served on the seminary faculty through these trying years, perhaps understated O'Connell as having "too narrowly focussed an eye, and too heavy a hand," and he "seemed often a less kind father than he might have been."[18] O'Connell's relentless enforcement of rules has given rise to numerous stories of expulsion for minor infractions and instances of the rector and faculty shielding students from the cardinal's wrath.

The seminaries of New York under Cardinal Hayes and Boston under Cardinal O'Connell are two important and perhaps extreme examples of narrow seminary policies. Both seminaries reflected the views and fears of their respective archbishops, against whom there was no countervailing authority. The archbishops ordinarily had to account to no one for their actions. Their attitudes could be found in varying degrees among other bishops in the conduct of seminaries here and there. By contrast, the diocesan seminaries conducted by Sulpicians, Vincentians, and Benedictines were characterized by internal exchanges of views about clerical formation among those responsible so that evaluation and adjustment of practices were likely to take place. In the case of Vincentians and Sulpicians, seminary personnel were regularly transferred within their network of seminaries, thereby giving members an experience of the problems at several institutions.

All the communities of priests conducting diocesan seminaries maintained traditions of their own as they came to terms with aspects of Roman direction. For example, the Sulpicians continued their tradition of having students perform limited ministerial tasks outside the seminary through their St. Camillus societies. As noted later on, Benedictines brought their liturgical interests to seminary training; and the western Vincentians had their traditions of evangelization to promote. Though seminaries varied in degrees of isolation from local surroundings and rigidity of personal discipline, no seminary permitted a large degree of personal freedom and initiative to seminarians.

Strict discipline and isolation from the world is not the entire story of seminary life during the era. The logical question was sometimes raised about the appropriateness of training priests for ministry in isolation not only from the world but from the life of the local church. As Chicago priest James A. Magner described the situation in 1935: "Until the day before his ordination, he [the seminarian] is regarded merely as a boy with a vocation and some theological knowledge. Then suddenly he is released into the full stature of the priesthood, to face the world with the front and bearing of a man of experience."[19] Others recognized the need for training seminarians in the practical tasks of everyday ministry and making them familiar with the larger issues of church life. Modest but significant changes began to develop in selected areas in the 1930s that looked beyond seminary isolation to the life of the local church and to practical training for the tasks of ministry.

Efforts to introduce seminarians to wider ideas often took place in isolation from the ordinary life of the church. For instance, Milwaukee seminarians took up summer residence in their archdiocese's seminary villa, where priest alumni or Marquette University professors conducted courses and seminars on pedagogy, speech, mental health, and social problems.[20] And Edward G. Murray, the rector of St. John's Seminary in Boston in the 1940s, devised a program of talks to seminarians of the third and fourth years of theology given by visiting diocesan officials. On these occasions the school superintendent addressed issues of school organization, the Catholic charities director outlined the archdiocesan social service programs, officials of the marriage tribunal discussed marriage and family issues, and so forth.[21] When these programs were adopted in the 1940s, it apparently would have been unthinkable to bring seminarians to the problems being discussed or give them direct experience of working in these areas.

Catechetical work had been regarded as a task suitable for seminarians to perform and provided a legitimate reason for introducing seminarians to some practical work outside the seminary. Involving seminarians took on greater importance as catechetical programs were organized in parts of the country where parochial schools were few. During the 1920s Edwin V. O'Hara, director of the National Catholic Rural Life Conference (NCRLC) and soon to be an influential bishop, developed a program of summer vacation schools for Catholic children in rural areas where there were no parochial schools. The conference developed a curriculum with instructional materials and recruited instructors among the teaching sisterhoods, Catholic public school teachers, and seminarians. The summer schools were conducted at small parishes and Catholic missions, normally in the Middle West and West. Despite the challenges of securing funding and personnel, the movement grew. In 1930 the flourishing program was transferred to the Confraternity of Christian Doctrine (CCD), also an agency of the National Catholic Welfare Conference, which by 1945 sponsored 8,000 vacation summer schools for 700,000 children. Seminarians continued to share in the work of these schools.[22]

Under the CCD's sponsorship, the role of organized catechetics in the seminary expanded, especially after World War II. The 1949 convention of diocesan directors of the CCD passed a resolution that a course in confraternity methods be studied in seminaries. The bishops' committee on the confraternity approved the resolution of the diocesan directors and appointed Bishop William P. O'Connor of Madison as episcopal chairman of the seminary committee of the CCD. O'Connor contacted rectors of the major seminaries of the country and recommended the establishment of a CCD unit in each seminary, headed by a seminary professor who was to cooperate with the diocesan director of CCD. The aim of the seminary unit was to provide instructions for seminarians in catechetics and to coordinate a program of teaching children. The general chairman of the CCD's seminary committee, Monsignor Rudolph G. Bandas, rector of St. Paul Seminary, acknowledged the presence of two schools of thought among seminary officials of the 1950s in permitting the students to leave the seminary for periods of catechetical work. One school held that the seminarian should not be distracted from studies or leave the enclosure of the seminary before ordination; the other school, which Bandas identified as a majority opinion, held that the benefits of limited absences from the seminary for practical catechetical work during the week far outweighed any disadvantages. He found that seminarians returned with a renewed interest in their studies and a desire for finding practical applications to subject matter.[23]

In the 1950s, accordingly, courses in catechetics advanced in the seminary, and seminarians engaged in a variety of activities outside the seminary in accordance with local arrangements: vacation summer schools, Sunday school instruction in institutions, and weekday instruction in schools. Few seminarians, diocesan and religious, were left untouched by the catechetical movement.

The Vincentians were responsible for another type of seminary activity on behalf of religious instruction. Members of the Congregation of the Mission pursued their traditional work of evangelization in rural areas in the Middle West and West throughout their history in the United States. In the 1930s one aspect of their work was street preaching by means of organized "Motor Missions" of traveling Vincentian priests in largely non-Catholic areas of rural Missouri and Oklahoma. Deacons from Kenrick Seminary participated in these activities during the summer. As an extension of the effort to maintain contact with potential converts, Lester Fallon, professor of dogmatic theology at Kenrick, developed a correspondence course for instructing the contacts. The basic text of the course was the popular contemporary manual *Father Smith Instructs Jackson* by Bishop John F. Noll. Beginning in 1937, the Kenrick students of second and third theology were organized to participate by each one taking responsibility for one or two of the course's students. Each seminarian answered questions and corrected tests under the supervision of seminary professors. Kenrick's faculty came to value the work as an opportunity for seminarians to translate textbook learning into a simple and practical explanation of the Catholic faith. The correspondence courses became a familiar extracurricular activity at the other Vincentian seminaries in the West in the 1940s and 1950s. Unlike the CCD programs, the correspondence courses did not oblige seminarians to leave the seminary, but like the latter programs, it permitted them to practice skills before ordination and enlarged their perspective to the wider activities of pastoral life beyond the seminary.[24]

Catholic missionary activity advanced rapidly through the world during the twentieth century. In the United States the Catholic Students Mission Crusade (CSMC) was organized in 1918 by Monsignor Francis Thill of Cincinnati (where it had its headquarters) to spread interest in missionary activity in Catholic schools and colleges. The CSMC movement organized local affiliates in high schools, colleges, and seminaries which sponsored programs of information, visits of missionaries on leave to speak about their experiences, and modest fund-raising activities for the missions. The Crusade organized annual national conventions of representatives from the affiliates. The example of Cardinal O'Connell in ending the organized activities of his seminary mission society notwithstanding, most seminaries had a mission club affiliated with the Crusade. By the 1950s the Crusade's national publication, *The Shield*, had a college and seminary edition to record the local activities of affiliates.[25] The formation of missionary clubs in seminaries encouraged a wider view of church activity and a sense of active responsibility for the missionary work of the church.

The interest in catechetical and missionary work represented a limited attempt to direct seminarians' attention to the life of the church beyond the seminary. At the same time new theological developments had far-reaching consequences in reexplaining basic aspects of Catholic belief and ultimately altering approaches to the priesthood and seminary. These interrelated developments related to ecclesiology in their renewed emphasis on the church as the Mystical Body of Christ, to worship as expressed in the liturgical movement, and to social thought through papal encyclicals whose influence was reinforced by the impact of current economic and social problems. All these movements enjoyed the highest official approval. The vitality of innovative ideas and the movements that accompanied them by the 1930s contrast sharply with the aspects of Catholicism projected by the oath against modernism, the neoscholastic approach of a theology of fixed ideas, and the continuities within the seminary curriculum that reflect a conformity to textbook theology. In the following decades the seminaries, to a degree, became the vehicles both for the continuity of traditional ideas and for the exploration of innovative new ones.

The view of the church as an institution governed by a fixed hierarchical order that traditionalists favored competed with a recovery of St. Paul's conception of the church as the Mystical Body of Christ. Jesus' discourse on the vine and the branches was another element to support this idea of the organic unity of the members of Christ's body. The concept had been revived in the nineteenth century by the German theologians Möhler and Scheeben and was mentioned occasionally by Pope Leo XIII. The Jesuit theologian Emile Mersch was most active in promoting

Mystical Body ecclesiology in the early twentieth century. In the United States, John Gruden of St. Paul Seminary in 1936 published the influential volume, *The Mystical Christ*, that brought the ideas closer to the American church.[26] Pope Pius XII's encyclical *Mystici Corporis* of 1943 accorded the concept the highest official endorsement.

The liturgical movement dated from the efforts of the French Benedictine Dom Prosper Guéranger in the 1840s to recover the purity of the Roman liturgy and to suppress the numerous local customs and nonliturgical rites and music that often obscured the historic liturgy. The movement advanced slowly in the Catholic Europe of the nineteenth century as church authority endorsed various devotional forms that had the effect of competing with the official liturgy. The motu proprio *Tra le sollecitudini,* issued by Pope Pius X in 1903, is considered the official charter of the movement. The decree strengthened the liturgical movement by promoting Gregorian chant in the sung liturgy in order to eliminate the more recent and operatic church music. In the recovery of chant it was made clear that the sung liturgy was not intended to be a theatrical spectacle for a passive audience. Successive popes followed up with additional legislation on restoring ancient liturgical music in the celebration of the liturgy.

In the 1920s the liturgical movement was launched in the United States, principally through the efforts of the Benedictine Virgil Michel of St. John's Abbey in Minnesota, the Jesuit Gerald Ellard, and the St. Louis diocesan priest Martin Hellriegel. In 1925 Michel began the periodical *Orate Fratres* (renamed *Worship* in 1951) as the organ of the liturgical movement in the United States.

The liturgical movement adopted the insights of the Mystical Body theology and placed emphasis on the corporate nature of liturgical worship and its centrality in Catholic life. The movement did not directly attack the plethora of nonliturgical devotions and pious practices that surrounded the prayer life of many Catholics, but the implications of the movement were clear. The Mass and the hours of the Divine Office were the church's official prayer, the rest was not essential. The movement was dedicated to making the Mass intelligible to participants and promoted the use of the vernacular translations of the Roman Missal for Catholics to follow during Mass instead of devotional works unrelated to the Mass. And reformers sought the active participation of all attending Mass with spoken responses or chant. The liturgical movement was promoted by seminars and national conferences through the era, during which St. John's Abbey and later the University of Notre Dame became leaders.[27]

The implications of the corporate explanation of Catholic worship extended to areas of social reform. Liturgical activists were concurrently social reformers. The community that was united in worship had mutual obligations in charity. The modern impulse for social reform among Catholics had been launched by the encyclical *Rerum Novarum,* issued by Pope Leo XIII in 1891. The call for social reform was reinforced in the encyclical *Quadragesimo Anno*, issued by Pope Pius XI in 1931 to commemorate the fortieth anniversary of *Rerum Novarum*. In the 1931 encyclical Pius XI laid down a program of social and economic reform that called for the reorganization of society along lines of vocational groups rather than conflicting camps of capital and labor. Though a reorganization of society along lines suggested by the encyclical was not altogether realistic, still its corporative aspect served to emphasize Christians' mutual responsibilities in society. The rise of the Catholic Action movement in Europe was a practical manifestation of a program of bringing the ideals of Christian social and political reform to society.

The message of Mystical Body theology, the liturgical movement, and Catholic Action activities were likely to be lost on Catholics, lay and clerical, who were accustomed to view the church as primarily a hierarchical institution, public worship as an occasion for private prayer, the Mass as the action of the priest before a passive audience, and social action only as donations to charity. The new movements began an uphill struggle to overcome practices and attitudes of questionable theological basis and to promote an adherence to the official message of the church in these areas. A part of the challenge of spreading some of these movements was their origin in the Middle West, largely among German-American Catholics.

In the application of the new movements within the Catholic seminary, Reynold Hillenbrand of Chicago stands out as a figure enjoying notable success and influence. Hillenbrand was born in Chicago in 1906 to a middle-class Catholic family with origins in German Catholic Wisconsin. Young Reynold followed his older brother, Frederick, through Cardinal Mundelein's new Chicago seminary system, first at Quigley Preparatory Seminary and then at St. Mary of the Lake Seminary. Reynold was ordained a priest in 1929 and continued his studies at the Chicago seminary, where he obtained the doctorate in theology in 1931. Cardinal Mundelein then sent him to Rome for a year of desultory study as a kind of "finishing" to his education. In Rome during the year of the issuance of *Quadragesimo Anno,* he came under the influence of contemporary movements in the church. Back in Chicago in 1932, Hillenbrand lived with a large community of diocesan priests at the rectory of the Cathedral of the Holy Name, whose peripatetic rector, Monsignor Joseph Morrison, made the cathedral parish a local center for liturgical and social action activities. Hillenbrand took part in these activities, taught at Quigley Preparatory Seminary, and preached with Chicago's group of priests conducting parish missions. Cardinal Mundelein, who had favored the young

Hillenbrand with opportunities for a variety of experiences, appointed him rector of St. Mary of the Lake Seminary in the spring of 1936. The new rector was only thirty-one years old. The cardinal personally presented the new rector to the seminarians and aptly stated, "I've brought you a man with imagination."[28]

As rector, Hillenbrand made a decisive impact on the spirit of seminary life without altering the forms of clerical formation. At St. Mary of the Lake the Jesuits continued to teach the academic courses. The seminarians led a highly controlled life of discipline and pious exercises. Their clerical identity was reinforced by the wearing of the cassock and spending nearly the entire year, including summers, in the company of priests and other seminarians. However, within the context of seminary traditions, Hillenbrand opened a broader vision of the Catholic world to the students of St. Mary of the Lake in three undertakings: teaching a class in the liturgy and implementing liturgical reforms, conducting a course in social problems to the deacon class, and inviting some of the leading Catholic thinkers and activists of the period to lecture to the seminarians.

Hillenbrand implemented some of the leading practices of the contemporary liturgical movement. The first was the dialog Mass. The students attended daily low or recited Mass in their residence hall, at which they answered the Mass responses and recited the proper parts. He transformed the Sunday High Mass into a genuine community Mass with a homily—that is, a commentary on the readings, as favored by the liturgical movement, instead of a topical sermon. He restored prominence to the official liturgy of Holy Week and abolished such nonliturgical customs as the *Tre Ore* on Good Friday. Though Jesuits taught academic courses, the rector customarily taught a course in pastoral theology to the deacons. Hillenbrand imparted the most up-to-date and official ideas to the deacons on the liturgy, social thought, and catechetics.

Hillenbrand broadened the seminarians' outlook by inviting guest speakers of contemporary importance. The visiting lecturer in Catholic seminaries was a common practice and bishops, visiting missionaries, Catholic apologists, and literary figures appeared regularly on the seminary circuit. However, Hillenbrand invited lecturers who were on the cutting edge of contemporary ideas, especially major figures of the liturgical movement. Maurice Lavanoux, founder of the Liturgical Arts Society and editor of the magazine *Liturgical Arts,* was the first liturgical activist to appear in the fall of 1936. In the following years, Virgil Michel spoke; Gerald Ellard, S.J., spoke and conducted retreats. Donald Attwater, leader of the liturgical movement in England, lectured.

Hillenbrand gave equal prominence to vital questions of the day with speakers who lived out the theoretical premises of the church's social teachings. The years of the economic depression saw a flowering of Catholic social activity at various levels and from several perspectives. Women lecturers appeared, probably for the first time before a Catholic seminary audience, when Dorothy Day, the leader of the Catholic Worker movement spoke; Catherine de Hueck soon followed. John Gilliard, an influential priest of the Society of St. Joseph, spoke on his society's work among blacks; John LaFarge, S. J., spoke on Catholic Interracial Councils. Monsignori John A. Ryan and Francis Haas spoke on economic and labor questions. Luigi Ligutti spoke on the National Catholic Rural Life Conference. Bishop Robert Emmet Lucey, then of Amarillo, Texas, addressed labor problems in the Southwest. The stress on progressive social thought corresponded to Cardinal Mundelein's own ardent support for the New Deal.

By hammering away at the leading religious and social issues of the time, Hillenbrand formed a cohort of Chicago priests during the years of his rectorship who began their careers with a strong desire to implement liturgical reform and act on social questions. There was an element of controversy in his rectorship as young priests were assigned to Catholic parishes where older priests were either unaware of, or unmoved by, contemporary Catholic thought. The young rector's aims to redirect aspects of the seminarians' education also created tension with the Jesuit faculty, which had the ordinary responsibility for formal instruction. Hillenbrand resigned the seminary rectorship in 1944 for reasons that are not altogether clear and was appointed pastor of Sacred Heart Church in the Chicago suburb of Hubbard Woods. He left at the seminary a record of giving seminarians a lively awareness of the church beyond the seminary, in which they were to take an active part after they were ordained. Though the element of the seminarians' physical isolation from the world was present at St. Mary of the Lake, as at other seminaries of the period, yet the church beyond and the vision of the active life of the priest were constant realities under the imaginative Hillenbrand regime.

Through the years of his rectorship and afterward, Hillenbrand was a leader in various movements that have been designated "specialized" Catholic Action. These took their cue from the model of Catholic Action of the Belgian Canon Joseph Cardijn. The canon proposed the idea of "like ministering to like" in which supporters of Catholic Action were organized along vocational lines, in other words farmers would relate to other farmers, workers to workers, and students to students. The so-called "cell" technique was adopted in which small groups of six to ten workers or students met regularly for study of Catholic social thought and to act upon Cardijn's three-step method of "see-judge-act" as activists addressed their common environment and explored ways to improve it. The work of active Catholics in dealing with the immediate and the local was considered the key to reestablishing a Christian social order and resisting secularism. The European movement resulted in the formation of Catholic Action movements along vocational lines, such as those for workers, students, and farmers. Cardijn's method and the movements associated with it enjoyed official endorsement from Roman authority.[29]

Hillenbrand and like-minded priests, notably Louis Putz, C.S.C, of the University of Notre Dame, were active in promoting a Catholic Action movement among priests in the United States. Catholic Action study weeks for priests were first held at the Milwaukee seminary in 1938. These led to the gradual formation of separate movements for workers and students in the United States. The formal national organization of a priests' Catholic Action movement resulted from Hillenbrand's convening of a meeting of some twenty-five priests from ten dioceses at Childerly Retreat House in Wheeling, Illinois, in August 1942. The return of a number of young American priests and seminarians whose studies in Europe were interrupted by the war was an important element in advancing Catholic Action in local settings. These young men had been attracted to Catholic Action methods in Europe and were eager to carry them out in the United States.

Hillenbrand's priests' conference of 1942, followed by a similar one also at Wheeling, in October 1943, began the efforts of Catholic Action chaplains to start cells among students and workers. At the meeting of 1942 it was decided to promote the cell technique in seminaries and two young priests of the Congregation of the Holy Cross, Theodore M. Hesburgh and Charles Sheedy, and a seminarian, Thomas Reese, of the Theological College at Catholic University, were designated to promote the movement for seminarians. Thereafter, the Seminarians' Catholic Action Movement took off. Reese was a capable promoter of study cells among the students at Theological College and was at the center of organizational efforts conducted by mail among seminaries across the country where like-minded activists were organizing study cells. Theodore Hesburgh, whose studies in Rome had been cut short by the war, was a graduate student in theology at Catholic University. His short volume *Theology of Catholic Action* was one of the basic study texts of the movement along with Cardijn's.[30]

The Seminarians' Catholic Action Movement was a noteworthy organizational success with study cells established in some sixty diocesan and religious order seminaries in the United States by 1948. It was particularly strong at the Catholic University and its affiliated houses of studies, in St. Mary's at Baltimore, and at seminaries in the Midwest. The seminarians' movement held summer gatherings, first at the University of Notre Dame in the summer of 1946 and again at a general convention of Catholic Action groups at Montreal during the summer of 1947 at which Canon

Cardijn himself was in attendance. The seminarians' movement published for several years from St. Meinrad's Abbey Press the occasional periodical *Forum,* which reported on local Catholic Action activities.

The Catholic Action thought which enjoyed the Holy See's official blessing found its way into the seminary curriculum of the period. In a report submitted to the Catholic Theological Society of America in 1948, thirty-two diocesan and religious order seminaries were found to include it in the classroom. Of these, nineteen seminaries offered a distinct course ranging from a brief one-semester course in the second year of philosophy to a more thorough treatment of one or two hours per week in the third and fourth years of theology. Thirteen other seminaries treated Catholic Action explicitly in courses in social encyclicals, sociology, economics, apologetics, dogmatic theology, pastoral theology, or liturgy.[31] The approach was thereby becoming internalized among seminarians and priests of the era. The 1940s and 1950s saw the growth of organized lay Catholic activity with such movements as Young Catholic Students, Young Catholic Workers, and the Christian Family Movement — all of the latter organized locally in cells with a local chaplain and having national headquarters in Chicago, close to their national chaplain, Reynold Hillenbrand. The Catholic Action movement had an important effect in extending the diocesan priest's range of activity with the laity and in enlarging the laity's sense of responsibility for the work of the church.

A fresh re-envisioning of the diocesan priest was likewise being approached from a different angle during the period. Again the source of new ideas was France, where the contemporary religious situation was the catalyst. The writings of several French theologians addressed the diocesan priesthood, including *De l'éminente dignité du sacerdoce diocèsain* (1938) by Canon Eugene Masure and the successive works, *Le clergé diocèsain* (1941), *Mission du clergé* (1942), the *Nature et spiritualité du clergé diocèsain* (1946) by Gustav Thils. The reconsideration of the priest's role was taken up by the assembly of French archbishops in 1944 in which Archbishop Emile Guerry of Cambrai presented a report later published under the title, *Le clergé diocèsain en face de sa mission actuelle d'évangelisation.*[32] Though these works were not available in English to American readers until the 1960s, Joseph Clifford Fenton took up issues related to the diocesan priesthood in his role as editor of the *American Ecclesiastical Review* during the 1940s. He reported on these European developments in the *Review* and published a series of articles on the diocesan priesthood in the 1940s that were collected in a volume titled *The Concept of the Diocesan Priesthood* (1951).

Fenton, who ordinarily viewed his function as elaborating and defending official church teaching, was in this instance the broker for new ideas emanating from European but non-Roman sources on the nature of the diocesan priesthood. As Fenton reports, the origins of a reconsideration of the diocesan priesthood resulted from differences of opinion concerning the spirituality appropriate for the diocesan priest. Much of the literature on the subject available for diocesan priests in recent centuries was written by members of religious orders. Some French clerical writers objected to this literature directed to diocesan priests as if the latter were somehow incomplete friars, monks, or vowed religious. The concern for developing a spirituality appropriate to the diocesan priest caused an exploration of the meaning of the diocesan priesthood.

Exploring the history of the diocesan priest lends itself to a consideration of the theology of the local church. Fenton regarded the existing theological treatments on the nature of the church as too preoccupied with the hierarchical constitution of the church, with particular stress given to defending the prerogatives of the Roman pontiff. He found that the reigning dogmatic manualists, Tanquerey and Hervé, shared that preoccupation. Missing from all such treatments was a theology of the local church. With reliance on the church fathers, especially on St. Ignatius of Antioch, the French writers and in turn Fenton found meaning for the diocesan clergy in the historical recovery of the ancient church. For Fenton, the local church consists of the faithful of a given territory gathered around their bishop, the "head and father" of the local clergy or *presbyterium*. The function of this local clergy is "to act as the instrument of the bishop in the liturgical, doctrinal, and administrative direction of the diocese." Fenton "cannot insist too strongly upon the corporate or collegiate nature of the *presbyterium*." The priests of the local church in fact "constitute a real brotherhood or social unit."

Fenton elaborates several ways in which the *presbyterium*'s corporate dimension was then exercised. He describes its goals as fourfold: (1) doctrinal ministry in order to provide members of the local church with an accurate knowledge of the church's teachings; (2) missionary function to edify the local church, which itself grows in holiness and charity so that those outside of it will want to join; (3) the building of unity among the faithful of the local church into a family bound by mutual charity; and (4) bringing each member to the fullness of divine grace. These themes he finds reflected in the encyclical *Mystici Corporis*, "the most important papal pronouncement of our time."[33]

Fenton identifies as one of the most important aspects of the local church its special mission to the poor and the suffering. On the one hand, this mission is directed to the alleviation of physical needs of the unfortunate. But the diocesan priest is not to consider himself exempt from personal activity among the poor because the church's organized charities may already be tending to their needs. If the priest is personally inaccessible to the poor, then that priest is obstructing the perfection of charity in the local church. On the other hand, the priest's mission includes those who are poor and deprived in a spiritual sense. The priest has a direct responsibility to instruct the poor, that is, those outside the church community, in the teachings of Jesus Christ and to bring them into the local church.[34]

Joseph Fenton, either by his own views or those borrowed from the French authors, implicitly and at times explicitly calls into question the existing ideas of spirituality for seminarians and pastoral practices. Fenton's views are directed to the priest's activities beyond the membership of the immediate parish community and the prescribed round of the ministry of the sacraments. The priest's duties have an integral relationship to building up the community of the local church. In this regard, Fenton makes many explicit references to the theology of the Mystical Body and the aims of contemporary movements such as Catholic Action. In other areas, Fenton joins the French authors in calling into question the ideas of the past. Diocesan seminarians should be instructed on their future duties from a sound theology of the local church. He questions the value of books on affective piety directed to individual holiness written in the language of the past.

In the era after World War II, the French church implemented innovative approaches to come to terms with secularization in French society. In particular to bridge the widening separation between the church and the working class, which had increasingly given up formal religious practices, the French bishops approved the worker priest movement in which selected priests became factory workers in order to come into contact with workers in their ordinary environment. The movement was controversial in theory and practice. Nevertheless, the Archbishop of Paris, Cardinal Emmanuel Suhard actively supported it as an appropriate outreach to assist in stemming the dechristianization of modern France. Suhard's eloquent writings, particularly his pastoral letter on the priesthood that was published in English under the title *Priests Among Men,* explained the works of the priest for the contemporary times. He strongly disapproved of the exaggerated explanations of the priesthood common in the traditions of French Catholicism, such as viewing the priest as superior to angels or describing his powers as somehow magic. Instead Suhard applied the insights of Mystical Body theology to explain the responsibilities of the priest within the Christian family.[35]

The new ideas and practices in pastoral activity in Europe produced a literature that was available to those who thought about these matters in the United States. In addition to Suhard's works, George Michonneau's volume on the life of a Paris parish, *Revolution in a City Parish,* appeared in 1950 with a foreword by Archbishop Richard Cushing of Boston. From Germany, the English edition of Josef Sellmair's volume *Priest in the World* appeared in 1953. Sellmair criticized the exaggerated supernaturalism often applied to the priest and explored the proper relationship of the priest to pastoral activity, to modern learning, and to contemporary culture.[36]

Because of the high level of religious practice among Catholics in the United States, the European literature directed to building up religious practice in a secularized population did not have an urgent attraction. Nevertheless, there were important beginnings to scientific analysis of parish life. In 1951 Jesuit sociologist Joseph Fichter produced a study of a New Orleans parish titled *Southern Parish* and, in 1954, *Social Relations in the Urban Parish.* In 1960, another Jesuit sociologist, Joseph B. Schuyler, produced a study of a New York City parish entitled *Northern Parish.*[37]

These groundbreaking sociological studies in parish life paralleled a concern among Catholic sociologists as to how to promote the study of sociology in seminaries in order to make available to seminarians the new sociological knowledge. As one priest sociologist put it: "Surely a priest, and a seminarian preparing to be a priest . . . should know as much as possible about the human heart and mind, the human personality, the environment and social milieu in which humans are born, mature, marry, earn a living, raise a family, grow old and die."[38] By the 1950s the American Catholic Sociological Society had a standing committee to study and promote the teaching of sociology in seminaries. In 1956 the committee surveyed social studies in Catholic seminaries and found that of the 108 responding major seminaries about half, or fifty-two, offered sociology courses while twenty-six permitted taking courses at a college nearby. These courses were normally introductory level with one additional course addressing some other interest such as marriage or the family, urban sociology or rural sociology, Christian social teachings, and so forth. Most seminary sociology instructors had formal training but did not have a degree in sociology. The common conclusion to such surveys was the importance of improving social studies in seminaries.[39]

The Jesuit Joseph B. Schuyler, who was particularly active in the cause, cites statements of recent popes on the importance of formal preparation for the church's social mission. Schuyler also endorsed scientific social studies in the seminary on the threefold basis: (1) the value of such studies in the formation of the future priest as an intelligent human being; (2) their direct relevance to effective pastoral work; and (3) because of the moral effects of social problems on the Catholic community.[40]

By the 1950s the various efforts to involve seminarians in activities outside the seminary, the changing concepts of the priesthood, and the new impetus for sociology were in circulation but were not intended to have the effect of greatly changing the classic traditions of seminary life. The controls of clerical formation remained as reflected in each seminary's rule book that outlines a lifestyle aimed at safeguarding the seminarians' vocation in isolation from the world. Thomas Dubay's *The Seminary Rule,* (1954), was a classic exposition of seminary life.[41] While formerly such explanations were written in a more declarative mode, Dubay adopts a more apologetical style that implicitly recognizes some questioning of traditional seminary discipline. Yet the book continues the longstanding assumption that an exacting rule of life pursued in isolation from the world was the means of personal sanctification, that faithfulness in small observances presaged responsibility in large matters, and that a docile and even cheerful obedience to the minutiae of seminary rules was indicative of suitability for priesthood.

An unquestioning devotion to these assumptions is strikingly evident in the diary of Thomas Mulligan, Sulpician rector of St. Patrick's Seminary at Menlo Park, California. Written between 1944 and 1957, the diary reveals Mulligan's devotion to the daily regimen of the seminary, which as a faithful Sulpician he kept along with his charges.[42] The seminary routine, as carefully recorded here, was the primary end of the seminary. That there were innovative approaches in pastoral ministry being discussed elsewhere, that the seminary program might benefit from reevaluation, and that new ideas were enlarging the concepts of ministry were beyond the rector's interest or concern.

Notwithstanding the outlook of Thomas Mulligan and those of like mind, the shifting of emphasis between the traditional concern for personal sanctification and the interest in training the seminarian for his future functions as priest emerges as a noticeable development. In 1961 Joseph Fichter's sociological study of the Catholic church's personnel outlines the many problems of Catholic priests and religious. Among the issues the author addresses is the training of church professionals for holiness as though it were strictly separate from other concerns. In view of the few opportunities for seminarians to take responsibility for any but personal matters in the years of training, Fichter finds validity in the often repeated expression that "the seminary makes boys out of men."[43] He approves Pope Pius XII's views on this subject in *Menti Nostrae*: "it is necessary to diminish gradually and with due prudence the separation between the people and the future priest in order that when he receives Holy Orders and begins his ministry, he will not feel himself disorientated—a thing that would not only be harmful to his soul but also injure the efficacy of his work."[44] Fichter describes as "curious" and a "paradox" the "common notion that training in personal perfection is one thing and professional preparation for the apostolic role is another thing."[45] In all other professions, the entry into professional activity is preceded by some kind of practical training or internship. But this was not the case with the priesthood, in which the newly ordained priest was expected to step fully into all the roles of his office on the day of his ordination.

An awareness of the dichotomy between formation for holiness and professional preparation was emerging openly by the early 1960s. Roman authority sent mixed signals on this problem. The views of Pope Pius XII in *Menti Nostrae* provided an authoritative basis for seminary reform, while, as discussed at the conclusion of Chapter 12, the Sacred Congregation of Seminaries and Universities expressed fears concerning the erosion of spirituality and the adoption of new methods in seminaries. In the following years, negotiating the competing claims of holiness and professional preparation would be among the major problems confronting seminary education.

16. Clerical Studies in Transition

I n the early twentieth century seminary studies achieved a pattern of
organization that was to remain generally in effect for the subsequent
six decades. A principal feature was the course of six years of study for
minor and major seminaries. In the major seminary, the leading courses
were dogmatic and moral theologies. Other subjects received proportion-
ately less attention. The Code of Canon Law named the courses of seminary studies and left the impression that authority determined clerical
learning. The oath against modernism and official endorsement of neoscholastic thought conveyed a powerful sense to faculty and seminarians
that the content of seminary learning was not subject to change. However,
within these broad characteristics, seminaries differed in the numbers of
courses and hours assigned to each subject. During the 1930s Roman authority strengthened the formal preparation of seminary faculties by reorganizing studies at pontifical universities to relate advanced learning to
research. Official approval for new biblical and theological scholarship gave
impetus to the redirection of selected aspects of seminary studies. These
developments paralleled the founding of learned societies among seminary
educators. The societies participated in the dissemination of new ideas
within academic disciplines and had the effect of raising questions about
the methods of traditional seminary pedagogy. Seminary studies were
thereby making a gradual transition from the methods of the early twentieth century so that by 1962 the ground was prepared for further reform.

The Code of Canon Law and the decrees of the Sacred Congregation of Seminaries and Universities did not establish a precise plan of studies
to be followed in all Catholic seminaries. While the code listed the courses
to be offered in the major seminary course of six years, there was no prescribed number of years of study or classes per week assigned to each subject. The Holy See's development of the Italian regional seminary system
through the early twentieth century to supplant the many small diocesan
seminaries also introduced a model course of studies. A. M. Micheletti,

professor of pedagogy at the Apostolic College in Rome, devised the course of studies. After the introduction of the Code of Canon Law in 1918 and pursuant to directives of the Holy See, Micheletti updated his course of studies. His plan might be considered a semiofficial standard for Catholic seminaries. It represented what was prescribed for Italy and thus has a basis in official thinking but was not given universal application. For those who desired a Roman plan of studies, the *Ordinamento* issued in 1921 for Italian seminaries was the closest to an official standard.[1]

For American seminaries, the Roman queries of 1906, as noted, brought about the long-postponed compliance with the six-year course for the major seminary. However, beyond the official concern for the length of the seminary course, there was no inquiry thereafter into the number of days in the academic calendar, the number and length of courses, or the class hours per course. Likewise, Roman authority did not address the American seminary's legal status or its relationship with the educational system of the country, which will be discussed in chapter 17. The Holy See periodically decreed that courses in particular subjects be taught and required triennial reports that reminded seminary officials of their accountability to higher authority. However, the Holy See adopted a laissez faire approach to the actual organization of studies, which differed widely among American seminaries. Force of local habits and informal administrative structures within American seminaries insured that there was slight evaluation and reconsideration of how effectively seminary studies were organized. Through the era the papers presented at annual meetings of the seminary departments of the Catholic Educational Association (CEA), known after 1927 as the National Catholic Educational Association (NCEA), provide a major source for tracing the evolution of ideas on seminary studies. These papers often reveal a questioning of the curricular status quo that is surprising for an era given to deference to official influence.

As early as the CEA meeting of 1913, Herman Heuser, one of the most influential seminary figures of his time, raised serious questions about methods of learning dogmatic theology. He questioned the value of the traditional apologetic method of dogmatic textbooks that had long been the hallmark of Catholic seminary instruction:

> the textbooks used in class are loaded down with arguments that are often purely artificial, and — to make a bold but true statement — are sometimes hurtful to the sense of honesty and truth. Deductions from Scripture and the interpretations of the Fathers which are unsound because they rest upon a defective and imaginary exegesis; illustrations appealing to supposed historical facts that are in reality legends; syllogisms that are built upon a symbolism lacking the logic

of just inference, because the images employed belong to another world of thought and feeling, are features of our present text-books of which, if I dared weary my hearers' patience, I could give definite instances. Such things beget not merely confusion; they create also an unhealthy state of mind which mistakes the dicta of the past for the experiences of truth, and confuses individual statements with the sum of authority.[2]

He expected these defects to be corrected in the future. However, he was more concerned at this point with the elimination of the superfluous from the course of seminary studies. He proposed a rearrangement of topics to avoid the repetitions that were rife. For instance, particular sacraments were treated variously in courses in dogma, moral theology, church history, and liturgy. Some theological controversies of the distant past that had no contemporary relevance were treated at length in dogma when they could have been summarized briefly in the church history course. Such tracts as *De Creatione,* treated at length in dogma, might more profitably be moved to the exegesis course. Heuser recommended a three-step program of reform: first, the coordination of the various subjects in the seminary course to avoid repetition and the resulting loss of time; second, elimination of formerly valuable information that had lost significance in modern times, such as refutations of ancient heresies and rehearsing controversies that were no longer controversial; and finally, the coordination of the content of courses so that "topics of a kindred nature, and likely to illustrate one another, are taught in a simultaneous course."[3]

In 1914 Heuser renewed the theme of reform of seminary studies with proposals for relocating Scripture studies. He proposed that the Scripture course should precede theological studies so that in the first year of philosophy the students should follow a program of Bible reading and in the second year a course of general introduction should be given. His plan assured that the student would have a general familiarity with the Scriptures before the beginning of dogma studies. Heuser's audience expressed qualified approval for his views, but there was slight interest in implementing them.[4]

Proposals along Heuser's lines were periodically raised at the CEA seminary department's annual meetings. In 1924 Charles Cremin of St. Mary's Seminary, Baltimore, returned to the theme of reorganizing seminary studies to eliminate repetition of the same topics in various classes. He further proposed the rewriting of textbooks and a close coordination of course matter among the faculty themselves to eliminate wasteful overlapping in their teaching. More radical for the time was Cremin's idea that theology be taught in the vernacular because of the confusion Latin inevitably caused in seminary instruction.[5]

In 1925 the seminary department's survey of seminary studies reported the defects of textbooks on the grounds that they were "crowded with matter extraneous to the respective sciences" and contained too much "antequated and useless matter and are sadly lacking in the actual questions and problems of the day and in those which are of vital importance in this country." The report concluded by calling for new textbooks to eliminate the superfluous and to deal with contemporary questions.[6] Another critic of seminary studies observed in 1931 that seminary studies lacked "coordination, cooperation, system, uniformity of program, understanding between the members of the same faculty, between seminaries generally, between the colleges generally, between the seminaries and the colleges. . . ."[7] But the proposals for reform in the previous two decades made slight headway in gaining support.

The status quo had its defenders, such as John M. Nevins of St. Mary's Seminary, Baltimore, who believed that for the most part the treatment of the same topics in the various disciplines was unavoidable and even desirable.[8] The many papers delivered at annual meetings in which educators described how they taught their subjects attest to the loyalty to the traditional division of subject matter. It was unlikely that a rearrangement of course offerings was possible, though the question had been raised.

Despite complaints, loyalty to teaching by the prescribed manual remained a principal characteristic of seminary learning. One textbook defender was the Sulpician Anthony Vieban, who conducted his society's year-long formation program or "Solitude" from 1921 to 1933 and served as rector of the Sulpician Seminary/Theological College from 1933 to 1944. In addition to providing spiritual direction, Vieban gave lectures on seminary pedagogy to Sulpician candidates. He defined the purpose of major seminary instruction as imparting a sound knowledge of church doctrine, which priests would be responsible for passing on to the Catholic faithful. As Vieban believed: "Neither the limited time at his disposal, nor the limited talent of the majority of his students allow a Sem. Professor to go beyond the boundaries of elementary teaching."[9] The requirements of elementary instruction point to the undesirability of relying on the instructor's lectures. The student might misunderstand lecture material and take incorrect notes. In later years, the priest would also be less likely to consult old lecture notes, but a comprehensive textbook could be more easily consulted. For the Sulpician context, the superior general of the society was responsible to church authority for the doctrine taught by its members. Vieban wondered how the superior general could fulfill this responsibility if Sulpician instructors gave their own lectures. He believed the correct approach to seminary instruction was to have a textbook that set down the entire body of theology to be taught.

The first comprehensive survey of diocesan seminary studies in the United States reveals aspects of the adherence to traditional methods of seminary instruction and diversity of course arrangements. In 1935 Theodore Heck, of St. Meinrad Abbey and Seminary, submitted a doctoral dissertation in education at Catholic University that examined studies in the thirty-two seminaries training diocesan priests at that time. Heck first compares the standards of the semiofficial Roman model, that is, Micheletti's program of 1919 for Italian regional seminaries, with the number of hours and courses offered at seven American diocesan seminaries in 1920. Heck's findings indicate the lack of uniform course offerings among selected American seminaries and their divergence from the Roman model.

Heck then surveys course offerings of thirty (of the thirty-two) diocesan major seminaries operating in the United States between 1932 and 1934. This detailed study provides a look at the seminary a quarter century after the condemnation of modernism, a decade after the promulgation of the Code of Canon Law, and after the initial years of Roman legislation pertaining to the seminary. Heck finds a continuation of diversity as seminaries offered a wide range of courses and class hours. In terms of total class hours of all subjects in the normal seminary course, the results vary from the highest of 5,215 hours required at St. John's Home Missions Seminary at Little Rock, Arkansas, to the lowest, 3,239 hours required at St. Vincent's Seminary at Latrobe, Pennsylvania. Course offerings varied, as some seminaries offered such additional courses as bookkeeping, apologetics, sociology, and modern languages. Among courses offered at all seminaries there were wide variations in numbers of hours given to homiletics, chant, canon law, Hebrew, and ascetical theology.[11]

Through the diversity of courses, the study of dogma received the greatest number of hours at most seminaries. At only two seminaries (St. Mary's at Baltimore and St. Francis Seminary at Loretto, Pennsylvania) moral theology slightly exceeded the number of hours given to dogma. Though dogmatic theology dominated seminary studies, there were wide variations in numbers of hours. The Jesuits at St. Mary of the Lake Seminary provided Chicago seminarians 1,078 hours of dogmatic theology, the highest number of hours, while St. Benedict Seminary, Atchison, Kansas, offered the lowest number with 480 hours. Twenty-one seminaries offered between 600 and 760 hours of dogma. St. Francis Seminary, Loretto, Pennsylvania gave 858 hours of moral theology while St. Benedict's Seminary, Mt. Angel Seminary, and St. Francis Seminary in Milwaukee offered

SEMINARY CURRICULAR OFFERINGS IN 1920[10]

Seminaries:*	NUMBER OF SEMESTER HOURS							
	M	A	B	C	D	E	F	G
Courses								
Sacred Scripture	32	26	24	24	16	42	36	24
Dogmatic Theology	32	40	48	40	40	48	40	40
Moral Theology	32	40	36	34	48	40	38	22
Pastoral Theology	16	—	6	2	4	2	6	—
Ascetical Theology	8	—	—	—	—	—	8	—
Canon Law	16	6	12	12	—	16	12	18
Patrology	8	4	—	6	4	4	4	4
Apologetics	6	—	—	—	—	4	4	8
Homiletics	8	16	10	6	8	8	12	8
Church History	16	12	12	18	12	18	18	12
Hebrew	4	8	8	8	8	4	6	6
Greek	16	4	4	16	—	4	4	2
Latin	12	—	8	8	—	4	4	—
Vernacular Tongue	12	—	4	6	—	4	8	6
Philosophy	54	20	36	28	24	26	28	20
Civil History	12	—	—	—	—	—	—	6
Mathematics	6	—	—	—	—	—	—	—
Sciences	12	16	8	12	6	14	8	14
Natural History	6	—	—	—	—	—	—	—

Subjects not recorded by Micheletti in the 1919 program

Liturgy		8	2	8	8	16	8	8
Gregorian Chant		6	—	8	8	8	8	4
Foreign Languages		8	—	12	—	—	—	6
History of Philosophy		—	4	8	8	2	4	—
Archeology		—	—	2	—	4	2	4
Bookkeeping		—	—	2	—	2	2	2
Pedagogy		—	—	8	—	—	—	12
Sociology		—	—	—	2	—	6	6
Catechetics		—	—	—	—	2	2	—

*M stands for Micheletti program; A is St. Mary's Seminary, Baltimore; B, St. Vincent's Seminary, Latrobe, Pa.; C, St. John's Seminary, Collegeville, Minn.; D, Pontifical Josephinum, Columbus; E, St. Meinrad Seminary, Indiana; F, St. Francis Seminary, Milwaukee; and G, St. Benedict Seminary, Atchison, Kans.

360 hours. Most seminaries offered between 500 and 700 hours of moral theology.[12]

The practice of offering dogma and moral courses in cycles prevailed at diocesan seminaries. At nine diocesan seminaries the cycle of dogma courses was offered over a four-year period, that is, a single dogma course per year was offered to the entire student body in four consecutive years. Thus a seminarian might take the course in fundamental dogma in the second, third, or fourth year of theology instead of the first year. In eleven seminaries, a course of fundamental dogma was offered annually for first-year students and the remaining courses of dogmatic theology were given over a three-year period. Three seminaries offered dogma in two two-year cycles. A similar arrangement prevailed in moral theology. Six seminaries offered a cycle of courses over a four-year period, though fourteen annually offered a course in fundamental moral theology and gave the remainder over a three-year cycle. Seven seminaries gave two cycles of two years, and only one seminary offered separate courses in each of the four years of theology.[13]

Use of Latin had been the subject of repeated exhortations of Roman authority. Its use in classroom instruction seems largely confined to dogmatic theology. Heck reports that only six seminaries made exclusive use of Latin in the dogma course, while sixteen reported Latin usage for only the major portion of dogma presentation. Fifteen seminaries required students to give oral responses in Latin, while fourteen required written responses in Latin. Heck did not inquire about Latin usage in other courses, many of which had English-language textbooks and were presumably conducted in English.[14]

The use of Latin textbooks in dogma and moral theology remained a major characteristic of seminary learning. For the study of dogmatic theology, Heck's survey of thirty diocesan seminaries indicates that a consensus had formed by the 1930s around one dogmatic author, Adolphe Tanquerey. The dogmatic authors and texts are given with the number of seminaries in which the text was in use:[15]

22 Adolphe Tanquerey, *Synopsis Theologiae Dogmaticae,* 3 vols. (1894)

4 Christian Pesch, *Compendium Theologiae Dogmaticae,* 4 vols. (1913–1914)

3 Jean Marie Hervé, *Manuale Theologiae Dogmaticae,* 4 vols. (1926)

2 John MacGuinness, *Commentarii Theologici,* 3 vols. (189?)

1 R. Hermann, *Institutiones Theologiae Dogmaticae,* 2 vols. (1897)

1 Edouard Hugon, *Tractatus Dogmatici,* 3 vols.

Tanquerey's strong influence continued from the previous period and weathered the condemnation of modernism. The Irish Vincentian MacGuinness was favored at seminaries conducted by Vincentians. The German Jesuit Pesch based his *Compendium* on his longer dogmatic series published in the 1890s. Thus the textbooks were either published or, in the case of Pesch, had their origins in the late nineteenth century before the condemnation of modernism, after which few ventured to write new dogma textbooks. The manual of the French Canon Jean Marie Hervé, professor of dogma at the major seminary of St. Brieuc, France, was recent. Its organization closely parallels that of Tanquerey. All the dogma authors were Europeans, though, as previously noted, Tanquerey taught eighteen years at St. Mary's Seminary at Baltimore.

Moral theology either equals or ranks second in emphasis in the number of course hours; it remained important as a preparation for hearing confessions. Heck's study surveys the choices of thirty-two diocesan seminaries: [16]

> 12 Jerome Noldin and A. Schmitt, *Summa Theologiae Moralis,* 3 vols. (1902)
> 10 Luigi Sabetti and Timothy Barrett, *Compendium Theologiae Moralis* (1884)
> 8 Adolphe Tanquerey, *Synopsis Theologiae Moralis et Pastoralis,* 3 vols. (1902)
> 1 Edouard Genicot, *Institutiones Theologiae Moralis,* 3 vols. (1896)
> 1 Dominik Prümmer, *Manuale Theologiae Moralis,* 3 vols. (1914)

The survey reveals a consensus forming around two authors, the Italian Jesuit Sabetti and the Austrian Jesuit Noldin, whose moral volumes were subsequently revised by their respective junior colleagues, the Jesuits Barrett and Schmitt. The Belgian Jesuit Genicot and the German Dominican Prümmer also appear.

The study of Sacred Scripture ranks behind dogma and moral theology in the number of class hours. The variation in number was also wide. The Pontifical College Josephinum offered 858 hours of Scripture, while St. Benedict's Seminary at Atchison offered 240 hours. Sixteen seminaries required between 500 and 660 hours of Scripture. [17] There were no predominant manuals to lend unity to the instruction. As Heck finds, "there are, probably, no seminary classes so frequently referred to, so severely criticized, and so variously taught as are those dealing with the biblical subjects." [18] In the absence of an influential textbook embracing the entire field, except for the actual Bible itself, Heck records the variety of books that were in use: [19]

> 4 Charles Grannan, *A General Introduction to the Bible,* 4 vols. (1921)
> 4 M. Seisenberger, *Practical Handbook for the Study of the Bible* (1911)
> 4 Adriano Simon, *Praelectiones Biblicae,* 2 vols. (1930)

3 Charles J. Callan, *The Four Gospels* (1918)
3 Rudolph Cornely, *Historia et Critica Introductio in U.T. Libros Sacros* (1885)
3 Cornely-Merck, *Introductio in Sacrae Scripturae Libros Compendium,* 2 vols. (7th ed., 1910)
2 Andrew Breen, *A Harmonized Exposition of the Four Gospels,* 4 vols. (1899–1904)
2 *Cursus Pontificalis Institutionis*
2 Francis E. Gigot, *General Introduction to the Study of the Holy Scripture* (1900)
2 Francis E. Gigot, *Outlines of New Testament History* (1898)
2 H. Hoepfl, *Introductionis in U.T. Libros Compendium,* 3 vols.
2 Ferdinand Prat, *Theology of St. Paul,* 2 vols. (5th ed., 1922)
2 Henry Schumacher, *A Handbook of Scripture Study,* 3 vols. (1922–1925)

Sixteen other volumes are listed as texts and references in use in seminaries.

Church history offerings varied from a high of 858 hours at Boston's St. John's Seminary to the very low offering of 69 hours from the dogma-minded Jesuit faculty at St. Mary of the Lake Seminary. Seventeen seminaries offered between 180 and 360 hours of church history.[20] Church history was conveyed by the medium of the textbook, of which the leading manual was *A Manual of Church History* by Franz Xavier Funk, in use at eight seminaries. Funk's volume, which first appeared in 1886, parallels the previous manuals of church history with its emphasis on institutional developments. Other manuals dating from the previous period were still in use, but there were also recent and less comprehensive volumes. In an allied development, seminaries showed an interest in a separate course of patrology, as offered in eighteen seminaries. Thirteen of these used the English version of *A Handbook of Patrology* by Jean Tixeront.[21]

Canon law instruction varied from 432 hours at St. Francis Seminary at Loretto, Pennsylvania, to the 70 hours given at St. John's Home Missions Seminary at Little Rock. Eighteen seminaries offered between 150 and 300 hours in canon law. Heck attributes the wide variations in hours to the fact that canon law often entered into the presentations in moral theology courses.[22]

Homiletical theory was conveyed by the influential manuals of the period including the nineteenth-century classic *Sacred Eloquence* of Thomas Potter. *Manual of Sacred Eloquence* of Bernard Feeney and *Preaching* by William B. O'Dowd were cited as frequently used treatises. The hallmark of homiletic instruction was the practice sermon. Here, too, practices varied, but Heck finds that most seminaries required the writing of two to four sermons per year and the delivery of one per semester.[23]

Ascetical theology was offered in twenty-five seminaries with the number of hours varying widely from 270 at St. Patrick's Seminary at Menlo Park to between 30 to 35 hours at nine seminaries. Adolphe Tanquerey's new textbook, *The Spiritual Life,* published in English in 1930, was the prescribed textbook in twelve seminaries. The Sulpician Tanquerey naturally favored the methods of the French school. His influential work helped to extend the influence of baroque spirituality for priests into the twentieth century.[24]

Pastoral theology was offered as a formal course in all but two seminaries and comprised between 30 and 72 hours. Instruction was likewise conveyed through the medium of the textbook. Frederick Schulze, who lived until 1931, published new editions of his *Manual of Pastoral Theology.* Versions of his text were in use at sixteen of the twenty-seven seminaries that reported the use of a textbook for pastoral theology. The unrevised manual of William Stang was used in four seminaries.[25]

The findings of Heck's survey reveal that seminaries adhered for the most part to the methods and textbooks that were in general use at the beginning of the century. Years of Roman direction may have had an impact on the doctrinal content of courses, in particular perpetuating the thought of St. Thomas Aquinas, but it had not touched the organization of seminary studies. The array of minor courses such as church history, patrology, education, catechetics, liturgy, homiletics, social problems, Hebrew, Greek, and modern languages, seem to grow with varying class hours. These seminary subjects, with the possible exception of modern languages, were not offered as electives. Seminarians had to take all the courses the seminary offered. The number of courses pay tribute to the expectation that the priest should have elementary training for a range of ministerial tasks.

Heck finds that seminary educators expressed unfavorable criticisms about the organization of studies. Many complained that seminary courses were "over-taught" in that they gave detailed classroom explanations that students could acquire on their own. Too much memory work was expected of the students and little independent study. Heck himself recommends a greater use of assignments, private study, collateral reading, and prepared discussions and reports to make seminary learning correspond to the learning methods in a contemporary college or university. He asserts that seminarians should not have twenty to twenty-four hours of class time per week, as in most seminaries, but fifteen to eighteen hours per week, as in a university. Less actual class time would enable seminarians to prepare properly for classes. In fact Heck points to the "disintegration" of the seminary curriculum into too many classes and courses as a hindrance to learning and properly calls for the coordination of studies, the elimination of the obsolete matter, and the end to repetition.[26]

Heck's views on seminary learning repeat the calls for the reorganization of subject matter to eliminate overlapping that other critics had made in the previous decades. His views also echo John Fenlon's 1922 address on the contemporary state of clerical education, in which he acknowledged the shortcomings of "spoon-fed" learning with its reliance on textbook and professor, the overcrowded curriculum, and the lack of opportunity for independent study. The closest Fenlon came to proposing a remedy for the priest's intellectual shortcomings was to point to the importance of a sound literary education and training in modern languages to develop in the priest the habits of reading and independent study throughout life.[27]

The dissatisfaction with the program of studies was not great enough to develop a reform movement. Given the hierarchical order within the church, reform came about through orders from the top. There was little disposition for reform through soliciting ideas for reorganization from below. The practice of triennial reports which had begun in the 1920s and the apostolic visitation of the late 1930s provided church authority with the means to inquire and to make recommendations, but official inquiry was limited to questionnaires on minimum standards. There was slight interest in an evaluation of programs based on the views of seminary instructors and seminarians.

In the 1930s there were, however, developments beginning to take effect that would have an impact on practices in seminary instruction in the following decades. The entering wedge for reform was improvement of graduate training for seminary instructors and ongoing professional activities thereafter. Heck did not survey the training of seminary faculties, but he notes with disapproval instructors' lack of formal preparation in some subject matter and general lack of training in teaching methods on the part of seminary faculties.[28]

By the 1930s the precedents for Roman training of talented American seminarians and priests destined for seminary teaching, as previously noted, were firmly established. From the early twentieth century onward virtually all major seminary instructors in dogma, moral theology, or Scripture who were beginning their teaching careers had earned the S.T.D., usually from a Roman or European theological faculty, as canon law recommended. Those who taught Scripture increasingly had a licentiate in Sacred Scripture (S.S.L.) in addition to a theology degree. The apostolic constitution *Deus Scientiarum Dominus* of 1931 greatly strengthened pontifical degrees by requiring dissertations entailing original research for the licentiate and doctorate. These new requirements had far-reaching consequences in redefining the purpose of academic activity in pontifical universities. With the implementation of the provisions of the apostolic constitution, a new generation of seminary instructors trained at pontifical universities would henceforth not only be apologists, they would be trained in the methods of research. The seminary instructor after the 1930s was therefore making the transition from apologist to scholar.

The effect of advanced research degrees was to encourage an interest in the developing scholarship of each discipline. The move toward research degrees at least implicitly recognizes that each academic discipline is in the state of ongoing development. Theology and other seminary disciplines are not fixed subjects whose content is timeless. As trained scholars, many seminary instructors believed in the importance of keeping up with developments in their particular discipline. Thus the new generation of seminary teachers took an interest in founding learned societies.

In the United States a strong tradition of learned societies was developing since the late nineteenth century. Professional scholars in several disciplines, who were usually associated with universities, formed a series of societies, such as the American Historical Association (1884), American Society for Church History (1887), American Economic Association (1892), American Psychological Association (1892), American Philosophical Association (1901), and thereafter other groups. These societies sponsored annual conventions where standards of research were discussed and promoted. They published learned journals for their respective disciplines in which research findings were disseminated.

In the generation following the formation of the learned societies, Catholic scholars began to form cognate societies for themselves. Though the attitude toward Catholics varied among the learned societies, Catholic scholars believed their distinct set of educational and religious values would be better respected and promoted by the formation of their own learned societies. Academics associated with the Catholic University of America were most prominent in their founding, but the expansion of Catholic colleges, universities, and seminaries in the early twentieth century provided a growing body of potential members.

Catholic University's church historian, Peter Guilday, initiated learned activities among Catholic historians with the formation of the *Catholic Historical Review* in 1915. In 1919 he issued invitations to Catholic historians attending the American Historical Association convention to form an association of Catholic historians to meet annually with the society. This initiative resulted in the formation of the American Catholic Historical Association. Likewise, John Montgomery Cooper, also of Catholic University, founded the Catholic Anthropological Conference in the 1920s and began the publication of the conference's review, *Primitive Man*.[29]

Catholic University's leading philospher, Edward A. Pace, and his junior colleague James H. Ryan organized the founding meeting of the American Catholic Philosophical Association in 1926 with representatives of forty Catholic colleges, universities, and seminaries in the United States. The association sponsored the quarterly *New Scholasticism,* initially edited by Pace and Ryan and published at the Catholic University. The philosophers' organization aimed "to promote study and research in the field of philosophy with special emphasis on Scholastic Philosophy." The association was active in impressing the neoscholastic revival on American Catholic educational life in the following years.[30]

These sectarian learned societies of historians, philosophers, and anthropologists were sustained by Catholic scholars — clerical, religious, and lay — engaged in teaching at Catholic colleges, universities, and some seminaries. In the following years, other learned societies were formed, such as the American Catholic Sociological Society (1938), Catholic Economic Association (1941), and the American Catholic Psychological Association (1947). A student of these professional movements finds that they shared a common interest for an apologetic approach to Catholic belief within each discipline. Yet at the same time the societies promoted the methodologies and scientific approach of each discipline within the growing constituency of Catholic higher education.[31]

While the forementioned societies engaged the interests of lay and clerical scholars, several societies were formed that pertained to disciplines taught in the major seminary. They therefore were of interest almost exclusively to priests, especially those serving on seminary faculties. The first of these societies was concerned with the practical tasks of catechetical work. The Confraternity of Christian Doctrine, an agency of the National Catholic Welfare Conference and hence an official activity of the American bishops, held its National Catechetical Congress in New York in October 1936. At this meeting, chaired by Bishop Edwin V. O'Hara of Great Falls, Montana, the Catholic Biblical Association was formed in order to provide a revised version of the Douay-Rheims translation of the New Testament for use in the Confraternity's work of religious instruction. The association's initial membership consisted of the fifteen biblical scholars on the committee of revision chaired by Edward Arbez of the Sulpician Seminary at Washington. Arbez became the first president of the association, whose members were subsequently drawn from priest scholars of religious orders and diocesan seminaries. The association's announced purpose was to provide the bishops with a body of biblical scholars "to work out questions on Sacred Scripture" and "to afford an opportunity for those interested in Scripture to advance their knowledge of it."[32]

In 1939 the association began publication of the *Catholic Biblical Quarterly,* then the only Catholic scholarly review on the Bible in the English-speaking world. Its first editor, Sulpician Wendell S. Reilly, announced that its purpose was to encourage biblical scholars to write and discuss subjects of common interest and to serve students of the Bible "who are not enclosed by the walls of seminaries and scholasticates." Reilly looked to the international and ecumenical dimensions of scholarship: "We shall look for light in works published in other languages and even in non-Catholic publications. We shall try not to be controversial, but to seek and communicate the truth in a peaceable way."[33]

The observance of the fiftieth anniversary of the Catholic University of America in 1939 was the occasion for the organizational meeting of canon lawyers. The university's successful School of Canon Law had produced hundreds of alumni since its creation in 1924. These canon lawyers served as officials of dioceses and religious orders across the country, though many taught in seminaries. They all had a professional interest in following developments in their field. The canon lawyers formed the Canon Law Society of America, which was closely associated with the School of Canon Law, and held annual meetings. In 1941 the society's quarterly review, *The Jurist,* published at Catholic University, made its appearance.[34]

Though outside the direct involvement of diocesan clergy, religious orders started theological reviews. The Dominicans' Province of St. Joseph launched the quarterly *The Thomist* in April 1939 with emphasis on neoscholastic philosophy. The theological faculties of the country's Jesuit seminaries founded *Theological Studies,* the first serious Catholic theological review to appear in the United States since the demise of the *New York Review.* The publication first appeared in February 1940, and its contributors initially were mostly Jesuits.

The formation of a professional organization for Catholic theologians had been talked about at the Catholic University in the early 1940s. Late in 1945 the editorial board of the *American Ecclesiastical Review,* who were all members of the Catholic University faculty, namely, Eugene Burke, C.S.P., Edmond Benard, Joseph C. Fenton, Francis J. Connell, C.SS.R., Alfred C. Rush, C.SS.R., and Thomas O. Martin, laid plans for the formation of a theological society. The founding meeting of the Catholic Theological Society of America (CTSA) was held in New York City on June 25 and 26, 1946. The meeting brought together 104 founding members, all priests, from the United States and Canada, and virtually all were theology professors in seminaries or at the Catholic University. Francis J. Connell was elected the first president and Joseph C. Fenton secretary. The CTSA constitution announced as its purpose: "to promote an exchange of views among Catholic theologians and to further studies and research in Sacred Theology. Its secondary object shall be to relate theological science to current problems."[35] The society published *Proceedings* of its annual meetings, although many members published articles of a generally pastoral nature in the *American Ecclesiastical Review* and others in the Jesuits' *Theological Studies*. The Catholic Theological Society of America remained the leading professional organization for theology instructors in Catholic seminaries thereafter.

After organizing itself, the CTSA made its first major item of business the drafting of a petition to Pope Pius XII in favor of the definition of the Assumption of Mary as a dogma of faith. The high tide of interest in Marian devotion and theology during Pius XII's years was further reflected in the formation of another professional organization, the Mariological Society of America, in October 1949. Juniper Carol, O.F.M., of Holy Name College in Washington, a Franciscan seminary, organized the association devoted to scholarly Marian studies. It was largely composed of theology instructors in the seminaries and houses of studies surrounding Catholic University. Carol served as first president and other officers included Fenton and Connell. It published the first issue of its journal, *Marian Studies,* in 1950.[36]

The professional societies provided annual meetings and either quarterly journals or annual proceedings for scholarly presentations and articles. By so doing, societies at once reflected the new importance of research in seminary-related disciplines and the subsequent sharing of new ideas. Seminary educators had available the professional culture that other scholars enjoyed through their learned organizations. The societies of biblicists, canon lawyers, and theologians, nearly all of whom were priests during the period, belonged to many dioceses and religious orders. The societies brought together priests from a number of seminaries and represented a step toward overcoming the isolation of the seminary instructor, who had been accustomed to dependence on the authority structure of his own diocese or religious order for direction. The societies provided educators with a point of reference and a fund of ideas beyond the immediate context of the seminary environment. The growing number of seminaries and the increasing size of seminary faculties provided a pool of members to insure the organizational success of each society.

The learned societies were founded at a time of a generally positive climate for Catholic theological activity. As noted, the encyclicals *Divino Afflante Spiritu* of 1943, *Mystici Corporis* of 1943, and *Mediator Dei* of 1947 had given official endorsement to developments in biblical studies, ecclesiology, and liturgical studies that were under way. The new scholarship in these areas was largely developing in western Europe. The meetings and publications of the learned societies provided a means of diffusing theological ideas among seminary educators in North America. By so doing, some effects of the absence of original theological activity in the United States were being overcome. The advancement of theological learning through reforms in the training of seminary faculties, the developments in Catholic thought in Europe, and the diffusion of an academic culture through learned societies began to inform approaches to seminary studies by the 1940s.

An indication of a greater appreciation of advancements in biblical and theological learning was a renewal of criticism of traditional methods of seminary pedagogy, especially in relation to the leading seminary subject, dogmatic theology. The dogma textbooks had been openly attacked by John Lancaster Spalding in 1884 when he described their style as "barbaric." And in 1913 Herman Heuser had called attention to the misuse of evidence from Scripture and tradition in the standard textbooks of the day. The shortcomings of dogmatic instruction were raised again in 1941 in a British publication for priests written — appropriately enough for ideas then rather controversial — by the anonymous "Paedagogus," who attacked the effect of the traditional apologetic approach on the student's understanding:

> He [the student] begins not with a problem, but with an answer, not with the loosely expressed testimonies of early writers, but with the elaborate conclusion of the theologians; and so his interest is never kindled, and he remembers nothing unless he learns the book by heart; a course that is sometimes even recommended by his professor. How much more admirable is the procedure of writers of detective stories, who though they must know the answer to their mystery before they begin to write, nevertheless refuse to let the cat out of the bag before the end of the book.[37]

Paedagogus proposed the revision of dogma manuals to reverse the order of presentation in order to trace the development of doctrinal evidence through the centuries leading to the church's teaching.

In the United States, biblical scholars began to address the role of Scripture study in seminaries from the early years of the Catholic Biblical Association. Scripture instructors cooperated in a survey of seminary Scripture courses that appeared in the first issue of the *Catholic Biblical Quarterly* in 1939. The findings reveal the same diversity in years of study, types of courses, class hours, and Greek and Hebrew requirements that Heck had found. Scripture instructors seemed to agree only that the courses should be taught in English. Their suggestions for improvement of the seminary course were too numerous to be published.[38]

Biblical scholars also addressed the role of Scripture in the seminary course at the 1941 meeting of the Catholic Biblical Association, at which they complained that the Bible was not used sufficiently in seminary studies. Their criticism focused on dogmatic theology, in which Scripture's subordination was "epitomized in dogmatic text-books which devote pages to arguments from reason and crowd the scriptural argument into a few lines or verses." And these were "callously" taken out of context.[39] The discussions centered so much on criticizing the dogma course that there was no time for suggestions for reform. They merely expressed the hope for a more positive use of Scripture in the theology course.

At the 1948 meeting of the Catholic Biblical Association, Edward F. Siegman, C.Pp.S., of St. Charles Seminary, Carthagena, Ohio, presented a detailed inquiry into the misuse of Scripture as proofs in dogma textbooks under the threefold heading of mistranslations, texts torn out of context, and reading into the texts. He generally found fault with the use of Scripture passages as proofs, though he acknowledged "no danger of wholesale perversion." He then posed the larger question: "Is the method of presenting Scripture in our textbooks of dogmatic theology satisfactory?" Siegman found an increasing dissatisfaction among his colleagues with the method of presentation in manuals and in it the basis of apathy of priests and seminarians toward theology. The recent centuries of theological controversy had had "disastrous effects on all theology." Much time was expended on controversies that presently had little contemporary interest, except to historians of theology. The apologetical agenda to prove a point had eliminated the importance of exposition. Siegman called instead for a biblically based theology and as an approach to dogmatic instruction, he recommended: "Our attitude should be, not as found expressed thus in commentaries, 'The dogmaticians use this text to prove so and so,' but 'This passage contains the revelation of truth which the Church has crystallized in the following formula.'"[40]

Catholic theologians began to share the concern about the treatment of Scripture in dogmatic theology. At a series of discussions at the 1949 meeting of the Catholic Theological Society of America, the members discussed the proper uses of Scripture in theology instruction. They too questioned the inherited uses of textbook proofs drawn from piecemeal quotes from Scripture and patristic literature. The dogma instructors expressed hope for cooperation with the instructors of Scripture and patristics.[41]

The 1951 instructions of the Pontifical Biblical Commission proposed that seminary instruction be aimed to impart a love for the Scriptures and to promote them as basic for spiritual life. At their 1954 meeting, the Catholic biblical scholars endorsed these aims for the seminary Scripture course, to balance what they called "information and formation." It was generally agreed that to some extent the approach to Scripture study was to be theological, "since exegesis in the fullest sense must include biblical theology" while avoiding the extremes of looking at the Scriptures as proof texts. Other members also insisted that the scientific approach must not be neglected. They desired that the instructor cite examples of how Scripture is studied according to scientific methods and the resulting beneficial results. This approach was to be done even in the face of opposition. "It was pointed out that many older priests had so little of the scientific approach that they would label much of what we now teach as heretical."[42]

The shortcomings of dogma instruction prompted James Laubacher, the influential rector of St. Mary's Seminary in Baltimore, to propose to his colleagues in 1956 that the whole issue of the unsuitability of the apologetical approach of the textbooks be discussed at the annual Sulpician retreat. He cited the growing criticism of Tanquerey's classic textbook on the familiar grounds of defective use of sources. He pointed out that instructors needed to correct Tanquerey's treatment of sources in their class presentation or provide a supplement to issues that are not found therein.[43] Alternative ideas were discussed in the following years about revising Tanquerey and improving dogmatic instruction.

At the 1960 NCEA major seminary meeting, the biblicist Bruce Vawter addressed the by now familiar theme that there were no dogmatic manuals which "consistently employ correct historical methodology in handling the Scripture." And he knew of no dogma professor who used the manual "uncritically." Vawter laid the problem in the lap of the dogmatist who had the responsibility to incorporate the best scientific learning in dogma courses, because the textbooks would be around for the forseeable future.[44] In a similar vein, at the 1962 NCEA meeting Sulpician Edward J. Hogan, a professor of dogma, urged that Scripture be made the basis of dogmatic instruction and not merely for proof texts. He allowed that the approach was less orderly than the old apologetic approach, but it would have to be done in view of the advancement of scientific information in the preceding generation.[45]

By 1962, those speaking to the issues related to such essential disciplines in the seminary curriculum, dogmatic theology and Scripture, had called into question aspects of the inherited seminary pedagogy. Scientific understanding of the Bible had so improved since the 1930s that it could no longer be subordinated to apologetical purposes in the dogma course.

There were no seminary academics who spoke out to defend the tradition of the dogma manuals as they had been used in the seminary in the previous centuries. Accordingly, some of the basic aspects of Catholic seminary learning had apparently reached a point of crisis.

A serious interest in coming to terms with current seminary studies lay behind the general survey of seminary studies sponsored by the Department of Education of the National Catholic Welfare Conference in 1962. John C. Boere, a priest and graduate student in education at Catholic University, agreed to undertake the project as a thesis for the M.A. Its results provide a follow-up on the Heck study published twenty-seven years previously, and it therefore points out some of the continuities and changes taking place in seminary studies. Coming as it does a half century after the antimodernist crisis and in the year of the opening of the Vatican Council, the study describes the academic life of the seminary at the end of an era.

Boere's survey attempts to study the curriculum of some 171 major seminaries of dioceses and religious orders for the school year 1962–1963. Not all seminaries responded to the survey and responding seminaries did not always supply complete information. The tabulated results of Boere's detailed questionnaires did not distinguish between seminaries of dioceses and those of religious orders. However, the larger proportion of major seminarians, that is, 4,673 or 57 percent were enrolled in thirty-three diocesan seminaries, while 3,525 or 43 percent were seminarians of religious orders enrolled in 129 seminaries and houses of studies.[46]

Boere's survey of the organization of the curriculum reveals wide variations in the organization of studies, such as number of class days, length of class periods, number of classes per week in individual subjects, and number of hours per week available for study.

Boere reports the continuing practice of offering courses in cycles. Twenty-six seminaries cycled the four years of theology courses; only seven seminaries did not resort to cycled courses. The more common pattern was to offer a first-year course and then cycle the remaining years as was done in 64 seminaries, though 33 of these also offered a separate fourth-year course of studies. Boere takes up the rather controversial issue of the language of instruction, which by frequent and even vehement Roman command was supposed to be Latin in dogma and moral theology. Of the seminaries reporting, 39 or 38 percent used Latin, 45 or 44 percent did not use Latin, and 18 or 17 percent used some Latin. It appears that contemporary Roman fears concerning the abandonment of Latin were indeed well founded.[47]

In the study of dogmatic theology, the diversity of emphasis continued as some seminaries offered as much as 64 or as low as 28 semester hours.[48] Most seminaries offered about 40 semester hours. The continuities in the ways of seminary pedagogy are most striking in the reported use of manuals as the basic medium of instruction. Boere's study of diocesan and religious order seminaries records not only the faithfulness to the tradition of the manuals but a strong adherence to manuals a half-century or more in use. The reporting seminaries used the following dogma textbooks:[49]

28 J. M. Hervé, *Manuale Theologiae Dogmaticae*
19 Tanquerey, *Synopsis*
10 Spanish Jesuits, *Sacrae Theologiae Summa*
 8 Thomas Aquinatis, *Summa Theologica*
 3 X. Ab Abarzuza, *Manuale Theologiae Dogmaticae,* 3 vols.
 2 M. Daffara, *Cursus Manualis Theologiae Dogmaticae*
 2 F. Diekamp, *Theologiae Dogmaticae Manuale,* 4 vols.
 2 M. Heinrich, *Theses Dogmaticae*
 2 Parente-Piolanti, *Collectio Theologica Romana,* 7 vols.
 1 G. Van Noort, *Opera Dogmatica,* 9 vols.

Several manuals had been recently published, but Hervé's volumes were in their forty-seventh edition by 1953. The older manuals of Tanquerey, Hervé, Diekamp, were used along with the newer manuals of Abarzuza, Daffara, and Parente-Piolanti. Textbook authorship had turned from the generation of French and German manualists to Spanish and Italian writers. By the 1950s Spain and Italy apparently provided the theological climate for the writing of new manuals according to the traditional methods. But still Hervé and Tanquerey dominate the field, for their volumes, when taken together, were in use at 47 seminaries.

If dogma manuals were in continued use, they were not always used with the same apologetical purposes for which they were written. Boere raises the question of different emphases in dogma instruction, a question which would not have been asked at the time of Heck's study. In the generation that had elapsed since the 1930s, seminary instructors generally had a richer preparation through better graduate training. They were presumably informed about recent developments in biblical studies, Mystical Body ecclesiology, and liturgical studies. Boere devises four categories to survey the different approaches to dogma instruction: speculative, biblical, kerygmatic, and practical. Boere does not define these terms but lets dogma professors describe their approach to teaching in these terms, either singly or in combination:

EMPHASES IN DOGMATIC INSTRUCTION[50]

Aspects Emphasized	Frequency
speculative-biblical	26
speculative only	17
no special emphasis	11
speculative-biblical-kerygmatic-practical	10
speculative-practical	10
speculative-kerygmatic-biblical	9
speculative-kerygmatic-practical	6
practical only	3
speculative-kerygmatic	2
biblical only	2
kerygmatic only	2
biblical-kerygmatic	1
biblical-kerygmatic-practical	1

These findings bespeak more varied approaches than the straight apologetic one that Anthony Vieban advocated decades before. By the early 1960s, the consensus on the use of manuals remained, but the way they were used could be altered according to the dispositions of seminary instructors.

In the study of moral theology, seminaries offered as high as 43 or as low as 16 semester hours; most offered 32.[51] Again the use of textbooks remained unaltered. Boere's findings of 95 seminaries in 1962 indicates continuities in the use of authors:[52]

50 J. Noldin, *Summa Theologiae Moralis,* 3 vols.
11 E. Genicot, *Institutiones Theologiae Moralis,* 2 vols.
 8 D. Prümmer, *Manuale Theologiae Moralis,* 3 vols.
 7 B. Merkelbach, *Summa Theologiae Moralis,* 3 vols.
 5 Aertnys-Damen, *Theologiae Moralis,* 2 vols.
 4 T. Jorio, *Compendium Theologiae Moralis,* 3 vols.
 3 A. Tanquerey, *Synopsis Theologiae Moralis et Pastoralis,* 3 vols.
 1 L. Fanfani, *Manuale Theorico-Practicum Theologiae Moralis,* 3 vols.
 1 Regatillo-Zalba, *Theologiae Moralis Summa,* 3 vols.
 1 A. Vermeersch, *Theologia Moralis,* 3 vols.
 1 M. Zalba, *Theologiae Moralis Compendium,* 2 vols.

Boere's queries on emphasis were posed to instructors in moral theology. Unlike the situation in dogmatic theology, questions about pedagogy in moral theology had generally not been raised among seminary educators in the 1940s and 1950s. Its study aimed at practical preparation for hearing confessions. As James W. O'Brien summarizes in a report to the Catholic Theological Society of America: "Moral theology, in contradistinction to dogmatic theology, is considered almost entirely as a practical science. . . ." In other words, "practical problems, in the estimation of many, means [sic] sins."[53] When queried on emphasis in moral theology, instructors' replies were overwhelming in favor of the practical with 86 respondents so describing their approach either alone or in combination with another category:

EMPHASES IN MORAL INSTRUCTION[54]

Aspects Emphasized	Frequency
practical	33
speculative-practical	31
no special emphasis	16
kerygmatic-practical	10
speculative-kerygmatic-biblical-practical	6
speculative-kerygmatic-practical	4
speculative-biblical-practical	2
speculative-biblical	1
speculative	1

In biblical studies, seminaries offered as many as 32 or as few as 16 semester hours, though 24 hours was more frequent.[55] Diversity can again be found in the basic texts in use in the early 1960s. The basic text, as Scripture instructors often asserted, was the Bible itself. Few seminaries had manuals to cover the entire course but used several texts. Boere reports 52 seminaries having one or more prescribed texts; thus the total "frequency of use" exceeds the number of seminaries:[56]

20 Edmund F. Sutcliffe and John B. Orchard, *A Catholic Commentary on Holy Scripture* (1953)

9 Andre Robert and A. Tricot, *Guide to the Bible,* trans. by Edward P. Arbez and Martin R. P. McGuire, 2 vols. (English ed., 1960)

9 John Steinmuller, *A Companion to Scripture Studies,* 3 vols. (1941–1943)

5 Simon-Prado, *Praelectiones Biblicae,* 2 vols.

5 A. Wilkenhauser, *New Testament Introduction*

3 H. Hoepfl, *Introductionis in Veteris Testamenti Libros Compen-
    dium*, 3 vols.
3 Peter Ellis, *Men and Message of the Old Testament*
2 R. T. A. Murphy, *The Sunday Gospels*
1 Charles Charlier, *The Christian Approach to the Bible* (English
    ed., 1958)
1 Stephen Hartdegen, *A Chronological Harmony of the Gospels*
    (1950)
1 J. Renie, *Manuel d'Ecriture Sainte*
1 Robert-Feuillet, *Introduction à la Bible*, 2 vols.
1 Burton-Hamilton-Throckmorton, *Gospel Parallels*

Boere's survey again raises the question of emphases and offers three choices: text criticism, Bible history, and biblical theology. Of 113 seminaries responding to the question, 78 noted biblical theology either alone or in combination with another category; 51 checked Bible history, and 41 noted text criticism.

EMPHASES IN STUDY OF SACRED SCRIPTURE[57]

Aspects Emphasized	Frequency
Bible history-biblical theology	27
biblical theology	19
biblical theology-Bible history-text criticism	17
biblical theology-text criticism	14
no special emphasis	13
text criticism-Bible history	5
text criticism	5
Bible history	1
Bible history-biblical theology (and exegesis)	1
(exegesis)	1

Church history commanded as many as 24 or as few as 8 semester hours, though 12 hours was more frequent.[58] In contrast to the developments in such an essential field as biblical studies, history was not the object of much official solicitude. The Sacred Congregation of Seminaries and Universities did not decree specific academic requirements for instructors in church history. The doctoral program in church history had been started at the Gregorian University only in 1934, and few American priests had sought to earn an advanced degree in such a slightly regarded field. Many instructors in church history had theology degrees. Furthermore, the importance of church history had seldom been discussed in annual meetings of the NCEA seminary department in the 1940s and 1950s. The subject was taught in most seminaries, but the offerings varied. In the ninety-three seminaries for which Boere had data, the courses ranged from two-year to four-year sequences and were usually given in cycles. The textbooks of general church history in greatest use by numbers of seminaries were:[59]

17 Charles Poulet, *A History of the Catholic Church,* trans. S. A. Raemers, 2 vols.
15 Philip Hughes, *A History of the Church,* 3 vols.
13 Neill-Schmandt, *History of the Catholic Church*
11 Joseph McSorley, *An Outline History of the Church by Centuries*
 6 Bihlmayer-Tuechle, *Church History*
 5 Newman C. Eberhardt, *A Summary of Catholic History,* 2 vols.

Other seminaries used a range of textbooks treating specific periods and several listed the use of books on the Catholic Church in the United States such as *American Catholicism* by John Tracy Ellis, *Catholic Church in the United States* by Theodore Roemer, and *The Story of American Catholicism* by Theodore Maynard. In a 1952 article John Tracy Ellis raised the issue of teaching American Church history in seminaries. He noted that only a few seminaries offered a course in American Church history. At Catholic University, Ellis presided over the graduate program in American Church history, but he had relatively few priest students who were preparing to teach the subject in seminaries. He pointed out that most American priests began their ministry knowing little or nothing about the history of the Catholic Church in their own country.[60]

Historical interest coincided with theology in the study of patrology, which was a required course in fifty-eight seminaries. Of these, twenty-one seminaries used the *Manual of Patrology* and *History of Theology* by F. Cayre (2 vols.), seventeen used the text *Patrology,* (3 vols.) of Johannes Quasten, and eleven assigned *Patrology* by B. Altaner.[61]

Courses in canon law varied from a high of 24 to a low of 6 semester hours, with 12 hours as a more frequent offering.[62] In other words, canon law was accorded about as much emphasis as church history. Unlike church history, the canon law instructor required graduate training in the field. In addition to the text of the code and the many commentaries and reference works available in the field, twenty-six seminaries assigned Bouscaren-Ellis, *Canon Law: A Text and Commentary* and ten prescribed Ulric Beste, *Introductio in Codicem.*[63]

Offered in 83 seminaries, the ascetical or mystical theology course varied from a high of 8 hours to a low of one hour with 4 hours the more frequent offering.[64] The subject was taught through the medium of comprehensive treatises. The classic textbook still in use was *The Spiritual Life* by Adolphe Tanquerey, required in thirty-one seminaries; its influence exceeded that of the author's famous dogmatic manuals, whose use had been in gradual decline.[65] The volume conveyed in a concise, clear manner classic doctrines of the spiritual life from all ages and schools but favored the French school's methods of meditation. It seems to be the most important published work for continuing the heritage of the French school into the twentieth century. Tanquerey's manual enjoyed this ascendancy during a period of wide choice of treatises on the spiritual life.

After nearly four decades of the liturgical movement's activities in the United States, seminary courses in liturgy reflected the transition from emphasis on mastery of liturgical rubrics to an understanding of the theology of worship. The transition is evident in the use of recent liturgical treastises in the liturgy courses among the reporting seminaries:[66]

 23 John H. Miller, *Fundamentals of the Liturgy* (1959)
  6 Josef Jungmann, *Public Worship: A Survey* (1958)
  5 William J. O'Shea, *The Worship of the Church; a Companion to Liturgical Studies* (1957)
  4 Adrian Fortescue and J. B. O'Connell, *The Ceremonies of the Roman Rite Described*
  3 Josef Jungmann, *The Mass of the Roman Rite: Its Origins and Development* (1959)
  3 Joseph Wuest, *Matters Liturgical: The Collectio Rerum Liturgicarum*

The more recent volumes of Miller, Jungmann, and O'Shea reflect contemporary developments in liturgical studies, while the volumes of Fortescue-O'Connell and Wuest are new editions of older volumes on rubrics. Courses in liturgy varied from a high of 16 hours to a low of 1 hour, with 4 semester hours more frequent.[67] The subject seems to have supplanted formal courses in pastoral theology about which Boere did not inquire.

In Boere's survey, homiletical textbooks were those introduced since Heck's survey. The leading volumes used at the reporting seminaries were:[68]

 11 Thomas V. Liske, *Effective Preaching* (1951)
  8 Sylvester F. MacNutt, *Gauging Sermon Effectiveness* (1960)
  6 Albert Dolan, *Homiletic Hints* (1942)
  4 John K. Sharp, *Next Sunday's Sermon* (1936)

These volumes, written by American priests, borrow from the general traditions of eloquence and public speaking in outlining effective methods of preaching. John K. Sharp introduces the student to the historical antecedents of homiletic theory before describing practical applications.

Albert Dolan, a member of the Carmelite order, stresses detailed preparation and writing out of sermons. Thomas V. Liske, a Chicago priest and teacher of speech at Quigley Preparatory Seminary, approaches homiletics from the background of a speech teacher. The sermon and homily are not distinct forms, separate from nonreligious speeches. Liske stresses such practical aspects as the preparation, the voice, and the effective use of gestures. Sylvester MacNutt, a Dominican priest, balances theory with instructions on preparation and delivery.

According to the historian of homiletics, the aforementioned figures from the 1930s to the 1960s were not influenced by contemporary ideas of pastoral theology that developed in Europe as the result of theological movements in ecclesiology, liturgy, and catechetics.[69] In the interest of improving homiletics in the American church, a homiletic activist, Joseph M. Connors, a priest of the Society of the Divine Word and professor of homiletics, initiated a learned society to advance homiletics. He brought together a group of priests, of whom many were seminary homiletic instructors, to form the Catholic Homiletic Society at New York City in December 1958. Connors hoped to advance the professional training of homiletic instructors and coordinate the sharing of ideas on homiletic instruction.[70]

The state of seminaries in 1962 reveals many areas of continuity with the earlier practices covered in Heck's study of 1935. In most subjects, especially dogma and moral theology, instruction was closely related to the textbook, though criticism was mounting as to the value of this approach. As noted, methods of dogma and Scripture instruction commanded lively discussion among seminary educators. Improvements in other areas of learning were also noticeable. The liturgical movement had eventually moved the approach to liturgy instruction away from such exclusive attention to rubrics. There was a new stirring in the long neglected field of homiletics. In other areas, there was little questioning of the status quo. Moral theology, church history, and other subjects did not yet merit reconsideration of content or methods of instruction.

A notable continuity was the great diversity among seminaries in the amount of time given to various seminary subjects, as Boere concludes, "there are hardly two seminaries alike" in terms of school days, courses, and hours.[71] Since 1935, the practice of imparting a large number of subjects had not changed. The seminarian was caught in a routine of too many courses and too many hours in the classroom listening to lectures. One clerical educator described the problem in a 1960 criticism of seminaries:

Seminary classes are numerous: five or six meetings a week in the major subjects with twenty-five or -six hours of total attendance. This tends to give the impression that the essence of teaching is getting everything said once. The faculty can not in conscience assign extended readings or papers to students whose major expenditure of energy is devoted to so much listening. Because of certain understandings in seminaries on the relative importance of the disciplines, a professor whose course meets only twice or three times weekly may be nudged by his colleagues or rector if he approaches matters as he might in a course of equal scope in a graduate school.[72]

This burdensome organization of studies geared toward listening scarcely provided a coherent learning experience. Little had changed since the 1930s when Heck raised the objection that because there was no time for reading and independent study related to course work, the seminarian could not acquire the habits of private study to serve him throughout life.

At the end of the era, several figures addressed the issue of the fragmentation of seminary learning. The issue of reorganizing studies was raised in a fashion more drastic than the proposals earlier in the century by Herman Heuser and Charles Cremin. The new critics suggested themes around which to organize related issues and disciplines.

For instance, at the 1959 meeting of the NCEA seminary department, Francis Gaydos, of St. Thomas Seminary, Denver, proposed scrapping the existing division of seminary instruction by traditional fields such as dogma, moral, ascetics, Scripture, history, canon law, and patrology. In their place, he proposed teaching four topical fields: (1) the church, (2) God, including the Trinity, Christology, and redemption, (3) grace, virtues, and precepts, and (4) sacraments. His approach would bring together faculty from the various fields to teach these courses, in which there would be unified presentations. "Scripture, history, and dogma will be a unified whole, as they necessarily must be if theology is to be a science." The ensuing discussion among seminary educators was described as "explosive," which can be readily understood, as they defended the boundaries of their respective disciplines, though most acknowledged valid points in the proposal.[73]

The Benedictine seminary educator Conrad Falk proposed an alternate principle to organize the theological curriculum at the 1960 major seminary meeting.[74] He took issue with the Aristotelian ideal of knowledge reflected in the neoscholastic worldview with its "ordered body of principles and conclusions." Instead, he found the liturgy as an "integrating principle" appropriate for unifying the academic program "by providing a focus of convergence for the other parts which is in conformity with the historical nature of revelation." Parts of the liturgy touch on dogma, morality, Scripture, and so forth, but Falk did not develop a detailed practical program for executing his idea.

At the 1962 meeting of the major seminary department, Catholic University's theologian Eugene Burke spoke on the broader question of developing an intellectual tradition in seminaries. He reacted strongly to the separation of the theological enterprise from the world in stating "all too long we have lived in a climate (not totally through our own fault) where the whole temporal order has been viewed with a mistrust bordering on hostility." He characterized the seminary and its learning:

> Thus, we have forgotten that however high we build the seminary walls the world, the flesh and the devil walk in through the front entrance with us and our students; stone and brick cannot keep them out, nor does the refusal to develop an incarnational view of the temporal order to combat or confront them as we ought. In any case, if we are to develop an intellectual tradition we must see all things through the prism of the Incarnation.

To introduce his incarnational approach to seminary learning, Burke designated history—a discipline that had scarcely merited reconsideration in the previous discussions of seminary educators—as the starting point. Though he stopped short of proposing history as the integrating principle for the entire theology course, he advocated an "overhaul" of the church history course by amending its chronologies of the names, dates, and heresies as arranged in textbooks and making it the course that embraces Christian culture. As a "truly effective instrument in the development of an intellectual tradition," the study of church history as Christian culture could integrate theology with philosophy, literature, the arts, and the history of society and its institutions.[75]

At the end of the era, then, discerning seminary educators were seriously questioning the status quo in the organization of seminary studies, which had been isolated from genuine reform for decades. It was left to leaders in the era of the Vatican Council and after to study and adapt seminary studies to the advancement of learning over the previous decades. In any case, seminary studies through the first six decades of the twentieth century had not been altogether changeless. Limited transitions had been made in response to developments in scholarship. These changes were but one aspect of the transformation that the seminary itself had been undergoing during the period.

17. Transforming the Seminary

The seminary canons of the Code of Canon Law and the regulations issued by the Sacred Congregation of Seminaries and Universities assumed that ordinarily the Catholic seminary existed in isolation from local Catholic and civil education systems. Neither the code nor the Sacred Congregation offered directions to relate the seminary to contemporary educational standards. Accordingly, bishops either individually or collectively were not obliged to consider raising their seminaries to the level of current educational standards. The rapid development of the minor seminary through the period forced seminary educators to come to terms with contemporary standards for the high school and college programs. With uneven support of church authorities, seminary educators aimed to overcome selected aspects of the seminary's isolation from contemporary education. Seminary leaders worked toward successive goals of obtaining state recognition for bachelor of arts degrees for liberal arts studies, then accreditation for seminary college programs, and finally degrees for theological studies. Thus the idea of the Catholic seminary as a program of spiritual and pastoral formation conducted solely according to church law became gradually transformed to an academic and professional institution subscribing to educational standards outside of church control.

At the beginning of the period, isolation characterized the seminary at several levels: seminarians were isolated from secular activities; the seminary was separated from the life of the local church; and the seminary had limited contact with contemporary educational standards. Furthermore, Catholic seminaries were greatly isolated from each other in the absence of formal direction to cooperate. The lack of a horizontal interaction among seminaries and seminary educators was only gradually overcome through the decades. The founding of professional societies of biblical scholars, canon lawyers, and theologians as treated in chapter 16 represents one aspect of overcoming the isolation of seminary instructors.

The annual meetings of seminary educators at the CEA or, after 1927, the NCEA convention provided the forum for seminary educators to express views regardless of affiliation with minor or major seminaries or of dioceses or religious orders. The gatherings of the seminary educators at annual NCEA conventions attracted representatives of only about fifteen to twenty seminaries up to the 1930s, so that its discussions did not touch a majority of seminaries. However, by the 1950s, the representation of seminaries increased. At any time, the most articulate and farsighted seminary educators attended and made their views known on a range of issues touching all seminaries, diocesan or religious. As a voluntary organization having few claims on the consideration of ecclesiastical authority, the resolutions passed at meetings had no binding force. But as the only forum available to seminary educators, the members' ideas, complaints, and exhortations reflected the state of Catholic seminary education and hopes for the future.

From the beginning of the period, seminary educators regularly addressed the goal of bringing the seminary into a relationship with the educational world beyond it. As early as the 1911 meeting, Bishop Joseph Schrembs pointed out the obvious fact that seminaries were isolated from each other. He called for more unity among seminaries and urged seminary educators to abandon any aloofness and to support the activities of the Catholic Educational Association.[1] At the same meeting, Catholic University's Edward A. Pace warned that the seminary could not avoid general educational problems "without hampering or even impairing its own efficiency."[2] Pace and Schrembs perhaps addressed the wrong audience; their concerns might better have been expressed to higher ecclesiastical authorities.

One approach to ending seminary isolation was to establish academic standards for the seminary to parallel the standards of contemporary education. Establishing standards was an ongoing issue among educators at all levels in the early twentieth century. Catholic educators carried on lively discussions of the purposes and standards of Catholic education within their educational association. The CEA's college and secondary education department attempted to devise quantitative standards of minimum numbers of hours, faculty, and equipment for Catholic colleges, but there was no means of enforcing these voluntary standards on member institutions.[3]

The seminaries, especially minor ones, could not subscribe to the minimum standards proposed for colleges because they were organized to offer a six-year course of studies. This European model of a *gymnasium* or *lycée,* providing in American terms four years of high school and two years of junior college, was neither a high school nor a junior college in a complete sense. Thus its organizational form insured the minor seminary's isolation from the debate on standards for Catholic high schools and colleges. To address the minor seminary's problems a separate minor seminary department of the CEA was organized in 1919.[4] Thereafter minor seminary educators met in their own sessions to hear papers and discuss issues bearing on studies and internal life of the lower levels of the seminary.

That the minor seminary was an educational anomaly in the United States was not lost on some seminary educators. As early as 1919, Sulpician Charles Schrantz, of St. Charles College in Maryland advocated the abandonment of the minor-major seminary divisions of six years each and the adoption of the American plan of four years each for high school, college, and the theological seminary. He argued that the six-six arrangement isolated the seminary from contact with the whole system of education. It made people wonder "what those clerical students are doing in their strange schools, and why it takes them so long to learn how to read the Mass."[5] Despite this early plea for reorganizing the seminary, the traditional arrangement had its defenders. At the 1921 meeting the minor seminary department approved a resolution affirming that the minor seminary differed from other institutions and called six years a proper period of training.[6]

However, precedents were established in the 1920s for reorganizing seminary education along American lines. At the 1929 NCEA meeting a Franciscan religious superior described his province's reorganization of seminaries along the lines of four years each of high school, college, and theology. In the same year, a Benedictine seminary educator proposed that minor seminaries be reorganized into distinct high school and college divisions.[7] The Cincinnati seminaries were organized to provide a single theological seminary with a course of four years at Mount St. Mary's of the West, and the separate St. Gregory's Seminary comprised four years of high school and four of college.

The idea of the seminary granting academic degrees was likewise discussed. At the 1922 CEA meeting a leading Benedictine seminary educator advocated the organization of minor and major seminary curricula so that the course of studies would lead to bachelor degrees. He identified the common assumption that a degree "was a useless appendage to a priest's name, yes, was even thought to smack of vanity." Instead, he favored degrees as a means of raising seminary standards, eliminating weak candidates, and giving the priest greater influence in his ministry.[8] The minor seminary department, accordingly, gave "unqualified endorsement to a program of studies arranged to lead to a degree."[9]

The idea of the seminary granting bachelor degrees for liberal arts studies came up regularly during the 1920s for several reasons. One seminary educator noted the surprise among non-Catholic educators when told that a priest could pass through years of study in seminaries without any recognition in the form of a degree.[10] In clerical journals the lack of degrees for priests was periodically raised. One priest compared the ecclesiastical promotions given to American priests educated abroad and holding degrees with the slower advancement of degreeless priests trained in American seminaries. Another clerical writer related the incident of his futile attempt to obtain a teaching position in a Catholic high school for an able former seminarian. Despite years of classical education, the young man was regarded as unqualified to teach without a degree.[11] The diocesan priest's role in teaching and administration of parish schools and in diocesan high schools occasionally drew attention to the importance of seminaries offering degrees. By 1931, 1,025 diocesan priests were teaching or administering in high schools.[12]

The discussions of standards and degrees corresponded to actual developments in this area. The seminaries affiliated with lay colleges such as St. Vincent's in Pennsylvania, St. John's in Minnesota, Mount St. Mary's in Emmitsburg, and Immaculate Conception Seminary in New Jersey had long had degree-granting powers from their states, thereby enabling seminarians to obtain bachelor's degrees. Older freestanding seminaries had not been accustomed to granting degrees and began to take a look at their old charters of incorporation obtained from state governments in the nineteenth century to determine if degrees could be granted. St. Charles Seminary in Philadelphia had a Pennsylvania charter since 1838 permitting the granting of degrees and at last in 1927 began to use that power to confer the bachelor's degree.[13] At St. Francis Seminary in Milwaukee, the old 1877 charter from the state did not include the power to grant degrees. The longtime rector, Joseph Selinger, had resisted periodic efforts to grant degrees, but Archbishop Sebastian Messmer had St. Francis Seminary's articles of incorporation amended in 1920 to include powers to grant degrees.[14] The Pontifical College Josephinum also began to grant bachelor's degrees to selected students of its collegiate course in 1915 based on its state incorporation.[15] St. Joseph's Seminary at Yonkers granted bachelor's degrees under its affiliation with the Regents of the State of New York since 1909. The seminary was empowered to grant masters' and doctoral degrees in 1921 but apparently did not do so.[16] Denver's St. Thomas Seminary at the time of the construction of its new building in 1926 obtained incorporation and powers to grant degrees from the state of Colorado.[17]

In Cincinnati, Archbishop John T. McNicholas integrated the seminaries with other components of local Catholic secondary and higher education under a corporation called the Athenaeum of Ohio in 1928. St. Gregory

Seminary, comprising the high school and college program, was empowered by the state to confer the bachelor's degree, while Mount St. Mary's Seminary of the West conferred master's degrees in scholastic philosophy on the relatively few students who chose to seek them.[18]

St. John's Seminary in Boston obtained a revised charter from the Commonwealth of Massachusetts in 1941 that strengthened its degree-granting powers to include courses of study other than those in divinity and philosophy.[19]

Many seminaries remained aloof from the move to grant degrees. St. Mary's Seminary in Cleveland and Immaculate Conception Seminary in Huntington, New York declined to offer bachelor degrees to seminarians. Seeking the approval of authority outside the Catholic church did not set well with some seminary leaders. Thomas W. Plassmann, a leading Franciscan educator, complained forcefully at the 1930 NCEA seminary meeting on the dangers of conforming seminaries to secular standards. He expressed the view that degrees were not compatible with the seminary curriculum "which must be a *cursus passivus*" — a course of passive learning. Ambitions to earn degrees would harm the fraternal charity in the seminary community. He affirmed that there were "in the School of Christ grades and degrees which alone should be recognized in our seminaries, if indeed they desire to maintain their original ideals. These are the seven degrees of the sublime Sacrament of Holy Orders."[20] It is likely that opposition to degree-granting and accreditation had a basis in attitudes similar to Plassmann's.

State charters to seminaries were but one aspect of degree-granting authority. Most state governments did not oversee the quality of education in the many private colleges for which incorporation was granted. Likewise the federal government had no ministry of education to develop and impose standards on colleges and universities. It was left to voluntary associations of educators to develop a consensus on standards and then to accredit colleges and universities that met these accepted standards. In the initial decades of the twentieth century, six regional associations of colleges and universities developed to determine standards in such areas as achievement of the students, qualifications of the faculty and administrators, suitability of the curriculum, library holdings, laboratory equipment, adequacy of physical facilities, and stability of financial support. The associations sent qualified educators to visit a college or university to determine whether minimum standards were observed, and, if so, the school was placed on the association's list of accredited colleges and institutions. The degrees granted by accredited institutions commanded more respect than those of unaccredited schools.

The most active and influential of the six regional associations was the North Central Association of Colleges and Universities, which accredited universities, colleges, and high schools in the central part of the country. In the 1920s officials of the North Central Association invited the participation of several leading Catholic educators to assist in devising standards to meet the specific characteristics of Catholic higher education, after which Catholic colleges began to seek accreditation with the North Central Association.[21] The issue of accrediting seminaries with North Central and other associations in due course arose in the annual meetings of the minor seminary department. At the 1928 meeting the members passed a resolution that minor seminaries "take steps to become standardized" and asked the major seminaries to grant a degree of Bachelor of Arts "which is recognized by any standardizing agency."[22]

As with other reforms proposed, such as accreditation, raising seminary standards depended on the ability to influence bishops or religious superiors in such a course of action. The lack of any national Catholic authority in seminary matters or formulation of a national policy by the bishops meant that there would not be a concerted movement among seminaries to seek accreditation. The administrative committee of the bishops' National Catholic Welfare Conference discussed the seminary issue when the practice of submitting triennial reports to the Sacred Congregation of Seminaries and Universities began in the late 1920s. In 1928 a bishops' committee on seminaries was formed pursuant to a motion of Bishop Joseph Schrembs. Archbishop McNicholas, chairman of the committee on education, was appointed to chair the committee on seminaries. In 1931 a general discussion of seminaries took place at the annual bishops' meeting. A major difficulty emerging from the discussion was the lack of accurate information about the academic life of seminaries. The bishops approved a resolution authorizing Archbishop McNicholas's committee to make a study of the curriculum of seminaries and report the findings at the following year's meeting.[23]

McNicholas subsequently requested that the NCEA's minor seminary department formulate recommendations for the problems of the seminaries. At their 1932 meeting the minor seminary educators duly formulated resolutions in which they complained about such problems as the "mediocrity of teaching traceable to untrained professors" and the problem of "certain seminaries" which were "often forced to change or lower their standards in particular cases, by the interference of higher ecclesiastical authority." The seminary educators recommended that qualified priests be appointed to seminary faculties, that ecclesiastical authority give full support to scholastic and disciplinary standards, and that high standards be set for clerical formation and the requisite financial support be extended to seminaries.[24] The content of the recommendations did not reflect well on bishops, and McNicholas apparently did not pass on the recommendations to the bishops as formulated. In the 1933 bishops' meeting McNicholas reported on a wide number of issues related to Catholic education but stated that five or six years would be needed for a thorough report on seminaries.[25] Seminary studies as an issue of the bishops' collective concern seems to have died there for the period. McNicholas, as discussed in chapter 14, was absorbed in affairs of the Catholic University of America during the 1930s. In 1936 he persuaded his fellow bishops to make the committee on seminaries a subcommittee of the committee on education. Bishop John Peterson of Manchester was appointed to chair the new subcommittee, and discussion of seminary studies did not subsequently take place at the bishops' meetings.[26]

Seminary educators were left to themselves to raise the status of the seminary. In the 1930s, for instance, a few seminaries conducted by communities of priests sought and obtained accreditation: the college department of Mount Angel Seminary, St. Benedict, Oregon (Northwest Association) in 1933; the high school department of St. Meinrad Seminary, Indiana (North Central Association) in 1934; the college department of St. Edward Seminary, Seattle (Northwest Association) in 1937; and St. Charles College, Catonsville, Maryland (Middle States Association) in 1939.[27] The modest movement for accreditation focused on the minor seminary or college program. Thus the interest in accreditation and degree granting pertained only to the nontheology portion of seminary studies. Degrees for theological studies, regarded as the function of pontifical degrees, was simply not raised through the 1920s and 1930s. By contrast, in the 1930s the consensus among Protestant seminary educators reached a point in 1934 in which the American Association of Theological Schools was formed as an accrediting body for seminaries. In Protestant theological education the granting of the bachelor of divinity degree became the focus of training for ministry.[28]

Several additional instances of organized professional activities among Catholic educators in the interwar years also touched on the interests of seminary education. The Jesuit, Franciscan, and Benedictine religious orders formed educational conferences for their own members, which held meetings and published journals. Jesuits and Franciscans conducted a variety of educational institutions. Their seminaries were primarily intended for training their own members, though their journals included articles on current seminary ideas.

The National Benedictine Educational Association was formed in 1918, and seminary education for diocesan clergy was a prominent issue in their annual meetings and volumes of proceedings until 1943, when the meetings came to an end.[29]

The Vincentians of the western province became most active in attempting to bring coherence to their various educational enterprises, including their diocesan seminaries. They laid plans for an educational conference of their members as early as 1936, but the organization was not implemented until 1946 and met annually thereafter. The conference was in part the outgrowth of an attempt to plan for graduate training of the province's members to meet their many educational commitments. Papers and discussions at annual meetings often focused on seminary standards and policies for the province's high-schools, colleges, and theologates. The Vincentians' concerns often paralleled the problems aired at annual NCEA seminary meetings.[30]

World War II and its consequences forced new issues on the operation of Catholic seminaries. As described in chapter 14, the war had a great impact on the Catholic University of America, which enjoyed for several years a monopoly on graduate studies in theology and canon law for American priests cut off from opportunities for graduate study in Europe. Likewise, promising seminarians could not be enrolled in the American colleges at Rome and Louvain. The most talented seminarians enrolled in American seminaries and added to the quality of seminary studies. Seminaries responded to the federal government's orders to colleges and universities to "accelerate" their courses so that degree candidates quickly made progress toward graduation. Though not legally required to do so, the American bishops with the approval of the Holy See introduced "acceleration" in seminaries which were then in operation throughout the year. By keeping seminaries operating during the summer, seminarians were shielded during the normal vacation time from any expressions of resentment that their draft-exempt status shielded them from the consequences of the war. Acceleration of studies and the resulting earlier ordinations permitted more priests to be released from ordinary work in dioceses or religious orders to serve as chaplains in the Armed Forces while maintaining a sufficient number of priests at home.[31]

The seminaries returned to their normal academic schedule in 1946, but the aftermath of war required seminaries to come to terms with a new issue. The Serviceman's Readjustment Act of 1944, commonly known as the G.I. Bill, provided veterans of the Armed Forces with benefits to finance higher education and professional training. The G.I. Bill had a profound impact on American colleges and universities by greatly enlarging their enrollments. Catholic seminaries were influenced because the federal government needed a list of approved institutions from the Catholic church for the seminarians who were veterans to receive their benefits. The Catholic church in the United States had no list and no accrediting organization such as other professions had for evaluating training programs according to professional standards. On the other hand, Protestants had the American Association of Theological Schools to list qualified institutions. Furthermore, most Catholic seminaries did not belong to the regional accrediting bodies, so that approval as recipients of benefits could not be obtained on the basis of accreditation. The issue raised by the G.I. Bill again focused attention on the Catholic seminary's lack of recognition within contemporary education. As Monsignor Frederick Hochwalt, general secretary of the National Catholic Educational Association, told members of the seminary departments in 1947:

> The long arm of government has reached out and touched the seminary whether it wanted it or not. The returning G.I. who has chosen the religious life has brought a certain amount of red tape with him for, when he seeks out a seminary and has the bishop or religious superior adopt him, the voice of the government is bound to inquire — what kind of a seminary is it? And is it on the approved list?[32]

In fact seminarians who were veterans received benefits if the seminary they attended was on an approved list supplied by state education departments.

The annual meetings of the NCEA seminary departments resumed in 1946, and seminary educators continued to address the traditional topics related to seminary life and learning. In addition to the problems related to the G.I. Bill, the issues of the Catholic seminary's standing in the educational world were regularly raised. Bishop William Mulloy of Covington keynoted the postwar era in the 1946 meeting by repeating the call to seminaries to come out of their isolation and show what Catholic seminaries were doing. He cited the recent accreditation of St. Paul Seminary in Minnesota as an example for a positive relationship with the educational world. St. Paul's accreditation in 1946 was the first major seminary accredited by the North Central Association, regarded as the most demanding of the regional accrediting associations. Mulloy's mention of St. Paul's began a lengthy, impromptu discussion of how the seminary obtained accreditation.[33]

St. Paul Seminary granted the bachelor's degree for the collegiate course, but it was rather unique among Catholic seminaries in providing an opportunity to gain recognition for theological studies through an optional master of arts degree in church history.[34] St. Paul's master's degree program raised the possibility of degree work for theological studies when obtaining accreditation, an issue that had not previously been raised.

Pontifical degrees became available to seminaries during the 1940s through the affiliation program with the Catholic University. However, as indicated in chapter 14, only a limited number of seminaries enlisted in the program, and some of the largest seminaries showed no interest. The idea of individual diocesan seminaries acquiring pontifical faculties to grant degrees seems to have died out after St. Bernard Seminary and St. Vincent Seminary acquired the privilege earlier in the century and then in effect lost the privilege in the 1930s pursuant to the apostolic constitution *Deus Scientiarum Dominus.* Nevertheless, the activist rector of St. John's Seminary in Boston, Edward G. Murray, with the blessing of Archbishop Richard J. Cushing, undertook negotiations in the 1940s with the Sacred Congregation of Seminaries and Universities to secure pontifical recognition. In the summer of 1947 the Sacred Congregation approved St. John's constitution for a pontifical seminary to grant degrees, including the doctorate. Boston's archdiocesan newspaper announced the granting of the pontifical faculties, but within weeks the Sacred Congregation asked Archbishop Cushing to delay implementing the pontifical brief pending final approval of the pope. But the matter died without a public explanation, and the Boston seminary never obtained its pontifical faculties.[35]

If the interest in degrees for theological studies was at first limited in the postwar era, a more immediate issue was the relationship of the seminary alumni with the other levels of Catholic education. Catholic education officials regularly addressed the major seminary department meeting on the issues facing Catholic schools in the postwar period of expansion. In 1948 and 1949 diocesan school superintendents reminded seminary educators of the importance of the parish priest knowing the issues of modern Catholic education. While the diocesan superintendent was responsible for setting education policies in parish schools, the pastor was usually responsible for implementing them. Pastors of an older generation at times had no understanding of the professional aspects of education and ignored diocesan school policies. School superintendents urged that seminarians be instructed in modern educational theory so that they might respond favorably to diocesan policies when they became pastors.[36] The need to educate future priests to the issues of the modern Catholic school was restated periodically.[37]

The expanding role of priests as high school teachers and administrators was another aspect of the school issue. In the 1950s the young diocesan priest might spend the first decade or more of his career in high-school teaching or administration before a pastorate became available. Sometimes high-school work was done unwillingly. Or, as a leading Catholic educator described clerical career expectations, "many young seminarians have their hearts set on big pastorates and sometimes consider teaching temporary condemnation to the lions."[38] Regardless of individual preferences of young priests, they were expected to perform school work in large numbers, and the seminary was called on to prepare them.

At the 1954 major seminary department meeting, a diocesan school superintendent, Anthony Egging, proposed course offerings of at least fourteen hours in education, to include history of education, teaching methods, educational psychology, and school organization and administration. Egging hoped that the seminary would therefore be able to confer a master's degree in education and urged seminary leaders to conform to their state's laws on teacher training.[39]

In the 1955 major seminary meeting, the influential Franciscan educator Pius Barth proposed that the model of Christ the teacher be impressed on seminarians. He hoped thereby to create a favorable attitude toward teaching for future priests. To meet the increasing requirements of state laws for high-school teaching certification, Barth proposed that seminarians take at least fifteen or twenty hours of education courses at neighboring Catholic colleges and universities. He expected that diocesan priests would be teaching a range of high-school subjects, not just religion. He urged seminary officials to establish working relationships with their state departments of public instruction concerning requirements for teacher training in the seminary.[40]

Many seminaries responded to the demand for teacher training programs according to state requirements during the 1950s, and gradual progress was made toward accreditation of seminary college programs. However, the idea of a Catholic accreditation body for theological studies was raised from a non-ecclesiastical source. In 1954 officials of the Department of Health, Education, and Welfare suggested to Monsignor Hochwalt that the department would welcome the creation of an accrediting body for Catholic seminaries similar to that of the American Association of Theological Schools. A Catholic accrediting body would assist in fulfilling the department's responsibilities in distributing federal benefits to veterans attending seminaries. A series of meetings in February 1955 brought together selected seminary educators and federal officials to discuss the matter. The federal officials disclaimed any intention of dictating standards to Catholics but instead wanted to see the formation of an agency representing the interests of seminaries themselves, as other professions had. The issue of a Catholic accrediting body was discussed at the seminary department's annual meeting in 1955, however, such an unprecedented idea to relate Catholic seminaries to each other was not taken up immediately.[41]

As issues concerning seminary standards were under consideration, the Catholic community in the United States was stirred by the controversy set off by the address of Catholic University's church historian, John Tracy Ellis, given at the meeting of the Catholic Commission on Intellectual and Cultural Affairs at St. Louis in 1955. Ellis's address on "American Catholics and the Intellectual Life" pointed out the absence of an intellectual tradition among American Catholics despite their large numbers and the many Catholic Colleges and universities. Though the ensuing debate touched on the deficiencies of Catholic higher education, Ellis was particularly concerned about the absence of intellectual interests among Catholics generally.[42]

In the 1957 meeting of the Catholic Commission on Intellectual and Cultural Affairs, the distinguished Jesuit theologian Gustave Weigel spoke on "American Catholic Intellectualism — A Theologian's Reflection." Weigel took Ellis's idea a step further and found that the "general Catholic community in America does not know what scholarship is." Weigel defined intellectual activity as consisting of the "contemplation of the truth, finite or infinite" within a particular discipline. However, he found that American Catholics had "an obsession with the apologetic defense of Catholic positions, ever looking to verbal debate with opponents who are only projections of subjective fear."[43] He delineated many distortions arising from apologetical obsessions in the teaching of philosophy along the lines of verbal formulae, tutiorism, and the distorted idea that any bright young Catholic was to be urged to become a priest or religious. The ensuing discussion among his listeners focused on the intellectual shortcomings of priests. There was general agreement that the average priest did not have respect for learning. The isolation of the seminary made communication with minds outside the church unlikely. The high value assigned to docility in seminary life was translated into intellectual conformity for priests. Moreover, the laity normally demanded clear answers to pastoral questions. Too often priests readily supplied oversimplified responses.[44]

Others joined Ellis and Weigel in a critique of Catholic intellectual life with references to the priest. Catholic layman Thomas F. O'Dea, sociology professor at Fordham University, published an extended inquiry into the various aspects of American Catholic intellectual life from the perspective of a social scientist. He raised questions about the reliance on authority and the passivity that was expected of students in Catholic educational life. In the discussions of relations between clergy and laity, he complained of the excessive emphasis on authority in Catholic life and the need to balance the latter with more creative thought.[45] George N. Shuster, president of Hunter College and one of the few Catholics influential in secular higher education of the era, joined the debate on the intellectual life of parish priests. He commended the superior education of priests of some religious orders, such as the Society of Jesus, but he lamented that the average American Catholic parish was "almost anti-intellectual in practice if not in spirit." He found that the training of parish priests was "too drastically separated" from the university and all its "manifold intellectual interests." He called for seminaries to be conducted within the context of schools of theology at universities.[46]

The unfavorable criticism of Catholic intellectual life in the United

States and the related aspect of the intellectual shortcomings of the seminary and the priests it produced corresponded to the strictures on the content of theology courses described in chapter 16. The NCEA provided a response to the need for seminary reform within the context of its overall response to the expansion of Catholic education in the postwar era. Monsignor Frederick Hochwalt, who had been executive secretary of the association since 1944, carried on an ambitious expansion of association activities and services. Through the 1950s he gradually established offices of full-time associate secretaries for separate departments of the association, including elementary school, secondary school, college and university, special education, and major and minor seminary.[47] In 1958, he engaged the Sulpician J. Cyril Dukehart, formerly president of St. Charles College at Catonsville, Maryland, to be full-time associate secretary for the major and minor seminary departments.

Dukehart was an articulate advocate for the improvement of Catholic seminaries along the lines suggested by reformers since World War II. His first address as associate secretary to the seminary educators in 1959 offered a critique and proposed solutions for the improvement of the seminary to meet new challenges. First, he identified what a searching self-evaluation of current seminaries revealed: (1) The absence of strong admissions procedures was the main reason for low standards of seminaries. The concern for the shortage of priests pressured seminaries into admitting mediocre students. (2) The priests teaching in preparatory seminaries and to a great extent in major seminaries were often not adequately trained either in content or method. (3) And he cited the "isolation of seminaries from the mainstream of current educational thought, method, and administration."[48] Their isolation was manifested by the seminary departments' poor record of support in attracting as institutional members only 52 percent of Catholic seminaries. No more than 10 percent of seminaries belonged to regional accrediting bodies. There was a general lack of public relations, so that the Catholic laity were ignorant concerning issues of seminary training. Likewise, government agencies and educational associations knew nothing about the Catholic seminary.

In view of the foregoing observations, Dukehart urged accreditation of seminaries with one of the regional accrediting bodies. This process would keep seminaries "on their toes" through self-evaluation and partially end their isolation from the educational world. Accreditation would give the seminary's degrees the respect that mere state approval did not confer, and it would eliminate the embarrassment of priests and former seminarians who did not have recognized credits or degrees when they applied for graduate or professional schools. In support of his views, he quoted Pius XII in *Menti Nostrae* to the effect that "literary and scientific education of future priests be at least not inferior to that of laymen who take similar courses of study. . . ."[49]

In view of his complaints about weak admissions policies, Dukehart recommended defined admissions procedures. He extended the criticism to include the way seminaries were administered. Few seminaries had printed statutes to place in the hands of faculty and administrators that defined the administration, the curriculum, the teaching, the finances, and other issues. The Catholic tradition of administration within religious institutions where all depend on the superior's authority did not favor such procedural clarity. But Dukehart found that "Internal peace and harmony as well as efficient administration depend in great measure on well-defined and published statutes."[50]

Dukehart expected his own office of associate secretary to be an important resource in the improvement of seminaries. He laid out a program of activities for the seminary department, such as publication of a newsletter and seminary directory and sponsorship of research projects on specific issues. To activate the members, he planned regional meetings of seminary educators with the view to preparing seminary officials for the accrediting process. And he proposed the formation of an Association of Roman Catholic Theological Seminaries, similar to the American Association of Theological Schools for the mainline Protestant seminaries. The Catholic seminaries would thereby have a professional organization to speak on their behalf to federal education officials and to the regional accrediting bodies.

Dukehart began at once to carry out some of his proposals. One of his initial activities was to gather information about Catholic seminaries. He contacted seminaries for statistical information and concurrently managed to raise institutional membership in the seminary departments. He disseminated information through the publication of a newsletter. The statistical data published in his first year in office impressed on Dukehart the challenges posed by the sheer number of seminaries. As he told a gathering of Catholic school superintendents in 1959, of the 381 minor and major seminaries in the United States operating in the 1958–1959 school year, more than 40 percent or 166 had fewer than fifty students. Dukehart questioned the ability of so many small seminaries to provide the facilities or faculty adequate for proper training. In view of the waste of facilities and manpower in small seminaries, he questioned the value of multiplying seminaries and suggested combining them. A related problem, Dukehart found, was the fast pace of seminary foundings. Of the 381 seminaries, 131 had been opened since 1945 or a 53 percent increase since the end of World War II. He asked whether sufficient planning had preceded the opening of so many seminaries. Though he questioned the value of the proliferation of small seminaries, he projected a steady increase in the number of seminarians in the following decade, that is, after 1959. Among the solutions he proposed for the educational problems of small seminaries was to affiliate seminaries with existing Catholic educational institutions.[51]

Dukehart launched as many activities for seminaries as the voluntary nature of the NCEA could reasonably sponsor. In addition to collecting and disseminating information, he developed contacts with accrediting bodies and planned for regional meetings of seminary educators with officials of accrediting bodies. These activities were all under way when Dukehart died unexpectedly on July 17, 1960—less than two years after his appointment as associate secretary. Though a successor could not be found for several years, the activities that Dukehart had established were carried on by the elected officers of the seminary departments and the staff of the NCEA.

By 1960 important changes were bringing the seminary out of isolation. Seminaries were being reorganized to correspond to the patterns of American education. Among diocesan seminaries forty-two reported adherence to the minor-major seminary format of six years each, while twenty had reorganized to offer four-year high-school, college, and theology programs.[52] The assumption that canon law required a seminary program of six years was eroding. One canonist found that the common law of the church permitted variation of the seminary organization and that the relevant Canon 1354 of the code did not impose a strict obligation of six years.[53] At the 1960 meeting of the seminary department Paul D'Arcy of Maryknoll Seminary delineated the advantages of organizing a seminary college of four years. Conforming to the patterns of American education, he found, facilitated the acquiring of a state charter for granting degrees and the elimination of difficulties for seminaries in obtaining accreditation.[54]

Dukehart stated in his last report to seminary educators in 1960 that there was "a great stirring" in the field of accreditation.[55] He cited the recent accreditation of three theology departments by the Middle States Association and stated that several others were in process. Before his death, Dukehart planned two regional meetings of seminary educators to discuss the problems of accreditation. The first was held in Chicago on October 3 and 4, 1960, and brought together eighty-seven registrants from nine states of the North Central Association's region. The program was devoted to the theme "The Liberal Arts Portion of Seminary Training," a topic that covered the interests of minor and major seminary educators. Two papers addressed the accreditation issue. In one paper, Pius Barth, a Franciscan educator who often worked with the North Central Association, reported that the association agreed to recognize seminaries with a single broad major, such as philosophy, provided the general education program was broad and the philosophy courses were not too narrow in scope and sequence. Another speaker, a diocesan school superintendent, spoke to the issue of preparing seminarians with courses in education. The trends in school legislation of most states was in the direction of raising standards that Catholic schools were required to meet. He favored the practice of every seminary affording seminarians the opportunity to earn a master's degree in education so that as priests they could take their places in the Catholic school system. A second regional meeting was held in New York City on February 7 and 8, 1961, for about a hundred seminary educators from states in the Middle States Association and the New England Association. The conferees heard papers that paralleled those given at Chicago on the importance of accreditation and the problems related in obtaining it.[56]

Through the early 1960s, seminary educators actively pursued a policy of relating the seminary to the standards of American higher education by seeking accreditation and, in some cases, by ending the minor and major seminary divisions and reorganizing seminaries in four-year components of high school, college, and theology school. By late 1961, ninety-five seminary divisions—that is, either high school, college, or theology divisions—had obtained regional accreditation. The regional pattern was:[57]

New England Association	9
Middle States Association	29
Southern Association	8
Northwest Association	5
North Central Association	38
Western Association	6

The levels of institutions accredited generally favored the seminary college, some of which had been reorganized as four-year institutions:[58]

High Schools	14
Junior Colleges	17
Colleges	42
Departments of philosophy	14
Departments of theology	8

The movement for accreditation, carried on to bring recognition for the education and degrees of the lower levels of the seminary training, especially the college, informed the goal of seeking recognition for theology studies. By 1961 only eight departments of theology were accredited. However, the emerging interest in accreditation had obviously extended into theology studies that for a long time seemed off limits to any noneccle-siastical purview. Advancement of the idea of accreditation and degrees for college studies eroded the older attitude that degrees for Catholic seminary students were necessary only for the brightest few. The degree was gradually becoming a mark of recognition of successful accomplishment of the ordinary course of studies. The precedent was thereby established, and future plans included the granting of degrees for theology studies. These degrees were granted on the basis of authorization outside the canonical channels of the Catholic church.

In the decades preceding Vatican Council II the Catholic seminary was touched by many new developments. As Eugene Burke of Catholic University told the seminary educators in 1962, the changes that had taken place in the past twenty-five years were "striking and extraordinary." He cited changes of an academic nature: the periodical literature, the library development, the foreign theological literature that was readily available in seminaries, the advancement of formal graduate training for seminary instructors. He cited the beneficial effects of the new prominence of the National Catholic Educational Association, the Catholic Biblical Association, and the Catholic Theological Society in producing interchange of ideas among seminary personnel.[59] He might also have cited the emerging movement for accreditation. These developments began to transform the Catholic seminary by drawing it out of its isolation and relating it to academic and educational standards that could no longer be ignored. The seminary's responses came about largely without recourse to a comprehensive plan thought out and promulgated by church authority. Seminary educators, with the sanction of local church authority, initiated responses to seminary issues that the demands of the times seemed to indicate. By the opening of Vatican Council II, their agenda of seminary reform was well underway. The following years would bring about the official reform that church authority itself would provide.

Epilogue:
Seminaries in Renewal,
1962 to the 1980s

On October 11, 1962 Pope John XXIII opened the Catholic church's ecumenical council for which the world's 2,500 Catholic bishops had assembled at the Vatican. Through sessions in four successive autumns the bishops or "council fathers" set the course for an extraordinary period of church reform and renewal as prescribed in the documents of the Second Vatican Council. The consequences are still unfolding at the time of this writing — a quarter of a century after the council's opening. Most conciliar enactments at least touched on issues of priesthood and seminary. Formulating the seminary decree, *Optatam Totius,* enabled bishops to consider the purposes and methods of seminary training to an extent that had not been possible in the half-century of Roman legislation preceding the council. The lack of distance from the council renders provisional historical judgment of its impact on the seminary. A full account of conciliar enactments that would interpret the contribution of various official bodies in drafting documents and take into account their implementation would require a volume. The following account offers highlights of major developments related to the seminary from the council to the pontifical visitation of American seminaries during the 1980s.

Pope John's aim for the council as expressed in the apostolic constitution *Humanae salutis,* issued December 25, 1961, to convoke the council formally, and in his speech at its opening was to address a world that had become increasingly removed from the supernatural. To fulfill an essentially pastoral purpose, he expected that Christian doctine "should be guarded and taught more efficaciously. That doctrine embraces the whole of man, composed as he is of body and soul. And, since he is a pilgrim on this earth, it commands him to tend always toward heaven."[1] Pope John

XXIII did not live long enough to direct the course of the council. He died on June 3, 1963, after its first period but before any documents were agreed to in final form and promulgated. Under his successor, Cardinal Giovanni Battista Montini, who took the name Paul VI, the council went forward as planned and was concluded.

The council's internal history conveys the human drama of differences among bishops in working out the council agenda. A noteworthy aspect of its history was the general rejection of the *schemata* drafted by preparatory bodies whose thinking represented the juridical and scholastic mentality of the Roman curia and its official theologians.[2] During the council, most draft texts were rewritten to represent the views of the episcopate. In so doing, Catholic scholarship as developed in the decades preceding the council became part of official teaching. From December 1963 when the Constitution on the Sacred Liturgy was issued until December 1965 when the council closed, the pope and bishops issued a body of documents consisting of four constitutions, nine decrees, and three declarations that touch upon most aspects of church life and the relations of Catholics to the world. Though the document on priestly formation specifically addresses the seminary, many conciliar acts had an impact on the priest's ministry and thereby carried implications for seminary formation.

The document that best captures the council's spirit is the Pastoral Constitution of the Church in the Modern World, *Gaudium et Spes*. The constitution was not planned by the council's preparatory process, which focused on internal church matters, but arose from the initiative of Cardinal Leon-Joseph Suenens, primate of Belgium, who told the bishops of the council's need to speak to the entire world. The document resulting from this initiative addresses the church's willingness to turn outward and come to terms with the political, social, intellectual, and moral situation as it exists in the modern world. It ended the church's posture of rigid aloofness from the world and its one-sided approach to addressing modern problems. In the spirit of engagement with the world, *Gaudium et Spes* commits the church to service in the world.[3]

The Dogmatic Constitution on the Church, entitled *Lumen Gentium,* considered the council's most important document, reexplains the church in the light of the understanding brought about by closer attention to biblical and patristic sources. The church is defined as the People of God, for whom baptism confers a common priesthood. This priesthood, though differing from the ministerial priesthood, provides a principle with profound implications in other aspects of church life.[4] The concept moves the idea of the church away from one whose members are hierarchically ranked and cultivating a strictly personal holiness.

The church's corporate aspects are elaborated in the explanation of the forms of ministry. After more than a century of expanding the powers of the papacy, the constitution restores some historic dimensions of the bishop's ministry in the life of the church. While juridicial preoccupations had the effect of reducing bishops to agents of Roman authority, the constitution affirms that bishops are successors of the apostles whose jurisdiction is derived from episcopal orders, not from appointment by the Roman pontiff. The constitution states that bishops form a college with the pope thereby recovering episcopal collegiality in the life of the church. In the Decree on the Bishops' Pastoral Office in the Church, *Christus Dominus,* this collegiality is given a concrete expression by endorsing meetings of bishops as they had flourished in the Catholic world until the late nineteenth century. National conferences of bishops were to be established where they did not already exist and were to meet regularly to decide issues of common concern for their respective countries.[5] In due course, the episcopal conference was to have an important role in seminary reform.

The Dogmatic Constitution on the Church delineates the concept of the local church, that is, the diocese, headed by the bishop assisted by priests who exercise ministry under his authority. The dependence of priests on the bishop moves the concept of the priest away from viewing him as a solitary figure representing Christ. By so doing, the council adopts the historic concepts of ministry as they had been recovered since the 1940s. Still, the constitution affirms the priest as "the image of Christ the eternal High Priest" and describes his duties "to preach the gospel, shepherd the faithful, and celebrate divine worship as true priests of the New Testament." The concept of ministry within the local church is further developed with the recovery of the diaconate, whose members "serve the People of God in the ministry of the liturgy, of the word, and of charity." The constitution provides for the restoration of the diaconate "as a proper and permanent rank of the hierarchy"—no longer just a transitional step on the path of ordination to the priesthood.[6]

The Decree on the Ministry and Life of Priests, *Presbyterorum Ordinis,* develops at greater length the ideas on ordained ministry contained in the dogmatic constitution. The theme of service threads through the decree as it describes aspects of the priest's ministry to teach, to administer the sacraments, especially the Eucharist, and to govern the People of God. New emphases flow from the recovery of the historic role of the bishop as leader of the local church, assisted by his priests. Foremost is the familial relationship uniting bishop and priests that reverses the former master-servant relationship. Priests with their bishop sharing the priesthood of Christ are united in a priestly brotherhood. Accordingly, bishops should be glad to hear the views of priests. For that purpose, a group or senate of priests was to be formed in each diocese. The priest's relationship with the laity is also influenced by the fact that he too shares membership with the laity in the People of God. The laity are to be treated with full consideration of their rights in the church: "Priests should also be confident in giving lay people charge of duties in the service of the Church, giving them freedom and opportunity for activity and even inviting them, when opportunity occurs, to take the initiative in undertaking projects of their own."[7]

Several conciliar decrees treat selected aspects of seminary training that later find their way into the Decree on Priestly Formation. The council's first document, issued in December 1963, was the Constitution on the Sacred Liturgy, titled *Sacrosanctum Concilium.* This document made normative the aims of the liturgical movement over the preceding century in its stress on the corporate nature of worship and the participation of the laity. It was the natural corollary to liturgical renewal that seminarians should have more effective training by instructors with advanced study in the subject. Liturgy, which had long been taught as a minor course in the practice of rubrics given shortly before ordination, was raised to the status of a principal seminary course. As the decree states:

> The study of sacred liturgy is to be ranked among the compulsory and major courses in seminaries and religious houses of study; in theological faculties it is to rank among the principal subjects. It is to be taught under its theological, historical, spiritual, pastoral, and juridical aspects. Moreover, other professors, while striving to expound the mystery of Christ and the history of salvation from the angle proper to each of their own subjects, must nevertheless do so in a way which will clearly bring out the connection between their subjects and the liturgy, as also the unity which underlies all priestly training. This consideration is especially important for professors of dogmatic, spiritual, and pastoral theology and holy Scripture.[8]

The liturgy was also to be the basis of the spiritual life of the seminarian.

The Constitution on Divine Revelation, *Dei Verbum,* stands with the Dogmatic Constitution on the Church among the most important council documents. The constitution clarifies the essential function of Scripture in the life of the church and as such reflects the advance of biblical scholarship in the previous decades. For theological learning, Scripture was described as the "soul of theology," not as subordinate to dogmatic theology as it had too often been in the past. Students for the priesthood were to be taught in a thorough manner so as to be able to proclaim the Word of God.[9]

Through the Decree on Ecumenism, *Unitatis Redintegratio,* the council commits the Catholic church to the restoration of Christian unity. As a corollary to this aim seminarians were to be instructed in an ecumenical perspective. They were to learn precise information about other Christian communions, not the outdated polemical approach.[10]

The Decree on the Eastern Catholic Churches, *Orientalium Ecclesiarum,* restates the rights and dignities of the various branches of Eastern Christianity that were in communion with the Roman See. Priests and seminarians of the Latin rite were to be carefully instructed in interritual matters. The Decree on Eastern Catholic Churches implicitly recognizes that the way of the Latin rite is not the only way to be Catholic, and that the Eastern churches have much to teach the Latin rite.[11]

The council's charter of seminary reform is the Decree on Priestly Formation, *Optatam Totius,* whose provisions bear the stamp of the experience of the episcopate in desiring a new approach to the seminary. The document's history parallels that of many other documents. The first draft presented to the Central Commission in June 1962 restated in detail the existing official thinking of the Sacred Congregation of Seminaries and Universities. Regarded as too long, the text of the schema was reduced to twelve pages of general principles and sent out to the bishops while the council was in recess in May 1963. During the summer of 1963, bishops and episcopal conferences sent in their *modi* or amendments to the schema. It was during this phase that bishops expressed their dissatisfaction with the existing forms of seminary education, especially its isolation and recommended the importance of training in personal responsibility, new methods of spiritual formation, and dealing with modern problems. Early in 1964 the Coordinating Commission, which expected the council to end in the fall of 1964, incorporated the bishops' suggestions in a schema reduced to a few propositions. The revised schema was sent to the bishops in May 1964 before the autumn session.

The revised propositions came up for discussion in the council on November 14, 16, and 17, 1964. The influence of progressive bishops was evident in the reforms represented in the draft. Italian conservatives such as Cardinals Bacci and Ruffini and the secretary of the Sacred Congregation of Seminaries and Universities, Archbishop Dino Staffa, expressed concern about relaxing discipline and altering studies. But such influential cardinals as Paul Leger of Montreal, Albert Meyer of Chicago, Julius Döpfner of Munich, Leon Suenens of Malines, and Archbishop Giovanni Columbo of Milan praised the draft in the debate. One of the most memorable council interventions was that of Archbishop Gabriel-Marie Garrone of Toulouse, France, who spoke in the name of seventy bishops. He strongly criticized the Sacred Congregation of Seminaries and Universities for its lack of information and contact with seminaries around the world. He called for a decentralization of its procedures and proposed that the Sacred Congregation should be staffed by personnel from many countries who are "true experts in every field of higher learning."[12]

Following the 1964 debates, the schema was revised and submitted to the council on October 11 and 12, 1965, with separate votes on each of its nineteen sections. The bishops approved the whole decree by a vote of 2,196 to 15. The pope and bishops gave final approval to the Decree on Priestly Formation in a public session on November 28, 1965.

The Decree on Priestly Formation consists of about three thousand words and is among the three shortest of the council's decrees. Accordingly, it speaks in very general terms. It is intended for the formation of diocesan priests, but seminaries for religious orders were to adopt aspects related to their situation. The very brief first chapter enunciates the key concept of decentralized responsibility for the implementation of the decree:

> Since the variety of peoples and places is so great, only general rules can be legislated. Hence in each nation or particular rite a "Program of Priestly Formation" should be undertaken. It should be drawn up by the Episcopal Conferences, revised at definite intervals, and approved by the Apostolic See. By it, universal laws are to be adapted to the special circumstances of time and place, so that priestly formation will always answer the pastoral needs of the area in which the ministry is to be exercised.[13]

This passage represents a significant reversal of practices of the previous half-century as it moves the Sacred Congregation of Seminaries and Universities away from its universal decrees that disregarded the different needs of various countries. It activates the bishops' newly recovered collegiality in order to devise a Program of Priestly Formation for their own country. And the program was not to stand as timeless, which was too often the assumption of church legislation in the age of the Code of Canon Law, but was to be reviewed at intervals and updated.

The decree addresses the concerns of promoting vocations to the priesthood through the Catholic school system, by means of the activities of priests, and with an understanding of modern techniques of psychology and sociology. All should respect the concept of vocation as a divine call and the freedom of individuals to respond to the call. In council discussions, the role of minor seminaries in vocation promotion had elicited some controversy. Many bishops questioned their value because they isolated students from family and home surroundings, created passivity, and compromised the student's freedom to choose a vocation. The decree called for a minor seminary program to conform to "laws of a healthy psychology" and to have an academic program similar to that of other schools.[14]

The minor seminary was not commended as a place of developing priestly formation but as a place of learning Christian maturity. The limited endorsement of the minor seminary effectively ends the Tridentine idea of sheltering youth from the entrapments of the world so that their vocations could be nurtured in isolation.

The greater part of the decree is directed to the major seminary, which is strongly affirmed "as necessary for priestly formation."[15] Candidates for ministry were to be readied in seminaries for the ministry of the word, of sacrament, and in the role of shepherd.

The spiritual formation of seminarians continues as an important element in order to develop in students a "familiar and constant companionship" with the Holy Trinity. Such formation of seminarians was to have a wide focus, starting with Scripture:

> They should be taught to look for Christ in many places: in faithful meditation on God's word, in active communion with the most holy mysteries of the Church, especially in the Eucharist and the divine Office, in the bishop who sends them, and in the people to whom they are sent, especially the poor, the young, the sick, the sinful, and the unbelieving.[16]

Exercises of piety handed down from the past were commended, but "care should be taken to keep spiritual formation from consisting solely in these things, and from producing unsubstantial religious feelings."[17] These instructions reverse aspects of the highly private cultivation of holiness practiced since the baroque period, and it is a summons away from the tradition of isolation with which seminaries had been conducted. The decree recommends to bishops that they consider interrupting the course of studies to give their seminarians an intense period of spiritual apprenticeship away from the routine of everyday life. It also commends the idea of raising the age for orders to permit a longer course and to have seminarians serve a suitable pastoral apprenticeship.

The revision of ecclesiastical studies combines elements of the old and the new. The study of philosophy is vigorously commended and its aim set forth "to detect the roots of errors and disprove them." Theology was to be taught so that "students will accurately draw Catholic doctrine from divine revelation." In the spirit of the Constitution on Divine Revelation, Scripture was to be the "soul of theology." Students were to be introduced to it, initiated into exegetical method, and draw inspiration from reading and meditating on it. In the study of dogmatic theology, biblical themes were to be introduced first, then the traditions of the church fathers of the East and West, and only then "by way of making the mysteries of salvation known as thoroughly as they can be" the students should learn "speculative reason under the tutelage of St. Thomas Aquinas." Such a procedure reverses the methods of manuals whose apologetical approach had lost its relevance in the minds of many seminary educators, as discussed in chapter 16. The decree affirms ideas first introduced in the council's earlier decrees. For instance, liturgy was to be taught as a principal subject in conformity with relevant articles of the decree on the liturgy. In keeping with ecumenical interests, greater attention was to be directed to a better understanding of the churches and ecclesial communities separated from the Catholic church. [18]

While the chapters on spiritual formation and seminary studies explicitly state the pastoral purposes of these aspects, the chapter on pastoral training, though brief, lists several purposes. Seminarians were to be trained in the tradition of spiritual guidance of souls. They should have the appropriate knowledge of pedagogy, psychology, and sociology to permit them to deal effectively with the laity. "Again, they should be trained with exactness to ignite and fan the apostolic activity of laymen." [19] The chapter affirms the desirability of having periods of pastoral practice away from the seminary during the course of training and during vacations.

Through the years of the council, issues of seminary reform were widely discussed in the United States. Among seminary educators who had been calling for reform since the 1950s, the period of the council and immediately afterward was a particularly exciting time. They had been airing views at meetings of the NCEA seminary departments or in articles published in professional journals normally read by priests and other seminary educators. Ideas formerly directed to limited audiences were now developed at greater length and to a wider audience in popular Catholic periodicals. Seminarians themselves caught on to new ideas articulated by seminary faculties. When seminary professionals discussed seminarians, they often spoke of the "New Breed" — a term that was used for a few years in the 1960s to describe seminarians who noticed the defects of traditional seminary training, questioned its practices, and were not inclined to accept seminary isolation and minute regulation as appropriate preparation for the active life of the priest.

As the number of published articles on the seminary reached a crescendo, books on seminary reform appeared for the first time since the publications of the Americanist figures decades before. The year 1965 was particularly productive with the publication of a volume by Stafford Poole and an anthology edited by James M. Lee and Louis J. Putz, C.S.C., and another edited by James Keller, M.M., and Richard Armstrong, M.M.

Stafford Poole's volume stands out as an active seminary educator's survey of the major issues facing the seminary. Poole, a Vincentian priest, was vice rector of Cardinal Glennon College in St. Louis at the time of publication. His book provides a synthesis of current progressive thought on renewal of the Catholic diocesan seminary, especially in ending its isolation. In the foreword, Bishop John King Mussio sets the tone by describing the ill effects of isolation on the seminarian: "If he is so secluded from his world that he becomes a stranger to it, then he has been successfully trained in uselessness."[20] Poole proposes the thesis that "if the seminary is to keep abreast of the modern world, it is going to have to be reunited organically with lay education." He expects the seminary to keep its character as a professional school but to become an integral part of the university. He designates the seminary as the "Achilles' Heel of American Catholicism" and finds seminary reform the key to the church's renewal: "Unless the training of priests keeps pace with other developments within the Church, then renewal will either remain the province of a minority, or else the layman's frustrated zeal will cause him to reject the guidance of the clergy altogether, and not without cause."[21]

Poole rehearses the familiar criticism of the seminary curriculum on the basis of its apologetical and nonintellectual academic aspects and the solitary and often nonliturgical dimensions to spiritual formation. In his chapter on "Freedom and Obedience," which draws on recent studies of Joseph Fichter, Andrew Greeley, Eugene Kennedy, Karl Rahner, and others, Poole questions the enormous stress on obedience in the seminary. The emphasis on obedience as a virtue and on the church's hierarchical organization created a mentality in which the superior's voice was equated with that of God. He finds that too often invoking obedience covered the unwise actions of those in authority and shielded subordinates from responsibility for their actions. It is instead necessary to respect the integrity and conscience of individuals. They must be free to communicate with authority. It is the duty of those in authority, Poole states, "to inspire and obtain spontaneous and free compliance" to leadership "for this is the kind [of obedience] that will be of the greatest service at the parochial level; it is the kind which is most human and most Christian."[22]

Issues of seminary reform are taken up in a collection of essays contributed by fourteen scholars, *Seminary Education in a Time of Change*, edited by James Michael Lee and Louis J. Putz, C.S.C., of the University of Notre Dame.[23] The contributors are well known in their respective fields; many are active seminary educators. Several contributors raise the question of whether the current seminary provided the proper environment for training clergy. The sociologist and priest Robert M. Brooks finds that unlike other professions priests and seminarians were not sufficiently studied from a sociological approach so that the problems of seminaries and seminarians could be better understood. George Hagmeier and Eugene Kennedy take up the psychological aspects of the seminary. They raise questions about the appropriateness of the seminary practice of isolating students from ordinary contact with the world and surrounding future priests only with priests and other seminarians. The emphasis on obedience and docility bred immature, passive, and apathetic personalities in seminarians.

Other authors treat the seminary's academic weaknesses that had been rehearsed since the 1950s. The distinguished Jesuit Scripture scholar John L. MacKenzie boldly states that too much time was devoted to spiritual formation and not enough to sound theology. Sergius Wroblewski summarizes the now familiar criticism of the absence of an intellectual climate in the seminaries and the bad effects of theological studies based on formulas, rote memorization, and a closed body of thought. He calls for a priest capable of dealing with the postmodern mind.

The essays of the co-editor, James Michael Lee, a professor of education, take up nearly a third of the volume. He gives a searching analysis of Catholic seminary administration and curriculum based on recent studies. However, he points out that scientific research on Catholic seminary education is still "miniscule, crude, and usually unrefined" compared to other areas of education because seminaries are surrounded by a "Kremlin-like cloak of secrecy."[24] He finds Catholic seminaries marked by many fundamental professional failings. For instance, seminary administrators ordinarily had the proper academic qualifications but no background in educational administration. The theological faculty also had academic qualifications but no formal training in teaching methods. Empirical studies of seminarians indicated that they found the seminary instructors often ineffective as teachers. The faculty in nontheological subjects, such as those at the college level, often did not have academic qualifications in the fields in which they taught. The nature of the seminary required nearly exclusive selection of priests for faculties, which too often meant that academically unqualified priests were appointed, and often priests burdened by outside duties. Lee also alleges that bishops often appointed priests to seminary faculties because the continuance of seminary life was thought to be good for them or because they were not suited for other duties.

Maryknoll priests James Keller and Richard Armstrong, the leaders of the Christopher movement, edited a volume of addresses presented at the Christopher Study Week in New York City in the summer of 1964 on the subject of seminary renewal in the light of the council.[25] The twenty-one contributors include clerical scholars from Europe and the United States, such as Avery Dulles, Bernard Häring, Peter Fransen, Myles Bourke, and Peter Grassi. They address the conference's theme of the convergence of spiritual and intellectual elements in seminary training. The occasion provided an opportunity for all contributors to describe and deplore the compartmentalization of knowledge, the separation of seminary theology from current theological developments, the weak relationship between the content of formal seminary learning and the themes appropriate for the priest's pastoral role in preaching and teaching, and the divorce between theology and spiritual formation.

Since the existing ways of conducting seminaries were seriously questioned, by 1965 there was a general assumption that renewal according to the conciliar thought would include an overhaul of the seminary. This assumption coincided with the close of the council at the end of that year and the beginning of the complex work of implementing renewal. To oversee seminary matters from Rome, Pope Paul VI appointed Archbishop Gabriel-Marie Garrone "pro-prefect" of the Sacred Congregation of Seminaries and Universities in 1966 to assist the aged Cardinal Pizzardo. Garrone and Pizzardo issued a letter in October 1966 authorizing seminaries to experiment with seminary reform according to the principles of *Optatam Totius*. They directed that seminary reform was to be undertaken with reference to the episcopal conference, and that reforms in individual seminaries were to be of a nature that they could be reversed if the national program of priestly formation so provided. The letter inaugurates the formal process of seminary renewal. The congregation was renamed the Sacred Congregation for Catholic Education in the general curial reorganization of 1967. Garrone resigned as archbishop of Toulouse and was made a cardinal in 1967. He became prefect when Cardinal Pizzardo was finally persuaded to resign in January 1968 at age ninety after twenty-eight years in office. Garrone remained prefect until 1980, and so his influence spans much of the period since the close of the council.

Following the council the bishops of the United States established the Committee on Priestly Formation at their November 1966 meeting to implement the provisions of *Optatam Totius*.[26] Bishop Loras Lane of Rockford, Illinois, chaired the committee until his death in 1968, when auxiliary Bishop James A. Hickey of Saginaw, Michigan (now archbishop of Washington), succeeded him. The Committee on Priestly Formation began work on the issuance of interim guidelines for American seminaries. With the consultation of many seminary officials, the committee forwarded a series of guidelines for the consideration of the bishops' conference. Once approved by the bishops' conference and routinely endorsed by the Sacred Congregation, guidelines were issued successively in April 1967 to seminary secondary schools, in November 1967 to the college that was now assumed to be a four-year program, and in December 1968 for the academic programs of both college and theologate and for spiritual formation, community life, and discipline in the theologate, and pastoral education, including field education. The guidelines reflect the implementation of the spirit of the council and the practices found in leading American seminaries.

As the American bishops' effort for a national plan for seminaries in the United States was under way, the first of the international synods of bishops, as provided by the *motu proprio* of Pope Paul VI, was held in Rome in October 1967. On this occasion Cardinal Garrone proposed to the synod several measures related to seminaries. The synod endorsed his main proposal that the Sacred Congregation draft a plan for seminaries according to the spirit of the Decree on Priestly Formation and as a guide to the episcopal conferences in drafting their own program of priestly formation. When the resolution was approved, Cardinal Garrone appointed a committee to draft the Basic Plan for Priestly Formation or *Ratio Fundamentalis*. The Sacred Congregation's plan was drafted, circulated to the national bishops' conferences, and amended in the following two years, and it received final ratification of Pope Paul VI on December 10, 1969.

The Basic Plan for Priestly Formation elaborates the provisions of the council's Decree on Priestly Formation as a basis for the further adaptation of seminary practices as needed by different countries but while providing for "that unity and that image of the Catholic priesthood which it demands of its very nature, and on which the Council earnestly insisted." With the council, the plan affirms that "seminaries are necessary" and that preparation for the priesthood is the proper goal of the seminary.[27] It outlines the basic elements of the seminary for the bishops' conferences to guide them in their national programs of priestly formation. In turn the seminaries of the respective countries are required to comply with that plan.

The plan acknowledges the minor seminary with a short section in which its purpose as a place where "initial signs" of a vocation could be recognized.[28] The plan is largely devoted to the major seminary, where formation for the priesthood takes place. It outlines the seminary officials: rector, vice-rector, spiritual director, prefect of studies, pastoral director, prefect of discipline, bursar, and librarian. These officials are presumably priests. Professors for the sacred subjects "as a general rule" should be priests, possess at least the licentiate, and should be trained in teaching methods. The basic elements of spiritual formation, academic life, and pastoral formation are then outlined. The plan for spiritual formation stresses the official liturgy as its basis. The document directs that the academic program of theology should last four years. The plan prescribes a pastoral formation that teaches seminarians "how to acquire the ability to involve themselves with true pastoral concern with the lives of the faithful."[29]

The American version of the plan is the Program of Priestly Formation, which was approved by the National Conference of Catholic Bishops in November 1969 and ratified by the Sacred Congregation on April 6, 1970, subject to minor changes in the wording of the text. After the final corrections were made and a section on ecumenism added, the Sacred Congregation approved the program in January 1971 for a period of five years. For the 1976 revision, the 1971 text was preserved and only a few new ideas added that were overlooked in the first edition.

The bishops' Program of Priestly Formation breaks new ground in addressing areas that had been severely criticized.[30] A major emphasis is that the seminary constitutes a community which in its human, faith, apostolic, and academic dimensions provides the most effective basis for priestly formation. This aspect is a decisive reversal of the older tendencies of the seminary as a kind of aggregation of individuals pursuing personal holiness and whose internal discipline and enforced silences kept seminarians apart from each other. The interaction of the community sustains the work of priestly formation. As a community of responsible men, it is assumed that an atmosphere of freedom will prevail as the demanding program of formation is pursued. The program states that there is no need for detailed regulations to govern everyday life. Building a sense of community and exercising freedom are sustained by frequent and frank communication among administrators, faculty, and students.

The program is noteworthy too for its attention to the structure of seminary administration. The bishop's authority remains central, but the program gives close attention to the requirements of adminstration by outlining duties of the rector, other administrative officers, faculty and their organizations, and a board of lay and clerical advisors. General principles for the students' admission, evaluation, and promotion to orders are outlined. The concern for administrative matters is a decisive move away from the unwritten and informal procedures of seminary governance in the past.

The purpose of the seminary program consists of formation of candidates for the priesthood in its spiritual, academic, and pastoral dimensions.

The spiritual program emphasizes the understanding of Scripture through study, reflection, and personal prayer as the starting point of formation. The program recognizes the value of traditional methods of meditation but also states the need to adapt them to current theology. The program recognizes the celebration of the Eucharist as the center of Christian life and growth and the importance of the divine office as liturgical prayer. The spiritual program aims to promote a concept of service, first in the immediate seminary community and in the larger church community.

The academic program outlines principles for curriculum renewal that take into consideration the new approaches of recent decades. Accordingly, the program recommends a proper balance of study of the Bible, historical development of theology, and fundamental doctrines through systematic theology. The text emphasizes historical consciousness in stating: "All courses must help the student develop a critical sense of history and an insight into the richness as well as the limitations of the varying cultural expressions of the Christian faith through the centuries."[31]

Aspects of seminary learning and spiritual formation have their fulfillment in pastoral formation. The program of pastoral formation proposes that every seminary have a field education program under the direction of a priest who is a member of the faculty. Field education is to be integrated with spiritual and academic aspects of the seminary. The experience of the seminarians in the parish is preferred, but other activities such as work in religious education, hospitals, and charitable and community organizations are recognized.

Official acts and policies launched the seminary on the path of renewal for the following years. Their formulation engaged the ideas and efforts of the Bishops' Committee on Priestly Formation, whose members were often former seminary officials. They were assisted by many active seminary officials. Official policies, of course, are not implemented in a vacuum. The general culture of the late 1960s and educational life outside the Catholic seminary influenced seminary educators and seminarians alike. In the successful implementation of seminary renewal, the wisdom and leadership skills of local bishops responsible for seminaries had to come to terms with the professional ideas of seminary educators and the rising expectations of seminarians. When the full history of seminary renewal is written, the record of the various levels of authority can be treated. For the present, only a few examples can be cited.

The discussions of seminary renewal and anticipation of the Decree on Priestly Formation naturally raised expectations in seminaries well before the council ended at the close of 1965. In the fall of 1964, Cardinal Joseph Ritter of St. Louis, an enthusiastic supporter of the council and in touch with the ideas that informed it, sanctioned a rather bold reform of the house rules for Kenrick Seminary. Kenrick's Vincentian rector Nicholas Persich and the faculty devised a simple internal rule that ended most of the personal restrictions of classic seminary life. Gone were the rules enforcing periods of silence, prohibitions of visiting private rooms, and bells for most activities.[32] The intended effect was to give seminarians responsibility for planning their own time outside of required common activities, such as classes, meals, and liturgy. The new house rules preceded the longer process of curriculum change and the process of obtaining accreditation. But Ritter's early approval of reform of internal seminary life recognized the importance of the issue of personal freedom among the "New Breed" and seminary educators favoring reform.

The case of Cardinal James McIntyre of Los Angeles provides a different reaction to current seminary reform.[33] McIntyre reacted angrily when he heard about the changes at Kenrick and the publication of Stafford Poole's controversial book on seminary reform. He feared the introduction of reforms in the Los Angeles seminaries that the Vincentians staffed and asked Vincentian officials for a statement of policy on the seminaries they conducted. He was apparently trying not only to forestall reform in his own seminaries but also to insure that other Vincentian-staffed seminaries would operate in as rigid a fashion as his own. The minutes of McIntyre's long discussions with Vincentian officials reveal that the cardinal had no understanding of seminary issues as they had developed in the previous twenty years. He had preconceived ideas that the classic seminary life was not capable of being changed. His principal desire was to preserve the traditional seminary life and that any reform be postponed until Roman authority issued decrees on numerous seminary-related issues after the council.

In seminaries staffed by diocesan priests, the bishop's leadership set the tone for a process of renewal, as was the case at Philadelphia's archdiocesan seminary under Archbishop John Krol. A canon lawyer by training, Krol began the process of seminary renewal early in 1966 by ordering a canonical visitation of the seminary to be conducted by several senior diocesan clergy. The seminarians of the theology department, where feelings were running high over recent disciplinary problems, prepared a synthesis of their views for the visitation. The students' report requested the kind of personal freedoms that had already been granted over a year earlier at Kenrick Seminary and were being routinely introduced at other seminaries. They requested liturgical changes, such as an altar facing the worshippers in the chapel, homilies at community masses, communal penance services, and more adequate spiritual direction. These reforms were already fairly standard practices at many seminaries and religious houses but not in the cautious local church of Philadelphia. The rather unremarkable requests contained in the students' report were leaked to the Philadelphia press, which published a summary. The disclosure caused Archbishop Krol to make an unannounced appearance before the seminarians to declare to them how much the leaking of the report had caused "resentment, disunity, and scandal" and he promised that any changes were to come from "directives of church law" rather than "personal whims or fancies of individuals."[34] In the following academic year (1966–1967) incidents of student unrest occurred after which seminarians were either dismissed or punished. Over the following several years, liturgical reform, expansion of personal freedom, and curricular reform were carried out at a gradual pace.

At Boston's St. John's Seminary, several issues, especially personal freedom, led to some rather dramatic student unrest.[35] In the early 1960s, St. John's longtime rector, Monsignor Matthew Stapleton, permitted seminarians the freedom to engage in off-campus social service activities and had arranged a stimulating series of lectures given by Catholic and Protestant scholars. When Stapleton retired in 1965, Cardinal Richard Cushing appointed as rector Monsignor Lawrence Riley, who reversed many policies of his predecessor, particularly by restricting off-campus activities and curtailing outside lecturers. Seminarians sent letters and petitions to the rector and cardinal, who ignored them. When Cushing attended a meeting of Boston pastors in the seminary library in April 1966, the frustrated seminarians picketed the building. In response, Cushing came outside and warned the Boston newsmen present not to report the unrest or they would not be welcome for interviews again. Naturally, the story appeared in the local papers and in national news magazines. Cushing later told a student delegation that they were injuring his reputation and even threatened to close the seminary.

At Cincinnati's Mount St. Mary's of the West, seminary reform was well under way by the fall of 1966. The seminary rector, Monsignor Joseph Schneider, implemented a relaxation of internal rules to allow greater personal freedom. The new liturgical program reflected the recent changes in the liturgy, the spiritual formation program became more flexible as students chose mentors from the entire faculty, and the academic program was moving in the direction of amalgamating courses, reducing the hours of classes, and increasing study time. In May 1967 an open letter signed by three-fourths of the students was sent to students' respective bishops to record general approval of the structural reforms enacted in the seminary, but it called for more open discussion of these issues. Seminary authorities viewed this very mildly worded letter with considerable alarm. The aged Cincinnati Archbishop Karl J. Alter professed to be "humiliated" before his suffragan bishops and found that the letter did "great harm" to the seminary.[36] Monsignor Schneider resigned.

In a period of highly publicized instances of campus unrest and civil disorder at leading universities in the United States during the late 1960s, these instances of seminarians expressing their views on seminary life to church authorities were indeed mild by comparison. Yet these instances seemed to have alarmed such prelates as Cushing, Krol, and Alter, whose view of church authority apparently assumed that directives for renewal were to be formulated from on high, then issued to those below. They did not recognize the need for genuine or ongoing communication with the seminary community. They continued to regard the seminary as an isolated world far from public view and became defensive when seminary matters were reported to the public. They apparently could not perceive that the era of renewal required more leadership skills than simply laying down the law.

Even after seminary renewal was rather well established, it was not always understood by bishops responsible for seminaries. Such an instance can be found at St. Patrick's Seminary at Menlo Park, California, where, in 1967, the Sulpician James Laubacher was appointed rector. Laubacher had been rector of St. Mary's Seminary in Baltimore since 1945 and was among the most respected Catholic seminary educators in the United States. However, he had a difficult relationship with San Francisco Archbishop Joseph McGucken, who objected to aspects of seminary renewal, especially the seminary's year-long deacon internship program. He could not understand the need for such a lengthy program though the rector pointed out its basis in official documents and the practices of other seminaries. McGucken asked an ad hoc committee of the NCCB to conduct a visitation at the seminary without prior consultation with seminary personnel. Though the visitation of January 1971 reported favorably on the seminary's program, Laubacher left the rectorship that spring.[37]

Thus, a smooth implementation of seminary renewal often depended on the bishop's grasp of relevant issues. Not all seminaries had problems of conflict between the local bishop and the seminary community. Diocesan seminaries conducted by communities of priests could often escape them. The other dimension of seminary renewal pertains to the leadership of seminary educators who continued to take initiatives through the years of the council and afterward to promote a raising of the seminary's stature as a professional school. Without the need for a comprehensive plan from church authority but with the sanction of individual bishops and religious superiors, seminary educators voluntarily planned for accreditation. Regional meetings of seminary educators had taken place before the council to prepare seminary officials and educators for the accrediting process with regional associations. Interest in accreditation was especially strong in the Middle West, where Catholic seminary educators representing thirty-four theologates in the region covered by the North Central Association met in Chicago in October 1964 to form the Midwest Association of Theological Schools (MATS). Their purpose was to assist member institutions in the accrediting process and to promote general excellence in seminary education. The first president of MATS was one of the leading activists of seminary reform, Benedict Ashley, O.P., president of the Dominicans' Aquinas Institute at River Forest, Illinois (for philosophy), and at Dubuque, Iowa (for theology). The Institute was one of the early theologates to be accredited with the North Central Association.[38]

The Midwestern example of seminary associations was in due course taken up by the other regions with the formation of the East Coast and West Coast rectors' conferences. These organizations supplemented the annual meeting of the NCEA seminary department, which remained without a full-time associate secretary for most of the 1960s. Leadership accordingly tended in the direction of regional groups as seminaries pursued accreditation with regional bodies through the period.

The interest in accrediting, particularly for college seminaries, extended to programs for theological degrees. The seminary educators who participated in the founding of MATS discussed the possibility of forming a Catholic accrediting body and drafted a proposal outlining the functions of an association. Eventually a series of contacts dating from the early 1960s between Catholic seminary educators, especially through the NCEA, and officials of the American Association of Theological Schools (AATS) produced another route for the accrediting of Catholic seminaries. The AATS had been composed of Protestant seminaries but had nothing in its founding documents that made the association necessarily Protestant. Academic criteria were the basis of accreditation, without regard to the doctrinal positions or church affiliation of member institutions. Accordingly, by 1968 fifteen Catholic seminaries joined the AATS as associate members.[39] Most Catholic seminaries then began the process of a thorough self-study according to the accepted criteria of educational and professional standards. After the self-study, the AATS assigned a team of seminary educators from peer institutions to conduct an on-site visit to evaluate the seminary. If the visiting team recommended accreditation, the seminary became a full member of the association. Accreditation with AATS, later known as the Association of Theological Schools in the United States and Canada or ATS, was sought and normally obtained by virtually all Catholic theological seminaries through the 1970s. In 1984 ATS listed forty-two Catholic accredited member institutions, three associate members, and four candidates for membership.[40]

ATS accreditation has brought many positive benefits not likely to occur when the seminary remains isolated from the standards of modern education. The process of a thorough self-study followed by evaluation forces the seminary's leaders to face the strengths and weaknesses of their institution. The seminary's stated purpose has to correspond with its own realities of adequate financial resources, physical facilities, personnel, and adminstrative procedures. If there are serious defects in these areas, the seminary is not able to fulfill its basic purposes. In the critically important areas of studies, the curriculum and faculty must be adequate to sustain the areas of study leading to degrees — normally the Master of Divinity degree for priesthood candidates.

By the late 1960s seminary catalogues began to record the profound change in the course of studies. In the early 1960s a few seminaries began to change from the old organization of dogmatic and moral studies according to the division of subject matter outlined in the classic seminary manuals. In the middle 1960s the reorganization of the curriculum ended the reliance on manuals rather long after their defects had become generally acknowledged. Though courses in dogmatic—now more properly called systematic—theology, moral theology, biblical studies, historical studies, liturgy, and homiletics remained, the hours were clarified so that course loads were more manageable.

Some of the most profound changes that took place in the Catholic seminary after the council relate to their number, enrollment, and composition. These changes are partially explained by the decline of so-called "ghetto" Catholicism during the 1960s and the entry of American Catholics in greater number into the middle class. The cultural supports to traditional Catholic life and values had thereby been weakened as the attitudes and behavior of Catholics began to parallel those of other Americans. Though there are indications of a decline of religious identification among Catholics, the religious behavior of those actively committed has changed. One indication of a change has been the sharp decline in the number of those offering themselves as candidates for the priesthood. In 1966 the number of students enrolled in major seminaries of dioceses and religious orders reached its highest level at 8,916. The enrollments then began a decline through the late 1960s and early 1970s to 5,804 in 1972 and 4,244 in 1984.[41]

The number of seminaries has declined drastically. The minor seminary system virtually collapsed in the years after the council as it became generally recognized that separating boys from a normal family and school environment was not suited to their personal development, that the number of priests produced from minor seminaries was very small, and that the costs of maintaining minor seminaries for small enrollments made their continuation unfeasible. The decline of theologates operated by religious orders for their own members has been very sharp as larger orders reduced the number of theologates, or religious orders both large and small joined together in unions or consortia as at Washington, D.C., Chicago, or Berkeley.

The historic major seminaries located at large archdioceses and dioceses have survived the trend of closures and amalgamation, though some have dropped college programs and are hence better described as freestanding theologates. These are located at or near Baltimore, Boston, Buffalo, Chicago, Cincinnati, Cleveland, Denver, Detroit, Los Angeles, Miami, Milwaukee, Newark, New Orleans, New York, Philadelphia, Rockville

Center, St. Louis, St. Paul, and San Francisco. Thus, among archdioceses only the seminaries of Seattle and Dubuque have closed, while that of San Antonio has joined with a neighboring religious order seminary. The seminary of the diocese of Galveston-Houston has been joined to a neighboring Catholic university. The eastern Vincentians' Mary Immaculate Seminary at Northampton, Pennsylvania, enrolls diocesan students. Some new seminaries have been formed, such as Holy Trinity Seminary at Dallas (closed in the 1980s) and those offering seminary programs to older students or so-called "delayed vocations" such as Pope John XXIII National Seminary at Weston, Massachusetts; Holy Apostles Seminary, Cromwell, Connecticut; Sacred Heart School of Theology, Hales Corners, Wisconsin; and Mater Dei Institute, Spokane, Washington. The theologates of the Benedictines have continued at St. Meinrad and St. Vincent archabbeys and at St. John's and Mount Angel abbeys. Other interdiocesan seminaries have continued such as Mount St. Mary's Seminary, Emmitsburg, Maryland, the Pontifical College Josephinum, Columbus, Ohio, and Sts. Cyril and Methodius Seminary, Orchard Lake, Michigan.

The declining number of seminarians has been accompanied by the leveling off and then decline in the number of priests. The new openings for lay participation in nonsacramental aspects of ministry that priests formerly performed has led to the development of training for nonordained ministry. Such programs have opened up seminaries to men who do not seek ordination and to women who may not be ordained. In 1984 the forty-nine Catholic theologates belonging to ATS enrolled 2,905 students studying theology who are not candidates for ordination. Of these students, 22 percent were women. Women too have joined the faculty. In 1983–1984 there were 72 full-time and 137 part-time female faculty members in Catholic seminaries.[42] The 1981 edition of the Program of Priestly Formation includes for the first time general statements on programs for lay ministry that seminaries are increasingly offering.

Official statements continued to inform and direct aspects of priesthood and seminary through the 1970s. The responsibility of bishops' conferences to provide successive editions of the Program of Priestly Formation has not replaced or diminished the role of the larger Catholic church in matters of the priesthood and the seminary. For instance, the second General Assembly of the Synod of Bishops in 1971 addressed the issues surrounding the ministerial priesthood. The synod's document on the subject frankly acknowledges the many challenges of modern pastoral life posed by secularization, the need for the priest to have varied skills in a complex world, and the fact that many activities formerly reserved to priests were being taken up by lay workers.[43] In the midst of these challenges, the bishops affirmed the value of traditional aspects of the priesthood such as celibacy and the ministry of the sacraments.

In response to an improved historical understanding of the theology of ministry, Pope Paul VI adjusted some traditional categories of official ministry. The pope issued the *motu proprio Ministeria Quaedam* on August 15, 1972, reforming the categories of orders after consultations with the episcopal conferences.[44] Since minor orders were not always uniform in the early church and many of their functions were performed by the laity, the minor orders of porter and exorcist were abolished. The former minor orders of acolyte and lector were to be called ministries. The major order of subdeacon was abolished in the Latin rite and its functions annexed to the ministry of acolyte. Henceforth, the historic orders of deacon, priest, and bishop stand out more clearly as authentic degrees of the sacrament of orders.

The issue of women's ordination elicited increasing controversy during the 1970s. In October 1976 the Sacred Congregation for the Doctrine of the Faith issued its "Declaration on the Question of the Admission of Women to the Ministerial Priesthood." The congregation affirmed the prohibition on women priests based on the practice of the church since apostolic times and the need for the priest to be male to represent the male Christ.[45]

The responsibility of the episcopal conference did not diminish the role of the Sacred Congregation for Catholic Education in informing the content of seminary life and learning. After consultation with seminary experts and the episcopal conferences, the Sacred Congregation of Catholic Education under the signature of Cardinal Garrone periodically issued instructions dealing with certain areas of seminary life. Concern about neglecting or undervaluing philosophy caused the Sacred Congregation to issue a document on the "Study of Philosophy in Seminaries" in 1972. The encyclical *Sacerdotalis Coelibatus,* issued by Pope Paul VI in 1967, affirmed the value of celibacy for priests. As a follow-up to the encyclical and in view of the obvious fact that celibacy was not widely esteemed, the Sacred Congregation issued the "Guide to Formation in Priestly Celibacy" in 1974. As canon law had become undervalued in the wake of many new undertakings of the Second Vatican Council, the Sacred Congregation issued a short document "On the Teaching of Canon Law to Those Preparing to Be Priests" in 1975. A lengthy document, "The Theological Formation of Future Priests," was issued in 1976 as a reminder of the demands of theological teaching and to provide guidelines for the teaching of theology. The great importance of the liturgy is stressed in the "Instruction on Liturgical Formation in Seminaries," issued in 1979. The "Circular Letter Concerning Some of the More Urgent Aspects of Spiritual Formation in Seminaries," issued in 1980, stresses a fourfold emphasis on cultivating love for Scripture, on the Eucharist, the spirit of self-denial, and devotion to Mary.[46]

For advanced learning, the apostolic constitution *Sapientia Christiana,* under preparation since 1967, was completed and promulgated in 1979 to supersede *Deus Scientiarum Dominus.* The new constitution relates directly to the status of advanced theological studies and places pontifical faculties under the obligation to explain and defend official Catholic positions. Accordingly, the constitution's provisions relate to the theology faculty at the Catholic University of America, where issues of theological inquiry have stirred widespread controversy with the suspension of Charles Curran from the faculty in 1985.

The election in 1978 of the Polish Cardinal Karol Wojtyla, who took the name Pope John Paul II, has had a significant impact on theological issues and measures related to seminary training. His pontificate has been marked by a policy of reaffirming aspects of the Catholic tradition that have been questioned either in the course of Catholic theological inquiry, in pastoral practices in the years since the council, or in the area of Catholic political thought and activity.

The questioning of tradition has advanced steadily within the area of studies relating to the history and practice of ordained ministry. On this issue Edward Schillebeeckx's historical essay *Ministry: Leadership in the Community of Jesus Christ,* first published in 1980, stands in contrast to the official theology on the priesthood contained in the letter to Catholic bishops *Sacerdotium ministeriale,* issued August 6, 1983, by the Sacred Congregation for the Doctrine of the Faith. Though Schillebeeckx declared his adherence to *Sacerdotium ministeriale,* and wrote a clarified book on ministry, *The Church with a Human Face; A New and Expanded Theology of Ministry,* published in 1985, the Sacred Congregation was not satisfied with his views and issued another warning in 1986.[47]

The Holy See addressed issues of seminary education by ordering visitations of seminaries in Brazil and the Philippines. In September 1981, Archbishop John R. Roach, president of the National Conference of Catholic Bishops, announced that the Sacred Congregation for Catholic Education planned to conduct a visitation of seminaries in the United States. Unlike the pontifical visitation conducted throughout the world in the late 1930s, the visitation was announced to the public, conducted with the cooperation of the bishops' conference, and coordinated by an American, Bishop John Marshall of Burlington, Vermont. He was assisted by forty bishops, nineteen religious superiors, and fifty-seven priests who were experienced seminary educators. The bishops and seminary educators formed teams to conduct the on-site visits to seminaries across the country.

The seminaries were evaluated on the basis of adherence to the Program of Priestly Formation and other official standards. An evaluation "instrument" was devised to guide seminary officials and the visitation teams in examining current practices in seminary education. A visitation team visited and evaluated each seminary, gave the seminary officials an oral evaluation, and afterward submitted a written evaluation for the seminary and its episcopal or religious superior. The latter evaluation was forwarded to the Sacred Congregation and is confidential.

Cardinal William Baum, prefect of the Sacred Congregation for Catholic Education since 1980, issued a letter on October 5, 1986, analyzing the general state of the thirty-eight freestanding theological seminaries conducted by dioceses and religious orders. The cardinal states at the outset that "the picture that emerges so far is that the theologates of the United States are generally satisfactory. Some in fact are excellent, a few have one or more serious deficiencies and the majority are serving the church well in preparing candidates for the priesthood."[48] However, the current concerns of Pope John Paul II's policy of Catholic restoration can be seen in the recommendations for seminaries:

> Our most serious recommendations have been about the need to develop a clearer concept of the ordained priesthood, to promote the specialized nature of priestly formation in accordance with Vatican Council II's affirmation of seminaries, to deepen the academic formation so that it becomes more properly and adequately theological (with more convinced and convincing attention to the magisterium in some courses), and to ensure that the seminarians develop a good grasp of the specific contribution that the priest has to make to each pastoral situation. There are some confusions, lacunae and staffing inadequacies, but there are more strengths and accomplishments.

The letter raises questions concerning programs for lay ministries within the seminary. Cardinal Baum invokes the Vatican Council's affirmation of the distinctive purpose of the seminary to train priests. The mingling of the seminarians in courses with other students, who do not have the same prerequisite courses, would require instructors to make adjustments to the less thorough philosophical and academic preparation of the nonseminarians. The cardinal is also concerned that too many unordained faculty will alter the character of seminary. Priests should ordinarily teach so that they can draw from the experience of ministry in their teaching. He points out that the contemporary experience of the church throughout the world has been such that "priestly formation is best secured when the professors are mainly priests and when the students are predominantly seminarians: The vocational orientation of the group guides and feeds the intellectual accomplishment."

The evaluation of spiritual direction takes issue with the practice of offering as spiritual directors those who are not priests. The cardinal asks for a "realignment" of the programs of these seminaries to provide only priest directors. Hence, spiritual direction is to be "vocationally oriented." A seminarian needs to profit from the "experience and role modeling of his priest-director" and to appropriate "some of the special charisms of the sacrament of holy orders."

In academic matters, the general evaluation suggests considerable unevenness among the seminaries of the country. Several unnamed seminaries are congratulated for the quality, balance, and coherence of the course offerings. Other seminaries do not offer new courses apparently because of a lack of qualified instructors or resources to hire more personnel. Some seminaries have limited course offerings that compress large areas of study into only a few courses. These deficiencies result in a mediocre course of studies. In a few cases, some courses are described as "very thin" because they were found to be "a mere marriage between the Scriptures and contemporary reflection on the state of the world." The cardinal urges a greater attention to thorough theological preparation. Another concern is the historical dimension in systematic theology and in patristic studies. A deeper study of church history is recommended. The letter takes note of a renewed interest in canon law, biblical languages, and Latin.

In the area of pastoral formation, the letter notes the shift in emphases that have taken place since its introduction in the late 1960s, that is, from a stress on long periods of field work and a consequent deemphasis on academic life to the reformulation of practical training to include theological reflection. It notes that some seminaries have not yet found a proper balance of the elements of pastoral formation. Its recommendations for pastoral formation renew the emphasis on the role of the priest by urging bishops to have pastoral formation programs under the direction of experienced priests—not simply trained experts. It recommends that formation relate more closely to the priest's roles as minister of word and sacrament.

Cardinal Baum notes the obvious development that most priesthood candidates receive the Master of Divinity degree or, in a few cases, the Master of Arts degree. He concludes that the "battle" to improve the status of the seminary "has been won." But he reminds seminary educators that "in terms of its intellectual excellence for vocational purposes, there is much still to be done if the theologates are to match the very best graduate schools in the United States." While endorsing the value of accreditation with accrediting associations, the letter also urges bishops to affiliate seminaries with ecclesiastical faculties "in order to promote better standards in the study of theology and to reap the advantages of canonical degrees to the life of the church."

On the issue of interest to strident critics of the seminaries who fear that they are rife with heterodoxy, the letter states clearly: "Dissent, in fact, is not a major characteristic of U.S. free-standing theologates for the formation of diocesan priests. However, a more common phenomenon is not dissent from the magisterium but confusion about it." The cardinal calls for greater attention to presenting the church's position clearly, especially on moral questions. On this issue several seminaries "need to make a better assertion of the teachings of the magisterium as normative for preaching and pastoral practice." The emphasis on presenting official teachings appears to favor a return to the old apologetical approach to seminary learning. Though the letter often achieves a balanced wording on many other issues, there is no concern expressed that restoring the apologetical approach to learning will also restore this method's shortcomings and seriously compromise the intellectual quality of seminary teaching.

Cardinal Baum's letter of 1986 represents the first public response of Roman authority to the visitation and is to be followed by letters after the visitation teams evaluate college seminaries and the religious orders' theological unions. On October 9, 1987, Bishop John Marshall told a gathering of seminary educators that the Congregation for Catholic Education would not issue new norms at the ending of the visitation. Instead, the congregation expects the National Conference of Catholic Bishops to address the visitation's recommendations in the subsequent revision of the Program of Priestly Formation.[49] While the recommendations place limitations on the episcopate's freedom to direct the future renewal of seminary through the program, the bishops are still permitted to offer some degree of leadership related to seminary issues.

Through the years since the council, church leaders at the levels of Roman congregations, the National Conference of Catholic Bishops, organizations of seminary educators, and officials of individual seminaries have made varying contributions to seminary renewal. Those responsible for the great changes taking place in the seminary have not always thoroughly considered the important question that should be raised prior to seminary reform, that is, what is the model of the priest that should inform seminary education? This question, of course, is difficult to address and often elicits theological controversy.

For previous periods of seminary history, it is possible to link current ideas on the model priest to developments in seminary training. In antebellum America, there was scarcely an articulation of original ideas as to what the diocesan priest was to do in the American context beyond the duties of administering the sacraments and leading devotional activities. In the late nineteenth century, the priest was expected to perform in a more professional fashion all his duties, especially the highly visible roles of teaching, preaching, and representing the Catholic church to those outside the Catholic community. In the Roman period, official standards were deeply impressed on the practices of the priesthood and seminary, yet in new areas of theology and in matters that church authority did not address, such as seminary standards, there was a new scope for developing concepts of the priesthood and seminary. In the era since the Second Vatican Council official statements, new pastoral practices that expand the roles of the laity, and a developing theology of ministry have not yet yielded a new consensus as to how the priest's ministry is to be practiced. The formulation of clear ideas related to ordained ministry has yet to be fully addressed. The importance of this task has been recently recognized as the last decade of the twentieth century approaches. Coadjutor Archbishop Thomas J. Murphy of Seattle, a former chairman of the Bishops' Committee on Priestly Formation, has called attention to this theme that may engage church leaders as they deal with seminary education in the years ahead:

> The question, What is the priest? is of tremendous significance today because when we are able to articulate a theology of priesthood that is appropriated by the Christian community, then we will have a clearer idea of the direction of seminary education and formation today in its task of preparing ordained leaders for the church of tomorrow.[50]

Abbreviations

ARCHIVES

AAB	Archives of the Archdiocese of Baltimore
AABo	Archives of the Archdiocese of Boston
AAC	Archives of the Archdiocese of Cincinnati
AANY	Archives of the Archdiocese of New York
AAO	Archives of the Archdiocese of Omaha
ACUA	Archives of the Catholic University of America
ADR	Archives of the Diocese of Rochester
AMSM	Archives of Mount Saint Mary's College, Emmitsburg, Maryland
APF	Archives of the Society for the Propagation of the Faith (AUND)
AUND	Archives of the University of Notre Dame
AUSCC	Archives of the United States Catholic Conference
DRMA	DeAndreis-Rosati Memorial Archives, St. Mary's Seminary, Perryville, Missouri
KSA	Kenrick Seminary Archives, St. Louis
LSA	Leopoldinen Stiftung Archives (microfilm at AUND)
MUA	Marquette University Archives
PFA	Propaganda Fide Archives
SAB	Sulpician Archives Baltimore
SAP	Sulpician Archives Paris (copies at SAB)

PUBLICATIONS

AAS	*Acta Apostolicae Sedis*
AHP	*Archivum Historiae Pontificiae*
AER	*American Ecclesiastical Review*
CBQ	*Catholic Biblical Quarterly*
CEAB	*Catholic Educational Association Bulletin*
CER	*Catholic Educational Review*
CHR	*Catholic Historical Review*
CTSAP	*Catholic Theological Society of America Proceedings*
CUB	*Catholic University Bulletin*
DTC	*Dictionnaire de Theologie Catholique*

431

HPR   *Homiletic and Pastoral Review*
NCE   *New Catholic Encyclopedia*
NCEAB *National Catholic Educational Association Bulletin*
RACHS *Records of the American Catholic Historical Society*

Notes

PROLOGUE

1. A standard brief history of the Catholic seminary is John Tracy Ellis, "A Short History of Seminary Education," in James Michael Lee and Louis J. Putz, eds. *Seminary Education in a Time of Change* (Notre Dame, Ind.: Fides, 1965), pp. 1–81.

2. Bernard Cooke, *Ministry to Word and Sacraments* (Philadelphia: Fortress, 1976); Nathan Mitchell, *Mission and Ministry: History and Theology in the Sacrament of Order* (Wilmington, Del.: Michael Glazier, 1982); Edward Schillebeeckx, *The Church with a Human Face: A New and Expanded Theology of Ministry* (New York: Crossroad, 1985); Thomas Franklin O'Meara, *Theology of Ministry* (New York: Paulist Press, 1983); for reform movements, see Steven Ozment, *The Age of Reform: 1250–1550* (New Haven, Conn.: Yale University Press, 1980) and Jean Pierre Massaut, *Josse Clichtove, L'Humanisme et la Réform du Clergé* (Paris, 1969).

3. Henry J. Schroeder, ed., *Canons and Decrees of the Council of Trent* (Rockford, Ill.: Tan Books, 1978), p. 73 (reprint of the English portion of Latin-English version published by Herder in 1941).

4. Ibid., pp. 144–145.

5. Ibid., pp. 162–163.

6. Ibid., pp. 160–161.

7. Ibid., p. 163.

8. Ibid., p. 183.

9. James A. O'Donohoe, *Tridentine Seminary Legislation: Its Sources and Its Formation,* Bibliotheca Ephermeridum Theologicarum Lovaniensium, vol. 9 (Louvain, 1957), pp. 33–48.

10. Hubert Jedin, "Domschule und Kolleg: zum Ursprung der Idee des Trienter Priesterseminars," *Trierer Theologische Zeitschrift* 67 (1958), 214–216.

11. O'Donohoe, *Tridentine,* pp. 64–87.

12. Ibid., pp. 89–162.

13. Schroeder, *Canons,* pp. 175.

14. Hubert Jedin, "Le Concile de Trente a-ti-il créé l'image-modèle du prêtre?" in Joseph Coppens, ed., *Sacerdoce et Celibat: Etudes Historiques et Theologiques* (Louvain, 1971), pp. 111–131.

15. Antoine Degert, *Histoire des Séminaires Français jusqu'a la Révolution,* 2 vols. (Paris: Beauchesne, 1912), 1:35–38.

16. Hubert Jedin and John Dolan, eds., *History of the Church,* vol. 6: *The Church in the Age of Absolutism and Enlightenment,* (New York: Crossroad, 1981), pp. 157–158.

17. Degert, *Séminaires,* 1:58–80.

18. For the sources of Bérulle's ideas, see Jean Dagens, *Bérulle et les Origines de la Restauration Catholique (1575–1611)* (Tournai: Desclee, 1952); also Fernando Guillen Preckler, *"Etat" chez le Cardinal de Bérulle: theologie et spiritualité des "états" bérulliens,* Analecta Gregoriana, vol. 197 (Rome: Universita Gregoriana Editrice, 1974); and Anne Mansfield Minton, "The Figure of Christ in the Writings of Pierre de Bérulle (1575–1629)" (Ph.D. diss., New York University, 1979).

19. Henri Brémond, *A Literary History of Religious Thought in France,* vol. 3: *The Triumph of Mysticism* (New York: Macmillan, 1936), p. 19.

20. Ibid., p. 54.

21. Ibid., pp. 58–59.

22. Ibid., p. 62.

23. Ibid., pp. 536–572.

24. Paul Broutin, *La Réforme Pastorale en France au XVIIe Siècle: Recherches sur la Tradition Pastorale aprés le Concile de Trente,* 2 vols. (Tournai: Desclee, 1956), 1:111–127, 191–203.

25. Pierre Coste, *The Life and Works of Saint Vincent de Paul* (Westminster, Md., 1952); Maurice A. Roche, *Saint Vincent de Paul and the Formation of Clerics,* Studia Friburgensia, no. 39., (Fribourg: The University Press, 1964).

26. Vincent de Paul to Bernard Codoing, Paris, 13 May 1644, in Pierre Coste, ed., *Saint Vincent de Paul: Correspondence, Entretiens, Documents* (Paris, 1922), 2:459.

27. Edward Healy Thompson, *The Life of Jean-Jacques Olier, Founder of the Seminary of St. Sulpice* (London, 1886), pp. 3–33.

28. Brémond, *History,* pp. 243–308.

29. Eugene A. Walsh, *The Priesthood in the Writings of the French School: Bérulle, De Condren, Olier* (Washington: Catholic University of America Press, 1949), p. 114; see also Lowell M. Glendon, "Jean-Jacques Olier's View of the Spiritual Potential of Human Nature: A Presentation and an Evaluation" (Ph.D. diss., Fordham University, 1982).

30. Adolphe Tanquerey, *The Spiritual Life: A Treatise on Ascetical and Mystical Theology* (Tournai: Desclee, 1930), pp. 335–339.

31. Pierre Pourrat, *Father Olier: Founder of Saint Sulpice,* trans. Wendell S. Reilly (Baltimore, 1932), p. 162.

32. Pierre Boisard, *La Compagnie de Saint Sulpice: Trois Siècles d'Histoire* (Paris: private printing, 1959), pp. 38–44.

33. Stafford Poole, *A History of the Congregation of the Mission, 1625–1843* (private printing, 1983), p. 83.

34. Degert, *Séminaires,* 1:385–386.

35. Boisard, *Compagnie,* pp. 48–69.

36. Poole, *History,* pp. 29–43.

37. Degert, *Séminaires,* 2:300–305.

38. Yves M.-J. Congar, *A History of Theology* (Garden City, N.Y.: Double-day, 1968), pp. 177–181.

39. "Probabilisme," *DTC* 13:556–586.

40. Degert, *Séminaires,* 2:179–108.

41. Ibid., 2:237–267.

42. Ibid., 2:509–510.

43. Owen Chadwick, *The Popes and European Revolution* (Oxford: Clarendon Press, 1981), p. 114.

44. Ibid., p. 115.

45. "St. Alphonsus Liguori," *NCE,* 1:336–341.

46. Jedin and Dolan, eds., *Church,* p. 158.

47. Chadwick, *Popes,* p. 120.

48. Josef Muller, *Der Pastoraltheologisch-Didaktische Ansatz in Franz Stephan Rautenstrauchs "Entwurf zur Einrichtung der Theologischen Schulen"* (Vienna: Herder, 1969).

49. Heinz Marquart, *Matthäus Fingerlos (1748–1817; Leben und Wirken eines Pastoraltheologen und Seminarregenten in der Aufklärungszeit* (Göttingen: Vandenhoeck & Ruprecht, 1977).

50. Chadwick, *Popes,* p. 122.

1. BALTIMORE AND EMMITSBURG

1. Thomas W. Spalding, "John Carroll: Corrigenda et Addenda," *CHR* 71 (October 1985), 505–518 corrects errors in Carroll historiography; on Carroll's return to Maryland, see Peter Guilday, *The Life and Times of John Carroll, Archbishop of Baltimore (1735–1815)* (New York, 1922), pp. 54–56; James Hennesey, "An Eighteenth-Century Bishop: John Carroll of Baltimore," *AHP* 16 (1978), 171–204 summarizes Carroll's views on major issues.

2. For problems of governing the American Catholic church during the Revolutionary War, see Guilday, *Carroll,* pp. 163–177; for Carroll's views on a national church, see Hennesey, "An Eighteenth-Century Bishop," p. 189; and Carroll to Charles Plowden, Maryland, February 27, 1785, in Thomas O'Brien Hanley, ed., *John Carroll Papers* (hereafter *JCP*) (Notre Dame, Ind.: University of Notre Dame Press, 1976), 1:162–166.

3. Carroll to Charles Plowden, Maryland, September 26, 1783, *JCP,* 1:78.

4. Ibid.

5. John M. Daley, *Georgetown University: Origin and Early Years* (Washington: Georgetown University Press, 1957), pp. 36–63.

6. Carroll to Plowden, Baltimore, October 23, 1783, *JCP,* 1:390; see also Philip Gleason, "The Main Sheet Anchor: John Carroll and Catholic Higher Education," *Review of Politics* 38 (October 1976), 576–613.

7. Joseph William Ruane, *The Beginning of the Society of St. Sulpice in the United States (1791–1829)* (Baltimore, 1935), pp. 26–36; Charles Herberman, *The Sulpicians in the United States* (New York, 1916), pp. 53–75; superseding these

is Christopher J. Kauffman, *Tradition and Transformation in Catholic Culture: The Priests of Saint Sulpice in the United States from 1791 to the Present* (New York: Macmillan, 1988), pp. 38-54.

8. Quoted in Ruane, *Beginning*, p. 26.

9. Ibid., p. 36.

10. Annabelle M. Melville, *Louis William DuBourg: Bishop of Louisiana and the Floridas, Bishop of Montauban, and Archbishop of Besançon, 1766-1833* (Chicago: Loyola University Press, 1986), 1:82-102; James Joseph Kortendick, "The History of St. Mary's College, Baltimore, 1799-1852," (M.A. thesis, Catholic University of America, 1942), pp. 1-49.

11. Quoted in Kauffman, *Tradition*, p. 53.

12. Daley, *Georgetown*, pp. 121-153.

13. Ruane, *Beginning*, pp. 159-168.

14. A popular biography is Richard Shaw, *John Dubois: Founding Father* (Yonkers, N.Y.: United States Catholic Historical Society, 1983), pp. 1-42; Melville, *DuBourg*, 1:167-176.

15. Mary M. Meline and Edward F. X. McSweeney, *The Story of the Mountain: Mount St. Mary's College and Seminary, Emmitsburg, Maryland* (Emmitsburg, 1911) 1:23-40.

16. Dubois to Tessier, Mount St. Mary's, January 1816, AMSM.

17. Quoted in Ruane, *Beginning*, p. 181.

18. Dubois, Bruté, and Hickey to Tessier, Mount St. Mary's, May 25, 1818, SAB.

19. Ronin John Murtha, "The Life of the Most Reverend Ambrose Maréchal, Third Archbishop of Baltimore, 1768-1828," (Ph.D. diss., Catholic University of America, 1965), pp. 77-90.

20. Dubois to Maréchal, Mount St. Mary's, October 26, 1821, AMSM.

21. Dubois to Garnier, Mount St. Mary's, November 10, 1821, AMSM.

22. Murtha, "Maréchal," p. 83.

23. Dubois to Maréchal, February 15, 1823, AMSM.

24. Ruane, *Beginning*, pp. 211-213.

25. Matthew Leo Panczyk, "James Whitfield, Fourth Archbishop of Baltimore: the Episcopal Years, 1828-1934," *RACHS* 75 (December 1964), 43.

26. "Report on the Visitation of the Sulpician Institutions in Baltimore made in 1829 by Mr. Carrière, Director of the Seminary of Paris" [1829], p. 28, SAB.

27. Ibid., pp. 35-37.

28. Kortendick, "St. Mary's," p. 94.

29. "Visitation Report" [1829], p. 38.

30. Ibid., pp. 39-40.

31. John J. Tierney, "St. Charles College: Foundation and Early Years," *Maryland Historical Magazine* 43 (December 1948), 294-311.

32. Quoted in *Golden Jubilee of St. Charles College, Near Ellicott City, Maryland, 1848-1898* (Baltimore, 1898), p. 23.

33. "Divers points de discipline pour le Séminaire de Baltimore arrêtés dans la Visite de 1850 ou renouvellés de celle de 1829," SAB.

34. Eccleston to Louis de Courson, Baltimore, August 9, 1849, AAB.

35. See St. Mary's Seminary, Baltimore, *List of the Superiors, Professors and Students Ordained, 1791-1891* (New York, 1917), pp. 5–11.

36. See chap. 3, nn. 12 and 40.

37. Thomas W. Spalding, *Martin John Spalding: American Churchman* (Washington, D.C.: Catholic University of America Press, 1973), pp. 83–84.

38. Quoted in Ibid., p. 183.

39. Ibid., p. 182.

40. Ibid., pp. 184–185.

41. *Sadlier's Catholic Directory, Almanac, and Ordo* (New York, 1878), p. 65.

42. Meline and McSweeney, *Mountain,* 1:160–161.

43. Ibid., 1:162.

44. Ibid., 1:232–233.

45. Ibid., 1:234, 350–351.

46. Ibid., 1:311.

47. The meeting is described in Louis Deluol Diary, February 19, 1834, SAB; Deluol also wrote to Bishop Benedict Fenwick of Boston: "we had neither the power nor the will to take back the institution of the Mountain." Deluol to Fenwick, Baltimore, February 24, 1834, AABo.

48. Meline and McSweeney, *Mountain,* 1:351.

49. Dubois to Thomas Butler, New York, February 22, 1837, AMSM.

50. Ibid.

51. John Timon to Marc-Antoine Poussou, May 28, 1842, General Curia Archives, Congregation of the Mission, Microfilm, Reel 1, #440, DRMA; Meline and McSweeney, *Mountain,* 1:348.

52. Ibid., 1:372.

53. Ibid.

54. McCaffrey to Brownson, Emmitsburg, July 6, 1849, Brownson Papers, AUND.

55. *Official Catholic Directory* 1858.

56. McCaffrey to Brownson, Emmitsburg, July 6, 1849, Brownson Papers, AUND.

57. Martin Spalding to John Purcell, Louisville, January 26, 1858, AUND.

58. John McCaffrey, *A Catechism of Christian Doctrine, Intended for General Use, Made Short, Comprehensive, Easy and Clear* (Baltimore, 1865).

59. McCaffrey to Purcell, Mount St. Mary's, January 7, 1858, Cincinnati Papers, AUND.

60. McCaffrey to Francis McFarland, Mount St. Mary's, December 7, 1864, Hartford Papers, AUND.

61. McCaffrey to Purcell, Mount St. Mary's, July 11, 1855, Cincinnati Papers, AUND.

62. Same to same, Mount St. Mary's, August 14, 1857, Cincinnati Papers, AUND.

63. Same to same, Mount St. Mary's, August 22, 1856, Cincinnati Papers, AUND.

64. Same to same, Mount St. Mary's, May 15, 1857, Cincinnati Papers, AUND.

65. McCaffrey to Spalding, Mount St. Mary's, August 28, 1866, AAB.

66. McCaffrey to Francis McFarland, Mount St. Mary's, December 7, 1864, Hartford Papers, AUND.

67. Stephen V. Ryan to Jean-Baptiste Etienne, the Barrens, November 12, 1861, General Curia Archives, Microfilm Reel 2, #265, DRMA.

68. McCaffrey to Spalding, Mount St. Mary's, April 4, 1866, AAB.

69. *Catholic Directory,* 1879.

70. Robert Emmett Curran, *Michael Augustine Corrigan and the Shaping of Conservative Catholicism in America* (New York: Arno Press, 1979), pp. 64–67; John Tracy Ellis, *The Life of James Cardinal Gibbons, Archbishop of Baltimore, 1834–1921* (Milwaukee: Bruce, 1952), 1:182–184.

71. William Byrne and Charles Grannan, "Petition," no date, RG 26, Box 13, SAB.

2. LOCAL DIOCESAN SEMINARIES

1. Gerald Shaughnessy, *Has the Immigrant Kept the Faith? A Study of Immigration and Catholic Growth in the United States, 1790–1920* (New York: Macmillan, 1925), p. 262. The early chronicle of American Catholic seminary history can be found in Lloyd Paul McDonald, *The Seminary Movement in the United States: Projects, Foundations and Early Development (1784–1833)* (Washington, D.C.: Catholic University of America, 1927) and William Stephen Morris, *The Seminary Movement in the United States: Projects, Foundations, and Early Development, 1833–1866* (Washington: Catholic University of America, 1932).

2. Martin John Spalding, *Sketches of the Early Catholic Missions of Kentucky* (Louisville, 1844), p. 189.

3. Martin John Spalding, *Life, Times, and Character of the Right Reverend Benedict Joseph Flaget* (Louisville, 1852), pp. 101–102.

4. Accounts of life at the Bardstown seminary appear in Spalding, *Sketches,* pp. 221–228; M. Columba Fox, *The Life of the Right Rev. John Baptist David* (New York: United States Catholic Historical Society, 1925); and William J. Howlett, *Historical Tribute to St. Thomas Seminary at Poplar Neck near Bardstown, Kentucky* (St. Louis: B. Herder, 1906), pp. 1–58; Clyde Crews, *An American Holy Land: A History of the Archdiocese of Louisville* (Wilmington, Del.: Michael Glazier, 1987), pp. 80–87.

5. Spalding, *Sketches,* p. 252.

6. Jean David to Antoine Duclaux, St. Thomas Seminary, May 2, September 15, 1816, October 2, 1819; Flaget to Duclaux, June 27, 1814, RG 23, Box 13, SAB.

7. Spalding, *Spalding,* p. 19 (see above, chap. 1, n. 37).

8. See chap. 5 below.

9. Peter Guilday, *The Life and Times of John England, First Bishop of Charleston (1786–1842)* (New York: American Press, 1927), 1:474–516; see also Peter Clarke, *A Free Church in a Free Society: the Ecclesiology of John England, Bishop of Charleston, 1820–1842* (Hartsville, South Carolina: Center for John England Studies, 1982), pp. 170–174.

10. Sebastian G. Messmer, *The Works of the Right Reverend John England, First Bishop of Charleston* (Cleveland: Arthur H. Clark, 1908), 7:91.

11. Ibid., 7:97

12. Guilday, *England,* 2:79–110.

13. Ibid., 2:117.

14. Ibid., 2:257–261.

15. "Theological Seminaries," *Catholic Herald* (Philadelphia), September 5, 1833. This series of five articles appeared September 5, 12, 19, October 3, 10, 1833; they are not mentioned by England's biographer, Guilday, or included in compilations of England's writings, or noted by recent students of England's thought, Peter Clarke and Patrick Carey. I thank Thomas W. Spalding for bringing these articles to my attention.

16. Ibid., September 19, 1833.

17. Ibid., October 3, 1833.

18. Messmer, 7:157–158.

19. Guilday, *England,* 1:482.

20. Peter Guilday, *A History of the Councils of Baltimore* (New York: Macmillan, 1932), p. 106.

21. Theodore Roemer, *Ten Decades of Alms* (St. Louis: B. Herder, 1942), p. 221. Roemer compiled statistics of the societies' contributions to the American church, assigning a fixed value to foreign currencies regardless of the reporting year. He assumed that the fluctuations of currency values even out over time. His figures therefore have to be used with some caution. The history of the Society for the Propagation of the Faith is found in Edward J. Hickey, *The Society for the Propagation of the Faith: Its Foundation, Organization and Success* (Washington, D.C.: Catholic University of America, 1922). pp. 10–26.

22. Benjamin Blied, *Austrian Aid to American Catholics, 1830–1860* (Milwaukee; private printing, 1944), pp. 17–34; Roemer, *Alms,* p. 221.

23. Theodore Roemer, *The Ludwig-Missionsverein and the Church in the United States (1838–1918)* (Washington, D.C.: Catholic University of America, 1933), pp. 1–28; Roemer, *Alms,* p. 221.

24. Oscar Hugh Lipscomb, "The Administration of Michael Portier, Vicar Apostolic of Alabama and the Floridas, 1825–1829, and First Bishop of Mobile, 1829–1859" (Ph.D. diss., Catholic University of America, 1963), pp. 125–149.

25. *Annales de l'Association de la Propagation de la Foi* (hereafter *Annales*) 4:502f.

26. John H. Lamott, *History of the Archdiocese of Cincinnati, 1821–1921* (New York: Fredereick Pustet, 1921), pp. 184, 280–281, 288.

27. M. Edmund Hussey, *A History of the Seminaries of the Archdiocese of Cincinnati, 1829–1979* (Norwood, Ohio, 1979), pp. 12–14.

28. John E. Sexton and Arthur J. Riley, *History of St. John's Seminary Brighton* (Boston: Roman Catholic Archbishop of Boston, 1945), pp. 23–24.

29. "Lettre de Mgr. B. Fenwick, Evêque de Boston, à M. le redacteur des Annales," Boston, May 16, 1831, *Annales,* 5:435.

30. Sexton and Riley, *St. John's,* pp. 33–41.

31. Ibid., pp. 44–47.

32. "Lettre de Mgr. Dubois, évêque de New-York, à M. P***," Rome, March 16, 1830," *Annales,* 4:460.

33. Shaw, *Dubois,* pp. 154–155.

34. John Hughes to Leopoldine Foundation, New York, April 16, 1840, Reel 3, #69, Suppl, LSA.

35. Arthur J. Scanlan, *St. Joseph's Seminary, Dunwoodie, New York, 1896–1921, with an Account of the Other Seminaries of New York* (New York: United States Catholic Historical Society, 1922), pp. 8–23.

36. AUND, Cincinnati Papers, Francis Kenrick to John Purcell, Bardstown, June 24, 1830.

37. *Catholic Herald* (Philadelphia), September 27, 1833.

38. Accounts of the founding of the Philadelphia seminary in Hugh J. Nolan, *The Most Reverend Francis Patrick Kenrick, Third Bishop of Philadelphia, 1830–1851* (Philadelphia: American Catholic Historical Society of Philadelphia, 1948), pp. 148–156; George E. O'Donnell, *St. Charles Seminary, Overbrook* (Philadelphia: Jefferies and Manz, 1943), pp. 1–32; James Connelly, *St. Charles Seminary Philadelphia* (Philadelphia: St. Charles Seminary, 1979), pp. 19–51.

39. See chap. 5 below.

40. Maller to Marc-Antoine Poussou, Philadelphia, May 23, 1842; Maller to Etienne, Philadelphia, January 2, 1844, Archives of the General Curia, Rome (microfilm), Reel 1, #143, #144, DRMA.

41. Marshall Roy Larriviere, "Louisiana's First Seminary St. Vincent de Paul" (M.A. thesis, Notre Dame Seminary, New Orleans, La., 1963), pp. 13–49.

42. George Paré, *The Catholic Church in Detroit, 1701–1888* (Detroit: Gabriel Richard Press, 1951), pp. 652–654.

43. Peter Lefevere to Vincent Milde, Detroit, July 15, 1842, Reel 2, #33, Suppl., LSA.

44. Letter of Bishop Bruté, 19 January 1839, *Berichte,* 12 (1840), 7; Mary Carol Schroeder, *The Catholic Church in the Diocese of Vincennes, 1847–1877* (Washington, D.C.: Catholic University of America Press, 1951), pp. 42–43, 116–117.

45. "Pastoral Letter of 1840" in Peter Guilday, ed., *National Pastorals of the American Hierarchy, (1792–1919)* (Westminster, Md.: Newman Press, 1954), p. 147.

46. Guilday, *Councils,* p. 140 (see above, n.20).

47. Matthias Loras to Vincent Milde, Dubuque, 1841, Reel 1, #182, LSA.

48. Thomas Auge, "A Man of Deeds: Bishop Loras and the Upper Mississippi Valley Frontier" (unpublished manuscript), pp. 129, 239–243.

49. Victor F. O'Daniel, *The Father of the Church in Tennessee or the Life, Times and Character of the Rt. Rev. Richard Pius Miles, O.P.* (New York, 1926), pp. 249–250, 390–411.

50. James Henry Bailey, *A History of the Diocese of Richmond* (Richmond: Chancery Office, 1956), pp. 83–86.

51. Henry Szarnicki, "The Episcopate of Michael O'Connor First Bishop of Pittsburgh, 1843–1860" (Ph.D. diss., Catholic University of America, 1971), pp. 118–124, 139–146.

52. Morris, *Seminary,* pp. 74–76 (see above, n.1).

53. Ibid., pp. 26–28.

54. William Quarter to Vincent Milde, Chicago, November 27, 1846, Reel 6, #57, LSA.

55. Philip Gleason, "Chicago and Milwaukee: Contrasting Experiences in Seminary Planting" in Nelson Minnich, Robert Eno, and Robert F. Trisco, eds., *Studies in Catholic History in Honor of John Tracy Ellis* (Wilmington, Del.: Michael Glazier, 1985), pp. 149–174.

56. Josef Salzbacher, *Meine Reise nach Nord-Amerika im Jahre 1842* (Vienna, 1845), p. 357.

57. Guilday, *Pastorals,* p. 136.

58. Michael O'Connor to the Council of the Society for the Propagation of the Faith, Pittsburgh, February 24, 1845, Fribourg Papers, APF; also quoted in Szarnicki, "O'Connor," p. 122.

59. Michael O'Connor to James O'Connor, Warren, Pennsylvania, July 15, 1846, O'Connor Papers, AAO; quoted in Szarnicki, "O'Connor," p. 140.

60. Salzbacher, *Reise,* p. 358.

61. Stephen Dubuisson, letter in *Berichte,* 11 (1838), 26–27.

3. FREESTANDING SEMINARIES

1. Shaughnessy, *Immigrant,* p. 262 (see above, chap. 2, n.1).

2. Guilday, *Councils,* pp. 156–157.

3. The legislation of these councils is compiled in *Acta et Decreta Sacrorum Conciliorum Recentiorum. Collectio Lacensis,* vol. 3 [North America and British Empire 1789–1869] (Freiburg im Breisgau, 1875).

4. Anthony H. Deye, "Archbishop John Baptist Purcell of Cincinnati: Pre-Civil War Years" (Ph.D. diss., University of Notre Dame, 1959), p. 346.

5. Francis P. Kenrick to Peter Kenrick, Baltimore, November 21, 1851 in *The Kenrick-Frenaye Correspondence* (Philadelphia: Wickersham, 1920), p. 328.

6. John B. Purcell to Francis P. Kenrick, Cincinnati, November 20, 1851, Kenrick Papers, AAB.

7. Guilday, *Councils,* p. 180.

8. Peter Kenrick to John Purcell, St. Louis, February 15, 1853, Cincinnati Papers, AUND.

9. Guilday, *Councils,* pp. 207–208.

10. Deye, "Purcell," pp. 228–230, 299–300.

11. The account of the history of Mount St. Mary's of the West is drawn from Michael J. Kelly and James M. Kirwin, *History of Mt. St. Mary's Seminary of the West, Cincinnati, Ohio* (Cincinnati, 1894); Hussey, *History,* pp. 15–25; and Francis J. Miller, "A History of the Athenaeum of Ohio, 1829–1960" (Ed.D. diss., University of Cincinnati, 1964).

12. John Purcell to Joseph Carrière, Cincinnati, April 26, 1850, Angers, March 2, 1851, SAP (copies in SAB); Purcell initially desired three or four priests to start the faculty.

13. Deye, "Purcell," pp. 399–401; Hussey, *History,* p. 18.

14. Kelly and Kirwin, *History,* p. 302.

15. Maurice de St. Palais to Antoine Blanc, Vincennes, April 18, 1859, New Orleans Papers, AUND.

16. Schroeder, *Vincennes,* pp. 199–201 (see above, chap. 2, n.44).

17. Michael J. Hynes, *History of the Diocese of Cleveland, Origin and Growth (1847–1952)* (Cleveland: Diocese of Cleveland, 1953), pp. 95–99.

18. Crews, *Holy Land,* p. 162 (see above, chap. 2, n.4); Benjamin Webb, *The Centenary of Catholicity in Kentucky* (Louisville, 1884), pp. 550–551; the Preston Park Seminary produced forty-seven ordinands by 1881.

19. Sylvester Rosecrans to John Purcell, Columbus, April 22, 30, 1868, August 18, 20, 1870, Cincinnati Papers, AUND; Herman E. Mattingly "Saint Aloysius Seminary, Columbus, Ohio, 1871–1876" *Catholic Record Society* 7 (1981), 1–8.

20. Roger Baudier, *The Catholic Church in Louisiana* (New Orleans: Baudier, 1939), pp. 444–445, 463.

21. Ibid., p. 404.

22. Quoted in John E. Rybolt, "The Carondelet Seminary," *Missouri Historical Quarterly* 74 (1977), 399.

23. Ibid., p. 401.

24. Peter Kenrick to John Purcell, St. Louis, March 27, 1842, Cincinnati Papers, AUND.

25. Pastoral Letter quoted in Rybolt, "Carondelet," p. 408.

26. Ibid., p. 409.

27. John Rothensteiner, *History of the Archdiocese of St. Louis* (St. Louis: Herder, 1928), 2:134.

28. John E. Rybolt, "Saint Vincent's College and Theological Education" (unpublished paper), pp. 7–9, 15–16.

29. Samuel Miller, "Peter Richard Kenrick, Bishop and Archbishop of St. Louis, 1806–1896," *RACHS* 84 (March, June, 1973), 129.

30. Peter Leo Johnson, *John Martin Henni* (Madison: State Historical Society of Wisconsin, 1963), pp. 88–99.

31. The history of the Milwaukee seminary is given in Peter Leo Johnson, *Halcyon Days: Story of St. Francis Seminary, Milwaukee, 1856–1956* (Milwaukee: Bruce, 1956).

32. M. Mileta Ludwig, *Right-Hand Glove Uplifted: A Biography of Archbishop Michael Heiss* (New York: Pageant Press, 1967).

33. For Salzmann's Career, see Joseph Rainer, *A Noble Priest* (Milwaukee, 1903).

34. Johnson, *Halcyon,* pp. 67–68.

35. Ibid., p. 397.

36. Harry C. Koenig, "History of Saint Mary of the Lake Seminary" (unpublished manuscript) and Gleason, "Chicago and Milwaukee," pp. 149–174 (see above, chap. 2, n.55).

37. Scanlan, *St. Joseph's,* p. 23–24.

38. Margaret Carthy, *A Cathedral of Suitable Magnificence: St. Patrick's Cathedral New York* (Wilmington, Del.: Michael Glazier, 1984), p. 45.

39. Quoted in Scanlan, *St. Joseph's,* p. 26.

40. Ibid.

41. John McCloskey to Francis McFarland, New York, August 22, 1864, Hartford Papers, AUND.

42. Scanlan, *St. Joseph's,* p. 33.

43. See chap. 5.

44. Henry G. J. Beck, *The Centennial History of the Immaculate Conception Seminary, Darlington, New Jersey* (Darlington, 1962), p. 5.

45. Szarnicki, "O'Connor," p. 145.

46. M. Cecilia Murphy, "A Reevaluation of the Episcopacy of Michael Domenec, 1860–1877, Second Bishop of Pittsburgh and only Bishop of Allegheny" (Ph.D. diss., St. Louis University, 1974), pp. 307–308.

47. Morris, *Seminary,* pp. 10–11.

48. Amat to Sturchi, Philadelphia, January 10, 1852, General Curia Archives (microfilm), DRMA.

49. Nolan, *Kenrick,* pp. 363–367 (see chap. 2, n.38).

50. Michael J. Curley, *Venerable John Neumann, C.S.S.R., Fourth Bishop of Philadelphia* (Washington, D.C.: Catholic University Press, 1952), pp. 379–380.

51. Alfred C. Rush and Thomas J. Donaghy, "The Saintly John Neumann and His Coadjutor, Archbishop Wood," in James F. Connelly, ed., *History of the Archdiocese of Philadelphia* (Philadelphia, Archdiocese of Philadelphia, 1976), pp. 252–266.

52. Connelly, *St. Charles,* pp. 67–79 (see above, chap. 2, n.38).

53. Ibid., p. 338.

54. [James O'Connor], "Probable Causes of Bp. Wood's dissatisfaction with me," n.d., O'Connor Papers, AAO.

55. Connelly, *St. Charles,* p. 69.

56. Canon Peter Benoit, "Hasty Notes of a Journey to America," pp. 54–55; original copy in the Archives of the Society of St. Joseph, Baltimore. Benoit reported that the original estimate for the seminary's construction was $160,000.

57. Connelly, *St. Charles,* p. 338.

58. David J. Rothmann, *The Discovery of the Asylum: Social Order and Disorder in the New Republic* (Boston: Little, Brown, 1971).

4. SEMINARIES ABROAD

1. Quoted in Guilday, *Carroll,* 1:334.

2. Quoted in ibid., 1:336.

3. *JCP,* 2:249.

4. Guilday, *England,* 1:521–522.

5. Ibid., 2:361.

6. Brief accounts of the origins of All Hallows can be found in Richard J. Purcell, "Missionaries from All Hallows (Dublin) to the United States, 1842–1865," *RACHS* 53 (December 1942), 204–249; and Thomas O'Laughlin, "The Demand

and Supply of Priests to the United States from All Hallows College, Ireland, Between 1842 and 1860," *RACHS* 94 (March-December 1983), 39-60.

7. O'Laughlin, "Demand and Supply," p. 45.

8. Ibid., p. 44.

9. Jeremiah Cummings, "Our Future Clergy;—an Inquiry into Vocations to the Priesthood in the United States," *Brownson's Quarterly Review* (October 1860), p. 506.

10. Lipscomb, "Portier," pp. 210-211 (see above, chap. 2, n.24).

11. Salzbacher, *Reise,* pp. 371-372 (see above, chap. 2, n.56).

12. Willibald Matthäuser, "The Proposed Mission Seminary at Altötting, 1845," *Central Blatt and Social Justice Review* 28 (October 1935-January 1936), 213-215, 250-252, 323-324, 213-215.

13. James Connelly, *The Visit of Archbishop Gaetano Bedini to the United States of America, June, 1853-February, 1854* (Rome: Universita Gregoriana, 1954), pp. 5-15.

14. Quoted in John Peter Marschall, "Francis Patrick Kenrick, 1851-1863: The Baltimore Years" (Ph.D. diss., Catholic University of America, 1965), p. 129; Szarnicki, "O'Connor," pp. 303-306 contains a summary of the Heyden letter to Propaganda.

15. Connelly, *Bedini,* pp. 101-103.

16. Peter Kenrick to Purcell, St. Louis, February 9, 1854, Cincinnati Papers, AUND; quoted in Marschall, "Kenrick," p. 138.

17. Connelly, *Bedini,* p. 244-247.

18. Roger Aubert, *Le Pontificat de Pie IX* (Louvain: Bloud and Gay, 1963), pp. 288-289.

19. Marschall, "Kenrick," pp. 271-272.

20. Quoted in Robert F. McNamara, *The American College in Rome, 1855-1955* (Rochester: Christopher Press, 1956), p. 17.

21. Ibid., p. 17.

22. Ibid., pp. 21-24.

23. Peter Kenrick to John Hughes, St. Louis, January 2, 1856, Hughes Papers (microfilm), ACUA; quoted in McNamara, *College,* p. 25.

24. Blanc to Purcell, New Orleans, February, 15, 1856, Cincinnati Papers, AUND.

25. Quoted in McNamara, *College,* p. 692.

26. McNamara, *College,* p. 32.

27. Quoted in Marschall, *Kenrick,* p. 281.

28. McNamara, *College,* pp. 28-36, 57-61, 63-71.

29. Connelly, *Bedini,* p. 245.

30. Orestes Brownson, "American College at Rome," *Brownson's Quarterly Review,* April 1860, p. 256.

31. John Tracy Ellis, "The Formation of the American Priest: An Historical Perspective," in Ellis, ed., *Catholic Priest in the United States: Historical Investigations* (Collegeville, Minn.: Saint John's University Press, 1971), p. 23.

32. Maisie Ward, *The Wilfrid Wards and the Transition: The Nineteenth Century* (London: Sheed and Ward 1934), 1:66.

33. William Barry, "Roman Memories of 1870," *Dublin Review* 167 (July, August, September 1920), 234, 236.

34. William McCloskey to Francis McFarland, New York, December 2 and 7, 1865, Hartford Papers, AUND.

35. John Hughes to Bernard Smith, New York, December 23, 1858, Hughes Papers (microfilm), ACUA.

36. "Appeal to the More Wealthy among the Catholics of the United States," *Catholic World* 8 (January 1869), 563.

37. Quoted in McNamara, *College,* p. 163; Bayley to Spalding, December 21, 1868, Spalding Papers, AAB.

38. I counted 135 ordinands up to 1880 from "Student Register, North American College, Rome, Italy" (Rochester, 1961) revised and augmented by Robert F. McNamara to supersede the register that appears in [McNamara], *The American College in Rome, 1855–1955.*

39. Franzelin Ponenza, 252 (October 1883), 1086–1088, PFA.

40. For the American bishops' record at the council, see James Hennesey, *First Council of the Vatican: The American Experience* (New York, 1963), pp. 274–282.

41. Gerald Fogarty, *The Vatican and the American Hierarchy from 1870 to 1965* (Wilmington, Del.: Michael Glazier, 1985), pp. 36–37.

42. Quoted in John D. Sauter, *The American College of Louvain (1857–1898)* (Louvain: Publications Universitaires de Louvain, 1959), p. 18.

43. Ibid., p. 19.

44. Ibid., p. 29.

45. Ibid., pp. 31–32, 41–42.

46. Ibid., p. 43.

47. Ibid., p. 195.

48. Ibid., pp. 95–96, 114–119.

49. John M. Lenhart, "The Short-Lived American College at Münster in Westphalia, 1866–85" *Social Justice Review* 35 (1942), 58–60, 94–96, 130–131, 280.

5. RELIGIOUS COMMUNITIES AND DIOCESAN SEMINARIES

1. The following account is drawn from Frederick John Easterly, *The Life of Rt. Rev. Joseph Rosati, C.M., First Bishop of St. Louis (1789–1843)* (Washington: Catholic University of America Press, 1942); also Stafford Poole, "The Vincentian Seminary Apostolate in the United States" (unpublished manuscript); Stafford Poole, "The Founding of Missouri's First College: Saint Mary's of the Barrens, 1815–1818," *Missouri Historical Review* 65 (October 1970), 1–21; and Melville, *DuBourg,* 1:328–366; 2:507–534.

2. Robert F. Trisco, *The Holy See and the Nascent Church in the Middle West, 1826–1850* (Rome: Gregorian University Press, 1962), pp. 290–296.

3. Quoted in John E. Rybolt, "Kenrick's First Seminary" *Missouri Historical Review* 71 (1977), 140.

4. Ibid., pp. 141–151.

5. Rybolt, "Saint Vincent's College," pp. 7–9 (see above, chap. 3, n. 28).

6. Poole, "Apostolate," p. 9ff.

7. Amat to Sturchi, Philadelphia, January 10, 1852, #31, Reel 1, General Curia Archives (microfilm), DRMA.

8. Timon to Marc-Antoine Poussou, Philadelphia, May 28, 1842, #440; Timon to Etienne, Philadelphia, May 30, 1842, #441, Reel 1, General Curia Archives (microfilm), DRMA.

9. Timon to Poussou, St. Louis, July 19, 1842, #444; same to same, July 30, 1842, #446; Timon to Sturchi, New Orleans, December 3, 1843, #462, Reel 1, General Curia Archives (microfilm), DRMA.

10. Timon to Etienne, Philadelphia, June 1, 1844, #473; same to same, St. Louis, November 4, 1845, #489; Timon to Sturchi, St. Louis, November 6, 1845, #490, Reel 1, General Curia Archives, DRMA.

11. *History of the Seminary of Our Lady of Angels, Niagara University, Niagara County, N.Y., 1856–1906* (Buffalo: Matthews-Northrop, 1906), pp. 13–28.

12. Jerome Oetgen, *An American Abbot: Boniface Wimmer, O.S.B., 1809–1887* (Latrobe, Pa.: Archabbey Press, 1976) is the modern biography on which the following account is based.

13. Thomas Franklin O'Meara, *Romantic Idealism and Roman Catholicism: Schelling and the Theologians* (Notre Dame, Ind.: University of Notre Dame Press, 1982).

14. Colman Barry, *Worship and Work: Saint John's Abbey and University, 1856–1980* (Collegeville, Minn.: Liturgical Press, 1980), p. 418; Wimmer's article appears in its entirety in Appendix I, pp. 417–423.

15. Quoted in Felix Fellner, "Abbot Boniface and His Monks," (unpublished manuscript, Archives of St. Vincent's Archabbey, Latrobe, Pa.), p. 63.

16. The following account is based on Barry, *Worship,* pp. 15–99.

17. Anselm Anthony Ober, "An Historical Sketch of the Establishment and Development of St. Vincent Seminary" (B.A. thesis, St. Vincent College, Latrobe, Pa., 1938), pp. 74–76.

18. Ildephonse Wenninger, Isidore Botz, and Innocent Neikirk, "St. John's Seminary," *Scriptorium* 16 (April 1957), 13–35.

19. Albert Kleber, *History of St. Meinrad Archabbey, 1854–1954* (St. Meinrad, Ind.: Grail, 1954), pp. 17–204; the volume brings together much primary material but the author's interpretations are not always well founded.

20. Ibid., p. 31.

21. Joel Rippinger, "Martin Marty: Monk, Abbot, Missionary, and Bishop —I" *American Benedictine Review* 33 (September, 1982), 223–240.

22. Joseph E. Keller, S.J., to James O'Connor, St. Louis, September 24, 1878; Robert J. Fulton, S.J., to O'Connor, New York, June 23, ?; R.W. Brady, S.J., to Joseph Keller, S.J., Baltimore, September 20, 1878, O'Connor Papers, AAO.

23. Simon Barth, "The Franciscans in Southern Illinois," *Illinois Catholic Historical Review* 2 (January 1921), 260–267.

24. Mark V. Angelo, *The History of St. Bonaventure University* (St. Bonaventure, N.Y.: Franciscan Institute, 1961), pp. 1–19, 37–66.

6. FORMATION AND LEARNING

1. John Grassi, "The Catholic Religion in the United States in 1818," in Philip Gleason, ed., *Documentary Reports on Early American Catholicism* (New York: Arno Press, 1978), pp. 238-239.

2. For the development of parish missions and devotional life, see Jay P. Dolan, *Catholic Revivalism: The American Experience, 1830-1900* (Notre Dame, Ind.: University of Notre Dame Press, 1978); Ann Taves, *Household of Faith: Roman Catholic Devotions in Mid-Nineteenth Century America* (Notre Dame, Ind.: University of Notre Dame Press, 1986).

3. John Carroll to John Grassi, November 30, 1813, *JCP,* 3:243-244.

4. Guilday, *England,* 1:511.

5. William J. Barry, "Catholic Education in the United States," *Brownson's Quarterly Review* (Third New York Series) 2 (January 1861), 58.

6. Quoted in Hennesey, "Carroll," *AHP,* 16:184.

7. Guilday, *England,* 2:481.

8. Guilday, *Councils,* p. 90.

9. Quoted in Connelly, *Bedini,* p. 240 (see above chap. 4, n.13).

10. Ibid., p. 241.

11. Barry to Brownson, Mount St. Mary's of the West, April 11, 1861, Brownson Papers, AUND.

12. See n. 3 above.

13. Kenrick to Purcell, August 29, 1830, Mount St. Mary's Papers, AUND.

14. Guilday, *Pastorals,* pp. 39-59 (see above, chap. 2, n.45).

15. Timothy O'Mahony, *Joseph Carrière, St. Sulpice and the Church of France in His Time* (Dublin, 1865), pp. 144-145.

16. "Rules of Conduct," undated, no author but it appears to be in John McCaffrey's handwriting, AMSM.

17. *Directoire des Grands Séminaires confiés aux Prêtres de la Mission* (Paris, 1895).

18. Maller to Etienne, Philadelphia, January 2, 1844, General Curia Archives, DRMA.

19. *Manuele Alumnorum Seminarii Provincialis S. Josephi, Trojae, in Statu Neo-Eboraceno* (Troy, 1871), pp. 13-16, in ADR. An extant antebellum seminary rule is the handwritten "Rules of the St. Louis Theological Seminary," n.d., KSA.

20. J. H. Icard, *Traditions de la Compagnie des Prêtres de Saint-Sulpice* (Paris, 1886), pp. 199-270; the Sulpician daily schedule is taken from Ruane, *Beginning,* pp. 222-224; "Minutes of Visitation" [1829], pp. 50-54, SAB.

21. "Minutes of Visitation," p. 18.

22. "Divers Points," (1850), p. 174, SAB.

23. Connelly, *Bedini,* p. 240.

24. Scanlan, *St. Joseph's,* p. 27 (see above, chap. 2, n. 35).

25. Louis Tronson, *Conferences for Ecclesiastical Students and Religious* (London, 1878); Frederick Oakley, *The Priest on the Mission* (London, 1871).

26. John O'Hanlon, *Life and Scenery in Missouri; Reminiscences of a Missionary Priest* (Dublin, 1890), p. 13, 96.

27. Szarnicki, "O'Connor," pp. 143–145.

28. *Catholic Herald,* October 10, 1833.

29. N. J. O'Brien to John Fitzpatrick, Philadelphia, January 25, 1856, Fitzpatrick Papers, AABo.

30. Kelly and Kirwin, *Mount,* pp. 85, 88, 180.

31. Connelly, *Bedini,* p. 244.

32. Fellner, "Abbot Boniface," p. 164.

33. A discussion of Carroll's ecclesiology can be found in Hennesey, "An Eighteenth-Century Bishop," *AHP* 16:195–200; England's views are in Peter Clarke, *A Free Church in a Free Society: The Ecclesiology of John England, Bishop of Charleston, 1820–1842, a Nineteenth Century Missionary Bishop in the United States* (Hartsville, S.C.: Center for John England Studies, 1982).

34. There are several essays treating the development of Gallicanism in M. Nedoncelle, et al., *L'Ecclésiologie au XIXe Siècle* (Paris: Cerf, 1960), especially Y. Congar, "L'ecclésiologie, de la Révolution française au Concile du Vatican, sous le signe de l'affirmation de l'autorité," and J. Audinet, "L'enseignement 'De Ecclésia' à St. Sulpice sous le Premier Empire et les débuts de gallicanisme modéré."

35. "Louis Deluol," [Notes], n.d., RG 1, Box 13, SAB.

36. Austin Gough, *Paris and Rome: The Gallican Church and the Ultramontane Campaign, 1848–1853* (Oxford: Clarendon Press, 1986), pp. 195–198.

37. "Jean-Baptiste Bouvier," *DTC* (Paris, 1932), vol. 2, pt. 1, pp. 1117–1119; Benoit, "Notes," p. 256 (see above, chap. 3, n.56).

38. Gerald McCool, *Catholic Theology in the Nineteenth Century: The Quest for a Unitary Method* (New York: Seabury, 1977), p. 82.

39. McCaffrey to Purcell, Mount St. Mary's, October 1, 1849, Cincinnati Papers, AUND.

40. Hussey, *History,* p. 21 (see above, chap. 2, n.27); Johnson, *Halcyon Days,* p. 226 (see above, chap. 3, n.31).

41. Joannes Perrone, *Praelectiones Theologicae,* vol. IX: *De Sacramentis in Specie* (Regensburg, 1855), pp. 27, 34, 43.

42. Ibid., pp. 81, 88, 96, 104.

43. Ibid., p. 118.

44. Gerald P. Fogarty, "American Catholic Approaches to the Sacred Scripture," in Minnich, Eno, and Trisco, eds., *Studies,* p. 93 (see above, chap. 2, n.55).

45. Eccleston to McCaffrey, Baltimore, September 3, 1845, AMSM.

46. "St. Alphonsus Liguori," *NCE,* 1:336–341.

47. "Deluol," [Notes], SAB.

48. "Jean Pierre Gury," *DTC,* vol. 6, pt. 2, pp. 1994–1995.

49. Hussey, *History,* p. 21; Johnson, *Halcyon,* p. 226.

50. Joanne Petro Gury, *Compendium Theologiae Moralis* (Regensburg, 1874).

51. Joseph Delfman Brokhage, *Francis Patrick Kenrick's Opinion on Slavery* (Washington, D.C.: Catholic University Press, 1955).

52. See Mary Marcian Lowman, "James Andrew Corcoran: Editor, Theolo-

gian, Scholar (1820–1889)" (Ph.D. diss., St. Louis University, 1958), and Ludwig, *Heiss,* pp. 267–283 (see above, chap. 3, n.32).

53. Johannes Baptist Alzog, *Manual of Universal Church History,* trans. Franz Josef Pabisch and Thomas S. Byrne, 3 vols. (Cincinnati, 1874–1878); Benoit, "Notes," p. 291.

54. Quoted in Columba Halsey, "The Life of Samuel Eccleston, Fifth Archbishop of Baltimore, 1801–1851," *RACHS* 70 (1965), 83.

55. Henry J. Browne, ed., "The Archdiocese of New York a Century Ago: A Memoir of Archbishop Hughes, 1838–1858," *Historical Records and Studies* 49–50 (1950), p. 163.

56. Joseph Michael Connors, "Catholic Homiletic Theory in Historical Perspective" (Ph.D. diss., Northwestern University, 1962), pp. 242–288.

57. "Registre du Résultates Assemblées du Séminaire de Baltimore," October 19–21, 1874, pp. 330–332, SAB.

58. Browne, "Hughes," pp. 162–163.

7. THE THIRD PLENARY COUNCIL OF BALTIMORE

1. Mary Augustine Kwitchen, "Newspaper Comment on the III Plenary Council of Baltimore," *Jurist* 8 (January 1948), 95–104.

2. Gerald P. Fogarty, *The Vatican and the American Hierarchy from 1870 to 1965* (Wilmington, Del.: Michael Glazier, 1985), pp. 27–28.

3. Nelson J. Callahan, *A Case for Due Process in the Church: Father Eugene O'Callaghan, American Pioneer of Dissent* (Staten Island, N.Y.: Society of St. Paul, 1971).

4. *New York Freeman's Journal,* October 3, 1868, p. 4; the history of the priests' rights movement is treated in Robert Trisco, "Bishops and Their Priests in the United States," in John Tracy Ellis, ed., *The Catholic Priest in the United States: Historical Investigations* (Collegeville, Minn.: St. John's University, 1971), pp. 111–292.

5. Curran, *Corrigan,* pp. 1–14. (see above, chap. 1, n.70).

6. Barry, "Education," p. 469 (see above, chap. 6, n.5).

7. Barry to Brownson, Mount St. Mary's of the West, April 11, 1861, Brownson Papers, AUND.

8. Guilday, *Councils,* pp. 207–208.

9. Murtha, "Maréchal," pp. 112–113.

10. John Tracy Ellis, *The Formative Years of the Catholic University of America* (Washington, D.C.: American Catholic Historical Association, 1946), p. 49.

11. Ibid., pp. 54–60; Thomas Joseph Peterman, *The Cutting Edge: The Life of Thomas Andrew Becker* (Devon, Pa.: Wm. T. Cooke Co., 1982), pp. 247–253.

12. Ellis, *Formative,* p. 52.

13. John Lancaster Spalding, *The Life of the Most Rev. M. J. Spalding, D.D.* (New York, 1873), pp. 313–315.

14. David Francis Sweeney, "The Life of John Lancaster Spalding, First

Bishop of Peoria, 1840–1916" (Ph.D. diss., Catholic University of America, 1963), pp. 164–165.

15. Ibid., p. 162; Spalding to Elder, Peoria, August 19, 1880, Elder Papers, AAC.

16. John Lancaster Spalding, *Lectures and Discourses* (New York, 1882), pp. 149, 150–151.

17. Franzelin Ponenza (see above, chap. 4, n.39) 252:1237–1238, PFA.

18. Ibid. 252:1083–1084, 1087–1089, 1091–1092, 1408–1409.

19. Francis P. Cassidy, "Catholic Education in the Third Plenary Council of Baltimore I," *CHR* 35 (October 1948), 266–270; for original minutes of meeting of American bishops with cardinals, see *Relatio collationum quas Romae coram S.C. de P.F. Praefecto habuerunt Archepiscopi pluresque Episcopi Statuum Foederatorum Statuum Americae, 1883* (Baltimore, 1884), AAB; also translated in "Minutes of Roman Meeting Preparatory to the III Plenary Council of Baltimore," *The Jurist* 11 (January 1951), 121–131.

20. Cassidy, "Education," pp. 270–272; for original reports from the provinces, see *Relationes eorum quae disceptata fuerunt ab Illmis ac Revmis Metropolitis cum suis suffraganeis in suis provincis super schema futuri Concilii praesertim vero super capita cuique commissa* (Baltimore, 1884), AAB.

21. Cassidy, "Education," pp. 275–288; original schema in *Schema decretorum concilii plenarii Baltimorensis tertii* (Baltimore, 1884) and the final version is in *Concilii plenarii Baltimorensis III acta et decreta* (Baltimore, 1886).

22. John Lancaster Spalding, *University Education Considered in Its Bearings on the Higher Education of Priests* (Baltimore, 1884), pp. 16, 20, 23, 25.

23. Quoted in Ellis, *Formative,* p. 110.

24. Ibid., p. 110.

25. Guilday, *Councils,* pp. 230–233.

26. Quoted in Guilday, *Pastorals,* pp. 238–239.

8. NEW SEMINARIES

1. Kauffman, *Tradition,* pp. 154–168 (see above, chap. 1, n.7).

2. *Sadlier's Catholic Directory 1879* (New York, 1879), p. 60; *Catholic Directory 1903* (Milwaukee: Wiltzius, 1903), p. 15; St. Mary's Seminary, Baltimore, *List of the Superiors, Professors and Students Ordained* (New York: Encyclopedia Press, 1917).

3. SAB, Dyer Obituary.

4. Sexton and Riley, *St. John's,* pp. 51–75 (see above, chap. 2, n.28).

5. Kauffman, *Tradition,* pp. 168–177.

6. Ibid., pp. 188–192.

7. Scanlan, *St. Joseph's,* pp. 69–91 (see above, chap. 2, n.35).

8. Consultors' Minutes Book, AANY; I thank R. Emmet Curran and Christopher J. Kauffman for lending their copies.

9. See Curran, *Corrigan* for a full exposition of the McGlynn affair.

10. Kauffman, *Tradition,* pp. 200–206.

11. Scanlan, *St. Joseph's,* p. 182.

12. Ibid., pp. 63, 98–116.

13. John Sebastian McDonough, "St. Patrick's Seminary, Menlo Park, California, 1898–1948 with an account of the Earlier Seminaries in California" (unpublished manuscript in SAB), pp. 80–104.

14. James P. Gaffey, *Citizen of No Mean City: Archbishop Patrick Riordan of San Francisco (1841–1914)* (Washington, D.C.: Consortium, 1976), pp. 93–103.

15. McDonough, "St. Patrick's," p. 114.

16. Gaffey, *Riordan,* pp. 247, 252–253.

17. *Official Catholic Directory 1911* (Milwaukee: Wiltzius, 1911), p. 214; McDonough, "St. Patrick's," p. 415.

18. Poole, "Apostolate," p. 36ff.

19. Thomas J. Smith to James Gibbons, Perryville, January 11, 1892, Gibbons Papers, AAB.

20. Magnien to Smith, Baltimore, January 14, 1892, #11, Roll 3, Series B, Curia Correspondence (microfilm), DRMA; Smith to Magnien, Perryville, January 20, 1892, RG 39, Box 1, SAB.

21. A. Smith to Fiat, Perryville, Barrens, January 8, 1894, #372; same to same, #373, February 21, 1894; O'Callaghan to Fiat, Barrens, November 6, 1894, #378; Barnwell to Fiat, Barrens, March 23, 1897, #403; Smith to Fiat, Barrens, February 23, 1898, #417; Barnwell to Fiat, Barrens, June 24, 1898, #421; Roll 2, Series A, Curia Correspondence (microfilm), DRMA.

22. *Official Catholic Directory 1911,* p. 189.

23. Poole, "Apostolate," pp. 43–47.

24. Michael Cantley, *A City with Foundations: A History of the Seminary of the Immaculate Conception, 1930–1980* (privately printed, 1980), pp. 30–31.

25. Patrick H. Ahern, "A History of the Saint Paul Seminary," [1945], (unpublished manuscript in the Catholic Historical Society of St. Paul collections in John Ireland Library, St. Paul Seminary), pp. 1–8; for the early development of St. Thomas Seminary, see Joseph B. Connors, *Journey Toward Fulfillment: A History of the College of St. Thomas* (St. Paul: College of St. Thomas, 1986).

26. Albro Martin, *James J. Hill and the Opening of the Northwest* (New York: Oxford University Press, 1976), pp. 452–453.

27. *St. Paul Seminary Register, 1896* (St. Paul, 1896), p. 57.

28. Ahern, "Seminary," p. 40.

29. Pastoral Letter, August 21, 1881, ADR.

30. Bernard McQuaid, "Our American Seminaries," *AER* 6 (May 1897), 464.

31. Frederick J. Zwierlein, *The Life and Letters of Bishop McQuaid* (Louvain, 1927), 3:390–461 contains account of the founding of St. Bernard's Seminary; see also Robert F. McNamara, "St. Bernard's Seminary, 1893–1968," *The Sheaf* 15 (1968), 3–76.

32. Zwierlein, *McQuaid,* 3:390–461.

33. McQuaid to Smith, Rochester, July 10, 1896, John Talbot Smith Papers, ACUA.

34. Zwierlein, *McQuaid,* 3:441.

35. *Official Catholic Directory 1911,* p. 604.

36. Leo Miller, "Soldier and Immigrant (1836–1870)," and Joseph C. Plumpe, "Pomeroy," both in Leo Miller, et al., *Monsignor Joseph Jessing (1836–1899)* (Columbus: Carroll Press, 1936), pp. 3–178.

37. Colman J. Barry, *Catholic Church and German Americans* (Milwaukee: Bruce, 1953).

38. George J. Undreiner, "The Pontifical College Josephinum" in Miller et al., *Jessing,* pp. 291–340.

39. The account of the Polish seminary is drawn from Joseph Swastek, *The Formative Years of the Polish Seminary in the United States* (Orchard Lake, Mich.: Center for Polish Studies and Culture, 1985) which originally appeared in *Sacrum Poloniae Millenium,* vol. VI (Rome, 1959); and Frank Renkiewicz, *For God, Country, and Polonia: One Hundred Years of the Orchard Lake Schools* (Orchard Lake, Mich.: Center for Polish Studies and Culture, 1985).

40. Renkiewicz, *Orchard Lake Schools,* p. 35.

41. Ibid.

42. For Kolasinski's activities, see Lawrence D. Orton, *Polish Detroit and the Kolasinski Affair* (Detroit: Wayne State University Press, 1981).

43. Hussey, *Cincinnati,* pp. 25–30.

44. Johnson, *Halcyon,* pp. 90–91.

45. Joseph F. Martino, "A Study of Certain Aspects of the Episcopate of Patrick J. Ryan, Archbishop of Philadelphia, 1884–1911" (H.E.D., diss., Pontifical Gregorian University, 1983), pp. 312–315.

46. Meline and McSweeney, *Mountain,* 2:210 (see above, chap. 1, n.15).

47. Lawrence J. McCrank, *Mt. Angel Abbey: A Centennial History of the Benedictine Community and its Library* (Wilmington, Del.: Scholarly Resources, 1983), pp. 46–47, 60–61.

48. Paschal Baumstein, *My Lord of Belmont: A Biography of Leo Haid* (Belmont, N.C.: Herald Press, 1985), p. 85.

49. Robert James Wister, *The Establishment of the Apostolic Delegation in the United States of America: The Satolli Mission, 1892–1896* (Rome: Pontificia Universitas Gregoriana, 1981), p. 298.

50. See James Hitchcock, "Secular Clergy in Nineteenth Century America: A Diocesan Profile," RACHS 88 (March–December 1977), 31–62 (on St. Louis priests); Daniel P. O'Neill, "The Development of an American Priesthood: Archbishop John Ireland and the Saint Paul Diocesan Clergy, 1884–1918," *Journal of American Ethnic History* 4 (Spring 1985), 33–52; and for the role of a freestanding minor seminary in developing an American-born clergy, see Dolores Ann Liptak, *European Immigrants and the Catholic Church in Connecticut, 1870–1920* (New York: Center for Migration Studies, 1987), pp. 60–83.

51. *Sadlier's Catholic Directory . . . 1884* (New York, 1884), p. 506; *Official Catholic Directory and Clergy List . . . 1910* (Milwaukee: Wiltzius, 1910), p. 1025.

9. CATHOLIC UNIVERSITY

1. John J. Keane, "The Catholic Universities of France," *Catholic World* 47 (June 1888), 293.

2. For the expansion of American graduate training, see Laurence R. Veysey, *The Emergence of the Modern University* (Chicago: University of Chicago Press, 1965).

3. Ellis, *Formative,* pp. 147–174; Ellis relies on John Keane's handwritten "Chronicles of the Catholic University of America from 1885" in ACUA.

4. Patrick H. Ahern, *The Life of John J. Keane, Educator and Archbishop* (Milwaukee: Bruce, 1955).

5. Fogarty, *Vatican,* p. 42; Ellis, *Formative,* pp. 224–226.

6. Ellis, *Formative,* p. 226.

7. Curran, *Corrigan,* p. 166.

8. "University Education" in John Lancaster Spalding, *Education and the Higher Life* (Chicago, 1890), pp. 176, 178.

9. Ibid., pp. 196, 197.

10. Sweeney, "Spalding," pp. 247–248; Spalding did not keep personal papers, so it is not clear how much Roman reaction to his address came to his attention.

11. "The General Constitution of the Catholic University of America" in *Constitutions of the Catholic University of America* (Washington, D.C.: Catholic University of America, n.d.), pp. 5–8.

12. Ellis, *Formative,* pp. 336–338; "Special Constitutions of the School of Sacred Science in the Catholic University of America" in *Constitutions,* pp. 13–19.

13. Ellis, *Formative,* p. 321.

14. "Apostolic Letter of His Holiness Pope Leo XIII to Most Eminent and Most Reverend James Cardinal Gibbons" in *Constitutions,* pp. 3–4.

15. Sweeney, "Spalding," pp. 248–249 (see above, chap. 7, n.14).

16. Ellis, *Formative,* pp. 384–385; *Solemnities of the Dedication and Opening of the Catholic University of America, November 13, 1889, Official Report* (Baltimore, 1890), p. 75.

17. John Belford to Alphonse Magnien, Brooklyn, November 7, [1891], RG 6, Box 3, SAB.

18. Patrick H. Ahern, *The Catholic University of America, 1887–1896: The Rectorship of John J. Keane* (Washington, D.C.: Catholic University of America Press, 1948), p. 40.

19. Ireland to Keane, St. Paul, April 26, 1892, Rector's Office Correspondence—Hierarchy, Box 4, 1887–1896, ACUA.

20. Ahern, *Rectorship,* pp. 49, 57.

21. Ibid., p. 49.

22. *Third Annual Report of the Rector of the Catholic University of America, April 1892* (Washington, 1892), pp. 4–5.

23. Henri Hyvernat, "A Memoir on the Catholic University of America submitted to His Excellency the Most Reverend John Bonzano, Archbishop of Meli-

tene, Apostolic Delegate to the United States of America" [1922], p. 22, Hyvernat Papers, ACUA.

24. Ibid., p. 22.

25. Ibid., p. 24.

26. Ibid., p. 26.

27. Daniel F. Reilly, *The School Controversy, 1891–1893* (Washington, D.C.: Catholic University Press, 1943); Timothy H. Morrissey, "Archbishop John Ireland and the Faribault-Stillwater School Plan of the 1890's: A Reappraisal," (Ph.D. diss., University of Notre Dame, 1975).

28. Fogarty, *Vatican,* pp. 77–83.

29. Maurice Francis Egan, *Recollections of a Happy Life* (New York: George Doran, 1924), p. 189.

30. Gerald P. Fogarty, "The Quest for a Catholic Vernacular Bible in America," in Nathan O. Hatch and Mark Noll, eds., *The Bible in America: Essays in Cultural History* (New York: Oxford University Press, 1982), p. 173.

31. Fogarty, *Vatican,* p. 141.

32. Ahern, *Rectorship,* pp. 162–163.

33. Peter E. Hogan, *The Catholic University of America, 1896–1903: The Rectorship of Thomas J. Conaty* (Washington, D.C.: Catholic University of America Press, 1949), pp. 13–23; during his years at Worcester, Conaty became acquainted with G. Stanley Hall, founding president of Clark University.

34. Ibid., pp. 153–156.

35. Ibid., p. 66.

36. "Educational Conference of Seminary Presidents," *CUB* 4 (July 1898), 397–405.

37. Ibid., p. 400; John B. Hogan, "Seminary and University Studies," *AER* 19 (October 1898), 361–370.

38. Edgar P. McCarren, "The Origin and Early Years of the National Catholic Educational Association" (Ph.D. diss., Catholic University of America, 1966); James Howard Plough, "Catholic Colleges and the Catholic Educational Association: Foundation and Early Years of the C.E.A., 1899–1919" (Ph.D. diss., University of Notre Dame, 1971).

39. Colman Barry, *The Catholic University of America, 1903–1909: The Rectorship of Denis J. O'Connell* (Washington, D.C.: Catholic University of America Press, 1950), pp. 71–108.

40. "Pro Memoria, To the Most Eminent Cardinal Gibbons and the Most Reverend Trustees of the Catholic University of America" (translation) [1904], Gibbons Papers, AAB.

41. Barry, *O'Connell,* pp. 265–266.

42. Hyvernat, "Memoir," p. 44.

43. "Sacra Facultas Theologiae" (list of S.T.D. recipients), Rector's Files, 1913–1969, II General Administration: Sacred Congregation of Seminaries and Universities, ACUA.

44. Shaughnessy, *Immigrant,* p. 262 (see above, chap. 2, n.1).

45. Hyvernat, "Memoir," p. 21.

46. "North American College — Rome (1859–1909) Historical Chart I" and "Historical Chart II," Gibbons Papers, AAB.

47. Herman Heuser, "Education in Our Seminaries," *AER* 23 (September 1900), 226.

48. Camillus Maes, "The Catholic University of America," *AER* 29 (December 1903), 574–575.

49. John Farley to Philip Garrigan, New York, March 28, 1895, Rector's Office Correspondence, Box 3, ACUA.

50. John B. Hogan, *Clerical Studies* (Boston, 1898), p. 126.

51. Camillus Maes to John Keane, Covington, Kentucky, October 15, 1891, Rector's Office Correspondence — Hierarchy, Box 4, ACUA.

52. Patrick J. McCormick to Dear Bishop, Dunwoodie, April 16, 1904, McCormick Papers, Box 5, ACUA.

10. MODEL PRIEST AND MODEL SEMINARY

1. James O'Connor to James Gibbons, Omaha, November 10, 1886, Gibbons Papers, AAB.

2. [Herman Heuser], "Literature and the Clergy," *AER* 1 (January 1889), 15. *American Newspaper Annual* (Philadelphia: N. W. Ayer, 1906), p. 771, reported the *Review*'s circulation as 15,000 in 1906.

3. Kauffman, *Tradition*, p. 211; *Newspaper Annual* (1906), p. 608, reported *Homiletic's* circulation at 20,000 in 1906; the monthly is the predecessor of the current *Homiletic and Pastoral Review.*

4. James Gibbons, *Ambassador of Christ* (Baltimore: John Murphy, 1896), p. 136.

5. Ibid., p. 56.

6. Ibid., p. 169.

7. Ibid., pp. 249, 262.

8. Ibid., p. 285.

9. John Hogan Diary, November 19, 1884, SAB.

10. Quoted in Walter Elliot, *Life of Father Hecker* (New York: Columbia Press, 1891), pp. xvii, ix–xi.

11. John F. Duggan, ed., "The Education of a Priest. Archbishop Ireland's Talks to Seminarians. I. The Priest as Gentleman," *AER* 101 (October 1939), 295, 298.

12. John F. Duggan, ed., "The Education of a Priest. Archbishop Ireland's Talks to Seminarians. II. The Priest as Scholar," *AER* 101 (November 1939), 387, 388.

13. "Pastoral Letter," St. Bernard's Day, 1899, McQuaid Papers, ADR.

14. "Pastoral Letter," August 20, 1892, McQuaid Papers, ADR.

15. McQuaid, "Seminarians," *AER* 6:471.

16. Sauter, *Louvain*, pp. 184–186 (see above, chap. 4, n.42).

17. William Stang, *Pastoral Theology* (New York: Benziger, 1896), p. 32.

18. Ibid., pp. 35–42.

19. Ibid., p. 68.

20. "Rev. Frederick Schulze," *Salesianum* 26 (January 1931), 82–84.

21. Camillus Maes, "Preparatory Seminaries for Clerical Students," *AER* 14 (April 1896), 316–317.

22. Camillus Maes, "The Theological Seminary," *AER* 14 (May 1896), 437–438.

23. Ibid., 435.

24. Frances Panchok, "The Catholic Church and the Theatre in New York, 1890–1920" (Ph.D. diss., Catholic University of America, 1976), pp. 441–446.

25. John Talbot Smith, *Our Seminaries: An Essay in Clerical Training* (New York: William H. Young, 1896), p. 4.

26. Ibid., pp. 13, 14.

27. Ibid., pp. 17–18.

28. Ibid., p. 19.

29. Ibid., pp. 20–21.

30. Ibid., p. 22.

31. McQuaid to Smith, Rochester, July 10, 1896; Patrick Heffron to Smith, St. Paul, January 16, 1897, John Talbot Smith Papers, ACUA.

32. Henry Edward Manning, *The Eternal Priesthood* (New York, 1884).

33. *Kenrick Seminary Calendar, 1896–1897,* p. 20, Kenrick Seminary Library.

34. "St. Mary's Faculty Minutes," Visitation of June 25 and 26, 1886, p. 19, SAB.

35. Based on published seminary histories, the seminaries of New York, Philadelphia, Milwaukee, Baltimore, San Francisco, and Rochester had sisters as domestics during this period. Most of these were from a local sisterhood. The Benedictine seminaries had the services of lay brothers for domestic service. The practice of hiring sisters would increase in the twentieth century.

36. *Prospectus of St. Bernard Seminary, Rochester, New York, for the Scholastic Year 1902–1903,* p. 31, ADR.

37. "Faculty Minutes of St. Joseph Seminary, (copy) p. 31, SAB; original in the Academic Dean's Office, St. Joseph Seminary, Yonkers, New York.

38. Edward McSweeney, "Apologia pro Foedere Abstinentiae," *AER* 30 (March 1904), 248–249.

39. Joan Bland, *Hibernian Crusade: The Story of the Catholic Total Abstinence Union of America* (Washington, D.C.: Catholic University of America Press, 1951), p. 230.

40. McQuaid, "Seminaries," *AER* 6:472.

41. Smith, *Seminaries,* pp. 168–169.

42. Ibid., p. 188.

43. Ibid., pp. 189–190.

44. Stang, *Pastoral,* p. 332.

45. Francis V. Nugent to Antoine Fiat, St. Louis, December 13, 1900, General Curia Correspondence, DRMA.

46. John Hogan, *Daily Thoughts for Priests* (Boston, 1899).

47. English translations of Pope Leo's encyclicals are available in Claudia Carlen, ed., *Papal Encyclicals, 1878–1903* (Wilmington, N.C.: McGrath, 1981).

48. "St. John's Seminary Minutes Book" (copy), p. 21, SAB; original in AABo.

49. Ibid., p. 73.

50. "Faculty Minutes of St. Joseph Seminary," p. 56, SAB.

51. *St. Paul Seminary Register 1901,* p. 31, John Ireland Library, St. Paul Seminary.

52. Hubert Jedin and John Dolan, eds., *The History of the Church,* vol. 9: *The Church in the Industrial Age,* (New York: Crossroads, 1980), pp. 257–269.

53. William G. Cluse, "The Nature and Aim of the Priests' Eucharistic League," and Fintan [Mundwiler], "History and Present Status of the Eucharistic League in the United States," *AER* 11 (November 1894), 321–329. The November 1894 issue of *AER* was devoted to articles related to the League's activities.

54. The official quarterly journal of the Priests' Eucharistic League in the United States, *Emmanuel,* starting in 1895 published accounts of conventions and conferences around the country and membership lists.

55. Joseph H. Chinnici, *Devotion to the Holy Spirit in the United States* (New York: Paulist Press, 1985), pp. 17–34.

56. Quoted in Joseph C. Fenton, "Devotion to the Holy Ghost and Its American Advocates," *AER* 121 (December 1949), 486.

57. Otto Zardetti, *Special Devotion to the Holy Ghost; A Manual for the Use of Seminarians, Priests, Religious and the Christian People* (Milwaukee, 1888) explains the devotion and contains the relevant prayers and exercises.

58. Chinnici, *Devotion,* pp. 57–63.

59. "St. John's Seminary Minutes Book," p. 73, SAB.

60. "St. Mary's Seminary Minutes Book," p. 154, SAB.

61. "Observations relating to the Condition and Results of Seminary Training in the United States," c. 1899 (attributed to Francis P. Havey), pp. 20–21, SAP.

62. Quoted in Gibbons, *Ambassador,* pp. 53–54.

63. McQuaid, "Seminaries," *AER* 6:473.

64. "St. Mary's Seminary Minutes Book," Visitation of June 25 and 26, 1886, p. 3, SAB.

65. McQuaid, "Seminaries," *AER* 6:465.

66. Smith, *Seminaries,* p. 62.

67. Patrick Danehy, "The New Seminary of St. Paul," *CUB* 1 (April 1895), 219.

68. "Pastoral Letter," August 20, 1891, McQuaid Papers, ADR; McQuaid also encouraged baseball playing.

69. Smith, *Seminaries,* p. 74.

70. Rex to Dyer, Boston, December 24, 1892; RG 10, Box 23, SAB.

71. Richard Wakeham to Dyer, Boston, March 4, 1894, RG 10, Box 22, SAB.

72. Smith, *Seminaries,* p. 143.

73. Rex to Dyer, Boston, October 5, 1892, RG 10, Box 22, SAB.

74. Wakeham to Dyer, Boston, March 4, 1894, RG 10, Box 22, SAB.

75. McQuaid, "Seminaries," *AER* 6:477.

76. Anthony Vieban, "Charitable Work of Seminarians as a Preparation

for the Work of the Ministry," in Catholic Educational Association, *Report of the Proceedings and Addresses of the Second Annual Meeting,* (1905), 249–263.

77. Daniel T. McColgan, *A Century of Charity: The First One Hundred Years of the Society of St. Vincent de Paul in the United States,* vol. 2 (Milwaukee: Bruce, 1951), pp. 213–217, 247–249.

78. Fogarty, *Vatican,* p. 152.

79. John Tracy Ellis, ed., *Documents of American Catholic History,* vol. 2 (Chicago: Henry Regnery, 1967), p. 539.

80. Thomas T. McAvoy, *The Great Crisis in American Catholic History: 1895–1900* (Chicago: Henry Regnery, 1957), pp. 327–343.

81. Smith, *Seminaries,* p. 167.

82. Quoted in Elliot, *Hecker,* p. xiii (see above, n. 10).

83. Diary, July 5, 1908, Peter Guilday Papers, ACUA. Guilday led a committee to protest the retreat master's remarks to the rector but did not record the outcome of the protest.

84. Timothy Holland to James Driscoll, January 6, 1904, RG 10, Box 7, SAB.

85. Dyer to Rex, Baltimore, May 5, 1892, RG 4, Box 36, SAB.

86. Rex to Dyer, Colorado Springs, April 18, 1896, RG 10, Box 23, SAB.

87. "Observations" (Havey), p. 6, SAP.

88. Pierre Veuillot, ed., *The Catholic Priesthood According to the Teaching of the Church: Papal Documents from Pius X to Pius XII* (Westminster, Md.: Newman Press, 1958), p. 59.

11. CLERICAL LEARNING

1. *Catholic Mirror* (Baltimore), July 18, 1885; Michael Heiss to Gibbons, Milwaukee, April 29, 1886, Gibbons Papers, AAB.

2. *A plan of studies for the direction of those Institutions which educate youth for the Priesthood* (Baltimore, 1886), p. 13; the numbers on the table presumably refer to class hours per week.

3. Hogan, *Clerical,* p. iii (see above, chap. 9, n.50).

4. Ibid., p. 369.

5. Ibid., p. 374.

6. Ibid., pp. 5, 9.

7. Ibid., pp. 44–45.

8. Ibid., pp. 70–71, 77–78.

9. Ibid., p. 98.

10. Ibid., pp. 173–174.

11. Ibid., pp. 175–177.

12. Ibid., p. 179.

13. Ibid., p. 192.

14. Ibid., p. 374.

15. Ibid., p. 387.

16. Ibid., p. 430.

17. Ibid., p. 442.

18. Ibid., p. 354.

19. Ibid., p. 317.

20. Smith, *Seminaries,* p. 266 (see above, chap. 10, n.25).

21. Ibid., p. 268.

22. Ibid., p. 270.

23. Ibid., p. 271.

24. Ibid., p. 273.

25. Ibid., p. 274.

26. "Archbishop Ireland's Address" in *St. Paul Seminary Register 1896* (St. Paul, 1896), p. 49.

27. John Hogan Diary, November 20, 1884, SAB.

28. Rex to Dyer, Brighton, February 25, 1892, RG 10, Box 23; Hogan to Rex, Washington, October 20, [1892], RG 4, Box 36, SAB.

29. The data on length of courses and course offerings becomes more accessible in the 1890s with the appearance of printed catalogs. St. Mary's at Baltimore began to issue annual catalogs from 1894, as did St. Paul Seminary from 1895 and Kenrick from 1893. Rochester issued "prospectuses" in 1902 and 1908. New York had one "souvenir" of the seminary with course offerings in 1899. St. Meinrad had a catalog from the 1870s. The other Benedictine seminaries, Mount St. Mary's at Emmitsburg, and Our Lady of the Angels had short sections on the seminary within the catalog of their affiliated lay colleges since the 1870s. Philadelphia, Boston, and Cincinnati had no printed catalogs.

30. Barry, *Worship,* p. 181 (see above, chap. 5, n.14); Johnson, *Halcyon,* p. 227.

31. *Catalogue of St. Mary's Seminary, Baltimore, Maryland, 1894–1895,* pp. 20–21, SAB.

32. Ibid., p. 25.

33. See Spalding's remarks in chapter 8 above.

34. Herman Heuser, "The Course of Dogma in Our Seminaries," *AER* 19 (September 1898), 225–232.

35. Charles Rex to Edward Dyer, Boston, December 30, 1888, RG 10, Box 23, SAB.

36. Archbishop Austin Dowling of St. Paul, quoted in *A Garland of Affectionate Tributes to the Memory of the Very Rev. John Baptist Hogan, D.D., S.S.* (Boston, 1906), p. 33.

37. "Augustin Lehmkuhl," *DTC,* vol. 9, pt. 1, 172–173; "Anthony Konings," *Catholic Encyclopedia,* vol. 8, 689–690; "Aloyse Sabetti," *DTC,* vol. 14, pt. 1, 438.

38. "Hugues de Hurter," *DTC,* vol. 7, pt. 1, 332–333.

39. Anthony Vieban, "Father Tanquerey," *Voice* (1928); Obituary File, Adolphe Tanquerey, SAB. Tanquerey had a particular sensitivity to adapting to the Irish characteristics of his students at Baltimore. Though the term manic-depressive was unknown to him, Tanquerey noted this type of behavior in his students in a lengthy untitled report on American seminaries in SAP (copy at SAB), "USA Visits and Reports," no date.

40. Jodok Birkhaeuser, *History of the Church from Its First Institution* (New York, 1884).

41. Heinrich Brück, *History of the Catholic Church for Use in Seminaries and Colleges,* trans. by E. Pruent (New York, 1887).

42. See Carlen, *Encyclicals,* vol. 4 (see above, chap. 10, n.47).

43. Francis Gigot, *General Introduction to the Study of the Holy Scripture* (New York: Benziger, 1900), p. 5.

44. Micheal DeVito, *The New York Review (1905-1908)* (New York: United States Catholic Historical Society, 1977), pp. 25-37.

45. There is no available biographical sketch of Souvay, but his lengthy and frequent letters to Superior General Antoine Fiat can be found in General Curia Archives (microfilm), DRMA. These letters reveal his academic interests and censorious disposition.

46. Herman Heuser, "The Study of the Bible in Our Theological Seminaries," *AER* 31 (August 1904), 113-120.

47. James F. Driscoll, "The Study of Scripture in the Seminary," Catholic Educational Association, *Report of the Proceedings and Addresses of the Second Annual Meeting* (1905), 221-229; Francis E. Gigot, "The Study of Sacred Scripture in Theological Seminaries" *AER* 23 (September 1900), 227-235.

48. Ibid., p. 233.

49. *St. Bernard's Prospectus 1902*, p. 31.

50. Connors, "Homiletic," pp. 290-295 (see above, chap. 6, n.56).

51. Johnson, *Halcyon,* pp. 156-174; "Catholic University Literary Society Minutes, Organized 1889" (1889-1897), ACUA.

52. Innocenz Wapelhorst, *Sacrae Liturgiae Compendium* (New York, 1887).

53. Edward A. Dyer, "Organization of Classes and Studies in the Seminary" *AER* 23 (October 1900), 338.

54. "Voyage de Son Eminence le Cardinal Fr. Satolli, Pro-Délégué apostolique aux Etats-Unis (Am. du Nord) du 12 Fevrier au 13 Mars 1896," pp. 62-64; Original in the Archives of the Collegio Sant Anselmo, Rome. I thank Robert J. Wister for the use of his photocopy of Satolli's memoir.

55. "Observations" (Havey), p. 22, SAP.

56. St. Mary's Minutes Book, Visitation, 1904, SAB.

57. *St. Mary's Catalogue 1894-1895*, p. 30.

58. Hogan, *Conaty,* p. 66 (see above, chap. 9, n.33).

59. Wister, *Satolli,* p. 298; PFA, NS, Rubric 9, 1895, vol. 55, p. 200. Hogan to Ledochowski, February 26, 1895; I thank Christopher J. Kauffman for securing a copy of this at the Archives of Propaganda Fide; the Ledochowski letter addressed to Satolli rejecting the petition for degrees was handcopied in Alexis Orban to Charles Rex, Washington, September 12, 1895, RG 4, Box 36, SAB. Orban was librarian of the Catholic University.

60. Hogan, *Conaty,* pp. 65-66.

61. Zwierlein, *McQuaid,* 3:449-454 (see above, chap. 8, n.31).

62. Kauffman, *Tradition,* pp. 203, 210.

63. Oetgen, *Wimmer,* pp. 283-284.

64. Poole, "Vincentian," p. 33; Smith to Fiat, Barrens, July 26, 1897, #410, Roll 2, General Curia Archives (microfilm edition), DRMA.

65. Fogarty, *Vatican,* p. 191; English texts of the several decrees are in *Rome*

and the Study of Scripture (St. Meinrad, Ind.: Grail Publications, 1958), pp. 36–39; 117ff.

66. "Rapport de la Commission des Études, Lu et Approuvé dans l'Assemblée Generale de juillet 1901," pp. 1–6, SAB.

67. Kauffman, *Tradition,* pp. 207–208.

68. Ibid., pp. 212–214.

69. R. Scott Appleby, "American Catholic Modernism at the Turn of the Century" (Ph.D. diss., University of Chicago, 1985), pp. 237ff.

70. Kauffman, *Tradition,* pp. 217–220.

71. Veuillot, *Documents,* 46–47, 49.

72. DeVito, *Review,* pp. 248–296, 299.

73. Fogarty, *Vatican,* p. 261–263.

74. Kauffman, *Tradition,* pp. 230–231.

75. Ibid., pp. 231–234.

76. Ibid., pp. 235–237.

77. Veuillot, *Documents,* pp. 81–82.

78. "Annual Meeting of the Archbishops of the U.S." (Minutes), April 26, 1906, April 10, 1907, and May 8, 1908; Gibbons to Cardinal Prefect of the Propaganda, May 31, 1907, AAB. Gotti's original letter to Gibbons could not be located.

12. THE ROMAN WAY

1. John F. Broderick, S.J., ed., *Documents of Vatican Council I, 1869–1870* (Collegeville, Minn.: Liturgical Press, 1971), p. 58.

2. Frederick Dwight Sackett, *The Spiritual Director in an Ecclesiastical Seminary* (Ottawa: University of Ottawa, 1945), pp. 60–61.

3. Joseph Godfrey Cox, *The Administration of Seminaries: Historical Synopsis and Commentary* (Washington, D.C.: Catholic University of America Press, 1931), pp. 48–72.

4. Hubert Jedin, Konrad Repgen, and John Dolan, eds., *History of the Church,* vol. 10: *The Church in the Modern Age* (New York: Crossroads, 1981), p. 151.

5. *AAS* 7 (1915), 493–495.

6. Veuillot, ed., *Documents,* 1:94–101.

7. T. Lincoln Bouscaren, S.J., and Adam C. Ellis, S.J., *Canon Law: A Text and Commentary* (Milwaukee: Bruce Publishing Co., 1951), pp. 756–760; Cox, *Administration,* pp. 48–72.

8. Sackett, *Director,* pp. 121–135; Casimir M. Peterson, *Spiritual Care in Diocesan Seminaries: A Historical Synopsis and a Commentary* (Washington, D.C.: Catholic University of America, 1966), pp. 117–119.

9. Philip Eugene Kendall, *Intellectual Formation in the Major Seminary Curriculum: Principles and Considerations, A Canonical-Historical Study* (Ph.D. diss., Catholic University of America, 1971), pp. 426–430.

10. *AAS* 9 (1917), 439.

11. Ibid., 305–317; Veuillot, ed., *Documents,* 1:107–108.

12. *AAS* 12 (1920), 385–422; Veuillot, ed., *Documents,* 1:137–144.

13. Philip Hughes, *Pope Pius the Eleventh* (London: Sheed & Ward, 1938).

14. *AAS* 14 (1922), 449.

15. Veuillot, ed., *Documents,* 1:151–155.

16. *AAS* 15 (1923), 309–356.

17. *AAS* 16 (1924), 180–182.

18. *AAS* 18 (1926), 453–455.

19. *AAS* 22 (1930), 146–148.

20. *AAS* 17, (1924), 547–548.

21. Pietro Fumasoni-Biondi, "Copy of Letter Addressed to All the Ordinaries of the United States by Order of the Sacred Congregation for Seminaries and Universities," *AER* 79 (1928), 76.

22. Ibid., 80.

23. Robert E. Sullivan, "Beneficial Relations: Toward a Social History of the Diocesan Priests of Boston, 1875–1944" in Robert E. Sullivan and James M. O'Toole, eds., *Catholic Boston: Studies in Religion and Community, 1870–1970* (Boston: Roman Catholic Archbishop of Boston, 1985), p. 210; John T. McNicholas to Amleto Cicognani, Cincinnati, [November 1935], McNicholas Papers, AAC. McNicholas reported that at the trustees' meeting of Catholic University on November 12, 1935, O'Connell denounced Ruffini by name for the second time at a trustees' meeting.

24. Fumasoni-Biondi to Curley, Washington, June 1, 1928; Curley to Fumasoni-Biondi, Baltimore, June 13, 1928; Curley to Msgr. B. J. Bradley, Baltimore, December 11, 1928, Curley Papers, AAB.

25. *AAS* 14 (1922), 673–700; 17 (1925), 593–610.

26. *AAS* 20 (1928), 165–178.

27. *AAS* 24 (1932), 177–198.

28. *AAS* 23 (1931), 493–517.

29. *AAS* 29 (1937), 373–380.

30. *AAS* 17 (1925), 223–225; Veuillot, ed., *Documents,* 1:167–168.

31. *AAS* 21 (1929), 689–706.

32. *AAS* 23 (1931), 120–129. Thomas Raphael Gallagher, O.P., *The Examination of the Qualities of the Ordinand: An Historical Synopsis and Commentary* (Washington, D.C.: Catholic University Press, 1944), pp. 62–79, contains an extended discussion of the decree.

33. Pietro Fumasoni-Biondi to "Your Excellency," Washington, July 14, 1931, Roman Documents File, AAB.

34. Domenico Jorio, "A Confidential Instruction to the Most Excellent and Most Reverend Archbishops, Bishops, Local Ordinaries and to the Major Superiors of Orders, etc." December 8, 1938, SAB.

35. *AAS* 23 (1931), 263–280; James J. Markham, *The Sacred Congregation of Seminaries and Universities of Studies* (Washington, D.C.: Catholic University of America, 1957), pp. 47–101 contains an extended exposition of the provisions of the apostolic constitution.

36. McNamara, *St. Bernard's,* pp. 34–35.

37. [Curley to Bisleti], Baltimore, April 30, 1925, Roman Documents File, AAB.

38. Curley to Bisleti, Baltimore, October 24, 1932, RG 26, Box 14, SAB.

39. Bisleti to Curley, Rome, May 6, 1933; Curley to Bisleti, Baltimore, November 6, 1933, Curley Papers, AAB.

40. Cicognani to Curley, Washington, March 13, 1934, RG 13, Box 1; John Fenlon to Curley, Baltimore, March 23, 1934, RG 13, Box 14, SAB.

41. *AAS* 28 (1936), 6–53; Veuillot, ed., *Documents,* pp. 198–246.

42. Cicognani to "Your Excellency," Washington, February 12, 1936, Curley Papers, AAB.

43. Ibid.

44. Cicognani to "Your Excellency," Washington, August 20, 1938, Curley Papers, AAB; Cicognani does not list the names of the associate visitators. It appears that among them were bishops John Peterson of Manchester, Samuel Stritch of Milwaukee, Francis Beckman of Dubuque, Edward Mooney of Detroit, Aloysius Muench of Fargo, and Thomas O'Gorman of Reno. Peterson, Beckman, and Muench had been seminary rectors at Boston, Cincinnati, and Milwaukee respectively.

45. Fenlon to Pierre Boisard, Baltimore, October 6, 1938, RG 13, Box 1a, SAB; Boisard was then vice superior general of the Society of St. Sulpice.

46. Fenlon to John J. Mitty, Baltimore, January 10, 1939, RG 13, Box 1, SAB.

47. Fenlon to Boisard, Baltimore, October 6, 1938, RG 13. Box 1a, SAB.

48. Same to same, January 17, 1939, RG 13, Box 1a, SAB.

49. "Mount Saint Mary's Seminary, Emmitsburg," [Memo of John Fenlon], September 18, 1942, RG 13, Box 1, SAB.

50. Sacra Congregatio de Seminariis et Studiorum Universitatibus, *Elenchus Seminariorum* (Rome: Typis Polyglottis Vaticanis, 1934), and *Enchiridion Clericorum; Documenta Ecclesiae Sacrorum Alumnis Instituendis* (Typis Polyglottis Vaticanis, 1938).

51. Fenlon to Henri Cheramy, Baltimore, February 27, 1939, RG 13, Box 1a, SAB.

52. *AAS* 35 (1943), 193–248.

53. Ibid., 297–326.

54. *AAS* 42 (1950), 495–505.

55. *AAS* 39 (1947), 521–595.

56. *AAS* 40 (1948), 5–7; Veuillot, ed., *Documents,* 2:124–126.

57. *AAS* 42 (1950), 561–578.

58. *AAS* 37 (1945), 173–176.

59. *AAS* 41 (1949), 618–619.

60. *AAS* 48 (1956), 5–25.

61. Ibid., 309–353.

62. *AAS* 39 (1947), 137–155; 43 (1951), 577–582; 45 (1953), 577–592.

63. *AAS* 42 (1950), 657–702; Veuillot, ed., *Documents,* 2:187.

64. Ibid., 2:189.

65. *AAS* 46 (1954), 161–191; Carlen, ed., *Encyclicals,* 4:243.

66. "Circular Letter to the Most Reverend Ordinaries urging the carrying out of the investigation of students before they are promoted to orders," December 27, 1955, SAB.

67. Ibid.

68. *AAS* 51 (1959), 545–579; "Sacerdotii Nostri Primordia" (English translation), *Pope Speaks* 6 (Winter 1959–60), 31–37.

69. Cardinal Joseph Pizzardo, "Letter to the Episcopate in the Third Centenary Year of the Death of St. Vincent de Paul on Certain Problems of Ecclesiastical Formation," *Review for Religious* 20 (May 1961), 173–179.

70. "Latin in Seminaries" (English translation), *Irish Ecclesiastical Record* 40 (August 1958), 203–206.

71. "Veterum Sapientia" (English translation), *Pope Speaks* 8 (Winter 1962), 31–37.

72. Ibid.

13. SEMINARY EXPANSION

1. Kauffman, *Tradition,* pp. 244–246.

2. Dyer et al. to Gibbons, Baltimore, April 24, 1916, RG 10, Box 20, SAB.

3. Kauffman, *Tradition,* p. 246.

4. Ibid., pp. 262–264.

5. Ibid., pp. 264–268.

6. Minutes of Provincial Council Meetings, October 21, 1927, p. 35, SAB.

7. Ibid., January, 1931, p. 46.

8. Fumasoni-Biondi to Fenlon, Washington, June 1, 1928; Fenlon to Fumasoni-Biondi, Baltimore, June 21, 1928; RG 13, Box 1a, SAB; the same issue arose again in 1932 after the submission of the second triennial, in Fenlon to Fumasoni-Biondi, Baltimore, June 4, 1932.

9. Kauffman *Tradition,* pp. 282–283.

10. Ibid., pp. 280–281, 285–286.

11. Ibid., p. 279.

12. John David Burke, "The Seminary of St. Louis, 1818–1918: Foundation for Ordination" (M.A. thesis, St. Louis University 1966), pp. 146–174; Poole, "Apostolate," pp. 124–132 (see above, chap. 5, n.1); John T. Comes, "The Design and Equipment of the New 'Kenrick Seminary,'" *AER* 48 (1913), 662–667.

13. Joe Hartmann, "A Dream Expands," *Ambassador* (75th Anniversary Issue) 25, no. 1, (1981), 11–14.

14. "Pastoral Letter of Archbishop Cantwell," January 1, 1926, in Cantwell Papers, Archives of the Archdiocese of Los Angeles; the general history of the seminary in Francis J. Weber, *A Guide to Saint John's Seminary, Camarillo, California* (Los Angeles: Roman Catholic Archdiocese of Los Angeles, 1966), pp. 7–19.

15. Ibid., pp. 21–31.

16. St. John's and Assumption Seminary's Alumni Association, *Priest Forever: History of St. John's Seminary, San Antonio, Texas, 1915–1965* (San Antonio, 1966), pp. 13–38.

17. Marshall F. Winne, "Vincentians Invited to Take Charge of St. John's Seminary San Antonio," [memo], September 7, 1943, Marshall Winne Papers, DRMA.

18. *Priest Forever,* pp. 57–63.

19. Carlos E. Casteñada, *The Church in Texas since Independence, 1836–1950* (Austin: Von Boeckmann-Jones, 1958), pp. 271–274.

20. "Washington, House of Studies" [memo], Marshall Winne Papers, DRMA.

21. *Catalogue des Maisons et du Personnel de la Congregation de la Mission 1960* (private printing), pp. 142–145, DRMA.

22. James A. Fischer to Confreres, St. Louis, May 24, 1962, James A. Fischer Papers, DRMA.

23. Barry, *Worship,* pp. 263–279.

24. Ibid., pp. 295–296.

25. McCrank, *Mt. Angel,* pp. 64–66 (see above, chap. 8, n.47).

26. Edward E. Malone, *Conception: A History of New Engelberg College, Conception College, and the Immaculate Conception Seminary 1886–1971* (Omaha: Interstate Printing Company, 1973), pp. 178–179.

27. "Announcing the Opening of St. Bernard Seminary, Cullman, Alabama" [1952], pamphlet in Archives of the Diocese of San Diego; Barry, *Worship,* pp. 315–318.

28. Joseph Cada, *Czech-Americans, 1850–1920* (Lisle, Illinois: Center for Slav Culture, 1964), pp. 72–74.

29. John P. Doyle, *History of the Third Order Regular of St. Francis of Penance* (Loretto, Pa.: St. Francis College, 1947).

30. Charles E. Nolan, *Mother Clare Coady: Her Life, Her Times, and Her Sisters* (New Orleans: Academy Enterprises of New Orleans, 1983), pp. 38–44; "Notre Dame Seminary, Archdiocese of New Orleans, Most Rev. J. W. Shaw, D.D., Archbishop," (brochure), September 8, 1923, Archives of Notre Dame Seminary.

31. Baudier, *Louisiana,* p. 524 (see above, chap. 3, n.20).

32. The history of St. Mary of the Lake Seminary is based on Koenig, "St. Mary of the Lake Seminary," pp. 50–115; and Edward R. Kantowicz, *Corporation Sole: Cardinal Mundelein and Chicago Catholicism* (Notre Dame, Ind.: University of Notre Dame Press, 1983), pp. 99–114.

33. Kantowicz, *Corporation Sole,* p. 115.

34. Mary Kevin Gallagher, ed., *Seed/Harvest: A History of the Archdiocese of Dubuque* (Dubuque: Archdiocese of Dubuque, 1987), pp. 111–112; conversation with Rev. Benedict Ashley, O.P., Aquinas Institute, St. Louis, September 19, 1983.

35. *St. John's Home Missions Seminary, School of Theology, Catalog for*

Scholastic Years, 1963–1964, 1964–1965, pp. 10–11, Archives of the Diocese of Little Rock.

36. John K. Sharp, *History of the Diocese of Brooklyn, 1853–1857: The Catholic Church on Long Island,* 2 vols. (New York: Fordham University Press, 1954), 2:175–176; Cantley, *City,* pp. 10–27 (see above, chap. 8, n.24).

37. Francis J. Rigney, "Diocesan Seminaries," unpublished manuscript, and Wally Homitz, "How to Build an Educational Colossus: The University of San Diego Story," *San Diego and Point Magazine* (May 1959), 40–42, 102–107 (clipping) in the Archives of the Diocese of San Diego.

38. Hussey, *History,* p. 39 (see above, chap. 2, n.27).

39. Hynes, *Cleveland,* pp. 337–340 (see above, chap. 3, n.17).

40. *Josephinum Weekly,* December 26, 1931.

41. Beck, *History,* pp. 41–48 (see above, chap. 3, n.44).

42. "Diocese of Steubenville," *NCE* 13:707.

43. John P. Gallagher, *A Century of History: The Diocese of Scranton, 1868–1968* (Scranton: Diocese of Scranton, 1968), pp. 436–438.

44. *St. John Vianney Seminary Bulletin, 1970–1971, 1971–1972,* p. 21.

45. "Press Release," of Very Rev. Sylvester Taggart, C.M., Provincial of the Eastern Province of the Congregation of the Mission, June 23, 1958, in St. John's University Archives, Jamaica, New York.

46. Michael J. McNally, *Catholicism in South Florida, 1868–1968* (Gainesville: University Presses of Florida, 1984), pp. 186–189.

47. *The Official Catholic Directory and Clergy List for the Year of Our Lord 1911* (Milwaukee: Wiltzius, 1911), p. 1077.

48. National Catholic Welfare Conference, Department of Education, *Summary of Catholic Education 1962 and 1963* (Washington, 1963), p. 8; *Official Catholic Directory 1963* (New York: P. J. Kenedy, 1963), general summary table.

49. Ibid.; each seminary is listed under the relevant diocese.

14. CATHOLIC UNIVERSITY REFORM AND INFLUENCE

1. Cf. chap. 9, n.23.

2. Pius XI, "Apostolic Letter," *CUB* 28 (June 1922), 44–45.

3. Blase Robert Dixon, "The Catholic University of America, 1909–1928: The Rectorship of Thomas Joseph Shahan" (Ph.D. diss., Catholic University of America, 1972), pp. 242–256.

4. McNicholas to Cicognani [November 1935], McNicholas Papers, AAC.

5. Kantowicz, *Corporation Sole,* p. 109.

6. "Nation Hears Broadcast," *CUB* 1 (January 1933), 1–5 contains texts of addresses of Cardinal William O'Connell and Archbishops John Glennon of St. Louis, John Mitty of San Francisco, and John Gregory Murray of St. Paul, broadcast on fifty-seven CBS stations on November 20, 1932; Cardinals O'Connell and Hayes and Archbishop Murray delivered addresses on CBS radio on November 19, 1933; see *CUB* 2 (January 1934), pp. 3–7.

7. Curley to Karl J. Alter, Baltimore, July 14, 1942, Curley Papers, AAB.

8. H. Warren Willis, "The Reorganization of the Catholic University of America during the Rectorship of James Hugh Ryan (1928–1935)" (Ph.D. diss., Catholic University of America, 1971), pp. 16–18.

9. Michael J. Curley, "Five Years of Progress," *CUB* 1 (May 1933), 1–2; Ryan's organization of the successful university fund-raising efforts during the depression is described in "Organization against Depression Assists University Finances," *CUB* 2 (September 1934), 1–2.

10. Cicognani to Curley, Washington, September 9, 1934, Curley Papers, AAB.

11. Steven M. Avella, "Thomistic Apogee: John T. McNicholas (1877–1950)," paper delivered at spring meeting of the American Catholic Historical Association, John Carroll University, April 1986.

12. John A. Ryan to Ordinaries of the United States, Washington, July 24, 1933, Rectors' Files, 1913–1969, Schools and Departments, ACUA.

13. "Confidential Minutes of the Episcopal Visiting Committee at the Catholic University of America, December 15–18, 1935," McNicholas Papers, ACUA.

14. Fulton J. Sheen to Gerald P. O'Hara [1935], also quoted in Willis, "Reorganization," pp. 256–257, McNicholas Papers, ACUA.

15. Peter Guilday to McNicholas, Washington, April 20, 1935, McNicholas Papers, ACUA.

16. McNicholas to Gerald P. O'Hara, Cincinnati, March 1, 1935, McNicholas Papers, ACUA.

17. Same to same, March 2, 1935, McNicholas Papers, ACUA.

18. Willis, "Reorganization," pp. 259–260.

19. Curley to O'Connell, Baltimore, September 9, 1935; Curley to Paolo Marella, Baltimore, November 7, 1935, Curley Papers, AAB.

20. Cicognani to Curley, Washington, October 8, 1935, and Curley to Cicognani, Baltimore, October 28, 1936, Curley Papers, AAB.

21. McNicholas to Cicognani [November 1935], McNicholas Papers, AAC. O'Connell's remarks were quoted by McNicholas, who then stated: "I felt that His Eminence was doing the most he could to get me to speak and I felt that as a member of the Pontifical Committee any word I said would be interpreted or rather misinterpreted as the mens Commissionis. I never in my life had so much difficulty in remaining silent." Curley to Cicognani, Baltimore, November 20, 1935, Curley Papers, AAB, also describes the trustees' meeting.

22. Minutes of the Board of Trustees, 94th Meeting, November 12, 1935, ACUA.

23. McNicholas to Corrigan, May 16, 1936, McNicholas Papers, ACUA.

24. Roy J. DeFerrari, *Memoirs of the Catholic University of America, 1918–1960* (Boston: St. Paul Editions, 1962), p. 412.

25. "Report of the Episcopal Visiting Committee, August 19th–24th, 1935," McNicholas Papers, ACUA.

26. Corrigan to McNicholas, Rome, January 30, 1937, Rectors' Files, 1913–1969; McNicholas to Corrigan, Cincinnati, February 23, 1937, McNicholas Papers, ACUA.

27. Corrigan to McNicholas, Rome, March 23, 1937, McNicholas Papers, ACUA.

28. Copy of Contract between Catholic University and Society of St. Sulpice, RG 13, Box 1, SAB.

29. Corrigan to McNicholas, Rome, March 23, 1937, McNicholas Papers, ACUA.

30. *Statutes of the Catholic University of America* (Washington, D.C.: Catholic University of America Press, 1937); Cicognani to Corrigan, Washington, June 24, 1940, Rectors' Files: 1913–1969, II, General Administration, Sacred Congregation of Seminaries and Universities file, SAB.

31. See *Annual Report of the Rector of the Catholic University of America, 1943* and in the following years, ACUA.

32. "Visitation of the Pontifical Commission for Sacred Sciences of the Catholic University, May 20 and 21, 1944," McNicholas Papers, ACUA.

33. McNicholas to Francesco Lardone, Cincinnati, April 4, 1942, McNicholas Papers, ACUA, is an extended defense of the rector's performance. The Corrigan administration is difficult to study because the published annual report of the university rector lapsed during his rectorship. AAB contains Curley's extensive correspondence with bishops during 1942 to raise funds for the university to meet the financial emergency.

34. Pascal Parente, "The School of Sacred Theology: The Oldest School of the Catholic University of America," *CUB* 25 (October 1958), 8, 13.

35. John Rogg Schmidt, "Affiliation of Seminaries," *CUB* 33 (January 1966), 7–9.

36. "Relatio de Origine, Tractu, Statu, Modo Agendi, et Fructu Systematis Affiliationis Seminariorum et Domorum Studiorum cum Facultate Sacrae Theologiae Universitatis Catholicae Americae" [1954], Seminary Affiliation File, ACUA reports on the affiliation program from 1939 to end of the 1952–1953 school year; Beck, *History,* p. 49.

37. "Minutes, First meeting of representatives of Seminaries affiliated with the Catholic University of America, etc.," Cleveland, June 25, 1956, Seminary Affiliation File, ACUA; the new S.T.B. program was announced to seminary educators attending the annual meeting of the Catholic Theological Society of America.

38. Joseph C. Fenton, *The Concept of Sacred Theology* (Milwaukee: Bruce, 1941) and "The Church and the State of Siege" *AER* 112 (January 1945), 45–63.

39. Peter Thomas Bayer, "Joseph Clifford Fenton: A Theological Critique (M.Th. thesis, St. Bernard's Seminary, 1970), pp. 116–144, contains a bibliography of Fenton's works; Donald E. Pelotte, *John Courtney Murray: Theologian in Conflict* (New York: Paulist Press, 1975), pp. 27–73, discusses Murray's conflicts with Fenton and Roman authorities.

40. Robert Paul Mohan, "Father Connell: A Personal Portrait," *AER* 138 (June 1958), 418–423.

41. Joseph Clifford Fenton, "Father Connell and the *American Ecclesiastical Review*" *AER* 138 (June 1958), 424–430.

42. Leonard Swidler, *Freedom in the Church* (Dayton: Pflaum, 1969), pp. 40–41.

15. NEW DIRECTIONS FOR PRIESTHOOD AND SEMINARY

1. Jacques Millet, *Jesus Living in the Priest: Considerations on the Holiness and Greatness of the Priesthood* (New York: Benziger, 1901); John Cuthbert Hedley, *Lex Levitarum: or Preparation for the Cure of Souls* (Westminster, 1906) and *A Spiritual Retreat for Priests* (London: Burns and Oates, 1918); Edward J. Mahoney, *The Secular Priesthood* (New York: Benziger, 1930); Francis Bourne, *Ecclesiastical Training* (Westminster, n.d.); James Keatinge, *The Priest, His Character and Work* (New York: Benziger, 1903); Thomas O'Donnell, *The Priest of Today, His Ideals and Duties* (New York: Benziger, 1910); Adolphe Tanquerey, *The Spiritual Life: A Treatise on Ascetical and Mystical Theology* (Tournai: Desclee, 1930).

2. Bernard Feeney, "The Seminarist Instructed in Preaching, Catechizing and Pastoral Visitation," *AER* 45 (August 1911), 163.

3. Bernard Feeney, "The Seminary and Moral Training," *AER* 45 (October 1911), 460. Articles are compiled in Bernard Feeney, *The Ideal Seminary,* ed. Jeremiah C. Harrington (New York: Macmillan, 1923).

4. John J. Burke, "The Right Reverend William J. Kerby—An Appreciation, 1870–1936" *AER* 95 (September 1936), 225–233; a more extensive study is Timothy Michael Dolan, "Prophet of a Better Hope: The Life and Work of Monsignor William Joseph Kerby," (M.A. thesis, Catholic University of America, 1981).

5. William J. Kerby, *Prophets of the Better Hope* (Philadelphia: Dolphin Press, 1937), p. 19.

6. Ibid., pp. 10–16.

7. Ibid., p. 50.

8. Ibid., pp. 107, 115.

9. Ibid., pp. 66–68.

10. Ibid., p. 79.

11. Ibid., p. 86; see also William J. Kerby, *The Considerate Priest* (Philadelphia: Dolphin Press, 1978).

12. Philip J. Murnion, *The Catholic Priest and the Changing Structure of Pastoral Ministry, New York, 1920–1970* (New York: Arno Press, 1978), pp. 113–115.

13. Ibid., p. 127.

14. Ibid., pp. 16, 48.

15. Florence D. Cohalan, *A Popular History of the Archdiocese of New York* (New York: U.S. Catholic Historical Society, 1983) pp. 240–241.

16. Willliam H. O'Connell to John B. Peterson, Boston, May 17, 1911, St. John Seminary File, AABo.

17. Sexton and Riley, *St. John's,* p. 191.

18. Ibid., p. 229.

19. James A. Magner, "Some Objectives in Seminary Training," *AER* 93 (November 1935), 473–480.

20. Johnson, *Halcyon,* p. 323.

21. Edward G. Murray, "Training for Youth Work in the Major Seminary," *NCEAB* 37 (1941), 732.

22. Raymond P. Witte, *Twenty-five Years of Crusading: A History of the*

National Catholic Rural Life Conference (Des Moines: National Catholic Rural Life Conference, 1948), pp. 181–186; William T. Mulloy, "Religious Vacation Schools and the National Catholic Rural Life Conference," in *The Confraternity Comes of Age: A Historical Symposium* (Paterson, N.J.: Confraternity Publications, 1956), pp. 27–40.

23. Rudolph G. Bandas, "Catechetics in the Seminary" in ibid., pp. 170–189.

24. Lester J. Fallon, "A Laboratory for Ecclesiastical Students," *AER* 102 (January 1940), 43–48.

25. "CSMC in the Church-at-Work," *The Shield* (College-Seminary edition) 37 (November 1957), 20–21; "Action for CSMC Seminary Groups," *The Shield* (College-Seminary edition) 38 (November 1958), 16–17.

26. John Gruden, *Mystical Christ: An Introduction to the Study of the Supernatural Character of the Church* (St. Louis: Herder, 1936).

27. Paul Marx, *Virgil Michel and the Liturgical Movement* (Collegeville, Minn.: Liturgical Press, 1957) includes a survey of the liturgical movement.

28. Steven M. Avella, "'I've Brought You a Man with Imagination': The Life and Career of Reynold Hillenbrand until 1944," unpublished seminar paper, Department of History, University of Notre Dame, December 1, 1982.

29. Dennis Robb, "Specialized Catholic Action, 1936–1949" (Ph.D. diss., University of Minnesota, 1972).

30. "Catholic Action Study in U.S. Seminaries" in Seminarians' Catholic Action Papers, MUA, donated by Msgr. Thomas Reese. I thank Msgr. Reese of St. Mary's Seminary, Baltimore for a personal account of the seminarians' movement, March 1983.

31. Edward A. Wuenschel, "Catholic Action in Seminaries," *CTSAP* 3 (1948), 15–21.

32. Joseph C. Fenton, "The Spirituality of the Diocesan Priesthood," *AER* 116 (February 1947), 126–140 reviews the European background not treated in the following volume.

33. Joseph C. Fenton, *The Concept of the Diocesan Priesthood* (Milwaukee: Bruce, 1951), pp. 6, 20, 81, 95.

34. Ibid., pp. 104–122.

35. Emmanuel Suhard, "Priests Among Men," in *The Church Today: The Collected Writings of Emmanuel Cardinal Suhard* (Chicago: Fides Publishers, 1953), pp. 219–346.

36. Georges Michonneau, *Revolution in a City Parish,* foreword by Archbishop Richard J. Cushing (Westminster, Md.: Newman Press, 1950); Josef Sellmair, *The Priest in the World* (Westminster, Md.: Newman Press, 1954).

37. Joseph Henry Fichter, *Southern Parish* (Chicago: University of Chicago Press, 1951) and *Social Relations in the Urban Parish* (Chicago: University of Chicago Press, 1954); Joseph B. Schuyler, *Northern Parish: A Sociological and Pastoral Study* (Chicago: Loyola University Press, 1960).

38. Joseph B. Schuyler, "Parish Sociology: Vital Help Toward Pastoral Preparation in the Seminary," *NCEAB* 56 (1959), 56–57.

39. Sylvester A. Sieber, "Sociology in the Seminary," *HPR* 56 (December 1955), 224–225; "Report of the Committee on the Teaching of Sociology in High

Schools, Seminaries, Colleges, and Universities," *American Catholic Sociological Review* 17 (March 1956), 38–39.

40. Joseph B. Schuyler, "The Need for and Content of Sociological Study in the Seminary," *NCEAB* 55 (August 1958), 63.

41. Thomas Dubay, *The Seminary Rule: An Explanation of the Purposes behind It and How Best to Carry It Out* (Westminster, Md.: Newman Press, 1954).

42. See Diary of Thomas Mulligan, 1944–1957, special collections in Library of St. Patrick's Seminary, Menlo Park, California.

43. Joseph H. Fichter, *Religion as an Occupation* (Notre Dame, Ind.: University of Notre Dame Press, 1961), p. 94.

44. Ibid., p. 95.

45. Ibid., p. 110.

16. CLERICAL STUDIES IN TRANSITION

1. Ambrose Kohlbeck, "The Ideal Major Seminary — A Summary of the *Ordinamento* of the Congregation of Seminaries and Universities of April 26, 1920," *CEAB* 19 (1922), 494–503.

2. Herman J. Heuser, "Suggestions Toward a Uniform Plan of Studies in the Department of Theology for Seminaries in the United States," *CEAB* 10 (1913), 465.

3. Ibid., p. 471.

4. Herman J. Heuser, "The Study of the Bible in Our Theological Seminaries," *CEAB* 11 (1914), 378–389.

5. Charles L. Cremin, "The Pedagogical Coordination of Theological Studies," *CEAB* 21 (1924), 681–693.

6. Thomas Plassmann, "Report on a Survey of Seminary Curriculum," *CEAB* 22 (1925), 585–587; similar views are in John Harbrecht, "The Challenge of the Seminary Curriculum," *CEAB* 22 (1925), 589–600.

7. John E. Graham, "Rearrangement of the Seminary Curriculum," *CER* 31 (1933), 465–476.

8. John V. Nevins, "The Sacraments in the Seminary Curriculum" *CEAB* 22 (1925), 601–609.

9. Anthony Vieban, "Principles of Pedagogy applied to Teaching in Major Seminaries," undated typescript, SAB, RG 11, Box 2.

10. Theodore Heck, *The Curriculum of the Major Seminary in Relation to Contemporary Conditions* (Washington, D.C.: Catholic University of America, 1935), p. 35.

11. Ibid., pp. 67–69.

12. Ibid., p. 67; the published version of the study lists statistics on individual seminaries without naming them. I thank Rev. Theodore Heck, O.S.B., for lending an annotated copy of his study with the seminaries identified on the tables.

13. Ibid., pp. 44–46.

14. Ibid., p. 45.

15. Ibid., p. 45.

16. Ibid., p. 47.

17. Ibid., p. 67.

18. Ibid., p. 40.

19. Ibid., p. 43.

20. Ibid., p. 67.

21. Ibid., pp. 54, 56.

22. Ibid., pp. 50, 67.

23. Ibid., pp. 52-53.

24. Ibid., pp. 48, 67.

25. Ibid., p. 49.

26. Ibid., pp. 108-109.

27. John F. Fenlon, "The Present Status of Clerical Education in the United States" *CEAB* 19 (1922), 429-440.

28. Heck, *Curriculum,* p. 73.

29. David L. Salvaterra, "The Apostolate of the Intellect: Development and Diffusion of an Academic Ethos among American Catholics in the Early Twentieth Century," (Ph.D. diss., University of Notre Dame, 1983), pp. 229-235.

30. *Proceedings of the First Annual Meeting of the American Catholic Philosophical Association held at the Catholic University of America, January 5, 1926.*

31. Salvaterra, "Apostolate," pp. 228, 254-259.

32. "Educational Notes," *CER* 34 (November 1936), 561-562.

33. Wendell S. Reilly, "Editorial Notes," *CBQ* 1 (1939), 6.

34. "The Canon Law Society of America," *Jurist* 1 (January 1941), 92-93.

35. "The Foundation and Progress of the Society," *CTSAP* 1 (1946), 5-10.

36. "Foundation of the Society," *Marian Studies* 1 (1950), 11-15; Joseph C. Fenton, "America's Two Theological Associations" *AER* 125 (December 1951), 449-458.

37. Paedagogus, "The Teaching of Dogmatic Theology," *Clergy Review* 21 (1941), 10-11.

38. Edward J. Byrne, "The Curriculum of Scriptural Studies in Our Seminaries," *CBQ* 1 (1939), 214-222, 333-341.

39. Joseph O'Donnell, "Sacred Scripture and the Theology Course," *CBQ* 4 (1942), 45-50.

40. Edward F. Siegman, "The Use of Sacred Scripture in Textbooks of Dogmatic Theology," *CBQ* 11 (1949), 151-164.

41. Hubert P. Coughlin, "Scientific Teaching of Dogmatic Theology," *CTSAP* 4 (1949), 174-180.

42. Eugene Maly, Edward F. Siegman, John P. Whealon, "Methods of Teaching Sacred Scripture," *CBQ* 16 (1954), 46-51.

43. Lloyd MacDonald to John R. Sullivan, Baltimore, May 14, 1956, with undated and untitled memorandum of James Laubacher in SAB, RG 16, Box 11.

44. Bruce Vawter, "New Testament for Seminarians — Suggestions for an Improved Course," *NCEAB* 57 (1960), 82-88; a similar perspective is Roland Murphy, "Old Testament for Seminarians — the Purpose of the Course" in ibid., 89-93.

45. Edward J. Hogan, "Teaching the Dogma Course: Scripture and Authority of the Church," *NCEAB* 59 (1962), 65-69.

46. John C. Boere, "A Survey of the Content and Organization of the Curriculum of the Theological Departments of Major Seminaries in the United States of America" (M.A. thesis, Catholic University of America, 1963), p. 10.

47. Ibid., pp. 39–40, 47.

48. Ibid., p. 89.

49. Ibid., p. 65.

50. Ibid., p. 66.

51. Ibid., p. 89.

52. Ibid., p. 73.

53. James W. O'Brien, "The Scientific Teaching of Moral Theology," *CTSAP* 4 (1949), 193.

54. Boere, "Survey," p. 74.

55. Ibid., p. 89.

56. Ibid., p. 79.

57. Ibid., p. 80.

58. Ibid., p. 89.

59. Ibid., p. 82.

60. John Tracy Ellis, "Teaching American Catholic History in Our Schools," *NCEAB* 48 (May 1952), 13–14.

61. Boere, "Survey," p. 83.

62. Ibid., p. 89.

63. Ibid., p. 85.

64. Ibid., p. 89.

65. Ibid., p. 85.

66. Ibid., p. 87.

67. Ibid., p. 89.

68. Ibid., p. 88.

69. Connors, "Homiletic," pp. 414–452 (see above, chap. 6, n.56).

70. Joseph M. Connors, "Needed: A Catholic Homiletic Society," *HPR* 59 (December 1958), 254–258.

71. Boere, "Survey," p. 90.

72. Gerard S. Sloyan, "Seminaries in America," *Commonweal* 73 (October 7, 1960), 37–40.

73. Francis A. Gaydos, "Toward an Improved Theological Curriculum," *NCEAB* 56 (1959), 54, 65–66.

74. Conrad Falk, "Integration of the Seminary Academic Program through the Liturgy," (summary) *NCEAB* 57 (1960), 71–72.

75. Eugene M. Burke, "Developing an Intellectual Tradition in the Seminary," *NCEAB* 59 (1962), 58–65.

17. TRANSFORMING THE SEMINARY

1. Quoted in "Proceedings, Seminary Department" *CEAB* 8 (1911), 467.

2. Edward A. Pace, "The Seminary and the Educational Problem," *CEAB* 8 (1911), 470–483.

3. James Howard Plough, "Catholic Colleges and the Catholic Educational Association: The Foundation and Early Years of the C.E.A., 1899–1919" (Ph.D. diss., University of Notre Dame, 1967); Campion Robert Baer, "The Development of Accreditation in American Catholic Seminaries, 1890–1961" (Ph.D. diss., University of Notre Dame, 1963).

4. Ibid., pp. 124–125.

5. Charles B. Schrantz, "Our Clerical College," *CEAB* 16 (1919), 19–31.

6. "Proceedings, Preparatory Seminary Section," *CEAB* 18 (1921), 589.

7. Reginald Lutomski, "The Organization of Our Seminaries in the Four-Four-Four Plan," *NCEAB* 26 (1929), 808–815; Patrick Cummins, "Recognition by Standardizing Agencies of Credits Allowed and Degrees Granted by Our Seminaries, Major and Minor," *NCEAB* 26 (1929), 726–731.

8. Lambert Burton, "The Young Levite and His Degree," *CEAB* 19 (1922), 533–540.

9. "Resolutions," ibid., 531.

10. John R. Hagen, "Discussion of the Paper, 'Evaluation of Credits,'" *CEAB* 22 (1925), 511–512.

11. Walter L. Fasnacht, "Seminaries Here and 'Over There,'" *AER* 70 (March 1924), 303–312; Herbert Lull, "The Priest and Academic Degrees," *AER* 76 (May 1927), 532–535.

12. Edward A. Cone, "The Diocesan Clergy in Secondary Education" (M.A. thesis, Catholic University of America, 1935), pp. 22–23.

13. Connelly, *St. Charles,* p. 209 (see above, chap. 2, n.38).

14. Johnson, *Halcyon,* p. 226.

15. *Twenty-Eighth Catalog of the Pontifical College Josephinum of the Sacred Congregation for the Propagation of the Faith, 1915–1916* (Columbus, 1916), p. 44 lists the first two degree recipients.

16. Scanlan, *St. Joseph's,* p. 167 (see above, chap. 2, n.35).

17. Hartmann, "Dream," *Ambassador* 25:11–14 (see above, chap. 13, n.13).

18. Miller, "Athenaeum," pp. 345–346 (see above, chap. 3, n.11); Hussey, *History,* pp. 41–43.

19. Sexton and Riley, *St. John's,* p. 234.

20. Thomas Plassmann, "A Protest Against Seminary Standardization," *NCEAB* 27 (1930), 633–641.

21. Baer, "Accreditation," pp. 169–172.

22. "Resolutions," *NCEAB* 25 (1928), 663.

23. Minutes, Meeting of April 17, 1928, Administrative Committee, NCWC; Minutes, General Meeting of the Bishops, November 11, 1931, in AUSCC.

24. "Proceedings, Minor Seminary Section," *NCEAB* 30 (1933), 615–617.

25. Minutes, General Meeting of the Bishops, November 16, 1933, AUSCC.

26. Minutes, General Meeting of the Bishops, November 19, 1936, AUSCC.

27. Baer, "Accreditation," p. 195.

28. "Why the Seminary? An Introduction to the Full Report of the Auburn History Project," (unpublished manuscript, Lilly Endowment, Indianapolis, Indiana), pp. 95–96.

29. In 1947 the Benedictine abbots of the United States formed the Ameri-

can Benedictine Academy as a society to promote scholarship among Benedictines in the United States. Its purpose is broader than the educational association which was oriented to school issues. The Academy began publication of the *American Benedictine Review* in 1950.

30. An unpublished collection of papers and proceedings of the Vincentian Educational Association can be found in DRMA.

31. Eugene J. Butler, "Legal Status of Seminarians under the Selective Service Act," *NCEAB* 41 (1944), 490; Johnson, *Halcyon,* pp. 304–305.

32. Frederick Hochwalt, "Relationship of the Seminary with Voluntary and Governmental Agencies," *NCEAB* 44 (1947), 133; also see Eugene J. Butler, "G.I. Bill of Rights and the Seminarian," *NCEAB* 43 (1946), 109–123.

33. "Proceedings, Major Seminary Department," *NCEAB* 43 (1946), 62, 66.

34. *Saint Paul Seminary, Register, June, 1946* pp. 9, 11 and *Saint Paul Seminary, Register, September, 1947* pp. 11–12 announces M.A. requirements.

35. "Boston Seminary is Elevated to Pontifical Status," *Pilot,* September 9, 1948; see Sacred Congregation of Seminaries and Universities letters in AABo.

36. Felix Newton Pitt, "Relationship between Pastors and the Diocesan School Superintendent of Schools," *NCEAB* 45 (1948), 125–137; Carl J. Ryan, "Preparing the Future Priest for His Work in the Parish School," *NCEAB* 46 (1949), 81–87.

37. Edmund J. Goebel, "The Office of the Superintendent of Schools and Major Seminaries," *NCEAB* 53 (1956), 58–59; Timothy F. O'Leary, "The Superintendent of Schools and the Seminary," *NCEAB* 55 (1958), 48–53.

38. Pius Barth, "Preparation of Teachers for High Schools," *NCEAB* 51 (1954), 105.

39. Anthony Egging, "The Content of the Course in Education in the Major Seminary," *NCEAB* 50 (1953), 88–91.

40. Barth, "Preparation," *NCEAB* 51 (1954), 105–109.

41. "Proceedings, Major Seminary Department," *NCEAB* 52 (1955), 62–63.

42. John Tracy Ellis, "American Catholics and the Intellectual Life," *Thought* 30 (Autumn 1955), 351–388.

43. Gustave Weigel, "American Catholic Intellectualism – A Theologian's Reflection," *Review of Politics* 19 (July 1957), 275–307.

44. "Meeting of Catholic Commission on Intellectual and Cultural Affairs – held at University of Chicago – April, 1957" in NCEA Office Files, ACUA.

45. Thomas F. O'Dea, *American Catholic Dilemma: An Inquiry into the Intellectual Life* (New York: Sheed and Ward, 1958).

46. George N. Shuster is quoted from an address given at the Catholic Midwest Family Life Study Week at Chicago in the *Boston Pilot,* October 31, 1959.

47. Donald C. Horrigan, "Frederick G. Hochwalt: Builder of the National Catholic Educational Association, 1944–1966" (Ph.D. diss., Teacher's College, Columbia University, 1977).

48. J. Cyril Dukehart, "Our Seminaries: Their Commitments and Resources," *NCEAB* 56 (1959), 73.

49. Ibid., p. 73.

50. Ibid., p. 74; in the next few years, others expanded on the rather new

topic of the internal administration of seminaries: Bernard Siegle, "Model Statutes for the Seminary," *NCEAB* 57 (1960), 94–105, and Edward J. Riley, "An Analysis and Evaluation of Seminary Administration," *NCEAB* 59 (1962), 69–74.

51. "Paper read at the School Superintendents' Meeting, October 27, 1959, Washington, D.C., by the Rev. J. Cyril Dukehart, S.S., Associate Secretary Seminary Department, NCEA" in RG 16, Box 2, SAB.

52. *The Official Guide to Catholic Educational Institutions in the United States* (New York: Catholic Institutional Directory Co., 1959).

53. Basil Frison, "The 6-6 Program for Seminary Training," *The Jurist* 19 (1959), 503–511.

54. Paul D'Arcy, "The 4-4-4 Arrangement of Seminaries," *NCEAB* 57 (1960), 106–112.

55. J. Cyril Dukehart, "Report of the Associate Secretary of the Seminary Departments," in ibid., pp. 113–114.

56. Baer, "Accreditation," pp. 271–284; Frank M. Schneider, "Report on Regional Seminary Meetings of Seminary Departments," *NCEAB* 58 (1961), 59–65.

57. John Fogarty, "Accreditation of Catholic Seminaries by the Regional Agencies" (M.A. thesis, Catholic University of America, 1962), p. 52, quoted in Baer, "Accreditation," p. 294

58. Ibid.

59. Burke, "Tradition," *NCEAB* 59:58–59 (see above, chap. 16, n.75).

EPILOGUE

1. "Pope John's Opening Speech to the Council," in Walter M. Abbott and Joseph Gallagher, eds., *The Documents of Vatican II* (New York: America Press, 1966), pp. 713–714.

2. Standard histories of the council include: Xavier Rynne, *Vatican Council II* (New York: Farrar, Straus, and Giroux, 1968) and Ralph M. Wiltgen, *The Rhine Flows into the Tiber: The Unknown Council* (New York: Hawthorn Books, 1967).

3. *Gaudium et Spes,* nos. 2–3; instead of citing page numbers, the council documents' numbered sections, common to all editions and translations, are cited. The translation used in the text is that of Abbott and Gallagher cited above.

4. *Lumen Gentium,* no. 10.

5. Ibid., nos. 18–21; *Christus Dominus,* nos. 36–38.

6. *Lumen Gentium,* nos. 28–29.

7. *Presbyterorum Ordinis,* nos. 7, 9.

8. *Sacrosanctum Concilium,* no. 16.

9. *Dei Verbum,* no. 24.

10. *Unitatis Redintegratio,* no. 10.

11. *Orientalium Ecclesiarum,* no. 4.

12. Rynne, *Vatican,* p. 396; an account of the decree's history can be found in Josef Neuner, "Decree on Priestly Formation" in Herbert Vorgrimler, ed., *Commentary on the Documents of Vatican II* 2:373–378.

13. *Optatam Totius,* no. 1.

14. Ibid., no. 3.

15. Ibid., no. 4.

16. Ibid., no. 8.

17. Ibid., no. 17.

18. Ibid., nos. 15, 16.

19. Ibid., no. 20.

20. Stafford Poole, *Seminary in Crisis* (New York: Herder and Herder, 1966), p. 14.

21. Ibid., pp. 28–29.

22. Ibid., p. 143.

23. James Michael Lee and Louis J. Putz, *Seminary Education in a Time of Change* (Notre Dame, Ind.: Fides, 1965).

24. Ibid., p. 96.

25. James Keller and Richard Armstrong, *Apostolic Renewal in the Seminary in the Light of Vatican Council II* (New York: Christophers, 1965).

26. Emile Joseph Labbe, "A Canonical Study of Pastoral Preparation for Priestly Ministry, with Special Reference to the United States" [Canon Law Studies No. 497] (J.C.D. diss., Catholic University of America, 1978), pp. 257–302 describes the work of the bishops' committee and its interim guidelines.

27. Sacred Congregation for Catholic Education, "Basic Plan for Priestly Formation" in *Norms for Priestly Formation: A Compendium of Official Documents on Training Candidates for the Priesthood* (Washington, D.C.: National Conference of Catholic Bishops, 1982), p. 19.

28. Ibid., p. 27.

29. Ibid., pp. 30–31, 42, 48.

30. National Conference of Catholic Bishops, *The Program of Priestly Formation* (Washington, D.C.: National Conference of Catholic Bishops, 1971).

31. Ibid., p. 8.

32. "Los Angeles Seminary Crisis," James A. Fischer Papers in DRMA, consists of twenty-nine letters and documents pertaining to the Vincentians' relations with Cardinal McIntyre; it includes a discussion of the reforms at Kenrick Seminary.

33. Ibid.

34. Connelly, *St. Charles,* pp. 206–207.

35. "Reform in the Seminaries," *Time* 87:60, April 15, 1966; "Revolt in the Seminary," *Newsweek* 67:68–69, April 18, 1966; "Turmoil in Boston," *Commonweal* 84:68–70, April 8, 1966; the incident was not reported in Boston's archdiocesan newspaper.

36. Hussey, *History,* p. 57.

37. Kauffman, *Tradition,* pp. 305–306.

38. Benedict Ashley to John P. Cody, River Forest, Illinois, October 9, 1964, Seminary Department Files, NCEA Papers, in ACUA.

39. *Directory of Theological Schools* (ATS), 1968 edition, cited in T. Howland Sanks, S.J., "Education for Ministry since Vatican II," *Theological Studies* 45 (September 1984), 487.

40. Ibid.

41. *Official Catholic Directory 1966* (New York: P.J. Kenedy, 1963), general summary; Adrian Fuerst, ed., *CARA Seminary Directory* (Washington, D.C.: Center for Applied Research in the Apostolate, 1984), p. vi.

42. Sanks, "Education," *Theological Studies,* 45:486.

43. See "The Ministerial Priesthood" in NCCB, *Norms,* pp. 295–312.

44. See Odile M. Liebard, ed., *Clergy and Laity* (Wilmington, N.C.: McGrath Publishing, 1978), pp. 346–351.

45. "Vatican Declaration: Women in the Ministerial Priesthood," *Origins,* February 3, 1977, vol. 6, no. 33:517, 519–524.

46. The texts of these documents are available in NCCB, *Norms.*

47. See "The Minister of the Eucharist" [*Sacerdotium Ministeriale*], *Origins,* September 15, 1983, vol. 13, no. 14:229, 231–233; "Who Can Preside at the Eucharist," ibid., January 24, 1985, vol. 14, no. 32:523, 525–526; and ibid., October 23, 1986, vol. 16, no. 19:344.

48. The text of Archbishop Roach's letter is in "Study of U.S. Seminaries Launched," *Origins,* October 8, 1981, vol. 11, no. 17:263–264; the text of Cardinal Baum's letter is in "The State of U.S. Free-Standing Seminaries," ibid., October 16, 1986, vol. 16, no. 18:313, 315–325, from which the quotations in the following pages are drawn.

49. Bishop John Marshall's address is in "Strengths and Weaknesses of U.S. Seminaries," *Origins,* January 7, 1988, vol. 17, no. 30:522–528.

50. Archbishop Thomas Murphy, "Forces Shaping the Future of Seminaries," *Origins,* February 25, 1988, vol. 17, no. 37:637–640; see another proposal on the same subject in M. Edmund Hussey, "Needed: A Theology of Priesthood," ibid., February 4, 1988, vol. 17, no. 34:577, 579–583.

Index

479

About the Author

Joseph M. White is a freelance writer in Indianapolis. In addition to *The Diocesan Seminary in the United States,* he is editor of the recently published book *American Catholic Religious Life: Selected Historical Essays.* White holds advanced degrees from both Butler University and the University of Notre Dame, where he received his Ph.D. He formerly held a faculty fellow position at Notre Dame's Cushwa Center for the Study of American Catholicism.